MW00559062

Game
Programming
Gems 6

Game Programming Gems 6

Edited by
Mike Dickheiser

CHARLES RIVER MEDIA

Boston, Massachusetts

Cover Design: Tyler Creative

CHARLES RIVER MEDIA
25 Thomson Place
Boston, Massachusetts 02210
617-757-7900
617-757-7969 (FAX)
crm.info@thomson.com
www.charlesriver.com

This book is printed on acid-free paper.

Mike Dickheiser. *Game Programming Gems 6.*
ISBN: 1-58450-450-1

All brand names and product names mentioned in this book are trademarks or service marks of their
respective companies. Any omission or misuse (of any kind) of service marks or trademarks should not be
regarded as intent to infringe on the property of others. The publisher recognizes and respects all marks
used by companies, manufacturers, and developers as a means to distinguish their products.

Library of Congress Cataloging-in-Publication Data

Game programming gems 6 / [edited by] Michael Dickheiser.-- 1st ed.
    p. cm.
  Includes index.
  ISBN 1-58450-450-1 (hardcover cd-rom : alk. paper)
  1. Computer games--Programming. 2. Computer graphics. I. Title: Game
programming gems six. II. Dickheiser, Michael, 1970-
  QA76.76.C672. G3646 2006
  794.8'1526--dc22
                        2006002318

06 7 6 5 4 3

CHARLES RIVER MEDIA titles are available for site license or bulk purchase by institutions, user groups,
corporations, etc. For additional information, please contact the Special Sales Department
at 800-347-7707.

Requests for replacement of a defective CD-ROM must be accompanied by the original disc, your
mailing address, telephone number, date of purchase and purchase price. Please state the nature of
the problem, and send the information to CHARLES RIVER MEDIA, 25 Thomson Place, Boston,
Massachusetts 02210. CRM's sole obligation to the purchaser is to replace the disc, based on defective
materials or faulty workmanship, but not on the operation or functionality of the product.

Contents

Foreword

Mark DeLoura

madsax@satori.org

Welcome to *Game Programming Gems 6*. This sixth volume of the *Game Programming Gems* series has been explicitly designed with your current challenges in mind. As this series has grown, so have the demands on game programmers. With team sizes constantly expanding, developers are finding themselves pushed to become increasingly specialized. This makes it important to have cutting-edge material in your specialization at your fingertips, as well as resources at your disposal that you can call upon in case you need to work outside your area of expertise. I hope that in these instances you will turn to *Game Programming Gems*.

Since we're at the sixth book in the series, let's take a moment to think about what has come before. Examining the material in the previous *Gems* volumes gives us an interesting historical perspective; the issues that were most pressing during the creation of the original *Gems* volume in the year 2000 now seem substantially less troublesome. Implementing advanced shader effects, integrating real-time physics into game design, synchronizing multiplayer networked games, and finding artist- and designer-friendly scripting languages are all prominent issues that we now need to confront.

But the biggest issue facing all of us now is cost. The next generation of machines is upon us—PlayStation® 3, Xbox® 360, Nintendo® Revolution®, multicore PCs—and with the new capabilities come some new challenges. Our players will expect higher-fidelity models and animations, fancier physics and graphics effects, and more-intelligent AI. In order to create these, we'll build up our teams and lengthen our schedules, and ultimately spend a lot more money. If we can't increase the price of games (please, no!) or increase our market size (please, yes!) we'll be more pressed than ever to deliver compelling experiences on time and on a budget. Crunch time, here we come!

The Importance of Tools

Making the technology we develop easily accessible to the rest of our team has become one of the most important things we do as game programmers. After all, what's the use of having that fancy shader that we stayed up all night writing if our artists can't figure out how to use it? While it's true that our team sizes are growing quickly, most of the growth comes from the increasing number of artists. So if we can make their lives easier by making some simple tools, our games will not only likely wind up looking better, they will also be produced more quickly and inexpensively as well—all good things!

Fortunately in this platform-transition period, reusing tools is much easier than reusing engine technology. The front-end interface of a tool can remain relatively unchanged, while the underpinnings and output of the tool are altered to suit the new target. This makes tools one of the easiest things to amortize the cost of, since they can largely be reused for multiple titles or multiple teams over time.

Having tools available at the beginning of the development process for pre-production and early production work is very helpful, and practically *de rigueur* now in order to save time on the development schedule. Unfortunately at this time, we're seeing a reduction in the number of tools available on the middleware market. So if you don't already have your own tools, what should you do? Increasingly, studios are banding together into larger development groups or being bought out by publishers, and for them, the logical choice is the creation of a central technology group.

Collaboration

The thought of trying to convince many studios to work together on sharing common technology and to rely on others is not something most of us relish. But with our costs spiraling upward, distributing the development cost of a piece of technology across multiple platforms and titles is a smart decision. Frankly, some of the larger projects recently have become so expensive that they've gone from amortizing their cost across multiple platforms to amortizing them across multiple future sequels! The development costs are so expensive, this might be the only way they'll ever turn a profit. How else could one justify these huge expenditures, if not by seeking to establish a strong brand and then reusing the tools and technology across multiple games in a franchise? It seems crazy, but with a large risk comes the possibility of a large reward.

Another kind of collaboration that is increasingly useful involves globalizing your development. By turning to studios in regions that haven't previously been considered—such as Eastern Europe, China, and India—publishers and developers in Europe, North America, and Japan have discovered new ways to keep their costs down. Producers are learning to pull together resources for a game from locations around the globe, and having solid tools to rely on becomes extremely important in this scenario.

Parallelization

As console developers move onto the next series of machines, they're facing a new challenge: parallelizing their game engine. PC developers have a little more time before they're pushed in this direction, as well. The upcoming multicore systems require serious study and creative new techniques in order to be fully taken advantage of. While we've all gotten used to some parallelism (e.g., between the CPU and GPU), these new machines are forcing us to think in new ways. How will we deal with splitting our engine into many pieces that are easily parallelizable? Will we be able to rely on compilers and other tools that make programming these multicore machines easier, or will we have to create new tricks and techniques for maximizing performance on parallel architectures, ourselves? It certainly won't be a boring time for expert programmers.

One interesting side effect to the increasing complexity of dealing with the hardware is a bifurcation of programming roles at larger development houses. Many teams now have dedicated, platform-specific programmers who deal with interfacing the game engine to the hardware, while the majority of their programmers write platform-independent code. This never works quite as cleanly as it sounds, and with the differences between the various platforms, there's definitely a lot of job security for the low-level coders. But ultimately, this is yet another way costs can be kept down, since some of the high-level programmers can then be less experienced and therefore less expensive!

Acknowledgments

The *Gems* series provides an interesting glimpse into the recent evolution of technology in the games industry. There are other resources that address technical issues, such as *Game Developer* magazine, *gamasutra.com,* and the *Journal of Game Development,* but none of them cover as much material, and that as thoroughly. Thanks to all of the authors and editors who have contributed so much of their time and energy to the series. If you haven't yet contributed your unique perspective to *Gems,* please consider writing down some of your experiences to share in the future!

Finally, many thanks to Michael Dickheiser for being such a professional and crafting *Gems 6* with his tireless persistence. I think you'll find that Mike's unique perspective has created a very valuable volume, and I hope that it finds a place of honor on your bookshelf!

Preface

Mike Dickheiser,
Applied Research Associates, Inc.

mdickheiser@ara.com

This series is no longer for game developers. Or rather, it's no longer *just* for game developers. The past several years have seen a rise in the related industries of Game-Based Learning, Edutainment, and other "serious games." Admittedly, this is nothing new, and the buzz surrounding these developments has been steadily growing ever louder. However, the activity in the last year or so must be described as nothing less than an *invasion*.

A World Discovered

Computer game engines and tools are drawing attention on a scale that probably escapes most game developers too busy to look up from their coffee-stained keyboards. As someone who has recently left the industry to explore the other side, I can vouch for the fact that many, many eyes are looking eagerly at what this industry has produced. New companies are sprouting up everywhere like mushrooms after the rain. Focused entirely on the use of game technology for the creation of commercial and military training environments and simulations, they are coming en masse to claim their stake in the New World.

But it's not just industry that's moving in. The academic world is paying greater attention to our efforts as well. I'm not talking about computer game schools and courses—those are exciting developments that deserve their own discussion. I'm talking about the use of licensed game technology in extremely sophisticated, cutting-edge research. A brief inspection of the activities in progress at many major universities will reveal the use of our best engines as out-of-the-box tools for exploring human-computer interaction, cognitive modeling, intelligent agents, interactive narrative, auditory pathology, motor skill therapy, human information processing . . . the list goes on and on.

Affirmation at Last

One thing is clear: computer game technology is finally recognized as true *technology*. The best evidence of this is that game tech is no longer mostly restricted to the service of end-users. It has now become the gift-wrapped starting point for custom development in R&D firms and research labs across the globe.

The significance of this is that the outside world is starting to *feed back* into the game industry. Sure, as game developers we've always stripped what we could from the literature and GPL toolset to satisfy our own needs, but this has always been on our terms, at our whim. Now, soon, we will see our own technology change before our eyes at the hands of the *noobs*. Witness the number of authors and editors in this series alone who are no longer in the industry, but whose contributions continue to shape the future of it.

An Emerging Paradigm

In can be no coincidence that the rapid growth of interest from the outside has occurred simultaneously with the shift *inside* the industry towards better tools supporting high-level engine access and content creation. Indeed, the sophisticated authoring tools behind many of our products are often the biggest attraction cited by R&D companies and university researchers.

Personally, I think we're finally starting to really do things the right way. The era of hard-coded, closed systems is coming to an end. The *change-a-number-compile-test-and-repeat* cycle has just *got* to go away, and in fact it is, if just a little bit too slowly. We are on the brink of an industry-wide renaissance that will see high-level, component-based content *and gameplay* creation that only the top-tier games now exhibit.

The *Game Programming Gems* series would be remiss to not recognize this fact, and so we embrace it completely by presenting a brand new section dedicated to "Scripting and Data-Driven Systems." This new section focuses entirely on the growing trend of removing the programmer from the data-tweaking loop. But it's much more than that: the new paradigm entails a philosophy of workflow that simply translates into much faster turnaround on creative ideas and allows programmers, designers, and artists to speak the same language during development. Inevitably, that changes everything.

Ok, enough soapboxing. Let's get down to business…

Game Programming Gems 6

This sixth volume of the series offers more than fifty articles written by experts in game technology—and related disciplines—from many different backgrounds and over twenty countries. Each has worked closely with the editing staff to bring you a very wide variety of gems that are just waiting to be part of your next project. Some of the material is truly innovative. Some of it brings fresh perspective to familiar issues.

All of it exemplifies the hard work of some very bright people who represent the best of what this industry has to offer. I leave it to you to explore and find that *one* critical insight that you've been seeking. But first, allow me to whet your appetite and prepare you for the treats you'll find inside these pages:

General Programming

Adam Lake, Intel Software Solutions Group

The general section is traditionally the home for a menagerie of insightful and down-right clever programming tools of all kinds, and this time is certainly no different. Here you'll find coverage of everything from multiprocessor techniques, unit testing, and security fingerprinting to an extremely cool application of *real* computer vision. Rest assured, that's just the beginning: this diverse chapter sets the tone and pace for hundreds of pages just bursting with true programming gems.

Mathematics and Physics

Jim Van Verth, Red Storm Entertainment, Inc.

Death and Taxes. Add to that a desire to get just one more cycle out of the FPU, CPU, and GPU and you've got the set of things that are always certain to stick around. If there's one thing that can be said to be the lifeblood of game programming, it is, of course, math. But don't worry: this section isn't about writing countless lines of code to squeeze out just one last drop of power. Instead, it offers a nice mix of freshly treated standard topics along with clever applications that really should find a home in your next project.

Artificial Intelligence

Brian Schwab, Sony Computer Entertainment of America

Always one of the most popular sections, AI gets a solid treatment that won't let you down. Game AI is particularly subject to the influence of cutting-edge research in cognitive science and machine intelligence, and with a strong showing from academia, this edition covers some heavy material on behavior modeling that's presented accessibly enough to use in your next title, and all those that follow. Just to show off, we even demonstrate how to use AI techniques in other systems in the engine. Take that, graphics!

Scripting and Data-Driven Systems

Graham Rhodes, Applied Research Associates, Inc.

The inaugural edition of this section brings a tear to the eye. We simply couldn't let this series continue without bringing scripting and data-driven systems right into the light where they belong. Starting with a survey of some popular and emerging languages, this section will educate you to get your engine up and running with a backbone so flexible you'll impress the Circus. Read this section—and shame on you if you aren't already at least thinking about doing some of the things discussed within.

Graphics

Paul Rowan, Rho, Inc.

A great mix of classic and emerging technologies are covered this time in the "Graphics" section, with a new spin on a few things you think you know well, and some truly cool ideas you probably have never thought to try yourself. If it's improved spatial partitioning you're looking for to squeeze even more cycles out of your engine, you're covered. If it's a way to load up your scene with more lights than you can imagine, you got it. Want to have the sharpest road signs and billboards in the industry? You'll find it here. And that's just the beginning of the creative content this time around…

Audio

Alexander Brandon, Midway Home Entertainment

I bet you never thought of generating sound from deformable meshes, did you? Or how about using spatial analysis to determine PASes? (I'll let you discover what those are.) Well, now you know what to expect inside the audio section: some really cool ideas for more advanced uses of the audio system. Then again, the section has really cool ideas for all kinds of uses of the audio system, so hang on to your ears and get ready to replace your speakers.

Network and Multiplayer

Scott Jacobs, Virtual Heroes

There's nothing scarier to me than the problems faced by game network programmers these days. A jillion players scattered throughout the global community all plugged in at once is intimidating enough. Add to that the fact that the rest of us keep adding increasingly detailed and sophisticated content to every single thing sent across the pipe, and you've got a real mess. My hat goes off to the experts in this area that not only have time to sort out the issues but actually write about them as well. This time we offer several gems that address these problems, allowing the rest of us to sleep at night. Or at least play on the 'net until sunrise.

Conclusion

I started with a claim that I now realize is completely false. This series—this industry—*is* still for game developers, and in fact always will be. Nobody works as hard to produce *the magic*, and that's what makes it ours. Even as other industries discover and barter and sell our technology, it will always remain our domain. And yes, I still count myself in. My heart will always belong to games, and in fact, I see myself not as someone who has left the industry, but rather as an ambassador on assignment abroad.

So, whether you're a new game programmer starting out on this exciting path, a grizzled veteran of the industry, or a most welcome visitor, I sincerely hope this book will bring inspiration, insight, and at least one or two true gems to your world.

Acknowledgments

First, I'd like to thank the authors: the tireless people who write code and then take the time to write *about* code while countless other game developers keep their noses to the grindstone behind them. I extend thanks not just because the series needs them, but also because without them the industry would have a weaker voice that might not reach the outside world knocking on our doors. To the authors: your efforts are now permanently etched into the timeline of the industry, and you can rest assured somebody somewhere at some time will take what you've generously given and make the next Big Thing that validates and celebrates all your ideas, driving the industry ever forward.

Next, I can't express enough gratitude to Jenifer Niles for entrusting me with the care of the series, if only for a short while. I'm honored to have played this part and hope I've succeeded in helping the *Gems* series continue to prosper and bring useful information to thousands of game developers. Jen…forgive me for any stress I've caused you!

Also, special thanks goes to Mark DeLoura. Not just for his guidance and vote of confidence, but also for his dedication to the series in spite of being extremely busy with other pursuits. I say this as a reader of the series, and as a programmer who has found that perfect piece of code or insight at just the right moment on several occasions. Mark: six books! Can you believe it? Here's to six more…

Section editors. No, I haven't forgotten the section editors. That simply wouldn't be possible. From the outside it might seem like a trite tradition to thank the editing staff, but having taken on this task I now know that the expression of gratitude is of the utmost sincerity and is woefully insufficient. I liken it to a weak nod from an exhausted quarterback to a team that carried the project on its aching shoulders through to the end of a hard-fought overtime Super Bowl victory. Twice. Thank you, guys…drinks are on me. And thank your families for me, too. I know they miss you.

Finally, and most importantly, I thank my wife, Sukie, for her boundless patience and support, not to mention a well-deserved kick in the pants every now and then.

About the Cover Image

In this image, Soldier of the Future Captain Scott Mitchell™ surveys an urban battle-field in *Tom Clancy's Ghost Recon Advanced Warfighter*™. This image was created in Montpellier, France at Ubisoft's Tiwak studio using Adobe® Photoshop® and Autodesk® 3ds Max®.

Captain Mitchell's Integrated Warfighter System (IWS) gear is based off the real-life Future Force Warrior program being developed at the U.S. Army Natick Soldier Center. It is comprised of armor and uniform elements by Crye Precision, including their MULTICAM™ uniform fabric and Armored Chassis, BlackHawk HellStorm Fury gloves, and a helmet by Artisent Inc. The Modular Rifle-Caseless (MR-C) design is by Crye Associates.

The U.S. Army does not sponsor or endorse *Tom Clancy's Ghost Recon Advanced Warfighter*™.

Contributor Bios

Contains bios for those contributors who submitted one.

Luis Otavio Álvares

Luis Otavio Álvares is a professor in the Department of Applied Computing at Universidade Federal do Rio Grande do Sul (UFRGS), Porto Alegre, Brazil. He received his Ph.D. in informatics from Université Joseph Fourier (Grenoble, France) in 1988, and his M.Sc. in computer science from UFRGS in 1982. His research interests include artificial intelligence applied to computer games, multiagent systems, and data mining. He has served as an organizing committee member, reviewer, and technical committee member of several conferences and journals.

Takashi Amada

taka.am@gmail.com

Takashi Amada is a software engineer at Sony Computer Entertainment, Incorporated. He received his bachelor's degree in bioscience from Tokyo Institute of Technology in 2003, and his Master's degree in information science from Nara Institute of Science and Technology in 2005. His research interest is focused on virtual reality, real-time rendering, and physically based animation.

James Boer

author@boarslair.com

James Boer began his game development career by delving inside the mind of white-tailed deer in order to develop AI for the surprise hit game *Deer Hunter*. After his eventual capture, return to civilization, and re-education, he worked on a number of games, including *Rocky Mountain Trophy Hunter, Deer Hunter II, Pro Bass Fishing, Microsoft Baseball 2000,* Tex Atomic's *Big Bot Battles,* Digimon *Rumble Arena 2,* and *Lord of the Rings: Tactics.* His writing credits include a number of *Game Programming Gems* articles, co-authoring *DirectX Complete,* a few assorted articles in *Game Developer Magazine,* and his own book, *Game Audio Programming.* ArenaNet currently employs him as a network and server programmer for their new game, *Guild Wars.*

Alexander Brandon

abrandon@midway.com

Alexander Brandon has been involved in game audio since 1994. He has been a composer, sound designer, voice actor, voice director, voice caster, technology design specialist, and audio director, and has contributed to or overseen over a dozen high-profile games, including *Unreal*® and *Deus Ex*. He has lectured at the Game Developers' Conference for five years and has lectured at numerous colleges, as well as game and music industry events. He is the columnist for *Game Developer* magazine's "Aural Fixation" column and has written a book: *Audio For Games: Planning, Process and Production*. He continues to work as the audio manager for Midway Home Entertainment in San Diego, California.

Matthew Campbell

campbell@bmh.com

Matthew W. Campbell has been developing software in both professional and academic environments for the past six years. Having only completed his undergraduate studies two years ago, Matthew spent most of his academic time working on several projects involving clustered parallel rendering, with the intent of finding cheaper solutions for driving massive virtual environment simulations using display wall and CAVE Automatic Virtual Environment™ technology. During this time, Matthew also spent several months at The Institute for Scientific Research (ISR), integrating parallel rendering technologies into existing display-wall technology. His most recent efforts include several projects based on the open-source game engine, Delta3D (*www.delta3d.org*), which seeks to leverage the power of gaming technology to benefit military simulation and training. Matthew holds a B.S. in computer science from Virginia Polytechnic University (Virginia Tech) and is currently employed by BMH Associates, Incorporated (Norfolk, VA).

Erin Catto

erincatto@gphysics.com

Erin Catto has been developing physics engines for the past 10 years. He is currently a physics programmer at Crystal Dynamics, working on *Tomb Raider Legend*. Previously, he worked on dynamic simulation of proteins, mechanical simulation software for computer-aided design, and modeling and control of flexible robot arms. Earlier in his life, he programmed games on his HP48 calculator, including *Ant* and *Joust*. He holds a Ph.D. in theoretical and applied mechanics from Cornell University.

Waldemar Celes

celes@inf.puc-rio.br

Waldemar Celes is an assistant professor in the computer science department at PUC-Rio, Brazil. He is a researcher and senior project manager associated with Tecgraf, the computer graphics technology group of PUC-Rio, and is a former postdoctoral associate for the computer graphics program at Cornell University. His current research interests in computer graphics include real-time rendering, scientific visualization, physical simulation, and distributed graphics applications. He is also one of the authors of the Lua programming language.

Octavian Marius Chincisan

mariuss@rogers.com

Octavian graduated from the Technical University of Cluj-Romania in 1987 with a M.Sc. in electrical engineering. One year later, he graduated with a Post University Diploma in applied electronics and finalized a project to build a Z80-based personal computer that was compatible with Sinclair Spectrum. From 1988 to 1994, he worked as a C++ programmer for a financial institution. Octavian came to Canada in 1994, where he worked for different companies as a C++ senior software programmer. In 2000 another challenge arose: game programming. Octavian is entirely self-taught in this field; and the result of his knowledge, passion, and work is the creation of the Getic 3D Editor and Getic SDK, which is currently under development. Octavian currently works as a software consultant for General Electric, as well as part time as a software architect for Zalsoft, Incorporated.

Mike Dickheiser

mdickheiser@ara.com

After spending nearly 10 years in the game industry making computer-controlled characters and vehicles chase each other around, Mike switched paths and now spends the government's money simulating anything and everything that moves on *real* battlefields. Borrowing from experiences working on flight simulators and, more recently, vehicle AI in the *Ghost Recon* product line at Red Storm Entertainment, Mike now spends his daylight hours at Applied Research Associates looking for ways to inject his passion for game technology into the world of serious simulation. As if work, family, and book editing weren't enough to keep him busy, Mike spends absurd amounts of time working on his master's degree in computer science at North Carolina State University, in the relentless pursuit of the world's first truly intelligent machine—all this powered by caffeine, Indian food, and the unshakable belief that some day it will all be worth it.

Thomas Di Giacomo

thomas@miralab.unige.ch

Thomas Di Giacomo has published many papers on computer graphics and networks in international journals, and at conferences and workshops, and contributed to *Graphics Programming Methods* and *Game Programming Gems 4*. His main interests are in level-of-detail for animation and physically based animation.

Arjan Egges

egges@miralab.unige.ch

Arjan Egges has published many computer graphics articles in international journals, as well as for conferences and workshops. He is also the editorial assistant for *Computer Animation and Virtual Worlds* journal.

Luiz Henrique de Figueiredo

lhf@visgraf.impa.br

Luiz Henrique de Figueiredo is an associate researcher at the Institute for Pure and Applied Mathematics (IMPA) in Rio de Janeiro, Brazil. He is also a consultant at Tecgraf, the computer graphics technology group of PUC-Rio. His current research interests include computational geometry, geometric modeling, and interval methods in computer graphics. He is also interested in programming languages, and is one of the designers of the Lua language.

Dominic Filion

dfilion@hotmail.com

Dominic is currently working as a graphics engineer at a major game development studio in Orange County, California. Previously, he held the position of technical director at DC Studios, where he led the technology team to create the studio's in-house, cross-platform 3D engine. He had worked on four commercial 3D engines before, and was principal architect on two of them. He also worked at Artificial Mind & Movement, Microids, and Fun Key Studios. Feel free to drop him a note about the articles, or just for a friendly chat.

Martin Fleisz

Martin graduated from the University of Derby, England, with a B.S. degree in computer science. For three years, he has worked as a professional C++ programmer. He spends most of his spare time enlarging his knowledge about game- and graphics-related programming techniques. In the remaining time, he also enjoys playing video games and drums.

Chun Che Fung

lanceccfung@ieee.org

Dr. Lance C. C. Fung is currently an associate professor at the School of Information Technology, Murdoch University. He obtained his Ph.D. from the University of Western Australia and his M.Eng. and B.S. (first-class honors) degrees from the University of Wales, Institute of Science and Technology, U.K. His interest in simulation and games can be traced to his undergraduate study. His project was the simulation of a ship's behavior under automatic-pilot control during various sea conditions. He has been teaching artificial intelligence for a long time and has published many journal and conference papers. His research interests and expertise are in applications of intelligent techniques and systems to real-life problems.

Diego Garcés

diegogarces@gmail.com

Diego Garcés is currently working in several games as an AI programmer at FX Interactive, a startup in Spain. Ever since the first PC appeared in his life, he wanted to make games. He started building (programming and graphics) small games at school, and after some work experiences outside the game world, he decided to go back to his passion—games. In the university, studying computer engineering, he also became interested in research. For the time being, he tries to find time to finish his Ph.D. studies while working. So far, he has surprisingly managed to finish the first two years of the Ph.D. program without being fired.

Stephane Garchery

stephane@miralab.unige.ch

Stephane has published many computer graphics articles, book chapters in the *Handbook of Virtual Humans,* and a Ph.D. thesis in the field of 3D facial animation for real-time applications.

Julien Hamaide

julien.hamaide@gmail.com

Julien started programming a text game on his Commodore 64 at the age of eight. His first assembly programs would follow soon after. He has always been self-taught, reading all the books his parents were able to buy. He recently graduated as a multimedia electrical engineer at the Faculté Polytechnique de Mons (Belgium) at the age of 21. After two years working on speech and image processing at TCTS/Multitel (*http://tcts.fpms.ac.be; http://www.multitel.be*), he is now working on next-generation consoles at Elsewhere Entertainment (*http://www.elsewhere-entertainment.com*), a Belgium-based video game company.

Anders Hast

aht@hig.se

Anders Hast has been a lecturer in computer science since 1996 and an associate professor since 2004 at the University of Gävle. He received his Ph.D. from Uppsala University in 2004. He has published over 20 research publications and book chapters in the field of computer graphics.

Roberto Ierusalimschy

roberto@inf.puc-rio.br

Roberto Ierusalimschy is an associate professor at the Catholic University in Rio de Janeiro (PUC-Rio). He is the leading architect of Lua. His current research area is programming languages.

Pete Isensee

pkisensee@msn.com

Pete Isensee is the development manager of the Xbox Advanced Technology Group. He's a regular speaker at GDC and a regular contributor to the *Game Programming Gems* series. He enjoys discussing C++ performance issues, particularly over a glass of Bordeaux.

Scott Jacobs

scott@escherichia.net

Using game technology to develop simulation and training software, Scott Jacobs works for Virtual Heroes in Cary, North Carolina. To some, he tells of his current interests in testing frameworks, continuous integration, and multithreaded game engine design. If the listener's eyes glaze over, he changes the subject to mountain biking, producing and consuming Indian food, and horror films.

Toby Jones

thjones@microsoft.com

Toby Jones is a software design engineer in the Media Technology Group at Microsoft®. He is currently working on the next-generation multimedia pipeline for Windows® Vista. Toby does not want to attach "Senior" to his title because he is not yet 65. If he can stop playing Xbox 360, he hopes to finish his M.Sc. in computer science. Back in the day, Toby wrote cool systems code for *Sound Forge, Vegas Video,* and *Dead Man's Hand* on Xbox, and *Prey.* And yes, he finally married Jessica.

Chris Joslin

cjoslin@connect.carleton.ca

Chris Joslin is an assistant professor at Carleton University, Canada, working on interactive multimedia, dynamic media adaptation through context, and real-time collaborative virtual environments.

HyungSeok Kim

kim@miralab.unige.ch

HyungSeok Kim has published many research papers in the field of computer graphics and virtual reality, in international journals and for conferences. Major published articles are focused on multiresolution modeling, adaptation of 3D content, and real-time interaction models. HyungSeok is also an editorial assistant for the *Visual Computer* journal.

Yongha Kim

ysoyax@gmail.com

Yongha Kim received a master's degree from Pohang University of Science and Technology for his work on the fast VQ encoding algorithm for animated sprites. This algorithm enables the RTS *Kingdom Under Fire from Phantagram* to generate resources 20 times faster than via conventional methods. Subsequently, he participated in the development of MMORPGs at both Phantagram and NEXON, respectively. He is currently a project manager for a new MMORPG at NEXON. The games under his supervision are expected to do much toward love and peace in the world.

David L. Koenig

david@touchdownentertainment.com

David Koenig is currently a senior software engineer with Touchdown Entertainment (formerly LithTech). His main focus is on supporting, maintaining, and enhancing the Jupiter 3D Engine technology for both PC and Xbox. His work has contributed to many titles, including *Tron 2.0* (PC), *Tron 2.0: Killer App* (Xbox), *Gun Griffon* (Xbox), *Chicago Enforcer* (Xbox), and many others. He holds a bachelor's degree in computer engineering technology from the University of Houston. His personal homepage is at *http://www.rancidmeat.com.*

Adam Lake

adam.t.lake@intel.com

Adam Lake is a senior software engineer for the Software Solutions Group leading The Modern Game Technologies Project at Intel. Adam has held a number of positions during his seven years at Intel, including research in nonphotorealistic rendering and delivering the Shockwave3D™ engine. He has designed a stream programming architecture, including the design and implementation of simulators, assemblers, compilers, and programming models. Previous to working at Intel, he obtained a M.Sc. in computer graphics at UNC-Chapel Hill and worked in the computational science methods group at Los Alamos National Laboratory. More information is available at *www.cs.unc.edu/~lake/vitae.html.* He has several publications on computer graphics, and has reviewed papers for SIGGRAPH and IEEE, as well as several book chapters on computer graphics. In his spare time, he is a mountain biker, road cyclist, hiker, camper, avid reader, snowboarder, and Sunday driver.

Noel Llopis

llopis@convexhull.com

Noel Llopis spearheads the research and development of next-generation technology at High Moon Studios. He is a firm proponent of agile development, automated testing, and test-driven development. He is the author of the book *C++ for Game Programmers* and regularly contributes articles to the *Game Programming Gems* series and *Game Developer* magazine. Some of his past titles include *Darkwatch* and the *Mech-Assault* series. In his spare time, he enjoys exploring different and unexpected ideas on his Web site, Games from Within (*http://gamesfromwithin.com*). He obtained a B.S. from the University of Massachusetts at Amherst and a M.Sc. from the University of North Carolina at Chapel Hill.

Chris Lomont

chris@lomont.org

Chris Lomont is a professional tinkerer, having held jobs as a salesman, research scientist, video game programmer, and graduate assistant, among others, and hopes to start a Discover Channel show on destructive devices. He holds degrees in math, physics, and computer science, with a Ph.D. in algebraic geometry from Purdue. Besides having a love for computer graphics and algorithms, he currently does quantum computing research for an Ann Arbor company. Many more of his hobbies, projects, and interests can be found at *www.lomont.org.* (His latest project is an LED cube for artistic visualization; also check out the superballs video.) Email him with any questions about math or algorithms—he likes the challenge.

Jörn Loviscach

jlovisca@informatik.hs-bremen.de

Jörn Loviscach is professor of computer graphics, animation, and simulation at Hochschule Bremen (University of Applied Sciences), Germany. He is interested in real-time rendering, plug-in development for standard DCC software, audio processing, and user interfaces. Prior to joining the Hochschule, Jörn worked at several German computer magazines, among them *c't,* where he served for three years as deputy editor-in-chief. Having designed and built music synthesizers and rhythm computers on his own as a teenager, he elected to leave electronics and study physics, in which he gained a doctorate degree. He finds much too little time to make use of the assortment of musical instruments that he keeps.

Frank Luchs

gameprogramminggems@visiomedia.com

In 1983, Frank Luchs wrote his first music program for the Atari computer and started his dual music/programming career. His projects have ranged from producing and composing scores for movie and TV, to sound design and programming of custom applications and multimedia software. He has produced and composed hundreds of songs, jingles, and movie scores, including Germany's most-known crime serial, *Tatort.* Frank has written chapters for *Game Programming Gems 3, 4,* and *6.* He is the founder of Visiomedia, Ltd., a company specializing in virtual instruments. At Visiomedia, he designed the software synthesizer Saccara. The grain-based synthesis method has been adapted as open source for the book *Game Programming Gems 6.* Frank currently works in the movie business in Munich, Germany. When he's not programming, he enjoys making a lot of noise with his synthesizer gear and composing electronic symphonies.

Blake Madden

blake.madden@oleandersolutions.com

Blake Madden is a software engineer at Oleander Solutions, where he focuses on text and 2D graphics software. He is also currently working on a graphics extension library for wxWidgets as well as a 3D-based Euchre game. In his spare time, he enjoys digital photography, hiking, and roller coasters.

Nadia Magnenat-Thalmann

thalmann@miralab.unige.ch

Nadia has pioneered research into 3D virtual humans over the past 20 years. She has published more than 200 papers on many computer graphics topics in all major conferences. She is also editor-in-chief of the *Visual Computer* and the *Computer Animation and Virtual Worlds* (formerly *Journal of Visualization and Computer Animation*) journals.

Enric Martí

enric@cvc.uab.es

Enric Martí joined the computer science department of the Universitat Autònoma de Barcelona (UAB) in 1986. In 1991, he received a Ph.D. at the UAB with a thesis about the analysis of hand-made line drawings as 3D objects. He became associate professor in 1991. He is a researcher at the Computer Vision Center (CVC). His present research interests are mainly document analysis—and more specifically, Web document analysis, graphics recognition, computer graphics, mixed reality, and human computer interaction. He is working on text segmentation in low-resolution Web images (e.g., GIF, JPEG) using wavelets to extract text information from Web pages. Also, he is working on the development of a mixed-reality environment with 3D interfaces (data glove and optical lenses). He is also a reviewer for the *Computer & Graphics* and *Electronic Letters on Computer Vision and Image Analysis* (ELCVIA) journals.

Curtiss Murphy

murphy@bmh.com

Curtiss Murphy has been developing and managing software projects for 13 years. As a project engineer, he leads the design and development of several serious game efforts for a variety of government and military organizations. His goal is to help the government leverage low-cost, game-based technologies to enhance military training. Recent efforts include a half-dozen projects based on the open-source gaming engine, Delta3D (*www.delta3d.org*), and a public affairs game for the Office of Naval Research based on *America's Army*™. Curtiss holds a B.S. in computer science from Virginia Polytechnic University and currently works for BMH Associates in Norfolk, Virginia.

Viknashvaran Narayanasamy

viknash@hobbiz.com

Viknash received his bachelor's (hons.) in computer engineering from Nanyang Technological University, Singapore, in 2004. He is presently pursuing a Ph.D. in game technology from the School of Information Technology at Murdoch University, Australia. He has been developing casual games for many years out of self-interest, and has produced numerous game demos in the process. Viknash has previously worked on *StarLogo TNG*, an educational simulation game at the Massachusetts Institute of Technology, and is presently working on *Murdoch Grand Challenge*, an educational racing game at Murdoch University. His R&D interests include GPU algorithms for general-purpose and graphics applications in games, as well as complex systems modeling for games. As part of his research studies, he is presently working on complex systems design, modeling and engineering for MMP games. His homepage is at *www.viknash.com.*

Charles Nicholson

charles.nicholson@gmail.com

Charles Nicholson is a senior programmer on the R&D team at High Moon Studios. Prior to that, he worked in the financial sector of New York City doing networked server programming. He got his first taste of game programming as a lowly intern at the Disney VR Studios and hasn't looked back since. He'd be happy to hear that you recognize some of the games that he's worked on, which include *Darkwatch*, *Disney's Toon Town*^{SM} *Online*, and *Polaris SnoCross*. When he's not living the Southern California lifestyle with his beautiful girlfriend and pet fish, he feeds his mild obsession with the optimal organization and structuring of game assets.

Hugo Pinto

hugo@hugopinto.net

Hugo Pinto received a Master's degree in artificial intelligence from Universidade Federal do Rio Grande do Sul, Brazil, in 2005. In his research, he investigated the application of extended behavior networks (a robotic architecture) to the design of agents with simple personalities in *Unreal Tournament.* He has been developing commercial AI applications in international teams since 2000 and has been a member of IGDA's AIISC since 2002. He is interested in computer games, artificial intelligence, human-computer interaction, and human languages.

His research and work have spanned computer games, multiagent systems, natural-language processing, cognitive architectures, and machine learning. Nowadays, he spends most of his time at Vetta Labs developing hard-core AI applications. He also finds time to work as an independent consultant and lecturer on game AI, to learn German, Hebrew, and Arabic, and to train in martial arts. His current non-Vettical research focuses on RTS games, particularly on improving strategic AI using multiagent coordination and learning techniques. His Web site is at *www.hugopinto.net.*

Frank Puig Placeres

fpuig@fpuig.cjb.net

Frank Puig is the director of the virtual reality team at the University of Informatic Sciences, Cuba. He designed and implemented the CAOSS Engine and CAOSS Studios, which has been applied to two published games, and he was a contributor to

Game Programming Gems 5. He also has designed and produced several tools for game development that improve and simplify the treatment of motion capture data, advanced texture mapping, and animation blending, among other applications.

Armand Prieditis

prieditis@lookaheaddecisions.com

Dr. Prieditis is the CEO and Founder of LDI, a company devoted to real-time decision-making, and Locust Games, a developer of game AI and animation software. While at LDI, he was awarded a $2 million Advanced Technology Program grant from NIST (National Institute of Standards and Technology). Prior to founding LDI, Prieditis was a professor in the computer science department at the University of California–Davis. He co-chaired the Twelfth International Conference on Machine Learning and has served on the program, organizing committees, and review boards for other international conferences on machine learning and the National and International Joint Conferences on Artificial Intelligence.

Steve Rabin

steve_rabin@hotmail.com

Steve Rabin has worked in the games industry for 15 years and is currently a senior software engineer at Nintendo of America. He has written AI for three published games and was a significant contributor to the *Game Programming Gems* series, as well as the founder and chief editor of *Introduction to Game Development* and the *AI Game Programming Wisdom* series. He has spoken at the Game Developers Conference and is an instructor at both the DigiPen Institute of Technology and in the Game Development Certificate Program through the University of Washington Extension. Steve holds a B.S. in computer engineering and a master's degree in computer science, both from the University of Washington.

Arnau Ramisa

aramisa@iiia.csic.es

Arnau Ramisa graduated with a degree in computer science from the Universitat Autònoma de Barcelona, and now is working on a Ph.D. in computer vision and artificial intelligence at the Institut d'Investigació en Intelligència Artificial at the same university, working in visual invariants and object recognition. He is interested in computer vision, augmented reality, human-machine interfaces and, of course, video games.

Michael Ramsey

Mike Ramsey is a lead programmer at Blue Fang, Incorporated, where he is developing technology for the Xbox 360 and PlayStation 3. Mike has contributed to both the *Game Programming Gems* and *AI Wisdom* series. He has a B.S. in computer science from MSCD. Mike's publications can be found at *http://www.masterempire.com*. In his spare time, Mike enjoys playing wiffle ball with his daughter Gwynn.

Aurelio Reis

AurelioReis@gmail.com

For Aurelio, video games have always been a portal for him to visit and enjoy new and exciting worlds. Realizing it as a creative outlet, he decided to pursue it as a career, and has since dedicated his life to creating games that evoke awe in their graphical splendor, challenge in their gameplay, and elicit emotions that draw the player into the game. Aurelio is currently a senior programmer at Raven Software, where he specializes in gameplay systems as well as graphics technology. He's currently working on next-generation technologies on multiple platforms for one of Raven's next games. In his (occasional) spare time, he likes to compose music, play sports, and work on graphics demos, as well as design amateur, independent games. You can see some of his work at his personal Web site: *www.CodeFortress.com*.

Graham Rhodes

grhodes@gsrhodes.com

Mesmerized (as many were) by games played in arcades and on his high school's Apple II computer, Graham Rhodes began coding his own arcade-style games while still a teen. Early projects included a *Robotron*™ play-alike game for the Commodore VIC-20 and the singular *Lunar Craft* for Atari 8-bit home computers. In the 1990s, he led the development of a series of mini-games for the *World Book Multimedia Encyclopedia* on PC CD-ROM (1997–2000). Designed to teach basic physics to high school students, the mini-games included student-controlled, real-time physics simulations. Recently, Graham has led the development of action games for industrial safety training, built on a state-of-the-art 3D game engine, and is developing new 3D graphics technology for simulation and training. Relevant publications include contributions to three books by Charles River Media, as well as contributions to the *Game Programming Gems* series and a chapter in the recently released *Introduction to Game Development*. He is moderator of math and physics at *gamedev.net*, has contributed at the annual Game Developer's Conference, and is a member of both ACM/SIGGRAPH and the IGDA. Graham holds a Master of Science degree in aerospace engineering from North Carolina State University.

Paul Rowan

paul@rowandell.com

Paul has worked on games since the early 1990s. His first graphics engine was focused on getting top performance out of CPU access to a frame buffer in main memory. Just throwing some color up on the screen at 30 Hz was cause for celebration. Recently, his focus is on delivering features where they are needed the most—in the hands of artists and designers. On cold winter nights, he still performs inner-loop optimization as a parlor trick for entranced onlookers.

Sébastien Schertenleib

Sebastien.Schertenleib@epfl.ch

Sébastien Schertenleib is a research assistant and Ph.D. candidate at the VRlab, Swiss Federal Institute of Technology. He obtained his master's in computer science at the EPFL. His research interests are mostly confined to the areas of crowd simulations as well as platforms architecture for 3D real-time applications. He is currently working on virtual heritage simulations. He welcomes email at the above address to provide him feedback or exchange ideas.

Brian Schwab

brian_schwab@yahoo.com

Brian Schwab has worked in the game industry for over a dozen years, on everything from the Genesis to the PlayStation 3. During all this time, he has continued to push forward with gameplay and game AI, by never giving up and going home until it's cool. He is the author of *AI Game Engine Programming*.

Allen Sherrod

ProgrammingAce@UltimateGameProgramming.com

Allen Sherrod has a bachelor's degree in computer information systems from DeVry University. He has written for *Game Developer* magazine and also has an upcoming book due out in 2006 on DirectX® game programming. In his spare time, Allen works on his Web site, *www.UltimateGameProgramming.com*.

Larry Shi

ai_shaying@hotmail.com

Larry Shi has co-authored 15 papers on entertainment computing, silicon-based digital rights management, security, and cryptographic processes. His main research interests in entertainment computing include data distribution for online games, data mining of player-generated data, automated testing of simulation games, and gameplay rewards engineering. Larry worked for nVIDIA, where he participated in designing the network unit of the nForce platform and investigated using the state-of-the-art GeForce® GPU for general purpose computing.

Larry also worked for EA Maxis during the summer of 2004, where he contributed to the console title, *URBZ*. His recent focus is on designing a digital-rights solution for graphics applications, and designing new cellular services and infrastructures for the next generation of online handset games. Larry Shi received two master's degrees: one in computer science and one in psychology. He is expecting his Ph.D. in computer science in early 2006.

Marq Singer

marq.singer@redstorm.com

Marq has had a long and varied career. He spent the late 1980s and early 1990s working in the film industry on a variety of projects and roles, which ranged from general crew for TV commercials to special effects for horror films, including the minor cult-classic *Killer* (1989). He is co-author of *Java Applets and Channels... Without Programming,* and is a frequent games and technology guest lecturer at several universities. Since 1998, he has been working in the games industry, serving in a number engineering functions, including physics, animation, UI, and AI. Currently, he is primarily a physics programmer for Red Storm Entertainment, a division of Ubisoft, working with both the Havok engine and custom soft-body dynamics. His most recent titles include *Rainbow Six: Lockdown* for the PS2 and PC.

Vaclav Skala

skala@kiv.zcu.cz

Professor Vaclav Skala, PhD Czech Technical University, is currently responsible for the Center of Computer Graphics and Visualization (CCGV—*http://herakles.zcu.cz*) at the UWB and research and application projects with the Czech Academy of Sciences, Microsoft Research (U.K.), Skoda-Auto (Volkswagen Group), etc. The CCGV has many international research links and MSc. students of Computer Graphics usually spend a semester studying abroad as the CCGV has over 30 educational links with universities within the European Union under the Socrates/Erasmus project. His research interests are Algorithms for Computer Graphics and Visualization, Algorithms, and Data Structures. He is a member of Eurographics and Eurographics Executive Committee, ACM-SIGGRAPH, Computer Graphics Society, Computers & Graphics (Pergamon Press), The Visual Computer (Springer Verlag) Editorial Boards and many International Program Committees of established scientific conferences and workshops. He is an author or co-author of many research publications and the organizer of the WSCG conference (*http://wscg.zcu.cz*).

Peter Smith

peter@smithpa.com

Peter is currently a contractor working in the NETC Experimentation Lab at NavAir, Florida. His work has him concentrating on the use of new and emerging technologies in naval training. The primary focus of the lab has been the use of gaming technologies for training, including work on Delta3D, an open-source game engine for training applications, as well as work with other game-based training systems. Peter is also a Ph.D. student at the University of Central Florida (UCF), studying modeling and simulation. He has a master's degree in modeling and simulation from UCF, and a B.S. in computer engineering from Rose-Hulman Institute of Technology.

Roger A. Smith

gpg@modelbenders.com

Roger is a chief engineer with Sparta, Incorporated, and the president of Modelbenders, LLC. He develops simulation systems for the military, creates commercial courses on simulation and virtual world technologies, and writes a constant stream of technical papers for books, encyclopedias, journals, and conferences. He has presented several full-day tutorials at the Game Developers Conference, and teaches simulation and gaming courses at a number of universities.

Robert Sparks

sparks.robert@gmail.com

Robert Sparks has worked at Radical Entertainment (Vancouver, Canada) since 2001 and is currently programming sound for *Scarface: The World is Yours*. His past game credits include *The Simpsons: Hit & Run*, *The Simpsons: Road Rage*, and *The Hulk*. Robert's first exposure to embedded systems programming was with Doppelmayr Seilbahnen GmbH (Wolfurt, Austria) while working with ski lift safety control systems.

Ben St. John

ben.stjohn@siemens.com

Ben St. John got his start in the gaming industry back in 1997 at Electronic Arts, working on the *NHL Hockey* series for the PlayStation. Falling in love with a German prompted a move to Munich, where he eventually found a job with Siemens doing R&D for graphics, image processing, and gaming for mobile phones (including developing the camera-based game for phones, *Mozzies*). He's since moved into the central R&D department of Siemens and has less to do with gaming, but tries to keep a finger in the virtual world.

Chris Stoy

cstoy@nc.rr.com

Chris Stoy has worked in the gaming industry since 1997. He was a co-founder of Sinister Games, where he helped develop their first title, *Shadow Company: Left for Dead*, and later was lead on developing new technology. Recently, he has been working at Red Storm Entertainment on *Rainbow Six: Lockdown* for the PS2. Outside of work, Stoy is a member of the Raleigh IGDA advisory board and is active in the martial arts.

Jim Van Verth

jimvv@redstorm.com

Jim Van Verth is a senior programmer at Red Storm Entertainment, where he concentrates on 3D graphics and simulation. He is co-author of the book *Essential Mathematics for Games and Interactive Applications* and has been a contributor to the *Game Programming Gems* series. In addition, he organizes an annual tutorial on topics in math and physics at the Game Developer's Conference. Jim lives in a haunted house on the edge of a windswept outcropping at the edge of an Eldritch plain with his wife, daughter, and 500 hungry dogs. He also has been known to exaggerate on occasion (there's only one very hungry dog).

Enric Vergara

evergara@lsi.upc.edu

Enric Vergara is a computer engineer at the Universitat Autònoma de Barcelona and recently received a Master's degree in video games creation at Pompeu Fabra University. Now he is working on a Ph.D. at the MoViBio Research Group of the Universitat Politècnica de Catalunya, specializing in modeling and visualization of biomedical data.

Gabriyel Wong

gabriyel@gmail.com

Gabriyel Wong is the technical director of gameLAB, a research and development facility focusing on game technology, at Nanyang Technological University, Singapore. Prior to this, he worked as technical lead and a software developer with companies producing games, simulation, and virtual-reality software. At his own leisure, he enjoys babysitting his son, and coding and researching state-of-the-art rendering and interactive techniques in real-time applications.

Kok-Wai Wong

k.wong@ieee.org

Kok Wai Wong is working as a Lecturer in the School of Information Technology at Murdoch University. He received the Bachelor (Hons.) of Computer System Engineering and PhD from Curtin University of Technology in 1994 and 2000 respectively. He has worked in the field of AI for around 10 years. He is a founding member of the Game and Simulation Research Group within the School of Information Technology at Murdoch University, and also the conference co-chair for CyberGames 2006. His current research interests include Game AI, Complex Systems Modeling for MMP Game, Personalization for Game Play, and Collaborative Agent Theory for MMP Games.

GENERAL PROGRAMMING

Introduction

Adam Lake, Intel Software Solutions Group, 3D Graphics Research

adam.t.lake@intel.com

Game development is undergoing significant changes in every aspect of the development pipeline. Extracting performance in previous generations of hardware meant a focus on scheduling assembly instructions, exploiting small vector instructions—SSE, for example—and ensuring data remains in registers or the cache while processing. While these issues are still relevant, they are now secondary relative to the need to exploit the multithreaded hardware in next-generation consoles and PCs. To this end, we have included articles on tools and techniques that will help game programmers to take advantage of this new hardware: "Utilizing Multicore Processors with OpenMP" (1.2), by Pete Isensee; and "Lock-Free Algorithms" (1.1), by Toby Jones.

We have included two articles on spatial partitions: "Geographic Grid Registration of Game Objects" (1.4), by Roger Smith; and another with a detailed implementation of the popular binary space partitioning (BSP) approach—"BSP Techniques" (1.5), by Octavian Marius Chincisan. It's often possible to utilize different spatial partitioning schemes, depending on the context. For example, visibility may be resolved with a BSP, but object management may be performed using a quadtree or octree. These articles will provide the information necessary to build your own BSP or octree implementation.

We also have authors who have written about techniques they use to improve both the ease of maintenance and quality of code in their past projects. An article by Blake Madden, "Using CPPUnit to Implement Unit Testing" (1.7), includes a detailed implementation of a unit-testing suite, complete with test cases. There is also an article by Noel Llopis and Charles Nicholson on asset hotloading (1.10), which provides an implementation of a mechanism to enable real-time loading of assets as they are modified during development, ultimately resulting in a faster time to market for your game. Another article that will help some game developers shorten development cycles describes an algorithm for determining the closest string match: "Closest-String Matching Algorithm" (1.6), by James Boer. String matching is useful when artists and programmers mistakenly type incorrect filenames when saving or accessing resources created during development.

For those interested in new interaction techniques, we have an article showing how to use the computer vision library, OpenCV. In "Computer Vision in Games Using the OpenCV Library" (1.3), Arnau Ramisa (et al.) demonstrates the use of the library to capture the movement of the player's head peeking around a corner.

For security, we have an article by Steve Rabin, "Fingerprinting Pre-Release Builds to Deter and Detect Piracy" (1.8). The author describes the different mechanisms a developer may use to fingerprint a game and the tradeoffs of the different approaches, and recommends a combined approach for the most reliability.

In the area of performance, we have an article and sample implementation for reordering assets: "Faster File Loading with Access-Based File Reordering" (1.9), by David L. Koenig. This article is especially relevant, given the fact that today's game engines have ever-increasing load times.

Each of these authors brings to the table his own unique perspective, personality, and vast technical experience. My hope is that you benefit from these articles, and that these authors inspire you to give back when you too have a gem to share. Enjoy.

Lock-Free Algorithms

Toby Jones, Microsoft

thjones@microsoft.com

While game programmers have always driven CPUs to their limits, increasingly they are depending on parallelism to achieve maximum performance. Modern games are expected to take advantage of Symmetric Multiprocessing (SMP) and Chip Multiprocessing (CMP) in PCs and consoles, such as the Xbox 360.

One of the challenges of gaining maximum CPU efficiency is making sure all CPUs are crunching data at all times. One difficulty arises when the CPUs need to share data. While it is best if this is kept to a minimum, at times it can be unavoidable. The traditional techniques involve tools such as mutexes, semaphores, and critical sections to safely serialize access to data and resources.

Mutexes and other lock-based structures are double-edged swords. They allow multiple threads to safely access data, but they are not very scalable. Failing to acquire a lock could cause a thread to spin while waiting for the lock, wasting valuable cycles. In the worst case, they can cause an expensive context switch.

A more modern technique is to use lock-free algorithms. Lock-free algorithms allow access to shared data without needing a lock, but they may restrict what operations are allowed. These algorithms are not wait-free in the sense that all threads will progress immediately, but at least one thread is always able to make progress. Additionally, the algorithms are not necessarily fair; threads are not guaranteed access in order.

One of the primary advantages is that lock-free algorithms can provide a huge boost in speed when used in the right places. They are also invulnerable to deadlock, and terminating a thread in the middle of an operation will not affect the stability of other threads. There are other advantages, but game programmers will generally choose lock-free algorithms due to their speed advantages.

Compare and Swap, and Other Universal Primitives

Implementing a mutex or critical section correctly involves the use of certain atomic primitives, such as a test&set. A thread can repeatedly test&set a memory bit until it succeeds, which would guarantee the thread exclusive access to a resource until the thread clears the bit. However, test&set is not powerful enough for lock-free programming.

Herlihy showed in his seminal paper [Herlihy91] that not all atomic primitives are equal when it comes to choosing primitives for lock-free algorithms. Particularly, test&set, swap, and fetch&add are computationally inadequate. There are primitives that rise to the challenge, which we will call *universal primitives*. These are listed in approximate order of increasing power:

Compare and Swap (CAS):   Atomically compares a memory word with a known value, and swaps the memory word with another value if the comparison is equal.

Load Linked/Store Conditional (LL/SC):   LL loads a memory word. SC stores a word at the location LL loaded from, provided nothing has written to that location.

Compare and Swap 2 (CAS2):   Similar to CAS, CAS2 operates on a contiguous double word.

Double Compare and Swap (DCAS):   Similar to CAS2, except the comparison is made on two noncontiguous memory words.

Compare and Swap N (CASN):   A generalization of CAS2, which operates on an arbitrary number of contiguous memory words.

Multiword Compare and Swap (MCAS):   A final generalization of DCAS, which operates on an arbitrary number of noncontiguous machine words.

CAS can be implemented in pseudo-C code rather easily, as shown in Listing 1.1.1.

Listing 1.1.1

```
// this function is atomic
bool CAS(uint32_t * ptr, uint32_t oldVal, uint32_t newVal) {
    if(*ptr == oldVal) {
        *ptr = newVal;
        return true;
    }
    return false;
}
```

Universal Primitives in Practice

It would be wonderful if all universal primitives were available on all hardware. However, most hardware barely supports a subset of these instructions. Generally, one will have either LL/SC or CAS, and perhaps CAS2. This is unfortunate, because many lock-free algorithms require higher-order primitives, such as DCAS.

PowerPC implements two instructions for handling LL/SC. These instructions are Load Word and Reserve Indexed (lwarx), and Store Word Conditional Index (stwcx). lwarx loads a word from memory and stores the address of the word in a hidden register called a reservation. For every memory store, the address is compared against the reservation, and the reservation is cleared if the address matches. stwcx attempts to write to the address, but only succeeds if the reservation matches the address. The reservation is then cleared.

x86 supports primitives for CAS and CAS2 through the Compare and Exchange (cmpxchg) and Compare and Exchange 8 Bytes (cmpxchg8b) instructions.[1] These instructions will compare a memory value against a register (or registers for cmpxchg8b), and swap the memory for a second register if the values are equal.

One of the great things about modern C++ compilers is that they often include intrinsics that can be used instead of writing assembly. This can improve portability and still allow the compiler to optimize the code. In Microsoft Visual C++®, _Interlocked-CompareExchange() can be used as a direct replacement for CAS.[2] Other implementations of CAS and CAS2 are available on the CD-ROM.

ON THE CD

Compiler optimizers can cause some problems common to multithreaded code. Lock-free algorithms run in loops, and shared variables may need to be marked with volatile in order to be optimized correctly. If available, a better method may be to manually insert read-and-write barriers.

Now that we have some actual universal primitives to work with, we can begin building a lock-free algorithm.

A Lock-Free Parameterized Stack

The stack we will implement will be a general linked-list based stack. Each node will contain a value and a pointer to the next node as shown in Listing 1.1.2.

Listing 1.1.2

```
template<typename T> struct node {
    T value;
    node<T> * volatile pNext;

    node() : value(), pNext(NULL) {}
    node(T v) : value(v), pNext(NULL) {}
};
```

We will also define the container itself and a couple of primitive operations, Push() and Pop(), as shown in Listing 1.1.3.

---

[1]It should be noted that the algorithms presented are designed with a 32-bit processor in mind. There is no barrier to implementing a lock-free algorithm on a 64-bit processor (provided the proper universal primitives are available), but the code in this gem depends on the implementation detail that pointers are 32-bits wide. On x64, there is no primitive that allows for a 128-bit cmpxchg, so alternative techniques must be used for CAS2. One option is to use a 32-bit offset from a base address as a near pointer.

[2]Alternatively, this functionality may be built right into the platform. On Windows®, the InterlockedCompareExchange() function is available, but it still may be preferable to use the intrinsic.

Listing 1.1.3

```
template<typename T> class LockFreeStack {
    // NOTE: the order of these members is assumed by CAS2.
    node<T> * volatile _pHead;
    volatile uint32_t _cPops;

public:
    void Push(node<T> * pNode);
    node<T> * Pop();

    LockFreeStack() : _pHead(NULL), _cPops(0) {}
};
```

When we want to push a new node onto the stack, we need to update the new node to point at the node at the head of the stack. Then, we change pHead to point at the new node. The trick is to do this in a way that maintains the integrity of the stack, even if another thread attempts to push or pop another node (see Listing 1.1.4).

Listing 1.1.4

```
template<typename T> void LockFreeStack<T>::Push(node<T> * pNode)
{
    while(true)
    {
        pNode->pNext = _pHead;
        if(CAS(&_pHead, pNode->pNext, pNode))
        {
            break;
        }
    }
}
```

First, we set the node to point at the head of the stack. Next, we atomically check to see if the head has changed; if not, we point _pHead at our new node. If it has changed, then we start over by grabbing the new head.

Popping an item off the stack is simply the reverse. Get the pointer to the second node from the first node. Then point _pHead at the second node. The first node is now extracted and can be returned. Listing 1.1.5 shows that the implementation is straightforward, but there is a twist:

Listing 1.1.5

```
template<typename T> node<T> * LockFreeStack<T>::Pop()
{
    while(true)
    {
        node<T> * pHead = _pHead;
        uint32_t cPops = _cPops;
```

```
        if(NULL == pHead)
        {
            return NULL;
        }

        node<T> * pNext = pHead->pNext;
        if(CAS2(&_pHead, pHead, cPops, pNext, cPops + 1))
        {
            return pHead;
        }
    }
}
```

Here we see that the implementation is the reverse of the Push() method, with the exception of _cPops. The reason for this additional check has to do with the ABA problem.

The ABA Problem

A problem that comes up in CAS-based algorithms has to do with aliasing. Consider Figure 1.1.1. Suppose a thread is attempting to pop A. It gets a pointer to B, with the intent of making that the new head. If the thread is preempted at this point, right before the CAS, then the stack becomes unstable. A new thread could pop A and B, and then push A. Now if the original thread attempts its CAS, it will see that the head still points to A, so it will try to make B the new head. The problem is that B is not on the stack!

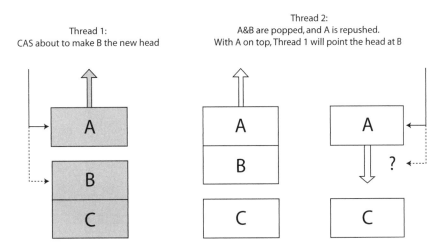

FIGURE 1.1.1   *CAS may see that the head is unchanged and consider the stack unchanged. This is the ABA problem.*

A solution is to tag the head with a version number. A simple tag counts the number of pops. If the count of pops does not match the expected value, then the head has changed and we must begin anew.

There are other ways to solve the ABA problem. Using LL/SC avoids the ABA problem entirely, as changing the head pointer in a competing thread will invalidate the linked reservation.

Lock-Free Techniques

At this point, the general idea of what is required for a lock-free algorithm may be evident. Work should be done offline in an object outside of the class. When done, CAS the pointer to the shared data. If the CAS fails, start over. The concept, though simple, is complicated in practice.

In the stack example, multiple threads can access the stack, but the content of each node is assumed to be accessed by only a single thread at a time. Allowing concurrent access to the content would require additional lock-free structures for each node, as well as handling the problem of memory management. Reclamation of freed objects is particularly tricky with lock-free structures, but this can be solved by using hazard pointers [Michael04b]. Some of these difficult areas are noted in the code on the CD-ROM.

ON THE CD

Making data access lock-free comes with some restrictions. Not every operation is available as in lock-based algorithms. For example, implementing iteration might be difficult. This would require that each node can be accessed by multiple threads and may require the use of primitives such as DCAS, which are not usually available. As processors begin to include more-powerful universal primitives, additional operations will become available.

What might not be obvious, but should be explained, is that lock-free algorithms cannot be built upon locks. It may be tempting to try, especially when the operations you want are not available.

A Lock-Free Parameterized Queue

A queue is among the most important multithreaded structures and is used in all kinds of situations. We can implement a singly linked lock-free queue with not much more complexity than the previously written stack. Listing 1.1.6 shows the basic container.

Listing 1.1.6

```
template<typename T> class LockFreeQueue {
    // NOTE: the order of these members is assumed by CAS2.
    node<T> * volatile _pHead;
    volatile uint32_t _cPops;
    node<T> * volatile _pTail;
    volatile uint32_t _cPushes;
```

```
public:
    void Add(node<T> * pNode);
    node<T> * Remove();

    LockFreeQueue(node<T> * pDummy) : _cPops(0), _cPushes(0)
    {
        _pHead = _pTail = pDummy;
    }
};
```

Here we have a typical definition of a simple queue container. We have pointers to the head and tail; and to avoid the ABA problem, we have version numbers for each end. The significant conceptual change is that we will now add new nodes to the tail of the list instead of the head. We also introduce an initial node into the queue, as suggested in [Michael96].

Adding a node to a queue is more complex than adding a node to a stack. Two operations must be done together. We need to point pTail at the new node at the same time that we point the old tail node to the new node. We are now witness to the complexity that comes with lock-free algorithms.

If we had DCAS, the algorithm could follow as in the stack case. Unfortunately, no modern hardware has support for DCAS, so a new method is needed. In this case, we will allow pTail to be incorrect, but the threads will cooperate to update pTail (in a lock-free way) until it is correct, before we attempt to add the node. This way, we only need to worry about updating the actual tail node atomically (see Listing 1.1.7).

Listing 1.1.7

```
template<typename T> void LockFreeQueue<T>::Add(node<T> * pNode) {
    pNode->pNext = NULL;

    uint32_t cPushes;
    node<T> * pTail;

    while(true)
    {
        cPushes = _cPushes;
        pTail = _pTail;

        // If the node that the tail points to is the last node
        // then update the last node to point at the new node.
        if(CAS(&_pTail->pNext, reinterpret_cast<node<T> *>(NULL),
            pNode))
        {
            break;
        }
        else
        {
            // Since the tail does not point at the last node,
            // need to keep updating the tail until it does.
```

```
                CAS2(&_pTail, pTail, cPushes, _pTail->pNext,
                                  cPushes + 1);
         }
    }

    // If the tail points to what we thought was the last node
    // then update the tail to point to the new node.
    CAS2(&_pTail, pTail, cPushes, pNode, cPushes + 1);
}
```

This approach forces Remove() to be aware of the tail pointer in the case that the queue is nearly empty. This is not a problem, as Remove() can simply update the tail pointer itself.

In Listing 1.1.8, there are a number of cases to consider. We need to make sure that we atomically retrieve all of the local variables. If the queue appears to be empty, we need to check if pTail is simply lagging behind, and retry if so. If the queue is ready to remove a node, it copies the value and attempts to adjust pHead.

Listing 1.1.8

```
template<typename T> node<T> * LockFreeQueue<T>::Remove() {
    T value = T();
    node<T> * pHead;

    while(true)
    {
        uint32_t cPops = _cPops;
        uint32_t cPushes = _cPushes;
        pHead = _pHead;
        node<T> * pNext = pHead->pNext;

        // Verify that we did not get the pointers in the middle
        // of another update.
        if(cPops != _cPops)
        {
            continue;
        }
        // Check if the queue is empty.
        if(pHead == _pTail)
        {
            if(NULL == pNext)
            {
                pHead = NULL; // queue is empty
                break;
            }
            // Special case if the queue has nodes but the tail
            // is just behind. Move the tail off of the head.
            CAS2(&_pTail, pHead, cPushes, pNext, cPushes + 1);
        }
        else if(NULL != pNext)
        {
```

```
                value = pNext->value;
                // Move the head pointer, effectively removing the node
                if(CAS2(&_pHead, pHead, cPops, pNext, cPops + 1))
                {
                    break;
                }
            }
        }
        if(NULL != pHead)
        {
            pHead->value = value;
        }
        return pHead;
    }
```

There is an optimization in [Fober05] that removes the need for a node copy at the expense of thread-killing immunity. For game objects that have expensive copy semantics, this may be important.

As you can see, the complexity and availability of certain lock-free algorithms depends greatly on the types of universal primitives that the platform provides.

A Lock-Free Parameterized Freelist

We now have a couple of fundamental algorithms for sharing data. Creating correct lock-free algorithms is very tricky, and often it is more productive to build complex algorithms on top of simple lock-free algorithms.

With these tools, we will build a lock-free freelist. A freelist is used by memory managers to keep track of memory blocks that the game can use. In this context, we will be constructing a fixed-size freelist that has attractive properties such as reduced memory fragmentation [Glinker04].

Our complete implementation in Listing 1.1.9 is a freelist that can create and destroy objects in a lock-free manner. The technique for implementing freelists in a lock-free manner is different from [Glinker04] in that we do not store a list of pointers to the free memory. Instead, we have our lock-free stack manage nodes that include our actual objects. Allocating or deleting objects is as easy as a push and pop!

Listing 1.1.9

```
    template<typename T> class LockFreeFreeList {
        LockFreeStack<T> _Freelist;
        node<T> * _pObjects;
        const uint32_t _cObjects;

    public:
        LockFreeFreeList(uint32_t cObjects) : _cObjects(cObjects)
        {
            _pObjects = new node<T>[cObjects];
            FreeAll();
        }
```

```
    ~LockFreeFreeList()
    {
        delete[] _pObjects;
    }
    void FreeAll()
    {
        for(uint32_t ix = 0; ix < _cObjects; ++ix)
        {
            _Freelist.Push(&_pObjects[ix]);
        }
    }
    T * NewInstance()
    {
        node<T> * pInstance = _Freelist.Pop();
        return new(&pInstance->value) T;
    }
    void FreeInstance(T * pInstance)
    {
        pInstance->~T();
        _Freelist.Push(reinterpret_cast<node<T> *>(pInstance));
    }
};
```

When a new object is allocated, we pop a node from the stack. Then we use the placement new() operator to set up the v-table and call the object constructor. FreeInstance() simply calls the destructor and pushes the node back on the stack.

If alignment is a concern, the node pointer could be overlapped on top of the object itself. This should not change the algorithm materially, but you may lose some type-safety.

Other Techniques

Under some circumstances, a lock-free freelist may be useful as an STL allocator. While a thread-safe allocator will not necessarily give you a thread-safe STL container, if the allocator is shared with other game subsystems, there may be some savings.

This freelist is good for allocating fixed-size objects, but there is the question of whether we can do general memory management in a lock-free manner. Object lifetime can be managed with techniques in [Michael04b]. [Michael04a] introduces an incredibly complex but lock-free memory allocator.

Conclusion

The basics of lock-free algorithms are easy to understand but terribly difficult to put into practice. Lock-free algorithms are powerful, but they come at a cost in complexity and restricted operations. Used judiciously, these techniques will allow game creators to squeeze the last bit of performance from their hardware.

When constructing a lock-free algorithm, it might be easiest to build on top of simpler lock-free structures, such as stacks and queues. However, when using low-level lock-free techniques, implement most operations on an outside object and CAS it in. CAS is the foundation of the universal primitives required to build lock-free structures. How these primitives are implemented on different processors may vary.

Lock-free algorithms encompass a new and quickly moving field. Almost monthly, new papers are published that improve techniques and change previous conceptions.

The future is very bright. Investigations are being done to add transactional memory and more powerful universal primitives to processors, which will open the door to more flexible algorithms. The C++ standards committee is also looking at proposals for multithreaded extensions [Alexandrescu04]. Undoubtedly, these proposals will include lock-free semantics.

References

[Alexandrescu04] Alexandrescu, Andrei, Hans Boehm, Kevlin Henney, Doug Lea, and Bill Pugh, "Memory Model for Multithreaded C++." C++ Standard Committee, WG21/N1680=J16/04-0120, September 2004.

[Fober05] Fober, Dominique, Yann Orlarey, and Stéphane Letz, "Optimized Lock-Free FIFO Queue Continued." Laboratoire de Recherche en Informatique Musicale, Technical Report TR-050523, 2005.

[Glinker04] Glinker, Paul, "Fight Memory Fragmentation with Templated Freelists." *Game Programming Gems 4,* Charles River Media, 2004.

[Herlihy91] Herlihy, Maurice, "Wait-Free Synchronization." *ACM Transactions on Programming Languages and Systems,* 13(1): pp. 124–149, January 1991.

[Michael96] Michael, Maged and Michael Scott, "Simple, Fast, and Practical Non-Blocking and Blocking Concurrent Queue Algorithms." 15th ACM Symp. on Principles of Distributed Computing, May 1996.

[Michael04a] Michael, Maged, "Scalable Lock-Free Dynamic Memory Allocation." The 2004 ACM SIGPLAN Conference on Programming Language Design (June 2004): pp. 25–46.

[Michael04b] Michael, Maged, "Hazard Pointers: Safe Memory Reclaimation for Lock-Free Objects." *IEEE Transactions on Parallel and Distributed Systems,* 15(6): pp. 491–504, June 2004.

Resources

[Grove04] Groves, Lindsay, Simon Doherty, Mark Moir, and Victor Luchangco. "A Practical Lock-Free Queue Implementation and its Verification." *FM in NZ,* 2004.

[Pugh90] Pugh, William. "Skip Lists: A Probabilistic Alternative to Balanced Trees." *Communications of the ACM,* 33(6):668–676, June 1990.

[Sutter05] Sutter, Herb. "The Free Lunch Is Over: A Fundamental Turn Toward Concurrency in Software." *Dr. Dobbs Journal.* March 2005.

1.2

Utilizing Multicore Processors with OpenMP

Pete Isensee, Microsoft Corporation

pkisensee@msn.com

CPU clock speeds are not improving at the rates we've become accustomed to over the past decade. The reasons are complex and best left to electrical engineers. The reality is that game players will have machines with multiple processors. Taking advantage of these new architectures requires multithreaded approaches to software development. Game developers now face the complex task of multithreading their game engines.

The high-performance computing industry has been dealing with this problem for some time. This industry often needs to schedule dozens and sometimes hundreds of independent processors that have a shared view of memory. One of their solutions is called OpenMP [OpenMP05]. OpenMP is a portable, industry-standard API and programming protocol for C/C++ that supports parallel programming. Many compilers used by game developers are integrating OpenMP technology. This gem provides a brief overview of OpenMP and examines how games can take advantage of this technology to improve performance.

OpenMP Example: Particle System

Suppose your game has a particle system that recalculates the positions of all particles once per frame:

```
for( int i = 0; i < numParticles; ++i )
    UpdateParticles( particle[i] );
```

On a multiprocessor architecture, it would be nice to split up the loop so that each portion is done on a separate hardware thread. For instance, if there are two threads, you'd like to accomplish something like the following:

```
// run half the loop on thread 0:
for( int i = 0; i < numParticles/2; ++i )
    UpdateParticles( particle[i] );
```

```
// run the other half on thread 1:
for( int i = numParticles/2; i < numParticles; ++i )
    UpdateParticles ( particle[i] );
```

OpenMP allows you to accomplish exactly that, using simple compiler #pragmas:

```
#pragma omp parallel for
for( int i = 0; i < numParticles; ++i )
    UpdateParticles ( particle[i] );
```

An OpenMP-enabled compiler generates code that automatically splits this for loop into multiple parallel sections, each of which executes independently. The number of parallel sections used depends on the hardware, the OpenMP runtime, and configuration settings that the programmer has established.

Benefits

There are some compelling features to note about this example. First, the technique is totally platform-independent. If the compiler is not OpenMP-enabled, it will ignore the #pragma. The code will still compile and work. If the compiler is OpenMP-enabled, the compiler will automatically inject the proper parallelizing constructs for the target architecture. If the target platform doesn't have multiple processors or hardware threads, the overhead of OpenMP likely will be very small.

Second, unlike typical multithreaded code, this code is readable. To the casual observer, it's very clear exactly what this loop is supposed to accomplish. Finally, only a single line of code was required to parallelize this task. Even in the best case with other methods, it would require dozens of lines of platform-specific code to make this loop multithreaded.

Clearly, OpenMP has some big benefits. It can even be used for last-minute optimizations because it's easy to add to existing code.

Performance

What kind of performance can you expect out of OpenMP? The answer depends on the compiler, the platform, and the code being parallelized. However, it's useful to examine a couple of cases to get an idea of potential gains. Consider the previous example. Suppose that numParticles is 100,000 and GetNewParticlePos takes a small fixed amount of time (see example code on the CD-ROM).

ON THE CD

Table 1.2.1 shows the performance metrics on two different systems using the Visual Studio® 2005 compiler. The first system is a desktop PC with dual Xeon® processors, each with two hyperthreads. The second system is an Xbox 360, which has three CPUs, each with two hardware threads.

Table 1.2.1   Particle System Gain with OpenMP

Hardware	OpenMP Threads	OpenMP Perf Gain	Windows Threads Perf Gain
Dual-core 2.3-GHz Pentium	4	2.9X	2.9X
Triple-core 3.2-GHz Xbox 360	6	4.6X	4.5X

The second column shows the number of hardware threads used by the OpenMP thread team. The third column shows the gain from parallelizing this loop in OpenMP. The gain was very significant: 3X–5X, depending on the target platform. Not bad for a one-line code change! The last column shows the performance when using standard threading techniques. Writing this particular example using Windows thread calls and synchronization primitives required over 60 lines of code (available on the CD-ROM), not to mention considerable debugging and tuning efforts.

ON THE CD

In the end, the performance gain was virtually the same as using OpenMP directly. In fact, on Xbox 360, the overhead of calling Windows synchronization primitives was higher than using OpenMP, because the OpenMP runtime is tuned to call kernel exports directly. What's clear from this simple experiment is that using OpenMP can provide major benefits with a very small investment.

Example: Collision Detection

Here's a more complex example showing how OpenMP could be used in a typical collision-detection loop. Because each iteration through the loop takes a variable amount of time depending on whether the objects actually intersect, dynamic scheduling is used to tell the compiler to schedule the thread team at runtime rather than simply dividing up the iterations evenly between the threads.

```
bool anyCollisions = false;

#pragma omp parallel for schedule( dynamic )
for( int i = 0; i < numObjects; ++i )
{
    for( int j = 0; j < i; ++j )
    {
        if( SpheresIntersect( obj[i], obj[j] ) &&
            ObjectsIntersect( obj[i], obj[j] ) )
        {
            anyCollisions = true;
        }
    }
}
```

It's more difficult to assess the performance of this example, because it depends on so many variables, including the number of objects intersecting and the time to compute each intersection. For the purposes of this example, we assume numObjects is 1,000; SpheresIntersect takes a small, fixed amount of time; and ObjectsIntersect takes 100 times as long as SpheresIntersect. We also assume a 10% sphere intersection rate and a 1% object intersection rate. Under these circumstances, Table 1.2.2 shows the resulting performance metrics.

Table 1.2.2   Collision Detection Gain with OpenMP

Hardware	OMP Threads	OpenMP Perf Gain
Dual-core 2.3-GHz Pentium	4	3.3X
Triple-core 3.2-GHz Xbox 360	6	5.4X

OpenMP typically adds very little runtime overhead in terms of either size or speed. The Visual Studio OpenMP DLL is only 60K. In this particular example, the performance approached the theoretical maximum. For instance, on Xbox 360, which has six hardware threads, the parallelized version ran 5.4 times faster than the serial version.

Thread Teams

OpenMP is based on a very simple concept: thread teams. Whenever the program enters a parallel section, the thread team goes to work. When the threads have finished their work, the team sits on the bench, waiting for the next parallel section. Because thread creation is somewhat expensive, most OpenMP implementations (including Visual Studio) create the thread team at first usage and then reuse that team throughout the program.

OpenMP allows nested parallel sections. Individual threads can spawn additional thread teams. The number of threads per team is also configurable programmatically. The "OpenMP Threads" heading in the performance tables represents the maximum number of threads in the team on the given platform. This number is programmatically available using the omp_get_max_threads() API.

Function Parallelism

Typically, OpenMP is used for data parallelism—that is, parallelizing loops as in the previous example. However, OpenMP can also be used for function-level parallelism. Consider the following implementation of QuickSort:

```
template< typename T >
void qsort( T* arr, int lo, int hi )
{
    if( hi <= lo )
        return;
    int n = partition( arr, lo, hi );
    qsort( arr, lo, n-1 );
    qsort( arr, n+1, hi );
}
```

Each of the recursive calls to qsort is completely independent of each other, because they operate on separate sections of the array. It's a perfect opportunity to parallelize those calls. One way is to split the independent recursive calls into their own OpenMP parallel sections:

```
#pragma omp parallel sections
{
    #pragma omp section
    qsort( arr, lo, n-1 );
    #pragma omp section
    qsort( arr, n+1, hi );
}
```

Each recursive call to qsort has been placed in its own OpenMP section. To execute the calls in parallel, they're wrapped in braces so that OpenMP knows what portion to run in parallel. On most platforms, however, the overhead of the recursive parallel sections is likely to outweigh the benefits. A better solution is to calculate a handful of partitions, then do a high-level parallelization on the resulting partitions. Given a decent partition function, each partition will be roughly the same size, and the resulting performance gains can be worth the effort.

```
template< typename T >
void qsortParallel( T* arr, int lo, int hi )
{
    if( hi <= lo )
        return;
    int n = partition( arr, lo, hi ); // 1st-level partition
    int m = partition( arr, lo, n-1 ); // 2nd-level partitions
    int q = partition( arr, n+1, hi );

    #pragma omp parallel sections
    {

        #pragma omp section
        qsort( arr, lo, m-1 ); // serial qsort

        #pragma omp section
        qsort( arr, m+1, n-1 );

        #pragma omp section
        qsort( arr, n+1, q-1 );
```

```
                    #pragma omp section
                    qsort( arr, q+1, hi );
            }
    }
```

The performance measurements for this function, given an array of random integers of size 1,000,000, is shown in Table 1.2.3.

Table 1.2.3 qsort Gain Using OpenMP

Hardware	OMP Threads	OpenMP Perf Gain
Dual-core 2.3-GHz Pentium	4	1.5X
Triple-core 3.2-GHz Xbox 360	6	1.4X

Gotchas

Like any technology, OpenMP has its flaws. First, OpenMP is not designed to solve all multithreading issues. Complex multithreading scenarios and synchronization are best done using native thread techniques. If you're writing a new engine, using OpenMP is probably not the way to go.

Second, OpenMP-enabled compilers typically don't check to ensure that your code will parallelize correctly. For instance, suppose we naively try to parallelize the partitioning from the qsort example:

```
// Evil OpenMP code; don't do this
int n, m, q;

#pragma omp parallel sections
{
    #pragma omp section
    n = partition( arr, lo, hi );

    #pragma omp section
    m = partition( arr, lo, n-1 ); // oh no! n probably undefined

    #pragma omp section
    q = partition( arr, n+1, hi ); // oh no! n probably undefined
}
```

Most compilers will compile this code without errors. The problem is that the second and third sections rely on the top section first completing with a valid value for n. OpenMP, however, makes no guarantee about the order in which parallel sections are executed. The results of this snippet are undefined, and it's likely the application will crash. *It's up to the programmer to ensure that OpenMP is only applied to constructs that are not order-dependent.* This applies not only to parallel sections, but also to loops that have order dependencies. Verify that the results given when your code is executed in a parallel environment match the results in a single-threaded environment.

Another gotcha is debugging. When the compiler encounters an OpenMP block, it generates custom code that calls into the OpenMP runtime. Unfortunately, the internals of OpenMP are a black box. This can make debugging devilishly difficult, depending on your compiler and debugger.

Finally, using OpenMP does not guarantee that you will improve performance on multiprocessor systems. Depending on your usage, the runtime overhead of OpenMP can dwarf any benefits. For instance, when `numParticles` in the first example was on the order of 100, performance gains were negligible. As with any optimization technique, profile to verify improvements.

Conclusion

OpenMP is a quick and useful technique for utilizing multicore and hyperthreaded processors. It's easy enough to be used for last-minute optimizations, yet flexible enough to use in cross-platform code. It's not without flaws; but used properly, OpenMP can be an excellent tool in your multithreading arsenal.

Potential applications of OpenMP in games include particle systems, skinning, collision detection, simulations, pathfinding, vertex transforms, signal processing, procedural synthesis, and fractals.

Even though OpenMP has been around for a while, it's a new technology for most game programmers. The best resource is the OpenMP specification, which is available at *http://www.openmp.org*. The specification is concise and surprisingly readable. The next best resource is typically your compiler documentation.

Reference

[OpenMP05] OpenMP C/C++ specification. Available online at *http://www.Openmp.org*.

Resources

[Chandra00] Chandra, Rohit, *Parallel Programming in OpenMP*, Morgan Kaufmann, 2000.

[Gaitlin05] Gaitlin, Kang Su and Pete Isensee, "Writing Multithreaded Applications with OpenMP in Visual Studio 2005," *MSDN Magazine* (Oct 2005): pp. 78–91.

[Isensee05] Isensee, Pete, "Effective Use of OpenMP in Games," Game Developer Conference 2005, available online at *http://www.c,pevents.com/Sessions/GD/EffectiveUse.ppt*.

[Sutter04] Sutter, Herb, "The Free Lunch Is Over: A Fundamental Turn Toward Concurrency in Software," *Dr. Dobb's Journal,* March 2005: pp 16–22, available online at *http://www.gotw.ca/publications/concurrency-ddj.htm*.

1.3

Computer Vision in Games Using the OpenCV Library

Arnau Ramisa, Institut d'Investigació en Intelligència Artificial, CSIC (Spanish Scientific Research Council)

aramisa@iiia.csic.es

Enric Vergara, Departament d'Informàtica Gràfica, Universitat Politècnica de Catalunya

evergara@lsi.upc.edu

Enric Martí, Centre de Visió per Computador—Department de Ciències de la Computació, Universitat Autónoma de Barcelona

enric@cvc.uab.es

Introduction

Digital cameras have become more affordable, and thus have become a common computer peripheral in many homes in the past five years. However, these *eyes* for our computers are used only as videoconferencing tools; we've failed to take advantage of their capacity as input devices. Fortunately, initiatives such as the Sony® EyeToy™ (*http://www.eyetoy.com*) or Camgoo (*http://www.camgoo.com*) are beginning to change this.

Computer Vision in Games

In the emerging computer-vision games market, all the attention is given to games played solely with Webcams, and traditional input devices are ignored. This is reasonable; this new interface involves (or can handle) the player's whole body. However, games played with keyboard, mouse, or game-pad can also benefit from the rich source of information a digital camera can provide. Face identification, tracking, and gesture recognition are rapidly developing areas that are waiting for someone to think of a way to apply them to computer games. This, along with the rapid improvements that digital cameras are experiencing these days, opens up an immense field of possibilities—widening the ways in which humans interact with machines in general, and with computer games in particular.

To illustrate the applicability of computer vision to traditional games, and to introduce the reader to the OpenCV library, we provide a simple example.

Open Computer Vision Library

Intel's Open Computer Vision Library (OpenCV) is a powerful, fast, and easy-to-use collection of algorithms and data types written in C/C++, which were created to aid in the development of real-time computer vision applications [OpenCV04].

Some of the areas covered by the library are: image statistics, mathematic morphology, contour detection and processing, histograms, optical flow, gesture recognition, and many more. The project, which comes with full source code, documentation, and examples, is hosted by Sourceforge.net at *http://www.sourceforge.net/projects/ opencvlibrary.* In addition, there is a very active Web group at Yahoo Groups (*http:// www.yahoo.com*) for sharing information, bugs, experiences, and questions and answers about the library.

One of the main drawbacks of using computer vision in a game is the computational cost associated with it. The OpenCV library is designed to use Intel's Integrated Performance Primitives [IntelIPP], and it is optimized for the Intel® Pentium® processor family. Therefore, simple but robust computer-vision applications should not cause a drop in the game's frame rate.

A Simple Computer-Vision Application for Games

Many games offer the option to discreetly lean around a corner to see if an enemy is on the other side. Unfortunately, the high number of keys that are used in these kind of games make it difficult to fully take advantage of this feature. Using the head to map the same action that is performed in the game increases the involvement of the player. In fact, many times we actually move our heads and bodies when we are immersed in our gameplay. We propose a simple computer-vision algorithm that uses the player's head to activate this action.

The proposed algorithm detects the pixels with skin color in the image to segment the player's head and return a value corresponding to its position in the Webcam's image. The algorithm is based on the OpenCV "camshiftdemo.c" sample program, but is simplified for our purposes.

The algorithm can be summarized as follows: First, we build a histogram from a captured calibration frame to learn the color values of the player's skin. We choose three different areas of consideration for improved fidelity. Then we find the probability for every pixel of the following frames of being part of the player's skin as the histogram value of the bin corresponding to the pixel's color. Using this information, the less-probable pixels are discarded. Finally, the number of filtered pixels in the three considered areas of the image is computed, and the area with the highest value is chosen.

Keeping in mind that we want to use this algorithm in a game, it is a good idea to encapsulate all the code and variables in a class to make it more portable and easier to use. Also, given the characteristics of this application, a singleton class is ideal: We want only one object that uses the camera, and it is useful to have it accessible from anywhere in the project. While the example provided here is presented as a standalone program, an object-oriented implementation can be found on the CD-ROM.

ON THE CD

Prior to writing the program, we should install the OpenCV library and start a project with all the libraries and header files required. A Visual C++ 7 configured workspace can be found on the CD-ROM.

To test the code provided here, a simple C++ project in console mode is adequate. The project configuration is as follows: The OpenCV headers needed are cv.h, cxcore.h, and highgui.h, and the directories where they reside should be added to the project's additional include directories. Also, the cv.lib, cxcore.lib, and highgui.lib must be included as additional libraries, and its directory added as an additional libraries directory. Finally, the files cv.dll, cxcore.dll, and highgui.dll must be copied to the project directory.

In the first lines of the program, we must declare the global variables needed, the function prototypes, and start the main function.

```
#include "cv.h"
#include "cxcore.h"
#include "highgui.h"
#include <iostream>

#define ESC_KEY 27

CvCapture* capture = NULL;
IplImage* image, *frame, *mask, *HSVimage, *h_plane, *s_plane,
    *v_plane, *backProj;
CvHistogram* hist = NULL;
int userPos;
bool flag=true;
```

```
void paintEllipse();
void calcHistogram();
bool detectionLoop();
void showImage();

int main()
{
```

Next we need to set up the Webcam and start capturing frames. The HighGUI library from OpenCV has some nice functions to do this. Capture from a camera is as easy as the following:

```
int numCam=-1;
if( !(capture = cvCaptureFromCAM( numCam )) )
{
    std::cout<<"ERROR: Camera can't be initialized."<<std::endl;
    return -1; //error
}
```

The variable numCam in the previous code sample refers to the identification number of the Webcam we want to use. The typical value is 0, but if there is only one Webcam, or if it does not matter which one to use, we can set it to -1. Once we have initialized our Webcam, we can start capturing frames:

```
//DECLARATIONS BLOCK
cvNamedWindow("WEBCAM",1);

//FIRST CAPTURE BLOCK (INITIALIZATION OF VARIABLES)
frame = cvQueryFrame( capture );
if( !frame ) return false;
image = cvCreateImage( cvGetSize(frame), IPL_DEPTH_8U, 3 );
//CreateImage( Image sizes, pixel depth, channels)
image->origin = frame->origin;

//MAIN LOOP BLOCK
for(;;)
{

    frame = cvQueryFrame( capture );
    if( !frame ) return false;

    cvCopy( frame, image, 0 );

    paintEllipse();

    cvShowImage( "WEBCAM", image );

    char c;
    c = cvWaitKey(10); //Wait 10 ms for a key
    if( c == ESC_KEY )
        break;
```

```
}

calcHistogram();

detectionLoop();

//CLEANUP BLOCK
cvReleaseCapture(&capture);
cvDestroyWindow("WEBCAM");
cvReleaseImage(&image);
cvReleaseHist(&hist);
cvReleaseImage(&HSVimage);
cvReleaseImage(&h_plane);
cvReleaseImage(&v_plane);
cvReleaseImage(&s_plane);
cvReleaseImage(&backProj);

return 0; //no error
}
```

The main loop will take a frame from the camera and display it in the window named WEBCAM we have created until we press the Escape key. The function cvQueryFrame returns a pointer to the last frame from the camera, and we copy it to the image variable, because the returned frame cannot be modified or deleted.

The next thing we want to do is to get a sample of the player's skin to build the histogram against which all of the pixels of the following frames will be compared. To keep things simple and avoid using mouse events or callback functions, we propose a rudimentary method based on centering the user's face in an ellipse printed in the image. A more sophisticated method can be found in the "camshiftdemo.c" sample that comes with OpenCV.

The following function will take care of it:

```
void paintEllipse()
{
    cvEllipse(image,cvPoint(image->width/2,image->height/2),
        cvSize(image->width/6,image->height/3),0,0,
        360,CV_RGB(255,0,0),2);
    cvFlip(image,NULL,1); //flip the image for easiest
        //visualization
}
```

A red ellipse will appear at the center of the image. The player should then place their face inside the ellipse. It is important that no pixel from the background appears within the ellipse, and is also a good idea to keep any hair outside of the ellipse. When the player is ready, the Escape key can be pressed. An example of this process in action is shown in Figure 1.3.1 and Color Plate 1 (top).

FIGURE 1.3.1 *Building the histogram via player skin sampling.*

Now that we have our sample image, we will build the histogram as shown in the following function:

```
void calcHistogram()
{
    //HISTOGRAM CALCULATION BLOCK

    cvFlip(image,NULL,1); //flip the image back to normal
    mask=cvCreateImage(cvGetSize(image),IPL_DEPTH_8U,1);
    cvZero(mask);
    mask->origin = image->origin;
    cvEllipse(mask,cvPoint(image->width/2,image->height/2),
        cvSize((image->width/6)-5,(image->height/3)-5),0,0,
            360,cvScalar(255),CV_FILLED);

    HSVimage=cvCreateImage(cvGetSize(image),IPL_DEPTH_8U,3);
    HSVimage->origin=image->origin;

    cvCvtColor( image, HSVimage, CV_RGB2HSV );

    h_plane=cvCreateImage(cvGetSize(image),IPL_DEPTH_8U,1);
    s_plane=cvCreateImage(cvGetSize(image),IPL_DEPTH_8U,1);
    v_plane=cvCreateImage(cvGetSize(image),IPL_DEPTH_8U,1);
    h_plane->origin = image->origin;
    s_plane->origin = image->origin;
    v_plane->origin = image->origin;

    cvCvtPixToPlane( HSVimage, h_plane, s_plane, v_plane, 0 );
    IplImage* planes[] = { h_plane };
```

```
    int h_bins = 32;
    int hist_size[] = {h_bins};
    float h_ranges[] = {0, 180};
    float* ranges[] = {h_ranges};

    hist=cvCreateHist(1,hist_size,CV_HIST_ARRAY,
        ranges,1);
    cvCalcHist( planes, hist, 0, mask );
}
```

The `mask` image created at the beginning is used to filter out the pixels of the image that we do not want to consider, which are those outside the ellipse.

Next, we change the color representation from RGB to HSV. The HSV color space [HSVspace] can be thought of as a cylinder, and each color is defined by three values: hue, saturation, and value. The *hue* is the color type, which is the dominant wavelength (e.g., red, green, yellow) at an angle from 0° to 360°. (In the OpenCV library, this value is divided by two, to fit in 8 bytes.) The *saturation* is the purity, or the amount of gray that is present in the color; in the color space this is represented by the distance from the center of the cylinder. Finally, the *value* is the brightness of the color, or the height of the color in the cylinder.

The justification for changing the color space is that in the RGB representation, illumination changes affect the three values R (red), G (green), and B (blue), making it impossible to compare with the reference histogram. However, in the HSV color space, the hue is invariant to illumination [Sandeep02] [Sedláček04].

In the following code segment, the three channels of the HSV image are divided into three images of a single plane, one for each color component. Then the histogram is created; the number of bins (`h_bins`) corresponds to the possible values of a dimension in the histogram. Here we are using 32 bins. This means that the H values of the pixels will be sampled in groups of four. Sampling the pixel's values is interesting, because considering a range rather than a concrete value allows us to handle small variations in the hue, and thus enables a more robust representation. `h_ranges` corresponds to the range of values that a pixel can take in the image. In our case, the range is [0,180] (recall that the hue is an angle divided by two to fit it in 8 bytes). Finally, the histogram is allocated and filled with the values of the H plane, filtered with the mask.

Now we can start the detection part:

```
bool detectionLoop()
{
    //DETECTION LOOP BLOCK
    backProj=cvCreateImage( cvGetSize(image), IPL_DEPTH_8U, 1 );
    backProj->origin = frame->origin;
    char c;

    for(;;)
    {
```

```
frame = cvQueryFrame( capture );
if( !frame ) return false;

cvCopy( frame, image, 0 );
cvCvtColor( image, HSVimage, CV_RGB2HSV );
cvCvtPixToPlane( HSVimage, h_plane, s_plane, v_plane, 0 );
IplImage* planes[]={h_plane };

cvZero(backProj);
cvCalcBackProject( planes , backProj, hist );

CvScalar mean=cvAvg( backProj );
cvThreshold( backProj,backProj,floor(mean.val[0]),
    255, CV_THRESH_BINARY );

int vol[3]={0,0,0};
cvSetImageROI( backProj,cvRect(0,image->height/4,
    image->width/3,image->height*3/4) );
vol[0]=cvCountNonZero( backProj );

cvSetImageROI( backProj,cvRect(image->width/3,
    image->height/4,image->width/3,image->height*3/4) );
vol[1]=cvCountNonZero( backProj );

cvSetImageROI( backProj,cvRect(image->width*2/3,
    image->height/4,image->width/3,image->height*3/4) );
vol[2]=cvCountNonZero( backProj );
cvResetImageROI( backProj );


if(vol[0]>vol[1] && vol[0]>vol[2]) userPos=-1;
else if(vol[1]>vol[0] && vol[1]>vol[2]) userPos=0;
else userPos=1;

//VISUALIZATION BLOCK
showImage();
c = cvWaitKey(10);
if( c == ESC_KEY ) break;
if( c == 'b' ) flag=flag?0:1;
    }
}
```

Again, frames are captured using the cvQueryFrame function and copied to image. Next, we convert it to the HSV color space and separate the image into planes. The cvCalcBackProject function assigns to each pixel of backProj the histogram value of the corresponding bin, given the value of the same pixel in the h_plane image. In short, the more frequently the hue value of the pixel appeared in the reference image, the higher the value assigned in the backProj image. To avoid noise and outliers, a threshold is applied to the back projection image to discard all pixels below the average value of backProj. Then we compute the valid pixels in the three defined windows (left, center, and right). Figures 1.3.2 and 1.3.3 illustrate these steps of the process.

FIGURE 1.3.2 *HSV color space image of author's face.*

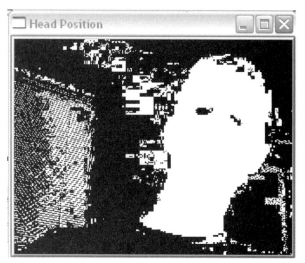

FIGURE 1.3.3 *Back projection image of author's face.*

The pixels in the lowest quarter of the image are not considered to avoid computing the shoulders of the player. Next, the calculated values are sorted, and the highest one is said to correspond to the player's head position.

Finally, to see the output of the algorithm, we call the following function, which produces results similar to those displayed in Figure 1.3.4 and the bottom image of Color Plate 1.

FIGURE 1.3.4   *The player's face is detected.*

```
void showImage()
{
    cvRectangle( image, cvPoint(0,image->height/4),
        cvPoint(image->width/3,image->height), CV_RGB(0,0,255) );
    cvRectangle( image,cvPoint(image->width/3,image->height/4),
        cvPoint(image->width*2/3,image->height), CV_RGB(0,255,0) );
    cvRectangle( image, cvPoint(image-> width*2/3,image>height/4),
        cvPoint(image->width,image->height), CV_RGB(255,0,0) );

    switch(userPos)
    {
    case -1:
        cvCircle( image, cvPoint(50,190),40,
            CV_RGB(0,0,255),CV_FILLED );
    break;
    case 0:
        cvCircle( image, cvPoint(159,190),40,
            CV_RGB(0,255,0),CV_FILLED );
    break;
    case 1:
        cvCircle( image, cvPoint(270,190),40,
            CV_RGB(255,0,0),CV_FILLED );
    break;
    }

    if(flag)
    {
        cvFlip(image,NULL,1); //flip image for easiest
                              //visualization
        cvShowImage("WEBCAM", image);
    }
    else
```

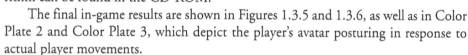

```
    {
        cvFlip(backProj,NULL,1); //flip the image
        cvShowImage("WEBCAM", backProj);
    }
}
```

To see if the player's skin is correctly segmented, the b key can be pressed to switch between the Webcam's image and the back-projected image.

Due to the nature of the method, objects in the scene with a similar color to the player's skin may be misclassified and affect the final result, so it is a good idea to remove them from the scene. Also, abrupt illumination changes can be dangerous.

ON THE CD

When used in old or low-quality cameras, or if the lighting conditions are inadequate, this algorithm has proven to be more robust when building the histogram using both the H and the S planes. The implementation of this variation of the algorithm can be found in the CD-ROM.

The final in-game results are shown in Figures 1.3.5 and 1.3.6, as well as in Color Plate 2 and Color Plate 3, which depict the player's avatar posturing in response to actual player movements.

FIGURE 1.3.5 *The player leans left.*

FIGURE 1.3.6   *The player returns to center.*

The object-oriented version of this algorithm has been used in a third-person action shooter computer game with good results. The game is the final project toward a degree in video game creation, and can be found at *http://www.iua.upf.edu/~evergara*.

Future Work

Even though the results of the presented algorithm are satisfactory in controlled environments, it can be improved in many ways—for example, using optical flow, detecting connected components, using background subtraction, refining the skin-color detection method [Vezhnevets03], or using any of the abundant techniques present in the computer-vision literature. Furthermore, the reader is encouraged to research the world of computer vision and explore ways to extend concepts for playing computer games.

This work is partially supported by the Spanish Ministerio de Ciencia y Tecnología under grant TIC2003-09291. Also, we would like to thank the Audiovisual Institute of the Pompeu Fabra University (*http://www.iua.upf.edu*) for their support.

References

[HSVspace] Wikipedia article on the HSV color space. Available online at *http://www.en.wikipedia.org/wiki/HSB_color_space*.

[IntelIPP] More information about the Intel Integrated Performance Primitives is available online at *http://www.intel.com/cd/software/products/asmo-na/eng/perflib/ipp/index.htm* and *http://www.support.intel.com/support/performancetools/libraries/ipp/sb/cs-010656.htm*.

[OpenCV04] Intel's Open Computer Vision Library beta 4 (August 13, 2004). Available online at *http://www.sourceforge.net/projects/opencvlibrary*.

[Sandeep02] Sandeep, K. and A. N. Rajagopalan, "Human Face Detection in Cluttered Color Images Using Skin Color and Edge Information." 2002. Available online at *http://www.ee.iitb.ac.in/~icvgip/PAPERS/166.pdf*.

[Sedláček04] Marián Sedláček, "Evaluation of RGB and HSV models in Human Faces Detection." 2004. Available online at *http://www.cg.tuwien.ac.at/student work/CESCG/CESCG-2004/web/Sedlacek-Marian*.

[Vezhnevets03] Vezhnevets, V., V. Sazonov, and A. Andreeva, "A survey on pixel-based skin color detection techniques." Graphicon-2003, Moscow, 2003.

1.4

Geographic Grid Registration of Game Objects

Roger Smith, Modelbenders, LLC

gpg@modelbenders.com

Introduction

Most game objects are interested in two questions: "Whom can I see?" and "Whom can I shoot?" When these questions are asked by a game-controlled object (an AI or NPC), they present the problem of determining which objects are within range. Unfortunately, this can sometimes mean searching through the entire list of objects in the game and subjecting each to a Line-of-Sight (LOS) or range check. This is hugely inefficient and completely unnecessary.

In virtual worlds, the primary organizing characteristic for interactions between objects is geographic location. Objects tend to interact with those in close proximity; this includes sensor detection, weapon engagement, communication, and the exchange of supplies.

Game programmers must manage lists of dynamic (i.e., living, breathing, moving) objects so as to retain the geographic relationships between them. The commonly used linked lists and tree structures do not retain this information. A linked list usually manages all of the objects, but does so in a nearly generic manner, so that the order of the list does not contain any useful information. Trees may have some useful information embedded in the data structure, including geographic location. However, implementations like quadtrees are generally applied to static terrain rather than dynamic objects. This gem describes a simple method for managing object lists using geographic grids as a means of significantly reducing the computational work required for range and line-of-sight decisions. Managing objects geographically can reduce the number of line-of-sight and other related geographic checks on a large battlefield from one million or more to a few dozen.

Some games enjoy a naturally occurring grid system for managing their objects. When the game level represents the inside of a dungeon, building, or space station, the world is naturally divided into rooms. A *portal engine* will take advantage of this to identify near objects according to the room where they are located. Visible or inter-actable objects exist only in the local room or an adjacent room with a portal leading to it. Though the game may actually contain several hundred objects, only two or three may be in the room with the object that is looking for targets. This significantly reduces the amount of work required to identify objects with which to interact.

Unfortunately, not all games are so nicely structured. Large, open battlefields or spacefields can contain hundreds or even thousands of objects. When there are no walls, mountains, or forests to separate them, all objects effectively exist in the same room. This presents a difficult computational problem for an AI agent (or any other game sys-tem) that is trying to identify the closest or most desirable targets. Svarovsky described this problem very briefly in the first volume of *Game Programming Gems* [Svarovsky00]. In this gem we explore it more deeply, explain why these open spaces are so difficult to deal with, and present a relatively simple solution that has been implemented in a num-ber of simulations. Pritchard also explored tile-based LOS in *Game Programming Gems 2* [Pritchard01]; but he limited his discussion to detectability from the perspective of the human player, leaving the actual detection outcome to the graphic-rendering engine and the human eye. This gem includes complete detection decisions for AI agents who rely on range and LOS calculations entirely in the game engine, and of course extends this to use for any system in the game that needs to make similar queries.

Quadtrees and Octrees

Graphics programmers are very familiar with quadtrees. These structures nicely divide a two-dimensional space into four smaller *child* spaces. This process can be continued from generation to generation until the entire 2D space is divided into small squares that contain the terrain data (see Figure 1.4.1). A sensor-viewing frustum overlays a

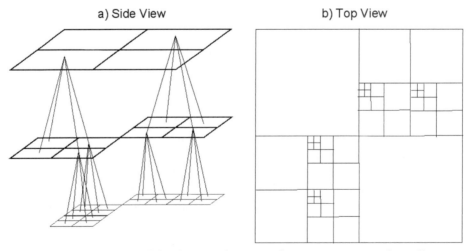

FIGURE 1.4.1   *Quadtrees subdivide a two-dimensional space into increasingly smaller areas.*

specific subset of these squares and identifies which grids need to be drawn. Therefore, it is not necessary for computer hardware to render the entire terrain database when only a fraction of it is viewable by a sensor [Ferraris01].

Octrees implement this same idea in three-dimensional space [Kelleghan97]. When the world cannot be simplified into a 2D surface, the subdivision of a 3D world results in eight adjacent spaces, creating data trees with eight children rather than four (see Figure 1.4.2).

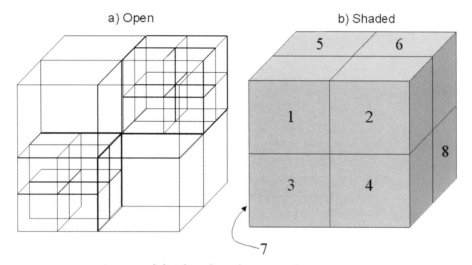

FIGURE 1.4.2   *Octrees subdivide a three-dimensional area into smaller volumes.*

Because terrain, buildings, rivers, and forests usually reside at fixed geographic locations, managing them in a geographic grid has always been a natural approach. Quadtrees and octrees can rapidly identify the pieces of the terrain that need to be drawn for a specific scene.

There is a close parallel to this approach for optimizing object-to-object detection for spaceships, trolls, and soldiers—objects that are moving around in the game world.

Object Organization

In this gem, object grid registration refers to the need to manage dynamically moving objects within the same type of grid that is used for terrain data. In some cases, these objects may actually use the very same grid system.

Dynamic objects are constantly changing their locations as well as other state variables. Individuals and groups of soldiers move from one position to another—advancing and retreating from the enemy. Therefore, from one moment to the next, the list of objects that can be seen or engaged is changing. In a brute-force approach to this problem, the game engine will constantly recalculate LOS or range for every pair of objects in the game. As long as the number of objects is relatively small, this approach can be tolerated. For example, if the world contains only 10 objects fighting each other, then the number of LOS calculations is merely 90—each of the 10 objects calculates LOS to the remaining 9 objects (see Figure 1.4.3). This is usually referred to as an *order n-squared problem,* or $O(n^2)$. Though the solution is complete in terms of performance and scalability, it is the worst possible approach. If the number of objects increases to 100, the number of range calculations jumps to almost 10,000. If there are 1,000 objects in the game, calculations jump to nearly 1 million.

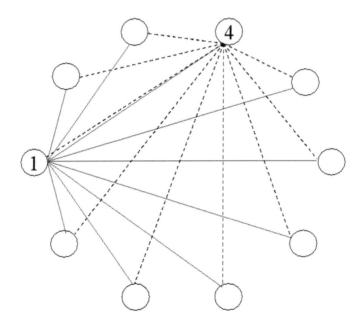

Brute Force = 10 objects * 9 detections = 90 computations

Pair Memory = 9+8+7+6+5+4+3+2+1+0 = 45 computations

FIGURE 1.4.3   *Brute-force object-to-object detection is an order n-squared problem.*

One simple improvement is to implement a pairing scheme in which the range calculated from Object 1 to Object 4 is used immediately to determine the visibility or sensor detection from Object 1 to Object 4, and from Object 4 back to Object 1. This means that objects only need to calculate range for the other objects that are later than them in the list of objects. This cuts the number of ranges calculated in half, as shown in Figure 1.4.3.

These calculations may be performed at each time step if there is not some other mechanism at work. Additional filters are often used to mitigate this problem, such as keeping track of the last time that an object changed position in order to avoid unnecessarily recalculating the range between the same two positions. But this requires retaining some information about the previous range calculation between specific pairs of objects and falls short of significantly reducing the complexity of the problem.

Line-of-sight is a geographic question. Arriving at an efficient solution requires a geographic approach to the problem, just as quadtrees have been used for static terrain information.

Grid Registration

Moving objects must be registered into a geographic grid as they change locations. This means calculating a grid location in addition to their more universal position. As an object moves from one grid square to another—just as a chess piece changes grid positions—it must be registered into the new grid and unregistered from the old grid, as illustrated in Figure 1.4.4. The figure illustrates two lists, one for Grid(1,5) and another for Grid(1,8). At time 1234, both of these grids contain two objects. However, at time 1235, Object 1 (O1) has moved to a new position. Therefore, the grid registration process must change O1's registration to Grid(3,6). The additional computational overhead associated with managing the grid location is much smaller than the computations required to perform all of the range computations described previously. One part of this savings is due to the simpler problem of determining grid location versus the more complex calculation of range or LOS. However, a far greater portion of the savings is due to the dramatically reduced number of operations that have to be performed.

Object grid registration is an order n problem—$O(n)$. LOS is an $O(n^2)$ problem. Therefore, a game that has 100 objects in it will require at most 100 grid registrations during each time step. Without the grid (and disregarding other detection filters), these 100 objects would require nearly 10,000 range calculations at each time step. So grid registration exchanges nearly 10,000 range calculations for 100 simpler registration operations.

Weapon or Sensor Footprint Overlay

Grid registration does not entirely eliminate range or LOS calculations. It simply limits it to a much smaller number of objects. As shown in Figure 1.4.5, the sensor of the searching object overlays a small number of the grids. These grids can be identified in a number of ways, as described in other articles on quadtrees and terrain database management [Frisken03]. Once this list of grid squares is identified, only objects that are registered within these grids need to be considered for detection or engagement. However, simply because an object is registered into one of these grids, there is no guarantee that the object also falls into the sensor footprint. In Figure 1.4.5, it is clear

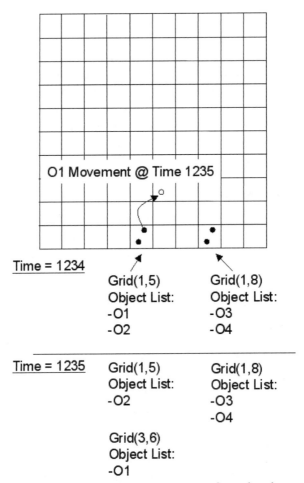

FIGURE 1.4.4   *Grid registration is performed each time an object's updated position is in a new grid square.*

that in many cases the sensor does not cover all of a grid square. Objects in the partially covered grids may not actually be within range of the sensor and may need to be excluded from the list of potentially detectable or engageable objects. Therefore, a separate range or LOS calculation must still be done for the much smaller group of objects found in these grids.

The programmer can implement the sensor footprint overlay algorithm such that it clearly differentiates the grid squares that are entirely within the sensor footprint from those that are only partially inside. For some games, this can entirely eliminate the need for a range or LOS calculation for objects in grid squares that are entirely contained in the sensor footprint [Pritchard01]. However, for games where 3D terrain is an essential part of the visibility decision of AIs or NPCs, it will remain necessary to perform a sep-

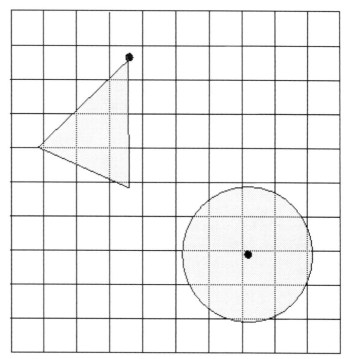

FIGURE 1.4.5   *Sensor footprints overlay the grid and identify which squares are potentially in the detection field of the sensor.*

arate LOS calculation for each object found in the contained grid squares. Although the grid system can identify which objects are within range of the sensor, it cannot determine whether there is a clear LOS vector from the sensor, through the terrain and obstacles, to the selected object.

Exaggerating the Footprint

Our goal is to minimize the number of objects that must be considered to be viewable by the querying system. However, in doing this, we must also be careful that we do not inappropriately eliminate moving objects that are on the edge of the sensor footprint. In most games, an object moves from point A to point B along a constant vector during a single time step. It is possible for the movement of an object to carry it across the edge of the sensor footprint such that it does not exist within that footprint during either of the two discrete times at which calculations are performed (see Figure 1.4.6a).

To capture these cases, the size of the footprint is usually exaggerated slightly. This allows the sensor to grab objects in grids that are immediately adjacent to the footprint, and which may potentially move across its edge. The size of the footprint exaggeration is determined heuristically based on the size of the grid squares, the maximum speed of game objects, and the length of the time step. The exaggeration must incorporate all grid squares for which an object can reach the edge of the footprint in a single time step. In games where movement precedes detection, the exaggeration will find the objects at their ending position and will use reverse dead-reckoning to calculate the path followed to reach that ending position, and determine whether that path crossed the sensor footprint.

There are often two or three instances of footprint exaggeration. The first is an exaggeration of the size of the footprint, as was just described. The second is the fact that the grid system is composed of squares, and the footprint may be shaped like a wedge or a circle. The process of *squaring the circle* brings in area that is not really within the footprint. Finally, the *squared circle* will not necessarily fall exactly along grid boundaries, so it is further exaggerated to include all of the area of the *squared-in* grid squares (see Figure 1.4.6b).

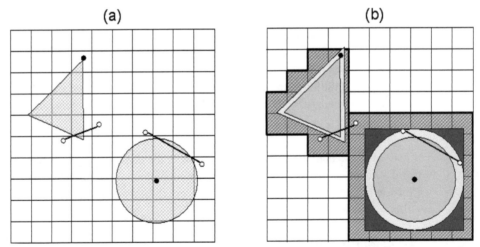

FIGURE 1.4.6   *Footprint exaggeration captures objects whose movement vector crosses the edge of the sensor footprint in a single time step.*

Conclusion

The method described in this gem is not complex. Once described, it seems to be an obvious approach to creating a more scalable detection algorithm. However, the number of projects that continue to rediscover this approach to the problem, and other variations of it, is scandalously high. It is captured here in an attempt to save future programmers from repeating the work of the past.

The goal is to manage dynamic object locations in a manner that is similar to that used for static terrain objects. These objects enter and leave the game, change positions frequently, and sometimes straddle two or more grid squares. All of these actions make the management of these objects more challenging, but the payoff in terms of saved processing time far exceeds the cost of implementing geographic grids to reduce LOS and range calculations, which are some of the most repetitive calculations in a game.

References

[Ferraris01] Ferraris, Jonathan, "Quadtrees." GameDev.net. January 2001. Available online at *http://www.gamedev.net/reference/articles/article1303.asp.*

[Frisken03] Frisken, S. and R. Perry, "Simple and Efficient Traversal Methods for Quadtrees and Octrees." *Journal of Graphics Tools,* Vol. 7, Issue 3. May 2003.

[Kelleghan97] Kelleghan, M., "Octree Partitioning Techniques." *Game Developer,* July 1997.

[Pritchard01] Pritchard, M., "A High-Performance Tile-Based Line-of-Sight and Search System." *Game Programming Gems 2,* Charles River Media, 2001.

[Svarovsky00] Svarovsky, Jan, "Multi-Resolution Maps for Interaction Detection." *Game Programming Gems,* Charles River Media, 2000.

1.5

BSP Techniques

Octavian Marius Chincisan, Freelancer

mariuss@rogers.com

ON THE CD

This gem presents a fully functional Binary Space Partition (BSP) compiler. It incorporates new algorithms for automatic portal generation and potentially visible set computation currently used in the Getic 3D® Editor and BSP compiler (*www.zalsoft.com*). This gem also comes with a full implementation of the BSP compiler on the accompanying CD-ROM.

What is a BSP and Why a BSP?

A BSP technique hierarchically partitions a 3D space into convex subspaces. Partitioning is performed by a given plane, which divides a given space into two subspaces that are roughly equal in size. Each subspace is then divided by a given plane, which creates two smaller subspaces. The partitioning process on each subspace continues until a pre-established condition is met.

BSP styles can be different, depending on how partitioning is performed and how the geometry is stored in the BSP. The algorithms explored in this gem can be used to develop different styles, such as the K-D tree, AABB tree, and beam tree. Originally, a BSP was used to sort back-to-front rendered polygons, and back-to-front sorting is still necessary, even with current video card technology. First, the use of translucent faces and blended objects in a game scene forces the engine to sort the polygons in back-to-front order to perform correct blending operations in the frame buffer. Second, collision detection is faster when performed against a BSP versus the whole scene. This is demonstrated in the collision-detection implementation which includes object-to-scene intersection, dynamic lighting, dynamic shadowing, fogging, corona effects, network traffic visibility zones, and others.

In the second part of this gem, the computation of potentially visible sets on a solid-leaf type of BSP is explored. Potentially visible sets provide an increase in performance and frame rate by eliminating unseen geometry from processing in a simple Boolean flag test. Some BSP techniques are examined in the following sections.

Node-Based BSP

A BSP is a binary tree, which is defined as a structure that stores two links in each node to children of the same type. Each node also stores polygons from the same scene. Hence, it is called a node-based BSP. The following code illustrates a node structure. Each node instance stores front and back node pointers, along with scene geometry, which are the polygons and the splitter plane.

```
NODE{ NODE front, back, parent
     List polygons;
     Plane plane;
};
```

The back node and front node are called the two children nodes. The node instances are linked to one another by each front and back node, until the whole partitioned space geometry is represented. The node-based BSP algorithm is illustrated in the following listing, and the whole routine can be found in the source code on the CD-ROM.

ON THE CD

```
Node BuildBSP(List polygons, Node& node)
{
    if(polygons.IsEmpty())
        return null;
    List front_list,back_list;
    Polygon polygon = Pick_Splitter_AndRemove(polygons);
    node.plane = polygon.GetPlane();
    node.polygons.Add(polygon);
    for_each (polygon in polygons)
    {
        if(polygon is on front of node.plane)
            front_list.Add(polygon);
        else if(polygon is on back of node.plane)
            back_list.Add(polygon);
        // split the polygon with the splitter plane
        // and add the polygon fragments accordingly
        else if (polygon is not coplanar with node.plane)
        {
            Polygon front_polygon, back_polygon;
            SplitPolygon(polygon, &front_polygon,
            &back_polygon);
            back_list.Add(back_polygon);
            front_list.Add(front_polygon);
        }

        // add all coplanar polygons into this node
        else
            node.polygons.Add(polygon);

    }
    BuildBSP(front_list, node.front);
    BuildBSP(back_list, node.back);
}
```

For a more detailed explanation, the algorithm is separated into different steps and demonstrated, starting with Figures 1.5.1 and 1.5.2:

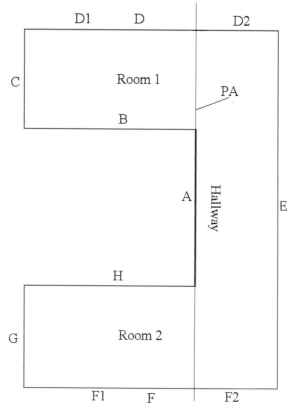

FIGURE 1.5.1 *A sample scene to be processed.*

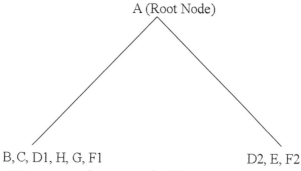

FIGURE 1.5.2 *Step one in the BSP process.*

Polygons A to H define a simple scene with two rooms and a hallway. Before starting, a function must be implemented for picking a partition plane. The function must do two things: keep the tree balanced, and keep the polygon count as close as possible to that of the initial scene (in this case, eight polygons). If a pre-established ratio balance of front/back polygons versus split polygons is reached, then it returns to the potential partition plane. The formula for the ratio balance in typical BSP compilers is usually as follows:

```
abs(front_count-back_count)+(both*balance_vs_cuts);
```

The first splitter A's plane is chosen. This yields the first glimpse of the BSP, as we saw in Figure 1.5.2. From back-list polygons B, C, D1, H, G, and F1, B's plane is chosen to be the next splitter; and from front-list polygons D2, E, and F2, E's plane is chosen to be the splitter.

After partitioning all polygons from the front and back spaces against B on the back side and E on the front side, the result is a BSP as shown in Figure 1.5.3. The next step is to partition all of the polygons. Partitioning occurs until there are no polygons left in both subspaces. At this stage, all polygons are stored in BSP nodes. All the intermediate steps in building the BSP are shown in Figures 1.5.3 through 1.5.5.

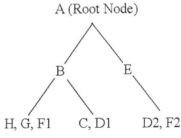

FIGURE 1.5.3   *BSP step two.*

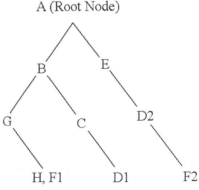

FIGURE 1.5.4   *BSP step three.*

A (Root Node)

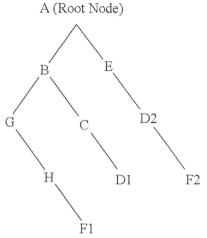

FIGURE 1.5.5 *The complete BSP.*

Rendering a Node-Based BSP

After partitioning, rendering is an easy process. The camera (point of view) is classified against the splitting node's plane, starting from the root node, and continuing to
each and every single node. If the camera is on one side of the splitting node, then the
other side of the node is rendered. Next, the current node and current side is rendered. The simplified rendering code is listed in following pseudo code:

```
void Render(Point camera_position,
    NODE& node=ROOT_NODE)
{
    //camera is on front of the node's plane
    if(Distance(camera_ position, node.plane)<0)
    {
        Render(camera_position, node.front) //render front
        Render(node.polys);                 //render current
        Render(camera_position, node.back)  //render back
    }

    //camera is on back of the node's plane
    else
    {
        Render(camera_position, node.back)  //render back
        Render(node.polys);                 //render current
        Render(camera_position, node.front) //render front
    }
}
```

Node-Based BSP (No Split)

Another approach for a node BSP is to avoid the polygon cut during the partitioning. This is performed by eliminating the cuttings done on the D and F polygons; instead, the polygons are added to both lists. The tree shown in Figure 1.5.6 is the result of such a procedure (Figure 1.5.7 shows the area or our scene).

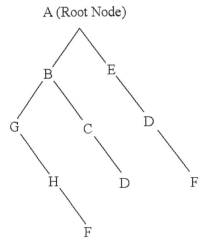

FIGURE 1.5.6   *BPS with no split.*

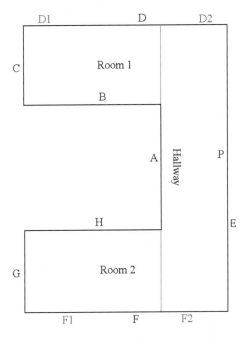

FIGURE 1.5.7   *The walking area of the scene.*

According to the BSP graph in Figure 1.5.6, polygons D and F are found in more than one node. The solution is to increment a counter every time the rendering function is called. Every rendered polygon will be flagged with this counter. If a polygon with the current frame counter is found, it is simply ignored.

Convex Leafy BSP

As the name implies, a leafy BSP stores the polygons in leaf nodes. Each leaf will define a convex region, meaning that they do not fall by bending in an edge formed by two polygons. This allows the BSP to be represented as a graph, where the leaves are connected by portals. This graph representation of the BSP will make the Potentially Visible Set (PVS) calculation possible. Before going into the example scene, we review the leafy BSP construction briefly described in the following pseudo code:

```
Node BuildSolidleafBSP(List polygons, Node& node)
{
    List front_list, back_list;

    // Pick a splitter from polygons. Avoid picking a
    // polygon that was already flagged as a splitter
    Polygon polygon = Pick_Splitter(polygons);

    // Flag the polygon being a splitter
    FlagAsSplitter(polygon);
    front_list.Add(polygon);        // Add it to front list
    node.plane = polygon.GetPlane(); // Store it in the node

    for_each (polygon in polygons)
    {
        // partition all the polygons against the splitter
        if(polygon is on front of node.plane)
            front_list.Add(polygon);
        else if(polygon is on back of node.plane)
            back_list.Add(polygon);

        //Split the polygon with the splitter plane
        else if (polygon is not coplanar with node.plane)
        {
            Polygon front_polygon, back_polygon;
            SplitPolygon(polygon, &front_polygon,
                &back_polygon);
            back_list.Add(back_polygon);
            front_list.Add(front_polygon);
        }
        else if(polygon is coplanar with node.plane)
        {
            if(polygon is facing as node.plane)
                front_list.Add(front_polygon);
            else
                back_list.Add(back_polygon);
        }
    }
```

```
    if(IsConvex(front_list) or
        AllPolygonsAreSPlitters(front_list))
    {
        // Front node is a leaf storing all the polygons
        // They form a convex space bordered by leaf polygons
        node.front.polygons = front_list;
    }
    else
        // Continue with the partitioning process
        BuildBSP(front_list, node.front);

    If(IsEmpty(back_list))
    {
        // Back leaf is null indicating a solid space
        node.back = 0;
    }
    else
    {
        // Continue with the partitioning process
        BuildBSP(back_list, node.back);
    }
}
```

The resulting solid, leafy BSP tree that we will see in Figure 1.5.10 was built using the same splitters as in the previous node tree. Here is the step-by-step build and explanation of the leafy BSP in the scene in Figure 1.5.1: The splitter plane is PA, and the polygon on which it was selected is flagged as a splitter. D and F polygons are being cut in D1 and D2, and F1 and F2, respectively. D and F fragments are added according to their relative positions in respect to the splitter. D2 and F2 go to the front list, and D1 and F1 go to the back list.

The first step in BSP tree construction is shown in Figure 1.5.8. Later, a test for convexity is run on the front list. This process is performed by partitioning all polygons from the front list against one another. If partition iterations yield any other polygon that is in front of any other polygon, they delimit a convex region. The front list polygons—D2, E, A, and F2—are in front of each other; therefore they define a convex region. Remember that all faces are inward. In this case, the node being processed is flagged as a leaf, and all the polygons are added to it. The back list consisted of polygons D1, C, B, H, G, and F1; B's plane PB is chosen to be the next splitter. All the polygons are partitioned in respect to this splitter. Figure 1.5.9 shows the next step in our BSP construction.

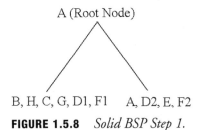

A (Root Node)

B, H, C, G, D1, F1   A, D2, E, F2

FIGURE 1.5.8   *Solid BSP Step 1.*

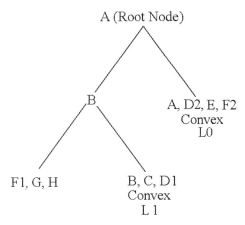

FIGURE 1.5.9   *Solid BSP Step 2.*

The front list of polygons is tested for convexity, and the back list is used to continue the BSP-partitioning process. On the front list, B, C, and D1 are in front of each other. The next step is to build a leaf-type node, where all of the polygons are added. The BSP tree at this stage is shown in Figure 1.5.9. Polygon G's plane is chosen as the next splitter on the back list. Continuing on yields the final BSP tree graph, as shown in Figure 1.5.10.

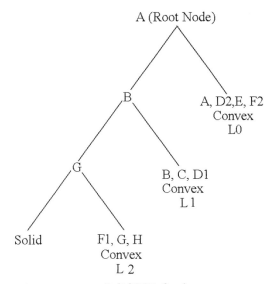

FIGURE 1.5.10   *Solid BSP final.*

All of the scene polygons have been pushed as convex regions on front of the BSP nodes. These regions are called empty or convex leaves. There is only solid space (Figure 1.5.10) on the back nodes. The walkable area will always be inside of the BSP in front of the F, G, and H polygons (leaf L2), B, C, and D polygons (leaf L1), and A, D2, E, and F2 polygons (leaf L0), as we saw in Figure 1.5.7.

Convex, Leafy BSP Portal Generation

Portal generation is an intermediate step for automatic PVS computation and portal information for portal-based engines. Portals are virtual polygons built between two adjacent empty leaves. These can also be seen as passageways between two convex regions. An automatic portal-generation algorithm involves two simple steps. (See [Getic], 3D Editor development.) The algorithm is much simpler and faster than any other known algorithm for automatic portal generation. The algorithm is as follows:

```
//find all leaves pairs that are touching together
void FindPairTouchingLeaves()
{
    for_each(leaf1 in leaves)
    {
        for_each(leaf2 in leaves)
        {
            if(leaf1==leaf2) continue;
            if(leaf1.box.Touches(leaf2.box))
              {
            // find common parent of both leaves and build
            // there a huge polygon. This the initial
            // portal.
            Node node = FindCommonParent((Node)leaf1,
                (Node)leaf2);
                Portal portal = CalculateInitialPortal(node);

                // clip initial portal with both leaf sides
                ClipWithLeavesides(leaf1, portal);
                ClipWithleavesides(leaf2, portal);

                // remaining polygon are valid portals
                listBSP_tree.Portals.Add(portal);
            }
        }
    }
}
```

ON THE CD The detailed implementation of portal generation can be found in the accompanying CD-ROM source code.

Two pairs of touching leaves are found after running the algorithm on the BSP (Figure 1.5.7)—leaf L0 with leaf L1, and leaf L0 with leaf L2. The BSP happens to only have one common node (root node) for both pairs of leaves, as shown in Figure 1.5.11. Initial portal PrA, shown in Figure 1.5.12, is built on the root node's plane.

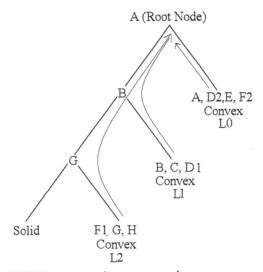

FIGURE 1.5.11   *A common node.*

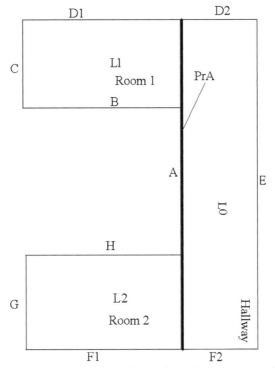

FIGURE 1.5.12   *Initial portal on the common node.*

To find the portal P1 lying between leaf L0 and leaf L1 (Figure 1.5.13), clip the initial portal PrA against leaf L1 and against leaf L0 polygons. To find portal P2 lying between leaf L0 and leaf L2 (Figure 1.5.13), clip initial portal PrA against leaf L2 and against leaf L0 polygons. This completes portal determination. The portal P1 separates leaf L1 (Room 1) by leaf L0 (Hallway), and the portal P2 separates leaf L2 (Room 2) by leaf L0 (Hallway).

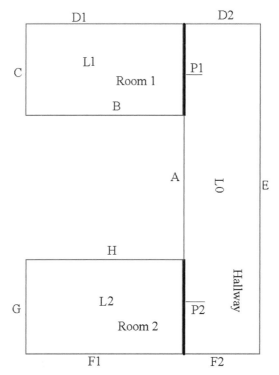

FIGURE 1.5.13   *The resulting valid portals.*

Convex, Leafy BSP Potentially Visible Sets

To describe the algorithm for convex leafy BSP PVS, consider the scene where two extra rooms are added (Figure 1.5.14). Adding additional rooms creates a more complex scene, where a more realistic PVS can be created. The new rooms form two additional leaves (leaf L3 and leaf L4), and of course another two portals (portal P3 and portal P4). The first step in the PVS calculation is to duplicate all the portals in the BSP. In order to accomplish this, all the portals are duplicated by making a straight copy and then reversing the vertices. This leads to duplicate portals sharing the same space but facing in opposite directions (Figure 1.5.14).

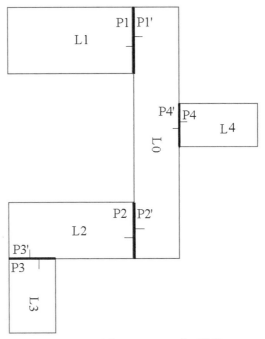

FIGURE 1.5.14 *The new scene for PVS.*

The second step is to attach each portal to the leaf on its back. This way, the leaf automatically becomes the portal's owner. Each portal now is owned by a leaf. Leaf L0 owns portal P1, P4, and P2; leaf L1 owns portal P1'; leaf 2 owns portal P2' and P3; leaf L3 owns portal P3'; and leaf L4 owns portal P4'. The preparation for PVS calculation is now complete. A leaf can now see what its own portals can see.

Leaf L4 can see what portal P4 can see. For example, imagine that leaf L4 spreads full light in all directions through its portal (Figure 1.5.15). If the light touches any other portal in the BSP, then it means that leaf L4 can see the touched portals' owner leaves, which in our case are leaf L2 and leaf L1. Leaf L4 can definitely not see portal P3, because it is in a shadow. Therefore, portal P3's owner is leaf L3.

The goal in this section is to use a simple algorithm that will produce 80%–95% PVS-accurate data. This algorithm is based on portal-to-portal relative position and orientation visibility (Figure 1.5.16) combined with portal-to-portal line-of-sight visibility (Figure 1.5.17). In Figure 1.5.16, portal P1 can never see portal P2, because portal P2 is completely in front of portal P1, and they are not facing one another. The reverse is also true—portal P3 cannot see portal P1 because portal P1 is completely behind portal P3, and they are not facing each other. Additionally, portal P3 can never see portal P4, regardless of its orientation, because they are in the same plane. However, portal P4 can see portal P1 because they are in front of each other, and they are also facing one another.

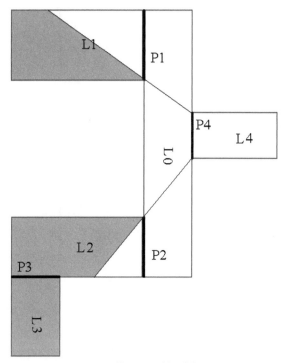

FIGURE 1.5.15   *Full view of leaf four (L4).*

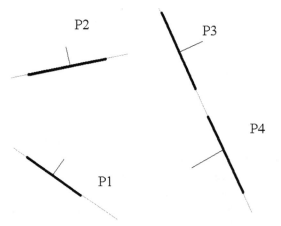

FIGURE 1.5.16   *Portal-to-portal orientation.*

Now that the basics have been covered, the line-of-sight visibility check can be done. In Figure 1.5.17, the task is to find at least one segment fired from any point of a portal to any point of a second portal, which does not collide with the BSP (solid space). If at least one such segment is found, the two portals can then see each other.

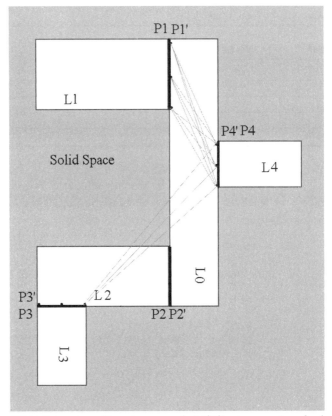

FIGURE 1.5.17 *Portal-to-portal visibility intersection check.*

If the portals can see each other, the owner leaves see each other, too. In real life, not all segments can be fired from one portal area to another portal area because our algorithm would be incredibly slow. Therefore, only a few chosen segments can be fired and equally spread over a portal's area (Figure 1.5.17).

Figure 1.5.17 shows the visibility test used between portal P1' and portal P4', and between portal P3' and portal P4'. Portal-to-portal intersection tests lead to the following results: Portal P1 can see portal P4 because at least one segment between them did not hit the BSP. Portal P3 cannot see portal P4 because none of the segments fired from portal P3 hit portal P4.

PVS data is allocated as follows: Five visibility flags are allocated for each leaf. These flags represent the PVS per each leaf. If leaf L1 can see leaf L2, then the visibility flag of leaf L1 for leaf L2 is set to 1. In the sample, leaf L4 can see leaf L1, L2, and L0, because leaf L4's portal P4' can see leaf L1's portal, leaf L2's portal P2', and leaf L0's portal P4. The result of these repeated procedures is shown in Table 1.5.1.

Table 1.5.1 PVS, Leaf by Leaf

Leaf	Vis L0	Vis L1	Vis L2	Vis L3	Vis L4
0	1	1	1	1	1
1	1	1	0	0	1
2	1	0	1	1	1
3	1	0	1	1	0
4	1	1	1	0	1

The final PVS set is built by placing all data in one chunk of memory and then linking the leaves to their PVS sets. Rendering by PVS is usually as shown in following pseudo code:

```
void Render(Point camera_pos)
{
    leaf current_leaf = Get_Camera_Curent_leaf(camera_pos,
        ROOT_NODE);
    for_each(leaf in leaves)
    {
        BYTE* pPvs = leaf.pPVS;
        If(pPvs[current_leaf.leaf_index])
            Render_leaf(leaf);
    }
}
```

The Get_Camera_Curent_leaf() function classifies the camera against the BSP until it reaches the current leaf. From the current leaf, all other leaves are tested for a PVS value to decide whether or not their polygons will be rendered. A closer look at the PVS-rendering algorithm reveals that back-to-front rendering was completely ignored, similar to the node BSP technique. This approach is not always desirable, even though the solid-leaf BSP painting routines can perform classic back-to-front painting. The tree can be walked from the given leaf and flag all nodes with the visibility flag. This technique extends the PVS from the leaf level up to big clusters of leaves, helping to reject, by PVS, whole branches of the BSP.

Each time the camera moves from one leaf to another, it performs the following: Increment a visibility counter and flag all of the PVS leaves of the current leaf with the current value of the visibility counter. Climb from each leaf in the PVS up into the BSP tree to reach the root node. While climbing up, flag all the nodes encountered with the current visibility counter. When a previously flagged node is found while traversing to a new PVS leaf, stop climbing. This way, the PVS has been extended from the leaf level to entire BSP branches. There is no need to reflag all visible leaves or to reflag the parent nodes as long the position hovers in one leaf. This gives a good performance boost to the BSP rendering.

PVS Compression

The popular bitwise PVS formula from the *Quake*® engine is given here [Abrash97]:

```
Pvs[i_>>3] & (1<<(i_&7)) or Pvs[i/8] & (1<<(i&7))
    // For unsigned char aligned PVS buffer and

Pvs[i_>>5] & (1<<(i_&31)) or Pvs[i/32] & (1<<(i&31))
    //For unsigned long aligned PVS buffer
```

Above is a simple PVS bit test for leaf i, which is similar to Pvs[i] in the byte-by-byte version. The PVS was already compressed eight times. Instead of using 25 bytes, for safety it is recommended to use 25/8, rounded up to the closest byte:

```
PvsSz = ( (sz + 7) / 8 );
```

This scene consists of five leaves yielding one byte per leaf. After calculating the size, allocate a continuous buffer to store the PVS data, and make each leaf remember its PVS index in the continuous PVS buffer.

Next, we show how to store a bit at a given offset in the PVS buffer. The first part of the bitwise PVS formula shows the byte offset (i/8), and the second part shows the bit within the byte. So for an i between 0 and 8 on the left side, the formula yields Pvs[0]; an i between 8 and 16 yields Pvs[2], and so on.

The second part of the bitwise PVS formula, (1<<i&7) rotates our bit up to its index from left to right in within the byte. The i&7 is i modulo 7 and holds the range within 0–7. The Pvs [leaf/8]&(1<<leaf&7) for five leaves always points to the first byte (one per leaf). Rather than test the Pvs for leaf i by the byte index, test it by checking the bit at index i and apply the bit-oriented PVS formula. Finally, combine back-to-front rendering, potentially visible sets, and frustum culling in one final painting routine.

```
// Back to Front Rendering of PVS and Frustum
void RenderBack2Front(Vertex camera_pos, NODE node)
{
    leaf current_leaf = Get_Curent_leaf(camera_pos,
        ROOT_NODE);
    if(current_leaf != _cached_cam_leaf)
    {
        frame_counter++;
        _cached_cam_leaf = cam_leaf;
        BYTE* pPvs = current_leaf.pPVS;
        for_each(leaf in leaves)
        {
            index = leaf.index;
            if(pPvs[index >> 3] &
               (index<<( index & 7)))
            {
                leaf.frame = frame_counter;
                while(node = leaf.parent)
                {
```

```
                    if(node.frm_counter ==
                        frame_counter)
                       break;
                }
                node.frm_counter = frame_counter;
            }
        }
    }
    Recurse_B2F_Render(camera_pos, node, current_leaf);
}

void Recurse_B2F_Render(Point camera_pos, NODE node)
{

    // Reject PVS clusters
    if(node.frm_counter != frame_counter)
        return;
    if(Out_Of_Frustrum(camera_pos,::BoundingBox(node)))
        return;
    if(::Isleaf(node))
    {
        Render_leaf(node);
        return;
    }
    side = node.plane.GetSide(camera_pos) >=0;
    Recurse_B2F_Render (camera_pos, side ?
        node-> node->pNodeFront:
        node-> node->pNodeBack);
    Recurse_B2F_Render (camera_pos, side ?
        node-> node->pNodeBack):
        node-> node->pNodeFront);
}
```

Terrain BSP

This gem concludes with a discussion on creating a BSP over a terrain environment. Although it is not a common practice, a BSP over terrain will accelerate the rejection of unseen geometry by performing frustum rejection, see Figure 1.5.19 (image taken from Getic BSP Editor). For terrain, the BSP compiler generates virtual splitter planes by alternating them on the X and Z axes. Virtual splitters are always introduced for dividing a terrain's largest extent.

The partitioning process follows the same algorithm as the one used in the node BSP section. The process is repeated for front and back lists until the polygons count reaches a pre-established polygon-count limit per leaf/node. At the point where the outer limit is reached, the splitting plane is chosen as the remaining geometry to be in front of this plane. This occurs by building the last splitter on one of the leaf bounding-box faces that is facing the leaf center. All of the polygons are stored in a leaf node. Figure 1.5.18 shows visible leaves inside the frustum. Figure 1.5.19 shows the splitting process for a single branch over a terrain mesh. The BSP compiler on the accompanying CD-ROM covers all aspects of the BSP explained in this gem.

ON THE CD

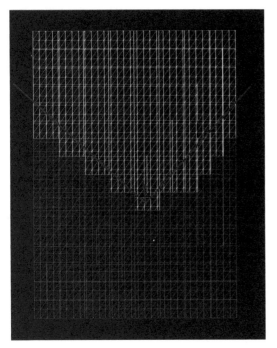

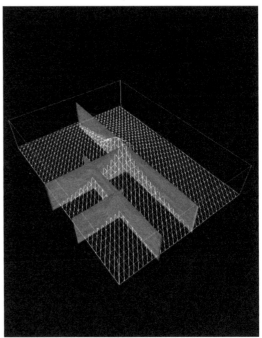

FIGURE 1.5.18 *Leaf rejection by the frustum.*

FIGURE 1.5.19 *Splitter process applied to the terrain.*

Conclusion

Even with the clipping technology that video cards have today, BSPs remain one of the primary partitioning algorithms used in many game engines, so be sure to browse and play with the complete BSP compiler on the CD-ROM.

References

[Abrash97] Abrash, Michael, *Graphics Programming Black Book.* Coriolis Group Books 1997.

1.6

Closest-String Matching Algorithm

James Boer, ArenaNet

author@boarslair.com

In this gem, we'll demonstrate an algorithm that can be used to find how closely any two strings match. More importantly, we'll demonstrate how this function can be utilized at the heart of a handy error-reporting mechanism wherever data is indexed and sorted by string-based IDs. When no exact string ID is found, this error-reporting mechanism can give the user a best guess as to which string should have been used instead. One of the best examples of this technology in action is the Google™ search engine. We'll examine a way to bring a very simple version of this functionality to a game database.

The Problem with String-Based ID Lookups

As game developers embrace data-driven methodologies, it can become increasingly difficult to manage the interface between code and data. When creating human-readable data elements, strings are often used as a self-descriptive form of identification for data elements of all types. During the development process, it is easy to make a mistake when typing in one of these identifiers in a script or data table. For reasons of efficiency, exact string matches are typically required for these sorts of data lookups. As such, any small error will cause the string lookup to completely fail. This will cause the developer to search for and replace the errant string value with the correct one.

Unfortunately, there are a near-infinite number of ways to make subtle mistakes. A human can see that when `SallyExample` was entered, the most logical match is `SillyExample`. But this only is only obvious to a human when presented with a very small data set. Humans are not good at tracking large amounts of data. For instance, making an error such as entering `BrightRedMagicFlash` when you meant to enter `LightRedMagicFlash` will make it difficult to resolve the problem. An alphabetized key list will provide little help, since the first letters do not even match.

The Problem Defined

The solution for this ID-lookup problem was simply devised. If a specified string was not found, a closest-string matching algorithm can be used to scan through all available ID strings and indicate which one was the closest match. Although a simple concept in practice, fuzzy string-matching turns out to be a somewhat difficult problem to solve efficiently. Consequently, a good deal of research is devoted to solving this problem in an efficient manner.

Most solutions tend to require allocation space for the core algorithm or require that the search space be organized in a particular manner. Our particular problem, however, was better suited for a solution that was not necessarily optimal in terms of run-time efficiency, but rather in terms of resource allocation and code size.

The design requirements favored a simple function that, given two normal C-style null-terminated strings, would return a floating-point value from zero to one as an indication of how closely the strings matched. Ideally, the function would also be run-time efficient, requiring no storage space (beyond a bit of stack space for a few variables) or run-time allocation. This is because the algorithm is expected to perform many small searches instead of traditional searches over a large data set. The cost of an allocation would end up outweighing the cost of the search algorithm itself.

Some Existing Solutions

What we are in fact looking for is a more practical implementation of the *Levenshtein distance formula* [Wikipedia05]. Invented by the Russian scientist Vladimir Levenshtein in 1965, this formula describes how closely two strings match by determining how many edits are required to transform one string into another.

In the case of our requirements, this formula alone would not suffice, as we need a ratio of similarity in order to be able to set a meaningful threshold. However, it is simple enough to turn this formula into a ratio, since we can define the upper bounds as the size of the largest string.

One potential contender for our consideration is the *Bitap algorithm*—also known as the *shift-or* or *Baeza-Yates-Gonnet* algorithm. The Bitap algorithm creates bit masks representing matching string values as a measure of adherence to the Levenshtein distance formula. While quite fast, this algorithm requires the allocation of a bit array equal to the size of the comparison string. We have opted to attempt to create a solution that requires no additional storage penalty, even at the cost of a bit of run-time efficiency at the algorithmic level. Additionally, we wanted a solution that could weigh incorrect case matches differently than a normal mismatched character pair.

Our Custom String-Matching Solution

How, though, do we define a *close match?* Let's examine our hypothetical key of `BrightRedMagicFlash` and compare it to `LightRedMagicFlash`. Here are the basic rules our algorithm uses to determine a match.

Matching Rules

We first determine the larger of the two strings and use this as a baseline value for length calculations. In this case, that value is 19. Each matching letter then represents 1.0 divided by the baseline length value, which works out to a value of roughly 0.0526 per letter in this case. Each letter that matches adds this value to a total score. For this particular match attempt, we see that we get a match value of 0.947, indicating a fairly close approximation.

For capitalization errors, we can add a percentage of the normal value of a match. In our implementation, we've chosen a value of 90% for a capitalization error. Incorrectly placed text is implicitly calculated at half value, since the last discovered match will be discarded in favor of a previous subset match. This seems to be a fair valuation, allowing a reasonable number of misplaced characters.

Finally, missing or additional characters create a decrease in the accuracy value proportional to the size of the set of characters to the correct key value. In other words, if the correct key had 10 characters and a potential match only had 9 of those 10, the resulting match would be 90%.

You may note that this set of rules is very similar to the Levenshtein distance formula. In our estimation, it was not necessary to follow the exact rules to the letter, so long as we remain faithful to the original intent.

The Algorithm

Let's examine the function stringMatch() and see how it works:

Listing 1.6.1 The stringMatch Function.

```
const float CAP_MISMATCH_VAL = 0.9f;

// This is the actual string-matching algorithm. It
// returns a value from zero to one indicating an approximate
// percentage of how closely two strings match.
float stringMatch(char const *left, char const *right)
{
    // get the length of the left, right, and longest string
    // (to use as a basis for comparison in value calculations)
    size_t leftSize = strlen(left);
    size_t rightSize = strlen(right);
    size_t largerSize = (leftSize > rightSize) ?
        leftSize : rightSize;
    char const *leftPtr = left;
    char const *rightPtr = right;
    float matchVal = 0.0f;
    // Iterate through the left string until we run out of room
    while(leftPtr != (left + leftSize) &&
        rightPtr != (right + rightSize))
    {
        // First, check for a simple left/right match
        if(*leftPtr == *rightPtr)
```

```
{
    // If it matches, add a proportional character's value
    // to the match total.
    matchVal += 1.0f / largerSize;
    // Then advance the pointers if there is room to do so
    if(leftPtr != (left + leftSize))
        ++leftPtr;
    if(rightPtr != (right + rightSize))
        ++rightPtr;
}
// If the simple match fails,
// try a match ignoring capitalization
else if(::tolower(*leftPtr) == ::tolower(*rightPtr))
{
    // We'll consider a capitalization mismatch worth 90%
    // of a normal match
    matchVal += CAP_MISMATCH_VAL / largerSize;
    if(leftPtr != (left + leftSize))
        ++leftPtr;
    if(rightPtr != (right + rightSize))
        ++rightPtr;
}
else
{
    char const *lpbest = left + leftSize;
    char const *rpbest = right + rightSize;
    int totalCount = 0;
    int bestCount = INT_MAX;
    int leftCount = 0;
    int rightCount = 0;
    // Here we loop through the left word in an outer loop,
    // but we also check for an early out by ensuring we
    // don't exceed our best current count
    for(char const *lp = leftPtr; (lp != (left + leftSize)
        && ((leftCount + rightCount) < bestCount)); ++lp)
    {
        // Inner loop counting
        for(char const *rp = rightPtr; (rp != (right +
            rightSize) && ((leftCount + rightCount) <
            bestCount)); ++rp)
        {
            // At this point, we don't care about case
            if(::tolower(*lp) == ::tolower(*rp))
            {
                // This is the fitness measurement
                totalCount = leftCount + rightCount;
                if(totalCount < bestCount)
                {
                    bestCount = totalCount;
                    lpbest = lp;
                    rpbest = rp;
                }
            }
        }
        ++rightCount;
    }
```

```
            ++leftCount;
            rightCount = 0;
        }
        leftPtr = lpbest;
        rightPtr = rpbest;
    }
}
// clamp the value in case of floating-point error
if(matchVal > 0.99f)
    matchVal = 1.0f;
else if(matchVal < 0.01f)
    matchVal = 0.0f;
return matchVal;
}
```

The function is a little long to take in at one glance, so let's divide and conquer as we analyze how it works. (You can also view all the code on the accompanying CD-ROM.)

To start with, you'll notice that we first calculate the largest of the two strings, which will be used when determining how much value to assign each potential character match. Each character's value is one/(maximum characters).

```
float stringMatch(char const *left, char const *right)
{
    // get the length of the left, right, and longest string
    // (to use as a basis for comparison in value calculations)
    size_t leftSize = strlen(left);
    size_t rightSize = strlen(right);
    size_t largerSize = (leftSize > rightSize) ?
        leftSize : rightSize;
    char const *leftPtr = left;
    char const *rightPtr = right;
    float matchVal = 0.0f;
```

Now that the housekeeping is done, we'll start our main loop. The while loop continues until the left or right iterating pointers are pointing to the end of the string.

```
// Iterate through the left string until we run out of room
while(leftPtr != (left + leftSize) &&
    rightPtr != (right + rightSize))
{
    ...
}
```

Our first test is the simplest of cases—a perfect match. In this case, the value of a single character match is added to the comparison value total, and both the left and right pointers are advanced. We need not worry about over-running the array bounds, since this is checked at the top of every loop.

```
// First, check for a simple left/right match
if(*leftPtr == *rightPtr)
{
    // If it matches, add a proportional character's value
    // to the match total.
    matchVal += 1.0f / largerSize;
    // Then advance the pointers if there is room to do so
    if(leftPtr != (left + leftSize))
        ++leftPtr;
    if(rightPtr != (right + rightSize))
        ++rightPtr;
}
```

If the perfect match fails, we can then try a case-insensitive comparison. This time, if we match, 90% of a single character match is added to the comparison value total, and the left and right pointers are advanced.

```
// If the simple match fails,
// try a match ignoring capitalization
else if(::tolower(*leftPtr) == ::tolower(*rightPtr))
{
    // We'll consider a capitalization mismatch worth 90%
    // of a normal match
    matchVal += CAP_MISMATCH_VAL / largerSize;
    if(leftPtr != (left + leftSize))
        ++leftPtr;
    if(rightPtr != (right + rightSize))
        ++rightPtr;
}
```

Now that the first two match checks are complete, we move into what could be considered the true heart of the algorithm. This code attempts to advance the two character pointers to the most optimal next matching pair. (Note that we do not distinguish case in this match, as it would have needlessly complicated the algorithm.)

It does this by cycling through all new match combinations using an outer and inner loop to advance left and right experimental pointers. A fitness value is calculated by determining how far we had to travel down each of the left and right strings for a match. We then add these two values together for the final score. *This prevents a potentially bad match wherein a single extraneous letter is matched against a character in another string that just happens to be near the end.* This match would be marked with a low fitness, and any more sensible match closer to the front of both strings would be favored.

```
char const *lpbest = left + leftSize;
char const *rpbest = right + rightSize;
int totalCount = 0;
int bestCount = INT_MAX;
int leftCount = 0;
int rightCount = 0;
```

```
// Here we loop through the left word in an outer loop,
// but we also check for an early out by ensuring we
// don't exceed our best current count
for(char const *lp = leftPtr; (lp != (left + leftSize)
    && ((leftCount + rightCount) < bestCount)); ++lp)
{
    // Inner loop counting
    for(char const *rp = rightPtr; (rp != (right +
        rightSize) && ((leftCount + rightCount) <
        bestCount)); ++rp)
    {
        // At this point, we don't care about case
        if(::tolower(*lp) == ::tolower(*rp))
        {
            // This is the fitness measurement
            totalCount = leftCount + rightCount;
            if(totalCount < bestCount)
            {
                bestCount = totalCount;
                lpbest = lp;
                rpbest = rp;
            }
        }
        ++rightCount;
    }
    ++leftCount;
    rightCount = 0;
}
```

We also take advantage of the best current match to avoid searching any deeper
into a string than we have to. While this does not improve the worst-case condition of
this algorithm when there are no matches, it does speed up the matching process on
average by limiting the typical search depth.

```
for(char const *lp = leftPtr; (lp != (left + leftSize)
    && ((leftCount + rightCount) < bestCount)); ++lp)
{
    for(char const *rp = rightPtr; (rp != (right +
        rightSize) && ((leftCount + rightCount) <
        bestCount)); ++rp)
    {
```

When the match with the best fitness score is determined, these pointers are
copied to our primary iterating pointers, and the loop is repeated.

```
leftPtr = lpbest;
rightPtr = rpbest;
```

Finally, we make sure we clamp the final result between 0.0 and 1.0 to eliminate
any potential floating-point error.

```
    if(matchVal > 0.99f)
        matchVal = 1.0f;
    else if(matchVal < 0.01f)
        matchVal = 0.0f;
    return matchVal;
```

Potential Optimizations

This is no doubt a sub-optimal algorithm. While some basic optimizations have been made, there are many ways in which to arrive at a solution in a more efficient manner. However, there are two basic hindrances in applying some of the classic string-matching algorithms and techniques.

To begin, we wished to utilize an algorithm that imposed no additional storage requirements or dynamic allocation. Moreover, the proposed algorithm would not be allowed to use advanced techniques, such as creating data hashes of the index values. This severely limits our available options, as algorithmic states must be confined to a fixed number of variables in code.

Quite frankly, optimal performance of the algorithm was never a primary concern, as the code would only be run during exceptional circumstances and should never be called during normal execution of the game. It is left as an exercise for the reader to further optimize if deemed necessary.

Applying the Solution

The original intent was not to create a fuzzy string-matching algorithm as an academic exercise. It was to assist in providing more meaningful errors when a string-based identification key does not match exactly. Listing 1.6.2 demonstrates a simple template-based function that can be used with any STL map that uses std::string as a key.

Listing 1.6.2 The closestMatch Function.

```
template<class _InIt> inline
_InIt closestMatch(_InIt _First, _InIt _Last, char const *val,
    float limit)
{
    float maxVal = limit;
    InIt _max = _Last;
    for (; _First != _Last; ++_First)
    {
        float newVal = stringMatch(_First->first.c_str(), val);
        if (newVal > maxVal)
        {
            maxVal = newVal;
            _max = _First;
        }
    }
    return (_max);
}
```

This particular function performs a linear search through a map's keys and returns an iterator to the closest match with at least a value of `limit`. A meaningful error message can then be reported, such as:

The object ID 'Key Word' was not found. Did you perhaps mean 'keyword'?

If no match of at least the value of `limit` was found, then the code can resort to a more generic error message.

Conclusion

By employing a reasonably simple mechanic, we are able to provide better debugging feedback for any portion of an engine that utilizes string-based ID lookups. If an ID is misspelled, a reasonable suggestion can be offered, and the substitution can easily be made. While some solutions do exist for this problem, many were not suitable for the requirements of our project.

With a bit of work, we can incorporate and extend this basic error-handling mechanism so that it becomes an easy matter to ensure that any simple spelling errors, when looking up a string ID, will quickly be corrected.

References

[Wikipedia05] "Levenshtein distance." September 20, 2005. Available online at *http://en.wikipedia.org/wiki/Levenshtein_distance*.

Using CppUnit To Implement Unit Testing

Blake Madden, Oleander Solutions

blake.madden@oleandersolutions.com

In the realm of quality assurance, there are two basic domains of testing: black box and white box testing. Black box testing refers to a Quality Assurance (QA) team's testing of a fully integrated system, which includes such techniques as script-based functional testing and manual testing (either unstructured or following a test plan). In contrast, white box testing is quality validation performed by the development team prior to the QA team's testing efforts. White box testing traditionally includes peer reviews and unit testing, the latter of which we will discuss in this gem. Essentially, unit testing is the use of automated tests to verify the results and behavior of smaller components of a software system at the developer's level, regardless of how the component is normally used.

Although unit testing sounds very similar to automated functional testing, these are actually quite different methods of testing that are meant to complement each other. Whereas functional testing is strictly a high-level, full-system method of testing, unit testing is a low-level, modular method of testing that allows us to test specific classes and functions on a more isolated level—that is, you can test a function without regard to how it is used throughout the rest of the system, and without regard to how other classes and functions interact with it.

Overview of Unit Testing

As with high-level automation tests, it's best to create small applications that are separate from the actual game's code base, sometimes referred to as a test harness. These test harnesses should contain all of your test cases, as well as run them and review their results. This way you can create small, localized test programs that include only the files from your code base that are needed. This is also important so that unit testing code is not mixed into the actual game, especially the release product.

Unit tests are collections of small functions that test every possible scenario for a given function and verify that it not only behaves as expected under normal circumstances, but also robustly handles potentially disastrous error conditions. The main benefit of unit testing is that because it is separate from the rest of the system, you can easily set up these tests and pass any sort of data to the functions that you are testing without having to actually step through the entire game with real-world data. The other benefit of unit testing is that your test harness not only runs your test cases, but also compares the results and creates a report of any conflicts or unexpected errors that occur. In this respect, unit testing can almost be thought of as an intelligent debugger that does most of the work for you (see Figure 1.7.1).

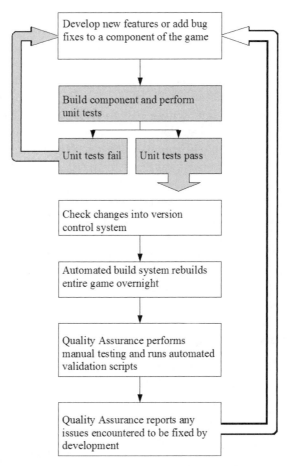

FIGURE 1.7.1   *How unit testing fits into the testing process.*

Unit tests can either be written for already existing functions, or they can be written prior to any other code. The latter technique is popular in test-driven environments where unit testing is set up while the rest of the system is still being designed. For the sake of simplicity, this gem will assume that you will be creating unit tests for an already existing code base.

Overview of CppUnit

CppUnit is a unit-testing library for C++, which is freely available online [CppUnit05]. It offers a framework for writing, organizing, and running unit tests for your functions, as well as numerous output reporting methods to enable you to easily review your test results. CppUnit has numerous features, such as easy-to-use condition-checking macros that handle all of the error logging and reporting for you, thus making test-case writing far more productive than writing them from scratch.

Including CppUnit

To include CppUnit into your testing application, you first need to build the CppUnit libraries, and then include cppunitd.lib (debug) or cppunit.lib (release) as library dependencies. Reference these header files in your main header file:

```
#include <cppunit/TestCase.h>
#include <cppunit/extensions/HelperMacros.h>
#include <cppunit/ui/text/TestRunner.h>
#include <cppunit/XmlOutputter.h>
#include <cppunit/TestResultCollector.h>
#include <cppunit/CompilerOutputter.h>
```

Finally, you need to set your runtime libraries to "multi-threaded DLL" if you are compiling on Windows.

Creating Test Cases

In CppUnit, you first create a test fixture class, which is derived from CppUnit:: TestFixture. A test fixture is a container class for organizing all of the test cases for a particular function or class. An empty test fixture will look something like this:

```
class MathTest : public CppUnit::TestFixture
{
public:
    CPPUNIT_TEST_SUITE(MathTest);
    CPPUNIT_TEST_SUITE_END();
};
```

The CPPUNIT_TEST_SUITE macro section is where you declare all of the test cases that you want this fixture to run. Say, for example, that this test fixture is testing a math class, and you want to have a test case for checking the math class's ADD function. You can create a test-case function to accomplish this as such:

```
void TestAddFunction()
{
    math my_math;
    CPPUNIT_ASSERT(my_math.add(2,2) == 4);
}
```

In this test case, we call the math class's ADD function with (2,2), and then use the CppUnit CPPUNIT_ASSERT macro to verify that the result is 4. If ADD does not correctly return 4, then CppUnit will log this error and output it for you, depending on how you set up your reporting output. After writing the test case, you just need to add it to the test fixture and add it to the CPPUNIT_TEST_SUITE section, like so:

```
class MathTest : public CppUnit::TestFixture
{
public:
    CPPUNIT_TEST_SUITE(MathTest);
    CPPUNIT_TEST(TestAddFunction);
    CPPUNIT_TEST_SUITE_END();

    void TestAddFunction()
    {
        math my_math;
        CPPUNIT_ASSERT(my_math.add(2,2) == 4);
    }
};
```

Running Test Fixtures

Now that you have your test cases and have organized them into a test fixture, you will want to set up a test harness to actually run the test fixture and output the results. You do this by creating a CppUnit::TextTestRunner object, add your test fixtures to it, set its output method, and then run it.

For this example, you will route the output to an XML file, which will use a style sheet to nicely display the results for easy review. The first step is to create the test runner, a CppUnit::TextTestRunner object, like so:

```
CppUnit::TextTestRunner runner;
```

Next, create the stream to the XML file to which you want to write the results. You can simply use a std::ofstream to do this:

```
std::ofstream ofs("tests.xml");
```

Next, create a handler for the XML file (a CppUnit::XmlOutputter object), set its style sheet, and then set the test runner to route its results to the XML handler:

```
CppUnit::XmlOutputter* xml =
    new CppUnit::XmlOutputter(&runner.result(), ofs);
xml->setStyleSheet("report.xsl");
runner.setOutputter(xml);
```

Finally, add all test fixtures that you want to perform to the test runner object, and then run it:

```
runner.addTest( LoadModelTest::suite() );
runner.run();
```

ON THE CD

After you run the test program, open "tests.xml" for a report of how many tests were run, how many passed and failed, and detailed information about any of the test cases that may have failed. An example report and style sheet are included on the CD-ROM.

It is recommended to run your test programs prior to committing your changes into your version-control system. For convenience, you could even integrate your test programs into your build process using a simple shell/batch file or a more feature-rich system, such as CruiseControl (available online at *http://cruisecontrol.sourceforge.net/*).

Using CppUnit To Test a Model Class

Let's demonstrate unit testing with a simple example of a model-loading class. Say that you are using a custom model file format in your game engine, and you write a class to load and render these models. Here is the prototype of this class:

```
class model
{
public:
    void load_file(const char* file_path);
    void render();
    void animate(float speed, bool loop = true);
    //Utility functions used to load model file
    void parse_header_section(char* file_text);
    void parse_triangle_section(char* file_text);
    void parse_mesh_section(char* file_text);
    void parse_material_section(char* file_text);
    void parse_animation_section(char* file_text);
    void prepare_joints();
    //Loads texture from file (BMP supported)
    void load_texture(const char* file_path);
    //File info functions
    double get_version() const
        { return m_version; }
    model_type get_type() const
        { return m_model_type; }
```

```
            const char* get_name() const
                { return m_name; }
            const char* get_author() const
                { return m_author; }
            //Data information functions
            size_t get_number_of_vertices() const
                { return m_number_of_vertices; }
            size_t get_number_of_triangles() const
                { return m_number_of_triangles; }
            size_t get_number_of_meshes() const
                { return m_number_of_materials; }
            size_t get_number_of_materials() const
                { return m_number_of_materials; }
            size_t get_number_of_joints() const
                { return m_number_of_joints; }
    private:
            //Private data
            double m_version;
            model_type m_model_type;
            char* m_name;
            char* m_author;
            unsigned short m_number_of_vertices;
            unsigned short m_number_of_triangles;
            unsigned short m_number_of_meshes;
            unsigned short m_number_of_materials;
            unsigned short m_number_of_joints;
            vertex_t* m_vertices;
            triangle_t* m_triangles;
            mesh_t* m_meshes;
            material_t* m_materials;
            joint_t* m_joints;
    };
```

More than likely, all that will be exposed of this class via automation would be the load_file, render, and animate functions, because the utility functions are not really of any interest to either the QA team or the player creating a mod. As you develop this class, you will be making many changes and bug fixes to these utility functions; and as you make these changes, you will be traditionally faced with two ways to handle testing these changes:

• Integrate your changes into your local build of the game and test with various model files prior to checking everything into your source-control system.
• Simply check in your changes to your source-control system, and QA will test your changes the next day, either through manual game-play testing or perhaps through scripted testing.

The first option is rather time consuming, given that you will need to rebuild at least one part of the system (e.g., the DLL or SO file) and step through the debugger while booting up the entire game just to get to where the model-loading takes place. The second option is risky, because QA may not be aware of your changes and will spend a good deal of time tracking down the problem when a core action like loading a level or character model causes the entire game to crash immediately. Also, once they report this problem to you, the time that you spend debugging and the time that you spend rebuilding a new image with the bug fix is time wasted for QA, because they have an unusable build for the rest of the day.

This is where unit testing comes to the rescue. Unit testing will allow you to validate the behavior of small core changes without having to debug the whole system. It also gives you the ability to perform some fairly in-depth sanity testing so that you can verify your changes prior to checking them in without worrying about them breaking other parts of the game.

Let's look at some examples of how to unit test the utility function `parse_header_section`. The first thing to do is to mentally step through the expected behavior of a function and then take inventory of everything that can go wrong, including passing invalid arguments to it. Let's start with the model file's header section, which looks like this:

```
<HEADER>
    <VERSION>1.1</VERSION>
    <TYPE>WorldLevel</TYPE>
    <NAME>Character Select Gallery</NAME>
    <AUTHOR>Blake Madden</AUTHOR>
</HEADER>
```

The `parse_header_section` function should load such information as the model's type, name, author, and file format that it is based on. The file-format version and type are necessary information, and if either is not found, then the function should throw a `model_invalid_version` or `model_invalid_type` exception, respectively. The model's name and author are optional values, and if not found, then the function should still load the version and type information, and not throw any errors. Finally, if the structure of the header section is ill-formatted, then the function should throw a more general `model_invalid_header` exception. With this knowledge, let's start creating test cases for this function.

The first case should be a simple test of passing bad arguments to the function—in this case a NULL pointer. Because you expect this function to throw a `model_invalid_header` exception if the header text passed to it is invalid, then your test case will pass a NULL pointer to `parse_header_section` and verify that it throws a `model_invalid_header` exception using the CppUnit `CPPUNIT_ASSERT_THROW` macro. Here is what this test case will look like:

```
void TestInvalidHeaderNullValue()
{
    model my_model;
    CPPUNIT_ASSERT_THROW(my_model.parse_header_section(NULL),
        model_invalid_header);
}
```

As you can see, you create a model object and then call the parse_header_ section function, and pass NULL to it to force a model_invalid_header exception. You wrap this call inside of the CPPUNIT_ASSERT_THROW macro, where the first parameter is your function call and the second parameter is the exception type that you are expecting to be thrown. If your function call does not throw the expected exception, then CppUnit will log this error as a failed test case that you will be able to review later.

Another test case would be to test passing a poorly formatted header section where you would also expect the function to throw a model_invalid_header. This test case looks like this:

```
void TestInvalidHeaderIllFormatted()
{
    model my_model;
    CPPUNIT_ASSERT_THROW(my_model.parse_header_section(
        "<HEADER"
        "<VERSION>1.1</VERSION>"
        "<TYPE>WorldLevel</TYPE>"
        "<NAME>Character Select Gallery</NAME>"
        "<AUTHOR>Blake Madden</AUTHOR>"),
        model_invalid_header);
}
```

Note that this header test is missing a ">" after the first HEADER and is also missing the terminating </HEADER>.

The next test case should test how the function behaves if the header section is missing either a version section or a type section, which, as mentioned earlier, are necessary and will respectively throw model_invalid_version and model_invalid_type exceptions if not found. Our test case for verifying a missing version number or entire version section looks like this:

```
void TestInvalidHeaderInvalidVersionSection()
{
    model my_model;
    //Version section is missing the version number
    CPPUNIT_ASSERT_THROW(my_model.parse_header_section(
        "<HEADER>"
        "<VERSION></VERSION>"
        "<TYPE>WorldLevel</TYPE>"
        "<NAME>Character Select Gallery</NAME>"
        "<AUTHOR>Blake Madden</AUTHOR>"
        "</HEADER>"),
        model_invalid_version);
    //Version section is missing
    CPPUNIT_ASSERT_THROW(my_model.parse_header_section(
        "<HEADER>"
        "<TYPE>WorldLevel</TYPE>"
        "<NAME>Character Select Gallery</NAME>"
        "<AUTHOR>Blake Madden</AUTHOR>"
        "</HEADER>"),
        model_invalid_version);
```

```
            //Ill-formatted version section
            CPPUNIT_ASSERT_THROW(my_model.parse_header_section(
                "<HEADER>"
                "<VERSION>1.2"
                "<TYPE>WorldLevel</TYPE>"
                "<NAME>Character Select Gallery</NAME>"
                "<AUTHOR>Blake Madden</AUTHOR>"
                "</HEADER>"),
                model_invalid_version);
    }
```

A similar test case should also be created to verify that invalid type sections throw a `model_invalid_type` exception, but we will omit this for brevity.

Just as important as testing a function for failure conditions is to test it with data that should actually work, and to see if the results are correct. To test a condition, you use the `CPPUNIT_ASSERT` macro, which is almost identical to the standard `ASSERT` macro. In this example, you will create a test case that calls the `parse_header_section` function with valid text, and verify the version and type information are correct afterward. Our test case looks like this:

```
    void TestInvalidValidHeader()
    {
        model my_model;
        //Perfectly valid header
        my_model.parse_header_section(
            "<HEADER>"
            "<VERSION>1.2</VERSION>"
            "<TYPE>WorldLevel</TYPE>"
            "<NAME>Character Select Gallery</NAME>"
            "<AUTHOR>Blake Madden</AUTHOR>"
            "</HEADER>");
        CPPUNIT_ASSERT(my_model.get_version() == 1.2);
        CPPUNIT_ASSERT(my_model.get_type() == world_level);
        CPPUNIT_ASSERT(strcmp(my_model.get_name(),
            "Character Select Gallery") == 0);
        CPPUNIT_ASSERT(strcmp(my_model.get_author(),
            "Blake Madden") == 0);
        //Author and name are not included
        my_model.parse_header_section(
            "<HEADER>"
            "<VERSION>1.2</VERSION>"
            "<TYPE>WorldLevel</TYPE>"
            "</HEADER>");
        CPPUNIT_ASSERT(my_model.get_version() == 1.2);
        CPPUNIT_ASSERT(my_model.get_type() == world_level);
        CPPUNIT_ASSERT(strcmp(my_model.get_name(), "") == 0);
        CPPUNIT_ASSERT(strcmp(my_model.get_author(), "") == 0);
    }
```

In this example, you pass a perfectly valid header section and then confirm that the version, type, name, and author values were all correctly loaded. If any of these items fail, then CppUnit will log this as an error.

Recall that the file specification for the header section states that the name and author are optional; you should also test this function with a header that omits these, and then verify that the author and name values are set to empty values. This last part is important because you want to be certain that if this function cannot find either the name or author in the header section, then it will appropriately set these values to blank strings, resetting any values that were in the class before from a previous-model loading call. To test this, append the following to your `TestInvalidValidHeader` test case:

```
//Author and name are not included
my_model.parse_header_section(
    "<HEADER>"
    "<VERSION>1.2</VERSION>"
    "<TYPE>WorldLevel</TYPE>"
    "</HEADER>");
CPPUNIT_ASSERT(my_model.get_version() == 1.2);
CPPUNIT_ASSERT(my_model.get_type () == world_level);
CPPUNIT_ASSERT(strcmp(my_model.get_name(), "") == 0);
CPPUNIT_ASSERT(strcmp(my_model.get_author(), "") == 0);
```

From here, you can continue making more test cases for all of the other functions from this class in the same way. For example, additional test cases can be created to test the animation-parsing function to verify that it correctly loads the right number of animations, that the animations have all of their frames and speeds loaded correctly, and that erroneous triangle data is handled robustly.

Now that your model-loading test cases are written, you will now organize all of them into a test fixture. In CppUnit, create a test fixture class derived from `CppUnit::TestFixture`. Here is what your empty test fixture will look like:

```
//Unit test for loading a model file
class LoadModelTest : public CppUnit::TestFixture
{
public:
    CPPUNIT_TEST_SUITE(LoadModelTest);
    CPPUNIT_TEST_SUITE_END();
private:
    Model m_model;
};
```

You will need to declare each test case that you want the fixture to run by adding them to the test fixture's `CPPUNIT_TEST_SUITE` section, as demonstrated here:

```
CPPUNIT_TEST_SUITE(LoadModelTest);
    CPPUNIT_TEST(TestInvalidHeaderNullValue);
    CPPUNIT_TEST(TestInvalidHeaderIllFormatted);
    CPPUNIT_TEST(TestInvalidHeaderInvalidVersionSection);
    CPPUNIT_TEST(TestInvalidValidHeader);
CPPUNIT_TEST_SUITE_END();
```

Now add the test cases to this fixture as member functions. Your test fixture will now look like this (test case bodies are excluded for brevity):

```
//Unit test for loading a model file
class LoadModelTest : public CppUnit::TestFixture
{
public:
    CPPUNIT_TEST_SUITE(LoadModelTest);
        CPPUNIT_TEST(TestInvalidHeaderNullValue);
        CPPUNIT_TEST(TestInvalidHeaderIllFormatted);
        CPPUNIT_TEST(TestInvalidHeaderInvalidVersionSection);
        CPPUNIT_TEST(TestInvalidValidHeader);
    CPPUNIT_TEST_SUITE_END();

    void TestInvalidHeaderNullValue();
    void TestInvalidHeaderIllFormatted();
    void TestInvalidHeaderInvalidVersionSection();
    void TestInvalidValidHeader();
};
```

Unit-Testing Private Functions

You may have noticed that in the previous example, the model class appears to be poorly encapsulated, because it has all of its utility functions (e.g., parse_header_ section) publicly available. However, if you actually declare these functions as being private or protected, then the test fixture will not have access to them, so that is why they were declared as public. This is a caveat with unit testing in general, because in most object-orientated languages, external classes can't access the private functions of other classes. The common solution is to break encapsulation, although C++ offers another workaround if you must keep your utility functions private: the friend keyword. Simply forward-declare the test fixture class before the class being tested, and then make the test fixture a friend, like so:

```
class LoadModelTest; //forward declare

class model
{
public:
    friend LoadModelTest; //make the test fixture a friend
    void load_file(const char* file_path);
    void render();
    void animate(float speed, bool loop = true);
private:
    //Utility functions used to load model file
    void parse_header_section(char* file_text);
    void parse_triangle_section(char* file_text);
    void parse_mesh_section(char* file_text);
    void parse_material_section(char* file_text);
    void parse_animation_section(char* file_text);
    void prepare_joints();
```

```
            //Loads texture from file (BMP supported)
            void load_texture(const char* file_path);
            ...
    };
```

Now the `LoadModelTest` test fixture will have full access to your model class.

Using CppUnit To Test Low-Level Functionality

It is important to emphasize the depth that unit testing gives you. Take the example of implementing a custom memory allocator in your game to optimally manage memory. There is no direct way for any manual or automated tests from QA to be able to validate this part of the system. Although the QA team may be inadvertently testing the memory manager simply by playing the game, there is no way for them to test the robustness of the memory manager for potential problems that are bound to appear eventually throughout the system. Problems such as the system not deallocating memory properly, failing to allocate memory under certain situations, and even allocation overlap in memory are bound to happen without proper testing. Unit testing is the tool that you use to run test case scenarios such as these on smaller pieces of your system (e.g., a memory manager) to validate their robustness even before these concerns can become an issue.

As mentioned before, the first step to unit testing is to understand the full behavior of the component and then take an inventory of everything that can go wrong. In this example, your memory manager controls a single, global heap and allocates piecemeal from it. If the heap is too fragmented when an allocation is requested, then it will allocate from the operating system's free store (via `new` or `malloc`). When you request to deallocate a pointer, it will correctly free the proper block of memory from its own heap (or from the operating system's free store). Finally, your memory manager should be intelligent enough to not delete a pointer if it is not one that it originally allocated. This could be accomplished by keeping track of all the pointers currently allocated and checking against this list when a deallocation is requested.

Now that you understand the expected behavior of this class, make a short list of possible issues that can occur:

- Requesting a block of memory too big from an already fragmented heap may cause the memory allocator to crash or not correctly get the memory from the operating system (OS). It may fail and return `NULL`.
- Deallocating memory that the manager had to get from the OS will not be freed like it should.
- Making allocation requests that might accidentally return overlapping pointers.
- Requesting an allocation of zero may cause a crash or unexpected behavior. In this case, you expect the memory manager to not allocate a memory block of zero and instead throw a `std::bad_alloc` exception.

- Passing a pointer that does not match any pointer returned from a previous allocation to the memory manager's deallocate function might be erroneously freed.

With these concerns in mind, you can now create some simple functions that test these scenarios and verify that the expected behavior occurs. Before you start writing your test cases, first create a test fixture with a few constants and a memory manager object that the test cases will use. The skeleton of this test fixture will look like this:

```
//Unit test memory allocation manager
class HeapAllocatorTest : public CppUnit::TestFixture
{
public:
    CPPUNIT_TEST_SUITE(HeapAllocatorTest);
    CPPUNIT_TEST_SUITE_END();
private:
    /*Memory manager used for all test cases
    (max heap size is 1000 bytes)*/
    heap_allocator<char, 1000> m_memory_manager;
    //Allocation sizes
    static const size_t FIRST_ALLOCATION_SIZE = 500;
    static const size_t SECOND_ALLOCATION_SIZE = 400;
    static const size_t THIRD_ALLOCATION_SIZE = 300;
    static const size_t TOO_BIG_ALLOCATION_SIZE = 1100;
};
```

In CppUnit, when you use a member object throughout different test cases, it may be necessary to run some general cleanup before each test case is called. In this case, the memory manager class has a `clear` function that needs to be called to zero out its heap memory. CppUnit provides two virtual functions, `setupUp` and `tearDown`, which are called before and after each test case is run, respectively. Add a public overload of the `tearDown` function to your test fixture, like so:

```
void tearDown()
{
    m_memory_manager.clear();
}
```

Next, begin writing test cases for the allocation and deallocation routines. Although in the previous example you created a test case function for each test, it is possible to include more than one test in a single function. Along with the CppUnit `CPPUNIT_ASSERT` macro, there is also a `CPPUNIT_ASSERT_MESSAGE` function that allows you to embed a diagnostic message with an assertion if it fails. This way, you can create more-generic test functions with numerous tests cases in them and still retain a fair amount of verbose error-messaging. The only possible drawback is that the first assertion that fails in a particular test-case function will cause the function to terminate, and the test fixture will skip to the next test case. This is because if a particular test assertion fails, then CppUnit will assume that what caused the assertion to fail may inadvertently cause false positives with the proceeding assertions. This is a safe assumption for your allocation tests, because if an allocation appears to be NULL or has corrupt data, then any further tests will yield undefined behavior.

With this knowledge, add a test case for the scenarios involving allocations. Request a few allocations (including a zero-size request) to fragment the memory manager's heap, and then request an allocation that will be more than it can handle. To verify that everything went well, test the pointers that the memory manager returned to make sure that they are not NULL, and then confirm that none of the allocations overlap each other. Your test case will look like this:

```
void TestAllocation()
{
//Data that we will copy into our allocated arrays
char data1[FIRST_ALLOCATION_SIZE];
std::memset(data1, 'a', FIRST_ALLOCATION_SIZE);
char data2[SECOND_ALLOCATION_SIZE];
std::memset(data2, 'b', SECOND_ALLOCATION_SIZE);
char data3[THIRD_ALLOCATION_SIZE];
std::memset(data3, 'c', THIRD_ALLOCATION_SIZE);

/*Allocate arrays, verify that the allocations worked
and fill with data*/
char* array1 =
    m_memory_manager.allocate(FIRST_ALLOCATION_SIZE);
CPPUNIT_ASSERT_MESSAGE("First allocation returned NULL",
    array1);
std::memcpy(array1, data1, FIRST_ALLOCATION_SIZE);
char* array2 =
    m_memory_manager.allocate(SECOND_ALLOCATION_SIZE);
CPPUNIT_ASSERT_MESSAGE("Second allocation returned NULL",
    array2);
std::memcpy(array2, data2, SECOND_ALLOCATION_SIZE);
//This request will be too big for the allocator's fragmented heap
char* array3 =
    m_memory_manager.allocate(THIRD_ALLOCATION_SIZE);
CPPUNIT_ASSERT_MESSAGE(
    "Requesting too much memory returned NULL", array3);
std::memcpy(array3, data3, THIRD_ALLOCATION_SIZE);

/*Try to allocate a zero size-size array and
verify it throws a bad_alloc exception*/
CPPUNIT_ASSERT_THROW(m_memory_manager.allocate(0),
    std::bad_alloc);

/*Test the integrity of the allocated memory to make sure that the
returned pointers don't overlap*/
CPPUNIT_ASSERT_MESSAGE(
    "First allocation's data is corrupt."
    "Allocations may overlap.",
    std::memcmp(array1, data1, FIRST_ALLOCATION_SIZE) == 0);
CPPUNIT_ASSERT_MESSAGE(
```

```
                    "Second allocation's data is corrupt."
                    "Allocations may overlap.",
                    std::memcmp(array2, data2, SECOND_ALLOCATION_SIZE) == 0);
                CPPUNIT_ASSERT_MESSAGE(
                    "Third allocation's data is corrupt."
                    "Allocations may overlap.",
                    std::memcmp(array3, data3, THIRD_ALLOCATION_SIZE) == 0);

                //Free everything
                CPPUNIT_ASSERT(m_memory_manager.deallocate(array1,
                    FIRST_ALLOCATION_SIZE));
                CPPUNIT_ASSERT(m_memory_manager.deallocate(array2,
                    SECOND_ALLOCATION_SIZE));
                CPPUNIT_ASSERT(m_memory_manager.deallocate(array3,
                    THIRD_ALLOCATION_SIZE));
            }
```

Finally, create test cases for the deallocation concerns. Because data corruption is not a concern with deallocations, create separate functions for all of the different deallocation test cases. Our first test case will perform a simple allocation and make sure that the deallocation works, along with a simple test to ensure that the memory manager doesn't deallocate NULL pointers:

```
    void TestDellocationSimple()
    {
        char* array1 =
            m_memory_manager.allocate(FIRST_ALLOCATION_SIZE);

        //Free it
        CPPUNIT_ASSERT(m_memory_manager.deallocate(array1,
            FIRST_ALLOCATION_SIZE));
        CPPUNIT_ASSERT_MESSAGE(
            "Allocation deallocated a NULL pointer.",
            m_memory_manager.deallocate(NULL, 1) == false);
    }
```

The next test case will make sure that the memory manager cannot deallocate memory that it did not originally allocate:

```
    void TestDellocationFromFreeStorage()
    {
        //Allocate array outside of the memory manager
        char* array1 = new char[FIRST_ALLOCATION_SIZE];

        /*Allocator should not free this out because it did not
        allocate it*/
        CPPUNIT_ASSERT_MESSAGE(
            "Allocator deallocated a pointer that it did not"
            "originally allocate.",
            m_memory_manager.deallocate(array1, FIRST_ALLOCATION_SIZE)
                == false);
        delete [] array1;
    }
```

Finally, you can add a test case to verify that a memory block larger than the manager's internal heap will still be deallocated properly:

```
void TestDellocationFromUnmanagedPointer()
{
    //This request will be bigger than the allocator's heap
    char* array1 =
        m_memory_manager.allocate(TOO_BIG_ALLOCATION_SIZE);

    /*Although allocator creates this from outside its own heap,
    it should still be able to deallocate it*/
    CPPUNIT_ASSERT_MESSAGE(
        "Allocation larger than managed heap wasn't deallocated.",
        m_memory_manager.deallocate(array1,
        TOO_BIG_ALLOCATION_SIZE));
}
```

Once you are finished writing your test cases, add them to the definitions section of the test fixture, like so:

```
CPPUNIT_TEST_SUITE(HeapAllocatorTest);
    CPPUNIT_TEST(TestAllocation);
    CPPUNIT_TEST(TestDellocationSimple);
    CPPUNIT_TEST(TestDellocationFromFreeStorage);
    CPPUNIT_TEST(TestDellocationFromUnmanagedPointer);
CPPUNIT_TEST_SUITE_END();
```

Our final test fixture will look like this (function bodies are omitted for brevity):

```
//Unit test memory allocation manager
class HeapAllocatorTest : public CppUnit::TestFixture
{
public:
    CPPUNIT_TEST_SUITE(HeapAllocatorTest);
        CPPUNIT_TEST(TestAllocation);
        CPPUNIT_TEST(TestDellocationSimple);
        CPPUNIT_TEST(TestDellocationFromFreeStorage);
        CPPUNIT_TEST(TestDellocationFromUnmanagedPointer);
    CPPUNIT_TEST_SUITE_END();
public:
    void tearDown();
    void TestAllocation();
    void TestDellocationSimple();
    void TestDellocationFromFreeStorage();
    void TestDellocationFromUnmanagedPointer();
private:
    //Allocation sizes
    static const size_t FIRST_ALLOCATION_SIZE = 500;
    static const size_t SECOND_ALLOCATION_SIZE = 400;
    static const size_t THIRD_ALLOCATION_SIZE = 300;
    static const size_t TOO_BIG_ALLOCATION_SIZE = 1100;
};
```

Now add this test fixture to your test runner (as previously discussed) and run your test program. All of the failures that occur with the memory manager will then be logged to an XML report for your review.

Conclusion

As you have seen in this gem, unit testing is a preventive method for testing smaller components prior to system integration. Along with offering an extra level of confidence with low-level code changes, it also allows you to test isolated parts of the program in an automated fashion—hence, saving you from many labor-intensive debugging sessions just to test a small handful of functions.

CppUnit further enhances unit testing by offering an easy-to-use framework that greatly simplifies setting up and running test cases. Also, the CppUnit reporting capabilities organize and present your test results for quick, easy review.

Reference

[CppUnit05] CppUnit. Available online at *http://cppunit.sourceforge.net/cgi-bin/moin.cgi*.

1.8

Fingerprinting Pre-Release Builds To Deter and Detect Piracy

Steve Rabin,
Nintendo of America, Inc.

steve_rabin@hotmail.com

No one wants to see their game pirated, but it is especially heartbreaking when this happens to your game before it has been released. It's one thing when you've sold your game to a million people and it's open season on your copy protection, but it's another thing when an insider leaks a pre-release build. So the big question is: What can be done about this?

The solution is twofold. First, you must deter those who have access to pre-release builds from leaking them in the first place. Second, if a build is leaked, you must somehow detect who is responsible so that they can be held accountable. The truth is that if the build gets out, you've lost the war, but it's important to be able to *detect* the guilty party so as to put teeth into your deterrence strategy.

This article will briefly discuss deterrence and then delve deeply into methods for detection through the use of embedded digital fingerprints.

Deterrence

The trick to deterrence is to make everyone involved realize that it would be personally very bad for them if they happen to leak a build. For the primary developers of a project, this generally isn't a problem, because they have a personal stake in the success of the game. However, for peripheral individuals, such as testers or game reviewers, the success of the game isn't a strong motivator.

The only effective deterrence for people on the periphery is to make them think that any build they touch is marked with their *fingerprint*. They must realize that they're on the hook should the game get leaked. This threat can either be real or imagined, as long as each person truly believes it. Thus, a significant part of deterrence is a strong warning that individuals will be held accountable should a build in their possession get leaked.

Your warning to these individuals is like putting a sign outside your house warning would-be burglars that you have an alarm—make sure everyone knows that the product is rigged to tattle on them. However, you might not actually *need* an alarm, because if you make your sign prominent enough, this will scare most people into not risking a leak. Of course, if there is in reality no alarm, this knowledge must be a closely guarded secret!

Other than clearly telling people that their fingerprint is embedded in a given build, it's wise to also erect a sign within the game to display this fingerprint (perhaps on the intro screen). This provides a constant reminder that they're on the hook. However, this must not be the only place the fingerprint is embedded, since it is likely easy to remove. The true fingerprint must be hidden deep within the game and should be nearly impossible to detect or remove.

Here is an example of a message that could be displayed on an intro screen:

> *Prerelease build signed out to Steve Rabin.*
>
> *Do not share or distribute this build. Steve Rabin's digital signature has been embedded directly into the build's assets and executable for the purpose of tracking down a leaked build.*

This simple warning should put significant fear into anyone thinking of distributing a build. In fact, even if you don't do anything else to the build, this might get 99% of the security effect you're after.

Detection with Watermarks and Fingerprints

On paper currency, a watermark is a design that identifies the currency as legitimate to anyone who inspects it, yet the design is extremely difficult to fake or reproduce. For example, on a U.S. five-dollar bill, if you hold the bill up to the light, you'll see a faint image of Lincoln's face on the front-right side. This watermark is an assurance that the bill is authentic.

With music, images, and movies, visible or invisible watermarks can be placed within them. For example, a museum might place an invisible watermark on any reproductions or digital images of a painting that they own in order to prove their ownership. Likewise, the recording industry has employed schemes to digitally watermark music to prove ownership.

A fingerprint employs the same techniques as a watermark, but it encodes the end-user's information on the item, instead of the original owner's. For software fingerprinting of pre-released builds, the goal is to have an undetectable fingerprint; yet if needed, the developer can clearly identify to whom the build was originally given. Instead of an image like a traditional watermark, a digital fingerprint is really just a rearrangement or addition of bits, but it should be difficult or impossible to remove without making the game unplayable.

Software fingerprints can be placed on textures, 3D models, animations, music, sound effects, and executable code. The trick is to alter the original so that the fingerprint is unnoticeable, undetectable, unalterable, and doesn't interfere with the gameplay or experience of the game.

Fingerprinting Workflow

As a practical matter, it would be a waste of time for programmers or artists to be involved with fingerprinting each build that was distributed. Therefore, any fingerprinting solution must be quick and easy.

The best solution would be to apply the fingerprint to a completed build as the very last step of burning an image. However, depending on the method chosen, this might not be possible, and the fingerprint might need to be applied before compiling and packaging a build. In any event, nontechnical people should be able to apply the fingerprint through a simple process.

Security of the Fingerprinting Process

Ideally, the fingerprinting process should adhere to Kerckhoffs' law, which states that a system should be secure even if everything about the system is public knowledge (with the exception of the key). Unfortunately, there is no known method to achieve this level of security for digital fingerprints. The attacker simply needs to corrupt the fingerprint—not decipher it—to defeat the security. If the attacker knows where the fingerprint is, it can be altered and made unreadable.

Consequently, the best security we can achieve is *security through obscurity*, which relies on the fingerprinting process being a well-kept secret. To ensure this secret, it is recommended that no more than two people should know all of the details about how a build is actually fingerprinted.

One tactic is to build a fingerprinting program that performs the magic on a finished build. This program should be password protected so that only a select few are allowed to fingerprint builds. For added security, the fingerprint should also encrypt the name of the person who applied the fingerprint.

Obviously, anyone who has knowledge of how to fingerprint builds or has permission to fingerprint builds can fake a fingerprint, which is a liability. For this reason, only extremely trusted individuals should be involved in this process, such as the lead programmer and producer. For example, don't have your intern fingerprint the builds!

Fingerprinting Strategies

The following are strategies for fingerprinting a build. What's important to notice with each method is the difficulty of implementation versus the resulting difficulty of fingerprint detection. Once the fingerprint is detected, it can be corrupted or destroyed, so an important goal is to make the fingerprint virtually undetectable in the first place.

Name on the Intro Screen

This strategy is mainly for visibility and deterrence, so it's obviously going to be easy to detect and easy to remove. However, this can be extremely easy to implement, given that it only requires a text change or an image change.

Add Extra Files

This strategy consists of adding one or more extra garbage files to the build that are not used by the game. The mere existence of each file is the fingerprint. What makes this technique so ingenious is that it is very easy to implement and extremely difficult to detect, especially given that most games have thousands of files. This technique is like sticking a marked needle in a haystack.

Adobe Photoshop CS Digimarc

Fingerprinting textures within a game can be simple with the use of the Photoshop Digimarc filter. This feature allows you to embed a number between 1 and 16,777,215 into the image at four different levels of durability. The more durable the mark, the harder it is to destroy with the application of a simple filter to the image. Regardless of the durability, anyone with Photoshop can read the mark if they know which texture to test. On one hand, this is a very weak form of fingerprinting, since everyone has access to the software that can read or write the mark. However, since a game might have hundreds or thousands of textures, fingerprinting two or more would make it a sufficiently arduous detection task.

Custom Algorithm To Fingerprint an Image

Since Photoshop's Digimarc filter is a widely available tool, an alternative is to create your own algorithm for fingerprinting images. Combined with the needle-in-a-haystack strategy of only fingerprinting a few images, it should be virtually impossible to detect this fingerprint.

Custom Algorithm To Fingerprint a 3D Model, Animation, or Sound Effect

It is possible to fingerprint models, animations, and sounds by subtly altering the data. If you know what the original should look like, then a fingerprint can be embedded through minor tweaks of the data. This will effectively introduce noise to the data and shouldn't noticeably alter the look or feel if done correctly. Unfortunately, this can be more difficult to implement, but it can be nearly impossible to detect.

Fingerprint the Executable

The techniques so far have concentrated on altering the game's assets; however, the executable code can be one of the best places to hide a fingerprint. While it would be trivial to place a fingerprint in a dead area of the code before compilation, this would complicate the workflow of embedding a fingerprint. Ideally, the fingerprint should be applied as a post-process to an already compiled executable.

One method would involve declaring some static data within the code, consisting of a unique key and some dead space—for example, a 24-byte marker followed by 32 bytes of garbage. As a post-process, a tool can read in the executable, detect the 24-byte marker, and then overwrite the 32-byte garbage area with an encrypted fingerprint. Reading the fingerprint back would be as simple as looking for the 24-byte marker and decrypting the next 32 bytes. In order to make this fingerprint as invisible as possible, care should be taken to make it look similar to other bytes in the static data section.

A more devious method for embedding an undetectable fingerprint is to rearrange critical instructions. Consider that there are likely to be places in the code where the order of instructions is unimportant (after all, this is how out-of-order processors obtain a great deal of speed). If you can find a series of five such instructions, then you can come up with 120 different permutations of these instructions. Thus, by simply rearranging existing code, you can invisibly fingerprint a number between 1 and 119 (notice that you can't fingerprint zero, since that would leave the order unchanged). While technically more complex to implement, it would be nearly impossible to detect such a fingerprint.

Combining Multiple Strategies

While each technique is reasonably effective, they become even more powerful and undetectable when used together. This dramatically increases the chances that at least one of the techniques will survive so that you can correctly identify a leaked build. Since many of these techniques are easy to implement, it would be smart to combine several for your own personal strategy. Table 1.8.1 shows a summary of each and compares their ease of implementation with how difficult they are to detect.

Table 1.8.1   Summary of Fingerprinting Techniques

Strategy	Simple to Implement	Difficult to Detect
Name on Intro Screen	Extremely	Not Very
Add Extra Files	Extremely	Very
Adobe Photoshop CS Digimarc	Extremely	Somewhat
Fingerprint Image File	Very	Extremely
Fingerprint 3D Model, Animation, or SFX	Not Very	Extremely
Fingerprint Executable	Somewhat	Extremely
Combining Multiple Strategies	Varies	Extremely

Defeating the Fingerprint

Defeating the fingerprint, without inside information on how it's implemented, would be extremely difficult for an attacker. However, if two attackers with individually fingerprinted builds colluded, they could compare their images and quickly pinpoint the differences [Wu04]. Since the differences are the fingerprint, they could corrupt or remove the fingerprint. For example, they could take the average of the two fingerprints, which would likely destroy any evidence of their collective identities.

While there is no foolproof way to counter a collusion attack, this is an active area of research that is still largely unexplored. For more insight into this area, please see [Wu04].

As a final note, it should be realized that the same fingerprint should always be given to the same person. Otherwise, the person could collude with themselves by comparing two builds that they received at different points during development.

Conclusion

Protecting pre-release builds might seem paranoid, but when there is so much at stake, it is worth the cost to prevent a catastrophe. Many large publishers implement some kind of fingerprint process, but it would benefit many smaller developers to do the same. As discussed, there are a variety of ways to fingerprint a build, ranging from complex to trivial.

Remember that a crucial part of the strategy is deterrence. Everyone involved should understand that they are personally responsible for any leaked builds. However, you'll want to put some teeth into your deterrence and adequately fingerprint the build by using some type of super-secret method.

The ideal realization of this fingerprinting process is to have a single program that can embed and read fingerprints from a final image of the game. Only one or two key people should know how it works and have permission to fingerprint builds. If individuals understand that each build they receive is fingerprinted through this process, then you can be reasonably confident that no one will attempt to leak your game before it's officially released.

References

[Wu04] Wu, Min, Wade Trappe, Z. Jane Wang, and K. J. Ray Liu, "Collusion-Resistant Fingerprinting for Multimedia." *IEEE Signal Processing Magazine,* March 2004. Available online at *http://www.ece.umd.edu/~minwu/public_paper/ Jnl/0403FPcollusion_IEEEfinal_SPM.pdf.*

1.9

Faster File Loading with Access-Based File Reordering

David L. Koenig,
Touchdown Entertainment, Inc.

david@touchdownentertainment.com

Most games face the requirement of loading resources from media. Operating systems can be fairly slow when obtaining file handles for a large number of files. Most games load their resources from packed resource files as an optimization. These are large file databases that contain a full directory hierarchy as a single file or small group of files. Resource files effectively solve this file-handle overhead issue. However, another problem exists: The order of resource files is generally a mirror of the directory structure on disk. Games rarely access resources in the order they appear within the directory structure. Instead, they tend to jump around within the resource file. This can be a major bottleneck. Resources will always load faster when accessed sequentially. Modern games use a large enough data set to show this weakness within the resource file layout. All games exhibit some pattern of resource usage. The next step in optimizing load times is to gather data on how the game uses resources. We can then examine those usage patterns to provide an optimized file order within the resource file. This gem explains a potential solution to this common problem.

The Problem

The chain is only as strong as its weakest link. In terms of speed, the current weakest link is mass storage in the form of hard drives, CD-ROM drives, and DVD-ROM drives. Mass storage is among the slowest piece of hardware in the PC or console, and the slowest to gain improvement. Hard drives today run at roughly the same speed as they did four years ago, but video cards are many times faster. That improved speed isn't worth much if you can't get your content onto it in a reasonable amount of time. See [History03] for a chronology of hard-disk storage.

Solutions

So, what options are there? The answer lies in the project requirements. All projects have different resource needs. Developers should identify what those needs are early in the development cycle. Here is a brief list of possible methods for improved loading times. This is by no means a definitive list of possible optimizations.

Solution One: Custom File Formats

Create content formats that contain all dependencies within each file itself. Basically, you could save an entire scene graph as one file. Alternatively, you could select individual objects and export them, plus all resource dependencies as one file. This would allow the resources to load in order. The problem with this method is redundant data. If any resources are shared across several objects, they will both contain the dependency, and thus make your deliverable larger than it needs to be.

Solution Two: One Resource File Per Level

Pack resources for each given level into their own resource file. What this does is shorten the distance that the disk head will need to jump when the files are out of order. This may cut the time down slightly. The upside to this solution is that it may be fairly easy to implement closer to the end of a project. The downside is that, depending on your project, there may not be much gain.

Solution Three: Reorder the File List

Rearrange the order that resources are loaded according to how they are packed within the resource files. This works best in situations where you load a known set of files at a given time. A perfect example of this is loading a standard set of weapon models before the player enters the game world. This is very common in first-person shooters. Generally, there is a common weapon set of around 10 to 20 models with textures or materials. All the developer needs to do in this situation is log the file pointer position when loading each file in this set. The load order can then be sorted in the order they appear within the resource file. Theoretically, the resources should load faster. Results will vary with each project.

Solution Four: Reorder the Resource File

To obtain optimal loading performance, resources need to be loaded as close to sequential as possible. The ideal situation is the complete elimination of fragmented file loading. This isn't always possible. What can be done is to reorder groups of files that are commonly loaded together into a more optimal layout. When files are grouped in this manner, the most likely optimal situation is presented. When the game switches to a new state, such as loading the front end-user interface, those files are loaded sequentially in order. This means that only one large file-pointer jump is required. The file system can make the jump and read the group in. It can then jump to another data group. This is a big improvement over jumping for each individual file loaded.

How Access-Based File Reordering Works

Step One: Run the Game and Collect Data

Run the game using a standard packed resource file. Log the file access and load times to a text file. The log should contain a list of files as they are accessed by the game. It might be a good idea to split the log into sections based on how the game transitions to different states. This could effectively offer hints to the file-order optimizer on which files are grouped together. The variations are unlimited. It all depends on how the game project uses resources. The load times should be logged as well so that later results can be compared to this baseline result.

Step Two: Parse the Data and Optimize the Order

ON THE CD

Run the file access log through a packing-order optimizer. This step is highly project-dependant. The associated code sample on the CD-ROM takes a *level*-oriented approach.

Common data is loaded as well as resources specific to one of the levels. The packing order is optimized for one specific level. A more robust approach would be to organize groups of files loaded in sequence. This requires that the game is able to log file access based on which system is accessing each resource, and when. A perfect place to start for optimization is any section that is common to all levels. Examples of this might be in-game UI, a standard weapon set, or a common shader library.

Step Three: Repack the Resource File

The resource-packing tool should have the ability to pack the resource file in a pre-determined order, specified by an input file. Pack the resource file based on the optimized order.

Step Four: Run the Game Again and Collect Data

We need to verify that our optimized resource file actually improves the load times. Run the game with the newly packed file and log the loading times. Compare the new data with the initial load data. Does the game load faster? If not, keep reading for possible issues that can affect the results.

Results

ON THE CD

Table 1.9.1 shows results obtained from the sample data contained on the CD-ROM.

Table 1.9.1 Sample Data Load Times

File System	Time To Load in Milliseconds
Windows File System (NTFS)	6077.858499
Resource File	1443.543244
Optimized Resource File	795.332088

As you can see, the optimized file loads the data almost twice as fast as the standard resource file. The actual numbers here are quite small, as the sample data set itself is quite small. In the preliminary tests with large files (>1GB), results as high as 20–50 times speed increase could be seen in certain cases when using an optimized resource file as opposed to a directory-traversed resource file layout—a difference of 200 milliseconds to 10 seconds—a huge difference in load times. The best results come from loading patterns that initially accessed the files in a fragmented manner, which meant a great deal of disk jumping. Reordering the resource file corrects the issue.

Factors That Can Affect the Results

The results are just numbers. Sometimes they don't tell you the whole story. There are several things that can affect the validity of the results.

Hard-Drive Caching

This is the number-one cause of invalid results and a tough problem to combat. All that is required to see this in action is to run the sample code. Run it a second time, right away. You will see a huge difference in the results due to the sectors being cached. The method to combat this problem depends on the device. One universal option is to reboot the machine. Another option is to load from a different media source.

File Fragmentation

Suppose the operating system actually stored the optimized resource file in several fragments instead of one contiguous file. The results might even show that the optimized file loads slower than the standard resource file. This exact issue was encountered while writing this gem. Once the defrag application was run on a hard disk partition, the problem was corrected. This is an issue that can affect the end user as well. Generally, this will not be a problem on CD-ROM or DVD-ROM media, as you have full control over the physical mapping of the files.

Potential Issues

Packing order can affect areas that you might not think about during the development cycle. One potential performance hit is for the mod community. If you pack the resources in the order that your storyline uses them, you lock the peak file system performance into your content. When an end user creates a new level using content from your game, they may find that the loading system performs worse than if no optimization was done. Currently, this is more of a problem for PC games than console games, but it is certainly something to consider.

General Loading Best-Practices

There are a number of standard optimizations that developers can use to speed up the loading of resources. These are not new ideas, but more of a review of current techniques.

Sequential Access

Read the file data incrementally. This is the number-one key issue for file-loading performance. Accessing files sequentially takes advantage of the hardware caching that occurs on your mass-storage device. Generally, mass-storage devices read a little ahead of the section that is currently being requested. This is in anticipation of those sections being requested by the application. The only way to fully take advantage of this feature is to load data in sequential order.

Preprocess Your Data

Data loading in general is faster when the data can be loaded straight into memory without conversion. A single data-type conversion might seem small on the surface, but can grow quickly with an increasing data set. As an example, consider that the end user has a low-end machine with a small amount of system and video RAM. Rather than down-sampling the data at load time, consider shipping a precreated *low-end* data set that has a smaller memory footprint. See [Olsen00] for more information.

Cache Files in Memory

Don't load a file more than once if you can help it. If the game world uses the same texture on multiple polygons, the resource management system should not load the file every time it is referenced in the world file. Store files in a common resource bank so that fast lookups can be done to avoid unnecessary file loading.

Data Compression

The less time the game spends loading data, the more time it can spend doing something interesting with it. Consider using some form of compression on large files that are easily compressed, such as large text files. There is an excellent compression library called zlib that is freely available online (see [Zlib05]).

Know the Hardware

Mass-storage devices generally have an optimal load size of data chunks. In the case of the Xbox DVD player, the optimal chunk size is 128k bytes (see [Mansur05]). This may differ from system to system. If you are working on a known platform, make sure you load data according to its specifications. If you're working on a PC title, you may not have access to this information, since there is no standard PC hardware set. As a general rule, it is least optimal to load data from media one byte at a time. Try to avoid doing so.

Conclusion

Optimizations are highly specific to the project at hand. Think about how your project uses resources in order to determine what optimization will work best for your needs. Like any optimization, don't wait until the end of the project to think about it. Loading-speed optimization needs to be planned before production starts, when you have the most flexible development time. Consider whether your title can take advantage of access-based file reordering. It might just cut your load times in half, or better. Remember that your game is constantly telling you exactly what it needs in order to run at optimal performance. Listen to it. For a simple example of this solution, take a

ON THE CD

look at the source code sample on the CD-ROM.

References

[History03] "The History of Computer Data Storage: The timeline :)" available online at *http://www.usbyte.com/common/history_of_storage.htm*, 2003.

[Mansur05] Mansur, Mark, "DVD Layout and Load-Time Tips and Tricks," available online at *https://xds.xbox.com*, March, 18, 2005.

[Olsen00] Olsen, John, "Fast Data Load Trick." *Game Programming Gems 3,* Charles River Media, 2002.

[Zlib05] zlib, 2005. Available online at *http://www.zlib.net.*

1.10

Stay in the Game: Asset Hotloading for Fast Iteration

Noel Llopis and Charles Nicholson, High Moon Studios

llopis@convexhull.com,
charles.nicholson@gmail.com

When it comes to making a polished game, practice really does make perfect. But even though the final quality of the game largely depends on the skill of the content creators, their efforts to perfect the game are often hampered by a painful workflow. Just to see the results of a one-line change to an AI script, a designer might have to quit the game, rebuild a several-hundred-megabyte resource file, and relaunch. Enabling artists and designers to quickly and painlessly iterate will result in better content, more experimentation, and ultimately a better game.

Asset hotloading is the process by which assets are automatically reloaded into the game while it is running, without stopping or restarting a level. Hotloading can be done with many types of assets: textures, models, level geometry, scripts, game object data, sounds, animations, and so on; and it can reduce iteration times to just a few seconds, even when working with game consoles. Not only will asset hotloading make a huge impact on the quality of your game, but you'll also earn the eternal gratitude of your content creators.

Hotloading Workflow

The following is a typical scenario showing how asset hotloading is integrated into the workflow and how the different parts of the system interact with each other. The steps are illustrated in Figure 1.10.1.

1. An artist modifies a texture in Photoshop.
2. The artist presses the custom Export button, which saves the source texture and triggers the asset converter, which in turn converts the TGA file into an optimized binary format. The asset converter can also do more-complex

operations, such as changing bit depth and compression formats, or generating mipmaps with the correct filtering.

3. The file monitor (which was running in the background all along) detects that one of the files it was keeping an eye out for has changed (the new texture file created by the converter). It contacts the runtime through a network channel and notifies it of the particular file that needs to be reloaded.

4. The runtime receives a message through the network. It retrieves the filename of the asset from the message and starts the actual reloading.

5. The texture is loaded in memory. No conversion is necessary, because it was already converted into binary format as soon as the texture was exported.

6. The old texture that is out of date is removed and the new texture takes its place.

7. In the next frame, the new texture is used for rendering.

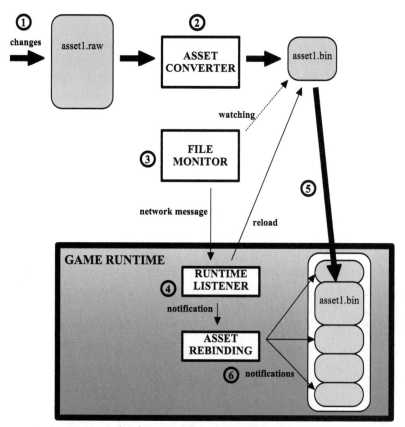

FIGURE 1.10.1 *Hotloading workflow integration.*

The total time elapsed from the time the artist pushes the export button until the new texture is displayed in the game can be extremely short. It can take as little as one second or less (conversion time + network communication time + load time). In the case of large assets or expensive conversions, the time can be a bit longer, but it's rarely more than just a few seconds.

Anatomy of Asset Hotloading

There are four main elements in the asset-hotloading process: the asset converter, file monitor, runtime listener, and asset rebinding.

Asset Converter

The asset converter takes assets in their raw or intermediate format and creates a binary, platform-ready format that the runtime can load directly. This step is not strictly necessary (the runtime could load the source format directly), but it has several advantages:

- It detects any errors or inconsistent data early on in the pipeline, so the content creator can get feedback right away. From this point on in the pipeline, the data can assumed to be correct.
- It removes the need to add lots of complex loading code to the runtime. Instead, the runtime loads one block of memory, and the asset is ready to be used. This is even more important if multiple types of source assets can be used (e.g., several texture formats, such as TGA, TIFF, PNG, etc.). The runtime can simply load one type and leave the conversion up to the asset converter. This results in extremely fast loading times, because the runtime simply has to load the data and use it without any parsing, memory allocation, and so on.

The asset converter is the same tool that you already use for all of your asset building in the game, so it's not something that needs to be created just to support asset hotloading. The only difference is that here it is invoked on a single asset as soon as an artist or designer modifies it, instead of as a batch process on a large amount of assets at once.

Converting assets can be more complicated than simply changing their formats. Complex resources depend on other resources, so the asset converter tool might also do some dependency-checking and build anything that needs to be rebuilt.

File Monitor

The file monitor's job is to monitor the built asset directory and notify the runtime listener whenever any file changes. When the asset converter builds a source asset into its final platform-specific form, the output file is put into the directory being watched by the file monitor. The file monitor, which is constantly watching this directory, notices that a file-write operation took place, and sends the file over the network to the runtime listener.

The cleanest and most efficient way of implementing the file monitor is through OS-specific file event hooks. Instead of constantly monitoring the state of some files, the file monitor can register itself to receive an event whenever any file in a certain directory changes.

A Win32 implementation of the file monitor can use the `ReadDirectoryChangesW` function. Other platforms have their own file event notifications, such as the Linux `dnotify/inotify`.

The documentation for `ReadDirectoryChangesW` looks complicated, but it boils down to associating a directory with an event to signal when any file operations occur. The monitor polls this event for completion every 200 ms, using `GetOverlappedResult`. When it returns `true`, it means that a file in our target directory has changed. The set of changed files is returned in the form of a large `char` buffer, which has to be cast to a `FILE_NOTIFY_INFORMATION` structure. Only the entries that have the `FILE_ACTION_MODIFIED` attribute turned on are processed, meaning that they have just been written to disk.

Since it is common to change many files in a short time period, the list of pending changed filenames is cached locally for one second before transmitting them over the network. This results in fewer batches and also has the side effect of dealing with the more-curious behaviors of `ReadDirectoryChangesW`: It will often report duplicate notifications for the same file, and the number of notifications per file seems dependent on the total number of changed files!

Once all the file changes have been sent over the network and dealt with, it is necessary to call `ReadDirectoryChangesW` again to restart the listening process. Conveniently, we can reuse the `Event` object, so only one is needed over the lifetime of the application.

If the target platform uses a different file system than the development platform (as is the case with Xbox), the file monitor should also copy the changed files to the target platform, or at least trigger another program to do the copying, before notifying the runtime of the changes.

Runtime Listener

The runtime listener constantly listens on a specific network port for notifications from the file monitor. Whenever a notification comes in, it triggers a reload of the specified asset.

For the listener to do its job correctly, it needs to know the filename of the asset to reload and what asset to replace in the runtime. In the simplest case, the runtime knows about all the filenames, and that's all the information it needs to load a new one. Other times, if the runtime doesn't already have a map between filenames and resources, we might need to pass in the asset ID along with the filename. In that case, the file monitor will need to know about the asset IDs, probably in the form of a map file created during asset creation or some asset file for the game that it can access.

The runtime listener is the only part of the asset-hotloading system that needs to be added to the game runtime; this is very convenient, because asset hotloading is something we only want to do during development. Therefore, one of the goals of implementing asset hotloading is to disturb the runtime code as little as possible. The amount of new code added to the runtime should be kept to a minimum and should be easy to remove with some simple `#ifdefs` when shipping the game.

Asset Rebinding

Games have many different kinds of assets. A typical game will have textures, models, animations, sounds, music, object definitions and instances, scripts for control and AI, visible and physical static geometry, and a host of other game-specific types. Some of these assets fit very naturally into the hotloading paradigm, and others require a little more careful consideration.

Once the runtime listener is notified of a change, the game begins loading the new assets. This can be done synchronously or asynchronously. Doing it asynchronously has the advantage that the frame rate will not vary very much during the load, but the new asset might not be displayed for several frames. On the other hand, a synchronous load will cause a slight pause in the game, but has the advantages of being simpler to implement and, most important, not require extra memory, since we don't need to keep both the old and the new versions of the resource in memory. Since asset hotloading is something that is only used in development, unless you have a really robust asynchronous asset-loading system in place already, loading them synchronously is more than sufficient.

We often have no guarantees that the new asset will fit in the same amount of memory as the asset it's replacing, so it will most likely be located in a different memory address. Since we want the rest of the game to use this new asset instead of the old one, we either need to use some form of indirection (e.g., a handle or a weak reference), or we need to keep track of what parts of the code were pointing to the old asset and fix them to point to the new one.

Getting these newly changed assets loaded onto the target platform is only the first part of the battle. Once the new assets are in memory, they still have to replace their previous instances and be bound to some sort of resource management system. This process is called *rebinding,* and the end result of the process is that the new assets are visible and usable without having to restart the game.

The main problem with rebinding is that it's not always easy to figure out which objects are keeping references to the assets that are about to be swapped out. In C++, the native pointer type is not enough, because it can't be used to determine when targets are destroyed. This can lead to dangling pointers and the standard madness that ensues.

One solution to this problem is to disallow direct resource pointers and instead employ a resource-handle table. A handle table is a global table of all resources currently loaded by the game, and is probably owned by the primary resource manager object. If an object in the game needs to use a resource, it must access that resource through the handle table by way of an ID. A temporary pointer to the resource is returned, but not cached by the object. If the object wants to work with the same resource again at a later time, it must reacquire the resource pointer from the handle table. Then, if the resource ends up being replaced by a hotload, the resource manager simply updates the appropriate table entry with the new resource, and the ID remains unchanged. Subsequent queries of the table will return the newly loaded resource and the client code is none the wiser. For convenience, it is also possible to wrap the handle mechanism inside a smart pointer that behaves mostly like a native C++ pointer.

Textures are probably the simplest resource to rebind, as they have no external dependencies and maintain no state. They generally only have to be copied into memory and their references updated. Model geometry and particle data can be as easy as texture data; and animations are also on the easy end of the spectrum, as they're mainly composed of raw track data.

So far, the assets discussed here have all been simple. When the assets being reloaded become more fundamental to the definition of the game, the steps required to replace the assets at runtime can become increasingly more destructive. For instance, the hotloading of a level definition that contains the starting locations and states of all actors in a level presents a much more complex problem. The easiest (and perhaps only) way to make this new data visible is to destroy and reset the level itself. Similarly, memory constraints may make reloading the heavyweight static level geometry and textures completely impossible. If the level geometry is large enough, the time it could take to hotload it would be so close to the time it would take to simply reload the entire game that it may not be worth the time investment.

Even though asset hotloading is a great technique to reduce iteration time, it is not necessary to adopt it across all resources. If there are technical or time constraints, you can implement asset hotloading for the most common assets and get most of the benefit for a small amount of work.

Practical Considerations

Network Connection

Having a live network connection between the development computer and the target platform is extremely useful. The asset-hotloading commands are just the beginning of the possibilities. Such a connection can be turned into a full debugging console where states can be toggled, commands can be run, or variables can be queried and displayed. It works in a unified way on many different platforms and even on remote machines.

Memory Fragmentation

Constantly destroying and reloading individual assets can lead to memory fragmentation, and can eventually lead to running out of usable contiguous memory for new assets. One way to combat this problem is to reuse the existing asset if its size hasn't changed. Whenever that is not possible, memory fragmentation is a definite possibility.

One approach is to simply let memory fragmentation happen. This is something that is only done during development, and development kits typically have more memory than the target platform, so we should be able to spare some memory. If the game eventually runs out of memory after eight hours of straight hotloading, then we can simply reboot it and continue working.

Another alternative is to block off a large section of the extra memory in the development kit and try to manage that memory with some of the well-known heap-management algorithms. That should keep fragmentation to a minimum at the expense of some wasted space.

Finally, we can bite the bullet and compact our resources if we ever run out of memory. Again, since this is used only during development, it's not a problem if it takes a few seconds (and only happens every few hours). We already have the technology in place to move assets around, so this shouldn't be too much of a problem.

Resource Packfiles

If you load your assets through a large resource packfile that contains all the assets for a particular level, you need to make sure you can also load individual assets directly. It also means that the asset converter should not do the final step of packing the modified assets into a packfile, and should leave them as individual files instead.

Example Program

ON THE CD

The CD-ROM contains a sample application that implements hotloading textures. It includes the three parts described in this gem:

Asset converter: Converts TGA files into binary textures that can be loaded by OpenGL directly with a simple header format.
File monitor: Listens for file changes in a particular directory.
Viewer application (runtime): Simple GLUT application displaying three textured teapots. It listens on a port for notifications from the file monitor.

To test the asset hotloading, start by running the viewer application. Then run the file monitor, indicating the directory to monitor for changes and the network address of the runtime. Modify one of the "textureX.tga" files (or just copy another TGA file on top of them), and run Make to invoke the asset converter. This will trigger notifications from the file monitor and an instant reloading from the viewer.

Conclusion

Asset hotloading is a very powerful technique that can be implemented with little effort. This gem showed one possible implementation that offloaded as much work as possible to offline tools and minimized the changes to the game runtime. By adopting this strategy incrementally with the assets that change most frequently, or by implementing it across the board on all game assets, content creators will be able to stay in the game and create the best possible content for their projects.

Further Reading

Bloom, Charles, "The making of *Oddworld: Stranger's Wrath*." GameTech 2005. Available online at *http://www.cbloom.com/3d/game_tech_04.zip*.

Hawkins, Brian, "Handle-Based Smart Pointers." *Game Programming Gems 3,* Charles River Media, 2002.

Johnstone, Mark S., "The Memory Fragmentation Problem: Solved?" ISMM98.

Llopis, Noel, "The Beauty of Weak References and Null Objects." *Game Programming Gems 4,* Charles River Media, 2003.

MATHEMATICS AND PHYSICS

Introduction

Jim Van Verth,
Red Storm Entertainment, Inc.

jimvv@redstorm.com

Since at least the time of Isaac Newton, there has been an alliance between mathematics and physics. This partnership has sometimes been uneasy; Richard Feynman was no fan of mathematicians. However, without mathematics, there would be no physics; and without physics, perhaps the advances in mathematics that physics inspired would have happened much later. Certainly Newton would have found it difficult to demonstrate his theory of gravitation without the calculus he had helped develop years before.

This codependency continues into game development. The physical theories described by the math still stand; but without the mathematics, it wouldn't be practical to create a program demonstrating the theory. Most of the algorithms used to solve physical simulation problems on the computer come from numerical analysis, a branch of mathematics. Ultimately, it comes down to the formulas and their implementation in code. And so we bring these two wary allies together into one section.

We begin with fundamentals. In the idealized world of the mathematician, real numbers have infinite precision, and division by zero merely provides new avenues for investigation. In the hard, cold world of the digital computer, we are not so fortunate. However, we are fortunate to have Chris Lomont, who provides us with an article that introduces us to this cold world and demonstrates that with a little ingenuity, we can take the limitations of floating-point representation and use them to actually write more efficient code. By treating the bits of a floating-point word as an integer, there are a large number of floating-point operations that can be handled much more quickly, or at least in parallel in the integer pipeline.

One rarely thinks of homogeneous coordinates, solving linear systems, and cross products as related topics (other than all being part of computer graphics). Here we present two articles that cover the same techniques from two different perspectives. The first is by Vaclav Skala, and focuses on the relationship between homogeneous coordinates and linear systems, and how a clever use of the cross product can be used to find intersections of lines and planes, and improve the efficiency of clipping code. The second, by Anders Hast, expands more on the theme of using the cross product to solve linear systems. In particular, it examines how the same technique can speed up scan-conversion setup for triangle attributes and the inversion of small matrices.

When talking about the collections of objects that most games contain, such as player data, animated objects, or even technology graphs, most developers consider them from the data-management perspective rather than a mathematical one. Palem GopalaKrishna provides an alternate view, and shows how the techniques of sequence indexing can help. Sequence indexing tries to answer questions about enumerating and ordering sets and subsets of symbols, and can be used for cataloging, compressing, and generating behaviors and metrics for our data.

At this point, many people are familiar with the basic techniques for determining and handling collisions between rigid bodies. If your game world is bricks and pavement, this may be enough. However, 70% of the real world is covered in water, and so we would like our games to reflect that. Therefore, real-time techniques for managing interactions between rigid objects and fluids are becoming increasingly more desirable. In this section of *Game Programming Gems 6,* we are blessed with two fine articles. In the first, Erin Catto introduces a simple geometric technique for determining the buoyancy forces for a rigid polygonal body in a fluid. An approximate model for drag forces is also discussed. The closing article in the section, by Takashi Amada, provides the counterpoint. He discusses a method called smooth particle hydrodynamics, which is a particle-based (as opposed to the standard cell-based) method for simulating fluids and fluid interaction with rigid bodies.

2.1

Floating-Point Tricks

Chris Lomont,
Cybernet Systems Corporation

chris@lomont.org

Once upon a time, floating-point code in video games was rare. It was too slow compared to integer-based code, so people resorted to fixed-point tricks for software rasterization. Those days are over; floating-point has gotten fast. Furthermore, many processors have independent floating-point and integer pipelines, so interleaving floating-point code properly with integer-based code results in great performance gains. Modern game programming relies heavily on floating-point code, from GPUs to physics engines to sound processing to collision routines to intersection tests. Here's a prediction: In the future, games will start using real-time ray-tracing engines, at which time floating-point tricks will become even more useful. Unfortunately, many programmers are in the dark about the intricacies of floating-point programming, such as numerical analysis and error propagation, and they even make simple errors like comparing floating-point values with "==." This gem teaches some of floating-point basics while supplying a few nifty tricks to speed up floating-point code.

Most programmers, even very good ones, cannot even explain how floating-point values are stored on their platform of choice. An interesting experiment is to ask coworkers how integers are stored and how to perform arithmetic operations on them, and then do the same for floating-point values. Embarrassingly enough, more programmers can thoroughly explain the obscure Binary Coded Decimal (BCD) details in game programming than can explain floating-point details. You probably use floating-point code often in your work; when was the last time you needed BCD?

Just as in the integer case, the first step to mastering floating-point code is to understand how floating-point values are stored in terms of their bit representations. This article will explain in detail the floating-point storage format used on the majority of systems. Those rare systems not implementing this method almost always use a similar one with minor variations, so the knowledge gained by studying this article will benefit your algorithm development greatly.

One final note before we begin: An article similar to this one appeared in *Game Programming Gems 2* [King01]. This gem extends that article in several areas, offering many new tricks and at least one improvement. Now, let's learn floating-point bit representations!

The Floating-Point Format

Almost all floating-point values you will run across conform to IEEE 754, a floating-point format defining precisely how values are stored, how errors propagate in basic operations, and how to handle over/underflow, Not-a-Number (NaN) results, and infinities. Before IEEE 754 was standard across platforms, floating-point code was very nonportable, giving wildly different and incorrect results across platforms. For the story, check out the Father of Floating-Point, William Kahan [Kahan98].

Most likely, every floating-point format you will see, even those not conforming exactly to IEEE 754, is some minor variation of the IEEE 754 layout. IEEE 754-conformant examples include values stored on the PC and most current and (probably) future game consoles. 3DNow!™ and SSE/SSE2/SSE3 use the IEEE 754 layout, but they often have minor discrepancies when it comes to supporting other details, like rounding modes required by the standard. The nVIDIA® and ATI™ GPUs, and the PlayStation 2 game console also use bit-compatible floating-point formats; so understanding the bit representations is useful in many areas.

IEEE 754 Format Basics

One size IEEE 754 defines is the 32-bit floating-point format, which is the standard `float` datatype in many C/C++ implementations. It has the bit layout shown in Table 2.1.1.

Table 2.1.1   32-Bit Floating-Point Format

Sign Bit S	Biased Exponent E	Packed Mantissa M
1 Bit in position 31	8 Bits in positions 30–23	23 Bits in positions 22–0

The value represented is $(-1)^S \cdot 2^{E-127} \cdot (1 + M/2^{23})$, where M is a 23-bit unsigned integer. Let's break this down a bit.

The highest order bit in a 32-bit float is the sign bit S, where $S = 0$ for nonnegative values and $S = 1$ for negative values. The next eight bits in locations 23–30 hold the biased (by 127) exponent. *Biased* means to take the 8-bit value, think of it as an unsigned 8-bit integer E, and subtract the bias 127 to get the real exponent that gives the power of 2 above. This allows the representation of very large to very small values.

Finally (and this is the part most people get incorrect), the 23 bits in positions 0–22 represent the packed mantissa, which you can view as a 23-bit unsigned integer M. The bits represent a fractional value in [0,1), thus the division $M/2^{23}$.

Packed means there is an implied 1 before the mantissa, hence the $1 + M/2^{23}$. For shorthand, we'll write 1.*M* for this value. Numbers stored in this packed form are also called *normalized* numbers, since the leading 1 bit in the value is shifted to the implied position and then not written down. The exponent is correspondingly decreased to maintain a similar magnitude. This allows storing one more bit in the format than if numbers were not normalized. Throughout, we'll use M and E to represent the unsigned bit values in a floating-point format.

As an example, consider the bit pattern in Table 2.1.2, representing a `float`:

Table 2.1.2 Anatomy of a `float`

1	1000 0010	101 0000 0000 0000 0000 0000

What is the value? The sign bit is 1, so the value is negative. The exponent bits represent $E = 130$, so the exponent is $130 - 127 = 3$. The mantissa bits represent $M = 2^{22} + 2^{20}$, so the mantissa value $1.M$ is $1 + (2^{22} + 2^{20})/2^{23} = 1.625$. Thus, the `float` represented is $(-1)^1 \cdot 2^3 \cdot 1.625 = -13$.

Other floating-point sizes on a PC and most everywhere else follow similar layouts, with differences as shown in the Table 2.1.3.

Table 2.1.3 Floating-Point Sizes

Type	float	double	long double	Half-Float[1]	SPARC long double
Bits	32	64	80	16	128
Sign bits	1	1	1	1	1
Exponent bits	8	11	15	5	15
Exponent bias	127	1023	16383	15	16383
Mantissa bits	23	52	64	10	112
Packed	Yes	Yes	No	Yes	Yes
Digits precision	7	16	19	3	34

Note the 80-bit representation is not packed! The usually hidden 1 bit is explicitly given as the most significant bit in the mantissa. Another important note is that internally the x86 processor uses 80 bits for floating-point operations, so most formats are unpacked to 80 bits, used in computation, and then repacked on storage. Sadly, the 80-bit floating-point values cannot be accessed in current Microsoft C/C++ compilers, where the `long double` and `double` are treated as the same 64-bit type. If you need this much precision, the only option is use assembly language.

---

[1] Used in DirectX 9.0 and OpenGL 1.2, and for ATI and nVIDIA chipsets, among other places.

IEEE 754 Exceptions

Easy so far, right? Well, think through the rules given above, and try to represent some important values, such as zero. You'll find we cannot represent zero with this method, since there is always the implied 1 from the packed mantissa. So we will need exceptional cases to the above scheme, which get placed at extreme values of E. Other than zero, the IEEE 754 standard defines a few other exceptional values:

When $1 \leq E \leq 254$, the numbers are represented as above.

(Signed) zeroes ±0:   If $E = 0$ and $M = 0$, then the represented value is 0. However, the sign bit may be 0 or 1, giving two different bit patterns, both with floating-point value 0.

Denormalized numbers (also called subnormal numbers).   If $E = 0$ and $M \neq 0$, there is no longer any implied 1 bit. These represent very small values (close to zero), and allow graceful underflow. The price is that these patterns have fewer significant digits.

Infinities: If $E = 255$ and $M = 0$, then the sign gives the values $\pm \infty$.

Not-a-Number: If $E = 255$ and $M \neq 0$, this denotes NaN. If the first bit of M is 0, then this denotes a Signaling Not-a-Number (SNaN). If the first bit of M is 1, then this denotes is a Quiet Not-a-Number (QNaN). Intel only implements one NaN and calls it QNaN. Signaling NaN should trigger exceptions in the code, and QNaN does not (hence *quiet*).

The above rules completely describe all possible bit patterns for IEEE 754 32-bit floating-point numbers. They are defined to behave nicely—for example, $\infty + \infty = \infty$, $\infty - \infty = NaN$ and $1/0 = \infty$ (which is not strictly correct). Oddly, $\sqrt{-0} = -0$. Obviously, we can generalize this to set exceptional bit patterns for the other data sizes. For more details see [754Ref05a] and [754Ref05b].

Now we have the complete rules of how floating-point values are stored. It is helpful for later discussion to map the various bit patterns onto a real number line for easy inspection. Values go from the most negative to the most positive. Code to produce this table (see Table 2.1.4) is on the CD-ROM in the function `MakeNumberLine`.

ON THE CD

Table 2.1.4   Special Floating-Point Values and Their Representations

Value	Hex	Signed 32-Bit Int	Name
−1.#QNAN	FFFFFFFF	−1	Negative NaNs
−1.#QNAN	FFFFFFFE	−2	
...	...	...	
−1.#QNAN	FF800002	−8388606	
−1.#QNAN	FF800001	−8388607	
−1.#INF	FF800000	−8388608	$-\infty$

$\rightarrow$

Value	Hex	Signed 32-Bit Int	Name
−3.40282e+038	FF7FFFFF	−8388609	Negative Normalized
−3.40282e+038	FF7FFFFE	−8388610	
...	...	...	
−1.17549e−038	80800001	−2139095039	
−1.17549e−038	80800000	−2139095040	
−1.17549e−038	807FFFFF	−2139095041	Negative
−1.17549e−038	807FFFFE	−2139095042	Denormalized
...	...	...	
−2.8026e−045	80000002	−2147483646	
−1.4013e−045	80000001	−2147483647	
0	80000000	−2147483648	−0
0	00000000	0	+0
1.4013e−045	00000001	1	Positive
2.8026e−045	00000002	2	Denormalized
...	...	...	
1.17549e−038	007FFFFE	8388606	
1.17549e−038	007FFFFF	8388607	
1.17549e−038	00800000	8388608	Positive Normalized\
1.17549e−038	00800001	8388609	
...	...	...	
3.40282e+038	7F7FFFFE	2139095038	
3.40282e+038	7F7FFFFF	2139095039	
	7F800000	2139095040	+∞
1.#QNAN	7F800001	2139095041	Positive NaNs
1.#QNAN	7F800002	2139095042	
...	...	...	
1.#QNAN	7FFFFFFE	2147483646	
1.#QNAN	7FFFFFFF	2147483647	

One thing to note is that if we take nonnegative increasing floats and treat their bit patterns as signed integers, the results are also increasing. Similarly, negative floats are less than positive floats when treated as signed integers. Unfortunately, negative floats are decreasing—or in reverse order—when viewed as signed integers.

Another point worth mentioning is that Intel processors handle denormals, infinities, and NaNs much more slowly than AMD chips—as much as 900 times slower! See [Dawson05b] for a very interesting read about this. So when designing floating-point code that handles exceptional cases or small numbers, you'll need to profile your code on various machines.

We wrap up this discussion with some remarks about floating-point comparisons. We needed a representation for zero, but unfortunately we got two distinct bit representations: +0 and −0. These compare as equal when treated as `float`; but clearly, when treated as `int`, we have to be careful. Even when we're comparing floating-point values we can run into issues. For example, for any floating-point value v in C/C++, is it true that v == v? Or given two floats v1 and v2, is it true that at least one of the following will be true: v1 > v2, or v1 == v2, or v1 < v2? See the end of this gem for the surprising answers.

Designing Routines

We don't have space enough in this article to cover the numerical analysis of floating-point routines. Instead, we will only cover tricks that manipulate floating-point values, using their bit representations. These tricks, while not usually as robust and accurate as using the floating-point unit of your CPU, will often result in much faster code. When you need that extra 40% speed increase in a core routine, have exhausted every last algorithmic trick, and cannot pipeline your code any further, the tricks presented in this article may save your life and the lives of those (projects) you love. As with other optimizations, you will need to time the resulting code and make sure it works on your desired platform to the desired level of accuracy.

Since we can access the bits of the float by treating it as an int, we can manipulate the bits using the normal C++ Boolean and shift operations. In many cases, this will turn out to be faster than the floating-point routines, but usually at a little cost in precision or lack of proper denormal/exceptional value handling. However, there are cases where treating the float as an int will make our routines even more accurate.

Sometimes the tricks are not compatible across all platforms/architectures; we'll try to point out gotchas and places to watch. Finally, do not resort to using tricks such as these until you need them. They often result in nonportable and hard-to-maintain code. However, the possible performance gains cannot be gotten without using them.

Preliminaries

In order to access the bits, we will require that float and int are the same size: 32 bits. If this fails on your compiler, use an integer size that is equivalent. If you wish to fiddle with the bits in doubles in Visual Studio.NET, you can use the __int64 type, since both are 64 bits. Throughout the code, we'll use the variable name ival for the integer representation of the bits in the float fval.

ON THE CD

First, we create a routine that checks platform sizes to ensure the library will run well. The TestArchitecture routine in the code included on the CD-ROM returns true if the desired architecture features are supported: the float and int types are the same size, unsigned shifting works as we want it to, and casting behaves as we need it to. If it returns false, you should look through the routine and change supporting defines to create a version that works properly on your architecture.

We'll begin by covering a few ways to access the bits of the float directly using C/C++. The most common is a direct cast:

```
int ival = (*(int*)&fval);
```

On C++ compilers that don't optimize aggressively, it may be faster to use the following:

```
int& ival = (*(int*)&fval);
```

However, Falk Hüffner [Anderson05] points out that the new C99 ISO standard specifies undefined behavior for this, so then you might need to use:

```
memcpy( &ival, &fval, sizeof(int));
```

A third way, seen in [King01], is to use a union of a float and int, such as:

```
typedef union { float f; int i; } IntOrFloat;
```

A fourth way is to use inline assembly and simply read the memory for the float into a 32-bit register, and work with that.

ON THE CD

The first two methods are supported in the code on the CD-ROM, handled by #defines, and union is used a few places in the code.

The first method is the default one. Throughout the code, the macros _fval_ to_ival() and _ival_to_fval() are used, which resolve to the proper method. You need to understand your platform to know what works best for you. Sometimes the union method always generates a memory copy; sometimes memcpy on small values will not generate a function call and will optimize away completely, letting the compiler just use the memory location for the float directly. There is no way to tell beforehand without trying the various methods and looking at the resulting assembly code.

Other common operations require a bitmask of all 0s or 1s, depending on the sign of a float. [King01] essentially uses int mask = (ival>>31); but this may run into problems, since under the C/C++ standards, right-shifting signed int is implementation-defined, whether or not the sign is preserved. (See [Lomont05] for details.) On Intel architecture and the Microsoft compiler, it works fine. Right-shifting signed int is also tested in the routine TestArchitecture. So we define a macro to handle this:

```
#ifdef _SIGNED_SHIFT
#define SIGNMASK(i) ((i)>>31)
#else
#define SIGNMASK(i) (~((((unsigned int)(i))>>31)-1))
#endif
```

In order to construct and deconstruct floating-point values for testing, two routines, MakeFloat and SplitFloat, allow creating a float value—given a sign, exponent, and mantissa as unsigned int—and allow reversing this process. There is also a DumpFloat routine that outputs a float in various formats to an ostream.

A final point is that our routines do not handle infinities and NaNs properly, and often need special cases to handle denormals. But since most game code does not deal with these cases (except denormals), things work out fine.

Manipulating the Sign Bit

First we'll look at various tricks we can achieve by fiddling with the sign bit. For example, a fast absolute value routine is as follows:

```
float FastAbs(float fval)
{
    int ival;
    _fval_to_ival(fval,ival);
    ival &= 0x7FFFFFFF;    // strip sign bit
    _ival_to_fval(ival,fval);
    return fval;
}   // FastAbs
```

Another trick is to negate a value quickly by XORing the integer representation with 0x8000000, which flips the sign bit. We can also quickly query various aspects of the floating point value with the following:

```
#define FI(f) (*((int *) &(f)))     // float to int

// float to unsigned int
#define FU(f) (*((unsigned int *) &(f)))

#define LessThanZero(f)
    (FU(f) > 0x80000000U)
#define LessThanOrEqualsZero(f)
    (FI(f) <= 0)
#define IsZero(f)
    ((FI(f)<<1)==0)
#define GreaterThanOrEqualsZero(f)
    (FU(f) <= 0x80000000U)
#define GreaterThanZero(f)
    (FI(f) > 0)
```

There are also function versions, but the call outweighs the benefits. Note that since these are macros, you can only call them on variables. You cannot compile, for example, IsZero(0.0f). If you are on an architecture where the type punning[2] is not guaranteed, or you do not like polluting the global namespace, use the function versions:

```
bool LessThanZero(float fval);
bool IsZero(float fval);
bool LessThanZero(float fval);
bool LessThanOrEqualsZero(float fval);
bool GreaterThanZero(float fval);
bool GreaterThanOrEqualsZero(float fval);
```

---

[2]See *http://msdn.microsoft.com/library/default.asp?url=/library/en-us/dndeepc/html/deep06012000.asp*, or *http://www. google.com* for type punning and read up. A type pun is when a memory location has two different meanings, like an English pun.

Clamping

Another series of useful routines clamps floating values to a specified range. The following routines are supported in our library:

```
// clamp a float to [0,1]
float Clamp01(float fval);
// clamp a float to [A,B] (requires A<B)
float ClampAB(float fval, float A, float B);
// clamp a float to [0,infinity)
float ClampNonnegative(float fval);
```

As an example how these work, consider clamping a float value to [0,1]. Usually, one might write:

```
if (fval < 0.0f) fval = 0.0f;
if (fval > 1.0f) fval = 1.0f;
```

In a pipelined architecture, the branches and comparisons will cost you performance. Using bit tricks, we remove the branching, with the potential to do this more quickly. The idea is to use the sign bit to make a mask to zero the value or leave it alone. Thus to clamp to 0:

```
int s;
IntOrFloat val;
val.f = fval;        // set floating value
s = SIGNMASK(val.i); // all 1's if sign bit 1 from int value
val.i &= ~s;         // 0 value if was negative
```

Next we clamp to 1. Note that [King01] has a similar routine, but the signs are incorrectly reversed.

```
// clamp to 1
val.f = 1.0f - val.f; // val > 1 goes negative
s = SIGNMASK(val.i);  // all 1's if sign bit 1
val.i &= ~s;          // 0 if was negative
val.f = 1.0f - val.f; // convert back
return val.f;
```

Whether this is faster than the comparisons depends on too many things to claim either is faster. Plus, the above can use the integer pipeline on x86 while other floating-point computations are executing. The other `Clamp*` functions are similar, and work by using floating-point shifts and scalings before the integer-based branchless clamping.

Conversions

Another family of useful tricks does fast `int-to-float` and `float-to-int` conversions. See [King01] for a detailed discussion of why these work. The rough idea is to add a value large enough to force the integral part to the mantissa, mask out the garbage exponent and sign, and subtract a constant to handle negative values. He provides the following two functions that work for integer values in $|fval| < 2^{22} = 4194304$.

```
float IntToFloat(int ival)
{
    IntOrFloat val,bias;
    val.i = ival;
    bias.i = ((23+127)<<23)+(1<<22);
    val.i += bias.i;
    val.f -= bias.f;
    return val.f;
} // IntToFloat

int FloatToInt(float fval)
{
    int ival;
    fval += (1<<23) + (1<<22);  // push integer to mantissa
    _fval_to_ival(fval,ival);   // convert
    ival &= (1<<23)-1;          // mask out garbage
    ival -= (1<<22);            // handle negative values
    return ival;
} // FloatToInt
```

Here is another version that extends this range to work for floating values in $|fval| < 2^{31} = 2147483648$. It works in the same manner as the more restricted versions, but uses a 64-bit double instead of a 32-bit float for conversions[3].

```
// convert a float to a long and vice versa.
// Valid for |fval| <= 2^31-1
long FloatToLong(float fval)
{
    // upcast to get enough bits
    // value is 0x59C00000 = 2^51+2^52
    double temp = fval +
        (((65536.0*65536.0*16.0)+32768.0)*65536.0);
    return (*(long *) &temp) - 0x80000000;
} // FloatToLong
```

Math Routines

What other tricks can we find? Well, note that the bit representation allows easy access to the linear part of the value in the mantissa and the logarithmic/exponential part in the exponent bits. One possible use for this is to look up values for various functions like sin and cos, using the float bits as an index. This is covered well in [King01], and so we will not do so here.

---

[3]As a side note, using doubles in your code is not much slower than using float in most cases (not on a PS2, however, where doubles are implemented in software). Test this and believe.

Another possibility is to use the exponent bits to find base 2 logarithms quickly à la [Anderson05]:

```
int IntLog2(float fval)
{
    // strip out exponent, remove sign, unbias
    assert(fval > 0);
    unsigned int ival;
    _fval_to_ival(fval,ival);
    return (ival>>23) - 127;
} // IntLog2
```

Note that this will fail on denormalized numbers, since the exponent $E = 0$ and the mantissa need to be scanned to get the exact value. In the code included on the CD-ROM, the slower `IntLog2Exact` is provided, which does extra work to find the correct log base 2 in the case where $E = 0$.

ON THE CD

Probably the most covered trick on the Internet (with `float` to `int` conversions running a close second) is finding fast square-root algorithms. Not to be outdone, here is one common version:

```
float FastSqrt2(float fval)
{
    assert(fval >= 0);
    float retval;
    int ival;
    _fval_to_ival(fval,ival);
    ival -= 0x3f800000; // subtract 127 from biased exponent
    ival >>= 1;         // requires signed shift to preserve sign
    ival += 0x3f800000; // rebias the new exponent
    _ival_to_fval(ival,retval);
    return retval;
} // FastSqrt2
```

As mentioned, many people recommend this routine. However, there is a nasty bug that is not mentioned anywhere else. What is the bug? Try to find a floating-point value that returns complete garbage, or see the end of this article for the answer.

So how does this routine work? The key is the right shift, which will divide the exponent bits by 2, effectively taking a square root of the magnitude. We shift the packed mantissa as well, since $\sqrt{1.M} \approx 1.(M/2)$. Subtracting and adding 0x3f800000 removes and adds the bias from the exponent, so the shift functions nicely. This routine will return the value 8.13152e-020 for $\sqrt{0}$—small but not zero. And if you want to really understand floating-point values, prove that the maximum relative error for this routine versus the correct square root is bounded by $\frac{3}{2\sqrt{2}} - 1 \approx 0.06$, or about 6%. A Newton-Raphson step like in the `InvSqrt` routine below will improve this accuracy at the cost of speed.

Before looking at another square-root implementation, let's try computing $1/\sqrt{x}$, the inverse square root:

```
float InvSqrt(float x)
{
    assert(x > 0);
    // to see why works, read [Lomont05]
    float xhalf = 0.5f*x;
    int i;
    _fval_to_ival(x,i);      // get bits for floating value
    i = 0x5f375a86 - (i>>1); // initial guess y0 w/magic number
    _ival_to_fval(i,x);      // convert bits back to float
    x = x*(1.5f-xhalf*x*x);  // Newton step, increases accuracy
    return x;
} // InvSqrt
```

To explain in detail how this routine works would take too much space for this gem. Roughly, we want the −1/2 power; so the shift, minus, and constant do this. The rest of the constant combines with the mantissa to give the best initial guess possible. Details, including deriving the magic constant 0x5f375a86, can be read online at [Lomont05], where a full discussion of this routine is provided.

ON THE CD

The second square-root function on the CD-ROM is then based on computing $x \cdot 1/\sqrt{x}$ for x > 0. This is fast and much more accurate than the previous square-root function. It also does not suffer from the (fixable) flaw in the previous version. It even returns zero for $\sqrt{0}$, since the InvSqrt function returns a large finite value for zero (which technically should be infinite), and then multiplies by x = 0.

Comparisons

Another area where bit tricks work is in comparisons. One of the first things a programmer learns about floating-point calculations is to avoid comparing floating-point values using code like:

```
if (fval1 == fval2) // ...
```

since it rarely does what the programmer intended due to rounding errors, internal representation error, or other issues. Instead many use code like:

```
if (fabs(fval1 - fval2) < tolerance) // ...
```

where tolerance is some small value. This leads to many hard-to-find bugs. In particular, once a tolerance is chosen, it does not scale with the values being compared as it should. (See the discussion in [Knuth97v2]; this is very important.) What one needs is code like the following:

```
if (fabs(fval1 - fval2) < max(fval1, fval2)*tolerance) ...
```

This scales a little better; however, this correct version can be up to five times as slow as the original (see [Lomont05]). After trying to solve this specific problem for a ray tracer, a few hours of thought led to a solution that is essentially the same as Bruce Dawson's [Dawson05]:

```
bool DawsonCompare(float af, float bf, int maxDiff)
{
    int ai,bi;
    _fval_to_ival(af,ai);     // get bits
    _fval_to_ival(bf,bi);
    if (ai < 0)
        ai = 0x80000000 - ai; // correct order
    if (bi < 0)
        bi = 0x80000000 - bi; // and again
    int diff = ai - bi;       // find the difference
    if (abs(diff) < maxDiff)  // is close enough?
        return true;
        return false;
}
```

And now the comparison check can go something like:

```
if (true == DawsonCompare(fval, aval, 1000)) // ...
```

where the 1000 replaces a tolerance and scales very well over the entire floating-point range. We now compare as "equal" any two floating-point values that are within 1000 of each other when their bits are viewed as int over the entire number range, which scales very well[4]. And it is faster than any of the previous methods! This is not the end of the story, though.

How does this work? The idea comes from the ordering discussed after viewing the floating-point number line. If both values are positive, we merely see if they are close as integers. If one or both is negative, some bit-twiddling needs done to correct the ordering. For more details, see [Dawson05].

By removing the branches, using some clever bit manipulation, the following faster code is obtained:

```
bool LomontCompare(float af, float bf, int maxDiff)
{
    // fast routine, portable across compilers
    // constant time execution
    int ai;
    int bi;
    _fval_to_ival(af,ai);
    _fval_to_ival(bf,bi);
    int test = SIGNMASK(ai^bi);
    assert((0 == test) || (0xFFFFFFFF == test));
    int diff =
        (((0x80000000 - ai)&(test)) | (ai & (~test))) - bi;
    int v1 = maxDiff + diff;
    int v2 = maxDiff - diff;
    return (v1|v2) >= 0;
}
    // LomontCompare
```

---

[4]The value 1,000 is a rough estimate, and it depends on how the values you are comparing were generated. You will need to experiment with your routines to find tolerances that suit your needs.

[Lomont05] details how this routine (and many prior variants) works. The bottom line is that it is equivalent to the `DawsonCompare`, but is faster on all machines tested[5]. It is much faster than the `KnuthCompare` and is stable across a large number range. Currently, this is used in a real-time Constructive Solid Geometry (CSG) ray-tracing engine that is still under development.

Future Directions

The above functions merely scratch the surface of what is possible. Some other tricks, which are left to you as exercises, include the following:

Fast inline swapping: Since you can view a `float` as an `int`, you can swap the two floats `af` and `bf` with integer representations `ai` and `ab`, with no `temp` variable, using the XOR trick: `ai ^= bi; bi ^= ai; ai ^= bi;`

Fast table lookup functions using the bit representation as a table index: This works well for `sin`, `cos`, and many other functions. [King01] covers this well.

Fast cube roots and other roots by clever exponent modification, followed by a fast mantissa approximation.

Fast divide and multiply by powers of 2, by working on the exponent: Just like you can shift integers to multiply by 2, you can do this to `floats` by adding to the exponent bits. This is similar to what we did with square roots.

Fast radix sorting, using the bits to select the bin: This gives a linear time-sorting algorithm. Remember though that the negative `floats` are order-reversed, so you need a trick like the one used in the `LomontCompare` function. You cannot instantiate templates on a `float`, but you can on an `int`. Thus, you can make a template that performs floating-point calculations at compile time for constants and other work. See [Rosten05] for a library that does exactly this.

Fast `memcpy` using the floating registers to move 64 or more bits at a time.

We should also add tricks yet to be discovered by us all to this list.

Conclusion

You have seen how floating-point values are stored. Now you realize the immense potential when using this knowledge as a last resort for creating fast (but obtuse) code. To go to the next level, you need to be able to analyze such routines and prove mathematically that they work, do worst-case and average-case error analysis, and do detailed performance-testing on the target platform. These tasks are hard and tedious. For an example of a detailed error analysis of the `InvSqrt` routine, see [Lomont05].

---

[5]Several current and older AMD and Intel PCs were tested, though not on consoles. Please email if you gather data.

And finally, a reward for anyone who's read this far—surprising answers to the questions posed throughout the article:

Can you assume for a `float` value v that `v==v` returns `true`? NO! This fails for NaN values. Usually, you should not get NaN in your routines; but it does happen, so do not rely on this assumption.

For two `float` values `v1` and `v2`, is it true that one of the clauses `v1>v2`, `v1==v2`, or `v1<v2` is `true`? Again, NO. All comparisons of any flavor fail if one operand is a NaN.

To see the weird bug in `FastSqrt2`, use what you have learned in this gem to compute `FastSqrt2` on the floating bit value for –0. The result is `2.76701e+019`, a very large value! To fix the routine, right after the `_fval_to_ival` conversion, insert `ival &= 0x7FFFFFFF` to mask out the sign before the shift.

Other places to learn about floating point include [Hecker96], [Hsieh04], and the wonderful book [Warren02].

ON THE CD

Finally, the code to do all of this and more is on the included CD-ROM. The Web site[6] for this gem will contain the code also, as well as future changes and versions. As we gather timing details for various functions, these will also be posted on the Web site.

References

[754Ref05a] Vickery, Christopher, "IEEE-754 References." Available online at *http://babbage.cs.qc.edu/courses/cs341/IEEE-754references.html.*

[754Ref05b] "IEEE Arithmetic." Available online at *http://cch.loria.fr/documentation/IEEE754/numerical_comp_guide/ncg_math.doc.html.*

[Anderson05] Anderson, Sean, "Bit Twiddling Hacks." Available online at *http://graphics.stanford.edu/~seander/bithacks.html.*

[Dawson05] Dawson, Bruce, "Comparing Floating-Point Numbers." Available online at *http://www.cygnus-software.com/papers/comparingfloats/comparingfloats.htm.*

[Dawson05b] Dawson, Bruce, "x86 Processors and Infinity." Available online at *http://www.cygnus-software.com/papers/x86andinfinity.html.*

[Hecker96] Hecker, Chris, "Let's Get to the (Floating) Point." *Game Developer Magazine,* February/March 1996. Available online at *http://www.d6.com/users/checker/pdfs/gdmfp.pdf.*

[Hsieh04] Hsieh, Paul, "Programming Optimization." Available online at *http://www.azillionmonkeys.com/qed/optimize.html.*

---

[6]See *http://www.lomont.org/Software,* or search for "Chris Lomont" on *http://www.google.com* to find the author and the code.

[Kahan98] Kahan, William, "An Interview with the Old Man of Floating-Point,"
1998. Available online at *http://www.cs.berkeley.edu/~wkahan/ieee754status/
754story.html.*

[King01] King, Yossarian, "Improving Performance with IEEE Floating-Point."
Game Programming Gems 2, Charles River Media, 2001.

[Knuth97v2] Knuth, Donald, *The Art of Computer Programming: Volume 2, Seminu-
merical Algorithms,* 3rd Ed. Reading, Massachusetts, Addison-Wesley, 1997.

[Lomont05] Lomont, Chris, "Taming the Floating-Point Beast," 2005. Available
online at *http://www.lomont.org/Math/Papers/2005/CompareFloat.pdf.*

[Rosten05] Rosten, Edward, "Floating point arithmetic in C++ templates," 2005.
Available online at *http://mi.eng.cam.ac.uk/~er258/code/fp_template.html.*

[Warren02] Warren, Henry S., Jr., *Hacker's Delight.* Addison-Wesley, July 2002.

2.2

GPU Computation in Projective Space Using Homogeneous Coordinates

Vaclav Skala, University of West Bohemia, Czech Republic

skala@kiv.zcu.cz

There are many examples in computer graphics where linear algebra is used to solve given problems—such as computing a line from two points, an intersection of two lines, or line clipping. In some cases, difficulties may occur if the given mathematical formula is applied directly. In particular, tests similar to $a == b$ are highly suspicious from the computational stability point of view. Even a very simple collinearity test between two lines is very unreliable due to limited computation precision.

There is another factor to be considered. In computer graphics applications, points are mostly represented in homogeneous coordinates—that is, in the real projective space [Ferguson01], [Hill01], [Shirley02]. Users and programmers mostly convert points in homogeneous coordinates into Euclidean coordinates using a division operation. This division can take a long time relative to other floating-point operations and might cause severe numerical instability or a fatal division-by-zero exception.

In this gem, we will show how common intersection computations can be performed directly using homogeneous coordinates. This approach results in higher numerical stability and, in some cases, a significant speed-up. The presented approach is especially convenient if vector and matrix operations are supported on the main processor, or for applications on a Graphics Processing Unit, or GPU.

Mathematical Background

Let us begin by reviewing some mathematical facts that are necessary for understanding the remainder of the gem.

137

Homogeneous Coordinates

Suppose we have a point in E^2 (or two-dimensional space) represented in Euclidean coordinates as $\mathbf{X} = (X, Y)$. It is well known that we can represent the same point in three-dimensional *homogeneous coordinates* as $\mathbf{x} = [x, y, w]^T$, where:

$$x = wX \quad y = wY, w \neq 0. \tag{2.2.1}$$

A common value for w is 1, so the point $\mathbf{X}$ is usually represented as $\mathbf{x} = [X, Y, 1]^T$. Note that since there are an infinite number of possibilities for w, $\mathbf{X}$ can be represented by an infinite number of points in homogeneous coordinates. Also, if $w = 0$, then the entity represented is not a point but a vector—that is, a *point at infinity*.

Given a point $\mathbf{x} = [wX, wY, w]^T$ in homogeneous space, the corresponding Euclidean coordinates (X, Y) are computed as:

$$X = x/w \quad Y = y/w, w \neq 0. \tag{2.2.2}$$

The homogeneous representation for points in E^3 (or three-dimensional space) behaves similarly.

Operations with Determinants

The determinant of a matrix $\mathbf{A}$ can be defined recursively as:

$$\det(\mathbf{A}) = |\mathbf{A}| = \sum_{j=1}^{n} a_{ij} (-1)^{(i+j)} \det(\tilde{\mathbf{A}}_{ij}), \tag{2.2.3}$$

where $\tilde{\mathbf{A}}_{ij}$ is the submatrix formed by removing the ith row and jth column from $\mathbf{A}$. For a 3×3 matrix, this can be computed as:

$$\begin{vmatrix} a & b & c \\ d & e & f \\ g & h & i \end{vmatrix} = a(ei - fh) - b(di - fg) + c(dh - eg). \tag{2.2.4}$$

We will be using two additional properties of determinants. The first is that scaling a single row by a factor q scales the determinant by the same factor q for $q \neq 0$. This can be represented as:

$$\begin{vmatrix} a_{11} & \cdots & a_{1n} \\ \vdots & & \vdots \\ qa_{k1} & qa_{k2} \cdots & qa_{kn} \\ \vdots & & \vdots \\ a_{n1} & \cdots & a_{nn} \end{vmatrix} = q \cdot \begin{vmatrix} a_{11} & \cdots & a_{1n} \\ \vdots & & \vdots \\ a_{k1} & a_{k2} \cdots & a_{kn} \\ \vdots & & \vdots \\ a_{n1} & \cdots & a_{nn} \end{vmatrix}. \tag{2.2.5}$$

The second property is that if the determinant is zero, then the rows or columns of the determinant matrix are linearly dependent; that is, you can create one row or column by scaling and adding the remaining rows or columns. Such a matrix has no inverse. Similarly, if the matrix is representing a system of linear equations, such a system has no solution.

Operations with Vectors

A dot product of two vectors $\mathbf{a} = [a_1,a_2,a_3]^T$ and $\mathbf{b} = [b_1,b_2,b_3]^T$ is defined as:

$$\mathbf{a}^T\mathbf{b} = \mathbf{b}^T\mathbf{a} = \mathbf{a} \cdot \mathbf{b} = \|\mathbf{a}\|\|\mathbf{b}\|\cos\varphi, \qquad (2.2.6)$$

where φ is the angle between vectors $\mathbf{a}$ and $\mathbf{b}$.

A *cross product* of two vectors $\mathbf{a} = [a_1,a_2,a_3]^T$ and $\mathbf{b} = [b_1,b_2,b_3]^T$ is defined as:

$$\mathbf{a}\times\mathbf{b} = \begin{vmatrix} \mathbf{i} & \mathbf{j} & \mathbf{k} \\ a_1 & a_2 & a_3 \\ b_1 & b_2 & b_3 \end{vmatrix}, \qquad (2.2.7)$$

where $\mathbf{i} = [1,0,0]^T$, $\mathbf{j} = [0,1,0]^T$, $\mathbf{k} = [0,0,1]^T$.

By Equation 2.2.4 above, this result is equal to:

$$\mathbf{a}\times\mathbf{b} = (a_2b_3 - a_3b_2)\mathbf{i} - (a_1b_3 - a_3b_1)\mathbf{j} + (a_1b_2 - a_2b_1)\mathbf{k}. \qquad (2.2.8)$$

This produces a vector perpendicular to $\mathbf{a}$ and $\mathbf{b}$. Note that this is only defined for vectors in three-dimensional space, and that $\mathbf{a} \times \mathbf{b} = -\mathbf{b} \times \mathbf{a}$.

We can introduce a cross product for the four-dimensional case as another determinant:

$$\mathbf{a}\times\mathbf{b}\times\mathbf{c} = \begin{vmatrix} \mathbf{i} & \mathbf{j} & \mathbf{k} & \mathbf{1} \\ a_1 & a_2 & a_3 & a_4 \\ b_1 & b_2 & b_3 & b_4 \\ c_1 & c_2 & c_3 & c_4 \end{vmatrix}, \qquad (2.2.9)$$

where $\mathbf{i} = [1,0,0,0]^T$, $\mathbf{j} = [0,1,0,0]^T$, $\mathbf{k} = [0,0,1,0]^T$, $\mathbf{1} = [0,0,0,1]^T$.

Similar to the three-dimensional case, this produces a vector perpendicular to $\mathbf{a}$, $\mathbf{b}$, and $\mathbf{c}$. This definition will be used later on.

Principle of Duality

The principle of duality states that any theorem remains valid when we interchange dual words in the theorem. For example, in the E^2 case, the words "point" and "line" are dual, together with "pass through" and "lie on," and "intersect" and "join." Similarly, in the E^3 case, a point is dual to a plane.

What does this mean in computer graphics? It is well known that a line p in E^2 can be defined as:

$$aX + bY + c = 0. \tag{2.2.10}$$

Based on this equation, we can state that a vector $\mathbf{a} = [a,b,c]^T$ in E^3 defines the line p. Furthermore, Equation 2.2.10 can be multiplied by any $w \neq 0$, and the line is geometrically the same. So the line p is actually dual to a homogeneous point (as we'd expect), and both are represented in the dual space by a vector $\mathbf{a}$. Understanding this is very important, as the principle of duality will help us to derive some formulas later on.

Computation in Homogeneous Coordinates

Now we will show how to use homogeneous coordinates to solve some simple linear systems. We will begin by concentrating on the E^2 case, and later on we will extend this to E^3.

The E² Case

Let us consider two lines, p_1 and p_2 in E^2:

$$p_1 : a_1X + b_1Y + c_1 = 0 \text{ and } p_2 : a_2X + b_2Y + c_2 = 0 \tag{2.2.11}$$

The intersection point of those two lines is defined as a solution of a linear system of nonhomogeneous equations:

$$\begin{bmatrix} a_1 & b_1 \\ a_2 & b_2 \end{bmatrix}\begin{bmatrix} X \\ Y \end{bmatrix} = \begin{bmatrix} -c_1 \\ -c_2 \end{bmatrix} \tag{2.2.12}$$

It is well known that the solution is given as:

$$X = \frac{D_x}{D} \qquad Y = \frac{D_y}{D}, \tag{2.2.13}$$

where $\quad D_x = \det\begin{vmatrix} -c_1 & b_1 \\ -c_2 & b_2 \end{vmatrix} \quad D_y = -\det\begin{vmatrix} a_1 & -c_1 \\ a_2 & -c_2 \end{vmatrix} \quad D = \det\begin{vmatrix} -a_1 & b_1 \\ -a_2 & b_2 \end{vmatrix}.$

However, since we are dividing by D, the solution becomes numerically unstable as $D \to 0$. Instead, note that Equation 2.2.12 can be rewritten using homogeneous coordinates:

$$\begin{bmatrix} a_1 & b_1 & c_1 \\ a_2 & b_2 & c_2 \end{bmatrix} \begin{bmatrix} X \\ Y \\ 1 \end{bmatrix} = \begin{bmatrix} 0 \\ 0 \end{bmatrix} \tag{2.2.14}$$

So an alternative is to express the solution of Equation 2.2.11 using homogeneous coordinates, as well:

$$\mathbf{x} = \begin{bmatrix} x, y, w \end{bmatrix}^T = \begin{bmatrix} D_x, D_y, D \end{bmatrix}^T \tag{2.2.15}$$

And using Equation 2.2.2, we can eventually compute X and Y as:

$$X = \frac{x}{w} = \frac{D_x}{D} \quad Y = \frac{y}{w} = \frac{D_y}{D} \quad D \neq 0, \tag{2.2.16}$$

which matches our solution in Equation 2.2.13. If $D = 0$ then the given lines are parallel or identical.

Examining the equations for D_x, D_y, and D, it can be seen that the homogeneous intersection point x can be computed as a cross product of two vectors, $\mathbf{a}_1$ and $\mathbf{a}_2$:

$$\mathbf{x} = \mathbf{a}_1 \times \mathbf{a}_2 = \det \begin{vmatrix} \mathbf{i} & \mathbf{j} & \mathbf{k} \\ a_1 & b_1 & c_1 \\ a_2 & b_2 & c_2 \end{vmatrix}, \tag{2.2.17}$$

where $\qquad \mathbf{i} = [1,0,0]^T, \mathbf{j} = [0,1,0]^T, \mathbf{k} = [0,0,1]^T$

Now let's look at the dual problem. As previously mentioned, the principle of duality in E^2 states that a line is dual to a point and vice versa. So for our situation, the dual problem is to determine a line given by two points. One way to solve this is via the following system of linear equations:

$$\begin{bmatrix} X_1 & Y_1 & 1 \\ X_2 & Y_2 & 1 \end{bmatrix} \begin{bmatrix} a \\ b \\ c \end{bmatrix} = \begin{bmatrix} 0 \\ 0 \end{bmatrix}, \tag{2.2.18}$$

where the two points are given as $\mathbf{x}_i = [X_i, Y_i, 1]^T$, and the line p is represented by the vector $\mathbf{a} = [a, b, c]^T$. Alternatively, we can use:

$$\mathbf{a} = \mathbf{x}_1 \times \mathbf{x}_2 = \begin{vmatrix} \mathbf{i} & \mathbf{j} & \mathbf{k} \\ X_1 & Y_1 & 1 \\ X_2 & Y_2 & 1 \end{vmatrix}. \tag{2.2.19}$$

So as with the intersection of two lines, this means that the line given by two points can be easily determined by the cross product.

However, suppose the points are given in homogeneous coordinates with nonunit w values—that is, $\mathbf{x}_i = [x_i, y_i, w_i]^T$? Normally, a division operation would be performed to convert the homogeneous coordinates to Euclidean coordinates, which we would then substitute into Equation 2.2.18. Instead, note that when using general homogeneous coordinates, we multiply the first row of the determinant in Equation 2.2.19 by $w_1 \neq 0$ and multiply the second row by $w_2 \neq 0$. Due to the identity defined by Equation 2.2.5, we can then write:

$$\mathbf{x}_1 \times \mathbf{x}_2 = \begin{vmatrix} \mathbf{i} & \mathbf{j} & \mathbf{k} \\ x_1 & y_1 & w_1 \\ x_2 & y_2 & w_2 \end{vmatrix} = \begin{vmatrix} \mathbf{i} & \mathbf{j} & \mathbf{k} \\ w_1 X_1 & w_1 Y_1 & w_1 \\ w_2 X_2 & w_2 Y_2 & w_2 \end{vmatrix} = w_1 w_2 \begin{vmatrix} \mathbf{i} & \mathbf{j} & \mathbf{k} \\ X_1 & Y_1 & 1 \\ X_2 & Y_2 & 1 \end{vmatrix} = w_1 w_2 \mathbf{a}.$$

(2.2.20)

The end result is that we have scaled our original vector $\mathbf{a}$ by $w_1 w_2$. However, as was stated, if $w_1 w_2 \neq 0$ the line represented by $w_1 w_2 \mathbf{a}$ is geometrically the same as the line represented by $\mathbf{a}$. So by using Equation 2.2.20, we can determine the line p directly using the general homogeneous coordinates of the given points, and without use of the division operation.

The E³ Case

The extension to the E^3 case is very simple. In this situation, a point is dual to a plane and vice versa. So we can write that:

- The intersection point $\mathbf{x}$ of three mutually non-coplanar planes can be computed as

$$\mathbf{x} = \mathbf{a}_1 \times \mathbf{a}_2 \times \mathbf{a}_3 = \begin{vmatrix} \mathbf{i} & \mathbf{j} & \mathbf{k} & 1 \\ a_1 & b_1 & c_1 & d_1 \\ a_2 & b_2 & c_2 & d_2 \\ a_3 & b_3 & c_3 & d_3 \end{vmatrix},$$

(2.2.21)

where: $\mathbf{a}_i = [a_i, b_i, c_i, d_i]^T$ represents a plane $\rho_i = a_i X + b_i Y + c_i Z + d_i$, $i = 1,\dots,3$, and $\mathbf{x} = [x, y, z, w]^T$ is the intersection point in homogeneous coordinates, and $X = x/w$, $Y = y/w$, and $Z = z/w$, are the Euclidean coordinates.
- As with the E2 situation, prior to the homogeneous divide, we can evaluate the coordinate w of the vector $\mathbf{x}$ and analyze singular or close-to-singular cases, which will represent coplanar or near-coplanar planes.
- The plane determined by three distinct (or non-coincident) points can be determined by:

$$\mathbf{a} = \mathbf{x}_1 \times \mathbf{x}_2 \times \mathbf{x}_3 = \begin{vmatrix} i & j & k & 1 \\ x_1 & y_1 & z_1 & w_1 \\ x_2 & y_2 & z_2 & w_2 \\ x_3 & y_3 & z_3 & w_3 \end{vmatrix}, \qquad (2.2.22)$$

where $\mathbf{x}_i = [x_i, y_i, z_i, w_i]^T$ represents the given points $\mathbf{x}_i$ and $i = 1,\dots,3$, and $\mathbf{a} = [a,b,c,d]^T$ represents the plane ρ determined by these three points—that is, $\rho = aX + bY + cZ + d$.

- We can evaluate the homogeneous coordinate w of the vector $\mathbf{a}$ and analyze singular or close-to-singular cases if $\mathbf{a} = [0,0,0,0]^T$, then the given points are not mutually distinct.

All four cases taken together mean that we have a very robust and simple method for determining:

- A line given by two points in the homogeneous coordinates in E^2
- The intersection point of two lines in E^2
- A plane given by three points in the homogeneous coordinates in E^3
- The intersection point of three planes in E^3

The presented approach is especially very efficient if vector/matrix operations are supported in the main hardware, or if a GPU can be used. An implementation of a 4D cross product used in high-level shader languages is presented in the Appendix A section of this article.

Line Intersection

There are many algorithms that are devoted to determining the intersection of a line or ray with an object. In some applications the line is in a parametric form, and the object is an implicitly described primitive (e.g., a line or plane). A typical example of such a situation is the CyrusBeck (CB) algorithm [Cyrus78] for line-clipping by a convex polygon in E^2 or by a convex polyhedron in E^3. The E^2 case is simple, but the E^3 case is a little bit tricky. One possibility is to define the line in E^3 using Plücker coordinates (see [Blinn77]), but the following approach is simpler.

Line-Plane Intersection

As the E^3 case is more complex, we will cover it in detail. Modification of the equations for the E^2 case is not very difficult and is left to the reader.

We define a line p in E^3 in the parametric form as $\mathbf{X}(t) = \mathbf{X}_A + (\mathbf{X}_B - \mathbf{X}_A)t$, where $\mathbf{X}_A = [X_A, Y_A, Z_A]^T$, $\mathbf{X}_B = [X_B, Y_B, Z_B]^T$ are given points in Euclidian coordinates. As before, we define a plane ρ as $aX + bY + cZ + d = 0$, where a vector $\mathbf{a} = [a,b,c,d]^T$ is a representation of the given plane. We can represent this in a slightly different form as $\boldsymbol{\alpha}^T \mathbf{X} + d = 0$, where $\boldsymbol{\alpha} = [a,b,c]^T$ is a normal vector of the given plane.

It is well known that the parameter of intersection of such a line and plane can be calculated as:

$$t = -\frac{\boldsymbol{\alpha}^T X_A + d}{\boldsymbol{\alpha}^T \left(X_B - X_A \right)}. \tag{2.2.23}$$

As we did with points, we can use homogeneous coordinates to represent t as $[\tau, \tau_W]$, where:

$$\tau = -\left(\boldsymbol{\alpha}^T X_A + d \right) \tag{2.2.24}$$

and

$$\tau_w = \boldsymbol{\alpha}^T \left(X_B - X_A \right). $$

By doing this, no division is needed immediately; it can be postponed in the modified algorithm.

This representation leads directly to a question: What happens if the points defining the line are given in the homogeneous coordinates in general? Usually, programmers convert the given points to Euclidean coordinates using the division operation. However, if we keep them in the homogeneous form, we can rewrite Equation 2.2.23 as:

$$t = -\frac{\boldsymbol{\alpha}^T X_A + d}{\boldsymbol{\alpha}^T \left(X_B - X_A \right)} = -\frac{\boldsymbol{\alpha}^T \dfrac{\boldsymbol{\xi}_A}{w_A} + d}{\boldsymbol{\alpha}^T \left(\dfrac{\boldsymbol{\xi}_B}{w_B} - \dfrac{\boldsymbol{\xi}_A}{w_A} \right)}, \tag{2.2.25}$$

where X_A, X_B, $\boldsymbol{\alpha}_T$, and d are as before; and $\mathbf{x}_A = [x_A, y_A, z_A, w_A]^T$ and $\mathbf{x}_B = [x_B, y_B, z_B, w_B]^T$ are the given points in homogeneous coordinates, $\boldsymbol{\xi}_A = [x_A, y_A, z_A]^T$, and $\boldsymbol{\xi}_B = [x_B, y_B, z_B, w_B]^T$.

Multiplying both sides of Equation 2.2.25 by $w_A \neq 0$ and $w_B \neq 0$, we get:

$$t = -\frac{w_B \left(\boldsymbol{\alpha}^T \boldsymbol{\xi}_A + w_A d \right)}{\boldsymbol{\alpha}^T \left(w_A \boldsymbol{\xi}_B - w_B \boldsymbol{\xi}_A \right)}. \tag{2.2.26}$$

So for the case where our line points are in homogeneous coordinates, we can rewrite Equation 2.2.24 as:

$$\tau = -w_B \left(\boldsymbol{\alpha}^T \boldsymbol{\xi}_A + w_A d \right) = -w_B \mathbf{a}^T \mathbf{x}_A \tag{2.2.27}$$

and

$$\tau_w = \boldsymbol{\alpha}^T \left(w_A \boldsymbol{\xi}_B - w_B \boldsymbol{\xi}_A \right). $$

If the proposed representation in homogeneous coordinates is used and basic arithmetic operations including comparison operations are properly optimized, we obtain more-robust algorithms. A speed up on the CPU can be expected, as well, due to the fact that the division operation is not needed.

In recent research, the proposed approach was applied to the CB algorithm. The modification of the CB algorithm in E^2 is faster for $N \geq 6$, where N is the number of edges of the given convex polygon. For $N \geq 500$, it is about 20% faster than the optimized, original CB algorithm. This means that for E^3, the performance will grow, as we can expect more polyhedron facets to be examined.

Conclusion

We have presented a new approach that uses homogeneous coordinates for some frequently used computations. There is a direct impact for algorithms that are convenient for GPU implementation. The main motivation of this work is to increase the robustness of algorithms, postpone the division operation to the very last moment, and enable direct computation in the homogeneous coordinates, if applicable. The presented approach has been already applied to line and line-segment-clipping algorithms, and led to a simpler and faster solution with increased robustness [Skala04] [Skala05].

The main advantages of the presented approach are:

- Graphical primitives are naturally represented in homogeneous coordinates.
- Elimination of division operations are possible if the result can remain in homogeneous coordinates.
- There is a significant speed-up if vector/matrix operations are supported in hardware.
- Short and compact code is realized for algorithms.
- Implementation is simple on current GPUs (see Appendix A and Appendix B).

Hopefully, the presented approach can lead to a new design of algorithms and computational models, as well.

Appendix A

The cross product in 4D defined as:

$$\mathbf{x}_1 \times \mathbf{x}_2 \times \mathbf{x}_3 = \det \begin{vmatrix} \mathbf{i} & \mathbf{j} & \mathbf{k} & \mathbf{l} \\ x_1 & y_1 & z_1 & w_1 \\ x_2 & y_2 & z_2 & w_2 \\ x_3 & y_3 & z_3 & w_3 \end{vmatrix} \qquad (2.2.\text{A1})$$

can be implemented in Cg/HLSL on GPU as follows:

```
float4 cross_4D(float4 x1, float4 x2, float4 x3)
{
    float4 a;

    a.x=dot(x1.yzw, cross(x2.yzw, x3.yzw));
    a.y=-dot(x1.xzw, cross(x2.xzw, x3.xzw));
    // or a.y=dot(x1.xzw, cross(x3.xzw, x2.xzw));
    a.z=dot(x1.xyw, cross(x2.xyw, x3.xyw));
    a.w=-dot(x1.xyz, cross(x2.xyz, x3.xyz));
    // or a.w=dot(x1.xyz, cross(x3.xyz, x2.xyz));

    return a;
}
```

or more compactly:

```
float4 cross_4D(float4 x1, float4 x2, float4 x3)
{
    return ( dot(x1.yzw, cross(x2.yzw, x3.yzw)),
            -dot(x1.xzw, cross(x2.xzw, x3.xzw)),
             dot(x1.xyw, cross(x2.xyw, x3.xyw)),
            -dot(x1.xyz, cross(x2.xyz, x3.xyz)) );
}
```

The code is simple and uses vector operations available on current GPUs. The cross-product in E^3 is supported directly by Cg/HLSL.

Appendix B

The line/plane intersection parameter defined as:

$$t = -\frac{w_B\left(\boldsymbol{\alpha}^T\boldsymbol{\xi}_A + w_A d\right)}{\boldsymbol{\alpha}^T\left(w_A\boldsymbol{\xi}_B - w_B\boldsymbol{\xi}_A\right)} \qquad (2.2.B1)$$

can be represented in a homogeneous form as:

$$\tau = -w_B\left(\boldsymbol{\alpha}^T\boldsymbol{\xi}_A + w_A d\right) = -w_B\mathbf{a}^T\mathbf{x}_A \quad \tau_w = \boldsymbol{\alpha}^T\left(w_A\boldsymbol{\xi}_B - w_B\boldsymbol{\xi}_A\right). \quad (2.2.B2)$$

Equation 2.2.B2 can be easily implemented on GPU using Cg/HLSL as:

```
float4 intersection_3D(float4 a, float4 xa, float4 xb)
{
    float4 t;
    t.x=-xb.w*(dot(a.xyz,xa.xyz)+xa.w*a.w);
    t.w=dot(a.xyz,xa.w*xb.xyz-xb.w*xa.xyz);
    return t;
}
```

It can be seen that the presented approach significantly benefits from vector/vector operations.

Acknowledgments

The author would like to express his thanks to students and colleagues at the University of West Bohemia for recommendations, constructive discussions, and suggestions that helped finish this work, especially to Ivo Hanak for hints in evaluation of hardware futures, Martin Janda for experimental verification within the Cyrus Beck algorithm, and Libor Vasa and Petr Lobaz for critical comments.

This work was supported by the Ministry of Education of the Czech Republic, project MSM 235200005, Microsoft Research, Ltd. (U.K.) Project No. 2004-360, and ATI Technologies Incorporated.

References

[Blinn77] Blinn, J. F., "Homogeneous Formulation for Lines in 3 Space." *Computer Graphics,* Vol. 11, No. 2, SIGGRAPH 77: pp. 237–241.

[Cyrus78] Cyrus, M. and J. Beck, "Generalized Two and Three-Dimensional Clipping." *Computers & Graphics*, Vol. 2, No. 1, pp. 23–28, 1978.

[Ferguson01] Ferguson, Stuart R., *Practical Algorithms for 3D Computer Graphics.* A. K. Peters, 2001.

[Hill01] Hill, Francis S., *Computer Graphics using OpenGL.* Prentice Hall, 2001.

[Shirley02] Shirley, Petr, *Fundamentals of Computer Graphics.* A. K. Peters, 2002.

[Skala04] Skala, Vaclav, "A New Line Clipping Algorithm with Hardware Acceleration." *cgi*, Computer Graphics International 2004: pp. 270–273.

[Skala05] Skala, Vaclav, "A new approach to line and line segment clipping in homogeneous coordinates." *The Visual Computer*, Vol. 21, No. 11, pp. 906–914, Springer Verlag, 2005.

Solving Systems of Linear Equations Using the Cross Product

Anders Hast, Creative Media Lab, University of Gävle

aht@hig.se

The most common uses of the cross product [Nicholson95] in computer graphics are to compute the normal of a polygon [Hearn04] and perhaps to compute the area of a polygon [O'Rourke98]. This article will show some lesser known applications for the cross product, which might be a surprise for those that are not experts in the field of clipping. In particular, the cross product can be used for solving systems of linear equations. For example, it can be used for computing the intersection of two implicit lines, as well as for computing the coefficients of an implicit line from two given points [Springall90]. We will also show how the setup for bilinear interpolation over a polygon can be computed efficiently using the cross product. Finally, we will show how the cross product can be used to compute the inverse of a 3×3 matrix. Since the cross product is implemented in hardware in both CPUs and GPUs, making careful use of these properties might lead to more-efficient code.

Introduction

Let us first examine how the cross product can be used to solve systems of linear equations. The cross product [Nicholson95] is defined as follows:

$$\mathbf{v}_1 \times \mathbf{v}_2 = \det \begin{bmatrix} \mathbf{i} & \mathbf{j} & \mathbf{k} \\ x_1 & y_1 & z_1 \\ x_2 & y_2 & z_2 \end{bmatrix}$$

$$= \begin{vmatrix} y_1 & z_1 \\ y_2 & z_2 \end{vmatrix} \mathbf{i} + \begin{vmatrix} z_1 & x_1 \\ z_2 & x_2 \end{vmatrix} \mathbf{j} + \begin{vmatrix} x_1 & y_1 \\ x_2 & y_2 \end{vmatrix} \mathbf{k}$$

$$= C_x \mathbf{i} + C_y \mathbf{j} + C_z \mathbf{k}. \tag{2.3.1}$$

Hence, it is clear that the cross product is nothing but a series of determinants. We shall use this fact in order to solve systems of linear equations with two equations and two unknowns. Such a system can be written as:

$$x_1 a + y_1 b = z_1$$
$$x_2 a + y_2 b = z_2. \tag{2.3.2}$$

We can write this system in matrix form as:

$$\mathbf{Mv} = \mathbf{k}, \tag{2.3.3}$$

where the coefficient matrix is:

$$\mathbf{M} = \begin{bmatrix} x_1 & y_1 \\ x_2 & y_2 \end{bmatrix}, \tag{2.3.4}$$

and the column of constants is:

$$\mathbf{k} = \begin{bmatrix} z_1 \\ z_2 \end{bmatrix}. \tag{2.3.5}$$

And finally, the vector containing the variables to solve for is:

$$\mathbf{v} = \begin{bmatrix} a \\ b \end{bmatrix}. \tag{2.3.6}$$

The solution to this system can be obtained in at least two ways. One is to rewrite the system as:

$$\mathbf{v} = \mathbf{M}^{-1}\mathbf{k}. \tag{2.3.7}$$

Here it is necessary to find the inverse of the matrix $\mathbf{M}$. Another possibility is to use Cramer's rule [Nicholson95], where the solution is found by:

$$a = \frac{\begin{vmatrix} z_1 & y_1 \\ z_2 & y_2 \end{vmatrix}}{\begin{vmatrix} x_1 & y_1 \\ x_2 & y_2 \end{vmatrix}}, \tag{2.3.8}$$

and

$$b = \frac{\begin{vmatrix} x_1 & z_1 \\ x_2 & z_2 \end{vmatrix}}{\begin{vmatrix} x_1 & y_1 \\ x_2 & y_2 \end{vmatrix}}.$$ (2.3.9)

This solution is found by first computing the determinant of the coefficient matrix, which gives the denominator. Next, the numerator for a is obtained by replacing the first column in the coefficient matrix by the column of constants. Similarly, the numerator for b is obtained by replacing the second column in the coefficient matrix by the column of constants.

If we change the order of the columns of the numerator in Equation 2.3.8, then the sign changes:

$$a = -\frac{\begin{vmatrix} y_1 & z_1 \\ y_2 & z_2 \end{vmatrix}}{\begin{vmatrix} x_1 & y_1 \\ x_2 & y_2 \end{vmatrix}}.$$ (2.3.10)

We can do the same for Equation 2.3.9:

$$b = -\frac{\begin{vmatrix} z_1 & x_1 \\ z_2 & x_2 \end{vmatrix}}{\begin{vmatrix} x_1 & y_1 \\ x_2 & y_2 \end{vmatrix}}.$$ (2.3.11)

These operations were done with a purpose. Now we can compute both the denominator and the numerator for a and b by the cross product as it is defined in Equation 2.3.1, since:

$$a = -\frac{C_x}{C_z},$$ (2.3.12)

and

$$b = -\frac{C_y}{C_z}.$$ (2.3.13)

If our system has a hardware-supported cross product, this can save us some time: one cross product, a divide, and two multiplies to solve a linear system versus six multiplies, three subtractions, a divide, and two multiplies.

In some cases, we will express the linear system implicitly, or in this form:

$$x_1 a + y_1 b + Z_1 = 0$$
$$x_2 a + y_2 b + Z_2 = 0. \tag{2.3.14}$$

Note that $Z_i = -z_i$, so the results of the determinants are already negated. Therefore, in this case we don't need to negate a and b. All we have to do is compute the cross product and substitute the Z_i values for the z_i values, and then divide by the resulting z component.

Implicit Lines

It is known that this cross-product technique can be used for computing the coefficients for an implicit line from two given points, as well as for computing the intersection of two implicit lines [Skala04], [Skala05]. We'll start by showing how an implicit line equation can be obtained from two points on that line, as shown in Figure 2.3.1.

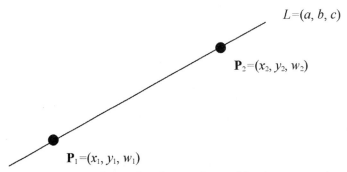

FIGURE 2.3.1   *The implicit line is obtained by the cross product of the two points defining the line.*

An implicit line in R^2 can be defined as:

$$ax + by + cw = 0. \tag{2.3.15}$$

This represents the points on the line where the dot product of a normal vector $\mathbf{n}$ and a point $\mathbf{p}$ are equal to zero, or:

$$\mathbf{n} \bullet \mathbf{p} = 0, \tag{2.3.16}$$

where

$$\mathbf{n} = (a,b,c)$$
$$\mathbf{p} = (x,y,w). \tag{2.3.17}$$

Some readers will recognize that by using three coordinates for points in R^2, we are representing the points in homogenous coordinates [Foley97]. Also note that there are an infinite number of equations defining the same implicit line, all scalar multiples of one another. That is, if we scale this equation by any $s \neq 0$, the geometry of the resulting line is the same—that is:

$$s(ax + by + cw) = 0 \tag{2.3.18}$$

is the same line as Equation 2.3.15.

Let two points in space be:

$$\mathbf{P}_1 = (x_1, y_1, w_1)$$
$$\mathbf{P}_2 = (x_2, y_2, w_2). \tag{2.3.19}$$

If we follow the usual case and set both w_1 and w_2 equal to 1, then to find the line that passes through both points, we have to solve the following system of equations:

$$ax_1 + by_1 + c = 0$$
$$ax_2 + by_2 + c = 0. \tag{2.3.20}$$

Since any scalar multiple of the line equation is valid, we can simplify things further by choosing the one where $c = 1$, or:

$$ax_1 + by_1 + 1 = 0$$
$$ax_2 + by_2 + 1 = 0. \tag{2.3.21}$$

This gives us two equations and two unknowns; and by using our cross-product method for solving linear equations, the coefficients for the line in Figure 2.3.1 can be computed as:

$$L = \mathbf{P}_1 \times \mathbf{P}_2, \tag{2.3.22}$$

and we then divide by the z value.

As it turns out, it is actually not necessary to compute the division. The reason is the same as when simplifying our equation: Any nonzero scale has no effect on the geometry of the resulting line; therefore, we can choose the one we get from the cross product directly.

The values a, b, and c are then just the results of the x, y, and z values of the cross product, respectively. However, if the z value of the cross product is zero (which would make the division invalid), then we know that no line exists. The two points are coincident.

Similarly, the intersection between the two implicit lines $L_1 = (a_1, b_1, c_1)$ and $L_2 = (a_2, b_2, c_2)$, as shown in Figure 2.3.2, can be computed using the cross product. To find the intersection, we have find the point (x, y, w) that lies on both lines, so we need to solve for:

$$a_1 x + b_1 y + c_1 w = 0$$
$$a_2 x + b_2 y + c_2 w = 0. \qquad (2.3.23)$$

Once again we use the cross product to solve the system, and the point can be computed as:

$$\mathbf{P} = (a_1, b_1, c_1) \times (a_2, b_2, c_2). \qquad (2.3.24)$$

This will yield a point in homogenous coordinates. So by dividing $\mathbf{P}$ with its third component, we get a point in the form $P_E = (x, y, 1)$. Again, if the third component is zero, there is no solution.

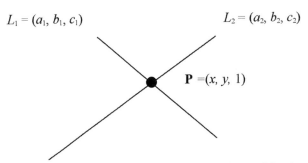

FIGURE 2.3.2 *The intersection point is obtained by the cross product of the two implicit lines.*

Efficient Scan-Conversion Setup

When polygons are rendered in software by the CPU, it is crucial to make the incremental computations over the polygon as fast as possible. The majority of these computations involve the interpolation of attributes set at each vertex, such as intensity for Gouraud shading [Gouraud71], the z-value for z-buffering, and texture coordinates for texture mapping [Hecker95]. Let us take Gouraud shading as an example. In this case, we need a setup that computes the coefficients for an equation defining the intensity over the surface, depending on the current coordinates. The intensity will form a plane, as will be explained later. Since the process is the same for each of the red, green, and blue components, for simplicity's sake, we will consider only generalized grayscale intensity.

The intensity is defined by:

$$\Phi(x, y) = ax + by + d. \tag{2.3.25}$$

For a particular triangle, the coefficients can be obtained by solving the following system of equations [Hast02] [Hast03] [Hast04]:

$$x_0 a + y_0 b + d = \phi_0$$
$$x_1 a + y_1 b + d = \phi_1$$
$$x_2 a + y_2 b + d = \phi_2, \tag{2.3.26}$$

where ϕ_0 is the intensity at (x_0, y_0), ϕ_1 is the intensity at (x_1, y_1), and ϕ_2 is the intensity at (x_2, y_2). The solution is as follows [Kugler96] [Narayanaswami95]:

$$a = \frac{(y_2 - y_0)(\phi_1 - \phi_0) - (y_1 - y_0)(\phi_2 - \phi_0)}{(x_1 - x_0)(y_2 - y_0) - (x_2 - x_0)(y_1 - y_0)} \tag{2.3.27}$$

$$b = \frac{(x_1 - x_0)(\phi_2 - \phi_0) - (x_2 - x_0)(\phi_1 - \phi_0)}{(x_1 - x_0)(y_2 - y_0) - (x_2 - x_0)(y_1 - y_0)} \tag{2.3.28}$$

$$d = \phi_0. \tag{2.3.29}$$

The computation of the solution obviously involves quite a lot of subtractions and multiplications. However, we can use the proposed technique instead and reduce all of them into two vector subtractions and one cross product. Nevertheless, the two divisions are still necessary.

The system in Equation 2.3.26 can be solved by using the proposed technique with relative coordinates, keeping in mind that we need to start from (x_0, y_0) with the intensity ϕ_0, and therefore $d = \phi_0$. The relative coordinates and intensities are as follows:

$$X_1 = x_1 - x_0$$
$$X_2 = x_2 - x_0$$
$$Y_1 = y_1 - y_0$$
$$Y_2 = y_2 - y_0$$
$$\Phi_1 = \phi_1 - \phi_0$$
$$\Phi_2 = \phi_2 - \phi_0. \tag{2.3.30}$$

The necessary computation can be done using two vector subtractions. If the components of the vectors are set to:

$$\mathbf{v}_0 = \begin{bmatrix} x_0 \\ y_0 \\ \phi_0 \end{bmatrix}, \ \mathbf{v}_1 = \begin{bmatrix} x_1 \\ y_1 \\ \phi_1 \end{bmatrix}, \ \mathbf{v}_2 = \begin{bmatrix} x_2 \\ y_2 \\ \phi_2 \end{bmatrix}, \tag{2.3.31}$$

and we define $\mathbf{V}_1 = (X_1, Y_1, \Phi_1)$ and $\mathbf{V}_2 = (X_2, Y_2, \Phi_2)$, then:

$$\mathbf{V}_1 = \mathbf{v}_1 - \mathbf{v}_0$$
$$\mathbf{V}_2 = \mathbf{v}_2 - \mathbf{v}_0. \tag{2.3.32}$$

The system to solve becomes:

$$X_1 a + Y_1 b = \Phi_1$$
$$X_2 a + Y_2 b = \Phi_2. \tag{2.3.33}$$

Using the proposed technique, we can take the cross product to get:

$$\mathbf{N} = \mathbf{V}_1 \times \mathbf{V}_2. \tag{2.3.34}$$

And the coefficients for Equation 2.3.25 are:

$$a = -\mathbf{N}_x / \mathbf{N}_z$$
$$b = -\mathbf{N}_y / \mathbf{N}_z$$
$$d = \phi_0, \tag{2.3.35}$$

where the subscript of $\mathbf{N}$ denotes position of the elements in the vector, starting with x and ending with z.

Let us examine what we have done so far. The cross product should still give us a vector that is orthogonal to two nonparallel vectors, as shown in Figure 2.3.3. What does this mean in our case? By computing the relative coordinates, we get two vectors $\mathbf{V}_1$ and $\mathbf{V}_2$, which lie in (x,y,Φ)-space. The polygon itself resides in screen space and has no z value, but it has intensity as its *third coordinate*. Therefore, we can say that this intensity plane resides in (x,y,Φ)-space, and Equation 2.3.26 is used to compute its normal, similar to what we would do in (x,y,z)-space.

We will now prove that $\mathbf{n} = (a,b,-1)$ is also a normal to the plane defined by Equation 2.3.25. This is quite obvious, since we computed a and b by dividing $\mathbf{N}$ by its negated third component $-\mathbf{N}_z$ in Equation 2.3.35. If we scale all three components of $\mathbf{N}$ by $-\mathbf{N}_z$, we get a result of -1 for the third component. However, we shall demon-

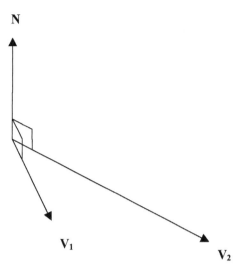

FIGURE 2.3.3 *The normal is orthogonal to the two vectors in* (x,y,Φ)-*space.*

strate this more formally by deriving Equation 2.3.25, using the well-known vector equation for a plane [Nicholson95]:

$$\mathbf{n} \cdot (\mathbf{P} - \mathbf{P}_0) = 0, \qquad (2.3.36)$$

where $\mathbf{P}$ and $\mathbf{P}_0$ are position vectors. We define the normal, the start point, and an arbitrary point on the plane as:

$$\mathbf{n} = (a,b,-1)$$
$$\mathbf{P}_0 = (0,0,d)$$
$$\mathbf{P} = (x,y,\Phi). \qquad (2.3.37)$$

Substituting this into Equation 2.3.36 gives us:

$$(a,b,-1) \cdot \big((x,y,\Phi) - (0,0,d)\big) = 0. \qquad (2.3.38)$$

Finally, we expand the dot product and get:

$$ax + by - \Phi + d = 0. \qquad (2.3.39)$$

This is obviously Equation 2.3.25 in its implicit form and fits what we know already about the coefficients of an equation defining a plane. The constant d is of course the value of the equation when the variables are all zero, and the coefficients of the variables make up the normal of the plane defined by the equation.

Solving Systems of Linear Equations with Three Unknowns

Here is one last trick you can do with the cross product, which can be used for solving systems of linear equations with three unknowns. It is obvious that we could use Cramer's rule once again, yielding a total of four determinants to compute three numerators (as we now have three unknowns) and one denominator. The determinant of a 3×3 matrix can be computed as:

$$\det(\mathbf{M}) = \mathbf{v}_1 \bullet (\mathbf{v}_2 \times \mathbf{v}_3), \tag{2.3.40}$$

where

$$\mathbf{M} = \begin{bmatrix} \mathbf{v}_1^T \\ \mathbf{v}_2^T \\ \mathbf{v}_3^T \end{bmatrix} = \begin{bmatrix} x_1 & y_1 & z_1 \\ x_2 & y_2 & z_2 \\ x_3 & y_3 & z_3 \end{bmatrix}. \tag{2.3.41}$$

The total cost would be four dot products, four cross products, one division, and three scalar multiplications. Moreover, we would need to swizzle the elements in the matrix for each determinant we compute.

Another way we could solve this system is by computing the inverse in Equation 2.3.7, using a variant of Cramer's rule, the adjoint formula [Nicholson95]:

$$\mathbf{M}^{-1} = \frac{1}{\det(\mathbf{M})} \operatorname{adj}(\mathbf{M}). \tag{2.3.42}$$

The adjoint of a matrix is the transpose of the matrix made up of the cofactors of the original matrix. The adjoint of a 3×3 matrix $\mathbf{M}$ is thus defined as:

$$\operatorname{adj}(\mathbf{M}) = \begin{bmatrix} y_2 z_3 - y_3 z_2 & y_3 z_1 - y_1 z_3 & y_1 z_2 - y_2 z_1 \\ x_3 z_2 - x_2 z_3 & x_1 z_3 - x_3 z_1 & x_2 z_1 - x_1 z_2 \\ x_2 y_3 - x_3 y_2 & x_3 y_1 - x_1 y_3 & x_1 y_2 - x_2 y_1 \end{bmatrix}. \tag{2.3.43}$$

If we examine the columns in this matrix, we will find that they are in fact cross products! It is easy to see that we have:

$$\operatorname{adj}(\mathbf{M}) = [\mathbf{v}_2 \times \mathbf{v}_3 \quad \mathbf{v}_3 \times \mathbf{v}_1 \quad \mathbf{v}_1 \times \mathbf{v}_2]. \tag{2.3.44}$$

Therefore, it is possible to compute the inverse using a total of four cross products, one dot product, one division, and one scalar-matrix multiplication.

Note that if our final goal is to solve the system of equations, this does not gain us anything. To do that, we also need to compute a vector-matrix multiplication, and the scalar-matrix multiplication can then be changed into a scalar-vector multiplication. This ends up being the same number of operations as using Cramer's rule, and we may need to be careful about numerical issues. However, either of these two methods can be useful, as they use operations implemented in hardware. And if we do need just an inverse, the latter method can be useful, since it involves just a few vector operations.

Conclusion

It is known that the cross product can be used for computing intersections of implicit lines as well as for obtaining the coefficients of implicit lines, at least for those who know clipping. In fact, the cross product is an important part of solving a system of linear equations. Cramer's rule was used to prove that the cross product could be used to solve systems of linear equations with two unknowns. It was proposed that the cross product could be used to compute the setup for bilinear interpolation over polygons, which is used for scan-converting Gouraud shading and other vertex attributes. It was also shown how the inverse of a 3×3 system could be computed efficiently by using the cross product. Since both CPUs and GPUs have specialized instructions in hardware for computing the cross product, this article might be useful for some applications.

Acknowledgments

I wish to thank Professor Václav Skala at the University of West Bohemia, Plzeň, Czech Republic for showing me how the cross product can be used to compute intersections of implicit lines and thereby giving me the inspiration to examine the cross product further.

References

[Foley97] Foley, J. D., A. van Dam, S. K. Feiner, and J. F Hughes, *Computer Graphics: Principles and Practice*, 2nd Ed. Addison-Wesley, 1997.

[Gouraud71] Gouraud, H., "Continuous Shading of Curved Surfaces." June 1971. *IEEE Transactions on Computers*, Vol., C-20, No. 6.

[Hast02] Hast, A., T. Barrera, and E. Bengtsson, "Improved Bump Mapping by using Quadratic Vector Interpolation." Eurographics '02 short/poster, 2002.

[Hast03] Hast, A., T. Barrera, and E. Bengtsson, "Fast Setup for Bilinear and Biquadratic Interpolation over Triangles." *Graphics Programming Methods*, Jeff Lander, Ed. Charles River Media, 2003: pp. 299–314.

[Hast04] Hast, A., "Improved Algorithms for Fast Shading and Lighting." Ph.D. Thesis, 2004.

[Hearn04] Hearn, D. and M. P. Baker, *Computer Graphics with OpenGL.* Pearson Education Incorporated, 2004.

[Hecker95] Hecker, C., "Perspective Texture Mapping, Foundations." *Game Developer Magazine,* April/May 1995: pp. 16–25.

[Kugler96] Kugler, A., "The Setup for Triangle Rasterization." August 1996. *Eleventh Eurographics Hardware Workshop '96,* Poitiers, France.

[Narayanaswami95] Narayanaswami, C., "Efficient Parallel Gouraud Shading and Linear Interpolation over Triangles." 1995. *Computer Graphics Forum,* Vol. 14, No. 1: pp. 17–24.

[Nicholson95] Nicholson, W. K., *Linear Algebra With Applications,* 3rd Ed. PWS Publishing Company, 1995.

[O'Rourke98] O'Rourke, J., *Computational Geometry in C,* 2nd Ed. Cambridge University Press, 1998.

[Skala04] Skala, V., "A New Line Clipping Algorithm with Hardware Acceleration." Computer Graphics International 2004: pp. 270-273.

[Skala05] Skala, V., "A new approach to line and line segment clipping in homogeneous coordinates." *The Visual Computer,* Vol. 21, No. 11, pp. 906–914, Springer Verlag 2005.

[Springall90] Springall, T. L. and G. Tollet, "A shading approach to non-convex clipping." July 1990. *APL 90: For the Future conference proceedings,* Vol. 20, Issue 4: pp. 369–372.

Sequence Indexing for Game Development

Palem GopalaKrishna,
Computer Science & Engineering Department,
Indian Institute of Technology

krishnapg@yahoo.com

Sequence indexing is the art of manipulating objects. It tries to answer one simple question: Given a collection of objects, how do we create, access, and identify various groups of objects drawn from that collection? Most games consist of large collections of objects, so it can be seen how understanding these concepts might be useful for game development.

Mathematically, we represent these collections of objects as a *sequence.* This gem presents the mathematical formulas for indexing and deindexing a few well-known sequences, such as:

- Range sequences,
- Permutation sequences, and
- Combinatorial sequences.

It also offers a few tips on how they can best be utilized in game environments for various tasks, ranging from simulating deterministic randomness to serializing game objects.

Terminology

Before discussing sequences, a few simple notations and definitions might be worth noting to eliminate any confusion over terminology.

Throughout this chapter, the symbol "#" will be used to denote the *size* of a set— for example, #{a,b,c} = 3, #{0} = 1, and #{} = 0.

A related operator is the symbol " $\perp$," which is used to denote the *position* (index) of a symbol within a set (array)—for example, $(b \perp \{a,b,c\}) = 1$ and $(a \perp \{a\}) = 0$. The assumption is that the symbol will be always present in the array (uniquely). Thus, $x \perp \mathbf{V}$ always satisfies the condition that $0 \leq (x \perp \mathbf{V}) < \#\mathbf{V}$.

The symbol "$n!$" will be used to denote the notion of *factorial*. In general $n! = n \cdot (n-1) \cdot (n-2) \cdot \ldots \cdot 3 \cdot 2 \cdot 1$—for example, $4! = 4 \cdot 3 \cdot 2 \cdot 1$, which is 24. This is quite useful in computing the value of the *choose* operator C_n^r, indicated by $\binom{n}{r}$, whose formula is given by $C_n^r = \left(\frac{n!}{r!(n-r)!} \right)$. Use of this and factorials will be covered below.

Sequences

A sequence is a series of terms, with each term representing an ordered group of symbols that satisfy some property particular to that sequence. We represent a sequence as an ordered set **S**, with the ith term in the set being represented as **S**[i] and the jth symbol of said term being represented as **S**[i][j]. So if

$$\mathbf{S} = \begin{cases} 1234 \\ 3467 \\ 4789 \\ 5789 \\ \vdots \end{cases}$$

represents a sequence, then **S**[0] = *1234*, **S**[1] = *3467*, **S**[2] = *4789*, **S**[3] = *5789*, . . . are its terms and **S**[0][0] = *1*, **S**[0][1] = *2*, . . . , **S**[3][2] = *8*, **S**[3][3] = *9*, . . . are its symbols. Here we present the elements of our sequence in italics to distinguish them as ordered groups of symbols and not necessarily representing numbers. The *length* of a sequence, represented as |**S**|, is the number of terms in that sequence. So if **S** is a sequence with **S**[0], **S**[1], . . . , and **S**[$m-1$] as its terms, then ||**S**|| = m.

Note that the symbols of our example sequence **S** satisfy the property that **S**[i][j] < **S**[i][$j + 1$] for all $0 \leq j \leq 3, i \geq 0$. This property, which is satisfied by all terms of the sequence when represented as a mathematical or logical expression, gives the *characteristic expression* of the sequence. By varying the characteristic expression, one can generate as many sequences as one wants. However, it should be noted that it is the characteristic expression that defines a sequence and not the individual symbols. In this regard, the sequences

$$\mathbf{S}_1 = \begin{cases} 1234 \\ 3467 \\ 4789 \\ 5789 \end{cases} \text{ and } \mathbf{S}_2 = \begin{cases} abcd \\ cdfg \\ dghi \\ eghi \end{cases}$$

are considered as one and the same (due to their characteristic expressions being the same, despite their symbols being different). This mechanism of abstracting out the individual symbols while refining their logical relations is one of the crucial factors behind the stepping-stones of many fields of computation: Pattern recognition, data compression, information theory, and AI are just a few examples.

While a characteristic expression defines a sequence uniquely and completely, it is not always possible to come up with appropriate logical /mathematical formulations for any given sequence of terms. (DNA sequencing is a well-known example of this.) In such situations, there is no way to refer to that sequence tersely, other than to explicitly state all of its terms. Thus, whenever characteristic expressions are available, they are compressed versions of their original sequences. For example, all programs are characteristic expressions of their instruction sequences[1]. A sequence without any known characteristic expression is said to be *uncompressible*. Uncompressible sequences are representatives of randomness and are of little use.

Finally, it is interesting to note that the individual symbols $S[0][0]$ or $S[0][1]$ need not necessarily be just integers or letters; they could as well be any complex data types, such as strings, mouse coordinates, event descriptors, or class objects. So what kinds of sequences can such complex symbols produce? And more importantly, how can games benefit from them? These are some of the questions the following sections try to answer.

Range Sequences

When the value of each symbol varies over a fixed range (independent of other symbols), the resulting terms form a *range sequence*. For example, the sequence

$$S_R = \begin{Bmatrix} a20 \\ a25 \\ a26 \\ b20 \\ b25 \\ b26 \end{Bmatrix}$$

is a range sequence of three symbols, with each symbol taking values from the sets {a,b}, {2}, and {0,5,6}, respectively. Their ranges are represented as $R[0] = \#\{a,b\} = 2$, $R[1] = \#\{2\} = 1$, and $R[2] = \#\{0,5,6\} = 3$.

---

[1]A program succinctly represents the detailed instructions that are to be carried out by the machine to achieve some functionality. For any typical program, the number of instructions executed by the machine on behalf of the program far exceeds the size of the program. For example, a simple program statement such as `for (i = 0; i < 10000; ++i)` represents no less than 10,000 run-time instructions for the CPU. Thus, the program is a compressed version of its actual run-time realization by the hardware. Languages that pack more meaning into their words require fewer sentences to express a fact on part of the source, but demand more processing power to understand that fact on part of the destination. The astounding compression ratio of 10,000:1 achieved by the C-language `for` loop here is nothing compared with the compression ratios an ordinary 10-year-old kid's daily sentences deal with—such as "come here," "look at that," and so forth. Reducing the complexity of these kinds of context-dependant instructions is one of the major hurdles AI programmers have to solve; and unfortunately, the interactivity of game environments is directly tied to this feat.

In general, for a given range sequence where each term has n symbols taking values from sets $V[0], \ldots, V[n-1]$ with corresponding ranges $R[0] = \# V[0], \ldots,$ and $R[n-1] = \# V[n-1]$, the sequence length is given by the formula:

$$\|S_R\| = R[0] \cdot \ldots \cdot R[n-1] = \prod_{i=0}^{n-1} R[i].$$

So the length of S_R can be calculated by multiplying the ranges together. For our example, $\|S_R\| = R[0] \cdot R[1] \cdot R[2] = 2 \cdot 1 \cdot 3 = 6$. Hence, our example has six terms in it, and any other term one can come up with (that satisfies the range properties) will be a duplicate of one of these six terms.

Given the index of any term, individual symbols of that term can be computed as follows. The jth symbol $0 \le j < n$ of the ith term of S_R, $0 \le i < \|S_R\|$ is given by:

$$S_R[i][j] = V[j] \left[\frac{i \% \prod_{k=j}^{n-1} R[k]}{\prod_{k=j+1}^{n-1} R[k]} \right].$$

Note that $\prod_{k=n}^{n-1} R[k] = 1$.

Conversely, given the symbols $t[0]\, t[1] \ldots t[n-2]\, t[n-1]$ of a term, the index i of the term can be calculated as follows:

$$i = \sum_{j=0}^{n-1} \left((t[j] \perp V[j]) \cdot \prod_{k=j+1}^{n-1} R[k] \right)$$

When coding the above expressions, one can avoid recomputing the products by maintaining a one-dimensional lookup array with the jth element of the array holding the value $\prod_{k=j}^{n-1} R[k]$. Pseudo code for this is as follows:

```
void PreComputeProducts(int Product[], int Range[])
{
    Product[NoOfSymbols] = 1;
    for(int k=NoOfSymbols-1; k>=0; --k)
        Product[k] = Product[k+1]*Range[k];
}
```

As an example, we can use this array when computing the term from an index:

```
TermType GetTerm(SymbolType Values[][], int TermIndex)
{
    TermType Term;
    for(int j=0; j < NoOfSymbols; ++j)
    {
        int i = (TermIndex % Product[j])/Product[j+1];
        Term[j] = Values[j][i];
    }
    return Term;
}
```

Implementation for the converse function is available in the accompanying source code on the CD-ROM.

Range sequences are quite useful for all programming purposes due to their being *universal* in their nature in the sense that almost any arbitrarily random set of terms can be grouped together and pronounced as being part of some (possibly new) range sequence. While this is true for some other kinds of sequences, too, the striking fact that the symbols in range sequences produce their values in an independent fashion makes these sequences a more obvious choice over others. This independence of symbol values offers a flexibility and generality for programmers that very few other kinds of sequences can offer. For example, consider the following hypothetical class:

```
class WildWestPerson
{
    enum Sex { Female, Male };
    enum Nature { Good, Bad, Ugly };
    enum Living { Dead, Alive };

    Sex m_SexVal;
    Nature m_NatureVal;
    Living m_LivingVal;
    BYTE m_RatingVal; //Valid values between [1,5];
};
```

This class has four member variables, each of which can take 2, 3, 2, and 5 values, respectively. All the possible unique objects that can be created for this class can be represented as a range sequence with four symbols, each symbol having ranges $\mathbf{R}[0] = \#\text{Sex} = 2$, $\mathbf{R}[1] = \#\text{Nature} = 3$, $\mathbf{R}[2] = \#\text{Living} = 2$, and $\mathbf{R}[3] = \#\{1 \ldots 5\} = 5$, respectively.

Analyzing the properties of this kind of range sequence often offers more insight into the game design than might be possible otherwise. For example, the maximum sequence length for the above example is $\Pi\mathbf{R} = 2 \cdot 3 \cdot 2 \cdot 5 = 60$, and thus there are at most 60 unique objects (personalities) offered by this class. This information can be used in conjunction with other elements of the game to analyze, understand, and/or create proper metrics for game behaviors such as liveliness, repeatability, and interactivity. Again using our example, if the aforementioned `WildWestPerson` class (and nothing else) controls the abilities of the main character of a game, then the player can have 60 different kinds of game styles before they are repeated[2].

In general, range sequences are quite useful for indexing a set of variables with well-known ranges, such as class objects or graph statistics. By examining the member variables of a given class instance and using the technique above, it is possible to assign

---

[2]The example described here is fictitious. However in real life, game worlds deal with hundreds of different range sequences that offer thousands and even millions of game variations. Most of the time, contribution to the variation in a game comes from the player's actions and reactions to the game events, rather than from within the game itself. Representing player action/reaction chains as sequences and exploiting their properties would greatly help in analyzing the player's behavior by forming standard behavioral metrics that can lead to improvements in the game design and play style.

a unique index that represents that instance's position among all other instances. Once the instances of any class are thus indexed, the possibilities are endless:

- Programmers can use the indexing as a hashing method to find or eliminate duplicates and store unique objects.
- The index associated with an object can be used as a communication token to transfer the state of the object across a network (without requiring any additional bit-packing routines).
- Similarly, one can use the indices to serialize the objects—for example, to quickly save the state of the game.
- Indices are also quite useful in performing complex functions directly on the objects instead of their member variables. For example, to compare two instances of `WildWestPerson`, one would normally write code that compares the individual member variables for the objects. The other possibility is to derive a characteristic expression for the object sequence and define comparison operators over that sequence instead—for example, preceding objects in the sequence are "less" than later ones. We can use this to do offline precomputation of the comparison results, which can be loaded and/or altered at runtime. This makes it possible to isolate the game data (policy decisions) from game concepts—an invaluable asset for every well-developed game.

Permutation Sequences

In mathematics, a *permutation* expresses the concept of arranging objects in various ways. For a given set of symbols, the exhaustive rearrangement of the symbols in all possible ways gives the *permutation sequence*, where each term of the sequence represents a unique arrangement of symbols. For example, with the ordered symbol set {a,b,c}, we can form the permutation sequence

$$\mathbf{S}_p = \left\{ \begin{matrix} abc \\ acb \\ bac \\ bca \\ cab \\ cba \end{matrix} \right\}.$$

The primary difference between range sequences and permutation sequences is that in a range sequence, each symbol within a term takes values independent of other symbols; whereas for a permutation sequence, the position of a symbol greatly depends upon (and is completely determined by) other neighboring symbols.

In general, given a set of symbols $\mathbf{A}$, the length of the permutation sequence formed out of $\mathbf{A}$ is given by $(\#\mathbf{A})!$. This matches what we saw above: The length of

S_p in our example is equal to $||S_p|| = (\#\{a,b,c\})! = 3! = 6$. S_p has six terms in it, each representing one particular arrangement. Any other arrangement we could think of would be just a duplicate of one of these.

As with range sequences, if we have the index of any term within a given permutation sequence, we can compute the individual symbols of that term. The jth symbol $0 \leq j < n$ of the ith term of S_p, $0 \leq i < ||S_p||$ is given by:

$$S_p[i][j] = A_j \left[\frac{i\%(n-j)!}{(n-j-1)!} \right], \text{ where } A_j = \mathbf{A} - \bigcup_{k=0}^{j-1} \{ \ S_p[i][k] \ \}.$$

ON THE CD

Here A_j represents the fact that we are whittling down our choices as we proceed from symbol to symbol within a term; it will be different for each term. For example, for $i = 2 : A_0 = [a,b,c]$, $A_1 = [a,c]$, and $A_2 = [c]$. Practically, we handle this through a series of swapping operations (see the included code for more details).

Conversely, given the symbols $t[0]\, t[1] \dots t[n-2]\, t[n-1]$ of a term, the index i of the term can be calculated as follows:

$$i = \sum_{j=0}^{n-1} \left[\left(t[j] \perp A_j \right) \cdot (n-j-1)! \right], \text{ where } A_j = \mathbf{A} - \bigcup_{k=0}^{j-1} \{ \ t[k] \ \}.$$

Permutation sequences are useful wherever there is an exhaustive rearrangement of any given set of symbols. For example, they are helpful in situations where a group of objects is subjected to a repeated sequence of actions, such as fight or animation sequences. Consider an animation sequence for a group of ships anchored at a bay. Despite the fact that the ships are mostly stationary, it is a common practice to display occasional movement in their masts or decks to make them look more realistic. A straightforward way to implement this is to pick a ship at random every few seconds and animate its masts. However, this kind of picking the ships at random has the potential and undesirable drawback of some ships never being selected and hence not animated.

Another option would be to pick the ships in a perfectly round-robin fashion. While all ships would be animated with this method, it looks less realistic. It would appear as if the wind is circulating around the ships and waving their masts in a perfectly predictable manner. A better method would be one that is deterministic but not determinable. Permutation sequences offer one such method in an easy and straightforward manner.

For example, consider four ships, a,b,c,d, which need to wave their masts every few seconds. The first time through, we select ship a and display its mast-waving animation. After a few seconds we select b, the next ship, and do the same. Next we handle c, and finally d. That completes one round. In the next round we once again start from a, followed by b; but this time we interchange the order of c and d, giving us an order of $abdc$. For the next round, we once again change the order and make it *acbd.* The next would be *acdb;* and the next *adcb*—and so on. In this way, one can keep changing the order for each round, making it look like the masts are being animated at random, while still being perfectly deterministic.

Beyond this, analyzing the properties of permutation sequences can offer more insight into the nature of deterministic chaos, which can greatly improve game realism. For example, consider three opponent archers/gunners *a,b,c* shooting at the player in the following sequence:

Table 2.4.1   Shooter Permutation Sequence

a,b,c,	*a,c,b,*	*b,a,c,*	*b,c,a,*	*c,b,a,*	*c,a,b,*	*a,b,c,*	*b,a,c,*	*b,c...*	...

Each shooter fires a round and ducks behind a pillar so that the player is not overwhelmed with all three opponents shooting at the same time. As per the above sequence (which obviously is a permutation sequence), *a* goes first and shoots, followed by *b,* followed by *c,* then *a* again, *and so on.* If observed carefully, one can find an interesting phenomenon in the sequence. Consider the Figure 2.4.1, which depicts the delays in successive shots for individual shooters.

...,b,**a**,c,b,c,**a**,c,b,**a**,c,**a**,b...a,**b**,c,a,c,**b**,**b**... ...,a,**c**,b,b,a,**c**,b,**c**,a,**c**,...

FIGURE 2.4.1   *Terms of a permutation sequence exhibit deterministic chaos.*

For an individual shooter, the gap between two successive shots is not always the same. For example, let's examine shooter *a.* In the interval between his first two shots there is a large gap compared with the interval between the next two shots. Nor is this gap the same for all shooters: Shooter *b* has two successive bursts without another shooter intervening, a privilege no one else enjoys in this sequence. Yet, there is regularity in the shots—no one is getting too many shots or too few. Every shooter is getting a chance in every round.

To the perspective of the player, this can have a natural effect. The regularity of the shots conveys the trained and determined nature of the opponent, while the varying intervals between shots suggest a lack of control that makes the enemy appear less robotic. The player, wanting to humanize the enemy, can interpret this last part in many ways. Perhaps the enemy is facing the occasional mishaps that are common for every battle, such as the need to reload ammo at critical times. Or perhaps he is uncertain of how to act because the tactic he was about to implement has just been broken by one of the moves of the player.

This feeling on the player's part will be even further enhanced if the delays between shots can be explained with interesting visual behaviors. For example, if an opponent has to be delayed for his shot in this round (as per the sequence) then he could do one of the following:

- Reload his ammo.
- Check to see if he was hit and bleeding.
- Try to throw a grenade, but find none in his arsenal. Cursing, he resumes firing with his original weapon.
- Move to another corner of the room (if that would provide some additional benefit for him). Possibly he finds that the situation has gone from bad to worse, and so he tries to move back.
- Try to retreat, but seeing that his companions are still firing, come back and renew his shots with rapid outbursts. This can occasionally explain the zero-gap successive shots, such as those of shooter *b*.

These are just a few options, and the total possibilities are endless. The exact choice of which option should be used is dependent on the length of the interval between shots. One can always precompute the terms of the sequence ahead of time in order to determine the interval between shots, and then use that information in deciding which behavior the character should exhibit to fill that gap.

Further improvements can be made to create much more complex behaviors. One possibility is to share a single permutation sequence across multiple groups of objects, instead of each group having its own sequence. Each group would use a different term of the sequence, resulting in behavior that is quite unique from all other groups. For example, if we had two groups using the sequence in Table 2.4.1, one group could use the terms indicated in dark gray, and the other group could use the terms indicated in light gray.

A measured exploration of these properties by game developers and designers can make the game a better experience for the players.

Combinational Sequences

Combinational sequences are the result of the selection of a few symbols out of many. Given a set of *n* symbols, the selection of *r* symbols from the set (where $r \leq n$) results in a combinational sequence. Each term of the combinational sequence represents a unique choice of symbols. For example, choosing two symbols out of an ordered set $\{a,b,c,d\}$ of four symbols would form the following:

$$S_C = \left\{ \begin{matrix} ab \\ ac \\ ad \\ bc \\ bd \\ cd \end{matrix} \right\}.$$

In general, given a set **A** of n symbols, the length of the combinational sequence formed by choosing r symbols out of those n symbols is given by:

$$\| S_C \| = \binom{n}{r} = \frac{n!}{r!(n-r)!}.$$

So the length of our example sequence is given by $|S_C| = \binom{4}{2} = 6$. The six terms each represent a unique choice; any other term one can come up with would be just a duplicate of one of these choices.

As before, given the index of any term, individual symbols of that term can be computed. The jth symbol $0 \le j < r$ of the ith term of S_C, $0 \le i < |S_C|$ is given by:

$$S_C[i][j] = A_j[q_j],$$

where:

$$q_j = \min\left\{ d \,\middle|\, \text{index}_j < \sum_{k=0}^{d} \binom{n_j - k - 1}{r_j - 1}, 0 \le d \le n_j - r_j \right\},$$

$$\text{index}_j = i - \sum_{l=0}^{j-1} \sum_{k=0}^{q_l - 1} \binom{n_j - k - 1}{r_j - 1},$$

$$A_j = \mathbf{A} - \bigcup_{k=0}^{j-1} \left\{ A_k[m] \,\middle|\, 0 \le m \le q_k \right\},$$

$$n_j = \# A_j, \text{ and}$$

$$r_j = r - j.$$

Conversely, given the symbols $t[0]\, t[1] \dots t[n-2]\, t[n-1]$ of a term, the index of the term can be calculated as follows:

$$\text{index} = \sum_{j=0}^{r-1} \sum_{k=0}^{p_j - 1} \binom{n_j - k - 1}{r_j - 1},$$

where $p_j = (t[j] \perp A_j)$, and A_j, n_j, and r_j are as before.

While these operations appear quite complex, especially compared with those for the other two sequences, the general concept is the same as the permutation sequence. As we generate the symbols for a term, we remove base symbols available to us, depending on the size of r and the index of the term. In both cases, this can be handled quite easily with a nested loop. Again, see the included code for more details.

ON THE CD

It should be noted that in contrast to permutation sequences where the position of symbols is important, combinational sequences only consider which combination of symbols are in a term, not their positions. For example, both *abc* and *bac* are treated as one and the same. Thus, a striking difference between these two types of sequences is that a term of a permutation sequence is made up of the same symbols as any other term in that sequence, while the symbols that make up one term of a combinational sequence will never be the same as that of any other term of that sequence.

Combinational sequences are quite useful wherever there is a notion of choice. For example, consider an RTS game where we want to choose five opponents out of eight possible civilizations. A common way to implement this notion of choice in games is to use seeded random number generators. However, while seeded random generators guarantee that the same sequence is generated every time the seed is the same, no such guarantee is provided for the contrary case. That is, one cannot be guaranteed that the random sequences will not be repeated *when we do not want them to be repeated*. This is primarily due to the lack of a pure random number generator. So when we randomize our choice, there exists no known efficient method that guarantees the choice to be unique from all past sessions of the game.

On the other hand, combinational sequences offer a bounded guarantee that no sequence it generates—up to a bounded number of instances—would be a duplicate of any other instance. This is primarily due to the nature of the sequence: No two terms are constructed from the same symbol subset. Up to the length of the sequence, all its terms are unique. Hence, in a game, all of the user's actions and choices made during gameplay can be indexed uniquely to express the game session in terms of combinational sequence indices.

Another useful application for combinational sequences is measuring the path complexity of a graph. The graph could be an abstract technology graph the player has to research in a game, or it could be a map of the terrain to be explored. The choices made by the player in traversing these graphs can be encoded as a combinational sequence that can be used to modulate the gameplay.

For example, consider the hypothetical technology graph shown in Figure 2.4.2. At each node, the player has a set of choices to choose from in order to progress toward the end node. Each choice results in a different path and causes different results. If we enumerate the list of all possible paths for that graph, the resulting sequence has the property that no two paths share the same set of choices—the fundamental property of a combinational sequence. Figure 2.4.2 shows this sequence of all possible paths, which is {*ad, aeh, bfh, cg*}. Note that while some terms of this

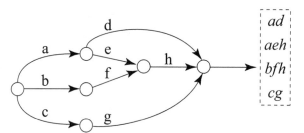

FIGURE 2.4.2   *Paths in a graph encoded using a combinational sequence.*

sequence have three symbols in them, others have just two symbols. However, this need not deter from the practicality of the sequence, for one can always append a dummy "don't care" symbol.

Note that the sequence does not contain all possible terms for a combinational sequence. For example, the term *abc* is absent in the list, because such a path is not valid for our graph. So the limited choices offered by the graph place restrictions on what terms will be present in the final sequence. Minimizing such restrictions results in a larger number of valid terms for the sequence, thus making the game more non-linear. This enumeration helps the designers create a metric for the game that measures the amount of nonlinearity offered to the player.

This notion of choice illuminates a major difference between range sequences and combinational sequences. Range sequences encode the game in terms of the programmer-defined objects, such as classes, while combinational sequences capture the game in terms of user choices and actions. For example, combination sequences are much better at representing the subset of quests completed from a full set of all possible available quests, or the subset of hidden treasures successfully collected from a full set of total available treasures. These choices, actions, and events are more closely related to the game concepts as viewed by the player than they are to the inherent programming logic as viewed by a programmer.

Similarly, the scope of combinational sequences can be thought of as being at the session level for a game. For example, in a game tournament where hundreds of game sessions are carried out between different players, each game session represents a unique term (made up of the choices and events carried out by a given player) in a big combinational sequence. As the choices vary from session to session for different games, so do the resultant terms. However, in each session there will be millions of game frames in which the game state at each frame can be represented as one term of a range sequence (made up of the class objects defined by the programmer). Thus, for each term of the combinational sequence at the session level, there will be millions of terms forming a range sequence at the frame level. In other words, combinational sequences are good at encoding the choice (at the macroscopic level), while range sequences are good at encoding the regularity (at the microscopic level).

This leads to one final application of combinational sequences: Encoding the player's *paths of choices* as terms of a combinational sequence allows the sequence to be analyzed for a better understanding of player tactics, which can help in modulating the gameplay to tune itself according to the player's expertise.

For example, a player who always follows one particular path of choices from session to session could be forced to adapt a different strategy by dynamically tuning the rewards or benefits for these choices. This could be quite useful in multiplayer games with features such as match-making, or for tuning the aforementioned strategy game with a technology tree. After the player's actions or choices are encoded as terms of a combinational sequence, each of the terms generated can be assigned a success or failure rating based upon how many players are able to win or lose when following that particular path as opposed to different paths. More often than not, certain choices will be more successful than others. This is either a reflection of the tactical strategy of the player or more likely points to a loophole in gameplay balancing. Addressing such issues could highly benefit the gaming experience for all players.

Conclusion

This gem covered the theory of sequence indexing, which deals with the notion of structured enumeration, or ordering and indexing objects based on their properties. In particular, it explained the mathematical properties of three important sequences that are quite useful for game developers and designers. Range sequences are useful for indexing variables with well-known ranges, such as class objects and graph statistics. Permutation sequences are suitable for indexing exhaustive rearrangements, such as those involving animation sequences and fight sequences. Combinational sequences are useful when choosing a subset of symbols out of many, such as player quest choices in a nonlinear game.

Further interesting possibilities for these sequences could be to use range sequences for bitmap font encoding, and permutation sequences to enumerate all branches in a script code for debugging and anagram manipulations. Combinational sequences could be used for implementing tasks that involve *selective ignorance,* such as *concept learning* in artificial agents (fixing a hypothesis for a set of observations by selectively ignoring some attributes of the observed facts) and random choice simulation.

With respect to the random choice simulation, it is worth noting that the seeded random number generation mechanism that is commonly in practice is just another variant of the general sequence indexing mechanism, where the seed becomes the index of the random sequence. Yet such random sequences are of a slightly different nature from the generalized sequences discussed above in that the deindexing functionality is not always possible for them. That is, one can compute a random sequence from a seed easily, but one cannot very easily compute the seed from a given random sequence. Hence, seeded random generators can be treated as one-way *partial indexers.*

For those who are interested in investigating sequence indexing further, some notes on implementation are important. While the mathematical formulas presented in this gem are quite straightforward and easy to implement, they nonetheless are not computationally efficient in their raw mathematical forms. This is because the mathematical formula for a particular $S[i][j]$ in its basic form does not explicitly refer to any other $S[x][y]$ values, whereas in reality the computation of $S[i][j]$ can highly benefit from the intermediate values obtained in previous computations, say that of $S[i][j-1]$. Thus, there is lot of scope for optimization. The accompanying source code for this article provides a medium level of implementation, thus leaving enough experimentation room for both advanced and basic readers.

ON THE CD

Another important point is the computation of *the factorial function*. For formulas that require factorial values, one should be aware that basic data types such as 4-byte integers cannot hold factorial values beyond 11! or 12!. Hence, any value beyond that requires *multiple precision arithmetic*, which is a mechanism that removes all precision limitations on arithmetic operations. The accompanying source code uses the Gnu Multiple Precision (GMP) library for this purpose. GMP is an open-source library that facilitates multiple precision operations on signed integers, rational numbers, and floating-point numbers. Refer to the source code for implementation details.

ON THE CD

Finally in this gem, only three types of sequences have been discussed. However, the theory of sequence indexing is much wider and deeper than has been explored here, and there remain countless variations to be discovered and utilized. Sequence indexing spans all branches of information sciences (e.g., encoding, compression, series analysis, etc.) and is a major contributor to the concept of *program as information source* [Kolmogorov65] [Li97]. Furthermore, it is also closely related to the concept of *deterministic chaos*, which is a natural property of all dynamical systems and modeling methodologies. More information on these can be gathered from [Atmanspacher91] and [Atmanspacher02]. Investigations in these fields can bring a complete new set of tools and perspectives to game development, making it an enjoyable experience for both developers and players alike.

References

[Atmanspacher91] Atmanspacher, H. and H. Scheingraber, H., Eds., *Information Dynamics*. NATO ASI Series, Plenum Press, 1991.

[Atmanspacher02] Atmanspacher, A. and R. Bishop, Eds., *Between Chance and Choice*. Academic, 2002.

[Kolmogorov65] Kolmogorov, A. N., "Three Approaches to the Quantitative Definition of Information." *Problems of Information Transmission*, 1965, No. 1: pp. 1–7.

[Li97] Li, M. and P. Vitanyi, *An Introduction to Kolmogorov Complexity and its Applications*. Springer, 1997.

2.5

Exact Buoyancy for Polyhedra

Erin Catto, Crystal Dynamics

erincatto@gphysics.com

Rigid body simulation brings many new capabilities and challenges. For example, imagine an impromptu raft created from the remnants of a collapsed building near a body of water. The player identifies a suitable chunk of wall and expects it to float in a believable manner. For this to happen, the game must simulate buoyancy realistically. It is obvious that increased realism in dynamic simulation naturally leads to increased expectations of emergence. Therefore, buoyancy is an important ingredient in a well-rounded rigid-body simulation system for games that include water in playable levels.

This gem describes an efficient method for computing buoyancy and drag forces on rigid bodies. The algorithm determines an exact buoyancy force for a polyhedron in a water volume. The central equations are in vector form to allow for SIMD optimization.

[Fagerlund] and [Gomez00] have provided similar investigations of real-time buoyancy. Fagerlund uses embedded spheres to approximate the submerged portion of an object. This requires an additional authoring step, and many spheres may be required. Gomez distributes points on the object's surface and attributes a portion of the surface area to each point. He computes vertical columns of displaced water at each surface point. His method also requires an additional authoring step and may require many points to be placed on the surface (e.g., 20 to 30 for a cube).

In contrast, the algorithm presented here requires no additional authoring step. In terms of geometric data, the algorithm only needs the vertices and triangles of the polyhedron; however, it is limited to flat water surfaces.

This algorithm is exact in the hydrostatic sense, because we neglect the inertia of water. This leads to somewhat unrealistic bobbing, but the approach is far simpler than a fully dynamic water simulation.

Buoyancy

Archimedes' principle states that the buoyancy force on a body immersed in water is equal to the weight of the water displaced by the body:

$$\mathbf{F}_b = \rho Vg\mathbf{n},\tag{2.5.1}$$

where ρ is the density of water, V is the volume of the submerged portion of the body, g is the acceleration due to gravity, and $\mathbf{n}$ is the up vector.

As shown in Figure 2.5.1, the buoyancy force counteracts the force due to gravity—for example, the weight of the object:

$$\mathbf{F}_g = -mg\mathbf{n}.\tag{2.5.2}$$

Here, m is the body's mass. The center of mass is $\mathbf{x}$, and the center of buoyancy is $\mathbf{c}$. If the body's average density is larger than the density of water, then the body will sink. On the other hand, if the body's average density is smaller than the density of water, then the body will float.

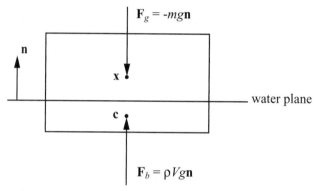

FIGURE 2.5.1   *Buoyancy and gravity forces acting on a body.*

The buoyancy force can also lead to oscillation or bobbing. If a body is dropped into water, its inertia force is added to $\mathbf{F}_g$, and it can displace a volume of water that exceeds the weight of the body. After dipping in too far, the body will accelerate back up, and the process will repeat until the kinetic energy is dissipated.

As shown in Figure 2.5.2, the buoyancy force may produce a torque about the center of mass. This happens because the center of buoyancy is at the center of the displaced volume, which doesn't necessarily coincide with the center of mass. The torque about the center of mass due to buoyancy is:

$$\mathbf{T}_b = \mathbf{r}_b \times \rho Vg\mathbf{n},\tag{2.5.3}$$

where $\times$ is the cross product and $\mathbf{r}_b$ is the radius vector directed from $\mathbf{x}$ to $\mathbf{c}$.

$$\mathbf{r}_b = \mathbf{c} - \mathbf{x}\tag{2.5.4}$$

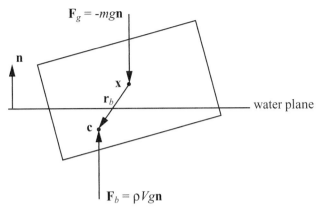

FIGURE 2.5.2 *Buoyancy torque.*

Buoyancy torque is the reason objects have some orientations that are more stable than others. Consider the set of all positions and orientations of the object where the displaced water has a weight equal to the weight of the body. A stable equilibrium configuration is an element of this set where the center of mass is at a (local) minimum height. This is why thin sheets of wood are more stable lying flat on the water than standing up on edge.

Polygon Area

The buoyancy computation for a polyhedron builds from the simpler problem of computing the area of a polygon, which builds on the notion of signed area. Therefore, we will discuss these simpler problems first.

Consider the triangle shown in Figure 2.5.3. The signed area of a triangle has a magnitude equal to the usual triangle area. The ordering of the vertices determines the sign. A Counterclockwise (CCW) order yields a positive sign, while a Clockwise (CW) order yields a negative sign. The edge vectors are defined as $\mathbf{a} = \mathbf{v}_2 - \mathbf{v}_1$ and $\mathbf{b} = \mathbf{v}_3 - \mathbf{v}_1$. Recall that the length of the cross product $\mathbf{a} \times \mathbf{b}$ is the area of the associated parallelogram. The area of the triangle is half the area of the parallelogram. If the plane of the triangle has the unit normal $\mathbf{k}$, then the signed area is:

$$A = \frac{1}{2}\left(\mathbf{a} \times \mathbf{b}\right) \cdot \mathbf{k}. \tag{2.5.5}$$

Thus, A is positive if the vertices have a CCW order and negative if the vertices have a CW order.

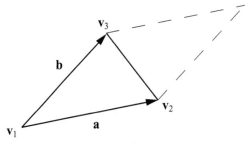

FIGURE 2.5.3   *A triangle.*

According to [O'Rourke98], the area of a polygon is the sum of the signed areas of all the triangles formed from each edge and an arbitrary point **p**. Thus, the area of the quadrilateral in Figure 2.5.4 is the sum:

$$A = A_1 + A_2 + A_3 + A_4$$
$$= A(\mathbf{v}_4, \mathbf{v}_1, \mathbf{p}) + A(\mathbf{v}_3, \mathbf{v}_4, \mathbf{p}) + A(\mathbf{v}_1, \mathbf{v}_2, \mathbf{p}) + A(\mathbf{v}_2, \mathbf{v}_3, \mathbf{p}). \qquad (2.5.6)$$

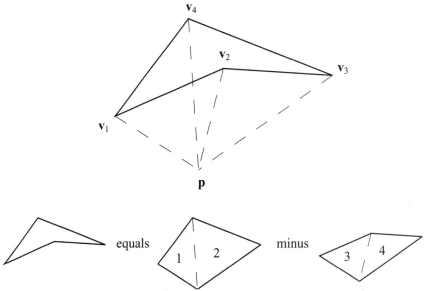

FIGURE 2.5.4   *Area of a polygon as a sum of signed triangle areas. The area of the original polygon is equal to the unsigned areas of triangles 1 and 2, minus the unsigned areas of triangles 3 and 4.*

Note that the first two triangles have positive area (CCW order), while the last two have negative area (CW order), and the overall sum is positive. Also note that each triangle is formed by connecting the CCW ordering of an edge with **p** as the last vertex.

The centroid of a single triangle is simply the average of the vertices, for example:

$$c_1 = \frac{1}{3}\left(v_1 + v_2 + p\right).$$ (2.5.7)

The polygon centroid is the area-weighted sum of the component triangles' centroids. Therefore, the centroid of the polygon in Figure 2.5.4 is:

$$c = \frac{1}{A}\left(A_1 c_1 + A_2 c_2 + A_3 c_3 + A_4 c_4\right).$$ (2.5.8)

Since we are using signed areas, some of the centroids have a negative weighting.

Polyhedron Volume

Assume for now that the polyhedron is fully submerged. Later, we will deal with the general case of a partially submerged polyhedron. The method for computing a polyhedron's volume is similar to the method for computing a polygon's area. A polygon's area is the sum of signed areas of triangles, while a polyhedron's volume is the sum of the signed volumes of tetrahedron. Each tetrahedron consists of a triangular face of the polyhedron and an arbitrary point **p**. The sign of the volume is positive if **p** is behind the face and negative if **p** is in front of the face, as shown in Figure 2.2.5.

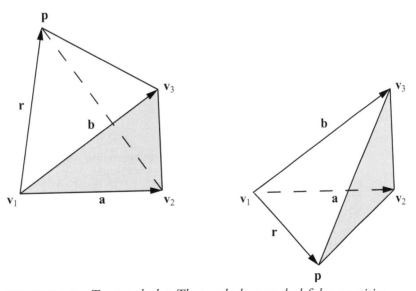

FIGURE 2.5.5   *Two tetrahedra. The tetrahedron on the left has a positive signed volume (**p** in back), while the one on the right has a negative signed volume (**p** in front).*

The formula of [Weisstein] is extended to obtain the signed volume of a tetrahedron:

$$V = \frac{1}{6}(\mathbf{b} \times \mathbf{a}) \cdot \mathbf{r}, \tag{2.5.9}$$

where $\mathbf{a} = \mathbf{v}_2 - \mathbf{v}_1$, $\mathbf{b} = \mathbf{v}_3 - \mathbf{v}_1$, and $\mathbf{r} = \mathbf{p} - \mathbf{v}_1$. Like a triangle, the centroid of a tetrahedron is simply the average of its vertices:

$$\mathbf{c} = \frac{1}{4}(\mathbf{v}_1 + \mathbf{v}_2 + \mathbf{v}_3 + \mathbf{p}). \tag{2.5.10}$$

See [Weisstein] for more details.

Similar to the two-dimensional case, the polyhedron volume is the sum of signed tetrahedron volumes, and the polyhedron centroid is the weighted average of all the tetrahedron centroids.

$$V = \frac{1}{6}\sum_{i=1}^{n}(\mathbf{b}_i \times \mathbf{a}_i) \cdot \mathbf{r}_i \tag{2.5.11}$$

$$\mathbf{c} = \frac{1}{V}\sum_{i=1}^{n} V_i \mathbf{c}_i \tag{2.5.12}$$

Since these formulas are in vector form, they are easy to optimize on SIMD hardware, as shown in Listing 2.5.1.

Listing 2.5.1   Code to Compute the Volume and Centroid of a Tetrahedron

```
float TetrahedronVolume(Vec3& c, Vec3 p, Vec3 v1, Vec3 v2, Vec3 v3)
{
    Vec3 a = v2 - v1;
    Vec3 b = v3 - v1;
    Vec3 r = p - v1;

    float volume = (1.0f/6.0f)*dot(cross(b, a), r);
    c += 0.25f*volume*(v1 + v2 + v3 + p);
    return volume;
}
```

Partial Submersion

Overview

First, consider the two-dimensional case of partial submersion, as shown in Figure 2.5.6. Vertices $\mathbf{v}_1$, $\mathbf{v}_2$, and $\mathbf{v}_3$ are submerged, while vertex $\mathbf{v}_4$ is above the water line. To compute the submerged area, it is necessary to clip the polygon against the water line. Clipping yields the new polygon shown in Figure 2.5.7.

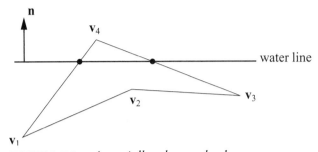

FIGURE 2.5.6 *A partially submerged polygon.*

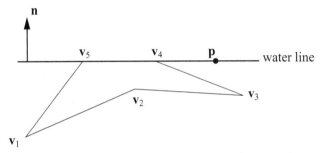

FIGURE 2.5.7 *Clipping the polygon along the water line.*

The area of the polygon in Figure 2.5.7 is the submerged area of the original polygon. To compute the submerged area, choose a point $\mathbf{p}$ that will form triangles with all the polygon edges. By placing $\mathbf{p}$ on the water line, the area of triangle $(\mathbf{v}_4, \mathbf{v}_5, \mathbf{p})$ becomes zero. This eliminates a term from the area sum, making the algorithm more efficient.

Since edges on the water line do not contribute to the submerged area, we can simplify the clipping algorithm. Clip each edge independently. An edge is either above the water line, below the water line, or crosses the water line. Edges above the water line do not contribute to the submerged area. Edges below the water line contribute directly to the submerged area. And finally, edges crossing the water line only contribute the portion that is below the water line.

In the three-dimensional case, clip each triangular face of the polyhedron against the water plane. The clipping process leaves a complex shape on the water plane; it may be several polygons, and the polygons may have holes. By placing $\mathbf{p}$ on the water line's plane, it is not necessary to consider the faces on the water plane. This greatly simplifies the three-dimensional algorithm.

Clipping

Each triangle belongs to one of three categories:

1. Above the water plane.
2. Below the water plane.
3. Intersecting the water plane.

Category 1 triangles do not contribute to the submerged volume. Category 2 triangles add directly to the volume computation. Category 3 triangles must be clipped against the water plane, resulting in one or two Category 2 triangles.

[Eberly01] presents an algorithm for clipping triangles against a plane. He presents the algorithm in the context of view frustum clipping for graphical rendering, but the algorithm also is well suited for buoyancy calculations. We use a modified version of the algorithm that is optimized for our buoyancy calculation.

Consider a triangle that intersects the water plane. There may be two configurations, as shown in Figure 2.5.8.

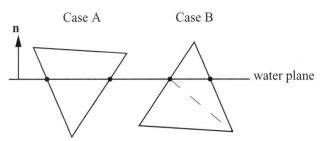

FIGURE 2.5.8   *Clipping configurations Case A and Case B.*

A. One vertex is below the water plane. This results in one Category 2 triangle.
B. Two vertices are below the water plane. This results in a quadrilateral with two Category 2 triangles.

For Case A, identify the two clipping points and process the resulting Category 2 triangle. For Case B, again identify two clipping points and process the resulting quadrilateral as two Category 2 triangles.

A typical graphics pipeline clips triangles against the view frustum and then adds the resulting triangles to the list of rendered triangles. In contrast, the buoyancy algorithm clips the triangles against the water plane and uses the resulting triangles immediately in the volume calculation. The algorithm does not update the list of triangles. This simplifies the code and uses less memory.

At the beginning of the volume calculation, the code computes the depth d of each vertex and stores them in an array. The main loop processes each triangle and examines the depths of the triangle vertices. If the code determines that the triangle is Category 2, then the vertices and their depths are passed to the triangle clipper, shown in Listing 2.5.2. The clipper determines the triangle configuration (Case A or B), performs the clipping via linear interpolation, and passes the resulting triangles to the tetrahedron volume function.

Listing 2.5.2   Code for Triangle Clipping

```
float ClipTriangle(Vec3& c, Vec3 p,
    Vec3 v1, Vec3 v2, Vec3 v3,
    float d1, float d2, float d3)
{
    Vec3 vc1 = v1 + (d1/(d1 - d2))*(v2 - v1);
    float volume = 0;

    if (d1 < 0)
    {
        if (d3 < 0)
        {
            Vec3 vc2 = v2 + (d2/(d2 - d3))*(v3 - v2);
            volume += TetrahedronVolume(c, p, vc1, vc2, v1);
            volume += TetrahedronVolume(c, p, vc2, v3, v1);
        }
        else
        {
            Vec3 vc2 = v1 + (d1/(d1 - d3))*(v3 - v1);
            volume += TetrahedronVolume(c, p, vc1, vc2, v1);
        }
    }
    else
    {
        if (d3 < 0)
        {
            Vec3 vc2 = v1 + (d1/(d1 - d3))*(v3 - v1);
            volume += TetrahedronVolume(c, p, vc1, v2, v3);
            volume += TetrahedronVolume(c, p, vc1, v3, vc2);
        }
        else
        {
            Vec3 vc2 = v2 + (d2/(d2 - d3))*(v3 - v2);
            volume += TetrahedronVolume(c, p, vc1, v2, vc2);
        }
    }
    return volume;
}
```

Robustness

Consider the case where a polyhedron is just barely submerged. The triangles produced by clipping may be thin slivers. Due to round-off errors, the sum of the tetrahedron volumes could produce a negative total volume. Also, the centroid may lie outside of the submerged portion of the polyhedron. While these errors may be minor, we consider it good hygiene to avoid spurious results.

The accuracy of the tetrahedron volume formula depends on the quality of the tetrahedrons. High-quality tetrahedrons have balanced interior angles. Low-quality tetrahedrons have interior angles that vary greatly in magnitude.

Consider the two-dimensional case shown in Figure 2.5.9. Notice that the triangle is of low quality, because the interior angles differ greatly. The area formula is:

$$A = \frac{1}{2}(\mathbf{a} \times \mathbf{b}) \cdot \mathbf{k}$$

$$= \frac{1}{2}\left(a_x b_y - a_y b_x\right)$$

$$= \frac{1}{2}\left[\left(L^2 + L\varepsilon\right) - \left(L^2 - L\varepsilon\right)\right] \qquad (2.5.13)$$

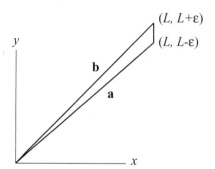

FIGURE 2.5.9   *A slender triangle.*

The exact area is $L\varepsilon$. Now, assume that L is large and ε is small. Then the cross product involves the difference of two large numbers, leading to a relatively small result. This computation is prone to a round-off error, since the L^2 terms dominate.

It is obvious that the tetrahedron quality depends on the placement of $\mathbf{p}$. We have already made the decision to place $\mathbf{p}$ on the water plane, but did not specify where $\mathbf{p}$ is located on the plane. An improvement in tetrahedron quality is possible by placing $\mathbf{p}$ directly above the submerged portion of the polyhedron. To achieve this improvement, project a submerged vertex up to the water plane. In our implementation, the projected vertex is chosen arbitrarily from the set of submerged vertices.

FIGURE 2.5.10   *Example of how the choice of **p** affects triangle quality in two dimensions. The choice **p₁** leads to a high quality triangle because the interior angles are well balanced. The choice **p₂** leads to a lower quality triangle because the interior angles are unbalanced. The choice of **p** in three dimensions has a similar effect on tetrahedron quality.*

Even with an optimal placement of **p**, the tetrahedron volume formula may still be inaccurate. Guards in the code can help to avoid erroneous results. First, abandon the buoyancy calculation if the submerged portion the polyhedron is small. Second, abandon the buoyancy calculation if the total computed volume is negative.

Drag Force

Recall that buoyancy forces coupled with gravity lead to oscillations. In nature, oscillations diminish due to drag forces. Drag forces also allow water currents to move objects.

The drag forces exerted by water on a rigid body are quite complicated. They depend on the surface characteristics and shape of the body. An accurate model of the drag forces requires a full dynamic water simulation. It is questionable whether such accuracy will add significantly to the visual realism, given the computational cost. Therefore, we use an approximate drag-force model that is inexpensive and uses the results of the buoyancy calculation.

Consider the following formula for drag force:

$$\mathbf{F}_d = \beta_l m \frac{V}{V_T}\left(\mathbf{v}_w - \mathbf{v}_c\right) \tag{2.5.14}$$

Here, β_l is a linear drag coefficient in units of one over time, m is the mass of the polyhedron, V is the volume of the submerged portion of the polyhedron, V_T is the total volume of the polyhedron, $\mathbf{v}_w$ is the velocity of the water current, and $\mathbf{v}_c$ is the velocity of the center of buoyancy. For simplicity, $\mathbf{F}_d$ is applied at the center of buoyancy.

The drag force $\mathbf{F}_d$ opposes the motion of the center of buoyancy relative to the water current. Equation 2.5.14 is one of many possible formulas, but it works well in practice.

The drag force $\mathbf{F}_d$ alone is not sufficient to dissipate angular velocity, particularly when the center of buoyancy is directly below the center of mass, and so it is useful to add a drag torque:

$$T_d = -\beta_a m \frac{V}{V_T} L^2 \boldsymbol{\omega}. \qquad (2.5.15)$$

Here, β_a is an angular drag coefficient in units of one over time, and L is the average width of the polyhedron. These parameters ensure that the units of torque are produced.

You can select the drag coefficients β_l and β_a through numerical experiments. First, set the drag coefficients to zero and run a buoyancy simulation with a representative polyhedron, such as a box. The box should oscillate in a stable manner. If not, then reduce the time step in your numerical integrator until the box is stable. Then begin increasing β_l until the bobbing dissipates after a few cycles. Next, drop the box, with an initial angular velocity, about the vertical axis. The box should continue to rotate after the bobbing has ceased. Finally, increase β_a until the rotation dissipates after a few rotations.

Source Code

ON THE CD
The source code and a demonstration program are available on the CD-ROM. The code emphasizes clarity over efficiency, so several optimizations are possible. Figure 2.5.11, Color Plate 4, and Color Plate 5 show screenshots from the demo.

FIGURE 2.5.11   *Buoyancy simulation of a concave polyhedron.*

Conclusion

This article has shown how to compute the exact hydrostatic buoyancy force for a polyhedron submerged in a water volume with a flat surface. Additionally, approximate models of drag force and drag torque were presented to simulate energy dissipation and current coupling. The algorithm is efficient, requires no extra authoring steps, is easy to implement, and integrates well into a physics engine.

Acknowledgment

The author would like to thank the team at Crystal Dynamics for supporting this effort.

References

[Eberly01] Eberly, David H., *3D Game Engine Design.* Morgan Kaufmann, 2001.

[Fagerlund] Fagerlund, Mattias, "Buoyancy Particles or Bobbies." Available online at *http://www.cambrianlabs.com/Mattias/DelphiODE/BuoyancyParticles.asp*.

[Gomez00] Gomez, Miguel, "Interactive Simulation of Water Surfaces." *Game Programming Gems,* Charles River Media, 2000.

[O'Rourke98] O'Rourke, Joseph, *Computational Geometry in C,* 2nd Ed. Cambridge University Press, 1998.

[Weisstein] Weisstein, Eric W., "Tetrahedron." Available online at *http://mathworld.wolfram.com/Tetrahedron.html*.

2.6

Real-Time Particle-Based Fluid Simulation with Rigid Body Interaction

Takashi Amada,
Sony Computer Entertainment, Inc.

taka.am@gmail.com

Realistic, real-time rendering of the motion of fluids is one of the ways to immerse the user into an interactive application, such as a computer game. The interaction of fluids with rigid bodies is important, because in real life, the motion of fluids and rigid bodies is affected by their influences on each other. Fluid simulation based on Computational Fluid Dynamics (CFD) is useful for rendering a visually plausible behavior for the fluid. However, the computational cost of many CFD techniques is often too great for real-time rendering of fluids, which requires fast simulation. Furthermore, many traditional techniques do not enable an easy simulation of fluids interacting with rigid bodies.

This article describes a way to use the smoothed particle hydrodynamics technique to simulate fluids that interact with rigid bodies, and vice versa. We also provide a fast implementation. The proposed method enables real-time simulation of water with rigid body interaction.

Fluid Simulation and Smoothed Particle Hydrodynamics

Basic Approaches to Fluid Simulation

You may have heard of the Naviér-Stokes equation that describes motion for generalized fluid flow. A version of this equation that is valid for incompressible fluids, such as water, is shown in Equation 2.6.1. This partial differential equation describes the conservation of momentum of the incompressible fluid and is equivalent to Newton's second law of motion.

$$\rho \frac{D\mathbf{v}}{Dt} = -\nabla p + \mu \nabla^2 \mathbf{v} + \rho \mathbf{f}$$

$$(2.6.1)$$

Here, ρ is the fluid density (a scalar), $\mathbf{v}$ is the fluid velocity (a vector), p is the fluid pressure (a scalar), μ is the coefficient of viscosity (a scalar, assumed to be constant here), $\mathbf{f}$ is an external force per unit mass on the particle (such as force due to gravity), ∇ is the vector *grad* operator defined in Equation 2.6.2, and ∇^2 is the Laplacian operator given by Equation 2.6.3.

$$\nabla = \mathbf{i}\frac{\partial}{\partial x} + \mathbf{j}\frac{\partial}{\partial y} + \mathbf{k}\frac{\partial}{\partial z}$$

$$(2.6.2)$$

$$\nabla^2 = \frac{\partial^2}{\partial x^2} + \frac{\partial^2}{\partial y^2} + \frac{\partial^2}{\partial z^2}$$

$$(2.6.3)$$

To simulate a fluid, you must simulate Equation 2.6.1, or one of many simplifications of it, along with other key governing equations, including continuity (conservation of mass) and conservation of energy. Unlike a rigid body whose motion can be represented in just six degrees of freedom (i.e., translation and rotation around three axes each), no matter how complex the shape, a fluid has an infinite number of degrees of freedom and cannot be represented as simply a rigid body. To actually simulate the governing equations of fluid motion, we must carefully consider the nature of a fluid.

Fluids, such as water, consist of a large number of molecules. There are so many molecules in even a very small volume of fluid that it is impractical in most cases to simulate a fluid by modeling it as a collection of individual molecules. Macroscopically, we can consider water and other fluids as a continuum where physical properties vary continuously throughout the fluid. The Naviér-Stokes equation was actually derived based on this view—that a fluid is continuous. When we take this view, it becomes possible to create realistic simulations that run in a reasonable amount of time on modern computers.

All fluid simulations can be categorized as either *Eulerian* or *Lagrangian*. In Eulerian simulations, the physical properties are represented at points that are fixed in a reference frame, and that do not move with the fluid (though they may move in space if the reference frame moves or deforms). The properties at a given point change as the fluid moves past that point. The typical approach to creating an Eulerian simulation of a fluid is to first create a mesh, such as the one shown in Figure 2.6.1—though the mesh need not be uniform or arranged in rows and columns. The fluid properties are stored at the vertices of the mesh. The governing equations are discretized on the mesh using various techniques, such as finite-difference or finite-volume methods. The simulation uses the discrete equations to update the properties from one frame to the next.

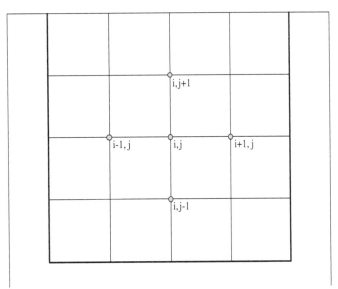

FIGURE 2.6.1   *A simple grid for a two-dimensional Eulerian fluid simulation of water in a reservoir.*

Developers have created Eulerian simulations for modeling fluids in games. For example, Jos Stam's famous Stable Fluids technique is an Eulerian simulation, though it uses particle tracing to achieve stability [Stam99]. Eulerian simulations have even been implemented on GPUs [Noe04].

Eulerian methods have some advantages. They can be easy to implement and yield smooth results. However, in some cases, the Eulerian approach is insufficient. While it is easy to implement a basic simulation, in practice it is difficult to perfect, especially when arbitrary boundaries are required or when arbitrary forces are applied to the fluid. The memory and computational cost can be prohibitive when it is desirable to resolve fine details in a flow, such as vortices or whirlpools. Eulerian methods also are not ideally suited to model fluids that splash or collect in pools, or for simulating two different types of fluid that mix together, or for fluids that interact with arbitrary rigid bodies.

In Lagrangian simulations, the physical properties are represented for a specific portion of the fluid and are tracked with that portion as it moves over time. It is possible to implement Lagrangian simulations using a mesh, similar to the Eulerian approach. Here, the mesh cells (triangles or quads for 2D, tetrahedrons or something else for 3D) would actually move with the fluid in such a way that the mass of each cell remains constant during the simulation. Grid-based Lagrangian simulators suffer some of the same difficulties as grid-based Eulerian simulators. For example, it can be difficult to deform the mesh cells in a way such that the mass within a cell is conserved, while at the same time satisfying the Naviér-Stokes equation and conservation of energy. In practice this can lead to the entire fluid failing to behave realistically.

Alternatively, it is possible to implement a Lagrangian simulation using a particle representation of the fluid. Conceptually, a particle-based Lagrangian simulation is similar to a particle simulation of individual molecules. Each Lagrangian particle represents a specific collection of molecules, such as a specific portion of the fluid, as illustrated in Figure 2.6.2.

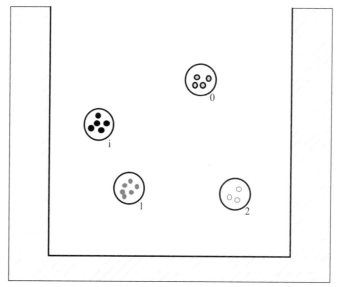

FIGURE 2.6.2   *Particle-based Lagrangian representation of a fluid.*

When a particle moves, it does so in a way that is representative of the molecules it conceptually contains. Statistically, the group of molecules represented by a given particle remains in the vicinity of the particle from frame to frame, as shown in Figure 2.6.3. Note that with particle-based Lagrangian methods, there is never any direct decision about how many molecules exist in each particle. The particles are just assigned an initial mass that is held constant from frame to frame. Continuity is naturally satisfied, so this governing equation can safely be ignored, and it is trivial to represent different types of fluids mixing together.

The governing equations were developed using the continuum assumption, but particle-based Lagrangian simulations do not fully treat the fluid as a continuum. You might think that a traditional rigid-particle-collision response could be used. And, of course, you could use a rigid-particle-collision response. But because of the presence of continuous pressure and viscous forces, fluids behave differently, and such an approach

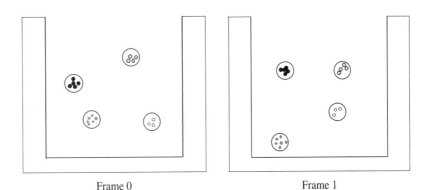

Frame 0   Frame 1

FIGURE 2.6.3 *Evolution of a fluid over time from the Lagrangian perspective.*

would not be realistic. To achieve realism, the interaction among the Lagrangian particles must be handled using some representation of the fluid as a continuum. A continuum representation generates derivatives of the properties present in Equation 2.6.1,
and these derivatives drive the simulation forward. The smoothed particle hydrodynamics method provides a simple way to compute the fluid properties and their derivatives as needed for the simulation, without the need for a grid.

Using Smoothed Particle Hydrodynamics to Simulate Fluids

As mentioned above, for the particle-based Lagrangian approach, the particles have
mass that is constant throughout the simulation, and so we can safely ignore the continuity equation. It is satisfied automatically. Furthermore, since we are assuming an
incompressible fluid with constant viscosity, we can safely ignore the energy equation;
it is decoupled from the pure fluid motion in this case.

The only equation that remains to be simulated is the Naviér-Stokes equation
(Equation 2.6.1). From a Lagrangian perspective, the $D\mathbf{v}/Dt$, term on the left side of
the Naviér-Stokes equation is the time rate-of-change of the velocity of a given fluid
particle—that is, it is simply the acceleration of a fluid particle. If for a given particle
we can compute the density and the terms on the right side of the equation, we can
compute the particle acceleration $D\mathbf{v}/Dt$, and then the total force on the particle. We
then can update the position of the particle using traditional particle dynamics techniques. This is the way Smoothed Particle Hydrodynamics (SPH) works.

Smoothed particle hydrodynamics is a simple CFD technique. Physical values of
the fluid are interpolated by summing kernel-weighted physical values of neighbor
particles. This is similar to how photon mapping works.

The SPH approach represents an arbitrary, interpolated value $A(\mathbf{r})$ at location $\mathbf{r}$,
using Equation 2.6.4. The domain of integration is the entire volume of the fluid.

$$A(\mathbf{r}) = \int A(\mathbf{r}')W\left(\mathbf{r} - \mathbf{r}', h\right) d\mathbf{r}' \qquad (2.6.4)$$

The property $A(\mathbf{r})$ can be any continuum fluid property, such as density or pressure. The function $W(\mathbf{r}, h)$ is a kernel function that has the following two features:

$$\int W\left(\mathbf{r} - \mathbf{r}', h\right) d\mathbf{r}' = 1$$
$$\lim_{h \to 0} W\left(\mathbf{r} - \mathbf{r}', h\right) = \delta\left(\mathbf{r} - \mathbf{r}'\right) \qquad (2.6.5)$$

Here, h is the valid radius of the kernel function, and δ is the delta function, which has a value of one when $(\mathbf{r} - \mathbf{r}')$ is zero, and has value zero otherwise. A simulation will use different kernel functions for different fluid properties, depending on the characteristics of the property being interpolated using Equation 2.6.4. For simplicity, Equation 2.6.4 can be evaluated using a simple summation over a discrete number of particles, rather than by evaluating the continuous integral.

Müller, et al. [Müller03] provides a solid introduction to SPH as applied to stable, fast, fluid simulation. Their article presents exactly the kernel functions and discrete summations that we recommend. [Müller03] is the basis for the extension supporting rigid-body interaction that we will describe.

We should note that although we are using the incompressible form of the Naviér-Stokes equation, during simulation the density of the particles will change. This is a consequence of the interpolation, and though technically inconsistent with the governing equations, this cannot be entirely avoided. All numerical methods contain numerical errors, and this is a disadvantage of the SPH method. But there are some cases where a density change is realistic, even when simulating incompressible fluids. For example, when mixing two different, incompressible fluids together, the overall fluid density will change, and so it is consistent for the density to change during simulation. This particular situation will prove quite useful for simulating the interaction of fluids with rigid bodies, as presented in the next section.

Extending SPH To Support Interaction with Rigid Bodies

The basic fluid simulation technique described in [Müller03] does not provide any suggestions as to how to simulate the realistic interaction between an SPH-simulated fluid and moving rigid bodies. The remainder of this article describes an extension to the SPH technique that enables fluid and rigid body interaction to be simulated quite easily.

There are two types of solid objects with which a fluid might need to interact inside of a game world. The first are the static objects, such as the world's level geometry, which cannot move. The second are the dynamic objects in the world—objects that might move, such as crates, characters, or vehicles. Static and dynamic objects are treated differently, as described in the following sections.

Interaction with Static World Geometry

When an SPH fluid particle interpenetrates a static solid object, an easy yet realistic approach is to compute a force in the opposite direction to force the particle back into the fluid region of the world. This is the *penalty force method,* and it works quite well for fluids interacting with static geometry. The penalty force causes the fluid particle to be moved outside of the solid object over a few simulation frames. There is no need to compute a force from the particle on the object, since the object cannot move.

When a fluid mass point interpenetrates a static object, a penalty force is applied (and added to the **f** term in Equation 2.6.1). Moore and Wilhelms [Moore88] provide a comprehensive introduction to the penalty force method. For our purposes, the penalty force applied to a fluid particle that interpenetrates a static object can be computed using Equation 2.6.6.

$$\mathbf{F}^{\text{col}} = k^{\text{s}} d\mathbf{n} + k^{\text{d}} \left(\mathbf{v} \cdot \mathbf{n} \right) \mathbf{n} \tag{2.6.6}$$

Here, d is the distance by which the particle has interpenetrated the static object, k^{s} is a spring constant, k^{d} is a damper constant, $\mathbf{n}$ is the normal vector at the point of collision, $\mathbf{v}$ is the relative velocity, and $\mathbf{F}^{\text{col}}$ is the collision response penalty force applied along the normal vector direction on the fluid particle. This collision force, divided by the particle mass (to achieve a force per unit mass), is added to the **f** term in the Naviér-Stokes equation for a given particle. Good values for the two constants can be found by experimentation. For each constant, start with small values and increase them slowly to achieve the effect you desire.

Interaction with Dynamic Rigid Bodies—Treatment

Dynamic rigid bodies (simply referred to as "rigid bodies" for the remainder of this article) are those that move during the game and that might need to interact with a fluid, such as water.

In our extension of the SPH method, we treat rigid bodies as a portion of the fluid. The initial density of the rigid body is required to be greater than the initial mass density of the fluid for this extension to work properly. We represent the rigid body as a collection of particles that are updated in the same manner as the fluid particles; the only special treatment occurs when computing the pressure contribution between fluid and rigid particles. The rigid particles exert a pressure that pushes the fluid away from the rigid bodies. Likewise, the fluid particles apply a pressure that results in a net translation and/or rotation of the rigid bodies.

The pressure applied on a rigid body particle is given by Equation 2.6.7, and the pressure at a fluid particle is given by Equation 2.6.8.

$$p = \begin{cases} k^{\text{rigid}} \left(\rho - \rho_0^{\text{rigid}} \right) & \rho \geq \rho_0^{\text{rigid}} \\ 0 & \text{otherwise} \end{cases} \tag{2.6.7}$$

$$p = \begin{cases} k^{\text{fluid}} \left(\rho - \rho_0^{\text{fluid}} \right) & \rho \geq \rho_0^{\text{fluid}} \\ 0 & \textit{otherwise} \end{cases} \tag{2.6.8}$$

Here, ρ_0^{rigid} is the rigid body's initial, or rest, density. Note that the density of individual rigid body particles will fluctuate due to interpolation and mixing, just as the density of individual fluid particles will fluctuate. The variable ρ_0^{fluid} is the initial, or rest density of the fluid. Equation 2.6.8 prevents fluid particles from penetrating into a rigid body because pressure is always positive, resulting in a repulsive force that moves fluid particles away from the rigid body particles.

By definition, rigid body motion is restricted to rigid translation and rotation around a center of mass. Since rigid bodies don't deform, at the end of a time step, the rigid particles must behave as a collection of simple mass particles that are rigidly linked together in the shape of the rigid body. In traditional rigid-body simulation, a net force and a net torque are applied the rigid body to cause the body to move as a whole. In our approach, pressure is applied individually to each rigid particle, causing them to move independently. Because of the independent, unconstrained update of rigid particles, the rigid particles do not necessarily conform to the shape of the rigid body after an update. To achieve an end result in which the rigid particles do conform to the proper rigid body shape at the end of a time step, we apply a correction step to enforce the rigidity of the rigid body particles. This process of updating the particles independently in a first step, then enforcing rigidity in a second step, is illustrated in Figure 2.6.4.

To enforce rigidity, we use the particle positions and motion after the particle update to compute a new location and orientation for the rigid body, as well as values for other key rigid body dynamics properties. We then update the rigid particle positions to be located at their correct location relative to the new rigid body configuration. In computing the new rigid body position and orientation, we treat rigid body motion in an approximate way that is a bit simpler than full rigid-body simulation, and achieve stable interaction with the fluid particles.

The total rigid body mass M is given by Equation 2.6.9.

$$M = \sum_j m_j \tag{2.6.9}$$

Here, m_j is the mass of a single rigid particle j, and the summation is computed over all of the particles in the rigid body. Assuming all of the rigid particles have the same mass, the velocity of the center of mass of a rigid body is given by Equation 2.6.10.

$$\mathbf{v}_g = \frac{1}{N} \sum_j \mathbf{v}_j \tag{2.6.10}$$

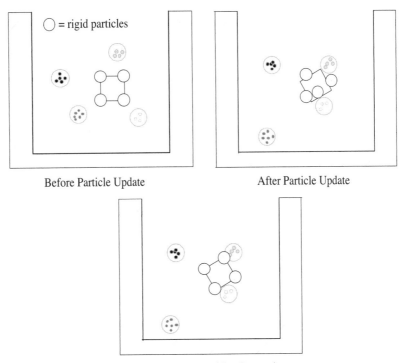

Before Particle Update   After Particle Update

After Applying Rigidity Constraint

FIGURE 2.6.4   *Illustration of rigid body particle positions after initial update and after rigidity is enforced.*

Here, N is the number of particles, and $\mathbf{v}_j$ is the velocity of a single particle j. The angular velocity of the rigid body $\boldsymbol{\omega}$ is approximated by Equation 2.6.11.

$$\boldsymbol{\omega} = \frac{1}{I} \sum_j \mathbf{q}_j \times \mathbf{v}_j \qquad (2.6.11)$$

Here, $\mathbf{q}_j$ is the location of a single rigid particle j, relative to its corresponding rigid-body center of mass $\mathbf{r}_g$. These quantities are defined by Equations 2.6.12 and 2.6.13. The rigid-particle location vectors $\mathbf{q}_j$ are computed in the local rigid-body coordinate system at the beginning of the simulation and are never recomputed. They represent the relative position where the rigid particles must be located to maintain the rigid body shape.

$$\mathbf{r}_g = \frac{1}{N} \sum_j \mathbf{r}_j \qquad (2.6.12)$$

$$\mathbf{q}_j = \mathbf{r}_j - \mathbf{r}_g \qquad (2.6.13)$$

The scalar variable I is related to a moment of inertia of the rigid body, divided by its mass, and is defined by Equation 2.6.14.

$$I = \sum_j \left|\mathbf{q}_j\right|^2 \tag{2.6.14}$$

The rigid body properties computed in Equations 2.6.9 through 2.6.14 can be used to obtain an updated position and orientation of the rigid body as a whole. For example, often in simulations, a rigid body's location will be defined by its center of mass, and so Equation 2.6.12 directly provides the updated position. We can compute the updated position and orientation as follows.

We store a rotation matrix $\mathbf{R}(t)$ and the center-of-mass $\mathbf{r}_g(t)$ for each whole rigid body. During the simulation, these are updated using Equations 2.6.15.

$$\mathbf{r}_g\left(t+\Delta t\right) = \mathbf{r}_g\left(t\right) + \Delta t \mathbf{v}_g\left(t+\frac{1}{2}\Delta t\right)$$

$$\mathbf{R}\left(t+\Delta t\right) = \mathbf{R}\left(t\right) + \Delta t \mathbf{Q}\left(t+\frac{1}{2}\Delta t\right) \tag{2.6.15}$$

Here, $\mathbf{Q}(t)$ is the time rate of change of the rotation matrix at time t, given by Equation 2.6.16. $\mathbf{Q}$ is evaluated at time $t + 1/2\Delta t$ by computing the new value of $\boldsymbol{\omega}$, using the particle velocities at time $t + 1/2\Delta t$, but using $\mathbf{R}(t)$ (since $\mathbf{R}(t + 1/2\Delta t)$ has not been computed yet).

$$\mathbf{Q}(t) = \begin{bmatrix} 0 & -\omega_z & \omega_y \\ \omega_z & 0 & -\omega_x \\ -\omega_y & \omega_x & \end{bmatrix} \mathbf{R}(t) \tag{2.6.16}$$

Once the rigid-body angular velocity and center-of-mass velocity are known, the kinematic velocity of each rigid-particle velocity constrained by rigid-body motion is computed with Equation 2.6.17.

$$\mathbf{v}_j = \mathbf{v}_g + \boldsymbol{\omega} \times \mathbf{q}_j \tag{2.6.17}$$

Interaction with Dynamic Rigid Bodies—Simulation Update

Updating Fluid Particle Positions and Velocities

The acceleration of a fluid particle $\mathbf{a}_j$ is exactly the $D\mathbf{v}/Dt$ term from the Naviér-Stokes equation, and therefore its computation requires that you evaluate the SPH equations described by [Müller03]. A force per unit mass due to gravity, or penalty due to collision with a static mesh object may be added to the **f** term, if desired. Once the acceleration is known, the other two particle kinematics properties, position and velocity, are updated using traditional particle simulation techniques. To update the position and velocity of fluid particles, one approach is to use the Leap-Frog Verlet numerical integration scheme shown in Equations 2.6.18.

$$\mathbf{r}_j\left(t+\Delta t\right)=\mathbf{r}_j\left(t\right)+\Delta t\mathbf{v}_j\left(t+\frac{1}{2}\Delta t\right)$$

$$\mathbf{v}_j\left(t+\frac{1}{2}\Delta t\right)=\mathbf{v}_j\left(t-\frac{1}{2}\Delta t\right)+\Delta t\mathbf{a}_j\left(t\right) \qquad (2.6.18)$$

The scheme requires that the particle velocity $\mathbf{v}_j$ be stored at time steps that are offset from the position $\mathbf{r}_j$ and acceleration $\mathbf{a}_j$ by half a time step Δt. It is easy to start the Leap-Frog method. Simply ignore the fact that the velocities are stored at offset time steps when you initialize the values for the particles—for example, just assign the velocity at time $=-0.5\Delta t$ to be the starting velocity for the particle, and proceed from there.

While the Leap-Frog Verlet scheme only computes the velocity at half-time steps, to compute the terms of the Naviér-Stokes equation for the SPH update, the velocity at t is needed. It can be calculated by using Equation 2.6.19. This value need not be stored. It can be quickly computed during the SPH update and then forgotten.

$$\mathbf{v}_j\left(t\right)=\frac{1}{2}\left\{\mathbf{v}_j\left(t-\frac{1}{2}\Delta t\right)+\mathbf{v}_j\left(t+\frac{1}{2}\Delta t\right)\right\} \qquad (2.6.19)$$

Of course, the Leap-Frog technique is not the only way that you might update the particle position and velocity. Feel free to try other schemes, such as the Verlet scheme without velocity.

Updating Rigid Particle Positions and Velocities

In our approach, the rigid body particles are updated in exactly the same way as the fluid particle, which enables implementations to be particularly elegant!

To enforce rigidity, after the rigid particle updates, we first compute the updated rigid body position and orientation as described in Equations 2.6.15. Once the overall rigid body's new position and orientation are known, it is possible to update the individual particles that make up the rigid body. The position of the each rigid body particle at the next time step, $t+\Delta t$, is given by Equation 2.6.20, which enforces the rigidity of the rigid particles.

$$\mathbf{r}_j\left(t+\Delta t\right)=\mathbf{R}\left(t+\Delta t\right)\left(\mathbf{r}_j\left(t\right)-\mathbf{r}_g\left(t\right)\right)+\mathbf{r}_g\left(t+\Delta t\right) \qquad (2.6.20)$$

Implementation Details

Neighbor Search

When updating the particles using the SPH technique, we interpolate the physical value of fluid properties at point **r** of the fluid by summing products of a kernel and a physical value of particles within the scope of a smoothing length h. Doing this requires searching for the surrounding particles that have a local influence. It is critical to implement the simulation in such a way that the search for neighboring particles is as fast as possible.

There are many spatial partitioning schemes that can enable extremely fast spatial searches. One simple approach is to divide the space into uniform voxels of size h and allocate each particle to the voxel that contains its center point. The neighborhood of a particle is then acquired by looking up particles in a $3 \times 3 \times 3$ voxel space: the voxel containing the particle and the 26 neighboring voxels. Figure 2.6.5 illustrates a voxel grid in 2D. In the 2D case, the array of neighboring voxels has dimension 3×3. Listing 2.6.1 shows pseudo code for allocating particles to voxels, and for locating the neighbors of a given particle i.

Listing 2.6.1   Partitioning Particles and Locating Neighbors

```
// allocate all rigid particles to voxels first
for each rigid particle i {
    allocate_to_voxel(i)
}

// Now locate the neighbors for fluid particle i,
// and allocate the fluid particle to the voxel grid
for each fluid particle i {
    for each neighbor voxel g {
        for each particle j in g {
            if h > distance(i, j)
                add_pair_to_list(i, j)
                // Collect neighbors of particle i
        }
    }
    allocate_to_voxel(i)
}
```

It is possible to reuse distances calculated at this neighbor-search step to reduce computation time for the next step. The simulation time can be shortened further by skipping the neighbor search in some cases where neighboring particle groups differ only slightly, depending on the scene situations.

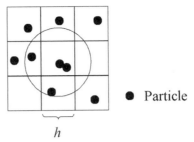

FIGURE 2.6.5   *Neighboring particles in 2D.*

Running the Simulation

A partial implementation of the simulation is listed below in pseudo code. Listing 2.6.2 shows the main entry point for the simulation, as well as the simulation loop. Listing 2.6.3 shows the function to locate neighboring particles. This is a variation of Listing 2.6.1. Listing 2.6.4 illustrates updated particle density computation. Listing 2.6.5 shows the wrapper code for computing forces on particles. Listing 2.6.6 shows pseudo code for updating the overall rigid-body motion properties. Finally, Listing 2.6.7 shows the update of the fluid particles.

Listing 2.6.2   Main Entry Point and Simulation Loop for the Simulation

```
procedure simulation_main {
    initialize

    while simulating {
        find_neighbors_of_fluid_particles

        compute_particle_densities
        compute_pressures  // including rigid/fluid interactions

        compute_all_forces // including static collisions
                           // and gravity

        // update position and velocity of each fluid particle
        // according to Leap-Frog scheme
        for each fluid particle i {
            update_position_and_velocity(i)
        }

        for each rigid body r {
        // perform initial rigid body particle update, and then
        // compute updated position and orientation of the
        // whole rigid body.
        compute_rigid_body_motion(r)
```

```
        // Now update the individual rigid particle positions to
        // to enforce rigidity.
        for each rigid particle i in r {

            // update position and velocity of each rigid particle
            // by Equation 2.6.20 to enforce rigidity
            update_rigid_position_and_velocity(i)
        }
    }
}
```

Listing 2.6.3   Locating the Neighbors of the Fluid Particles

```
procedure find_neighbors_of_fluid_particles {
    clear(grids)
    for each fluid particle i {
        // compute voxel index corresponding to particle i
        g = compute_index(i)

        for each particle j in neighborhood of voxel[g] {
            dist = compute_distance(i, j)
            if (dist < h) {
                // store neighbor particle and its distance
                add(neighbor_list[i], j, dist)
            }
        }

        // allocate particle to corresponding voxel
        add(voxels[g], i)
    }
}
```

Listing 2.6.4   Using the SPH Method To Update Particle Densities

```
procedure compute_particle_densities {
    for each particle i {
        for each particle j, dist in neighbor_list[i] {
            d = compute_density(dist, pos[i], pos[j])

            // add contribution to density of
            // one particle and another
            // because of symmetry of contribution
            density[i] += d
            density[j] += d
        }
    }
}
```

Listing 2.6.5   Computing Forces on Particles

```
procedure compute_all_forces {
    for each particle i {
```

```
                    for each particle j, dist in neighbor_list[i] {
                        // compute density contribution of
                        // one particle on another
                        f = compute_force(dist, i, j)

                        force[i] += f
                        force[j] -= f
                    }
                }

            function compute_force(float r, int i, int j) {
                // grad_spiky_coef and lap_vis_coef are
                // precalculated coefficients
                // of the SPH equations
                // grad_spiky_coef = -45.0f/(PI*h^6)
                // lap_vis_coef = 45.0f/(PI*h^6)

                if (is_rigid[i] or is_rigid[j])
                {
                    force = mass[j]*(h - r)/density[i]/density[j]*(-
                    0.5*(max(pressure[i], 0) + max(pressure[j],
                    0))*grad_spiky_coef*(h - r)/r + (vel[j] —
                    vel[i])*mu*lap_vis_coef)

                }
                else
                {
                    force = mass[j]*(h - r)/density[i]/density[j]*(-
                    0.5*(pressure[i] + pressure[j])*grad_spiky_coef*(h - r)/r +
                    (vel[j] - vel[i])*mu*lap_vis_coef)

                }

                return force
            }
```

Listing 2.6.6 Compute the Overall Rigid-Body Motion Properties

```
        procedure compute_rigid_body_motion(r) {
            for each particle i in rigid[r] {
                // update velocity of particle according to
                // force acting on it
                update_velocity(i)
            }

            // compute center of gravity and q[i]
            // by Equations 2.6.10 and 2.6.11
            // compute I by equation 2.6.12
            r_g = compute_gravity_center(r)
            for each particle i in rigid[r] {
                q[i] = pos[i] - r_g[i]
                I += length(q[i])^2
                omega = cross(q[i], vel[i])
            }
```

```
        omega /= I

        // compute updated rotation matrix
        // by Equations 2.6.18 and 2.6.19
        compute_rotation_matrix
}
```

Listing 2.7.7   Update the Fluid Particles

```
procedure update_position_and_velocity(int i) {
    // the simulation stores position, velocity,
    // velocity half stepped,
    // and acceleration for each fluid particle
    for each fluid particle i {
        // compute v(t + 1/2dt)
        vel_half_next = vel_half[i] + t*acc[i]

        // compute r(t + dt)
        pos[i] = pos[i] + t*v_half_next;
        // compute v(t)
        vel[i] = 0.5*(vel_half_next + vel_half[i])
        vel_half[i] = vel_half_next
    }
}
```

Optimizations

The computation of the right side of the Naviér-Stokes equation is performed using three kernel functions. It is possible to precalculate the coefficients of these kernels to achieve faster computation, since the effective radius of kernel h is a constant value.

The most naive implementation would compute equations containing particle interactions by iterating across all the particles each time. However, the effects of one particle on another particle, and vice versa, are symmetric. So for the sake of efficiency, compute the contributions first, and then compute interpolated physical values.

Conclusion

This article has shown an extension to the smoothed particle hydrodynamics technique of fluid simulation, which enables the interaction of fluid and rigid bodies. Any actual game application requires that the fluid be rendered. If the system is rendered as a particle system, then the particles will appear to behave like a fluid. The illusion is stronger if there are more particles, but of course this increases the cost of simulation. Alternatively, it is possible to generate a continuous fluid surface and render that surface using various water rendering techniques. The rendering can be implemented as follows:

1. Generate the implicit surface from the distribution of particles,
2. Triangulate the implicit surface by methods such as Marching Cubes [Bloomenthal94], and finally,
3. Shade the surface using any technique of interest.

The fluid can be rendered to look extremely realistic if you use hardware shaders to simulate both light reflection and refraction. Sample code for the methods discussed in this gem is available on the CD-ROM accompanying the book.

References

[Bloomenthal94] Bloomenthal, Jules, "An implicit surface polygonizer." *Graphics Gems IV,* Academic Press, pp. 324–349, 1994.

[Moore88] Moore, Matthew, and Jane Wilhelms, "Collision Detection and Response for Computer Animation." *Proceedings of the 15th Annual Conference on Computer Graphics and Interactive Techniques,* ACM Press: pp. 289–298, 1988.

[Müller03] Müller, Matthias, David Charypar, and Markus Gross, "Particle-based Fluid Simulation for Interactive Applications." *Proceedings of the 2003 ACM SIGGRAPH/Eurographics Symposium on Computer Animation,* Eurographics Association: pp. 154–159, 2003. Available online at *http://graphics.ethz.ch/Downloads/Publications/Papers/2003/mue03b/p_Mue03b.pdf.*

[Noe04] Noe, Karsten, "Implementing Rapid, Stable Fluid Dynamics on the GPU." 2004. Available online at *http://projects.n-o-e.dk/GPU_water_simulation/gpuwater.pdf.*

[Stam99] Stam, Jos, "Stable Fluids." *Proceedings of the 26th Annual Conference on Computer Graphics and Interactive Techniques,* ACM Press: pp. 121–128, 1999.

ARTIFICIAL INTELLIGENCE

Introduction

Brian Schwab, Sony Computer Entertainment of America

brian_schwab@yahoo.com

Artificial intelligence . . . Just what do we mean when we say that? To some it means machines that think like we do. To others it simply means that in-game characters perform actions listed in a script. With so much variation in what we're all after, it's no wonder that the field is not only hugely broad, but also quite confused and disorganized.

So many researchers, as well as working engineers and hobbyists, are working *within* the field of Artificial Intelligence (AI)—but all approaching it from not only different directions, but also with different tools, mindsets, and overall goals. While sometimes overwhelming, the sheer volume of material being produced in the name of advanced-game AI is truly exciting for those of us that work within the industry. In the past, the AI programmer might find an article or two on pathfinding optimization, or extensions to general state-machine architectures. But now, even a casual online search can deliver hundreds of references (many accompanied by professionally designed code) on dozens of advanced AI techniques: combat and terrain analysis, planning algorithms, AI learning, and the list goes on and on.

One thing we shouldn't forget in the shadow of all this available material, however, is that the AI tools we use in our games are just that: tools. You should pick the right tool for the current job you are working on and not get stuck thinking that any one AI technique will give you everything. Try to take into account the game you're working on, but also assess factors like your time schedule, the actual level of intelligence you're looking for, and the specific behaviors you'll require of your AI agents. AI, as has been said many times before, is not a simple problem; nor is it a singular problem.

The articles in this volume of *Game Programming Gems* are a varied toolset, indeed. Armand Prieditis gives us a gem detailing a model-based system for AI planning. Diego Garcés offers more tips and tricks on dealing with the issues of multiple unit coordination. Hugo Pinto and Luis Otavio Álvares give us a series of gems about using traditionally robotic AI systems within games. Julien Hamaide talks about achieving short-term memory with support vector machines. Michael Ramsey's gem explains the quantified judgement model for predicting combat outcomes. Sébastien Schertenleib guides us through the creation of a flexible AI engine, giving a specific application of issues covered within Section 4: Scripting and Data-Driven Systems. Hopefully one or more of these gems will provide you with insight into the particulars of the AI problems you're currently working on.

Another thing to consider as the AI programmer on a game team (or one of them, now that studios are seeing the need for more advanced systems and are hiring additional AI engineers), is to try to notice other areas of development that could use your AI-based tools, and apply your craft there. AI is just beginning to be used in nongameplay areas of game development, and this part of an AI programmer's job will only continue to grow as its usefulness is fully realized. Companies are using AI for automated product testing, streamlining the build process, tuning complex physics parameters offline to be used within in-game systems, and for many other applications. The gem by Gabriyel Wong actually discusses using fuzzy logic to handle level-of-detail determination by the graphics system of a game.

All in all, the job of an AI programmer is a double-edged sword. On the one hand, we are being given increasingly more quantity and quality of tools to put in our AI toolsets. But we are also being expected to find novel uses for these tools on each and every game we make. Continuing to break new ground in the areas of game intelligence and emergent behaviors should be our ever-constant focus.

We must continue to strive forward and experiment with novel uses of our technology in the direction of overall game development, but always return to our prime directive: the creation of fun game experiences. By instilling within the player the feeling that he's playing against another mind in some form or another, we can deliver the fun factor that gamers are clamoring for and continue to push ourselves as creators in the meantime.

3.1

Applying Model-Based Decision-Making Methods to Games: Applying the Locust AI Engine to *Quake*® *III*

Armand Prieditis, Lookahead Decisions Inc.

prieditis@lookaheaddecisions.com

Mukesh Dalal, Lookahead Decisions Inc.

mukesh@lookaheaddecisions.com

Developing good game Artificial Intelligence (AI) is difficult. The standard approach to developing game AI is based on rules. Unfortunately, rules are brittle, expensive, and time-consuming to develop, modify, and debug, and often result in unintelligent behavior. This gem describes a new approach to game AI, one based on models of the underlying game world—actions, their effects, and observations. The model-based approach is more robust, reduces development cost and time, eases modifications—and results in behavior that is more intelligent. Specifically, this article describes the preliminary results of applying the model-based approach as embodied in the Locust AI engine to *Quake III*. This article focuses on the impact on the game AI practitioner in terms of features and benefits, and presents a vision for the future of game AI development.

Introduction

As shown in Figure 3.1.1, modern computer games combine technology from graphics, physics, and AI to produce realistic gameplay. Realistic gameplay is difficult to define, but it roughly translates to a sense of immersion in the game world and a sense of intelligence behind the Non-Player Characters (NPCs). In realistic play, objects behave and look much as they do in the real world, and NPCs act rationally. The goal of game AI is not to create unbeatable opponents, but to create gameplay that is more immersive and interesting through NPC behavior that is more intelligent.

For example, in some cases it is possible to create an unbeatable opponent entirely without AI, namely through cheating. Consider the case where an NPC with developer-added cheating goes directly to the room in which you are hiding. An intelligent NPC would instead conduct a systematic and rational search of all rooms. The latter is more believable, and consequently more immersive and interesting. In fact, a truly intelligent NPC might have as its objective to maximize the interest and immersion of a human player, rather than trying to be unbeatable.

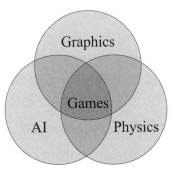

FIGURE 3.1.1 *Computer games are a combination of technologies.*

Game engine graphics and physics have both shown great progress in the past few years. In fact, stunning graphics from packages such as Maya® and 3ds Max are now the norm, rather than the exception. Physics packages such as Havok now let developers create physically realistic worlds. But good graphics and physics are no longer enough to differentiate a game product. As a result, game developers are now looking for other innovations in which to differentiate. Since game AI has not progressed as much as graphics and physics, it offers more room for differentiation and innovation. Moreover, the percentage of CPU cycles that developers are allowed to burn on AI computations has been steadily growing, because high-speed graphics cards are taking over ever more functions from the CPU. This article describes a new approach to game AI, one that takes advantage of these computational opportunities.

Current Game AI: Rule-Based

Current AI in games is primarily rule-based. A rule is of the form: Situation → Action. When the situation is matched, it causes the action to execute, where the action might be a single move, a script of moves, or a full animation clip.

For example, a rule can say that if the enemy is visible and health is low, or the enemy's weapon is better than the player's, then the player should retreat. The retreat action might simply be an animation clip that is played for a few seconds or until the next rule is selected based on the updated situation. Rules might contain multiple Boolean conditions for the situation; in this case, the Boolean is simply an OR.

Another popular rule, this one for pathfinding, specifies that an NPC should take the shortest path to a particular destination. This rule can work quite well in the absence of dynamic obstructions and other agents.

The way in which the rule is matched can vary greatly. It can be in the form of a decision tree, as shown in Figure 3.1.2, which combines common parts of the situation for a set of actions. Nodes in the tree correspond to a test on the current situation; the leaves of the tree correspond to the actions. For example, in the decision tree in Figure 3.1.2, the first node tests whether the NPC has a weapon; if so, the next test asks if the NPC is close to the enemy. If this final test succeeds, then the associated action is to attack. Of course, there is another path to attacking as well—if the NPC doesn't have a weapon and the enemy is smaller than the NPC.

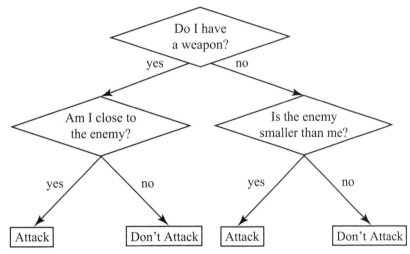

FIGURE 3.1.2   *A simple decision tree structure.*

In short, each path through the tree corresponds to a Situation → Action rule, where the situation is the set of tests for all the nodes along the path, and the action is the leaf at the end of the path. Although decision trees are a more compact way of storing rules and are somewhat easier to maintain than a set of rules, they are equivalent to standard rules in terms of decision-making power.

Another way to encode a set of rules is as a Finite State Machine (FSM). An FSM consists of a set of developer-defined states that correspond to some action, and arcs that correspond to test on the situation and lead from one state to another [Rabin02]. For example, in the FSM shown in Figure 3.1.3, the initial state might be IDLE, where the NPC does no action until the enemy is seen. When the enemy is seen, the action is to ATTACK (e.g., a clip of gunfire). Once the attack state is reached, if the NPC loses sight of the enemy, then a SEARCH behavior is engaged, which again might be an appropriate clip.

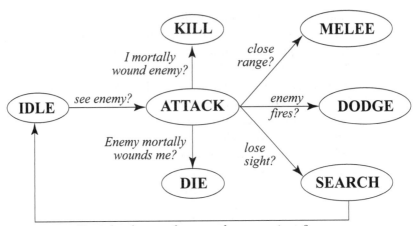

FIGURE 3.1.3   *A typical finite-state machine.*

As with the decision tree, an FSM is equivalent to a set of rules with flags that correspond to the states and that are set in the action part of the rule while also executing the associated action. While FSMs offer no more in terms of power than standard rules, they are somewhat more manageable, as they do not require explicit manipulation of flags and their associated states. For that reason FSMs are used in most commercial games, including *Age of Empires, Enemy Nations, Half-Life, Doom,* and *Quake.*

Other techniques can be used to encode rules. Fuzzy logic offers rules that have probabilistic methods of matching. Similarly, neural nets offer more-complex matching, but they encode rules nonetheless. These methods make it easier to express certain conditions in a more compact way than standard rules. They also make it possible to learn rules from examples. Expert systems combine a series of rules with an internal rule interpreter that can add its own internal symbols (i.e., symbols that do not directly appear in a situation) to allow for more-complex matching. While this method of matching can add significant run-time flexibility, it is considerably slower than other methods and is rarely used for games. Note that expert systems are equivalent to a set of rules since the interpreter can be used to *unwind* the set of rules that the expert system executes: The weakest preconditions for applying the rules correspond to a Situation, and the resulting action corresponds to an Action.

In sum, rules can appear in a variety of forms—some easier to modify, maintain, and understand than others—but all are equivalent to Situation → Action.

The Problem with Rules

While rules are often attractive as a first choice for game AI, they have several shortcomings. These are summarized below.

Rules often result in unintelligent behavior.   Rules have difficulty gauging the long-term ramifications of an action. This is because it may take several subsequent actions by several NPCs to discover that some initial action was wrong. For example, if all NPCs follow the shortest-path rule to a destination, congestion will result, because they will all vie for the same shortest-path route, resulting in a traffic jam.

Rules are expensive and time-consuming to develop.   This is because the game developer requires an extensive knowledge of the game before good rules can be developed.

Rules-based behavior is limited by the cleverness of the game AI developer. No intelligent behavior will emerge that the game AI developer has not already painstakingly programmed. Given a tight development deadline, it is often too much to expect that the AI developer will have enough time to develop enough expertise to endow each NPC with intelligence. Moreover, good programmers don't always make the best game players.

Rule-based behavior can destroy the immersive experience by creating disbelief. One of the most important factors in a game's success is the player's suspension of disbelief. Irrational behavior can also create disbelief in the game player. NPCs that cheat are even worse: Too smart actually appears too dumb, and the heavy hand of the developer is seen everywhere when this happens, also destroying immersion.

Rules are brittle: They break when they are even slightly outside of the situation for which they were designed.   For example, if an NPC normally takes a certain shortest path to a destination, and that path is temporarily blocked, the shortest-path rule breaks. Brittleness also occurs because rules have difficulty dealing with imprecise or parallel actions, actions involving time, positional uncertainty, or missing, noisy, or uncertain observations.

Rules are expensive to modify and debug, and lead to an inefficient *generate-and-patch* development process.   The usual fix to a brittle rule is to add an exception to it. As a result, the game developer is forced to continually add special cases to handle new situations. For example, consider the following rule: If the NPC's health is less than 50%, seek out a health power-up. The brittleness begins when the NPC stops attacking to chase a health power-up, and the NPC's enemy only has a sliver of life remaining. The NPC only needs to fire at its enemy for a few seconds to kill him, so it looks unintelligent when the NPC stops attacking so abruptly. So the patch to this brittle rule might say: If the NPC's health is less than 50% and it's not currently attacking an enemy whose health is less than 5%, go seek out a health power-up. That solves the immediate problem. The NPC will finish killing its nearly dead enemy before healing itself. But what if the NPC's ammunition is running very low, as well? It needs to know that it cannot continue to attack its enemy, even though the enemy's health is very low, because it will run out of ammo soon. This might be solved by adding an exception to the exception, like this: If the NPC's health is less than 50%, and it's not currently attacking an enemy whose health is less than 5%, unless the NPC's ammo count is less than 5%, go seek out a health power-up. This commonplace generate-and-patch method of rule development is not only inefficient, but it leads to spaghetti code that is difficult to maintain, and which is easily broken by new game features. The QA process of tracking down bugs is also painful, because complicated contexts and states mean that the bug may have originated many frames prior to its eventual appearance.

Rules are never done.   The generate-and-patch process—add a rule, test it in various scenarios until it breaks, then build a patch rule that handles the specific case that caused it to break—is pervasive in industry and invariably leads to an inherently incomplete AI product. This is because the generate-and-patch process usually continues until the production deadline date is reached, and then the product is shipped with fingers crossed and the hope that the game-playing end user will not discover the unpatched portions, most of which even the game AI developer is unaware of. Of course, the game player often delights in discovering where the rules break down, and takes pride in being the first to post these breakdowns on blogs and newsgroups, destroying all the positive PR and buzz surrounding what would otherwise be a good game.

Rules are unpredictable and unstable.   A patchwork system of rules not only becomes rapidly unmanageable, but unpredictable. An unplanned situation might bring the entire system down or create looping, insect-like behavior.

Rules don't scale up to multiple NPCs.   Controlling the behavior of a single NPC is hard enough with rules. The opportunities for brittleness and the complexity of rules increase exponentially as more NPCs are added, especially if these NPCs are to work in collusion or opposition.

Given these shortcomings in the dominant approach to game AI rules, it's no wonder that game AI has not progressed as much as game graphics and physics: The rule-based approach has hard limits that have long been reached by game AI developers.

The Model-Based Approach to Game AI

According to the rational model of decision theory, the best decision is one that max-imizes the expected outcome based on future decision sequences. For example, Figure 3.1.4 shows that we might be considering two decisions. And for each of these two decisions, there are two subsequent decisions, leading to some outcome. Nodes in this tree represent states or situations; directed arcs represent moves that result in a new state. The arcs emanating from the root node represent the actual choices at hand; those below represent future choices. The best choice is the one on the right, since it maximizes the expected outcome.

We call this approach to game AI *model-based,* because it contains a description of the high-level dynamics of the system: the set of legal actions and their results. Model-based decision-making can be summarized in the following three steps:

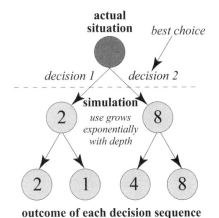

FIGURE 3.1.4 *Two possible decision sequences.*

1. **Simulate** the effects of each decision forward in time by building a look-ahead tree.
2. **Evaluate** the expected outcome of each decision sequence in that tree.
3. **Choose** a decision that results in the best expected outcome.

In the classic board game chess, the model is the description of each legal move, how the game ends, and who wins. In video games, the model is a description of each allowable action, its effects, and other events that can take place in the world. Note that the *rules* of the game should not be confused with a rule-based approach, which *prescribes* the actions that should be taken for a particular situation, rather than *describes* them as the model does in the model-based approach. Another way to look at the model-based approach is as the high-level physics of NPC behaviors.

Interface to the Game

The particular way in which a model-based decision-making system is interfaced to the game will vary, but the basic process is the same. For example, in the Locust game engine, the interface assumes four processes: Observe, Update, Decide, and Act (see Figure 3.1.5). Observation involves getting sensory information. Updating is the process of using the observations to change the beliefs about what is occurring. Deciding on a course of action involves using the current beliefs to choose a course of action that somehow is likely to improve the situation according to some measure. Acting means effecting change in the environment. This interface also assumes that the current state of the world is known by the decision-making engine. For example, it assumes that it knows the current location of all NPCs; the Update process takes into account changes to that current state.

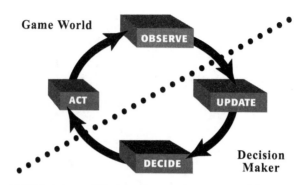

FIGURE 3.1.5   *The interface to the game world.*

As shown in Figure 3.1.5, this cycle of Observe → Update → Decide → Act continues indefinitely. The dashed line is the point of interface, separating the Locust engine from the game world where actions and observations actually take place. That is, Locust's internal belief structures and decision-making processes are separate from the world. In fact, its internal beliefs are generally an approximation of the game world and are dependent on the complexity of the representation of that world.

Real-time decision-making is an important aspect of this model. In any complex world, a planned course of action is rarely possible to execute in its entirety, because the world is unpredictable. For example, an A*-produced path, neatly showing how an NPC can navigate to its target destination, will rarely be applicable in its entirety, because other NPCs might get in its way or obstructions might suddenly appear.

Locust takes this into account, because decisions are interleaved with observations that monitor the effects of a decision. This allows for adjustment of a course of action. Of course this model allows for the decision-maker to have a detailed plan in mind, but in most applications, this plan will not be applicable in its entirety because of this unpredictability. Each decision-maker is always using an internal model of the beliefs about the world in terms of certain parameters, which are then updated based on what is observed.

Advantages and Implications for the Game AI Developer

The model-based approach to game AI, at least as implemented in the Locust game engine, offers several advantages to the game developer over the standard rule-based approach:

It results in behavior that is more intelligent.   This is because it takes into account the future impact of each decision. A Locust-powered NPC has logical and consistent goals that define what the NPC wants to accomplish, and the

NPC's moment-by-moment actions lead toward fulfillment of those goals. Locust seamlessly combines short-term tactical decisions with long-term strategic plans, and smoothly reprioritizes its goals in reaction to changes in its environment or status. The result is NPC behavior that is more intelligent.

It reduces development time and cost.   Getting a game shipped on time and on budget is crucial. Game developers know that AI programming can kill a development schedule. Often, the development team simply runs out of time before perfecting NPC behavior, and a game ends up shipped with AI that is just good enough, because the development team simply ran out of time. With Locust, the model can be built rapidly at a relatively low cost, without requiring great expertise. All that is needed is a description of the actions and their effects, and how observations are related to underlying states.

It results in emergent intelligent behavior.   This means that NPCs can exhibit intelligence not originally programmed in by the game developer. This is easy to understand with a simple analogy: The Deep Blue chess team used a similar model-based approach to developing their program, which beat the human, world-champion chess player Gary Kasparov. Yet, the Deep Blue team members were not world-champion chess players, themselves. Thus, the intelligence of the NPCs is not limited by the intelligence of the game developers. This frees the game developer to think about the creative aspects of NPCs—their personalities, weapons, sensors, and goals—rather than having to worry about developing rules.

It creates greater immersion.   When the NPCs do things that the player would do, the illusion of reality is maintained. Behavior that is more intelligent dramatically increases the game player's enjoyment of the game.

It is more robust.   Look-ahead is more robust than rules, because it is always situation-specific yet general-purpose. This makes it decidedly nonbrittle. When making a decision, Locust takes into account all factors, such as NPC health, enemy health, proximity to health power-ups, and ammo counts. Given these inputs, Locust always returns the best decision for a given time boundary. The more time, the better the decision, as more future implications of a decision can be taken into account. The Locust AI engine also works with complex terrains by automatically creating hierarchical waypoints.

It scales up to multiple NPCs.   Its underlying look-ahead technology is based on distributed decision-making, which reduces the exponential-branching factor traditionally associated with multiple NPCs. It can also be distributed onto multiple machines running over a network.

It makes modifications and debugging easy.   If other factors ought to play a part in an NPC's behavior, they are relatively simple to add. For example, if individual NPCs require differing personalities, the discounts on certain goal costs can simply be changed to reflect the NPC's propensities. A timid NPC would more deeply discount going for health power-ups as early as possible, whereas a bolder NPC might discount getting to its enemy, with less regard for its own health. A lazy NPC might add a surcharge to any movement whatsoever, thus encouraging it to stay near its starting location. The Locust approach is much simpler and nearly context-free, making maintenance easier and bugs quicker to find. Adding or changing behavior is simply a matter of modifying the NPC's simulation and goals. Locust sidesteps the spaghetti code of rule-based systems with its simulation-based look-ahead. In short, when the model changes, the decisions that result from it automatically change, with no additional effort.

It enables portable characters.   Gamers love to see similar personalities from game to game. Once the model is built for one NPC, it can be ported and easily adapted for an entirely different game. With the Locust AI engine, it is possible to create a library of characters based on their behavior, rather than their physical realization.

It offers greater product differentiation.   We mentioned that game AI is the last frontier for product differentiation. Yet rules create vanilla behaviors that offer little differentiation. The model-based approach, and Locust in particular, offers several advantages to the animator: When the game developer wants to control a small number of completely autonomous characters with high-level actions over a long period of time, and when the animator wants to control a large number of simple characters with low-level joint-control over a relatively short period of time. Model-based control of low-level locomotion is also possible with Locust. Flocking and crowd behavior is one of the simplest things in Locust, and is entirely embedded in the goal specification rather than in a control rule. Thus crowd behavior is emergent, rather than programmed.

The model-based approach has two disadvantages over the rule-based approach. First, it requires the construction of a model. However, this model is easier to develop than a set of rules, and it is possible to build the model from interaction. Second, creating the look-ahead tree is likely to be slower than the processing of a rule. However, the additional time taken to compute a better decision is worth it in most complex applications. We've found that Locust can make decisions in a few milliseconds for multiple NPCs. This provides more than enough time to react in real time to game changes, while exhibiting intelligent behavior.

Quake III Arena with the Locust AI Engine

This section describes the basics of *Quake III Arena* (*Q3A*), a multiplayer, first-person shooter game made by id Software. As we will see, real-time decision-making in this game is complicated: You have fractions of a second to react to nasty NPCs who are continually trying to kill you; you must reason about moving to gain health and weapons, and avoid certain NPCs; and you must choose from a diversity of weapons that you can find and fire, each of which has a best usage.

Players move throughout the map, or *arena*, to *frag* (the *Quake* word for kill) enemy players and score points based on the game mode. If your player's life reaches zero, then your character will die. Soon after, your character *respawns* at specific places throughout the map, but you lose all of the items that you had gathered previously. The game ends when a player or team reaches a specified score, or when a time limit has been reached.

Weapon systems are designed so that a good weapon exists for every situation. One of the primary decision-making tasks is to pick the right weapon. Weapons also spawn themselves at regular intervals at specified locations. You can gain a weapon simply by picking it up off the ground. All weapons come with a certain amount of ammo. Ammo boxes, sometimes hidden, are located throughout the game world.

When your health gets low, you can pick up health items in four categories: yellow recovers 25 health, orange recovers 50 health, green recovers 5 health (but can go over 100), and blue recovers 100 (and can go over 100). The maximum health you can get to is 200.

Movement in *QA3* is relatively simple: You can run, walk, crouch, or jump. Running is always on by default, though running everywhere isn't smart. Walking is useful, as you make no noise when you walk, allowing you to sneak up to an opponent. While crouching also deadens the noise made when moving, it makes you move more slowly. The advantage of crouching is it puts you lower to the ground, and therefore makes you a smaller target. This can be useful if you want to hide behind low structures or peek at something without creating a big target.

The Locust AI engine applied to *QA3* controls all NPCs—none use rule-based control. The actions it executes are as follows: Move forward a certain number of units at a certain angle, move backward a certain number of units at a certain angle, continue previous action, fire current weapon, and idle. We tried different levels of look-ahead depth and found that three to eight levels worked best. Beyond five levels, the improvement in performance leveled off. Locust sampled 20–30 whole-screen updates per second (most games feature 20+ frames or updates per second). During each update, Locust controlled two or three NPCs doing a full look-ahead. Locust made fast decisions, roughly 13 msec per NPC.

The original rules in *QA3* took six months to develop and 50,000 lines of code. The Locust version, stripped of all rules, took two weeks to develop and only 2,000 lines of code—a massive reduction in time and cost. Qualitatively, it resulted in NPCs that made more rational decisions, and more challenging and crafty opponents, thus improving the gamer's experience as well as the intelligence of the NPCs.

Related Work

Soar ([Laird00] and [LairdDuchi00]) is most closely related to the spirit of this work. Soar is unique in that it uses rules to make decisions, but yet uses backward chaining and subgoaling to resolve forward progress impasses, and to make choices among competing rules. For example, to control the human player's character, it used 715 rules,

100 operators (that change internal state), and 20 substates. Since Soar is a cognitive architecture it also includes models of human memory, such as a limited amount of working memory, symbol processing, and chunking. In contrast, our approach to game AI is more focused on performance, rather than modeling human cognition.

Conclusions and Future Work

The vision for the future is clearly to build a game AI that is as good as current graphics. Our research has found that the rule-based approach to game AI, as widely practiced today, will not get us to that point. Chess program developers recognized that in the early 1980s and completely abandoned the rule-based approach for the model-based approach, which resulted in a chess program that beat the human world-champion chess player (Gary Kasparov) in the 1990s. Game AI developers are beginning to recognize the same thing. In particular, this article has described a model-based approach to decision-making as embodied in the Locust AI engine. We found that Locust offers several significant advantages over the standard rule-based approach, while increasing decision-making performance.

References

[Laird00] Laird, J., "It Knows What You're Going to Do: Adding Anticipation to a Quakebot." AAAI 2000 Spring Symposium Series: Artificial Intelligence and Interactive Entertainment. AAAI Technical Report SS-00-02.

[LairdDuchi00] Laird, J. and J. Duchi, "Creating Human-like Synthetic Characters with Multiple Skill Levels: A Case Study using the Soar Quakebot." AAAI 2000 Fall Symposium Series: Simulating Human Agents.

[Rabin02] Rabin, Steve, "Implementing a State Machine Language." *AI Programming Wisdom,* Charles River Media, 2002: pp. 314–320.

3.2

Achieving Coordination with Autonomous NPCs

Diego Garcés, FX Interactive

diegogarces@gmail.com

In most modern action games, the player must face multiple AI-controlled enemies. As gamers become more exigent of the challenges games present to them, more complex behaviors are needed. It is not sufficient to only have individually complex behaviors; it is often more important to use each behavior at the appropriate time and in the right place. If behavior coordination is not addressed properly, NPCs will behave without taking into consideration other NPCs, even though they are all sharing a common goal: defeating the player while providing a fun gameplay experience.

To produce a real appearance of intelligence for the player, groups of NPCs must work together and perform behaviors cooperatively.

When a game agent tries to decide when, where, or how to apply a specific behavior, it has to take into consideration many different factors related to its internal state. Personality, health, armor, ammo, or current weaponry can all be deciding factors.

However, an even more important factor toward making the right decision is quite frequently what actions the other NPCs are doing. By taking this into account, they will all seem to collaborate to a common goal, instead of hindering each other. Blocking another one's line of fire, trying to attack from the same spot, or not being aware of what their partners are doing are common AI mistakes that can make the player forget about the individual behaviors (however perfect they may be) and just perceive stupidity in the enemies, ruining an otherwise fun gaming experience.

This article presents some mechanisms that can be easily added to autonomous NPCs to allow more-cooperative operation. Even though each NPC is deciding its behavior independently, the addition of some extra information and simple communication will make it seem that real coordination is happening.

Possible Solutions

Coordination, like most AI problems, can be solved in multiple ways. One solution is to not do it. Some game types can avoid the added complexity of coordinated behavior, since enemies are supposed to behave chaotically. However, this is usually not the case.

There are two traditional methods to solve the coordination problem: within a centralized game entity, and by giving more autonomous control to each game entity.

The Centralized Approach

The method traditionally applied in games is the centralized solution. In such a solution one agent, not necessarily representing a real game entity, analyzes the situation of the player and all the NPCs. After collecting all of this information, it performs the required calculations to obtain a coordinated strategy. To execute this strategy it then sends specific orders to each of the AI-controlled agents. If everything works as planned, the NPCs behave in a perfectly coordinated way, even though they are just following orders blindly.

Some games require strict control of NPC behavior directly by the designers. In such a case, a more fixed and less autonomous organization would be the best solution, so that the level of control that the designers request can be more easily realized.

In games that benefit from the use of autonomous agents, however, centralized solutions for coordination offer a system that is much easier to control. If designers need a concrete coordination action to be taken in some specific situation, it is possible to just insert a few tweaks directly within the centralized agent, which will be simpler than tweaking many different autonomous mechanisms to act in a specific manner under certain circumstances. Additionally, it is often easier with a centralized approach to debug and keep track of which actions are taken by different NPCs.

The main drawback to the centralized approach is that of scale: This kind of solution tends to get very big and complex as the size of the system increases. And how does the system grow in size? It does so with larger scenarios, increasingly more-complex agent behaviors, and a higher number of NPCs to manage. These are just some of the important features most games are asking for in the future. Furthermore, since this is a monolithic structure, it is difficult to adapt to changes that can and will happen between the computation of the strategy and the end of its execution.

In summary, centralized approaches do not scale well or adapt well to changing environments, and can consume a lot of CPU resources, possibly reducing NPC responsiveness. In addition, it is often difficult to deal with situations not foreseen at design time. The appearance of multicore processors in next-generation consoles and modern PCs add more obstacles to adopting a centralized organization, since splitting a process to make full use of multiple processors is not an easy task—and an even harder one if a variable number of processors are available.

The Autonomous Approach

Another solution [Orkin03] lies in looking into the well-established, distributed computing methodology. Many of the issues described above in the centralized approach are solved within distributed systems. Therefore, the solution proposed will be to distribute the coordination responsibility among all the agents. This organization provides a scalable and flexible structure; and with it, each agent can be assigned an independent thread of execution. These NPCs are thus autonomous in the sense that they decide what actions they will undertake. They are not just machines executing actions; they take active part in the decision process.

Coordination, instead of being explicitly programmed, will emerge by means of communication and sharing of information between multiple autonomous agents. When addressing simple local problems, it is easier to find a good solution for choosing the best behavior for each agent, and then to take care of the coordination as a separate problem. No global strategy is computed at any time. This allows a few behavior adjustments to respond to a large game-situation change, instead of having to recompute an entirely new global strategy.

Since each NPC is completely independent, this solution scales well as we need to increase the number of NPCs. Adding new NPCs to the system and letting them use the same coordination mechanisms is obviously much easier then getting a central entity to take into account additional new NPCs. A distributed solution also fixes the problems of use with multicore hardware, since each NPC can be assigned a different thread of execution. Multithreaded programming issues must still be faced, but task decomposition is already a given with this kind of architecture.

The responsiveness of any given AI-controlled entity is not an issue, because each agent decides what to do on its own, and its decision process will not take as long to compute as a global strategy in a centralized solution.

Despite these advantages, no system is perfect, and this is no exception. Coordinating a set of autonomous entities so that they all do what they are supposed to do is a big challenge. Moreover, fine-grained control over group behavior could be difficult without specific mechanisms for it.

NPC Structure

We are striving toward fully autonomous NPCs, so the system must provide them with all the capabilities to act in such a fashion. With that purpose in mind, a flexible architecture has been chosen to represent a game agent. It is composed of a number of controllers that will take care of the different tasks the agent must perform within the game.

A typical NPC should be able to play animations, move around the scenarios, sense the surrounding world, and perform actions on it. To address these tasks, the *animation*, *movement*, *sense*, and *behavior* controllers are defined (see Figure 3.2.1).

This article will cover the *behavior* controller specifically. The behavior controller is in charge of executing actions that will control what the agents do at each time slice within the game. Some of these actions are very simple, like jumping to avoid being hit, and some are complex, such as the attack routine of a level boss. They can also be organized in trees or hierarchies to build even more-complex actions from simpler ones. The controller contains a set of *active* actions that are being executed every frame and another set of *waiting* actions that continuously check upon a condition to see if they are ready to start executing.

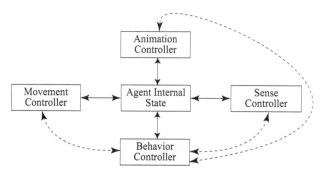

FIGURE 3.2.1   *NPC structure and the connection between controllers.*

This organization can be very useful and adds a great deal of flexibility to the system. It is possible to have more than one action active at a time, for example changing from one cover point to another while shooting, if possible. Waiting actions allow using behaviors that take some time to start (i.e., not necessarily deterministic), because old actions will be still active while the new one receives all the required data. Path computation is sometimes a time-consuming process, and behaviors requiring a path to start executing (e.g., going to cover) will not make the character stand still waiting for the pathing information; instead, the character will continue with its previous actions as expected, until the path is available.

Imagine an NPC designed to patrol around and perform certain attack actions when the player is within sight. This can be implemented with waiting tactics that will be executed under the condition that the player has been seen. We just have to set the patrol action as active and the attack action as waiting, and the NPC will take care of the rest.

These features relax some of the requirements of the coordination system. It will be possible to spend more time adjusting behaviors to achieve better coordination without worrying about frozen characters.

Coordination Mechanisms

At this point, each NPC is executing actions and evaluating waiting actions as a consequence of a decision made by the NPC, like attacking the player or running away. However, this is not enough to fully give the illusion of intelligence. If the NPCs are allowed to decide these things all by themselves, they will have completely chaotic behaviors. Now, how do we get all the NPCs to perform coherent actions that appear to the player as intelligent, coordinated, and challenging?

Since each NPC makes its own decisions, the best way is to give them mechanisms to exchange information. This way, each of them will have all the information necessary to make an informed decision when choosing what actions to perform and where to perform them.

The mechanisms proposed in this article that allow the exchange of information between NPCs are:

- Attack slots
- Exclusion zones
- Trigger systems
- Enemy events
- Player mutex
- Allowed zones
- Blackboards

These mechanisms do not try to build super-intelligent agents. They try to provide simple solutions that, when combined, can simulate the effect of multiple intelligent agents working together.

In the following sections, we are going to cover each of the above mechanisms, explain each conceptually, discuss the reasons that make each useful, and see how they can be used to give the impression of coordination.

Attack Slots

In most games today, there are multiple enemies attacking the player at any one time. If they make decisions as if they are alone, they could all decide that the best option is to attack the player from close distance. In that case, all the enemies will be surrounding the player, possibly blocking each other. Obviously, this is not a desired result. This situation originates because of the lack of information about the rest of the NPCs in the decision process.

As a general rule for gameplay, it is better to distribute all the enemies across the available space rather than crowding them around the player. The best option will be to build an NPC capable of performing a situational analysis, taking into account the scenario topology, positions of the rest of the NPCs, and the required game difficulty. It will then choose the optimal position(s) to attack from. However, it is not always possible to have such an agent, due to complexity issues or CPU time available for such calculations.

Attack slots try to solve the problem in a convenient fashion. A slot acts like a token and represents the minimum distance an NPC is allowed to attack the player from while possessing that token (see Figure 3.2.2).

They can be easily adjusted to distribute the NPCs, and they can be specific to each scenario or group of enemies. Each attacking NPC must possess one attack slot, and it cannot move closer to the player than the distance indicated by that slot.

Whenever an NPC looks for a point to attack from, it asks for the best attack slot available (the one with the shortest distance). With this slot in hand, it performs the necessary calculations to find a good attacking point that meets the requirements of this attack slot. When this attack is finished, the NPC tries to adjust its attack slot to the one least restrictive—that is, a far-away slot that is at least farther from the player

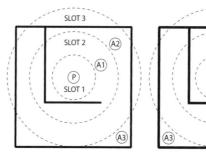

FIGURE 3.2.2   *In the left picture, three agents (A1–3) are attacking the player with one slot each. In the right picture, the agents have moved. A1 has moved correctly according to its slot, A2 has moved too close with its current slot, and A3 has moved to a correct location—although it had to pass through, closer to the player.*

than the current attack slot being used. If the new chosen attacking position results in a spot farther away then what was allowed by the best attack slot, the NPC will free this slot for the new, less-restrictive one—all of which will allow another NPC to use the old attack slot and get closer to the player if necessary.

Exclusion Zones

While attack slots do address some of the problems of crowding the player, they cannot solve everything, because they only set a minimum distance requirement. This is made especially clear with overlapping attack slots. With only a minimum distance constraint, two NPCs can choose to attack from the same spot if it is within legal distance for both attack slots, since they don't have another way of knowing that the position is already taken by another NPC.

Another typical problem with multiple-shooting enemies is line-of-fire blocking. One enemy is shooting from a spot, when all of a sudden another enemy breaks into the line of fire and stops to shoot, forcing the first enemy to stop shooting (since the second guy is in the way). This greatly reduces the impression of intelligence and also generates other issues, like an enemy being hit by friendly fire.

Exclusion zones are one way to face these issues, as they will add another constraint to the availability of zones or points within the scenario. They represent zones that are already occupied or will be occupied soon by some NPC. Thus, points within exclusion zones are off limits as attacking spots.

Each NPC registers the zone where it is attacking or is going to attack from, including the corresponding line of fire. This zone could be a circle around the attacking position or a zone the NPC is protecting alone.

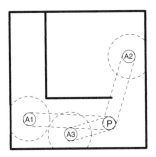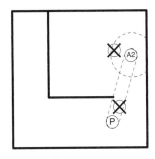

FIGURE 3.2.3 *Agents 3 and 1 (A3 and A1) cannot move to that location because the line of fire and the zone around A2 are registered, respectively.*

These zones are registered in a shared place so that the rest of the NPCs can access them. When looking for a new point to attack from (e.g., searching for a good cover point), positions within these exclusion zones will be excluded from the search process.

This mechanism ensures that two enemies will not choose the same place to attack. Furthermore, the topology, size, and shape of the exclusion zone can be custom configured to the enemy type, behavior, or scenario basis (see Figure 3.2.3).

Trigger Systems

Trigger systems have been widely used in the artificial intelligence of games. They have multiple uses, one of which is communication. To see details about how to build a trigger system for a game engine, take a look at [Orkin02].

Sometimes communication is based on location. In this type of communication, a trigger system can be very useful in the communication between game entities. It becomes especially handy for spoken announcements or sounds emitted by NPCs. For example, if an NPC discovers the player and shouts for them to stop, this shout should be heard by nearby NPCs so that they can go to help. Alerting behavior like this can be simulated easily with a trigger placed where the shout was emitted (see Figure 3.2.4). This form of communication between NPCs is very useful for giving the user the feeling of NPC intelligence, because some game event (in this case a sound) causes a realistic reaction in the game (in this case, another NPC coming to inspect or help). The reaction happening after the sound will seem much more realistic than a scripted affair that might not completely align with the player's movements.

Triggers are mostly used for sound effects (e.g., explosions, shots, door openings, or NPC dialogues). But triggers are not limited to explicit communication. Consider a dead enemy; it may want to "communicate" to anyone who can see the dead body that someone is around. Enemies that receive this communication can raise the alert and start hunting the intruder. This type of communication is handled much more easily with a trigger system than by manually checking all nearby NPCs to see if they are alive.

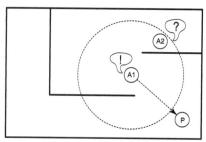

FIGURE 3.2.4   *Agent1 (A1) sees the player and sets a shout trigger. Agent 2 (A2) hears it and alerts itself.*

Enemy Events

The above mechanisms provide channels for implicit communication between NPCs. They expose their intentions by reserving an attack slot, registering an exclusion zone, or setting up a trigger to broadcast some event. With this kind of information, other NPCs can adjust their behavior accordingly.

However in some cases, more-direct communication is needed. For example, if an NPC is being blocked by another NPC, it can send a message directly to the blocking NPC to move aside.

A typical message-passing architecture can be used for this purpose. Messages can be sent to a specific NPC, to an entire group of NPCs, or broadcast to everyone. Treatment of messages will be done synchronously each frame, but this politic could be changed for specific needs. Upon receipt of a message, the NPC can change its behavior if the message is *accepted*. (Can the agent do anything about it? Does the incoming message have higher priority than the current action?) Consult [Rabin02] for details on message-passing architectures.

Enemy events can be combined with triggers. An example that could be very useful in some games genres is dynamic formation of groups. At some moment, an NPC decides to form a squad to attack. It spawns a trigger to announce to nearby units that a group request has been issued. NPCs that receive this trigger respond with an enemy event to the source (the group leader) that they are ready to be part of the group. The group leader can then process the responses received and decide which NPCs will be part of the group or retire the group call entirely (e.g., because of a new game situation or simply because of a lack of good group members), and switch to another tactic.

Player Mutex

Attack slots allow for separation of the NPCs at a distance by limiting the number of enemies that can get very close to the player. Sometimes this is not enough, and it is necessary to restrict the number of enemies that can attack the player at the same time. This is especially true with melee combat, where typically only one enemy is allowed to fight with the player, while other enemies wait or use their ranged attack. In fact, it is useful to picture some behaviors as having to require exclusive access to the player. Considering the player as a shared resource among the NPCs, traditional resource-access management in multithread environments can be used, specifically mutexes.

A *mutex* is a token whose possession gives access to a shared resource. In this case, the shared resource is the player. When an NPC wants to perform a melee attack, it tries to get the mutex. If it is available (i.e., no other NPC is already holding it), the mutex is captured by the NPC, and any other enemy that tries to perform a melee attack will have to wait until the current mutex owner is finished with its attack.

With this mechanism, you can control when the mutex is released—thus, giving you fine control over issues like letting the player recover after a melee attack. Furthermore, the mutex can be requested in advance, or a priority queue could be built so that enemies attack the player in turn. In general, all the traditional mechanisms to manage mutual exclusion can be used with this kind of mutex.

Allowed Zones

In some specific scenarios or tasks, it is important to distribute multiple NPCs over different areas. Imagine a few connected rooms like those shown in Figure 3.2.5. The designer may want a particular enemy to attack from one room, while another enemy is holding a different room. Without any additional restrictions, the enemy from the first room may want to get closer to the player or move outside his assigned room in search of a good cover point.

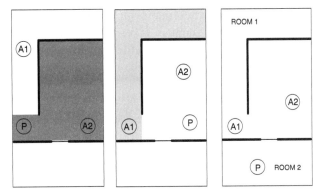

FIGURE 3.2.5 *Allowed Zones. (Left) Agent 2 (A2) protects its zone and the door, and it will not follow the player into Agent 1's (A1's) zone. (Center) A1 cannot enter; it will attack from there. (Right) The player can escape by entering Room 2; the enemies will not follow.*

To allow for this possibility, we should define zones where the enemy is allowed to move to, attack from, or generally perform any behavior. The NPC can pass through disallowed zones to reach a position inside its allowed zones, but no destination point can be outside the NPC's allowed zones.

Using allowed zones, the game designer can map out specific situations. This mechanism allows designers to add design-time knowledge directly to the coordination of the NPCs. Allowed zones can also be set by the NPCs—for example, the leader of a squad can decide to assign some zone to each of the squad members in order to distribute the space available and cover the level in the best way possible.

Blackboards

A blackboard system [Isla02] is an important tool for exchanging and exposing information among NPCs; it can also be used to achieve coordination. It is a centralized information-sharing facility—a common place where each NPC can publish information so that the rest can access it and change their behavior according to this new information. This results in an implicit coordination between the information publisher and the reader(s). All kinds of information can be published in the blackboard—from NPC intentions to perception values to action suggestions.

Since very different types of information will be stored within the blackboard, an ad-hoc version will not be very flexible, because it will require modifying the definition of the blackboard for each new information type added to the system. Blackboard systems are widely used in games as a powerful and simple communication tool. Therefore, it is worth investing some time in building a flexible system that allows reuse in other areas, or enables extending the agents without any changes in the blackboard's inner workings.

A generic property system provides a good solution. Properties can be of any type and can be accessed by name or ID for fast access. With this kind of system, it is very simple to add new information to the blackboard and serialize its state to disk. This kind of persistence can be used to allow for saved-game support or persistence between game levels.

Enhancements to traditional blackboard data can help it become even more useful. For example, an expiration time can be used to automatically take care of obsolete information and to avoid the problem of the blackboard growing very large in memory (e.g., filled with out-of-date information).

Example: Coordinated Search for the Player

In this section, we will cover a typical example of multiple enemies searching for the player within a game level. It will make use of some of the mechanisms explained above.

Inside the game engine, precise information about the location of the player is available. However, it will be unrealistic to send the enemies directly to the player's hiding spot if no NPC has seen the player hide there. If we are developing an infiltration game (where the player is supposed to sneak around and remain hidden), cheating NPCs that always know where the player is, or NPCs that never find the player can completely ruin the game experience.

One possible way to organize a search within a level is to separate NPCs so that they can cover more terrain in less time. Each NPC can register an exclusive, allowed zone to search within. Each level can be divided into simple zones by the designer or by using a simple navigational mesh scheme.

As the NPC registers a search zone, it moves to the closest point of that zone and continues examining the zone. The NPC can then publish in the blackboard which points have been already examined, with some expiration time or any other design-specific data. The NPC can use this data to remember which points have been recently inspected unsuccessfully, and other NPCs can also have that information available. This is important since zones could overlap a bit, and NPCs can share the same zone if an NPC finishes inspecting their zone and moves on to the next (see Figure 3.2.6).

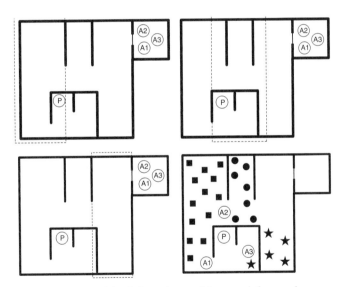

FIGURE 3.2.6 *Top left, right, and bottom left: search zones. Bottom right: explored points.*

If an enemy discovers the hidden player, it can raise the alert by setting a trigger at the enemy's location so that nearby NPCs can come and help. In addition, the NPC can also communicate with certain units if specific behavior is needed to face the player, like heavy warfare or a sniper. These kinds of communication can be performed through NPC events that request reinforcements.

Conclusion

In this article, we have presented several ways in which NPCs can be represented successfully as autonomous agents. There is no centralized system that distributes orders to each NPC. They choose which action to execute based on the information they have. This information is not always gathered from the environment; it can also be obtained from other NPCs, and this is what enables coordination between them. If NPCs have detailed information about what other NPCs are doing, they can make good action choices without hindering the other agents' interests.

Having autonomous agents in a game is becoming even more important with the multithreading requirements of next-generation games. You can have CPU-intensive computations like pathfinding or cover searching in separate threads that can be assigned to different processors, and let the behavior controller deal with nondeterministic wait times.

Since autonomous agents are independent from each other, it is also possible to distribute them among all the processors available. Agents will behave the same way; only the communication mechanisms will have to be adapted to exchange information between processors.

References

[Isla02] Isla, Damian, and Bruce Blumberg, "Blackboard Architectures." *AI Game Programming Wisdom,* Charles River Media, 2002.

[Orkin02] Orkin, Jeff, "A General-Purpose Trigger System." *AI Game Programming Wisdom,* Charles River Media, 2002.

[Orkin03] Orkin, Jeff, "Simple Techniques for Coordinated Behavior." *AI Game Programming Wisdom 2,* Charles River Media, 2003.

[Rabin02] Rabin, Steve, "Enhancing a State Machine Language Through Messaging." *AI Game Programming Wisdom,* Charles River Media, 2002.

Behavior-Based Robotic Architectures for Games

Hugo Pinto and Luis Otavio Álvares

hugo@hugopinto.net

Recently, interest in robotic architectures has grown in the game development community due to the similarities of the 3D action game domain and the domain of mobile robots.

A robot has to decide what do at each step, based solely on its perception of the environment and its built-in knowledge. It must make decisions quickly, function without supervision for hours, and deal with many possibly conflicting goals. It needs to do all its perception and decision-making with limited processing power. Acting in the real world, the robot is faced with a fast-changing environment populated with diverse entities.

The modern game action environment presents a similar scenario. The agent is situated in a 3D world with approximated, continuous properties. It has many actions available and interacts with several other entities in real time. Processing power is limited, and the agent has contradictory goals, such as killing enemies and keeping its safety. The major differences are that in a game, unless we explicitly want to, we do not have noise in the game robot sensors, and sensing is not expensive.

Agents that do not cheat are becoming increasingly popular due to their potential for believability. By not cheating, we mean that a bot has the same information that a player has, not more. It perceives only what is in its line of sight, hears only up to a distance, and knows only facts that it can deduce or know by asking, noticing, or being told. This leads to greater realism in its actions, which in turn leads to greater player immersion. We see that a noncheating game bot may be built as a robot; we provide it with sensors and actuators, and program its decision-making mechanism. The good news is that the field of robotics is mature and full of well-tested, proven solutions. We have a plethora of techniques available for straightforward adaptation and testing in the 3D game domain.

Professional developers and academics have investigated the application of robotic architectures in games, with encouraging results. [Yiskis03] and [Champandard03] have used the subsumption architecture [Brooks86], with the latter making a bot for *Quake II.* [Pinto05-a] has applied extended behavior networks [Dorer04] to the design of agents for *Unreal Tournament.* In this gem, we examine these architectures and their applications, present other promising techniques, and point extensions to the systems discussed.

Subsumption Architecture

The subsumption architecture [Brooks86] was proposed as a control mechanism for autonomous robots that have multiple goals, several sensing abilities, and need to be robust in face of noise and small system failures. It has been applied to the construction of several robots, including one that wandered through a real office collecting empty soda cans. In games, it has controlled bots in *Quake II* [Champandard03].

A striking feature of subsumption architecture design is that we split the agent not into layers corresponding to information flow, but rather make a decomposition based on the desired class of behaviors that we want the agent to have—its *competences.*

Suppose we want to build a simple agent that attacks its enemies. A decomposition based on program flow would be as shown in Figure 3.3.1. We have a module that translates the sensory information into a suitable representation for a planner. The planner sends a predetermined plan to executor modules that will carry out the actions in the sequence defined by the plan. A problem with this approach is that as new percepts and actions are added, the planner may face a combinatorial explosion. Another is that we need to replan often, using sophisticated heuristics, because the plan may become obsolete in the middle of its execution.

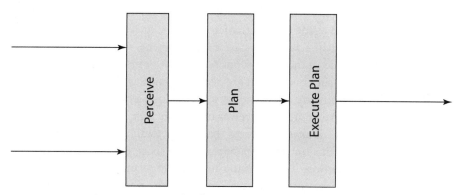

FIGURE 3.3.1   *Decomposition of a shooter agent based on program flow.*

A decomposition based on competences is shown in Figure 3.3.2. Here we have no problem adding more sensors; each layer uses just a few sensors and is directly connected to an output. Replanning is also not a problem, as the system is fast and all layers operate in parallel.

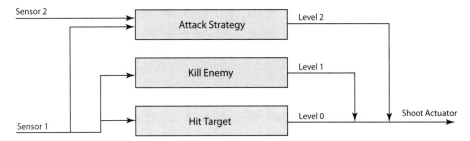

FIGURE 3.3.2 *Decomposition of a shooter agent based on competences.*

We see that each upper layer specifies a more specific class of behaviors for the agent, as well as includes the more general behavior layer below it. The Kill Enemy competence (Level 1) includes the target-hitting competence (Level 0). Likewise, employing an Attack Strategy subsumes the enemy-killing competence. Thus, the name *subsumption architecture;* upper layers subsume the layers below them.

Each layer may be composed of several behavior modules whose sequence up to an actuator makes up a competence. In Figure 3.3.3, we see that the Hit Target competence is made up of three behavior modules: Detect Entities, Pick Target, and Shoot.

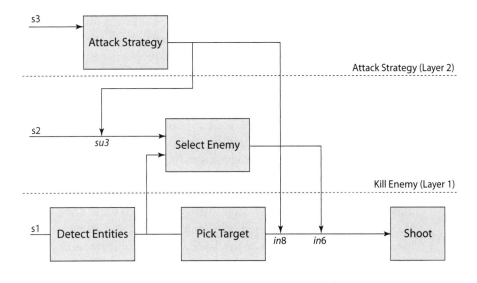

FIGURE 3.3.3 *Detailed subsumption architecture for a shooting agent.*

Modules in higher layers may replace the input of behavior modules in lower layers or suppress their output. Upper layers may receive input from any module in lower layers. Figure 3.3.3 shows how the layer Kill Enemy connects to the lower layer Hit Target, and how Attack Strategy connects to the two lower layers. Note that we have three sensors—s1, s2, and s3—and a single actuator—Shoot. Kill Enemy looks at the entities detected and eventually suppresses Pick Target's output with the coordinates of an enemy. Attack Strategy receives a strategy input (s3). It is able to replace the input to Select Enemy (s2) and inhibit Select Enemy's output. The overall behavior of this architecture could be summarized as follows: The Hit Target layer selects a random target to shoot. The Kill Enemy layer detects if there is an enemy in sight, and with other relevant info (from s2) selects an enemy as Target if there is one. The Attack Strategy layer is able to influence the Enemy Select behavior by replacing one of its inputs. It is also able to directly suppress the output of the lower layer.

There are three design issues worth mentioning. The first is that the behavior modules themselves are not altered after they have been implemented—that is, we work only on their inputs and outputs. The second is that each upper layer may depend upon a module in a lower layer, which leads to a bottom-up design. The third is that each behavior operates asynchronously, leading naturally to the exploration of parallel processing.

We see that the robustness of the mechanism comes naturally from its organization: If an upper layer stops functioning, the lower layers will continue to do their job. If our agent fails for some reason to lay an attack plan, it will still attack the enemies that it sees.

Ok, now we have an idea of what a subsumption architecture is, how it works, and how we may design one. Are there specific guidelines for its application to games? [Yiskis03] suggests that we build the lower layers to achieve immediate goals and the upper layers to achieve longer term goals. He proposes enforcing the condition that no upper competence bypass a lower one—that is, upper competences must achieve their goals only by issuing messages to the competences below it. [Champandard03] provides the guideline that lower competences should be the ones that are applied by default, and higher competences are exceptions to the default rule.

An example of an application for animation control is given in [Yiskis03]. The architecture has four layers from lowest to highest: Movement, Action, Behavior, and Strategy. The lower layer Movement is responsible for actually playing the animations and enforcing any necessary physical constraints. For instance, if the agent is running and bumps into an obstacle a "stop" followed by a "go back" animation is played. The Action layer has the building blocks for all actions, and its actions occur only for a given time limit. All actions of this layer are carried out by issuing commands to the Movement layer. Note that here we are applying the principle discussed above: All animation is made with calls to the lower layers, and no behavior in the Action layer will directly interact with the animation system. The Behavior layer contains behaviors that happen over an indefinite time period, usually some Action layer actions in a loop. The Tactical layer makes high-level plans.

A good feature of this organization is that animation integration is insulated in the first layer. As new layers are added, we do not have to worry about having to revise it.

[Champandard03] has applied the subsumption architecture to build a robot for *Quake II*. The architecture has seven layers, with their obvious meanings: Explore, Investigate, Gather, Attack, Hunt, Evade, and Retreat. Explore was the lowest. We see that it specifies a "coward" robot. Its code and further explanation are found in [Champandard03].

The robustness, speed, and modularity of the subsumption architecture make it an interesting candidate for the real-time action domain. The main limitations, when compared to other behavior-based architectures, are the need to explicitly specify every connection between modules and having a fixed hierarchy between competences. The next architecture addresses these issues.

Extended Behavior Networks

Extended behavior networks [Dorer04] were designed to be the action-selection mechanism of robots in the RoboCup. The team in which they were first applied was vice champion of its league [Dorer99], and in the following year they were once again used with success in the competition [Dorer00]. Besides being successful in robotic soccer, Extended Behavior Networks (EBNs) were applied with good results in *Unreal Tournament* [Pinto05-b].

Extended behavior networks are the latest evolution of behavior networks [Maes89], another behavior-based architecture that has been constantly evolving as shown by [Rhodes96], [Goetz97], and [Nebel03].

An extended behavior network can be viewed as a set of linked behavior modules and goals that spread activation energy among them, starting at the goals and flowing to the modules. The modules with higher energy and executability that do not use the same resources are selected for execution at each step.

The structure of an extended behavior network is composed of a set of behavior modules, a set of goals, a set of links that join modules to goals and other modules, a set of resources, and a set of control parameters. Figure 3.3.4 shows an example behavior network for an *Unreal Tournament* bot.

A goal is defined by a proposition that must be met, a strength value, and a disjunction of propositions that provide the context for that goal, called the *relevance condition*. The strength provides the static, context-independent importance of the goal, and the relevance condition provides the dynamic, context-dependent one. The use of two kinds of conditions in the goals enables us to express goals that become more or less important depending on the situation the agent is in. In Figure 3.3.4, the goal *HaveHighHealth* has strength 0.8 and context condition *NotHaveHighHealth*. The goal becomes more important as the robot's health lowers. The total strength of a goal at a

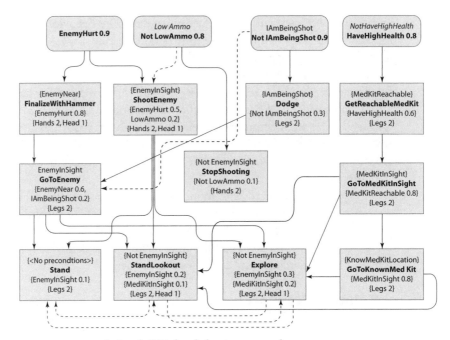

FIGURE 3.3.4   *A simple* UT *bot behavior network.*

certain instant is found by multiplying its dynamic and static importance values. All propositions in the network are real-valued, allowing the use of fuzzy concepts.

Each behavior module is specified by a conditions list, an action, an effects list, and a resources list. The first list is a conjunction of real-valued propositions that represent the needed conditions for the module to execute. The effects list is a conjunction of propositions (each possibly negated) whose values are the values that we expect them to have after the module's action execution. The resources list is made of pairs (i.e., resource, amount), each indicating the expected amount of a resource an agent uses to perform the action.

The links are made based on the effects of the modules, and the conditions of modules and goals. Predecessor links go from a module or goal B to a module A for each proposition in the condition list of B that is in the effects list of A, such that the proposition has the same sign (i.e., true (+) or false (–)) in both ends of the link. The link from goal *EnemyHurt* to module *ShootEnemy* in Figure 3.3.4 is an example. Conflict links go from a module or goal B to a module A for each proposition in the condition list of B that is in the effects list of A, such that the proposition has opposite signs at each end of the link. In Figure 3.3.4, the link from *NotLowAmmo* to *ShootEnemy* is a conflict link. Conflict links take energy away from their targets, and predecessor links input energy to their targets. This way a module or goal tries to inhibit modules whose execution would undo some of its conditions, and attempts to bring into execution modules whose actions would satisfy any of its conditions.

The goals are represented by round-cornered rectangles and behaviors by sharp-cornered rectangles. Straight lines represent predecessor links, dashed lines conflict links, and curved lines resource links. The directions of the arrows indicate the activation flow for both predecessor and conflict links. In resource links, they indicate the module's dependence on the resource.

Action selection is based in the mutual excitation and inhibition among the network nodes via activation spreading. The set of modules selected for execution at each time step are the modules with highest execution value, and which have all their needed resources available. The execution value of a module is the product of its activation and executability (i.e., the fuzzy logical AND of its conditions). The gem "A Goal-Oriented Unreal Bot" (Article 3.5) provides a detailed overview of EBN structure and the action-selection algorithm; so here we will focus on EBN properties and design issues.

Extended behavior networks have the same advantages as subsumption architectures: They are fast, modular, lend themselves to incremental design easily, and are robust. Also, action selection is done concurrently and asynchronously, allowing fast parallel implementations. Nonetheless, they have some advantages over subsumption architectures and address some of their limitations.

As each module is specified by pre- and post-conditions, and the architecture is linked based solely in this info, we do not have to hand craft the network connections as we did in the subsumption architecture. All we have to worry about is designing and implementing the goals and individual behaviors. Their interaction is automatically taken care of by the network linkage and action-selection algorithm.

The robustness of an EBN is greater. In a subsumption architecture, the robustness was based in the fact that the failure of an upper layer did not compromise the functioning of lower ones. However, the failure of individual behaviors in lower layers could compromise all other levels. As designers, we would have to hand code and foresee all interactions to prevent this from happening. In EBNs, if a module fails, the architecture will automatically use any other module capable of leading to the fulfillment of the goal condition.

Other advantages are context-dependent goals, the use of real-valued propositions, and the way the architecture deals with goal interactions. Context-dependent goals allow easier partitioning of the situation space and a more natural agent design. We are able to specify that a goal is not always important, but only given certain conditions. For instance, in Figure 3.3.4, we specify that the agent should worry about having a high health level only if it is not already with high health (goal *HaveHighHealth*). The same happens with ammo (goal *NotLowAmmo*); the agent does not need to concern itself with ammo preservation if it has plenty.

We do not have a crisp hierarchy between goals and behaviors, which allows greater adaptivity. Which modules execute is a function of activation accumulated and executability. Activation is a function of the agent's goals, what other modules exist, and the recent situations the agent has been in. The module hierarchy changes to adapt to the current activity of the agent. Real-valued propositions allow us to naturally deal with concepts that have a fluid nature, such as near, strong, and healthy.

To build a behavior network for an agent, we start by defining its goals. Next, we assemble modules that achieve the goals. Finally, we tune the activation-spreading parameters to achieve a desired overall behavior. Network definition and assembling is detailed in the gem "Constructing a Goal-Oriented Robot for *Unreal Tournament* Using Fuzzy Sensors, Finite-State Machines, and Extended Behavior Networks" (Article 3.4), and parameter setting is discussed in the gem "A Goal-Oriented Unreal Bot" (Article 3.5).

An interesting feature of EBNs is that changing a few global parameters that control activation-spreading—mainly how much activation a module retains from each previous step and the minimum execution value suitable for execution—we are able to drastically affect overall agent behavior. This allows the designer to make several different characters easily. This feature is discussed at length in the gem "A Goal-Oriented Unreal Bot" (Article 3.5) and in [Pinto05-b].

In the application of EBNs in *Unreal Tournament* [Pinto05-a], we have carried out experiments to assess action-selection quality and agent performance. In the latter, we compared an agent using EBNs to a purely hierarchical reactive agent. The EBN agent had a much better performance due to its better action-selection policy. The action selection displayed the properties of robustness, reactivity, chaining of actions, and proper combination of concurrent actions. This is illustrated in detail in the gem "A Goal-Oriented Unreal Bot" (Article 3.5).

Discussion

As we have pointed out the positive features of the subsumption architecture and extended behavior networks, as well as their specific limitations, now we will address a limitation common to behavior-based systems: their absence of variables.

The absence of variables leads to low generality of the modules; for each new weapon type, we need to create a whole new module. However, it is exactly this limitation that allows their low use of resources and speed. General inference and the ability to use variables come at the price of lower speed and greater processing demands.

Fortunately, we have come across some attempts to integrate the use of variables while retaining the interesting properties of behavior-based systems. [Horswill99] proposes an architecture that allows limited use of variables. We are unaware of their application to games, though there is mention of future applications in *Unreal Tournament*. Also, [Rhodes96] proposes a behavior network model that allows variables in a limited way. Combining this model with the extended behavior network model may result in a model with greater flexibility.

Conclusion

We have seen that the subsumption architecture and the extended behavior network carry out their positive features from the robotic domain to the domain of action games. These properties are robustness, reactivity, speed, and modularity. Both lend themselves to incremental design, modular development, and parallel implementations.

In a subsumption architecture, we have to specify every connection between modules and layers; while in the behavior network, the architecture itself takes care of behavior interaction.

Behavior hierarchy is fixed in a subsumption architecture, while in an EBN it is adaptive. The price for this adaptivity is a greater time needed for action selection, even though EBNs are fast, especially when compared to planning systems.

A distinctive feature of EBNs is that they allow us to build simple personality traits into the agent by means of simple constant tunings. The limited use of resources in behavior-based systems makes them interesting for the real-time strategy and action domains.

References

[Brooks86] Brooks, R., "A Robust Layered Control System for a Mobile Robot." *IEEE Journal of Robotics and Automation.* Vol. RA-2, No. 1., 1986.

[Champandard03] Champandard, A., *AI Game Development.* New Riders Publishing, 2003.

[Dorer99] Dorer, K., "Extended Behavior Networks for the Magma Freiburg Team." RoboCup-99 Team Descriptions for the Simulation League. Linkoping University Press: pp. 79–83, 1999.

[Dorer00] Dorer, K., "Concurrent Behavior Selection in Extended Behavior Networks." Team Description for RoboCup2000, Melbourne, 2000.

[Dorer04] Dorer, K., "Extended Behavior Networks for Behavior Selection in Dynamic and Continuous Domains." *Proceedings of the ECAI Workshop on Agents in Dynamic and Real-time Environments,* 22/23, August 2004, Valencia, Spain.

[Goetz97] Goetz, P., "Attractors in Recurrent Behavior Networks." Ph.D. Thesis, University of New York, Buffalo, 1997.

[Horswill99] Horswill, I. D. and R. Zubek, "Robot architectures for believable game agents." AAAI Spring Symposium on Artificial Intelligence and Computer Games, AAAI Technical Report SS-99-02, 1999.

[Maes89] Maes, P., "How to do The Right Thing." *Connection Science Journal,* Vol. 1, No. 3., 1989.

[Nebel03] Nebel, B. and Y. Babovich, "Goal-Converging Behavior Networks and Self-Solving Planning Domains, or: How to Become a Successful Soccer Player." s.l. *IJCAI03,* 2003.

[Pinto05-a] Pinto, Hugo, "Designing Autonomous Agents for Computer Games with Extended Behavior Networks: An Investigation of Agent Performance, Character Modeling and Action Selection in Unreal Tournament." Masters of science thesis, Universidade Federal do Rio Grande do Sul, Brazil, 2005.

[Pinto05-b] Pinto, H. and L. O. Alvares, "Extended Behavior Networks and Agent Personality: Investigating the Design of Character Stereotypes in the Game Unreal Tournament." *Proceedings of the Fifth International Working Conference on Intelligent Virtual Agents,* Kos-, Greece, 2005.

[Rhodes96] Rhodes, Bradley, "PHISH-Nets: Planning Heuristically in Situated Hybrid Networks." Masters of science thesis, Massachusetts Institute of Technology, Boston, 1996.

[Yiskis03] Yiskis, E., "A Subsumption Architecture For Character-Based Games." *AI Game Programming Wisdom II,* Charles River Media, 2003.

3.4

Constructing a Goal-Oriented Robot for *Unreal Tournament* Using Fuzzy Sensors, Finite-State Machines, and Extended Behavior Networks

Hugo Pinto and Luis Otavio Álvares

hugo@hugopinto.net

When we design an agent for a game, we need to tackle at least three issues: how it will decide what to do at each time step, how it will perceive its environment, and how we will design its basic behaviors.

Each of these factors restricts and influences the others: An agent is able to make decisions based on its knowledge and perception of the environment, and the behaviors of the agent must be amenable to the decision mechanism so as to be properly coordinated. Also, the perceptions of the agent often influence not just what behaviors are executed, but how they are executed; for instance, "attack weakest enemy" will be influenced by a perception of who among the enemies is the weakest.

Extended behavior networks [Dorer04] are a class of action-selection architectures designed to select good enough sets of actions for agent with many goals situated in dynamic and complex environments. They use real-valued conditions and modular behaviors, being especially suited to integration with fuzzy sensors. They have been successfully applied in the RoboCup [Dorer99] and in research using *Unreal Tournament* [Pinto05].

Fuzzy sensors have been successfully applied to various domains in which we have continuous properties and arbitrary categories, and with good results. For a game, they are especially suited to sense things like "enemy is near" and "enemy is strong," as near and strong are concepts better grasped by a continuous measure.

Finite-state machines are a well-known and well-established technique, both in academia and the game development community, that have been extensively applied in games. They are a good modeling technique for basic *competences* and *behaviors,* such as "go to home" and "shoot enemy."

In this article, we describe how we designed and integrated fuzzy sensors, finite-state machine behaviors, and an extended behavior network to build a robot for *Unreal Tournament.*

Extended Behavior Network Design

Extended Behavior Networks (EBNs) combine properties of traditional planners (i.e., chaining of actions based on preconditions and effects) and connectionist systems (i.e., activation spreading). They are specified by a static structure and an action-selection algorithm.

The structure of an extended behavior network is composed of a number of predefined sets. These are: a set of behavior modules, a set of goals, a set of links that join modules to goals and other modules, a set of resources, and a set of control parameters. A behavior module resembles a STRIPS operator [Nilsson71], having lists with both the expected effects of its action execution and preconditions for it becoming active. The links are made based on the effects of the modules, and the conditions of modules and goals.

Action selection is based in the mutual excitation and inhibition among the network nodes via activation spreading. The set of modules selected for execution at each time step are the modules with the highest execution value, and which have all their needed resources available. The execution value of a module is the product of its activation and executability (i.e., the fuzzy logical AND of its conditions). Details of the behavior network structure and action-selection algorithm are available in the gem "A Goal-Oriented Unreal Bot" (Article 3.5).

Extended behavior networks were designed as a control mechanism for situated agents. From an engineering perspective, this means that the abstractions used by the agent's *cognitive* system, such as propositions and representations of entities, are made relative to the tasks the agent performs, the environment he is embedded in, and its goals.

The environment of the agent is defined not only by the game features and game rules, but also by the primitive sensory-motor messages available to the agent for interacting with the game. Thus, when designing sensors, goals, and behavior modules, we take into account the GameBots [Kaminka02] package messages and commands.

Figure 3.4.1 illustrates the communication between the agent, GameBots, and *Unreal Tournament* server.

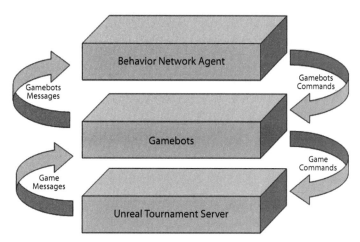

FIGURE 3.4.1   *Integration of the behavior network agent with the GameBots package and* Unreal Tournament *server.*

The *Unreal Tournament* server sends game messages to GameBots. In turn, Game-Bots sends its own messages to our agent. The agent's sensors process these messages, and updates the values of the conditions of the behavior network and the internal state of the agent. Action selection takes place, and the appropriate actions are carried out by sending commands to GameBots, which in turn sends low-level *Unreal Tournament* commands to the server.

So, let us see the design of a simple behavior network for an *Unreal Tournament* agent, which allows it to play Death Match in the map DM-Stalwart. We present the network as we have built it, step by step, showing the rationale behind each choice.

In the Death Match game, the basic concerns of an agent are killing as many enemies as possible and avoiding death. It must be able to detect, chase, and shoot enemies, as well as avoid being shot and replenish its health.

We start by defining the agent's goals. From the game rules, we see that it has to kill enemies and stay alive. To kill an enemy, the agent has to hurt the enemy until it dies; and to stay alive, the agent has to maintain its health and restore it when depleted. To fulfill the need to kill enemies, we give the agent the goal of hurting enemies (*EnemyHurt*). For its self-preservation we add the goals of avoiding being shot (*Not IAmBeingShot*) and having a high health (*HaveHighHealth*).

Now we must design the behaviors that will achieve these goals. To hurt an enemy, our agent must attack it. A sensible candidate would be the behavior *Attack-Enemy*, with precondition *EnemyInSight* and effect *EnemyHurt*. The problem with such a general behavior is that if we attack with a shooting weapon, we have to specify the additional effect of ammo decrease. If we attack with a contact weapon (Impact Hammer or Chainsaw) we need to be near the enemy, and behavior execution will have no effect upon the ammunition supply. Thus, we create two attacking behaviors instead of just one: *FinalizeWithHammer* and *ShootEnemy*. Figure 3.4.2 shows these behaviors linked to the goal *EnemyHurt*. Note that they use exactly the same resources, which makes them mutually exclusive (unless we use this network with a four-armed, two-headed agent).

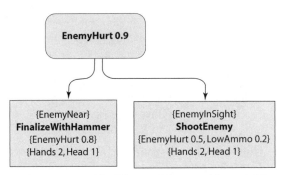

FIGURE 3.4.2   *Goal* EnemyHurt *and its satisfying modules.*

Now we need modules that make true *EnemyNear* and *EnemyInSight*. As the only sensing ability of the agent is vision, for it to tell if an enemy is near, it must first have perceived an enemy in sight. We have three ways to make *EnemyInSight* true: stand still and wait for an enemy to appear in front of us, stay were we are and look for an enemy around us, or actively explore the level to find an enemy. These three possibilities are reflected in behaviors *Stand, StandLookout,* and *Explore*, respectively. To stand in place, there are no preconditions; but we wish to explore or look out for an enemy only if there are no enemies in sight. If we are shot, we must stop exploring and find what is shooting us, so we add the precondition *Not IAmBeingShot* to behavior *Explore*. A module that has *EnemyNear* as an effect is what is left to complete the paths to the goal. A trivial solution is module *GoToEnemy* that has as precondition *EnemyInSight* and as effects *EnemyNear* and *IAmBeingShot*. We add *IAmBeingShot* as an effect, because going toward an enemy makes it likely to be shot. Figure 3.4.3 shows the network built so far, with only goal *EnemyHurt* included.

Now let us make modules to satisfy goal *Not IAmBeingShot*. The most basic way to avoid being shot, besides not fighting at all, is to dodge the bullets. We create behavior *Dodge* with precondition *IAmBeingShot* and effect *Not IAmBeingShot*. The agent needs to use only its legs to dodge. The network now is as shown in Figure 3.4.4.

Now let's see how to achieve goal *HaveHighHealth*. Health vials and medical kits in *Unreal Tournament* have fixed locations. With the game options we used in our tests, these kits, if taken, disappear for some time and then magically reappear at the same location. Thus, health items have fixed locations within a level, enabling us to store their locations and just go to a known medical item whenever we need one. A module *Get Known Medical Kit* with precondition *Know Medical Kit Location* and

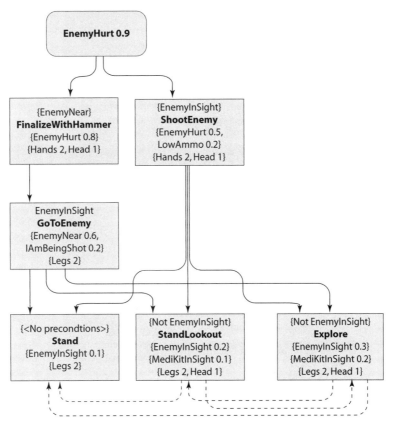

FIGURE 3.4.3   *Behavior network for goal* EnemyHurt.

effect *HaveHighHealth* would be our first solution. The problem with this module is that it is specified at too high a level of abstraction: Getting a known medical kit a hundred steps away is treated in the same module as getting a health vial in the immediate vicinity. Also, this module will have to contain checks to see if there is a way to get a medical kit (if it is reachable) as well as deciding which of the known kits to get. Could this module be made simpler by exploiting environmental or sensory information?

Examining the GameBots messages and protocol, we see that the robot receives primitive information about an item in sight: its position, its location, and whether it is reachable (i.e., if there is straight path to the item). If we exploit this information, we can then make three modules instead: *GetReachableMedKit*, *GoToMedKitInSight*, and *GoToKnownMedKit*. The first has as a precondition that there be a reachable medical kit and the effect *HaveHighHealth*. The second module makes a medical kit in

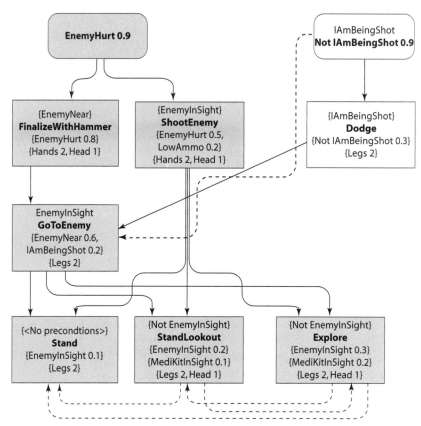

FIGURE 3.4.4   *Behavior network for goals* EnemyHurt *and* Not IAmBeingShot.

sight a reachable one. The last module makes *MedKitInSight* true by going to a known medical kit location. We see that either *StandLookout* or *Explore* may satisfy the precondition of *GoToKnownMedKit*, as both tend to lead to a known medical kit location. Figure 3.4.5 shows these modules incorporated in the network.

Our network seems ready, but we haven't mentioned additional modules needed for special tasks in *Unreal Tournament*. Whenever we tell the game to shoot a certain agent or position (command SHOOT) it will keep shooting until we tell it to stop (command STOPSHOOT). We could well treat this inside a module, but as the need to stop shooting in fact is embedded in the aim of not wasting ammo, we create a goal for it, *Not LowAmmo*. To stop shooting may be an independent, complete competence module, *StopShoot*, with preconditions *Not EnemyInSight* and effect *Not LowAmmo*. Figure 3.4.6 shows our complete network. We added the context condition *LowAmmo* to goal *Not LowAmmo*, as we want the agent to "worry" about having low ammunition as its ammo decreases.

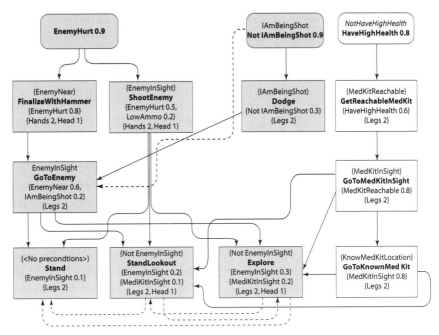

FIGURE 3.4.5 _Behavior network with health-related modules (white background) added._

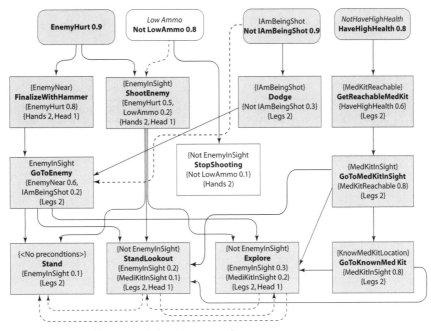

FIGURE 3.4.6 _Complete behavior network._

Now that we have our network ready, we are left with three questions: How will the network propositions be verified? How will each of the behavior actions be carried out? How will it all function together? In the next section, we address the first question and provide an overview of the agent's sensing mechanism.

Hierarchical Fuzzy Sensors

Before venturing into the exposition and discussion of our network's sensors, let us clarify what kind of sensors we are talking about. In the beginning of this gem we pointed out that agent perception is influenced by its internal state, its beliefs, and its current activity. Primitive sensory information is defined by messages from the Game-Bots package. This information includes robot position, robot velocity, robot rotation, robot ammo, robot health, enemies in sight, and items seen. The behavior network operates upon propositions whose value attribution comprises a form of high-level perception. It is this high-level perception that is done by the sensors discussed in this section. Our sensors act upon the information provided by the GameBots messages, and the knowledge of the agent to create the necessary information for action selection and behavior execution.

Each condition of the behavior network has a sensor associated to it. Each sensor has a membership function P and an internal state function I. Function P takes the current perceived state of the agent and returns a fuzzy proposition, corresponding to the condition, with a value in the range [0, 1]. Function I updates the internal state of the agent. Note that this functioning implies that the order in which the sensors are activated matters, as each activation may alter the internal state of the agent. Figures 3.4.7 and 3.4.8 illustrate how a high-level sensor *SensorEnemyInSight* operates.

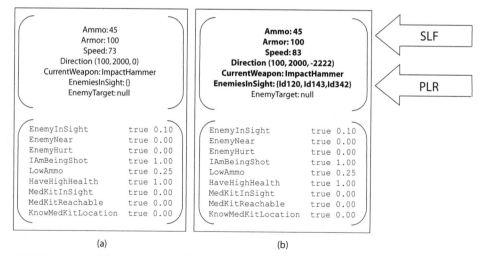

FIGURE 3.4.7 *(a) Agent internal state and propositions just before receiving GameBots messages. (b) Internal state and propositions after receiving GameBots messages SFL and PLR. Fields in bold signal what was changed by these messages.*

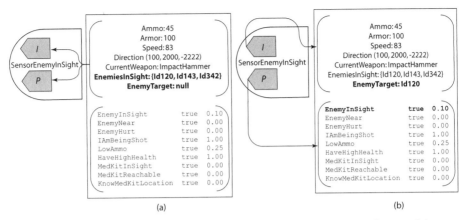

FIGURE 3.4.8 *(a) Sensor* SensorEnemyInSight *reads in the internal state of the agent. Both functions* I *and* P *receive the same input. The data in bold shows what is actually used by this sensor. (b) Sensor* SensorEnemyInSight *updates the internal state and the behavior network propositions. Function* I *sets the enemy target to Id20, and* P *sets the verity of* EnemyInSight. *What the sensor has changed is in bold.*

The cautious reader may now be asking himself why we keep only true propositions. Two reasons: simplicity and storage saving. The operator we use for negating a proposition p is $N(p) = 1 - p$, so we can always make a straightforward conversion between the value of a proposition and its negation.

To finish our exposition on sensors, let us proceed to examine how sensor *Sensor EnemyNear* operates, as it provides a good example of the importance of sensor ordering. As Figure 3.4.9 shows, *SensorEnemyNear* gets the target set by *SensorEnemy*

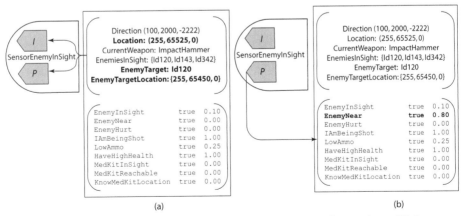

FIGURE 3.4.9 *(a) Sensor* SensorEnemyNear *reading internal state data. (b) Sensor* SensorEnemyNear *updating proposition* EnemyNear *value.*

InSight, the robot's own position, and the target position, and sets the verity of proposition *EnemyNear*. This sensor alters the propositions but leaves the internal state untouched. Note that it is crucial that *SensorEnemyInSight* operates first, because the assessment of nearness is done relative to the target set by this sensor. Figure 3.4.10 shows how *P* establishes the truth value of *EnemyNear*.

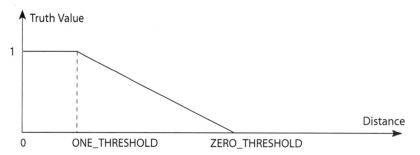

FIGURE 3.4.10   *Truth-value formula of* SensorEnemyNear. *ONE_THRESH-OLD is the distance in which, if less than a set value, we consider the enemy surely near. ZERO_TRESHOLD is the distance at which, if greater, the enemy is surely not near.*

Having seen the subtleties of agent sensing and how the network's propositions get their values, we are ready to examine the behavior modules.

Finite-State Machine Behavior Modules

The actions of the behavior modules are built around augmented Finite-State Machines (FSMs). When selected for execution, each behavior action has a certain amount of time to execute. The behavior module is responsible for monitoring its own action execution, and start, resume, and interrupt each state as necessary.

A behavior action may issue one or more primitive commands to the game when executing. All behaviors have access to the internal state of the agent. Figure 3.4.11 shows the sequence diagram of behavior *GoToEnemy*.

We see that the behavior is fairly complex, even though the high-level action is simple. The agent has to discover a path to the enemy, deal with obstacles that may appear in its way, and give up whenever it concludes that the target enemy is unreachable.

Let us follow some paths in the diagram to illustrate how the behavior relates to the perception and internal state of the agent, and how the behavior action relates to the primitive actions of the GameBots package.

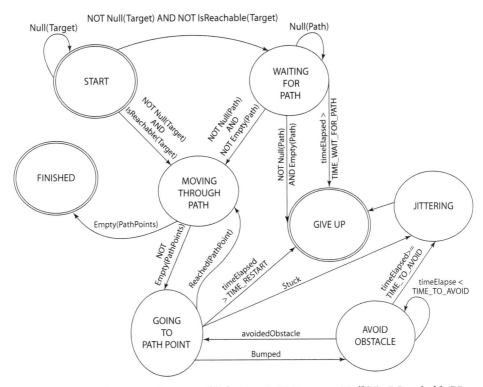

FIGURE 3.4.11   _Sequence diagram of behavior_ GoToEnemy. _Null(X), IsReachable(X), Reached(X), and Empty(X) are predicates. Stuck and Bumped are Boolean flags. Target, TimeElapsed, PathPoints, and PathPoint are variables. TIME_TO_AVOID, TIME_WAIT_FOR_PATH, and TIME_RESTART are constants used for the behavior self-monitoring. States START, FINISHED, and GIVE UP are terminal states. FINISHED is the successful reaching of the target; GIVE UP is desistence._

Let us start at state START. The variable target is the one set by sensor _Sensor EnemyInSight,_ as described in the previous section. If there is no target set (Null(target)), the agent does nothing. If the target is not immediately reachable, the module requests a path to it and enters WAIT FOR PATH. Upon receiving the path to the target, the agent starts moving (MOVING THROUGH PATH).

In state WAIT FOR PATH, the module sends a GetPath command to the game and waits for the corresponding path message (PTH). If the time of wait (time Elapsed) goes beyond the maximum allowed (TIME_WAIT_FOR_PATH), the agent gives up going to that target (state GIVE UP).

But what are these paths all about? *Unreal Tournament* levels are covered by graphs that span most of the level area. Each node of the graph is a possible destination and is called a navigation point (NavPoint). A navigation point may be the place of an item, a weapon, or just a point where the agent may move. We are able to give specific 3D coordinates for the agent to move, but more often we provide just a NavPoint ID. The response to the GetPath command provides a list of NavPoints to the target if there is a path to it, or *Null* is there is no path.

Let us continue following the diagram from MOVING THROUGH PATH. When the agent has no more points in its path, it goes to state FINISH and ends the behavior successfully. If there is a point to go to, it enters state GOING TO PATH POINT. If it encounters an obstacle while going to the desired NavPoint, it goes to state AVOID OBSTACLE. If after a certain time the agent has not managed to avoid the obstacle, it goes to state JITTERING. In this state, the agent tries some random action just to get away from where it is. It is a primitive heuristic to deal with occasions when the agent is stuck. A better implementation would be to make an internal map of the level and perform some reasoning on the possible stuck cases (e.g., crates that leave a space too narrow for the agent to go through, or holes, jumpable obstacles, etc.). After jittering, the agent always gives up (state GIVE UP). We decided to take this course of action because we consider that whenever the agent has failed to avoid an obstacle, there has probably been too much time since we started moving toward the target, and it is better to restart from state START.

The cautious reader may by now be wondering: How does the behavior actually execute? Does it go from state to state until reaching a terminal node? Can it be interrupted in the middle of a state?

This method receives as a parameter the internal state of the agent. By examining the internal state of the agent, including its propositions, each module decides what to do next. So, we see that the agent never interrupts a behavior; only the module itself may do it.

The case of interruption common to all behaviors is when it is in a nonterminal state, and too much time has elapsed since it was last executed. In this case, it is reset and begins anew from state START. Each call of the execute method makes at most one state transition. The system was built in this way to allow a great deal of flexibility in how behaviors are executed and scheduled.

Conclusion

In this article, we illustrated the integration of fuzzy sensors, behavior networks, and finite-state machines to build an agent for *Unreal Tournament*. We saw that behavior networks enable us to break down agent motivations and behaviors into self-contained modules, and that they have a simple, flexible, and robust structure. We were able to tackle one goal at a time, seeing that the network architecture took care of their interaction. We saw that fuzzy sensors are a straightforward way to calculate the network's propositions. Finite-state machines provide an interesting solution to the network's behavior modules.

In our exposition, the behavior network selected which modules would execute at each time step; but once selected for execution, a behavior module was responsible for monitoring and controlling its execution flow. It was a sensible separation between high-level decision-making and low-level acting.

One aspect of the design was missing: the setting of the global parameters of the network and the attribution of values for the goal strengths. These issues are discussed at length in the gem "A Goal-Oriented Unreal Bot" (Article 3.5).

References

[Dorer99] Dorer, K., "Extended Behavior Networks for the Magma Freiburg Team." RoboCup-99 Team Descriptions for the Simulation League, Linkoping University Press, 1999: pp. 79–83.

[Dorer04] Dorer, K., "Extended Behavior Networks for Behavior Selection in Dynamic and Continuous Domains." *Proceedings of the ECAI workshop Agents in dynamic domains,* U. Visser, et al. (Hrsg.) Valencia, Spain, 2004.

[Kaminka02] Kaminka, G., et al., "GameBots: a flexible test bed for multiagent team research." *Communications of the ACM,* Vol. 45, Issue 1: pp. 43–45, 2002.

[Nilsson71] Nilsson, N. J., "STRIPS: A New Approach to the Application of Theorem Proving to Problem Solving." *Artificial Intelligence,* 1971: pp. 189–208.

[Pinto05] Pinto, H. and L. O. Alvares, "An Extended Behavior Network for a Game Agent: Investigating Action Selection Quality and Agent Performance in Unreal Tournament." To appear in MICAI-2005, *Advances in Artificial Intelligence,* 2005. Alexander Gelbukh, Ed.

3.5

A Goal-Oriented Unreal Bot: Building a Game Agent with Goal-Oriented Behavior and Simple Personality Using Extended Behavior Networks

Hugo Pinto and Luis Otavio Álvares

hugo@hugopinto.net

In the design of a game-playing robot (or *bot*), one of the key concerns is how it selects its actions so as to exhibit goal-oriented behavior. When the robot has many possibly conflicting goals, this task gets more complicated. If the robot is also in a quickly changing environment and has to consider many factors at each instant, we have a hard problem to tackle. Search-based approaches turn impractical due to the large search space, and traditional planning is made much harder, as the environment may have changed when the agent finishes planning.

Behavior networks were proposed as an action selection mechanism to select good enough actions in complex and dynamic environments. They have been constantly evolving since their first appearance [Maes89], as shown by [Tyrrell93], [Rhodes96], [Goetz97], [Dorer99] and [Nebel03]. They have been applied to animal simulation [Tyrrell93], interactive storytelling [Rhodes96], the RoboCup [Müller01] and *Unreal Tournament* [Pinto05-a].

Extended behavior networks [Dorer04] represent state-of-the-art behavior network models. They use real-valued propositions for effects and conditions, allow the specification of situation-dependent goals, and select actions concurrently.

Good action selection is important, but how the agent selects its actions and how these actions affect its personality is also a concern in a computer game. Wouldn't it be interesting if while building an agent toward proper goal-oriented behavior we could take into consideration this aspect of agent design? Behavior networks enable just that. [Rhodes96] has applied a behavior network model, PHISH-NETs, to the design of character personalities, and we have applied extended behavior networks to the design of stereotypes [Pinto05-b].

First-person shooter games, such as *Unreal Tournament,* constitute a domain where the application of extended behavior networks is interesting. We have the agent situated in a 3D, continuous virtual environment, interacting in many ways with several entities in real time. The scenarios an agent may face are varied and complex. The agent has many weapons available, each with certain properties, and has several items to use. It moves over different landscapes and interacts with several other agents. The action repertory is large (e.g., run, walk, turn, crawl, shoot, change weapons, jump, strafe, pickup item, and use item, among others), and an agent may carry out more than one action simultaneously, such as shooting while jumping. Also, the agent has many possibly conflicting goals, such as fighting while staying safe.

For most game modes, simple, stereotypical personalities suffice, as we have mostly shallow characters. In this article, we present the extended behavior network model and the results of experiments to assess its action-selection quality, and we illustrate how we may tune and modify a behavior network so as to achieve different character personalities.

Extended Behavior Networks

An extended behavior network can be viewed as a set of linked modules and goals that mutually inhibit and excite each other via activation-spreading, starting at the goals and flowing to the modules. The modules with higher activation and executability that do not use the same resources are selected for execution at each step. In the next sections, we examine in detail the structure of the network and the action-selection algorithm.

Structure

An extended behavior network is defined by a number of predefined sets. These are: a set of behavior modules, a set of goals, a set of resources, and a set of control parameters. Figure 3.5.1 shows the specification of part of a behavior network used in our experiments. Figure 3.5.2 shows the network built from this specification, where *goals* are represented by round-cornered rectangles, *behaviors* by sharp-cornered rectangles, and *resource* nodes by octagons. Straight lines represent *predecessor* links, dashed lines *conflict* links, and pointed lines *resource* links.

A goal Gi is defined by a proposition that must be met, a strength value, and a disjunction of propositions that provide the context for that goal, called the *relevance condition.* The strength provides the static, context-independent importance of the goal, and the relevance condition provides the dynamic, context-dependent one.

The use of two kinds of conditions in the goals enables us to express goals that become more or less important, depending on the situation the agent is in. A context-independent goal is modeled leaving it without relevance conditions. Goal *Enemy-Hurt* in Figure 3.5.1 is an example of such a goal. Note that a goal without relevance conditions amounts to a goal that is always relevant—that is, its relevance is always maximal.

Module	Goal
name ShootEnemy	name EnemyHurt
precondtion EnemyInSight	Context <none>
action ShootEnemy	condition EnemyHurt
effects EnemyHurt 0.6	strength 1.0
LowAmmo 0.1	endGoal
using Hands 2 Head 1	
endModule	Goal
	name Not LowAmmo
Resource	context LowAmmo
name Legs	condition Not LowAmmo
amount 2 endResourse	strength 0.7
	endGoal
Resource	Parameters
name Head	name ActivationInfluence value 1.0
amount 1 endResource	name InhibitionInfluence value 0.9
	name Inertia value 0.5
Resource	name GlobalThreshold value 0.6
name Hands	name ThresholdDecay value 0.1
amount 2 endResource	endParameters

FIGURE 3.5.1 *Specification of a simple behavior network.*

Each behavior module is specified by a conditions list, an effects list, an action, and a resources list. The first list is a conjunction of real-valued propositions that represent the needed conditions for the module to execute. The effects list is a conjunction of propositions (each possibly negated) whose values are the values that we expect them to have after the module's action execution. The resources list is made of pairs (resource, amount), each indicating the expected amount of a resource an agent uses to perform the action.

Goals and modules are connected by two kinds of links. Predecessor links go from a module or goal B to a module A, for each proposition in the condition list of B that is in the effects list of A, such that the proposition has the same sign—true (+) or false (−)— in both ends of the link. The link from goal *EnemyHurt* to module *ShootEnemy* in Figure 3.5.2 is an example. Conflict links go from a module or goal B to a module A, for each proposition in the condition list of B that is in the effects list of A, such that the proposition has opposite signs at each end of the link. In Figure 3.5.2, the link from *Not LowAmmo* to *ShootEnemy* is a conflict link. Conflict links take energy away from their targets, and predecessor links input energy to their targets. This way, a module or goal tries to inhibit modules whose execution would undo some of its conditions, and attempts to bring into execution modules whose actions would satisfy any of its conditions.

Each resource is represented by a resource node and defined by a function $f(s)$ that specifies the expected amount of the resource available in each situation s. In addition to $f(s)$, each node has a variable *bound* that keeps track of the amount of bound resources, and a resource activation threshold $\theta_{Res} \in (0..\theta]$, where θ is the global activation threshold. In Figure 3.5.2, we see that the expected used amount of each resource is constant for all situations. This is not surprising, since our agent has the same number of body parts available in any situation (the game does not account for limb loss or similar gruesome events).

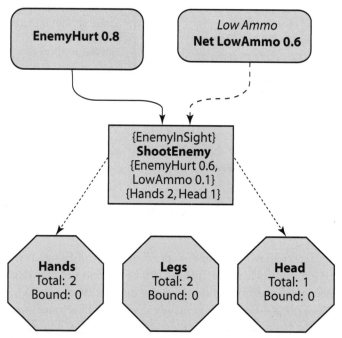

FIGURE 3.5.2   *Simple behavior network diagram.*

The modules are linked to the resource nodes via resource links. For each resource type in the resources list of a module there is a link from the module to the corresponding resource node.

The control parameters are used to fine-tune the network and have values in the range [0,1]. The activation influence parameter γ controls the activation from predecessor links. The inhibition influence δ is the negative activation from conflict links.

The inertia β, the global threshold θ, and the threshold decay $\Delta\theta$ have their straight-forward meanings. Their functions will become clearer in the next section.

Action-Selection Algorithm

The modules to be executed at each cycle are selected in the following way:

1. The activation a of each module is calculated.
2. The executability e of each module is calculated using some triangular-norm operation over its condition list.
3. The execution value $h(a,e)$ is calculated by multiplying a and e. Note that this value combines the utility of executing a behavior (activation) and the probability of executing it successfully (executability). This way, even modules with conditions that are not very satisfied may execute if they have high activation.
4. For each resource used by a module, starting by the last nonavailable resource, the module checks to see if it has exceeded the resource threshold and if there is enough of that resource for its execution. If so, it binds the resource.
5. If a module has bound all of its needed resources, it executes and resets the resources thresholds to the value of the global threshold.
6. Each module unbinds the resources it used.

The thresholds of the resources linearly decay over time, ensuring that eventually a behavior will be able to bind its needed resources, and that the most active behavior gets priority.

Formula 3.5.1 shows the activation that goes from a goal g_i to a module k through a predecessor link at instant t. Function f is a triangular norm that combines the strength and the dynamic relevance of a goal. The term ex_j is the value of the effect proposition that is the target of a link.

$$a_{kg_i}^{t}{}' = \gamma \cdot f\left(\iota_{g_i}, r_{g_i}^{t}\right) \cdot ex_j \qquad (3.5.1)$$

Formula 3.5.2 shows the activation that goes from a goal i to a module k through a conflict link at an instant t.

$$a_{kg_i}^{t}{}'' = -\delta \cdot f\left(\iota_{g_i}, r_{g_i}^{t}\right) \cdot ex_j \qquad (3.5.2)$$

Formula 3.5.3 shows the activation spreading from a module $succ$ to a module k at an instant t through a predecessor link.

$$a_{kg_i}^{t}{}''' = \gamma \cdot \sigma\left(a_{succ\, g_i}^{t-1}\right) \cdot ex_j \cdot \left(1 - \tau\left(p_{succ}, s\right)\right) \qquad (3.5.3)$$

p_{succ} is the proposition of the successor module, and a_{succ} the activation of the successor module. $\tau(p_{succ}, s)$ is the value of p_{succ} in situation s. The activation-spreading increases as the proposition at the start of a predecessor link becomes less satisfied.

Thus, we can see unsatisfied conditions as increasingly demanding subgoals of the network. Function 3.5.4 is used to make the behavior modules strong attractors [Goetz97] with a high probability. This reduces unnecessary behavior switches, as small changes in the percepts will be less likely to disrupt an ongoing behavior.

$$\sigma(x) = \left(1 + e^{k(\mu - x)}\right)^{-1} \tag{3.5.4}$$

Formula 3.5.5 describes the activation spread from a module through a conflict link. The terms a_{conf} and p_{conf} stand for the activation and proposition of the module that is the source of the conflict link, respectively.

$$a_{kg_i}^t{}'''' = -\delta \cdot \sigma\left(a_{conf\ g_i}^{t-1}\right) \cdot ex_j \cdot \tau\left(p_{conf}, s\right) \tag{3.5.5}$$

Formula 3.5.6 shows that the activation of a module k at an instant t is its activation in the previous time step $t-1$ weighted by the inertia constant β plus the sum of the activations retained by each goal i.

$$a_k^t{}' = \beta a_k^{t-1} + \sum_i a_{kg_i}^t \tag{3.5.6}$$

Formula 3.5.7 shows that a module retains just the activation of greatest absolute value from each goal. It amounts to keeping only the strongest path from a module to each goal.

$$a_{kg_i}^t = \text{abs}\left(\max\left(a_{kg_i}^t{}', a_{kg_i}^t{}'', a_{kg_i}^t{}''', a_{kg_i}^t{}''''\right)\right) \tag{3.5.7}$$

Action-Selection Quality

We made a series of experiments to assess the quality of action selection using the behavior network of Figure 3.5.3. We give a high-level description of the perceived state of the agent, the actions it executed, and the values of the control parameters of the network during the experiment. The default configuration for the network was: γ (ActivationInfluence) = 1.0, δ (InhibitionInfluence) = 0.9, β (Inertia) = 0.5, and θ (Global threshold) = 0.6. These parameters worked well in most cases. In a few experiments we tried extreme values for some parameters, especially the inertia β and the inhibition influence δ. Each of the discussions below was based in log analysis and direct observation of agent behavior.

Overall Behavior

The overall behavior of the agent could be described as follows: It started exploring the level and kept wandering until it found an enemy (*Explore*). Upon finding an enemy, it started shooting (*ShootEnemy*) and approaching the enemy (*GoToEnemy*), then switched weapons and used the more powerful weapon Impact Hammer (*FinalizeWithHammer*).

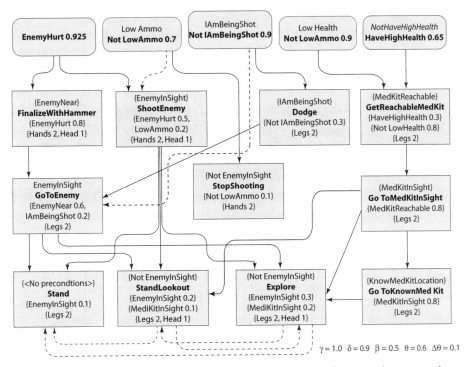

FIGURE 3.5.3   *Behavior network used in the investigation of action-selection quality.*

After the enemy died, it stopped shooting (*StopShoot*) and started wandering again. When shot repeatedly, it kept shooting; after a while, it stopped going to the enemy and started dodging subsequent shots. If the enemy stopped shooting, it would go toward it again. When the agent was hurt in combat, if it knew the location of a medkit (*GoToKnownMedKit* had a high truth value), it would go to it and restore its health after a while. If when approaching the enemy, the agent became very low in health, and if there was a reachable medical kit (*MedKitReachable*), the agent would stop going to the enemy and go to the medkit while maintaining fire—unless it was close to the enemy, in which case it attempted a killing with the hammer (*FinalizeWithHammer*).

Action Chaining

Three common action sequences were observed. The sequence {*StopShooting, Explore, GoToEnemy, ShootEnemy, FinalizeWithHammer*} was the usual attack sequence of the agent, and {*GoToKnownMedKit, GoToMedKitInSight, GetReachableMedKit*} was carried out when no enemies were in sight and health was not high. The long sequence {*Explore, GoToEnemy, ShootEnemy, FinalizeWithHammer, StopShooting, GoToKnown MedKit, GoToMedKitInSight, GetReachableMedKit*} is basically the two previous ones, one after the other, and was the most common overall behavior of the agent. We saw that the agent made reasonably long, consistent chains of actions, even though the agent made no formal planning.

Reactivity and Persistence

We can see the sequence of actions {*Explore, GoToEnemy, FinalizeWithHammer*} as a plan to fulfill the goal *EnemyHurt*. If while going to the enemy the agent was shot, it stopped behavior *GoToEnemy*, executed *BehaviorDodge*, and having evaded the shot, resumed *GoToEnemy*. We see that the agent reacted to an event in the environment and then got back to our perceived "plan." It exhibited a good compromise between reactivity and persistence. For large values of β (inertia), the agent took some time to dodge after perceiving a shot and only dodged when a sequence of shots happened.

Resolution of Conflicts

Take a look at Figure 3.5.3 again. We see that goal *EnemyHurt* tries to make behavior *ShootEnemy* execute, and goal *Not LowAmmo* tries to prevent *ShootEnemy* from executing. The goal *Not LowAmmo* has little influence until the agent starts to run short of ammunition. When this happens, the conflicting influence of *Not LowAmmo* makes the agent switch to the hammer weapon (*FinalizeWithHammer*), because Hammer does not need ammunition. It is an unusual, though sensible approach to ammunition-saving that emerged by the interaction of the goals. (Note that the "designed" way to save ammo is by using behavior *StopShooting*.)

Another case of conflict resolution happens with behavior *GoToEnemy*. To better fulfill *EnemyHurt*, the agent has to get near to the enemy; but to satisfy *Not IAmBeing Shot*, it should maintain some distance. The network deals with this conflict well, dodging when appropriate and resuming the approach after avoiding the shot.

Preference for Actions that Contribute to Several Goals

The network always preferred *StandLookout* and *Explore* to *Stand* when they had equal executability, even when we used larger expected values for the *EnemyInSight* effect of *Stand*. The reason is simple: Both *StandLookout* and *Explore* contribute to *EnemyHurt* and *HaveHighHealth*, while *Stand* just contributes to *EnemyHurt*. (In fact, it contributes to *ShootEnemy*, which in turn contributes to *EnemyHurt*.) The modules that contribute to more goals are able to accumulate more activation, and are selected more often.

Proper Combination of Concurrent Actions

We saw that the agent made good use of its resources and combined the actions properly. It shoots while dodging a bullet or running toward the enemy, it stops shooting while exploring or getting a medical kit, and even continues to shoot while getting a medical kit. All combinations of actions are reasonable, and all of the good action combinations we could conceive were physically observed, as the previous analysis attests.

The experiments of this section have shown that extended behavior networks provide a competitive solution to action selection for a goal-oriented game agent. Next we will investigate how to tune and modify behavior networks to achieve different personalities.

Personality Design

For an agent controlled by a behavior network, we have three approaches for building its personality: changing the global parameters, changing the goal strengths, and changing the network topology itself.

Working on the Global Parameters

Changing the global parameters allows us to control two key personality characteristics: thoughtfulness (through the activation threshold θ) and persistence (through the inertia β).

A high activation threshold θ leads to better action selection, as only actions that have a high activation may execute—that is, it requires on average more activation spreading cycles to decide what to do next and also requires higher executability of each module (remember that a module executes only when executability multiplied by its activation is above the thresholds of the resources it needs). To an external observer, this amounts to a thoughtful behavior, as an agent mostly does what seems effective and proper to achieve its goals.

A high β leads to a persistent behavior: An agent only changes its behavior if there is a large or long change in its sensory information. Suppose we need to build two characters for *Unreal Tournament:* the Veteran and the Novice. The Veteran is calm and rational, and tries to maximize all of its goals in the long run. He has great self-control and persistence, and wants to kill as many enemies as possible, but never at the expense of his life. The Novice aspires to be like the Veteran and has similar values, but still lacks the endurance and discipline to act properly. He is impulsive and frequently does not take the best action for a circumstance.

We notice that the personality requirements of the Veteran match the requirements of an agent built to maximize its score over a series of games. This is exactly the agent shown in Figure 3.5.3. Looking at the overall behavior description in the last section, we see that we have the personality of an archetypal combat Veteran: The agent is persistent when killing, heals itself when it is safe to do so, and has the endurance to keep fighting even when being shot at—and without "panicking."

So, how do we proceed to transform this Veteran into a Novice? To make the agent more impulsive, we lowered its inertia, making it far more reactive. The agent, when shot, immediately attempted to dodge. Also, if while pursuing an enemy the agent became very low in health, upon spotting a reachable medkit, the agent would immediately go to it. This resulted in poorer behavior; often the enemy was as hurt as the agent, and an attack with the hammer would deliver victory. The same could be said of the pursuit; dodging is good, but only to prevent being extremely damaged, as it is not guaranteed to succeed.

To augment the number of mistakes of the Novice, we lowered the global threshold. This way we decreased the quality of action selection, as many modules surpassed the threshold simultaneously; and among modules that are above the threshold, no one has priority over others. Now, often the agent shot the enemy even when it was very near and could hammer the foe. For the extremely low value of 0.1, the agent also often just stood still (*Stand*) instead of exploring the level (*Explore*).

The best parameters we found to bring forth the character of the Novice were $\gamma = 1.0$, $\delta = 0.9$, $\beta = 0.1$, $\theta = 0.25$, and $\Delta\theta = 0.1$.

Working on the Goal Strengths

Now suppose the game designer, overwhelmed by how easily we have created a new character out of the original Veteran, asks us to build another two characters: the Samurai and the Berserker.

The Samurai is cold, persistent, and aggressive. To die in battle is his highest honor, and he likes fair matches. Killing his opponent is his stronger goal, and he will try to achieve it even at the expense of his life. When in a fight with an enemy, he won't stop to attack another agent, nor will he be stopped by pain or danger.

The Berserker is aggressive, undisciplined, and nonpersistent. Once in the arena, he will attack opponents fiercely and in a mad frenzy. He is insensitive to pain, and most times will not stop attacking to heal himself or even to dodge bullets.

To transform the Veteran into a Samurai we worked on the goal strengths, because the Samurai is as persistent, experienced, and thoughtful as the Veteran. We set *EnemyHurt* to 1.0, *NotIAmBeingShot* to 0.6, *NotLowHealth* to 0.5, and *HaveHigh-Health* to 0.4. With these strengths, the agent will always approach the enemy instead of dodging bullets, and will not stop to get medkits if in a fight. We verified that whenever he found an enemy, he went toward it shooting and then attacked with the Hammer (*FinalizeWithHammer*) if the enemy had not died yet. If there were no enemies in sight, the Samurai would go after medkits to restore health. For a gamer, the Samurai displayed the exact behavior we desired: He was never disturbed by pain (low health) or danger (being shot at) in his pursuit of an enemy, and employed good tactics (shooting from afar and hammering when near).

To bring into being the mad Berserker, we started with the Samurai, because their goals are similar. We lowered even more the agent's sensibility to pain by decreasing the importance of the goal *LowHealth*. To bring forth his frenzy, we diminished both inertia and its global threshold. Lowering β made the agent too reactive, and lowering θ made the agent take insane actions, such as shooting instead of hammering at close quarters.

The overall behavior of the Berserker was as intended: He would not stop to dodge or heal while in combat, and he fought madly—hammering and shooting everything that was in his path.

Adding New Behavior Modules

One fundamental archetype in a combat scenario is missing: the Coward. His main goal is getting out of the combat alive and unhurt, so he will avoid confrontation and will prioritize maintaining and restoring health.

To bring forth the Coward, we started from the Veteran, lowered *EnemyHurt,* and raised *HaveHighHealth.* We left the global constants untouched, because like the Samurai, the Coward is as thoughtful and persistent as the Veteran.

The behavior of the Coward could be thus described: He started exploring the level until he found an enemy. With an enemy in sight, he started shooting. When fired upon, if the shots missed him, he would begin dodging for all subsequent shots. If he were actually hit by a shot, he would go and immediately get any reachable medkit. In the case that there were no reachable medkits, he would keep dodging and fighting until he had a very low health value. When that happened, he would flee combat and go restore his health, even if he had to go to a medkit that was very far away.

We see that even though the agent is far more concerned with its health and could not be described as brave anymore, a key point of its specification is missing: its active avoidance of engagement. To achieve this, we implemented a new module for the network: *GoAwayFromEnemy.* With this module added, when the Coward spotted an enemy, he would go away from the enemy while shooting (*GoAwayFromEnemy* and *ShootEnemy* were executed concurrently). Figure 3.5.4 shows the network of the Coward character. Note that adding a new behavior was a simple modular operation, dispensing adjustments. The network architecture handled the relation between the modules naturally.

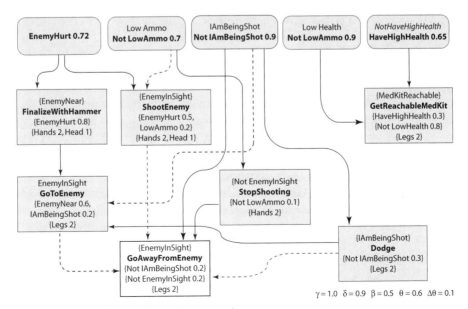

FIGURE 3.5.4   *Coward behavior network.*

Conclusion

We have seen that the extended behavior network is a good action-selection mechanism for a complex game agent with complex goals and actions situated in a dynamic and continuous environment, such as modern action games.

We verified the properties of a good-enough action selection mechanism in the 3D action game domain—namely, persistence, exploitation of opportunities, preference for actions that satisfy multiple goals, proper resolution of conflicts, performing of actions in sequences to achieve goals, and sensible selection of concurrent actions.

From an agent-design perspective, the strong points of extended behavior networks are its modularity and easy integration of new goals and behaviors. The designer can develop and test one module at a time, and build a library of basic behaviors. When designing an agent, we are able to just assemble the modules, leaving their interaction to be dealt with by the architecture. This relieves the designer from the burden of foreseeing every possible interaction and leads to interesting, immersive gameplay.

To build an agent, start by setting goals that reflect the character values and motivations. Next, proceed by assembling a set of modules capable of achieving those goals (i.e., modules that have the goal conditions as effects). Finally, by adjusting the goal strengths and global parameters, adjust the overall behavior of the agent so as to achieve the desired personality.

Our experiments in stereotype design show that for simple personas, extended behavior networks are a competitive solution; they are simple and enable us to make very different agents by the mere adjusting of constant values.

Finally, we must point out that extended behavior networks fulfill the requirements of a goal-oriented action-planning architecture, with the additional benefits of allowing the specification of situation-dependent goals, dealing well with conflicts among goals, and being a well-established technique in the robotics domain.

References

[Dorer99] Dorer, K., "Extended Behavior Networks for the Magma Freiburg Team." RoboCup-99 Team Descriptions for the Simulation League, Linkoping University Press, 1999: pp. 79–83.

[Dorer04] Dorer, K., "Extended Behavior Networks for Behavior Selection in Dynamic and Continuous Domains." *Proceedings of the ECAI workshop, Agents in dynamic domains,* U. Visser, et al. (Hrsg.) Valencia, Spain, 2004.

[Goetz97] Goetz, P., "Attractors in Recurrent Behavior Networks." Ph.D. Thesis, University of New York, Buffalo, 1997.

[Maes89] Maes, P., "How to do The Right Thing." *Connection Science Journal,* Vol. 1, No. 3., 1989.

[Müller01] Müller, K., "Roboterfußball: Multiagentensystem." February 2001. CS Freiburg, Diplomarbeit. University Freiburg, Germany.

[Nebel03] Nebel, B. and Y. Babovich, "Goal-Converging Behavior Networks and Self-Solving Planning Domains, or: How to Become a Successful Soccer Player." s.l. IJCAI03, 2003.

[Pinto05-a] Pinto, H. and L. O. Alvares, "An Extended Behavior Network for a Game Agent." Anais do Quinto Encontro Nacional de Inteligência Artificial, Brazil, 2005-a.

[Pinto05-b] Pinto, H. and L. O. Alvares, "Extended Behavior Networks and Agent Personality: Investigating the Design of Character Stereotypes in the Game Unreal Tournament." *Proceedings of the Fifth International Working Conference on Intelligent Virtual Agents,* Kos, Greece, 2005-b.

[Rhodes96] Rhodes, Bradley, "PHISH-Nets: Planning Heuristically in Situated Hybrid Networks." Masters of Science Thesis, Massachusetts Institute of Technology, 1996.

[Tyrrell93] Tyrrell, Toby, "Computational Mechanisms for Action Selection." Ph.D. Thesis, University of Edinburgh, U.K., 1993.

3.6

Short-Term Memory Modeling Using a Support Vector Machine

Julien Hamaide, Elsewhere Entertainment

julien.hamaide@gmail.com

Programming challenging artificial intelligence in games is one of the most interesting problems you can face. The key element is the learning process. The learning systems experience a lot of difficulties when the strategy of the player is changing continuously. Classical learning systems take time to forget the old rules and to learn the new ones. As a solution, this gem introduces a temporal concept for learning classifiers. The system can easily forget past events. Presented with Support Vector Machines (SVMs), this technique can be applied to other kinds of classifiers.

Introduction to Support Vector Machines

SVMs are learning classifiers, such as neural networks. But the concept they use is slightly different. SVMs are a generalization of linear classifiers. Their construction and training algorithms are the key aspects of their superiority over neural networks. A quick introduction of the key concepts is presented here. More information can be found in [Cristianini01]. The linear classifier is first introduced and then generalized to nonlinear problems. The kernel concept and training algorithms conclude this introduction.

Linear Classifier

The linear classifier splits the input space into two parts, class A and class B, with the help of a hyperplane. Every point that lies on the upper side of the hyperplane belongs to class A, while every point that lies on the lower side of the hyperplane belongs to class B. Figure 3.6.1 shows a classified data set. The plane D, defined by Equation 3.6.1, is the only parameter of the classifier. If the points x_i are divided into two classes A and B, and if the classifier is trained, the classification of the data is then realized with Equation 3.6.2 and Equation 3.6.3. $\langle x, y \rangle$ represents the standard dot product $\langle x, y \rangle = x_1 \cdot y_1 + x_2 \cdot y_2 + \dots.$

$$D \equiv \langle w, x \rangle + d = 0 \tag{3.6.1}$$

$$x_i \in A \Leftrightarrow \langle w, x_i \rangle + d > 0 \tag{3.6.2}$$

$$x_i \in B \Leftrightarrow \langle w, x_i \rangle + d < 0 \tag{3.6.3}$$

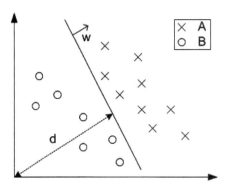

FIGURE 3.6.1 *Linearly separable data set.*

However, the training of a system composed of two constraints is not trivial. If Equation 3.6.4 and Equation 3.6.5 are posed, then the condition of classification becomes Equation 3.6.6.

$$y_i = 1 \Leftrightarrow x_i \in A \tag{3.6.4}$$

$$y_i = -1 \Leftrightarrow x_i \in B \tag{3.6.5}$$

$$y_i \cdot (\langle w, x_i \rangle + d) > 0 \tag{3.6.6}$$

The training thus consists in finding w and d such that Equation 3.6.6 is verified for each point. However, there exists an infinite number of splitting planes (see Figure 3.6.2). One of them needs to be selected. We will try to choose the plane that generalizes the classifier the most—that is, the plane that gives the better result with the data *not* included in the training set. Instead of Equation 3.6.6, we decide to use Equation 3.6.7. We now have two splitting planes, as shown in Figure 3.6.3. Each plane corresponds to a value of y_i (1 or −1). The distance between those planes is called the *margin*. One can show that this margin is proportional to $1/|w|$ [Moore01].

To have the more general classifier, we must maximize the margin, or minimize $|w|$. This will be used in the training algorithm.

$$y_i \cdot (\langle w, x_i \rangle + d) \geq 1 \tag{3.6.7}$$

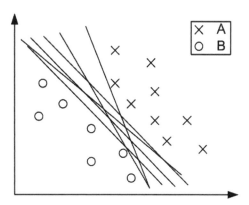

FIGURE 3.6.2   *Several planes splitting the data set.*

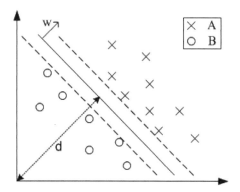

FIGURE 3.6.3   *Best splitting planes.*

The points x_i that verify Equation 3.6.8 are called the *support vector*. They are supporting the solution; they are on the limit plane and lie at the border of their class.

$$y_i \cdot (\langle w, x_i \rangle + d) = 1 \tag{3.6.8}$$

One can demonstrate that the vector w is a linear combination of support vectors [Burges98]. Equation 3.6.8 combined with Equation 3.6.9 can be rewritten as Equation 3.6.10. Now the classification condition is independent of training data.

$$w = \sum_j \alpha_j y_j x_j \text{ with } \alpha_j \geq 0 \qquad (3.6.9)$$

$$\sum_i \alpha_i y_i \langle x_i, x \rangle + d \geq 1 \qquad (3.6.10)$$

The training now consists in finding α_i and d. Coefficients α_i will be null for each point that does not verify Equation 3.6.8, thus moving it away from a solution. That is a goal to reach for the training. Support vectors and their respective coefficients are used as parameters of the classifier.

Figure 3.6.4 shows that the solution planes lie on the support vectors, with one condition: As they are sharing their normal w, the planes must be parallel. One can prove that removing a vector that is not a support vector does not change the solution. This is logical, as their α_i is null and cannot change the classifier parameters.

If we want to train the system with a new data set, it is not necessary to add the entire old data set. We just need the support vector of the old data set.

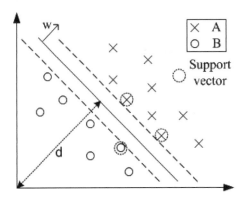

FIGURE 3.6.4   *Planes lie on support vectors.*

Extension to Nonlinearly Separable Data Sets

Data sets that are not linearly separable can become linearly separable if the input space is transformed into a higher-dimension space. Figure 3.6.5 shows the concept of the space transformation.

A concrete example is shown in Figure 3.6.6(a). If one tries to classify this data set with a linear classifier, no plane will ever succeed. If the one-dimensional space is transformed with the help of Equation 3.6.11 in a two-dimensional space, the data set is now linearly separable. Figure 3.6.6(b) shows the transformation and a successful splitting plane. This example, although simple, shows the power of such transformation into a higher-dimension space.

$$\Phi(x) = (x, x^2) \qquad (3.6.11)$$

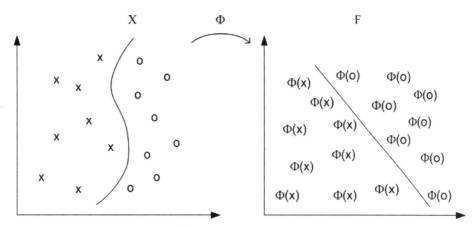

FIGURE 3.6.5   *Input space transformation.*

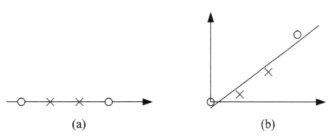

(a)   (b)

FIGURE 3.6.6   *Example of a solved problem by using transformation into a higher-dimension space.*

Kernel Function

If the transformation is applied to each vector x_i and to w, Equation 3.6.10 becomes Equation 3.6.12.

$\langle \Phi(x_i), \Phi(x) \rangle$ is the dot product of both transformed vectors. In spite of the high dimension of the transformed space, the return value will always be a scalar value. $\langle \Phi(x_i), \Phi(x) \rangle$ can then be considered as a simple function returning a scalar value. This function is called a *kernel* (K). Equation 3.6.13 shows the definition of $K(x,y)$. It is now not mandatory to know $\Phi(x)$. $\Phi(x)$ can now also transform data to an infinite dimension space (an exponential kernel is an example of such a transformation). As an example, the equivalent kernel of transformation represented by Equation 3.6.11 is computed in Equation 3.6.14. We can now rewrite our classifying condition to its last form in Equation 3.6.15.

$$\sum \alpha_i y_i \langle \Phi(x_i), \Phi(x) \rangle + d \geq 0 \qquad (3.6.12)$$

$$K(x,y) = \langle \Phi(x), \Phi(y) \rangle \tag{3.6.13}$$

$$K(x,y) = \langle \Phi(x), \Phi(y) \rangle = \left\langle \begin{pmatrix} x \\ x^2 \end{pmatrix}, \begin{pmatrix} y \\ y^2 \end{pmatrix} \right\rangle = x \cdot y + x^2 \cdot y^2 \tag{3.6.14}$$

$$\sum \alpha_i y_i K(x_i, x) + d \geq 0 \tag{3.6.15}$$

The kernel function must validate some conditions that can be found in [Burges98]. In this case, some $\Phi(x)$ matches the kernel function. Some interesting properties of kernel functions are displayed in Equation 3.6.16.

$$K(x,y) = K(y,x)$$

$$K(x,y) = K_1(x,y) + K_2(x,y)$$

$$K(x,y) = \alpha K_1(x,y) \text{ with } \alpha > 0 \tag{3.6.16}$$

$$K(x,y) = K_1(x,y) \cdot K_2(x,y)$$

$$K(x,y) = f(x) \cdot f(y)$$

$$K(x,y) = K_3(\Phi(x), \Phi(y))$$

Some classical kernels are presented in Equation 3.6.17. They can be combined with properties shown in Equation 3.6.16.

$$K(x,y) = \exp\left(-\|x - y\|^2 / 2\sigma^2\right)$$

$$K(x,y) = \langle x, y \rangle^n \tag{3.6.17}$$

$$K(x,y) = (\langle x, y \rangle + 1)^n$$

Training

As mentioned earlier, training consists of finding w and b under the constraints of Equation 3.6.7. With Equation 3.6.9, training now consists of finding α_i and b under the constraints of Equation 3.6.15. The goal here is to find the most general splitting plane. The margin must then be maximized, or $|w|$ minimized. The training algorithm becomes Equation 3.6.18. This is an optimization under constraints.

By applying Lagrange optimization theory, Equation 3.6.18 becomes Equation 3.6.19 [Cristianini01]. Equation 3.6.19 is a quadratic optimization problem. Quadratic optimization theory says that the problem is convex, and there exists no local minimum. In this optimization problem, the best result is always found. This is a key advantage of the SVM: The best solution is always found given the data set and the chosen kernel. Training the system several times gives exactly the same result. Many quadratic optimization algorithms exist, but these algorithms are far beyond the scope of this article. More information can be found in [Gould].

$$\min_{w} \frac{1}{2}\|w\|^2 \ with \sum \alpha_i y_i K\left(x_i,x\right) + d \geq 0 \tag{3.6.18}$$

$$\max_{\alpha} \sum_i \alpha_i - \frac{1}{2}\sum_{i,j} \alpha_i \alpha_j y_i y_j K\left(x_i,x_j\right) \tag{3.6.19}$$

Short-Term Memory Modeling

The classifier system is trained with the collected data set. In the case of a neural network, it is impossible to decide or to know when the network will forget the situations learned in the past. The classification within an SVM is characterized by support vectors and their coefficients, α_i (see Equation 3.6.9). These vectors are part of the collected data set. It is then possible to date each vector. One can then, after a fixed time step, cancel the effect of a vector by removing it from the solution set. The entire collected data set is then decreased by the oldest vector and increased with newest vector. Figure 3.6.7 shows the evolution of the solution when an out-of-date support vector is removed. Figure 3.6.8 shows the evolution of the solution when a new support vector is added.

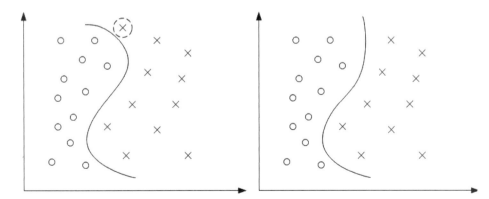

FIGURE 3.6.7   *Removal of an out-of-date vector.*

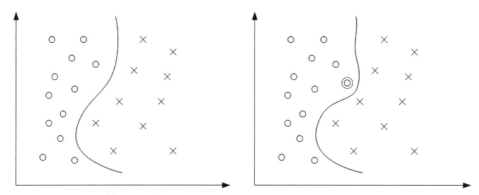

FIGURE 3.6.8   *Addition of a new support vector.*

On one hand, because the training gives exactly the same result as long as support vectors have not changed (or if no new or old data is a support vector), the solution won't change, and the training will be very fast. On the other hand, if a removed or added support vector exists, training will take more time; but it will be fast, because the data weights (α_i) of nonsupport vectors will remain at zero.

System derivation could be a problem, but in addition to support vectors and their coefficient α_i, the solution is conditioned by the choice of the used kernel. Although it can be an advantage, it is also a disadvantage, because the choice of such a kernel can be delicate.

This technique is interesting in a highly variable environment, because the knowledge learned in the past does not have an infinite influence. Indeed, in the case of neural networks, if the environment has changed, some decisions may not be valid anymore. We need to made several errors in order to reverse this tendency. In the case of SVM with dated vectors, only one error or a sufficient wait (i.e., out-of-date period of vectors) is needed.

Although this technique is presented in the case of SVM, it is obvious that it can also be applied to other classifiers that express their parameters with data from training data sets, such as K-Nearest Neighbors (KNN). This kind of SVM can, for example, replace neural networks in reinforcement learning.

CPU Consumption Limitation

To evaluate a point x, Equation 3.6.20 needs to be computed. This classification needs evaluation of $K(x,y)$ and two multiplications for each support vector. It is important to limit the CPU consumption of the classifier. The only way to lower it is to limit the quantity of support vectors, and to limit it to a fixed value. With this dated system, the oldest support vectors can be dropped from the evaluation when the quantity of support vectors is too high. However, dropped vector support must not be removed from the training data set. If so, the support vector will surely be replaced by another one. This action will decrease the effectiveness of the classifier. In games, it is important to limit the number of support vectors. The decrease of effectiveness is not always a disadvantage, as it introduces some noise in the decision.

$$\sum \alpha_i y_i K\left(x_i, x\right) \geq 0 \tag{3.6.20}$$

Conclusion

This article, in addition to introducing SVMs, also introduces aging data concepts. Although this concept can be used with the majority of the classifier systems, an SVM is a good candidate, because the parameters of the classifier are expressed with the training data set. It also gives a solution that limits the quantity of support vectors and CPU consumption.

References

[Burges98] Burges, Christopher, "A Tutorial on Support Vector Machines for Pattern Recognition." 1998. *Knowledge Discovery and Data Mining*, Vol. 2, No. 2: pp. 955–974.

[Cristianini01] Cristianini, Nello, "Tutorial on Support Vector Machines and Kernel Methods." ICML-2001 Tutorials. Available online at *http://www.support-vector. net/icml-tutorial.pdf*.

[Gould] Gould, Nick and Philippe Toint, "A Quadratic Programming Page." Available online at *http://www.numerical.rl.ac.uk/qp/qp.html*.

[Moore01] Moore, Andrew W., "Support Vector Machines." Available online at *http://www.autonlab.org/tutorials/svm.html*.

3.7

Using the Quantified Judgment Model for Engagement Analysis

Michael Ramsey

The Quantified Judgment Model (QJM) is both a model and a theory of combat. Originally developed to simulate historical battles and then later (upon further refinement) used for modern engagement prediction, it is an ideal system for predicting potential victors in a game. In this gem, we will describe the base QJM formula. The base formula can then be further expanded upon by adding models such as an attrition calculation, spatial effectiveness of units, and casualty effectiveness.

For as long as conflict has existed, there have been different theories governing war. Two of the most predominant figures that have contributed to this rich history of war theory are Henri Jomini [Jomini92] and Carl Von Clausewitz [Howard83]. While Jomini developed his combat theories relative to complex geometric patterns, Clausewitz approached combat from a more philosophical and qualitative angle. One of Clausewitz's precepts was the "Law of Numbers." This law of numbers was originally developed to deal with the simple relationship of two quantities with a random variance to basically account for the intangibles of engagements. It is this law of numbers that is both the spiritual inspiration and the fundamental foundation for the QJM and the theory behind it.

QJM provides a relatively simple framework in which two opposing forces are compared by evaluating and computing a series of variable factors. QJM was invented by T. N. Dupuy [Dupuy84], and was initially used to evaluate historical engagements for the armed services. The easiest aspects of military engagements to quantify are the weapons and their effects on combatants, terrain, and structures. The characteristics of a particular weapon are usually well defined, and they (usually) obey standard criteria. But during engagements, weapons do not usually perform per spec; QJM gives consideration to these "variable" factors by quantifying their weapon usage. Another aspect of the QJM process is the inclusion of factors often left out of other theories. One of these inclusions is that of behavior. This gem details the basic QJM formula, and how it can be used to predict combat results quickly, consistently, and efficiently.

The Basic Formula

The basic QJM formula is a fairly simple one that aggregates some complex variables. So instead of hiding the formula until the end of the article, we'll take a look at it right now, and then throughout the rest of the article dissect the details, and finally examine an example.

The basic QJM formula that generates a Combat Power (CP) value is:

$$CP = (ForceStrength(FS)) \times (VariableFactors(VF)) \times (CombatEffectiveness(CEV)) \quad (3.7.1)$$

It looks pretty simple, and it really is; but as with most mathematical formulas, it is the details that are interesting. Throughout this article, the basic formula will evolve into a succinct model, while at the same time identifying individual details of the various subformulas. Unless otherwise noted, all variables are defined between zero and one, inclusive.

Calculating the Force Strength

One of the components of the QJM is the Force Strength (FS)—the total firepower being brought to bear against an opponent. The force strength is modified by a plethora of variables. These variables can range from weather and terrain to logistical factors, as well as leadership. The base formula for calculating the force strength is:

$$S = (W_N \times V_N) + (W_G \times V_G) + (W_I \times V_I) + (W_Y \times V_Y) + (W_G \times V_L) + (W_O \times V_O) \quad (3.7.2)$$

where:

S is the calculated force strength.
W is the cumulative Operation Lethality Index (OLI) for weapons in a specific category.
V is the variable effect factors.

The subidentifiers for the cumulative OLIs and the weapon effect factors are:

N is the infantry weapons ID.
G is the artillery weapons ID.
I is the armor weapons ID.
Y is the air support weapons ID.
L is the anti-armor weapons ID.
O is the air defense weapons ID.

While the original QJM FS is defined in rigid real-world terms, there is no reason that the FS could not be altered or replaced with values that originate in a science-fiction setting or even a fantasy setting. We could easily even easily create a category for satellite weaponry. The only prerequisite is that this formula be used consistently among the engaged belligerents.

Calculating the Power Potential

The next step in the QJM process is to generate a Power Potential (P). The power potential uses the values assigned to various operational identifiers. Operational identifiers are not individual unit statistics, but are the average value as observed from an operational vantage point. This method helps to dampen the effect of one unit type over another. For example, one unit of an army may be an incredibly fast reconnaissance tank, while the majority of the forces are slower heavy tanks. We obviously want the speed of that one reconnaissance tank to be mitigated by the overall force composition. The base QJM formula also uses operational identifiers, such as the morale and training of the forces. One of the more interesting aspects of calculating the power potential, is that inclusion of all the base identifiers is not required; if you do not have a need for it, you don't need to use it. This really allows and exemplifies the natural plug-and-play aspect of the QJM system.

The formula for the power potential is:

$$P = S \times M \times L \times T \times U \times B \times US \times RU \times HU \times ZU \times V. \qquad (3.7.3)$$

The various components of the power potential are defined as:

P is the calculated power potential.
S is the calculated force strength from Equation 3.7.1.
M is the operational mobility value.
L is the operational leadership value.
T is the operational training value.
O is the operational morale.
B is the operational logistics identifier, which aggregates such concepts as supply and communication.
US is the operational posture.
RU is the operational terrain variance.
HU is the operational weather variance.
ZU is the operational seasonal factor.
V is the general operational vulnerability.

Modeling a Weapon's Effectiveness

The measure of weapon effectiveness is determined by its Operational Lethality Index (OLI). The OLI was initially developed to represent the comparative lethality of weapons based on a historical perspective. What this would allow for is the comparison of any historical weapon, such as a flintlock, with a modern-day M-16, or possibly even a futuristic weapon of some type. It is impossible to model an exact OLI, being that weapons have such a vast array of destructive capabilities. But what OLI provides is a consistent framework over varying weapons classes. The most basic aspects of this framework are included in the following variables: weapons rate of fire, reliability, accuracy, range, and number of targets per strike. These five variables are part of a consistent framework that defines the Theoretical Lethality Index (TLI). The resultant value from the TLI is expressed in casualties per hour. The TLI is converted into OLI by using a predetermined dispersion factor.

The formula for calculating the TLI is:

$$TLI = RF \times R \times A \times C \times RN. \tag{3.7.4}$$

The various components of the TLI are defined as:

RF is the rate of fire.
R is the reliability.
A is the accuracy.
C is the number of strikes per target.
RN is the range.

The TLI components are each determined a bit differently. The *rate of fire RF* is the number of effective strikes delivered against a target over period of time. The standard length of time that is normally defined is an hour. The *reliability R* of a weapon is the number of times it will fail. Failure includes everything from maintenance to general weapon failure. Weapons that are wielded as hand-to-hand weapons are deemed to be 100% reliable. The *accuracy A* of a weapon is determined free of human factors. A weapon should be considered sighted and bolted down. Then, using a predetermined rate of fire and length of firing time, exactly how accurate is the weapon when firing against a fixed target? The *number of strikes per target* (C) is calculated by using a predetermined target density to gauge how many potential targets a weapon can hit. A sword has a C of generally just one, while a bomb of any size is usually in the hundreds to thousands.

The dispersion factor is a value that defines the inherit capabilities of some weapon types to inflict greater amounts of damage over larger areas. Table 3.7.1 contains sample dispersion factors.

Table 3.7.1   Dispersion Factors for Different Military Eras

Period	Dispersion Factor (DF)
Early Man (stone weapons and clubs)	1
Medieval (bows, spears)	2
Napoleonic (age of gunpowder)	10
Civil War (rifles and cannons)	20
World War I	100
World War II	5,000
Early Twenty-First Century (nuclear)	10,000

To convert the TLI into a value that is usable at the operational level, it must converted into an operational lethality index. The formula for the OLI is:

$$OLI = \frac{TLI}{DF}.$$

(3.7.5)

OLI values need to be organized by class. The standard classifications are defined as: Infantry, Artillery, Armor, Air Support, Air Defense, and Anti-Armor weapons. There is nothing that precludes us from adding additional categories; but in general, new weapons should be evaluated to see if they fall into any of the pre-existing categories before adding an additional one. OLI values are calculated once and used over multiple engagements.

Obtaining a Theoretical Outcome

We can now obtain a theoretical outcome from an engagement by evaluating a simple ratio of two combat power ratings.

Power Potential Ratio (PPR) is:

$$PPR = \frac{(PowerPotentialForce1)}{(PowerPotentialForce2)}.$$

(3.7.6)

If the *PPR* is 1.0 or greater, then *Force*1 will be the theoretical victor. If the *PPR* is less then 1.0, then *Force*2 should be successful.

What About the CEV?

As we've stated before, the QJM allows for components to be added and removed. But can components such as the CEV be optional? The answer is yes. Even though the CEV is a component of the base formula, it is only used for prediction of future engagements when they have a historical counterpart. So if we were programming the Artificial Intelligence (AI) for a realistic World War II game, we would compare our results with results from an actual, historical battle. Further details can be found in [Dupuy85].

An Example of the QJM System

We will now step through an example that exemplifies the QJM system. This example will portray an engagement between two ancient armies on an open plain, with one of the armies physically and morally exhausted. Being set in an ancient time period, the dispersion factor will be 1.

We have two armies facing off against each other. The first army has 5,000 infantrymen with knives and hatchets, 5,000 infantrymen with spears, and 5,000 archers. The second army has 10,000 infantrymen with knives and 5,000 archers. The first step will be to calculate the TLI for the three different weapon types:

The TLI for infantrymen equipped with knives is: $60 \times 1 \times 1 \times 1 \times 1 = 60$.
The TLI for infantrymen equipped with spears is: $30 \times 0.5 \times 1 \times 1 \times 3 = 45$.
The TLI for infantrymen equipped as archers is: $20 \times 0.2 \times 1 \times 1 \times 20 = 80$.

The second step is to convert the TLIs into OLIs. This will convert the theoretical lethality index to operational lethality. As noted before, this is just dividing the TLI by the dispersion factor. Since this is a fantasy setting, the dispersion factor is defined as 1. So the OLIs are 60, 45, and 80 for the infantrymen with knives, spears, and archers, respectively.

The next step is to calculate *FS*. Since calculating the force strength also involves several variable factors, we must define these. The variable factors can include terrain, posture, season, and weather. For our example, we'll define just the terrain variable (see Table 3.7.2).

Table 3.7.2   Variable terrain factors for infantrymen. Terrain that is tougher for infantrymen to maneuver and fight on is given a value closer to zero.

Terrain Type	Variable (0.0 to 1.0)
Clear/Unobstructed	1.0
Forested	0.5
Mountainous	0.1

The force strength for the first army is:

$$((60 \times 5) \times 1) + ((45 \times 5) \times 1) + ((80 \times 5) \times 1) = 300 + 225 + 400 = 925.$$

The force strength for second army is:

$$((80 \times 5) \times 1) + ((45 \times 5) \times 1) + ((80 \times 5) \times 1) = 600 + 225 + 400 = 1225.$$

The next step is to calculate the power potential for each army. The values we'll use in our power potential calculation will be the army's leadership abilities, its morale, and the operational weather variance. Army one will have a leadership rating of 1.0, a morale rating of 1.0, and operational weather variance of 1.0. Army two will have a leadership rating of 0.2 (it's been beaten up in a few battles), a morale value of 0.5, and again an operational weather variance of 1.0.

The power potential for the first army is:

$$925 \times 1.0 \times 1.0 \times 1.0 = 925.$$

The power potential for the second army is:

$$1225 \times 0.5 \times 0.5 \times 1.0 = 306.$$

To finally obtain a theoretical outcome, we evaluate a power potential ratio:

$$\frac{925}{306} = 3.02.$$

As defined in the PPR, if the result is 1.0 or greater, then the first army will be the victor. As we see in this example, the first army is the decisive victor!

Limitations

While the QJM theory allows for accurate engagement prediction, there are areas for improvement. Since the QJM is essentially a formula built on of a system of equations, it does not allow for a truly clean extraction of potential unit losses at any particular time. In contrast, the Lanchester differential system allows for evaluation of data at specific times because it is a simpler, unified model. The Lanchester system definitely has its own limitations; the system and its limitations are discussed in *Game Programming Gems 5* [Bolton05].

Conclusion

This gem has provided an introduction to a unique combat-prediction formula: the QJM. The QJM not only can be used to replay historical engagements, but can also be used to be predict the outcome of engagements. The QJM also has plug-and-play capabilities that allow for the integration of concepts like attrition calculation or spatial effectiveness. The QJM can also be modified and extended to fit into other game systems.

References

[Bolton05], Bolton, John, "Using Lanchester Attrition Models to Predict the Results of Combat." *Game Programming Gems 5,* Charles River Media, 2005.

[Dupuy84] Dupuy, Trevor N., *The Evolution of Weapons and Warfare.* Da Capo, 1984.

[Dupuy85] Dupuy, Trevor N., *Numbers, Predictions and War.* Hero Books, 1985.

[Howard83], Howard, Michael, *On War.* Princeton, 1983.

[Jomini92], Jomini, Baron Antoine Henri, *The Art of War.* Greenhill Books, 1992.

3.8

Designing a Multilayer, Pluggable AI Engine

Sébastien Schertenleib,
Swiss Federal Institute of Technology,
Virtual Reality Lab
Sebastien.Schertenleib@epfl.ch

The purpose of this gem is to present an architecture for a data-driven AI engine capable of controlling large groups of autonomous characters that are responding to environment and user interactions in real time. The actual engine that we coded was used as a crowd-simulation system. This article will outline a fully realized data-driven AI system and show its pros and cons, and also compare and contrast this with more-traditional, code-based AI implementations.

In any game AI system, you can think of the AI as actually being two separate areas:

The logic layer, also known as the "engine" level: This is where the underlying systems that control AI characters within the game world are placed. This would include things like animation selection, pathfinding, obstacle avoidance, and the like.

The data layer: Here we describe the actual AI behaviors and decision structures necessary to move and progress within the game world. At this level we are describing things like specific actions to perform, places to which the AI should travel, or weapon selection.

Many AI game systems today still rely on entirely code-based implementations, or "monolithic architectures." In this system, both the logic and the data layers are written in code. Any change at the data level would require a system recompilation. This leads to a programming bottleneck in development, since a programmer is required to not only add to the system, but to rebuild the system so that changes can be tested. Also, as the system scales upward in complexity, a monolithic system tends to become increasingly more unmanageable and inefficient.

To prevent this, we must enforce a clear separation between these two basic AI levels. Each level will then be easier to implement and improve independently, as well as allowing for greater synergy between the two. If we perform this separation by having the data layer be defined by configuration files and/or scripts, then this is what is widely known as a data-driven architecture ([Grimshaw89], [Bilas02]), which have been proven to provide more-streamlined and effective results [Shumaker04]. One of the basic problems any data-driven system needs to address is manipulation of the flow of control from within the data. The system we present in this gem is built around a multilayer system, emphasizing minimization of functionality at the base level and allowing for dedicated, plug-in extension modules to take care of specific cases.

Related Work

In the past couple of years, the introduction of programmable Graphical Programming Units (GPUs), and therefore the advent of programmable shaders for real-time graphical applications [Lindholm01], has shown that with relatively little effort, great advances in the graphical quality of the average game can be achieved. The introduction of higher level programming languages for the creation of these shaders (e.g., [Cg04], [GLSL04], [HLSL05]) has demonstrated that even better graphical quality is achievable by providing more-powerful tools directly to the developers [Fernando03]. Through the same mechanisms, further improvements in the quality and complexity of artificial intelligence could be achieved with a higher level of abstraction in the AI definition language. Many researchers are convinced that dedicated hardware for AI accelerators will become available [Funge99]. Another possible inroad might be future hardware with multicore processors, which might allow AI applications to have a dedicated core.

These kinds of hardware evolution will allow for the creation and visualization of large crowd simulations with much better behavioral fidelity. In the past years, offline techniques have been elaborated in commercial systems [Koeppel02], [Moltenbrey04]. But now, researchers and middleware companies are trying to integrate offline techniques within interactive applications. [Champandard03] has developed the framework [Fear02] that allows for the creation of AI behaviors through XML configuration files. [Kruszewski05] describes their middleware [AI Implant00] and its integration in the next generation of gaming platforms. Similar data-driven architectures, like the one from [Bilas02], have been exploiting the approach for commercial products as well.

AI Engine Architecture

Principles

The system consists of multiple abstraction layers connecting every agent with both low-level (e.g., animation, physics, steering, etc.) and high-level functions (e.g., tactical senses, perceptions, memory, etc.) through consistent plug-in API interfaces. By separating the core AI engine from the other plug-in modules, we increase the ability to reuse the core engines for different projects. In fact, every plug-in module comes with its own set of constraints and specifications. They can be designed for speed, memory performance, high-fidelity rendering, or whatever else you require. Because of this level of flexibility, you have more freedom when choosing the proper module based on the current project requirements (due to license fees, scalability, platform, etc.). It becomes possible to develop different kinds of real-time applications using the same core AI functionality.

System Overview

Managing a crowd simulation with hundreds of highly customizable, distributed entities requires constant modifications and adjustments in the behavior rules in order to produce convincing results [Sung04]. Every agent must be able to accomplish different tasks, like walking or interacting with environmental objects. In order to define the agent's behaviors in a more intuitive way, you must use a higher level of abstraction and defer the details to a lower level system [Fairclough01]. In our system, this will be achieved by taking advantage of a script language for managing behavioral rules through prioritized tasks, and hierarchical Fuzzy State Machines (FuSMs), which will be explained later in this gem.

Behavioral Engines

The system architecture relies on C++ templates, using meta-programming techniques as described in [Abrahams04]. Each entity in the system is derived from a common core of template classes. They are combined using both inheritance and delegation through the property-design pattern [Gamma95]. Most entities share similar properties and derive from a dynamic property (e.g., for steering behaviors, etc.) and a physical property (e.g., things such as mass, gravity, etc.). The engine works on the entity's separate properties, using common interfaces to facilitate the plug-in functionality. Listing 3.8.1 shows a typical interface code snippet—in this case for the IAnimation class.

Listing 3.8.1 A Snippet for the Animation Pluggable Interface

```
Class IAnimation : public IPlugIn
{
    void defaultPosture() = 0;
    //key_frame
    kfActivate(const std::string& keyframeName)=0;
    kfSetTimeScale(vhtReal rTimeScale) =0;
    // ...
    // Walk Animation
    void walkSetDesiredFrontalSpeed(const vhtReal& rSpeed) =0;
    void walkSetPositionReachedTolerance(const vhtReal& rValue) =0;
    void walkSetDesiredPosition( vhdVector3 vecPos) =0;
    // ...
    //look
```

```
void lookSetTargetLocation(const vhdVetor3 & vecPos) =0;
void lookSetEyeBlinkParameters(vhtReal rCloseEyeAngle,
    vhtReal rPeriod,
    vhtReal rVariance)=0;
// ...
// other actions
// ...
};
```

When a new behavior goal is initiated, the request starts at the top level of the system. For instance, the animation module might indicate that it desires to move an arm to a certain position. The "animation module" in this example is actually the high-level, common interface level. The actual work will then be done by the plug-in implementation underlying the animation system, which we call the "concrete implementation." In this way, the AI engine is not bound to a dedicated animation or physics package. Each package is free to implement the common interface requests as it sees fit. A walking animation can be computed either using key frame animation or using physics-based dynamic walking. Figure 3.8.1 shows an overview of the architecture, clearly displaying the separation of the plug-in implementations from the AI engine. Each entity is in possession of its encoded private-behavior rules, and also has access to its default actions, but is not in direct control of its instanced world object.

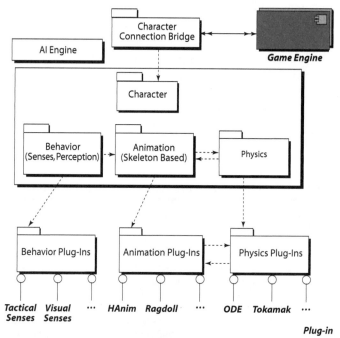

FIGURE 3.8.1   *Hierarchy of property and concrete body instances.*

Data-Driven Classes and Properties

In this engine design, the information required to update the state of each agent must not depend on the data itself. These different abstraction layers (see Figure 3.8.2) ensure this separation:

- The behavioral rules, and FuSM states are defined using Lua metatables [Ierusal-imschy96].
- Event propagation and world interaction is managed through Python micro-threads ([Hoffert98], [Python91]).
- The initial world description is set using XML configuration files.

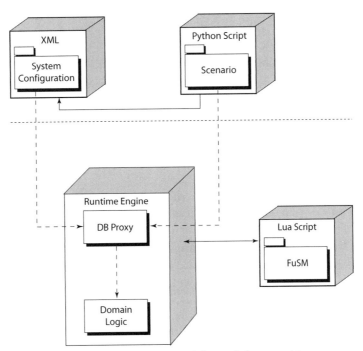

FIGURE 3.8.2   *System overview of the multilayer architecture.*

At each abstraction layer, we take advantage of each language's unique peculiarities. The logic layer is written in C++, and the data manipulation is done using script languages. The decision to use two different script languages is based on several reasons. First, Lua is generally a faster-interpreted language than Python [Bagley05]. So, we use Lua for manipulating and updating the different state machines for each entity; thus, we can maintain a level of efficiency while keeping a data-driven approach. Python, however, comes with more third-party components (notably for database and network management) that we can leverage.

Although the system is written such that each script language does not interfere with the other, direct communication between Python and Lua is possible using the two-way bridge solution from [Niemeyer03].

Hierarchical FuSM: Fuzzy-State Machine

FuSMs are a permutation of regular Finite-State Machines (FSMs), which use fuzzy logic rules instead of Boolean logic for decision-making [Kantrowitz97]. As a result, fuzzy states are not limited to being on or off, but can hold an intermediate value. A fuzzy-state system, unlike a finite-state machine, can have any or all of its states on to some degree. While this curious nature makes the construction of FuSMs slightly more complicated than the creation of a vanilla FSM, the existence of simultaneously active states greatly reduces the predictability of the resulting behaviors. It also dramatically reduces the complexity of the state machine, as a wider range of different behaviors can be encoded with fewer states.

In our case, the FuSM states and substates required by the application were defined within Lua metatables. In Lua, a metatable is an ordinary Lua table, but with additional specifications as to its behavior (and how it uses user-supplied data) under certain operations. In our case, these involved representing specific rules for dedicated states, allowing for scenario-based rules (e.g., different environments, number of entities, etc.) and for providing reference access to the C++ character entity data structure.

As shown in Listing 3.8.2, each state description requires four keys to be provided:

Name: Simply the name of the state.
Enter: The function for the entity to call upon for entry to this state.
Execute: The update function for the state.
Exit: To be called when exiting the specific state.

Listing 3.8.2   A FuSM State Described in Lua Metatables

```
-- create the State_PathBehaviorActivateGoal state
State_PathBehaviorActivateGoal = {}
State_PathBehaviorActivateGoal["Name"] = "PathBehaviorActivateGoal"
State_PathBehaviorActivateGoal["Enter"] = function(character)
    -- nop
end
State_PathBehaviorActivateGoal["Execute"] = function(character)
    character:walkTo(character:getDesiredPosition(), true)
    character:activateWalk()
    character:getPath():setNextWaypoint()
    if character:getPath():finished() then
        --done
        character:getFSM():changeState(State_PathBehaviorDone)
    else
        character:getFSM():
            changeState(State_PathBehaviorSelectGoal)
    end
end
```

```
State_PathBehaviorActivateGoal["Exit"] = function(character)
    -- nop
end
```

C++ and Lua Metatable Bindings

The core C++ engine contains a Lua interpreter and exposes its functionality using the [Luabind03] library to generate "glue" code (a term that refers to the code required to manage variable and/or class bindings between C++ and Lua). Luabind shares many things in common with the meta-programming approach of the Boost library [Boost98], as it offers a set of functions that expands the Lua script language with extended object-oriented mechanisms, like allowing Lua classes to derive from other Lua or C++ classes. Since Luabind uses meta-programming, it doesn't require a preprocessor compilation pass like the popular tool from [Manzur03]. The compiler simply generates the glue code automatically. However, the compilation of the binding code can be relatively slow. One trick in fighting this is to keep the binding code in separate object files, instead of in one huge binding depository. Listing 3.8.3 shows an example of C++ classes being exposed to Lua using the Luabind library.

Listing 3.8.3   Luabind Bindings

```
void iCharacter::registerWithLua(lua_State* pLua)
{
    //register the class into the module vhdEl
    luabind::module("vhdEl", pLua)
    [
        //indicate that the resulting Lua class
        //inherit from the exported base class
        .def(luabind::class_<iCharacter,
            luabind::bases<vhdEl::iBaseEntity> > ("iCharacter")
        .def(luabind::constructor<const std::string&>),
        .def("setWalkStyle" , &vhdEl::iCharacter::setWalkStyle),
        .def("setWalkSpeed" , &vhdEl::iCharacter::setWalkSpeed),
        .def("lookAt" , &vhdEl::iCharacter::lookAt),
        //...
        .def("performSensing" , &vhdEl::iCharacter::performSensing)
    ];
}
```

As you can see in Listing 3.8.3, many aspects of the engine can be exposed to the script language. In this system, the behavioral rules and FuSMs that drive the animation and entities' reactions are described within the Lua scripts. Every entity's state machine keeps an internal `luabind::object` facilitator, which serves as the connection between Lua objects and their C++ counterpart. This connection variable gives the user a straightforward hook to interact between the engine code and the Lua stack. By having each state contain its own binding facilitator, the system is not affected by the size or complexity of the FuSM in terms of access time. The engine can execute and update the agent's state without knowledge of the state itself. Listing 3.8.4 shows a small snippet of the state execution-control logic within the engine.

Listing 3.8.4   C++ Method for Updating the Active State Machine

```
void FSM::update()
{
    //luabind object point to the current Lua metatable
    if (_luaCurrentState.is_valid())
    {
        //_pOwner: pointer to the entity
        _luaCurrentState.at("Execute") {_pOwner)
    }
}

void FSM::change(const luabind::object& newState)
{
    //call exit on the active state
    _luaCurrentSate.at("Exit"){_pOwner);

    //change state
    _luaPreviousState = _luaCurrentState;
    _luaCurrentState = newState;

    //call the entry method for the new state
    _luaCurrentState.at("Enter")(_pOwner);
}
```

Prioritized Task Manager

The performance impact of using a script language can be minimized in a number of ways. One way is use a manager to handle the workflow of the FuSM system by assigning tasks among categories of states, thus avoiding updating unnecessary tasks. However, as the engine is not bound directly to the data, the designer must tag the different states with relevant category information to facilitate this.

AI Architecture Using Prioritized Tasks

To keep real-time performance high, any AI system needs to work within a budgeted time frame. It should constrain the number and/or complexity of the behaviors within the system to accommodate the available CPU time [Funkhouser93]. This should keep the AI system requirements relatively stable so as not to affect the gameplay through inconsistent frame rates caused by spiking CPU needs [Schertenleib02]. By providing a high-level approach that allows the designer to organize the different tasks within the system, we are able to separate each task's classification from the engine.

Among all the tasks that can be activated in a particular frame, we need to distribute their dispatch so that we can ensure that the per-frame workflow remains somewhat constant. To do this, we separate the different tasks into three categories: those that need to be updated every frame, those that can be updated on a periodic basis, and finally those tasks that will be executed only if processing time is available.

You might check certain tasks on a periodic basis for very different reasons. In the case of checking if a key frame animation has completed, you might use a periodic priority because it is unlikely to change on a frame-by-frame basis. Another reason to check certain tasks periodically is to introduce a certain amount of delay before the task propagates; such latency increases the sensation of AI presence by avoiding the situation in which the entity reacts immediately to every stimuli [Laird01]. The number of tasks that need to be updated each frame needs to be minimized, as this subtracts directly from the total time available in your AI performance budget.

By using categorized tasks, we can ensure that the engine will maximize efficiency. We do this by using configurable search rules (custom to each category of task) to help direct our search through each bank of behaviors. We can ensure that more-import tasks happen first, but that older tasks are not starved out of the system. Figure 3.8.3 shows a very simple overview of the task scheduler.

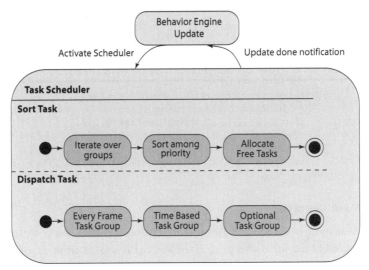

FIGURE 3.8.3   *Task scheduler management.*

Performance Issues and Techniques

There are a number of performance issues that can potentially arise in the system described in this gem; but with care, they can be handled properly or even avoided altogether. Here we discuss these issues and techniques for dealing with them.

Profiling

One common issue that somewhat plagues data-driven systems is that of performance, since executing scripted routines is almost always slower computationally then straight code. All data-driven engines must avoid unnecessary state updates by scheduling based on priorities, as well as limiting the work that is being done at the script level. Heavy floating-point operations or large search-type actions have to remain at the code level, while the scripts (usually) only set parameters where appropriate. Keeping the scripts limited in this way allows the benefits of data driving your system from being outweighed by the overhead.

In the system described here, information stored within C++ objects is bound to the script interfaces on demand. One problematic area is with task classification. Since the engine does not have control at the level of task complexity or duration, designers need the ability to provide hints to the system, like those described in Listing 3.8.5. A custom profiler may be necessary for collecting information about each task, like its resource usage over time. Depending on those profiled results, tasks can be assigned to the appropriate classification group.

For instance, tasks with small variance in performance are good candidates for constant, frame-rate-based execution (using the maximum time duration necessary to allow for the largest time-based category). The different Level of Details (LODs) for each task's management can benefit from predicators that will try to estimate the cost of each LOD based on heuristic functions.

Listing 3.8.5   Task Classifications May Differ in Their LODs

```
State_DoAction["Enter"] = function(character)
    -- hints for classifying tasks
    character.lod[0] = MaxTimeTask(0.01)
    character.lod[1] = MaxTimeTask(0.002)
    -- constant time
    character.lod[2] = ConstantTimeTask(0.0001)
end
```

Task Ordering

Managing and ordering all the different tasks comes at a cost. In this system, scheduling takes the form of a priority-linked list based on time. In order to reduce the complexity, we break each task into small chunks. Each chunk will be executed in order, providing a constant time-search function. The rescheduling is an $O(m)$ operation, where m is the number of tasks within a chunk. If the chunks are well defined, rescheduling will not occur very often.

Level of Detail

Similar to graphics engines that need to render multiple objects within the capacity of the current processor's power, the AI has to be able to provide different levels of abstraction for controlling its entities. When an entity is close to the player, we expect very smart, rich behaviors. However, offscreen and distant entities do no require the same attention to detail [Robbins03].

Determining the LOD classification for any given task depends again on several factors, like overall resource usage. In a graphical LOD system, the distance to the camera may serve to select the current LOD. Sound and behavior LOD systems may require much more specialized alternate heuristics. An AI LOD might take into account the computational complexity of performing the task. Animations within our system can be based on skeletal animation or use prerecorded gestures. In the former case, the computation would be based on the number of bones within the animation, whereas the latter would be a constant time task. Thus, the system will be able to provide more-accurate dispatching of available tasks based on their current LOD, as shown in Listing 3.8.5.

For ordering workflow, tasks need to be separated into different categories. One category contains tasks that need updating on a frame-by-frame basis. Another category holds periodic tasks, and another keeps tasks that are to be executed only when processing time is available. Some typical use cases of this last category are related to virtual characters that populate the world, but that do not directly interact with the player. Thus, if such a character is playing some idle animation and needs to update its behaviors, the task can easily be postponed for a few frames, without becoming too noticeable to the player. To some extent, some tasks can also use statistical information collected by the engine in order to be reassigned to a more appropriate category on the fly (e.g., notably for periodic tasks).

Tools

With today's system complexity, developing a library alone is not enough. A dedicated effort for building tools that will unleash the library's potential is also necessary. Coding thousands of states by hand can be a painful process. Thus, allowing the generation of the FuSMs in a graphical environment can provide an important productivity boost.

Offline Pipeline

Figure 3.8.4 shows a customized tool for setting up state transitions that then exports this data directly to their associated scripts. Open-source initiatives like the ones from [Darovsky05] or [Jacobs05] could serve as a good point of entry for interested readers.

In the FuSM editor shown in Figure 3.8.4, the core idea is to store this information into XML configuration files. Then, a compiler generates the different FuSMs within Lua metatables. The reason for using XML code within the intermediary files is to keep separate the authoring tool from the engine data structure. Figure 3.8.5 depicts this pipeline, showing that the runtime engine will transpose the Lua scripts into Lua byte code, which will in turn be used by the AI engine at runtime.

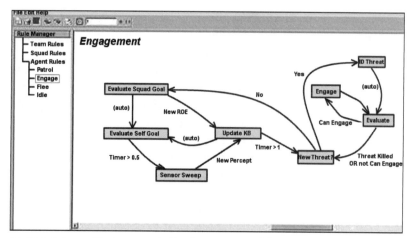

FIGURE 3.8.4   *Designer tools for the creation of the FuSM.*

FuSM AI Design Pipeline

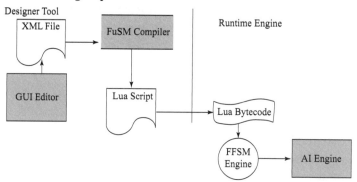

FIGURE 3.8.5   *Pipeline for generating the different FuSMs from the GUI editor to the runtime engine.*

Runtime Information

The development of 3D real-time applications featuring hundreds or more dynamic entities (like crowd simulations) is a difficult process. To construct believable worlds, designers need to interact directly with the virtual environments. Seeing general action from the onscreen characters is not enough; they also need to modify the simulation parameters at the entity level during runtime. The idea is to generate dynamic GUIs that can reflect the current data set based on the designers' needs. Figure 3.8.6 shows an example of such a GUI; it provides visual debugging information for the current navigation graph used for path-planning requests, as well as a set of widgets displaying feedback information for (among other things) controlling the simulation. Users can interact directly with the system, trigger events, or dynamically change system parameters.

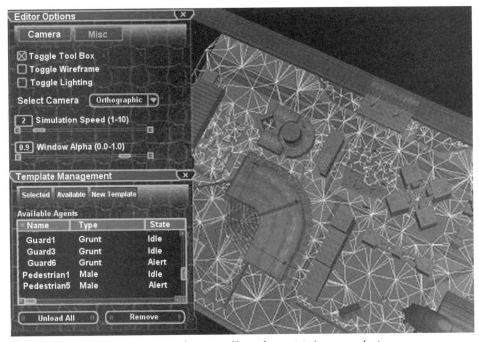

FIGURE 3.8.6 *Real-time GUIs for controlling the entities' state evolutions.*

Conclusion

This gem demonstrates design architecture for a data-driven AI engine. The system performance is able to handle large crowd simulations that are controlled completely via its data.

However, the system comes with some limitations. First, designers must help the system to order the different tasks among priority groups. Second, the multilanguage development environment adds an extra layer of complexity, notably in debugging across different programming and script languages. Nevertheless, the plug-in interface offers the system much greater flexibility, which enables designers to reuse core engines with a limited performance impact. The recent progress made in the graphical programming world, offering better tools and higher level languages, clearly demonstrates the benefit of data-driven systems. The AI field must still reach a level of standardization that would allow designers to focus on the behavioral aspects of the system, rather then the implementation. This article is an attempt toward this objective, but even more work is required to extend it with more-efficient tools and within the data-creation pipeline.

References

[Abrahams04] Abrahams, D., *C++ Template Metaprogramming: Concepts, Tools, and Techniques from Boost and Beyond.* A. Gurtovoy, 2004.

[AI Implant00] A.I.IMPLANT, "Middleware from BioGraphic Technologies for real-time crowd simulation." BioGraphic Technologies, 2000.

[Bagley05] Bagley, D., "The Great Computer Language Shootout Benchmarks." 2005. Available online at *http://shootout.alioth.debian.org.*

[Bilas02] Bilas, S., "A Data-Driven Game Object System." *Gas Powered Games,* 2002.

[Boost98] Boost, "Boost C++ Libraries." 1998.

[Cg04] Cg, "The Cg Shader Programming Language." nVIDIA, 2004.

[Champandard03] Chapandard, A., *AI Game Development, Synthetic Creatures with Learning and Reactive Behaviors.* New Rider, 2003.

[Darovsky05] Darovsky, A., FSME, 2005.

[Fairclough01] Fairclough, C., "Research Directions for AI in Computer Games." Technical Report TCD-CS-2001-29, Trinity College, Dublin, 2001.

[Fear02] Alex Champandard, "Fear Flexible Embodied Animat Architecture." 2002.

[Fernando03] Fernando, Randima and Mark J. Kilgard, *The Cg Tutorial.* Addison-Wesley, 2003.

[Funge99] Funge, J. D., *AI for Games and Animation: a Cognitive Modeling Approach.* A K Peters, 1999.

[Funkhouser93] Funkhouser, T. A., "Adaptive Display Algorithm for Interactive Frame Rates During Visualization of Complex Virtual Environment." C. H. Séquin, University of California at Berkeley, 1993.

[Gamma95] Gamma, E., et. al., *Design Patterns: Elements of Reusable Object-Oriented Software.* Addison-Wesley Professional, 1995.

[GLSL04] GLSL, "The Shader Programming Language for OpenGL," 2004.

[Grimshaw89] Grimshaw, A. S., "Real-Time Mentat: A Data-Driven Object-Oriented System." Proc. IEEE Globecom: pp. 232–241, 1989.

[HLSL05] HLSL, *The Microsoft DirectX High-Level Shader Programming Language.* Microsoft, 2005.

[Hoffert98] Hoffert, J. and K. Goldman, "Microthread: An Object for Behavioral Pattern for Managing Object Execution." Washington University, Distributed Programming Environments Group, 1998.

[Ierusalimschy96] Ierusalimschy, R., "Lua-an Extensible Extension Language." Software: Practice & Experience, Vol. 26, John Wiley & Sons, 1996.

[Jacobs05] Jacobs, S., "Visual Design of State Machine." *Game Programming Gems 5:* pp. 169–176, Charles River Media, 2005.

[Kantrowitz97] Kantrowitz, M., "Fuzzy Logic and Fuzzy Expert Systems." 1997. Available online at *http://www.faqs.org/faqs/fuzzy-logic/part1/.*

[Koeppel02] Koeppel, F., "Massive Attack." Popular Science, 2002. Available online at *http://www.popsci.com/popsci/science/d726359b9fa84010vgnvcm1000004eecbccdrcrd/5.html.*

[Kruszewski05] Kruszewski, P. A., "A practical system for real-time crowd simulation on current and next-generation gaming platforms." 2005.

[Laird01] Laird, J., "Toward human-level AI for computer games." Invited presentation, AAAI-2000. Available online at *http://ai.eecs.umich.edu/people/laird/talks/ Soar-games/index.htm.*

[Lindholm01] Lindholm, E. and M. J. Kilgard, "A User Programmable Vertex Engine." *Proceedings of SIGGRAPH 2001,* ACM Press/ACM SIGGPRAH: pp. 149–158, 2001.

[Luabind03] Luabind libraries for use with the Lua language, 2003.

[Manzur03] Manzur, A., *toLua++.* 2003.

[Moltenbrey04] Moltenbrey, K., "Digital artists re-create ancient Rome for the epic miniseries Spartacus." *Computer Graphics World,* 2004.

[Niemeyer03] Niemeyer, G. *Lunatic Python.* 2003.

[Python91] *Python Programming Language.* 1991.

[Robbins03] Robbins, J., "Simulation Level of Detail Or Doing As Little Work As Possible." Physically Based Modeling, Simulation, and Animation, 2003.

[Schertenleib02] Schertenleib, "Complex 3D Environments System Rendering and Consistent Frame Rate." 2002.

[Shumaker04] Shumaker, S., "Techniques and Strategies for Data-Driven Design in Game Development." Computer and Information Science, 2004.

[Sung04] Sung, M. and M. Gleicher, "Scalable behaviors for crowd simulation." *Eurographics* 23, 2004.

3.9

A Fuzzy-Control Approach to Managing Scene Complexity

Gabriyel Wong,
Nanyang Technological University

gabriyel@gmail.com

Jianliang Wang,
Nanyang Technological University

It is commonly known that games are designed around expected rendering-load ranges. Often, 3D artists work with level editors that are directly linked to the actual game engines, as this allows them to preview their work and to check if the content developed can be run at interactive frame rates. While this has become a norm, probably due to the way games are played by single-users in an expected manner, it is increasingly evident that dynamic environments, such as multiplayer gaming scenarios, are challenging this paradigm. In this article, we describe a fuzzy-control approach to managing scene complexity that addresses both performance and image quality, and is suitable for use in dynamic gaming environments.

The Key Idea

Given a fixed set of hardware resources, the objective in real-time computer graphics is to maximize visual acuity (quality) at interactive frame rates (performance). Although existing mechanisms, such as Level-of-Detail (LOD) control, visibility algorithms, and image-based techniques all strive to reduce geometrical complexity, it is undeniable that their performances vary with different scene content, and they are monolithic when it comes to dealing with the overall scene-geometry load control.

This article does not describe a new algorithm or heuristic for geometry reduction. Instead, it illustrates a novel approach to managing the geometry load of a scene using fuzzy-logic principles for LOD selection. By treating the rendering process as a "Plant," it is possible to establish a controller based on fuzzy logic that regulates the load that is to be sent to the Plant for rendering. With a feedback mechanism, this controller will be able to adjust the geometrical load using prebuilt rules derived from the developer's knowledge to effectively select the LODs of scene objects such that the load can be varied for performance-quality requirements.

Why Fuzzy Control?

There are several advantages in adopting fuzzy logic [FIDE1] in the context of controlling the rendering process. First, in contrast to conventional approaches for system control, fuzzy logic provides a design methodology that is fast and convenient. The rendering process is known to be complex, and hence exact modeling of it in its entirety could be nontrivial. Fuzzy techniques allow input-output rules to be built upon the expert's knowledge and used instead of possible mathematical models that could be tedious or impossible to derive. The implementation can be simplified to IF-AND-THEN statements that govern the input-output relationships. In addition, its linguistic nature provides a simple platform for developers and users to design and customize, since rules are derived from language descriptions rather than mathematical formulas. Furthermore, fuzzy logic provides an alternative solution to describing the nonlinearities in a system through the developer's intuitive understanding of the system. Thus, the aforementioned benefits make fuzzy logic an attractive option to be used as a basis for controlling a complex process, such as real-time rendering.

Tools

There are many tools available for the construction of Fuzzy Inference Systems (FISs). Some of them include the Fuzzy Logic Toolbox from MathWorks, INFORM's *fuzzy*Tech®, and Aptronix's FIDE™ (Fuzzy Inference Development Environment). The workflow to develop the FIS is similar across the gamut of tools. It basically involves the identification of the input variables, output variables, and the construction of the rule-set. In order for the FIS to work, it is necessary to "fuzzify" the inputs and outputs of the controller by mapping the linguistic descriptions (fuzzy sets) to simple mathematical extents (e.g., VERY LOW to 0, and VERY HIGH to 5, etc.). The above-mentioned tools usually provide various types of membership functions to assist input/output value-mapping to their corresponding linguistic descriptions. Figure 3.9.1 provides an illustration of the input and output membership-function concepts described here.

The rule-set basically describes the relationship between the antecedents (IF conditions) and the consequents (THEN outputs) of the FIS, based on the knowledge of the developer. Similarly, a good FIS design tool would provide an editor for easy construction and amendment to the rule-set (e.g., see Figure 3.9.2). It is important to note that the specification of the input-output parameters and rule-set does not mark the completion of the FIS development. Rather, putting the FIS to the test in the game application and tuning it over possibly several experiments certifies its validity and usefulness.

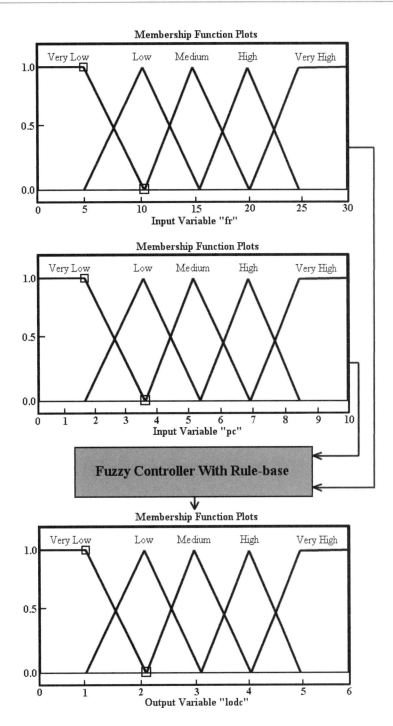

FIGURE 3.9.1 *Membership functions of the inputs and outputs of the FIS system.*

FIGURE 3.9.2   *An example rule-set that governs the input-output relationship of the FIS.*

System Design

Figure 3.9.3 illustrates the overview of a system with a Fuzzy Logic Controller (FLC). The system consists of a feedback branch from the Plant (rendering process) to the FLC. The frame rate and polygon count of the scene are selected as feedback information to the FLC. An important issue to address in designing such a system is configurability. Users' preferred frame rates and polygon counts could be set as references to which the application should behave. The feedback information is compared to these user-set target values, and the errors are retrieved as inputs to the FLC.

The FLC may be seen as a black box that computes the output via its rule-set, based on these inputs. Subsequently, this output is channeled into the Plant as a control variable for selection of the LOD, which eventually moderates the polygon load sent to the rendering pipeline.

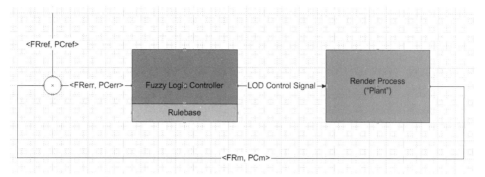

FIGURE 3.9.3   *The rendering system with a fuzzy logic controller.*

LOD is the primary mechanism by which the FLC controls geometrical load of the rendering system. While the FLC itself is not an algorithm or heuristic for reducing geometrical complexity, it rides on LOD mechanisms to achieve the same purpose, but for a global objective—that is, to control the overall scene geometrical load. [Luebke03] provided a very comprehensive insight into various LOD techniques and related issues on their usage in real-time graphics applications. Two very common schemes that are adopted in many games are discrete and continuous LOD control. A discrete LOD control scheme makes use of prebuilt models of the same 3D object, but of varying polygon counts at runtime. Usually based on distance or screen-space occupancy, a model will be selected to represent the 3D object in the scene. This method is straightforward and easy to implement. However, it has a strong dependency on the artist's skills, as the switching of LOD levels may create visual disturbances if the relative differences between successive LOD levels are not carefully moderated. The continuous LOD scheme (hysteresis) avoids this problem by smoothing the process of LOD-switching through a continuous reduction of polygons over different viewing distances. The advancement in multiresolution mesh algorithms (for continuous LOD objects) has also enabled complex objects to reduce in geometrical complexity, with little noticeable difference, even at very low polygon counts.

The rendering system described in this article employs the continuous LOD selection mechanism for 3D objects in the virtual world. The output of the FLC that acts as a control variable is also an LOD multiplier, such that the geometrical structure or polygon count of a 3D object does not depend solely on the distance factor, but also on this multiplier. To illustrate, the fall-off in terms of polygon count for a 3D object typically could be linear with respect to distance. By including this LOD factor from the output of the FLC as a multiplier, the fall-off could vary exponentially. Hence, a number of different fall-off patterns may be created easily by the developer, using the LOD control variable in accordance with the requirements of the application. The following code illustrates how this can be implemented:

```
void setCLODFalloff(float fallOffMultiplier)
{
    // For each mesh node in the scene
    {
        // Start doing some camera-object distance calculation

        // Compute near distance as ratio of viewing range
        float fRatio = (fDepth-fNear)/(fFar-fNear);

        // If nonlinear drop-off is required
        fRatio = Mathf::Pow(fRatio,2.0f);

        int newIndexCount = (int)(MaxIndex * fRatio *
                           (1.25/fallOffMultiplier));
        CLODObject->SetIndexCount() = newIndexCount;

        // ...
    }
}
```

By using continuous LOD, it is possible to achieve seamless transitions between the LOD levels of 3D objects, thereby reducing visual artifacts during runtime. This adheres to the design principle of the rendering system, since using this LOD mechanism could preserve the image-quality factor. An open-source graphics toolkit is used to construct this rendering system. The FLC is developed based on the FIS library (in C language) provided by Matlab®.

Adoption in Games

The Fuzzy Logic Toolbox from MathWorks [Matlab1] provides a good starting point for developing an FIS to be used in a game. There are a few points to note on any direct use of this FIS:

- The FIS provided contains rules pertaining to the polygon load and frame-rate relationship. They appear fundamental, but may not be optimized for different application or hardware settings.
- It is necessary to obtain a baseline assessment from the initial test results using this FIS to further tune the rule-set until it yields satisfactory results.

MathWorks provides a powerful tool for prototyping fuzzy logic application through its Simulink® environment [Matlab2]. The development process for such applications typically involves creating "building blocks" in Simulink and linking them together as a system. Even a simple Simulink model file illustrates the concept

of a controlled rendering process with the FLC in place. The different signal generators can be used to simulate the varying geometrical load conditions commonly
brought about by factor, such as camera motion (e.g., user movement) and the creation of new entities, or inclusion of new objects in the game. Instead of using the signal generators to serve the varying inputs, one possible way to assess the performance
of the FLC is to replace the Plant with the actual game application. This may be done
using the Simulink S-function structures to create wrappers around the game itself.

It is also noteworthy that no FLC can be built to handle load beyond the capability of the underlying hardware. The developer or user is free to set target frame rates
and polygon counts, as shown in Figure 3.9.3, but these values must be within the
limits of the aggregated computing power of the platform. Hence, it is advisable that
preliminary tests be conducted for assessment of the load-handling capability of the
target hardware platform in order to ascertain reasonable values for these parameters.

Assumptions

The approach to using fuzzy logic to manage scene complexity as discussed in this
article relies heavily on the assumption that scene complexity is almost completely
described by the geometrical load, alone. However, game development could realistically consist of many more processes, such as network, artificial intelligence, audio,
and physics calculations, which account for the time division in each frame. Furthermore, with advanced rendering techniques like shaders, it is now possible to decouple
the relationship between polygon count and surface details by using normal maps and
per-pixel shading algorithms.

Nevertheless, the central idea of using fuzzy logic still can be useful in the context
of controlling the various process elements (including the graphical and nongraphical
processes) in the game software during runtime. This can be achieved by associating
the information of these processes as inputs to the FLC and creating a new set of rules
relating the output to various combinations of the inputs, as described earlier. But
consequently, this also implies the requirement for adequate expert knowledge or delicate formulation of input-output rules in order for the FLC to be effective.

Implementation Considerations

While the continuous LOD mechanism may provide a means to a more accurate control of geometry load, it is important to note that the process for calculating and switching LOD may hamper the frame rate itself. Hence, it may not be advisable in general to
calculate the LOD per frame, but rather in alternate frames or according to some periodic cycle. Another good reason to support such an approach is that coherency between
successive frames in terms of scene content exists and therefore can be exploited for rendering efficiency. In contrast, careless handling of LOD switching for each frame may

even cause "flickering effects" that can be visually disturbing, especially if the switching distances are scaled to values near to the eye-point (in heavy loading conditions).

Another consideration that may be useful during implementation is the inclusion of continuous LOD objects. One of the commonly known weaknesses of the continuous LOD control scheme is the requirement to build vertex connectivity information for the 3D objects prior to sending them into the rendering pipeline. Although this can be done offline, it may reduce productivity if the frequency of testing or restarting the game application is high. Furthermore, since the computation overhead of continuous LOD selection is high, (obviously) for performance reasons, it may not be advisable to include all objects in the scene to be continuous LOD objects.

Tests and Results

We developed a test application consisting of a sample 3D world populated with numerous cows in an open terrain. Approximately 40% of these cows are constructed with continuous LOD, and thus they constitute the proportion of the total scene geometry that can be managed by the FLC. Naturally, this setting may be adjusted according to the nature of the scene content in different applications for optimum performance. For example, a geometrically complex and huge object that contains the bulk of the geometrical load may be better managed by the FLC than many small objects with low polygon counts (for the sake of building up the same proportion of load), as the latter will incur higher computation overhead.

The objectives of this test are to affirm that performance gains are derivable using a rendering system with FLC, and also to test the FLC's functionality and effectiveness in steering scene load toward its user-set targets when compared to the conventional approach of using only the Discrete LOD (DLOD) mechanism. A common camera path was constructed for running the tests using the two different approaches. The results are shown in Figure 3.9.4.

From the graphs shown in Figure 3.9.4, it can be observed that the rendering system with the FLC produces approximately 25% higher frame rates than the other one, which uses the conventional DLOD mechanism throughout the entire test. The two rendering systems were subjected to stress loading at the initial period of the test, when geometry beyond the processing power of the systems to render at 30 Hz was sent to them for rendering. The Triangle Count Gain graph shown in Figure 3.9.4 refers to the relative difference in polygon count per frame, using the two different rendering systems. Evidently, the system with FLC achieved significantly higher geometry savings during this stress period, even though the frame rates fell momentarily to approximately 22 Hz, and also at other periods of the test, depending on the scene composition. A sample screenshot of the test application is provided in Figure 3.9.5, as well as in Color Plate 6.

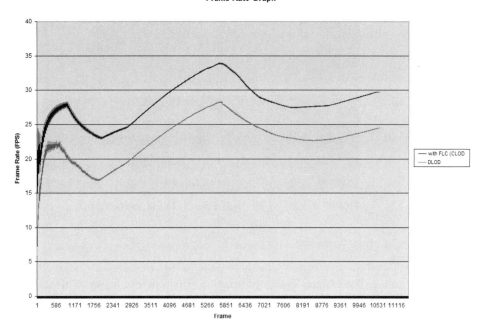

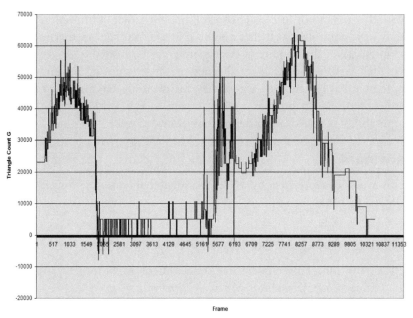

FIGURE 3.9.4 *A performance comparison of two different rendering systems.*

FIGURE 3.9.5   *A screenshot from the test application.*

Conclusion

This article advocates the use of fuzzy control in managing scene complexity for the purpose of achieving some form of macro-controllability in terms of the overall geometrical load of a scene. This is different from the common objective of optimization methods such as level-of-detail algorithms, visibility calculations, and image-based techniques, which lack global load sensitivity. In fact, it is possible to construct a software framework that ties in not just LOD control, but also other optimization techniques to the fuzzy logic controller such that a more powerful mechanism that meets the optimum performance-quality requirements in games may be created.

Finally, while artificial intelligence or soft-computing techniques such as fuzzy logic may have been used extensively for decision-making or combat scenarios in games, we hope to provide a new horizon to this field of study by unraveling its applicability in real-time rendering and games, as well.

Acknowledgment

This work is supported by DSO National Laboratories, Singapore, under grant DSOCL01144.

References

[FIDE1] FIDE, Fuzzy Inference Development Environment. Aptronix. Available online at *http://www.aptronix.com/fide/whyfuzzy.htm*.

[Luebke03] Luebke, D., et al., *Level-of-Detail for 3D Graphics*. Morgan Kauffman.

[Matlab1] Fuzzy Logic Toolbox. Matlab. Available online at *http://www.mathworks.com/products/fuzzylogic*.

[Matlab2] Simulink. Matlab. Available online at *http://www.mathworks.com/products/simulink*.

SCRIPTING AND DATA-DRIVEN SYSTEMS

Introduction

Graham Rhodes, Applied Research Associates, Incorporated

grhodes@gsrhodes.com

In the beginning, video games were simple and easy to make. The earliest games contained practically no art content, and were frequently the product of a single individual, invariably a programmer who knew how to write code in a traditional programming language, such as C or assembly. Any programming language would do; and those who were to become players didn't have any preconceptions about how the output ought to look, what it should sound like, or whether or not the character AI could pass a Turing test.

Simple games with clearly defined rules rarely need to be anything other than a closed system. That is as true today as it was in the beginning. But video games evolved. And so did the players. Fast-forward some 45 years since the very earliest computer games, to early 2006. Many games today are complex. It is not uncommon for the code base of a modern game to reach a million lines of code written in C++, developed by a team of programmers during a production cycle that might last a year or two. Art content for games and much of the game design is now created by people who are not programmers. Games have become data-driven products. Hardcore gamers today expect animations to be realistic. They expect dramatic audio effects to play when emergent events occur and for AI-controlled characters to behave as realistically as possible. The content of complex video games regularly exceeds the capacity of multiple CD-ROM disks, and contains 3D models, textures, and animations for hundreds or thousands of game objects and characters. Beyond coding the game engine, gameplay features, and behaviors, the management of such large numbers of game objects, from the point of view of artists and programmers alike, brings another complexity into the fold.

Scripting languages these days are commonly integrated into games for the benefit of all the people involved in making games, as well as the players themselves. Programmers, for example, can use an integrated scripting language to access engine features and debug a release build of the game, or debug on a computer where development tools or source code are not installed. They might also use scripting to more rapidly develop some functionality, such as a finite-state machine for an AI system, or a task-management system. A scripting language can have a far simpler syntax than C++, and the simplicity can enable a game designer to implement a gameplay feature without having to wait for the programming staff to find time to write a C++ function and rebuild the game application. Along the same lines, artists who know how to write scripts for digital content-creation tools such as 3ds Max or Maya can easily learn how to use game-integrated scripting to implement animation triggers and to play in-game cinematic sequences. Game players all over the world are even now writing game scripts to create their own custom mods for their favorite games.

Nowadays, scripting languages, like game engines, are ubiquitous. Gone are the days when the only way a studio could provide scripting support was to develop a custom scripting language system from the ground up. We are at the stage now where studios can pick and choose among several production-quality, off-the-shelf scripting systems, based on their need for high performance, mirroring of game engine objects within the scripting system, multithreading, networking, or simply—simplicity.

With all the options out there now, new challenges exist: How can a studio choose the appropriate scripting system, and how can developers best exploit the features of the system to maximize the benefits without introducing undue risk that the game application will break as a result? The scripting articles in this section provide a number of gems that will make it easier to meet these challenges.

First up, Diego Garcés provides a detailed survey of several scripting languages that are popular in game development circles, and gives advice about when a specific feature might be particularly beneficial or problematic. Next, Waldemar Celes, Luiz Henrique de Figueiredo, and Roberto Ierusalimschy offer a pair of articles that will help you with Lua development. First, they provide a detailed look at various approaches to binding C++ objects to Lua. Next, they discuss various practical uses of Lua co-routines, ranging from intuitive list iterators to the management of cooperate multitasking. Sébastien Schertenleib then presents an approach to using microthreads in Python, which facilitates robust development of cooperative multitasking code for games that need to manage hundreds of simultaneous tasks in real-time.

Scripting systems work best when the C++ engine they expose is written in an intuitive and optimal way. Because of the data-driven nature of modern games, it is important that game engines reflect the nature of the content in a natural way. It is not at all a trivial task to design the architecture for a game, and poor design decisions up front can lead to an escalation of development and QA costs, poor performance in the end, and even a failure to complete the project. There are two articles on data-driven architecture in this section, which discuss alternative approaches to representing game objects. Both of these articles describe engine architectures that can be mapped intuitively into a scripting system. Matthew Campbell and Curtiss Murphy present a framework for exposing the properties of game actors via proxy objects in a way that can readily integrate game engine objects into artists' tools (e.g., level editors and the like) or high-level runtime subsystems, such as messaging frameworks. Chris Stoy presents a game object component system that organizes and simplifies and the bloat of C++ objects that is often the result of ad-hoc or quick-and-dirty game engine design, and enables simpler runtime composition of objects.

The processes that studios apply toward developing games these days are more sophisticated than ever before; however, it seems many teams remain plagued by inadequate planning, delays, and an inability to react quickly when their publisher changes requirements. A well-designed, data-driven software framework combined with a flexible scripting system can enable your team to rapidly ramp up production, and to change direction when it becomes necessary. Use the gems contained herein during the planning or pre-production phase of your next game project to develop a new framework or improve your existing framework. The wisdom that these authors impart is guaranteed to improve your team's ability to deliver a quality title in time for the holiday rush!

4.1

Scripting Language Survey

Diego Garcés, FX Interactive

diegogarces@gmail.com

Why Use a Scripting Language?

Over the past several years, scripting languages have become popular tools in the development of computer and video games, and for good reason. Scripting languages can control multiple aspects of a game's execution. For example, they can control animated sequences, the behavior of an enemy NPC, or how an AI-controlled party member reacts to the player's instructions. These are parts of the game that are created by artists, designers, or players. Scripting languages can enable these team members to modify or create these behaviors.

Scripting languages also enable rapid prototyping, which is gaining popularity in the game community. Building an early prototype of your game allows testing gameplay issues and trying different approaches at the beginning of the development cycle. Following the same philosophy, scripting allows quick changes without long compilation times, and possibly without reloading the game.

Introduction

There are many scripting languages available. This article does not try to cover all possible options, but only a few of the most popular ones in game development, as well as a few that are emerging:

- Python™
- Lua
- GameMonkey
- AngelScript

Lua [Lua05] and Python [Python05] are part of successful commercial games, while GameMonkey [GameMonkey05] and AngelScript [AngelScript05] are young and still introducing themselves to the game community.

Scripting languages share some common characteristics, but when choosing a scripting language, you must consider the following:

Language coding: Language features and ease of coding.

Integration with C/C++:   Scripting languages are mostly extension languages to the main core in C++. It is important that data exchange between the core engine and the script does not require too much programming effort, and is powerful enough and efficient for project requirements.

Performance: Scripts are not used in performance-critical parts of the game. Still, too much memory consumption could be an issue on console platforms, and slow execution of certain tasks can have an impact on the game's frame rate.

Development-support features: Additional tools or facilities that simplify the use of the scripting language can dramatically increase a developer's productivity. Good debug, profiling, and logging tools can make a difference between fast problem solving and long crunch times.

Language Coding

Universal Features

Scripting languages all share some common characteristics, because they all have some similar goals in their design.

Scripting languages are interpreted languages. They are not compiled to machine code, and thus they need a virtual machine to execute them. This feature makes these languages slower. At the same time it adds flexibility, with the possibility of adjusting the code while the game is running, allowing fast tweaking of algorithms or game parameters. To reduce execution time, script code can usually be compiled to byte code (an intermediate binary form of the script), although this also has to be executed by the virtual machine.

Scripting languages are high-level languages. They make use of automatic memory management, making it possible to forget about pointers, access violations, and memory leaks. High-level structures like lists and tables allow programmers to focus their efforts on the algorithm instead of the data treatment.

Scripting languages provide flexibility in flow control. Flow control and iteration features are very similar among all the scripting languages; but they are always characterized by flexible and simple-to-use instructions (e.g., easy iteration over the elements of a list or table).

Features That Are Not Universal

Different design philosophies sometimes lead to scripting languages taking different approaches to solving the same problem. This section (by no means exhaustive) describes how the languages choose to approach several important problems. The complete list of features provided by complex languages like Python, with all its extensions, is far beyond the scope of this article.

Type Safety, Argument Passing, and Memory Management

AngelScript is a strongly typed language. Parameters and variables have a fixed type and cannot hold values of different types. Type-checking is performed when the script is compiled to byte code. A comparison of fixed versus dynamic typed languages is shown in Table 4.1.1.

The rest of the languages are dynamically typed. Both simple variables and containers can store values of different types. Even functions can be stored, as they are treated as first-class values. This has been traditionally a popular feature in functional programming with the Lisp language, widely used for academic AI research.

Table 4.1.1 Comparison of Fixed Versus Dynamic Typed Languages

Python	Lua/GameMonkey	AngelScript
f = 3.1415	f = 3.1415;	float f = 3.1415;
f = True	f = true;	f = true; // Error
f = "hello world"	f = "hello world";	

AngelScript requires the declaration of variables prior to their use, while Python, Lua, and GameMonkey create variables when they are first assigned. In Lua, you have to declare a variable as local if you do not want it to be global. In GameMonkey, you have to declare a variable as global, otherwise it is local.

Functions in Lua, Python, and GameMonkey can receive an arbitrary number of parameters, and return multiple values. In Lua, extra parameters are discarded, while parameters not supplied are assigned the *nil* value (a special value to represent the absence of value, which also serves as the Boolean value *false*). Table 4.1.2 gives examples of multiple-argument and return-value use among these languages.

Table 4.1.2 Examples of the Use of Multiple Arguments and Return Values

Python	Lua
```def f(a,b,c = False): if (c): return a+b,a*b else: return a-b,a/b,a+b```	```function f(a,b,c) if (c) then return a+b,a*b; else return a-b,a/b,a+b; endend```

Example Usage:
`d,e = f(2,4,True)`
`# Result is 6,8`
	Example Usage:
	`d,e = f(2,4,true)`
	`-- Result is 6,8`

`g,h,i = f(4,2)` `# Result is 2,2,6`	`g,h,i = f(4,2)` `-- Result is 2,2,6`
`g,h,i = f(4,2,True)` `# An error results`	`g,h,i = f(4,2,true)` `-- Result is 2,2,nil`
`j,k = f(2,4,True,20,30)` `# An error results`	`j,k = f(2,4,true,20,30)` `-- Result is 6,8`
`k = f(6,2)` `# Result is 4,3,8`	`k = f(6,2)` `-- Result is 4`
`k, l = f(4,2)` `# An error results`	`k,l = f(6,2)` `-- Result is 4,3`
`k = f(b = 2,a = 6)` `# Result is 4,3,8`	`k = f(b = 2,a = 6)` `-- Not possible`

Based on automatic memory management, all the languages discussed here offer some kind of dynamic container. Python has the largest variety of dynamic structures, with lists, tuples, sets, and dictionaries as built-in types. Tables are the data type used in Lua and GameMonkey to implement containers and objects, mimicking the behavior of maps, arrays, trees, or classes (see Table 4.1.3). AngelScript has a dynamic-array built-in type.

Table 4.1.3 Examples of Tuples, Lists, and Tables

Python	GameMonkey
```pot1 = HealPotion()pot2 = HealPotion()pot3 = ManaPotion()weapon1 = Sword()gold = 20.5```	```pot1 = HealPotion();pot2 = HealPotion();pot3 = ManaPotion();weapon1 = Sword();gold = 20.5;```

→

Python	GameMonkey
```bag = pot1, pot2, pot3``` `backpack = [weapon1, bag, gold]` `# bag is a tuple` `# backpack is a list`	```bag = {pot1, pot2, pot3};``` `backpack = {weapon1, bag, gold};` `// bag and backpack both tables`

Inheritance and Object-Oriented Programming

Scripting languages are often used to build quick prototypes of portions of a game, or even the whole game. Support in the scripting language for object-oriented programming is a great help, since most games nowadays are built upon objects. Only Python provides classic out-of-the-box object support. Easy definition and handling of objects are provided with single and multiple inheritance. As shown in Table 4.1.4, Lua and GameMonkey use tables to simulate classes. Since functions are first-class values, they can be stored in tables and act as methods. Inheritance is also possible in Lua, but requires some advanced programming with metatables (e.g., callbacks for some conditions, like access to nonexistent items). AngelScript, as an extension language, just provides access to C++ classes. Virtual functions are not generally an issue, because containers and functions can actually use derived values.

Table 4.1.4 Comparison of Native and Table-Based Object Programming

Python	Lua

```class Soldier:``` `    "Soldier base class"` `    def TakeDamage(self,iDamage):` `        self.iHealth-=iDamage;` `    iHealth=200` `    def Print(self):` `        print "Soldier Health:"` `        print self.iHealth`
 	
 `class Sniper(Soldier):` `    "Sniper derived class"` `    def Print(self):` `        print "Sniper Health:"` `        print self.iHealth`
	```Soldier={}``` `S_mt={__index=Soldier}` `function Soldier:new()` `    return` `        setmetatable({iH=200},S_mt)` `end`
	
	 `function Soldier:TakeDamage(iDamage)` `    self.iH = self.iH-iDamage` `end`
	
	 `function Soldier:Print()` `    print("Soldier Health:",self.iH)` `end`
	
	 `Sniper = {}` `Sn_base_mt={__index=Soldier}` `setmetatable(Sniper,Sn_base_mt)` `Sn_mt={__index=Sniper}` `function Sniper:new()` `    return` `        setmetatable(Soldier:new(),Sn_mt)` `end` `function Sniper:Print()` `    print("Sniper Health:",self.iH)` `end`

Language-Specific Issues

Lua has tail calls—a calling mechanism that allows the lightweight use of recursive algorithms. It reuses the same stack for the new function, thus eliminating most of the overhead of a new call. This is only possible if the call is the last expression of the current function, as illustrated in Listing 4.1.1.

Listing 4.1.1   Example of Using Lua Tail Calls

```
function Hanoi(n, sA, sB, sC)
    if (n == 1) then
        print("Move disk from",sA,"to",sB)
    else
        Hanoi(n-1,sA,sC,sB)
        print("Move disk from",sA,"to",sB)
        return Hanoi(n-1,sC,sB,sA) -- tail call: reuse of stack
    end
end
```

Metatables are callbacks executed upon certain operations with values. They are part of the Lua feature list, and at first were only available for tables and C objects. In version 5.1, every data type has its own metatable. Their main uses are helping in the binding of classes from C++ and providing support for objects based on tables; however, there are many other possible uses for metatables.

GameMonkey natively supports the concept of state, which is widely used in AI finite-state machines, and natively provides functionality to stop the execution of a function at any point, jump to another function, and simulate a state change.

Integration with C/C++

This section discusses how developers can integrate these scripting languages with C++. There are several aspects to consider in the integration:

- Global variable-sharing
- Using the script from C++ code
- Accessing C++ features from the script

General Description

Python

The Python/C API is provided to make data- and functionality-exchange possible, with functions to build Python values from C++, call Python functions, and register C++ callbacks to be called from Python. The process of binding standard Python with C++ is not a simple or easy task. A lot of code is needed, and it soon becomes very large and error-prone. It is often more convenient to use a system of automating the integration of Python into a C- or C++-based game. You could use a homemade system if you have enough time and resources, or use one of the freely available ones, like Boost.Python, or Swig.

Lua

The exchange of information between Lua and C++ is done via a virtual stack that the Lua runtime manages. Each function call has its own stack. This means that if you call a C++ function that calls a Lua function, a new stack will be created for this interchange of values. To provide more flexibility, it is not a pure stack, and its data can be accessed with indices. Positive indices access the stack from the bottom, while negative indices access it from the top.

AngelScript

AngelScript shares the calling convention of C++, as this is one of the goals in its design. Because of that, no proxy functions are needed to integrate scripts into C++ code, and this reduces the amount of effort required to share a function.

GameMonkey

GameMonkey supports easy integration with C++, as this was one of its design goals. Though GameMonkey supports limited object-oriented programming via the use of tables, it is not an object-oriented language and lacks support for class inheritance, polymorphism, and function overloads. Even so, class support can be implemented with extra programming; and if you do not need complex object-oriented programming, GameMonkey could perfectly satisfy your needs.

Global Variable-Sharing

Complete access to global variables defined in a script is possible in Lua, AngelScript, and GameMonkey. Lua and GameMonkey let you access a global table that contains global variables, while AngelScript offers API functions to retrieve a pointer to a global variable. Global constants in Python can be accessed from C++.

Variables defined in C++ can be registered easily for their access from script code in AngelScript. Lua and GameMonkey use the global table to store user data from C++ so that it can be accessible from script functions.

Using the Script from C++ Code

Scripting languages are used as an extension to the core C++ engine. From the C++ perspective, it is required to be able to call a script function. The process consists of passing arguments, starting execution, and retrieving returned values.

The Python programmer has to convert all parameters to Python objects and then group them in a tuple that will be passed as a unique argument. In Lua, parameters are stored on the stack, while in AngelScript and GameMonkey, they are added to helper classes, an `asIScriptContext` or a `gmCall`, respectively, which are initialized with the name of the function to be called.

In the case of Python and Lua, calling the function is performed with specific API calls. In AngelScript and GameMonkey, a method of their helper classes starts the script execution.

Once the function has finished, it is time to get the results. GameMonkey and AngelScript only can retrieve one returned value, which is done by accessing the helper classes again. Only one value is returned by the call to a Python function from C++, but it can be a tuple grouping several values. Lua also allows multiple return values. They will be pushed onto the stack, where they can be retrieved by the C++ function after the script execution. Table 4.1.5 compares methods for calling script functions.

Table 4.1.5   Methods for Calling Script Functions

Python	Lua

`d=PyModule_GetDict(module);`
`func=PyDict_GetItemString(d,`
`    "Attack");`
`arg=Py_BuildValue("si","Grunt",`
`    iDice);`
`res=PyObject_CallObject(func,`
`    arg);`
`PyArg_ParseTuple(res,"ff",`
`    &fDamageReceived,`
`    &fDamageInflicted);`
	`lua_pushstring(L,"Attack");`
	`lua_gettable(L,LUA_GLOBALSINDEX);`
	`lua_pushstring(L,"Grunt");`
	`lua_pushnumber(iDice);`
	`lua_call(L,2,2);`
	`fDamageInflicted=lua_tonumber(L,-1);`
	`lua_pop(L,1);`
	`fDamageReceived=lua_tonumber(L,-1);`
	`lua_pop(L,1);`

GameMonkey	**AngelScript**

`gmMachine m;`
`gmCall call;`
`call.BeginGlobalFunction(&m,`
`    "Attack"))`
`call.AddParamString("Grunt");`
`call.AddParamInt(iDice);`
`call.End();`
`call.GetReturnedFloat(fDmgRcvd)`
`// DamageInflicted cannot be`
`// obtained`
	`engine->CreateContext(&context);`
	`fID=engine->GetFunctionIDByDecl(`
	`    "module", "floatAttack(int,int)");`
	`context->Prepare(fID);`
	`context->SetArgDWord(0,GRNTID);`
	`context->SetArgDWord(1,iDice);`
	`context->Execute();`
	`fDamageReceived=`
	`    context->GetReturnFloat();`
	`// DamageInflicted cannot be`
	`// obtained`

Accessing C++ Features from the Script

Usually, the calling convention is different between scripting languages and C++. Because of that, proxy functions (see Table 4.1.6) need to be written for each function we want to call from a script. The exception to this rule is AngelScript, which was designed to simplify binding with C++ and shares its calling convention.

In Python, these proxy functions receive a Python object containing the parameters, and also return a Python object with the results. In Lua and GameMonkey, they receive a state structure—Lua_State and gmThread—that allows retrieving the parameters and sending the results back to the script, among other useful operations.

Table 4.1.6 Examples of Proxy Functions

Python	GameMonkey
```PyObject* AttackP(PyObject* self, PyObject* args) { PyArg_ParseTuple(args,"si", szEnemy,&iDice); Attack(szEnem,iDice, fDamageReceived, fDamageInflicted); return Py_BuildValue("ff", fDamageReceived, fDamageInflicted); }```	```int _cdecl AttackP(gmThread* th) { GM_CHECK_NUM_PARAMS(2); GM_CHECK_STRING_PARAM(szEnem,0); GM_CHECK_INT_PARAM(iDice,1); Attack(szEnemy,iDice, fDamageRec, fDamageInf); th->PushFloat(fDamageRec); th->PushFloat(fDamageInf); return GM_OK }```

The scripting virtual machine does not have any means to find a C++ function on its own. We have to tell it where to find this function and what its name will be in the scripting scope. Python and GameMonkey require the developer to fill in a structure for all the functions of a library or module, with the name and a pointer to the proxy function. The developer must then register them all with a single API call. Lua and AngelScript export global functions, registering each one individually, and without any intermediate structure. Table 4.1.7 compares these two registration methods.

Table 4.1.7 Comparison of Individual Versus Structure-Based Registration of Functions

Lua	GameMonkey
```lua_register(L,"Attack", AttackP); lua_register(L,"Attack2", AttackP);```	```static gmFunctionEntry s_AttLib[]= {"Attack",AttackP}, {"Attack2",Attack2P}, ... }; machine->RegisterLibrary(s_AttLib, sizeof(s_AttLib)/sizeof(s_AttLib[0]));```

AngelScript allows C++ methods to be registered with the same mechanism as global functions, without any modification. Python, Lua, and GameMonkey can only register static methods. This is because the address of a method can only be obtained if it is declared as static. These static methods can act as proxy functions that receive an extra parameter with the object instance to be used, and then use this instance to call the real method. Functionality is provided at the expense of a double indirection.

AngelScript easily exports classes to the script with a single call to the API. Python, Lua, and GameMonkey also have mechanisms to do this, but they require some extra programming that can be complex. These tasks are usually performed by means of binding tools.

Binding Tools

As we have seen, the exchange of data between C/C++ and the scripting language can be a complex task. For this reason, the Python and Lua communities have developed automatic wrappers to help in the integration of the scripting language. GameMonkey also has an automatic binding tool, but it's still in the early stages of development. To avoid a lot of copy-and-paste errors, it is important to invest effort in building a custom binding tool, or in learning how to properly use one of these tools, thus ensuring that you have a robust way of sharing features and data between C++ and script.

Python—Swig

Swig is a tool that acts as a C preprocessor. It takes as input an interface file, written by the developer, and outputs source files in C++ and Python, which must be included in the game compilation. This interface file describes all the C++ features that are being exposed to Python, such as functions, classes, and global variables.

Swig provides an automated mechanism to generate shadow classes out of C++ classes. These are Python classes that behave like their C++ counterparts. By using them, you can have clean Python code while using the C++ implementation. Since the shadow classes are real Python classes, they can also be used as base classes in an inheritance hierarchy.

Virtual calls overridden in Python are supported by Swig with the use of *directors*. These are intermediary objects that forward method calls to the appropriate implementation, whether it is in C++ or Python. They add considerable overhead in memory and CPU time. For this reason, they are only recommended when a Python override of a C++ method will be written.

Overloaded functions and operators are supported, except when Swig cannot distinguish between parameter types (e.g., between `int` and `short`).

Exceptions can be propagated and even generated from error values returned by C functions, but additional work is required in the interface file. Table 4.1.8 shows an example of a Swig interface.

Table 4.1.8 Example of a Simple Swig Interface

C++ Header File (soldier.h)	Swig Interface File
| ```
class Soldier
{
public:
    void TakeDamage(int iDamage);
    void Print();
}
``` | ```
%module Army
%{
#include "soldier.h"
%}
``` |

Python—Boost.Python

Boost.Python is a library that relies on meta-programming to help in the integration of C++ with Python. One of the goals of this system is to be as seamless as possible. This means that it won't require major modifications of the C++ code to export features to Python.

C++ classes can be exposed to Python by writing some C++ code, with a syntax very similar to Python, to describe the methods and data members we want to export. Listing 4.1.2 shows an example.

Listing 4.1.2 Exposing a C++ Class with Boost.Python

```
#include <boost/python.hpp>
BOOST_PYTHON_MODULE(Army)
{
    class_<Soldier>("Soldier")
        .def("TakeDamage", &Soldier::TakeDamage)
        .def("Print", &Soldier::Print);
}
```

Boost.Python also supports constructors with parameters and data members exported as properties. Properties will be seen from Python as public data members, but internally they make use of accessors.

C++ inheritance must be represented in the class definition and will have the expected behavior in Python code. New Python classes can be derived from wrapped C++ classes, but if we want to call virtually overridden methods in Python, we will have to build a dispatcher class that calls the Python function, if present. *Pyste*, a contributed extension, can be used to simplify this task.

Function overloads and operators are exported the same way as functions with default parameters—a separate registration for each overload, and the number of parameters, respectively.

Exceptions that occur while executing Python code called from C++ can be automatically propagated and translated.

Boost.Python provides some special features, including the ability to use C++ iterators from Python code like they were Python iterators, and some support for the reverse. The object interface, with its derived classes for Python common types, is part of the Boost.Python library, and encapsulates the use of Python data types within C++ code.

Lua—ToLua++

Like Swig, ToLua++ takes as input a package file (basically a list of header files) and outputs some C++ code that implements the binding for you. The difference is that with ToLua++, it is usually sufficient to include some extra comments in regular header files and include them in the package file.

Classes are exported by ToLua++ without much effort, requiring only a clean C++ definition of the class, with the methods and data members to export. The user can then use these classes as Lua classes and perform all the permitted operations with them. Single inheritance and polymorphism are supported transparently, but multiple inheritance requires specifying the extra base classes when accessing their members.

Overloaded functions and operators are supported, but operators must be part of a class; they cannot be external functions.

Lua—LuaPlus

LuaPlus does not try to solve the same problems as ToLua++. It is a wrapper to integrate C++, but also provides some extensions and modifications to the Lua core, including a modified version of the Lua distribution. Therefore, if you want to use the latest build of the official Lua distribution, LuaPlus may not be the best option.

LuaPlus does not provide complete C++ exporting power. LuaPlus lets the user register functions and class methods to be seen within Lua as global functions, building closures or functors automatically. However, LuaPlus doesn't provide support for cross-language inheritance or function overloading. The function-dispatching mechanism is not as powerful as ToLua++.

LuaPlus offers some extra utilities to ease the use of Lua from C++, which are not available in other binding solutions. These extra features are an encapsulation of the Lua state (`LuaState`) and Lua objects (`LuaObject`). With `LuaState`, the C++ programmer can initialize Lua, perform operations with the stack, and access global variables or the registry easily. `LuaObject` provides an encapsulation of Lua objects that is not based on the stack. With it, the C++ programmer can forget about the Lua stack, and the use of Lua objects from C++ code becomes extremely simple.

Performance Features

Memory Management

These scripting languages are high-level languages; and because of that, they all implement automatic memory management. Complex tasks, like allocating memory for structures, freeing memory when they are no longer used, or solving memory leaks or access violations, can be forgotten with these scripting languages. Still, careful consideration of memory issues applies. Freeing memory at inappropriate times can make an impact on frame rate. Too much memory consumption or memory fragmentation can be a performance killer in console platforms.

Reference Counting

Reference counting is a technique where each object stores the number of references to it held by other objects. If an object reference count reaches zero, it means that no other object needs to access it in the future, so it can be deleted from memory. Python and AngelScript rely on this mechanism for their memory management, though both have also implemented garbage-collection algorithms.

With reference counting, it is possible to create reference cycles that prevent objects from being freed. Figure 4.1.1 shows an example. In this particular case, even if all the external references to the Tank object are released, it will not be freed, since it has still one reference left (the one from Turret). The problem is that Turret is referenced by Soldier, so it will not be freed; and Soldier is referenced by Tank, which completes the cycle. None of them will ever be released, even when they are no longer used by any object outside the cycle. If no other automatic memory management system is provided, the script author must take care to avoid such cycles. Garbage collection, described in the next section, provides a way to automatically break reference cycles.

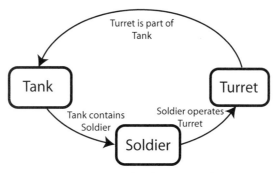

FIGURE 4.1.1   *Example of circular reference.*

Access to free a chunk of memory is a costly operation. Because of that, the advantage of reference-counting is that freeing memory is distributed over time. Each time an object becomes unreferenced, some time is lost, depending on the size of the object. Usually there is not a noticeable slowdown.

Garbage Collection

As an alternative to reference counting, garbage collection does not keep any extra information to know when an object is not referenced. This information is computed in each garbage collection cycle by traversing the entire object hierarchy from the root elements. Root elements (e.g., threads and global variables) store references to some other objects, which are also traversed until no new objects are found. Objects get a mark when a reference to them is found so that the scripting language runtime will not try to free them. When the traversing process has finished, all the objects with no mark can be garbage-collected. This traversing and freeing process is generally known as *mark and sweep*.

A simplified version of a typical war game's object hierarchy can be seen in Figure 4.1.2. The world is composed of a Tank, a Soldier, and a Squad that can also be further decomposed into smaller components, including Privates. In order to find out if a Private object can be deleted, the garbage collector must traverse the Squad object. The Private object will get a mark, and so will not be deleted. When the Private dies, an artificial-intelligence algorithm will remove its reference from the Squad object. Since no other object references it, the Private will not be marked by the next mark and sweep cycle, and thus it will then be deleted from memory.

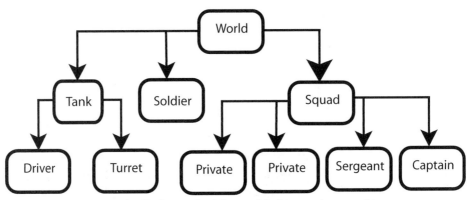

FIGURE 4.1.2   *Example of a hierarchy. The world object is the root object.*

If the mark-and-sweep process is performed in one step, it is called "full garbage collection." A full garbage collection cycle can take a lot of time, especially in a busy system, and is a traditional reason for not using garbage-collection languages in real-time applications like games. To solve this problem, incremental garbage collection was born. It consists of distributing the mark-and-sweep operation over several frames, minimizing the impact on frame rate produced by garbage operations.

As described in the previous section, reference cycles cannot be addressed only with reference counting, since all the objects within the cycle will have at least one reference and will never be freed. Garbage collection provides a solution to this problem. Python and AngelScript have implemented a small garbage-collection cycle to free objects that exist in circular reference cycles.

GameMonkey supports both full and incremental garbage collection. The garbage-collection process is customizable in the number of child objects to inspect per call, so that large hierarchies of objects to be marked will not block the system for long. It is also possible to configure memory limits to select when the garbage collector will run. A soft limit tells the virtual machine that when memory used surpasses this number, the incremental garbage collection is started. A hard limit adds a threshold to start a full garbage collection.

Lua, beginning with version 5.1, has available incremental garbage collection. It was a long-requested feature, since most of the performance problems with Lua were caused by the use of full garbage collection.

If incremental garbage collection isn't enough for our frame-rate requirements, GameMonkey and Lua provide functions to perform garbage collection immediately at the end of the logic tick, for example, to avoid possible freeze times in the middle of a frame.

Custom Memory Manager

Memory available on console platforms is limited. Because of this, memory issues like fragmentation of the system memory into small chunks can ruin performance, and the lack of sufficient contiguous memory can cause allocation failures. If the scripting language used in the game is allocating memory directly from the system, the complete control over memory allocations is lost, and fragmentation can lead to catastrophic application failures. To address these problems, console games often include a proprietary memory manager that allocates and frees memory independently from the operating system.

GameMonkey and AngelScript allow for easy integration of custom memory management, and provide callbacks when memory needs to be reserved or freed for an object. Adding custom memory allocation to Lua or Python is more complex. It requires changes to their internal code. Still, since they are both open-source distributions and well documented, it is a feasible task.

Profiling

Python offers the developer two modules in its standard library for profiling tasks. The *Profile* module allows running a function and storing profiling data about that execution. The *Pstats* module provides a means for inspecting the contents of these profiled data.

The latest versions of Python have replaced the *Profile* module with the *Hotshot* module, which is written in C and provides more-seamless operation. Other modules worth exploring are the *Trace* and *Timeit* modules, which trace execution of whole scripts and perform fine-grain timing measurements, respectively. In addition, some commercial profilers for Python are being developed and tested.

Profiling in Lua and AngelScript can be done using the hooks explained above to collect timings for functions or fragments of code. *LuaProfiler* is a package to profile Lua code. With it, it is very simple to obtain a log of function calls and time consumed by them.

Development Support Features

In this section we try to explain some important issues that a game developer must take into consideration, since they can really make the difference when working with a language.

Multithread-capable operating systems and CPUs are now the norm; however, developing optimum, robust multithreaded applications is a difficult task. Languages that provide features to facilitate multithreaded development can greatly improve a developer's productivity.

The availability of a debugger or profiler may be more important than any feature the language can offer. Good tools are a very important factor in completing a game project successfully, but game developers do not always have the time and resources to build good proprietary tools. A developer's coding time can be greatly reduced if the scripting language has good built-in support for memory management and multi-threading—both of which traditionally consume significant development time.

Multithreading

Python, in its current standard implementation, is not completely thread safe. It makes use of a global lock called GIL to block the access to shared resources. This exclusive access is required for a variety of operations, like accessing a global variable or calling a C function.

Both Python and Lua provide classes to simulate a multithread system. These classes are *Generators* in Python and *Coroutines* in Lua. They can facilitate the continued execution of other functions, but they cannot be scheduled out by the system. The same applies to GameMonkey and its native, cooperative thread support. GameMonkey thread support was one of the language design goals, and because of that, there is more support here than can be found in the other languages. Threads in GameMonkey can be blocked or set to sleep until a certain game or system event wakes them up.

If multiple scripts make use of different Lua states, they can be executed at the same time by multiple threads, so it may be possible to execute a Lua script for each game entity in parallel. GameMonkey can also support execution from multiple threads, because its functions are thread-safe. Still, the compilation of scripts, based on flex, is not thread-safe, and it is necessary to precompile the scripts or implement exclusive access to the script compiler in the game engine.

Debugging Facilities

Debugging has been traditionally forgotten by scripting languages, and looking for errors in scripts can be a hard and time-consuming task. As scripting languages are becoming widely used in the game environment, the requirement for good debugging tools is more important.

Python has some modules available, such as the *Logging* package, to help the programmer with debugging issues. The *Pdb* module supports setting breakpoints, stepping through code or inspecting stack frames. The class provided by this module is also extensible, letting the user customize the debugging functionality as needed.

In addition, it's possible to find external debuggers, HAP being the most famous. HAP was developed by game developer Humongous Entertainment™. HAP has a lot of features and has gained acceptance in the Python community, especially among game developers.

Lua doesn't provide any built-in debugging tools. Instead, the language provides hooks and helper functions to get information about the runtime stack, or to access local variables when the function is not active. There are hooks available to introduce custom behavior when a function is called, when a function returns, when a new line inside a Lua function starts to execute, and when a number of instructions have been executed. With these tools, it is not very difficult to build a custom debugger to perform simple tasks (and in fact, some third-party Lua debuggers currently exist). If we are using LuaPlus as the binding interface, we can make use of its remote debugger as an add-in to a widely used, Windows-based development environment.

GameMonkey has a native function to set a break point inside the code. Moreover, it is possible to set asserts inside GameMonkey code to ensure a certain condition is true, throwing an exception otherwise, which could be captured by the application and show a message or any other engine-specific task.

GameMonkey also provides callbacks for the virtual machine, which are called under certain conditions, like when an exception is thrown, garbage collection starts, a thread is created, or a thread is destroyed. An example debugger comes with the standard GameMonkey distribution. It is simple, but it can be extended with the mechanisms provided.

AngelScript relies on callbacks to provide debugging support. For each statement executed, a callback function can be called, and this function can perform any required debug treatment, like suspending execution for a breakpoint. Support for inspecting variable values will be possible in the near future.

Unit testing is another debugging mechanism that is gaining support nowadays. It has been implemented in Python and Lua. PyUnit is a framework that is now part of the Python standard library. Lunit and Luaunit are tools developed by the Lua community for unit-testing Lua programs. Luaunit is based in the PyUnit framework.

Conclusion

This article describes the differences between four scripting languages—Python, Lua, GameMonkey, and AngelScript—so that developers can choose the one best suited for their game project.

Python was not conceived to be just an extension language, while Lua, Game Monkey, and AngelScript were designed at first to be just that. This makes Python seem the most complete and complex language in terms of features provided by the language, though it is not very far away from Lua and GameMonkey in functionality. In any case, it is arguable and project-dependent whether such a rich set of features is really needed or worth paying the price for in memory or speed for the target platform.

GameMonkey and AngelScript have a C++-like syntax. This may add some extra complexity at first for nonprogrammers, who are usually more comfortable with pseudo-code syntax. But, the familiar syntax helps programmers to transition from C++ coding to scripting. Most complex scripts will require at least programmer assistance, and a change of syntax is prone to errors and slowdowns, which a game developer cannot afford when on a tight schedule. Depending on the role assignment in the studio, C++ syntax may be an important feature to consider.

Traditionally, script programming was associated with being a difficult and tedious task, due to the lack of proper tools. Today this no longer applies. Good editing, debugging, logging, and profiling tools are available for Python, Lua, and GameMonkey. AngelScript currently does not have many external tools. As the languages become more popular, better tools will make it even easier to write scripts for games.

References

[AngelScript05] Jönsson, Andreas, "AngelCode Scripting Library (AngelScript)." 2005. Available online at *http://www.angelcode.com/angelscript*.

[GameMonkey05] Riek, Matthew and Greg Douglas, "GameMonkey Script." 2005. Available online at *http://www.somedude.net/gamemonkey*.

[Lua05] Ierusalimschy, Roberto, Luiz Henrique de Figueiredo, and Waldemar Celes, "The Programming Language Lua." 2005. Available online at *http://www.lua.org*.

[Python05] van Rossum, Guido, "Python Programming Language." 2005. Available online at *http://www.python.org*.

4.2

Binding C/C++ Objects to Lua

Waldemar Celes, PUC-Rio

celes@inf.puc-rio.br

Luiz Henrique de Figueiredo, IMPA

lhf@impa.br

Roberto Ierusalimschy, PUC-Rio

roberto@inf.puc-rio.br

The use of scripting languages in games has become a standard practice. Scripting languages can play an important role in the development of games, and facilitate tasks such as data structuring, event scheduling, testing, and debugging. Scripting languages also allow artists and designers who are not expert programmers to productively code the game by means of a high-level, abstract scripting layer. Part of such an abstract layer can also be made available to the players for game customization.

From the programmer's point of view, a major issue when embedding a scripting language in a game is how to provide access to the host objects (typically C/C++ objects). Two features are critical when choosing a scripting language: ease of embedding and ease of binding. One reason for the success of Lua as a scripting language is that it is easy to embed; this was one of the original design goals of Lua. However, Lua does not come with tools for creating bindings automatically, because another design goal of Lua is to provide mechanisms, not policy.

As a consequence, there are multiple strategies for binding host objects to Lua. Each strategy has advantages and drawbacks, and game developers have to identify the best strategy to expose the desired functionality to the scripting environment. Some developers may map C/C++ objects as simple values, while others may need to implement mechanisms that allow runtime-type checking, or to extend the services provided by the host in Lua. Another important issue that must be addressed is whether to allow

Lua to control the lifetime of host objects. In this article, we explore different strategies to bind host objects using Lua's API [Ierusalimschy03].

Binding Functions

To illustrate the implementation of different strategies, let us consider the binding of a simple C++ class to Lua. The goal is to have access to the class in Lua, thus allowing the scripter to use the services provided by the host through the exposed methods. The same techniques can, of course, be applied to C code and to map more complex classes. The main idea here is to use a simple class to drive the discussion. The class under consideration represents the Hero of a hypothetical game, with a few illustrative public methods being mapped to Lua:

```
class Hero {
public:
    Hero (const char* name);
    ~Hero ();
    const char* GetName ();
    void SetEnergy (double energy);
    double GetEnergy ();
};
```

To bind the class methods to Lua, we have to write *binding functions*, using the Lua API. Each binding function is responsible for receiving Lua values as input parameters, converting them to the corresponding C/C++ values, calling the actual function/method, and then converting the returned values back to Lua. The Lua API and the auxiliary library, which come with the standard distribution of Lua, expose several handy functions that ease the conversion from Lua to C/C++ values, and vice-versa. For instance, the function `luaL_checknumber` converts an input parameter into the corresponding floating-point value (double). If the parameter does not correspond to a number in Lua, the function raises an error. Conversely, the function `lua_pushnumber` pushes a number that corresponds to the provided floating-point value on the top of the Lua stack. Similar functions exist to map other basic Lua and C/C++ types. Our main goal here is to present different strategies to extend the standard library and provide functions for converting C/C++-type objects. In order to use C++ parlance, let us create a concrete class named Binder to encapsulate the functions used to convert values between Lua and host environments, including functions to bind typed host objects. This class also provides a method to initialize the module (library) being exposed to Lua.

```
class Binder {

public:
    // Constructor
    Binder (lua_State* L);
```

```
// Module (library) initializer
int init (const char* tname, const luaL_reg* flist);

// Mapping methods for basic types
void pushnumber (double v);
double checknumber (int index);
void pushstring (const char* s);
const char* checkstring (int index);
...
// Mapping methods for typed host objects
void pushusertype (void* udata, const char* tname);
void* checkusertype (int index, const char* tname);

private:
    lua_State* L;
};
```

The class constructor receives the Lua state used for mapping the objects. The initializer function receives the name of the type being bound, which also represents the name of the library (a global variable name that represents the class table in Lua), and the list of binding functions. The methods to map basic types are implemented as direct calls to the standard Lua library. For instance, the methods to map a number to and from Lua can be implemented as follows:

```
void Binder::pushnumber (double v) {
    lua_pushnumber(L,v);
}

double Binder::checknumber (int index) {
    return luaL_checknumber(L,index);
}
```

The challenge is to implement the corresponding methods used to map user-defined typed objects: pushusertype and checkusertype. These methods have to map the objects in accordance with the binding strategy in use. Each strategy requires different procedures to set the library up, thus dictating different implementations of the initializer method, init.

Once we have an implementation of the binder class, the binding functions are easily coded. For instance, the binding function associated with the class constructor and destructor can be simply coded as follows:

```
static int bnd_Create (lua_State* L) {
    LuaBinder binder(L);
    Hero* h = new Hero(binder.checkstring(L,1));
    binder.pushusertype(h,"Hero");
    return 1;
}
```

```
static int bnd_Destroy (lua_State* L)
{
    LuaBinder binder(L);
    Hero* hero = (Hero*) binder.checkusertype(1,"Hero");
    delete hero;
    return 0;
}
```

Similarly, the binding functions associated with the GetEnergy and SetEnergy methods can be given by the following code:

```
static int bnd_GetEnergy (lua_State* L) {
    LuaBinder binder(L);
    Hero* hero = (Hero*)binder.checkusertype(1,"Hero");
    binder.pushnumber(hero->GetEnergy());
    return 1;
}

static int bnd_SetEnergy (lua_State* L) {
    LuaBinder binder(L);
    Hero* hero = (Hero*)binder.checkusertype(1,"Hero");
    hero->SetEnergy(binder.checknumber(2));
    return 0;
}
```

Note that the binder class encapsulates the strategy being used to map the objects: host objects are mapped using the corresponding check and push methods, which also receive the associated type name as the input parameter. After coding all binding functions, we can write the method to open the library:

```
static const luaL_reg herolib[] = {
    {"Create", bnd_Create},
    {"Destroy", bnd_Destroy},
    {"GetName", bnd_GetName},
    {"GetEnergy", bnd_GetEnergy},
    {"SetEnergy", bnd_SetEnergy},
    {NULL, NULL}
};

int luaopen_hero (lua_State* L) {
    LuaBinder binder(L);
    binder.init("Hero",herolib);
    return 1;
}
```

Binding Host Objects to Lua Values

The simplest strategy to bind a C/C++ object to Lua is to map its address as light user-data. A light userdata represents a pointer (void*) and is treated by Lua as an ordinary value. From the scripting environment, one can then get an object's value (its pointer), make comparisons (a light userdata is equal to any other light userdata with the same

C/C++ address), and pass it back to the host (e.g., by calling a host function that has been mapped to Lua). The corresponding methods of the binder class needed to implement this strategy are implemented by directly calling the function already available in the standard library:

```
void Binder::init (const char* tname, const luaL_reg* flist) {
    luaL_register(L,tname,flist);
}

void Binder::pushusertype (void* udata, const char* tname) {
    lua_pushlightuserdata(L,udata);
}

void* Binder::checkusertype (int index, const char* tname) {
    void* udata = lua_touserdata(L,index);
    if (udata==0) luaL_typerror(L,index,tname);
    return udata;
}
```

The function `luaL_typerror` used in the implementation above raises an error, indicating that the corresponding input parameter does not correspond to a valid object.

By using this strategy to map our class Hero, the following Lua code becomes valid:

```
local h = Hero.Create("my hero")

local e = Hero.GetEnergy(h)
Hero.SetEnergy(h,e-1)

Hero.Destroy(h)
```

There are at least three advantages to mapping objects as simple values: simplicity, efficiency, and small memory footprint. As seen above, the implementation is straightforward, and the communication between Lua and the host program is done very efficiently, because it does not involve any indirect access or memory allocation. However, as implemented, this simple strategy is not safe since any userdata value is accepted as a valid parameter; passing an invalid object may crash the host program!

Adding Type Checking

We can implement a simple runtime type-checking mechanism to avoid crashing the host program from the Lua environment. Of course, adding type checking to our binding code decreases performance and increases memory usage. If the scripting is used only during the development phase of the game, the type-checking mechanism can be turned off before releasing the product. On the other hand, if the scripting facilities are to be exposed to the end users, then type checking becomes crucial and has to be delivered with the product.

To add a type-checking mechanism to our binding-to-value strategy, we can create a table to pair the address of each object mapped to Lua with the corresponding type name. (In all the strategies presented in this article, we assume that the address uniquely identifies the host object.) The table uses light userdata as keys and strings (the type names) as values. The initializer method is responsible for creating this (initially empty) table and making it visible to the mapping methods. However, it is important to preserve its privacy: access to the table from the Lua environment must not be allowed; otherwise, it would still be possible to crash the host from Lua scripts. One option to ensure privacy is to store the table using the *registry table*, a global table accessible solely from the Lua API. However, since the registry table is unique and global, using it to store our mapped objects would also prevent other C libraries from using it for implementing other control mechanisms. A better scheme is to provide access to the type-checking table only for the binding functions. Until Lua 5.0, this could be accomplished by passing the table as an *upvalue* to the binding functions. With Lua 5.1, there is an even better (and more efficient) approach: the use of the *environment table* associated with C functions. We set the type-checking table as the environment table of the binding functions. Then, within the functions, we can efficiently access the table. Each function registered to Lua inherits its environment table from the current function. Thus, it suffices to change the environment table associated with the initializer function—and all registered binding functions will have the same associated environment table.

We can now code the methods of the binder class to perform type checking:

```
void Binder::init (const char* tname, const luaL_reg* flist) {
    lua_newtable(L); // create table for type checking
    lua_replace(L,LUA_ENVIRONINDEX); // set table as env table
    luaL_register(L,tname,flist); // create libtable
}

void Binder::pushusertype (void* udata, const char* tname) {
    lua_pushlightuserdata(L,udata); // push address
    lua_pushvalue(L,-1);            // duplicate address
    lua_pushstring(L,tname);        // push type name
    lua_rawset(L,LUA_ENVIRONINDEX); // envtable[address] = tname
}

void* Binder::checkusertype (int index, const char* tname) {
    void* udata = lua_touserdata(L,index);
    if (udata==0 || !checktype(udata,tname))
        luaL_typerror(L,index,tname);
    return udata;
}
```

This code uses a private method to perform the type checking:

```
int Binder::checktype (void* udata, const char* tname) {
    lua_pushlightuserdata(L,udata);    // push address
    lua_rawget(L,LUA_ENVIRONINDEX);    // get envtable[address]
```

```
        const char* stored_tname = lua_tostring(L,-1);
        int result = stored_tname && strcmp(stored_tname,tname)==0;
        lua_pop(L,1);
        return result;
    }
```

By doing so, we achieve a binding strategy that is still very efficient. Also, memory overhead is quite low—just one table entry for each bound object. However, to avoid inflating the type-checking table, we have to release the corresponding table entry in the binding function that destroys the object. Inside the bnd_Destroy function, we have to add a call to the following private method:

```
    void Binder::releaseusertype (void* udata) {
        lua_pushlightuserdata(L,udata);
        lua_pushnil(L);
        lua_settable(L,LUA_ENVIRONINDEX);
    }
```

Binding Host Objects to Lua Objects

Binding host objects using light userdata, although simple and efficient, is very limited. Because host objects are mapped to ordinary Lua values, we cannot treat them as objects; we cannot use object-oriented syntax to invoke methods, and we cannot use Lua to manage the lifetime of objects. (Lua has garbage collection, and we can set Lua to automatically destroy a C/C++ object when it is no longer referenced.) To treat host objects as Lua objects, we have to use a different binding strategy. Instead of using light userdata, we can map objects to full userdata. The Lua API offers the lua_newuserdata function that allows us to create a raw block of memory and to map it to Lua as an opaque object (of type *userdata*). In Lua, one cannot distinguish a light userdata from a full userdata. However, the host can associate a *metatable* with full userdata, thus defining specific behaviors. A different metatable will be set for each different type of object, and, accordingly, objects of the same type will share the same metatable. The type-checking mechanism can then be built using the support already provided by the auxiliary library, through the functions luaL_newmetatable and luaL_checkudata. For each created metatable, the auxiliary library adds an entry in the registry table, mapping the type name to the metatable. Then, given a type, we can easily access the corresponding metatable.

In our case, the userdata will be created with the size of a pointer to store the address of the object being bound. We can then program the userdata to inherit from the library table. (It suffices to assign the library table to the metatable __index field.) Thus, whenever a userdata is indexed, the corresponding library table will be accessed. This allows us to use object-oriented syntax in the scripts, as shown in the code below:

```
local h = Hero.Create("my hero")

local e = h:GetEnergy()
h:SetEnergy(e-1)
```

Moreover, we can also program the garbage-collection meta-event (the metatable __gc field) to destroy the corresponding host instance; no explicit call to the *Destroy* method is needed in the script. Lua automatically triggers the associated meta-event whenever it collects the userdata.

The use of full userdata to represent each bound object imposes a new challenge. We cannot create a new userdata each time an object is mapped to Lua. We have to ensure uniqueness. If the same object is being mapped to Lua a second time, the same userdata has to be used. If we used a different userdata, we would have inconsistency: two different objects in Lua representing the same host object. It would be inefficient, too, because each mapping would request the creation a new dynamic object. Therefore, we need to keep track of all objects mapped to Lua. Again, this can be done by using the environment table associated with the binding functions. This table can relate each object address to the corresponding full userdata. To allow Lua to still automatically collect the userdata representing host objects, we have to set this table as having *weak values*—that is, the table keeps *weak references* to its values (the userdata). If this table were an ordinary table, the userdata would never be collected, because it would be always referenced by the table itself. Weak references are not considered by the garbage collector.

The initializer function now receives an extra parameter: the binding function to destroy the object, which is associated with the garbage-collection event (__gc).

```
void Binder::init (const char* tname, const luaL_reg* flist,
                   int (*destroy) (lua_State*)) {
    lua_newtable(L); // create table for uniqueness
    lua_pushstring(L,"v");
    lua_setfield(L,-2,"__mode");      // set as weak-value table
    lua_pushvalue(L,-1);              // duplicate table
    lua_setmetatable(L,-2);           // set itself as metatable
    lua_replace(L,LUA_ENVIRONINDEX);  // set table as env table
    luaL_register(L,tname,flist);     // create libtable
    luaL_newmetatable(L,tname);       // create metatable for objects
    lua_pushvalue(L,-2);
    lua_setfield(L,-2,"__index");     // mt.__index = libtable
    lua_pushcfunction(L,destroy);
    lua_setfield(L,-2,"__gc");        // mt.__gc = destroy
    lua_pop(L,1);                     // pop metatable
}
```

The function to push a userdata onto the Lua stack first checks to see if the object has already been mapped. If not, it creates a new userdata and maps it in the environment table. If the object already exists in Lua, the function simply returns the corresponding userdata stored in the environment table. The function to check the type of a given userdata is straightforward and uses the function `luaL_checkudata` provided by the Lua auxiliary library.

```
void Binder::pushusertype (void* udata, const char* tname) {
    lua_pushlightuserdata(L,udata);
    lua_rawget(L,LUA_ENVIRONINDEX);     // get udata in env table
    if (lua_isnil(L,-1)) {
        void** ubox = (void**)lua_newuserdata(L,sizeof(void*));
        *ubox = udata;                  // store address in udata
        luaL_getmetatable(L,tname);     // get metatable
        lua_setmetatable(L,-2);         // set metatable for udata
        lua_pushlightuserdata(L,udata); // push address
        lua_pushvalue(L,-2);            // push udata
        lua_rawset(L,LUA_ENVIRONINDEX); // envtable[address] = data
    }
}

void* Binder::checkusertype (int index, const char* tname) {
    void** udata = (void**)luaL_checkudata(L,index,tname);
    if (udata==0)
        luaL_typerror(L,index,tname);
    return *udata;
}
```

Binding host objects as Lua objects brings several benefits, especially because host objects are treated like any other object in Lua. We use the same syntax and rely on the garbage collector to free the allocated memory. Moreover, the performance penalty is only significant when mapping an object for the first time (because a new userdata has to be created). The memory footprint is also kept under reasonable limits: a userdata (to store a single pointer) and a table entry (to ensure uniqueness) for each mapped object.

Adding Inheritance

Let us now consider the existence of a base class, Actor, from which our Hero is derived. To illustrate the discussion, we have moved the GetName method to the base class:

```
Class Actor {
public:
    Actor (const char* name);
    ~ Actor ();
    const char* GetName ();
};

class Hero : public Actor {
    ...
};
```

After binding the two classes to Lua, we naturally desire to access methods of the base class from instances of the derived class. So, it should be valid to write the following Lua code:

```
local h = Hero.Create("my hero")
local n = h:GetName()
```

If we applied the binding code discussed so far, the system would report an error on the call to the GetName method: an object of class Actor was expected, and a Hero would be received. Our type-checking mechanism is not taking into account the class hierarchy. Nevertheless, it is quite easy to add support for polymorphism and inheritance in our binding code.

First, we modify the initializer function: It now also receives the base-type name (bname). Next, we store the metatable associated with the base class in the metatable of the derived class—for instance, using a _base field. This is needed for the type-checking mechanism. Finally, we set the library table to inherit from the base library table— that is, an object now inherits from its library table and then from the base library table. These additional settings are coded by extending the initializer function shown previously.

```
...
lua_pushcfunction(L,destroy);
lua_setfield(L,-2,"__gc");          //mt.__gc = destroy
if (bname) {
    luaL_getmetatable(L,bname);
    lua_setfield(L,-2,"_base");      //mt._base = base mt
}
lua_pop(L,1);                        //pop metatable
if (bname) {
    lua_getfield(L,LUA_GLOBALSINDEX,bname);
    lua_setfield(L,-2,"__index");   //libtable.__index = baselib
    lua_pushvalue(L,-1);            //duplicate libtable
    lua_setmetatable(L,-2);         //set itself as metatable
}
}
```

For checking the type of a given parameter, we can no longer use the function provided by the auxiliary library, because on fail, we have to check to see if the method belongs to a base class, and follow the chain of base classes coded in the _base field of the metatables. This can be coded as follows:

```
void* Binder::checkusertype (int index, const char* tname) {
    lua_getfield(L, LUA_REGISTRYINDEX, tname); // get type mt
    lua_getmetatable(L,index); // get associated mt
    while (lua_istable(L,-1)) {
        if (lua_rawequal(L,-1,-2)) {
            lua_pop(L,2);
            return *((void**)lua_touserdata(L,index));
        }
        lua_getfield(L,-1,"_base"); // get mt._base
        lua_replace(L,-2); // replace: mt = mt._base
    }
    luaL_typerror(L,index,tname);
    return NULL;
}
```

The ability to inherit from base classes also illustrates the strength of binding host objects to objects in Lua, instead of treating them as ordinary values.

Adding Extensibility

We can go one step further. Lua is a powerful scripting language because it provides easy-to-use, but sophisticated mechanisms to structure our code and also our data. The concept and implementation of several advanced data structures become trivial in Lua, mainly due to the use of *tables*: associative arrays that can be indexed with any value (except `nil`). The use of tables, in fact, greatly facilitates the description of complex data, and it would be extremely beneficial if we could add this ability to our binding system. The goal is to allow the scripter to treat host objects as associative arrays: One can attach new attributes to the object, redefine existing methods, or extend the object behavior:

```
local h = Hero.Create("my hero")
h.myFactor = 2     -- stores an extra attribute
h.GetEnergy =      -- redefine the GetEnergy method
    function (h)
        return Hero.GetEnergy(h) * h.myFactor
    end

h:GetEnergy()     -- call the modified method
```

We can provide such extensibility by associating a Lua table with our object. To allow the attachment of new fields to the object, we treat the corresponding meta-event (the `__newindex` event) to store the new field in the associated table. Also, we modify the accessing meta-event (the `__index` event) to first look for the field in the associated table, which inherits from the library table (and then from the corresponding base library tables). With Lua 5.1, the associated table, which stores the extra fields, can be set as the environment table associated with the userdata. Initially, any new userdata inherits the environment table from the current C function. The idea is to attach a new environment table to the userdata whenever the first `__newindex` event is triggered. With this strategy, we only create a new table if the script really uses it. This event treatment can be coded as follows:

```
static int newindex (lua_State* L) {
    lua_getfenv(L,1);            //get env table
    if (lua_equal(L,-1,LUA_ENVIRONINDEX)) {
        lua_newtable(L);         //create new table
        lua_pushvalue(L,-1);     //duplicate it
        lua_setfenv(L,1);        //set as env table to udata
        lua_pushvalue(L,-1);     //duplicate env table
        lua_setmetatable(L,-2);  //set itself as metatable
        lua_getfield(L,LUA_ENVIRONINDEX,"__index"); //get libtable
        lua_setfield(L,-2,"__index"); //envtable.__index=libtable
    }
```

```
        lua_pushvalue(L,2);
        lua_pushvalue(L,3);
        lua_rawset(L,-3); //store key in env table
        return 0;
    }
```

One disadvantage of this strategy is that it imposes a performance penalty on accessing the host methods, because we have to check first whether the field also exists in the environment table. The __index meta-event cannot be directly mapped to the library table, but has to be coded by a function to access the corresponding environment table:

```
    static int index (lua_State* L) {
        lua_getfenv(L,1);
        lua_pushvalue(L,2);
        lua_gettable(L,-2);      // access env table
        return 1;
    }
```

Binding Host Objects to Lua Tables

There is a simpler and more natural strategy for binding the host objects when an application needs to frequently attach extra fields. This strategy binds host objects to Lua tables. Instead of creating a new (full) userdata for each object, we create a table for each object. The reference to the host object is then stored in the table by a light userdata assigned to a pre-defined field (for instance, _pointer). Because tables are treated as objects in Lua, all features discussed for userdata can also be applied to tables—such as use of object-oriented syntax, automatic garbage collection and, mainly, storage of extra attributes, which is naturally handled. We also have to ensure uniqueness, resulting in a code quite similar to the strategy using full userdata. The initializer function is exactly the same as the one used for full userdata without extensibility—that is, there is no need to program __index and __newindex events. The main differences reside in the functions to push and check objects (more precisely, in the way the object pointer (void*) is stored and retrieved):

```
    void Binder::pushusertype (void* udata, const char* tname) {
        lua_pushlightuserdata(L,udata);
        lua_rawget(L,LUA_ENVIRONINDEX);      // get object in env table
        if (lua_isnil(L,-1)) {
            lua_newtable(L);                 // create table to be the object
            lua_pushlightuserdata(L,udata);// push address
            lua_setfield(L,-2,"_pointer"); // table._pointer=address
            luaL_getmetatable(L,tname);    // get metatable
            lua_setmetatable(L,-2);        // set metatable for table
            lua_pushlightuserdata(L,udata);// push address
            lua_pushvalue(L,-2);           // push table
            lua_rawset(L,LUA_ENVIRONINDEX);// envtable[addr]=table
        }
    }
```

```
void* Binder::checkusertype (int index, const char* tname) {
    lua_getfield(L, LUA_REGISTRYINDEX, tname); // get type mt
    lua_getmetatable(L,index);          // get associated mt
    while (lua_istable(L,-1)) {
        if (lua_rawequal(L,-1,-2)) {
            lua_pop(L,2);                  // pop string and mt
            lua_getfield(L,index,"_pointer"); // get address
            void* udata = lua_touserdata(L,-1);
            return udata;
        }
        lua_getfield(L,-1,"_base");    // get mt._base
        lua_replace(L,-2);             // replace: mt = mt._base
    }
    luaL_typerror(L,index,tname);
    return NULL;}
```

The only drawback of this strategy, compared to the use of extensible full userdata, is that it allocates more memory to bind an object in the case that we do not
attach extra attributes to it. (The memory footprint of a table is larger than the memory footprint of a userdata to store a single pointer.)

Conclusion

We have discussed different strategies to bind host objects to Lua. There is no best
strategy. Each application has to identify its specific needs in order to compare and
weigh different options. Lua provides mechanisms, but does not impose any policy.
Nevertheless, any comparison of binding strategies has to take into account at least
three main issues: flexibility, efficiency, and memory requirement. To help the evaluation of an appropriate binding strategy, we have made a set of comparisons relating
these three issues among the strategies presented in this article.

First, in Table 4.2.1, we summarize the features provided by the different strategies. Of course, all strategies provide raw access to the bound object from the script
environment. A safe access can only be provided if the strategy performs type checking. Strategies that bind host objects to objects allow the use of object-oriented programming (with inheritance) on the Lua side. Finally, two strategies allow using the
bound objects as associative arrays, thus implementing extensible objects.

Table 4.2.1   Table of Features Supported by Each Presented Binding Strategy

Strategy	Access	Type-Checking	OO	Extensibility
Light userdata	✓			
Typed light userdata	✓	✓		
Full userdata	✓	✓	✓	
Extensible userdata	✓	✓	✓	✓
Table	✓	✓	✓	✓

To test efficiency, we have measured the time spent by each strategy to invoke simple methods. We also compared the efficiency for holding extra attributes, which is supported by the last two strategies. We should emphasize that these times should not be interpreted as definitive results. Take these results just as a hint; they will probably be slightly different on your machine. The tests were run decoupled from an actual application. Therefore, the real impact on an actual application performance is not considered. All the time spent on the binding procedures (e.g., method access, type-checking, and mapping) may be negligible when compared to the time spent to perform the actual method on the host side. The times reported in Table 4.2.3 were achieved by running the pieces of code shown in Table 4.2.2, with N set to 1 million.

Table 4.2.2 Piece of Code Used To Test the Efficiency of the Different Strategies (with N set to 1,000,000)

Method Invocation		Extra Attribute Access
For Binding Objects To Values	**For Binding Objects To Objects**	**Extra Attribute Access**

<pre>for i = 1, N do
    Hero.SetEnergy(h,i)
    if Hero.GetEnergy(h)~=i
    then
        error("failed")
    end
end</pre>
	<pre>for i = 1, N do
	    h:SetEnergy(i)
	    if h:GetEnergy()~=i
	    then
	        error("failed")
	    end
	end</pre>
		<pre>for i = 1, N do
		    h.myattrib = i
		    if h.myattrib~=i
		    then
		        error("failed")
		    end
		end</pre>

Table 4.2.3 Elapsed Time (in Seconds) To Invoke Methods, Executing the Loop 1 Million Times

	Time	
Strategy	**Method Invocation**	**Attribute Access**
Light userdata	0.52	N/A
Typed light userdata	0.77	N/A
Full userdata	0.97	N/A
Extensible full userdata	1.42	0.61
Table	1.53	0.16

Finally, Table 4.2.4 shows a comparison of memory space required by each strategy. In this table, U denotes a (full) userdata to store a single pointer, T denotes an initially empty table, and E denotes a table entry.

Table 4.2.4 Memory Comparison

Strategy	Memory Consumption	
	Per Object	**Extra Attributes**
Light userdata	—	N/A
Typed light userdata	E	N/A
Full userdata	U + E	N/A
Extensible full userdata	U + E	T + E per attribute
Table	T + E	E per attribute

A final, but important remark: The list of strategies presented in this article is not an exhaustive one. Many other different strategies could be examined, especially for performing type-checking with class hierarchies. The main goal of this article was to present the basic ideas needed to bind C/C++ objects to Lua and provide some useful strategies for the actual binding. We encourage developers to try different strategies, taking into account the needs of their own games. The complete code for all the strategies presented here is available on the companion CD-ROM.

ON THE CD

Reference

[Ierusalimschy03] Ierusalimschy, R., "Programming in Lua." Lua.org, 2003. Available online at *http://www.lua.org.*

4.3

Programming Advanced Control Mechanisms with Lua Coroutines

Luiz Henrique de Figueiredo, IMPA

lhf@visgraf.impa.br

Waldemar Celes, PUC-Rio

celes@inf.puc-rio.br

Roberto Ierusalimschy, PUC-Rio

roberto@inf.puc-rio.br

Coroutines are powerful mechanisms for game programming. A coroutine is similar to a thread in a multithreaded system, in the sense that it represents a line of execution with its own local execution stack, but it shares the global environment with other coroutines. Unlike regular threads that are managed by the operating system and conceptually run concurrently, only one coroutine can be running at a given time, just like regular functions. However, unlike functions, coroutines can be suspended and resumed later, at will. Thus, coroutines provide the illusion of parallel execution without the costs and burden of managing critical sections. This can simplify the program structure significantly.

The Lua programming language implements stack-full coroutines: we can suspend a coroutine from inside any number of nested function calls. Lua coroutines allow the programmer to implement several advanced control mechanisms, such as filters, iterators, and cooperative multitasking. Coroutines are also very useful for implementing incremental algorithms, a very common task in game programming.

In this article, we describe how to use Lua coroutines to implement some advanced control mechanisms in games. We focus on the use of coroutines from the Lua side, without using the C API. For a brief example of managing Lua coroutines from the host side, see [Harmon05]. A detailed discussion on the facilities provided by Lua coroutines can be found in [deMoura04] and [Ierusalimschy03].

Lua Coroutines

Coroutines are first-class values in Lua. This means that a coroutine can be treated just like any other value: it can be assigned to variables, passed as a function argument, used as a key or value in table entries, and so forth. Lua provides functions to manipulate coroutines in the coroutine module. We create a new coroutine by calling `coroutine.create`. This function takes as input a function that will become the *main function* of the coroutine and returns the newly created coroutine.

Lua coroutines can be in three different states: *suspended*, *running*, and *dead* (see Figure 4.3.1). Just after its creation, a coroutine is *suspended*—that is, not executing. To start the execution of a coroutine, call the function `coroutine.resume`, and pass the coroutine as its first argument. The coroutine's state then switches to *running*. A coroutine can be suspended by calling the function `coroutine.yield` during its execution (provided there are no pending C calls). The control then goes back to the function that resumed the coroutine. A suspended coroutine can be resumed later by calling `coroutine.resume` again, and its execution continues at the return point of the last call to `coroutine.yield`. When the main function of a coroutine returns, the coroutine becomes *dead* and can no longer be resumed; control returns to the caller as expected. At any moment, we can query the status of a coroutine by calling the function `coroutine.status`.

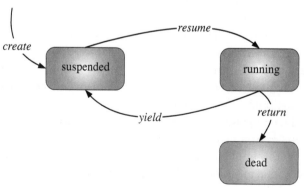

FIGURE 4.3.1   *States of Lua coroutines.*

Lua implements *asymmetric coroutines* because there are two different functions to transfer the control to and from a coroutine: resume and yield. A coroutine is subordinated to its caller (i.e., the function that resumed it), and the control is always transferred back to the caller. Asymmetric coroutines, which at first seem to be a limited mechanism, are actually powerful and easy to use. For instance, symmetric coroutines can be easily implemented on top of Lua coroutines [deMoura04].

Lua also provides a useful way to exchange data between the coroutine and the caller. All arguments passed to yield are used as return values of the corresponding resume call. Reciprocally, all arguments passed to resume (except the first one, which indicates the coroutine to be resumed) become the return values associated with the last yield executed. As a special case, the first time a coroutine is resumed, those arguments become the main function arguments.

Filters

A simple but significant use of coroutines is to implement filters. A *filter* processes a stream of data: It transforms a sequence of input data, generating a modified sequence of output data, as illustrated in Figure 4.3.2.

FIGURE 4.3.2   *Schematic representation of a filter.*

Although this seems trivial, filters actually are a part of a producer-consumer link, a classical computing problem. What makes this problem nontrivial is that the producer and the consumer work at different speeds. Coroutines come into play to manage this speed difference in a natural way.

Event-handling is a simple example of a filter in games: External events need to be translated into game events. Consider an illustrative loop to process each game event in order:

```
while true do
    local ev = GetNextEvent()
    ...     -- handle event
end
```

The function GetNextEvent is responsible for mapping external events into game events. When each external event corresponds to a single game event, the implementation is straightforward. The implementation is also straightforward if we have to process more than one external event to compose one game event: Within the function, we keep processing external events until they translate to one valid game event.

The challenge appears when one external event is translated into more than one game event, because `GetNextEvent` can only return one event at a time. To keep the code simple, the event-handling loop should not be aware of how each game event is generated. This is where coroutines become useful. What we need is a mechanism to return a value (one game event), preserving the internal state of the function to be able to return the next event(s) already generated—and that is exactly what coroutines are good for. We can then code an event filter as a coroutine. The example below handles the following situations: (a) one external event mapped to one game event; (b) two external events mapped to one game event; and (c) one external event mapped to two game events.

```
local EventFilter = function ()
    while true do
        local curr = GetExternalEvent()
        local kind = ClassifyEvent(curr)
        if kind == "one-to-one" then
            coroutine.yield(TranslateEvent(curr))
        elseif kind == "two-to-one" then
            local next = GetExternalEvent()
            coroutine.yield(CombineEvent(curr,next))
        elseif kind == "one-to-two" then
            local ev1, ev2 = SplitEvent(curr)
            coroutine.yield(ev1)
            coroutine.yield(ev2)
        else
            return nil
        end
    end
end

local GetNextEvent = coroutine.wrap(EventFilter)
```

The coroutine is created by calling the function `coroutine.wrap`, which creates the coroutine and returns a function that resumes the created coroutine each time it is called. By doing so, the event-handling loop is coded exactly as if there was a call to a regular function.

Iterators

The implementation of iterators is another problem that frequently appears in the development of games and where, again, coroutines can be very handy. Iterators represent a means for traversing (visiting) all elements stored in a data structure. A *true iterator* is a high-level function that traverses the data structure and allows the client to process each visited element by calling a given function. Because functions in Lua are first-class values, the implementation of a true iterator is straightforward. Just to illustrate the discussion, let us consider a very simple array of strings:

```
local weapons = {"knife", "sword", "gun", "knife", ...}
```

The simplest implementation of a function to traverse an array (i.e., an array iterator) can be coded as follows. The function receives the array and a callback function to be called on each element of the array.

```
local iterator = function (array, cb)
    for i = 1, #array do
        cb(array[i])
    end
end
```

Because Lua provides full lexical scoping, closures, and anonymous functions, it is easy to write the appropriate callback functions needed by such iterators. For instance, a function to count the number of occurrence of a given element in the data structure can be coded using the iterator above, as follows:

```
local count = function (container, elem)
    local n = 0
    iterator(container, function (value)
        if value==elem then
            n = n+1
        end
    end)
    return n
end
```

Although valid and useful, such an iterator is not flexible. For instance, it is not possible to traverse two data structures simultaneously (e.g., to compare or merge their elements). Moreover, the code itself looks unnatural. Programming languages offer loop constructs for iterating on a set of elements, and it would be more natural and flexible if we could use such regular constructs to iterate over any data structure. For that reason, in programming languages such as C++ and Java, an iterator is an object that provides access to the "next" element of the data structure. In Lua, such an iterator is represented by a function that returns the next element each time it is called. Using this scheme, we can rewrite the function count above as follows:

```
local count = function (container, elem)
    local n = 0
    local itr = elements_of(container)
    local value = itr()
    while value do
        if value == elem then
            n = n + 1
        end
        value = itr()
    end
    return n
end
```

Here, the function `elements_of` is responsible for creating and returning the iterator (`itr`). With the generic *for* construction provided by Lua, this code can be written in a more concise way (the function call to the iterator is implicit in the loop):

```
local count = function (container, elem)
    local n = 0
    for value in elements_of(container) do
        if value == elem then
            n = n + 1
        end
    end
    return n
end
```

The implementation of `elements_of` is also straightforward in Lua. As coded above, the iterator has to store its current state to be able to continue the iteration each time it is called. This can be achieved in Lua using closures with lexical scoping:

```
local elements_of = function (array)
    local i=0
    return function () i = i+1 return array[i] end
end
```

All of these constructions are very simple. The challenge arises when we need to create iterators for complex hierarchical data structures. In such cases, the iterator has to keep track of complex states, and closures with lexical scoping cannot do the job. Here is where coroutines play their role. The execution of a coroutine can be suspended from inside any number of nested calls—including, of course, recursive calls. To illustrate the use of coroutines to iterate hierarchical data structures, let us consider a game that uses a *scene graph* to describe its virtual world. Such scene graphs can be naturally coded in Lua by means of table constructors, as illustrated below:

```
myscene = Scene {
    name = "my scene",
    LightSource {
        position = {0.0,5.0,0.0},
        cutoff = 60,
    },
    Transform {
        translation = {1.0, 0.0, 0.0},
        rotation = {45, 0.0,0.0,1.0},
        Entity {
            geometry = Sphere{radius=1.0},
            appearance = Texture{image="myimage.tif"},
        },
        ...
    }
    ...
}
```

With coroutines, creating a function that iterates over all nodes of the graph (e.g., scene, light sources, transforms, entities, etc.) is as easy as coding a recursive function that traverses the graph. Instead of calling a callback on each visited element, we simply yield the execution, passing the corresponding element value as argument:

```
local function traverse (graph)
    coroutine.yield(graph)
    for i=1,#graph do
        traverse (graph[i])
    end
    return nil
end
```

The iterator, itself, is given by a function that resumes the coroutine:

```
local nodes_of = function (graph)
    return coroutine.wrap(function () traverse(graph) end)
end
```

With such an iterator, the loop to visit all nodes in the graph follows a standard construction:

```
for n in nodes_of(myscene) do
    -- process node n
    ...
end
```

Task Schedulers

Another natural use of coroutines is to implement task schedulers. The idea is to create a scheduler object to which multiple tasks can be added. The scheduler thus provides a function that executes each registered task in turn. Each task is implemented as a coroutine, yielding its execution after performing a few computations. Coroutines implement nonpreemptive multithreading, hence the need for each task to suspend its execution explicitly. (Nonpreemptive multithreading has the advantage of eliminating the occurrence of synchronization errors—it suffices to yield the execution outside critical sections.)

The code below illustrates the implementation of a task scheduler on top of Lua coroutines. The scheduler is represented by an object that holds a set of registered tasks. We have opted to associate a name with each task.

```
local scheduler = {
    tasks = {}
}

function scheduler:addtask (name, task)
    self.tasks[name] = coroutine.create(task)
end
```

The main scheduler function loops over the tasks to execute them in turn and can be coded as follows. After executing each task, the scheduler checks to see if the corresponding task coroutine is *dead,* removing it from the scheduler in this case.

```
function scheduler:loop ()
    repeat
        for name,co in pairs(self.tasks) do
            coroutine.resume(co)
            if coroutine.status(co) == "dead" then
                self.tasks[name] = nil
            end
        end
    until not next(self.tasks)
end
```

Note that the order in which the tasks are executed is undefined, because `pairs` uses an arbitrary order. If we had to ensure a specific order of execution, we would have to store the tasks in an array.

The loop function can also be implemented as a coroutine, yielding its execution after iterating over all the tasks once. By doing so, we can add the loop function of one scheduler as a task to another scheduler, thus creating a hierarchical task scheduler.

Cooperative Multitasking

Coroutines allow the construction of more-elaborate control mechanisms. As an example, let us extend the standard states of Lua coroutines. The goal here is to implement cooperative multitasking. We use the data-exchange facilities of Lua coroutines to allow the transfer of messages between two tasks, a common requirement in game programming. For instance, a dialogue can be modeled as a transferring of messages between two actors.

In this illustrative implementation, a task can be in four different states: *awake, sleeping, waiting,* and *dead* (see Figure 4.3.3). A *Dispatcher* controls task executions. As in the previous section, a name is assigned to each registered task, and this name is used to identify the task in the data-transfer mechanism. At each iteration, the Dispatcher visits all registered tasks, executing them as needed. All tasks in the *awake* state are executed, and all tasks in the *sleeping* state are checked to see if they have to be awakened and then executed. Tasks in the *waiting* state are ignored.

Each task is again implemented as a coroutine. However, instead of using the standard yield function, the tasks use the following functions provided by the Dispatcher to suspend their executions:

Transfer (receiver, message): sends a message to the *receiver* task; the sender task remains in the *awake* state.

Sleep (dtime): tells the Dispatcher to ignore the task for a certain period of time; the task enters the *sleeping* state.

Wait ( ): tells the Dispatcher to ignore the task until it is explicitly awakened; the task enters the *waiting* state.

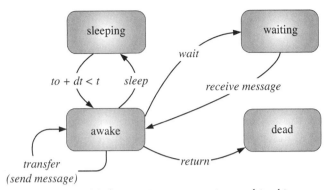

FIGURE 4.3.3   *Task states in a cooperative multitasking.*

If the main function of a task ever returns, the task becomes *dead* and is removed from the Dispatcher list. If a task is in the *waiting* state and receives a message, it is awakened and resumed in the next iteration.

Instead of creating a single Dispatcher object, we have opted for illustrating the creation of a library that provides support for the creation of multiple Dispatchers. The table `Dispatcher` emulates a Dispatcher class and is used as the metatable of each created `Dispatcher` object:

```lua
-- Exported Dispatcher "class"
Dispatcher = { }
Dispatcher.__index = Dispatcher

-- Create new Dispatcher object
function Dispatcher.create ()
    local obj = {
        reftime = os.time(), -- set initial time
        tasks = {}           -- list of tasks
    }
    setmetatable(obj,Dispatcher)
    return obj
end
```

The method used to register a new task to a `Dispatcher` receives the task name and its associated main function. Internally, each task is represented by a table that stores all information needed by the `Dispatcher` to control the task execution.

```lua
function Dispatcher:addtask (name, task)
    local t = {
        name = name,
        status = "awake",
        co = coroutine.create(task),
        wakeuptime = 0,
        sender = nil,
        message = nil,
```

```
        }
        self.tasks[name] = t
        self.active = t
        coroutine.resume(t.co,self)
    end
```

Note that the Dispatcher calls the task once passing itself as an argument. This will give the task a chance to do any setup needed. The task should then return control to the Dispatcher immediately. (See the examples at the end of the section.)

The loop that controls the execution of all tasks iterates over all registered tasks, executes the *awake* ones, and checks to see if *sleeping* tasks have to be awakened and executed.

```
function Dispatcher:loop ()
    repeat
        self.currtime = os.difftime(os.time(),self.reftime)
        for name,task in pairs(self.tasks) do
            if task.status == "awake" then
                self:execute(task)
            elseif task.status == "sleeping" then
                if task.wakeuptime <= self.currtime then
                    task.status = "awake"
                    self:execute(task)
                end
            end
            task.sender = nil
            task.message = nil
        end
    until not next(self.tasks)
end
```

The auxiliary method responsible for executing a task resumes the corresponding coroutine, passing as extra parameters: the name of the sender, and the message. This function also checks to see when the task becomes dead and removes it from the dispatcher.

```
function Dispatcher:execute (task)
    self.active = task
    local ok, errmsg =
        coroutine.resume(task.co,task.sender,task.message)
    if not ok then
        error (errmsg)
    end
    if coroutine.status(task.co) == "dead" then
        self.tasks[task.name] = nil
    end
end
```

An implementation of the methods used by a task to suspend its execution is presented below. The method to transfer a message to other task receives, as input parameters, the name of the receiver task and the message. The message and the sender name are stored, to be used upon resuming the corresponding receiver task. If the receiver is in the *waiting* state, it is awakened.

```
function Dispatcher:transfer (receiver, message)
    if receiver and self.tasks[receiver] then
        local task = self.active
        self.tasks[receiver].sender = task.name
        self.tasks[receiver].message = message
        if self.tasks[receiver].status == "waiting" then
            self.tasks[receiver].status = "awake"
        end
    end
    return coroutine.yield()
end
```

The method used to set a task in the *sleeping* state stores the wake-up time to be checked in the execution loop. Finally, the method to set a task as *waiting* simply marks its state.

```
function Dispatcher:sleep (dtime)
    local task = self.active
    task.wakeuptime = self.currtime + dtime
    task.status = "sleeping"
    return coroutine.yield()
end

function Dispatcher:wait ()
    local task = self.active
    task.status = "waiting"
    return coroutine.yield()
end
```

Note that the value of a message being transferred is not limited to a string. The message can represent any Lua value, thus allowing the transferring of complex data (e.g., tables or application-defined userdata).

To exemplify the use of cooperative multitasking on top of the code given above, consider the implementation of a game character. To keep things simple, assume that the character is passive and only answers questions addressed to it. Here is a simple character that reacts to some messages: "hi," "who," "advice," "sleep," and "bye." For the first three, the character sends back an appropriate reply. It reacts to "sleep" by entering the *sleeping* state for 10 seconds. While sleeping, the character is inactive and does not receive any messages. The character reacts to a "bye" message by exiting; it then becomes *dead* and is removed from the dispatch task list.

```
local character = function (dispatcher)
    local reply = {
        hi = "Hi",
        who = "I am a scripter",
        advice = "Try Lua",
```

```
        }
        local sender, message = dispatcher:wait()
        while message ~= "bye" do
            if message=="sleep" then
                io.write("(Zzz)\n")
                sender, message = dispatcher:sleep(10)
            else
                local answer = reply[message] or "Sorry?"
                sender,message = dispatcher:transfer(sender,answer)
            end
        end
    end
end
```

In an actual game, the behavior of such a character would be extended to incorporate more-complex interactions.

To test the behavior of this character, let's simulate a player as another agent in the task list. The player types messages to a console prompt and sees the replies.

```
local player = function (dispatcher)
    local sender, message = dispatcher:transfer()
    while true do
        if sender then
            io.write(sender,": ",message,"\n")
        end
        io.write("Player: ")
        local line = io.read()
        sender, message = dispatcher:transfer("Character",line)
        if line == "bye" then
            return
        end
    end
end
```

To make these two agents work together, we need to create a dispatcher, add them to the task list, and enter the dispatch loop:

```
local d = Dispatcher.create()
d:addtask("Character",character)
d:addtask("Player",player)
d:loop()
```

ON THE CD

All the code in this gem is available on the companion CD-ROM.

Conclusion

In this article, we presented some advanced control mechanisms that were programmed on top of Lua coroutines. Coroutines implemented in Lua are based on a few simple concepts, but provide a powerful programming tool. We encourage game programmers to use Lua coroutines for the construction of other control paradigms. Game programmers can also take advantage of Lua coroutines to implement solutions to a wide range of other common problems, such as incremental simulation, artificial intelligence, and text processing.

References

[deMoura04] de Moura, A. L., N. Rodriguez, and R. Ierusalimschy, "Coroutines in Lua." *Journal of Universal Computer Science,* 10(7): pp. 910–925, 2004.

[Harmon05] M. Harmon, "Building Lua into Games." *Game Programming Gems 5,* Charles River Media: pp. 115–128, 2005.

[Ierusalimschy03] Ierusalimschy, R., "Programming in Lua." Lua.org, 2003. Available online at *http://www.lua.org.*

4.4

Managing High-Level Script Execution Within Multithreaded Environments

Sébastien Schertenleib,
Swiss Federal Institute of Technology,
Virtual Reality Lab

sebastien.schertenleib@epfl.ch

The next generation of dedicated hardware, high-end PCs, and home consoles will provide a multicore architecture [DeLoura05] [Intel05] [Microsoft05]. Developing efficient code within a multicore environment is a complex task that few developers will be able to master completely. To allow developers to create and manipulate game simulations on multicore hardware, a dedicated effort is required to provide friendlier development environments. Therefore, game-development systems need to provide much better abstraction layers for high-level interactions, such as behavioral scripts.

This gem will describe how a component-based architecture can be adapted to benefit from scripting interfaces that provide a multitasking representation. A specific implementation based on the concept of microthreads [Hoffert98], described here, overcomes some limitations and performance overhead associated with the use of a distinct thread for each flow of control.

Component-Based Software and the Script Interpreter

Component-based software design provides a layered architecture style that divides system functionality into a hierarchy where each layer connects to the layers above and below it [Rene05]. This approach tends to promote reusability by keeping the application-specific code at the topmost levels, and allowing developers to easily reuse the lower layers. The bottom layers are generally low-level libraries that are optimized to run on specific platforms, while the upper layers are used for communication with the system. Here, an independent plug-in can communicate with any top-level services.

A plug-in architecture allows exposing engine functionality to scripting interfaces with ease. In this architecture, a scripting-language interpreter handles the binding of C++ objects to scripting-language objects. The C++ objects are reflected in the safer, scripting-language environment, and this frees developers from having to worry about common C/C++ issues like memory management or type checking. As a result, productivity levels can be greater, allowing more development time for experimentation with conceptual ideas and completing actual gameplay code.

The following sections will describe how a standard interpreter can be extended with more advanced features to meet the specific requirements of game systems. We present some implementation details based on the Python scripting language [Python05]; however, the general concepts are adaptable to other scripting languages, such as Lua [Lua05].

Coroutines and Microthreads

Ideally, when creating virtual worlds populated by individual entities, we expect every agent to react independently. Thus, the most intuitive approach is to dedicate a separate flow of control for each character. From a programming perspective, we can envision the allocation of a dedicated thread to every single agent. However, the overhead of thread context switches and memory latency makes this approach prohibitive. For optimal performance, the number of heavyweight threads should match the number of cores available. Moreover, developing and debugging within a multithreaded environment is much more difficult than within a single-threaded environment. Only a few team members may have the skills and knowledge required to develop multithreaded component-based systems. Therefore, a key objective is to provide a software architecture that can be manipulated through higher-level abstractions, while keeping real-time performance and a multitasking representation. It is desirable to greatly ease the development of cooperative multitasking and provide multithreading functionality to nonexperts, while removing the difficult job of debugging race conditions and other data-synchronization conflicts.

The concept of a coroutine, attributed to [Conway63], is one of the oldest proposals for a general control abstraction. The idea is to provide control behaviors in a concurrent context. The convenience of providing a programmer with this powerful control abstraction has been disregarded by general-purpose language designers. Recently, scripting languages like Python, Lua, and Perl have investigated cooperative task-management as an alternative to multithreading environments [Schemenaur01] [Adya02]. A restricted form of coroutine in the form of simple iterators or generators is called a microthread. A microthread represents a unit of execution that has its own private data and control stack, while sharing global variables with other microthreads. Due to a cooperative concurrency model, microthreads must explicitly request to be suspended before another microthread may run.

Within the Python environment, a microthread is a particular function that contains a `yield` statement [Schemenaur01]. When called, a microthread function must return a first-class object that can be resumed at any point in the program within the microthreads control stack. As microthreads do not suffer from expensive context switches, several thousand of them can run at a time without significant performance penalty [Tismer00].

Microthreads allow greatly simplified AI and object update code by moving much of the object state information into local variables, where it naturally belongs [Carter01]. Microthreads can be used to write functions that generate one result and yield back to the main program. The main program can then resume them later on, and they resume where they left off, with local variables intact. Since microthreads are based on cooperative multitasking, data synchronization is limited.

Microthread Manager

To simplify the use of microthreads for cooperative multitasking, we introduce a microthread manager that controls microthread execution. This manager is able to independently control each microthread's status (e.g., running, paused, or terminated). By communicating with the manager, an application can interact with the microthreads, changing their status on demand. During development, developers can break any scripts at runtime, which is useful for prototyping behaviors.

In the scenario illustrated in Figure 4.4.1, observe that microthread id1 receives control and continues its execution where it last yielded. When a *yield* statement is reached, it gives control back to the manager. Simultaneously an external event requires the termination of the microthread id3. The manager will send this information to the microthread, releasing all of its variables' states. When this operation is completed, the microthread id3 will send a message to the microthread manager, allowing the update of the current list of active and inactive microthreads. In the example, microthread id2 is currently inactive.

Implementation

The microthread manager has to keep a list of microthreads together with their status. It needs to handle creation, execution, and destruction of every active microthread. Listing 4.4.1 illustrates a partial implementation.

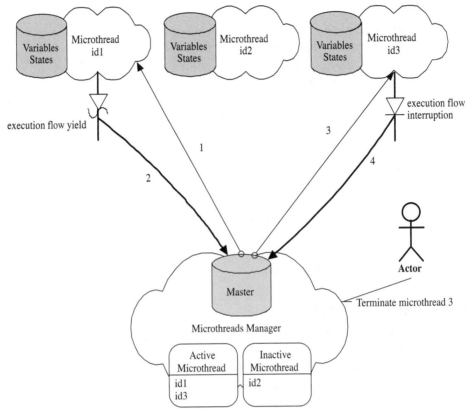

FIGURE 4.4.1 *Microthread execution model.*

Listing 4.4.1 Microthread Manager Implementation Details

```
#The manager is itself a Python generator.
def pyMicroThreadManager():

    '''
    To synchronize the Python micro thread manager with C++ code
    we yield at each iteration, leaving the C++ code triggering the
    .next() statement
    '''

    while 1:
      yield 0
      if (isMicroThreadManagerPaused()):
        # Pause this manager and wait until the app resumes it
        yield 0
      elif (isMicroThreadManagerMustDie()):
        # Break and terminate the microthread generator
        break
      else:
```

```
                # Safe removal of killed mircrothreads
                for i in range(len(g_pyMicroThreadToBeRemoveFromList)):
                    removeMicrothread(g_pyMicroThreadToBeRemoveFromList[i])

                g_pyMicroThreadToBeRemoveFromList = []

                # Manage each microthread status independently.
                for i in range(len(g_pyMicroThreadList)):
                    g_pyCurrentMicroThreadInRun=i
                    nameOfMicroThread=g_pyMicroThreadNameList[i]
                    if (not isMicroThreadPaused(nameOfMicroThread)):
                        # Handle script calling C++ code throwing exceptions
                        try:
                            # If it is already finished, throw exceptions
                            yieldResult = g_pyMicroThreadList[i].next()
                            if isMicroThreadMustDie(nameOfMicroThread)
                                or yieldResult==1:
                                pyEndOfMicroThread(nameOfMicroThread)
                        except ValueError:
                            print "Safely terminate the microthread"
                            pyEndOfMicroThread(nameOfMicroThread)
                # Check if an external event requires termination of the manager
                yield pyEndOfMicroThreadManager()

# First create the manager
g_pyMicroThreadManager=pyMicroThreadManager()

# Create the micro thread list
g_pyMicroThreadList=[]

# A parallel one with names not generator this time
g_pyMicroThreadNameList=[]

'''
Create a list of micro thread that have been killed, to be
safely remove in sync by micro thread manager
'''
g_pyMicroThreadToBeRemoveFromList=[]

'''
Create a variable which contains the ID in the list from the
last microthread called, in order to be able to remove it in case
of C++ throw Exception, we simply kill this microthread
'''
g_pyCurrentMicroThreadInRun=-1
```

Embedding Python

Configuration Modes

If the core-engine API is exposed to the scripting language, complex scripts can be developed. A typical use case is to write algorithms that need to run fast in C++, and to control them within a script. As every game has its own requirement, different configuration modes have been developed. All of them allow the script to execute in different ways.

Blocking Mode

In this mode, illustrated in Figure 4.4.2, the main thread waits until the interpreter finishes its update, which is performed using microthreads that are registered with the microthreads manager discussed above. The microthreads notify the microthread manager of their status. The Python microthreads update loop runs at a different frequency than the core C++ engine, allowing the execution of complex scripts without reducing the C++ core path performance.

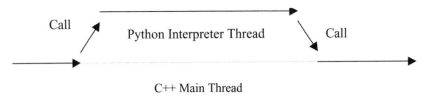

FIGURE 4.4.2   *Case 1, blocking mode.*

Cooperative Multitasking Mode

In this mode, illustrated in Figure 4.4.3, microthreads are used to run scripts via cooperative multitasking. This ensures that microthread updates do not run at a higher frequency than the C++ code path, avoiding microthread updates that run faster than necessary and use too many valuable system resources. In general, this is the most appropriate mode to use.

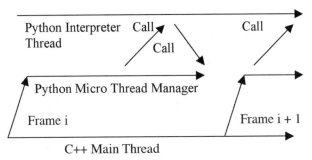

FIGURE 4.4.3   *Case 2, cooperative multitasking.*

Concurrent Multitasking Mode

In this mode, illustrated in Figure 4.4.4, the Python microthread manager runs in a thread created within the Python interpreter thread. This clear separation between the C++ and Python code paths makes it possible to prevent frame rate inconsistency when the overall scripting workflow differs on a frame basis.

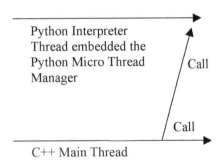

FIGURE 4.4.4 *Case 3, concurrent multitasking.*

Custom Preprocessor and Specific Keywords

One purpose of the system described here is to provide a higher level of abstraction for microthread usage. The concrete implementation must be hidden. The system should handle all variable/object creation and management. To facilitate the script-development process, we developed a custom preprocessor. Its purpose is to translate simple scripts with custom keywords into native Python microthread code. The use of custom keywords followed by an automated preprocessing step is meant to reduce mistakes made due to confusion when coding this logic by hand. This also allows the modification of the manager without breaking hundreds of scripts. The preprocessor also generates Python object references that bind to C++ objects at runtime. This removes the need to explicitly bind these objects to each microthread context.

To simplify script creation, two new keywords have been created: the vhdYIELD and vhdRETURN statements. The vhdYIELD keyword gives control back to the microthread manager, which will do the transition to the next microthread in the stack. To qualify as microthread, scripts need at least one mandatory vhdYIELD statement. Using this keyword enables long-running routines to be distributed across several frames. Developers can set this statement in key areas within long or unpredictable algorithms, like path-planning requests. The vhdRETURN keyword breaks and terminates the current microthread. By default, the last line of all microthreads must be the vhdRETURN statement.

To illustrate, let's investigate the script depicted in Listing 4.4.2.

Listing 4.4.2 A Basic Script

```
B=0
while (true):
    B=B+1
    if (B==10):
        vhdRETURN
    vhdYIELD
```

This sample script will be executed in 10 consecutive frames. Every time the Python interpreter reaches the keyword vhdYIELD, the microthread will yield back to the microthread manager, which will eventually process the next microthread in the queue. When B equals 10, the execution of vhdRETURN will notify the manager that this microthread must be terminated.

As these extra keywords are not parts of the Python language, it will not run within a standard Python interpreter. The custom preprocessor tool described above translates Listing 4.4.2 into the native Python code shown in Listing 4.4.3.

Note that from a runtime-performance perspective, the impact of parsing the scripts occurs only during development. For application deployment, all the scripts will be distributed as pure Python byte code.

Listing 4.4.3 Python-Compliant Script Based on Preprocessing the Script from Listing 4.4.2

```
# Microthread definition
def __PythonScript2123():
    '''
    Use a try-and-catch block to avoid that the script calls a
    C++ method to propagate the exception.
    Also, dump the traceback helping the end user
    '''
    try:
        # The original script begins here
        while (true):
            print B
            if B == 10:
                '''
                The preprocessor replaced vhdRETURN with this Python code
                '''
                yield pyEndOfMicroThread(
                    "__generatorObj__PythonScript2123")
            B = B + 1
            '''
            The preprocessor replaced vhdYIELD with this Python code
            '''
            yield 0
    except:
        traceback.print_exception(sys.exc_info()[0],
          sys.exc_info()[1], sys.exc_info())
        yield pyEndOfMicroThread("__generatorObj__PythonScript2123")
```

```
# Create the Python generator
__generatorObj__PythonScript2123=__PythonScript2123()

# Register the microthread
g_pyMicroThreadList.append(__generatorObj__PythonScript2123)
g_pyMicroThreadNameList.append("__generatorObj__PythonScript2123")
```

Our implementation of the preprocessing system has limitations and will not be able to discover when a long-running main loop needs to be split over several frames, or when the script author wants to explicitly terminate a microthread.

Authoring Tool

To facilitate the development process, authoring tools are mandatory. In our implementation, a Python Console GUI, based on a text editor (see Figure 4.4.5), provides the communication layer and interaction with the game engine. The editor gives feedback about the current state of each microthread and uses color syntax highlighting not only for the Python keywords, but also for specific game-engine objects as well.

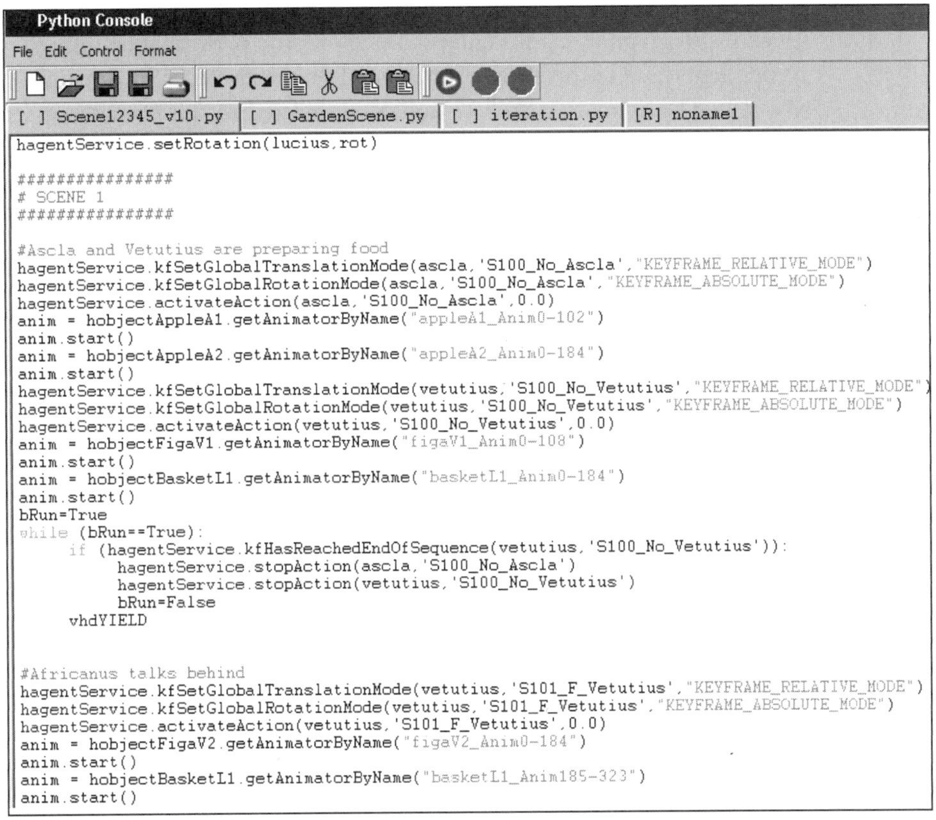

FIGURE 4.4.5 *Python Console.*

Experiments and Results

So far, our implementation of the microthread manager has been used for controlling dynamic components such as cloud simulations, particle systems, and also within agent simulations. However, the system is far from being perfect and comes with some limitations, notably coming from the Python microthreads model. For instance, it is not possible to interrupt a microthread outside of its running context. As a consequence, specific handling may be required in some circumstances. As a side note, the actual implementation of coroutines in Lua provides such functionality.

For analyzing the scalability of this architecture, several different testbed applications were built to test its viability for use in crowd simulations. One testbed features 800 individual agents running on dedicated microthreads. The purpose of this application was to control the agents' behavioral context objects wherein each entity keeps its own internal logic within a microthread. The distinct separation in the entity representation provides granularity on the entity level. Thus, the AI engine is able to control the scheduling of every active entity within the realtime constraints and change their inherent logic based on their current level of detail. It also provides higher flexibility in the flow execution.

Different use cases have served for benchmarking the system. Tests have been executed on a Pentium 4 Xeon at 2.2 GHz, with 1 GB of memory and an nVIDIA Quadro Pro graphics card. Figure 4.4.6 shows the performance impact of the major components used in this simulation. The 3D-rendering component is the most expensive task. The animation and AI update are related to the number of active entities, with the difference that nonvisible entity animation update remains a constant time-based function (e.g., only the skeletal root orientation and position are modified).

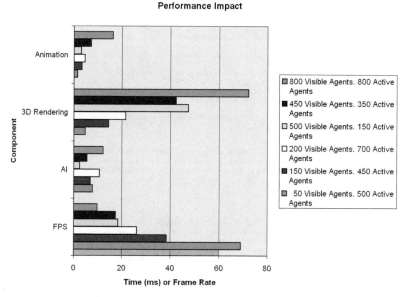

FIGURE 4.4.6   *Performance impact.*

Conclusion

This article demonstrates that a higher level of abstraction can be built on top of existing component-based platforms. The system is intended to provide dedicated tools that allow nontechnical users to control virtual worlds within multitasking environments. The advantage of having as many dedicated flows of control as desired provides a more intuitive representation of the world without sacrificing real-time performance.

There are plans to extend the flexibility of this model in the future by extending the current microthread manager with a control scheme for finer-grained microthreads management, as well as providing more tools to help in debugging the simulation.

References

[Adya02] Adya, A. and J. Howell, "Cooperative Task Management without Manual Stack Management." *Proceedings of USENIX,* Annual Technical Conference, Monterrey, California, 2002.

[Carter01] Carter, S., "Managing AI with Micro-Threads." *Game Programming Gems 2,* Charles River Media: pp. 265–272, 2001.

[Conway63] Conway, D., "Design of a Separable Transition-Diagram Compiler." CACM, 1963.

[DeLoura05] DeLoura, M., "CELL: A New Platform for Digital Entertainment." GDC, 2005.

[Hoffert98] Hoffert, J. and K. Goldman, "Microthread: An Object for Behavioral Pattern for Managing Object Execution." Washington University, Distributed Programming Environments Group, 1998.

[Intel05] Intel, "Intel Multi-Core Processor Architecture Development Backgrounder." 2005.

[Lua05] Ierusalimschy, R., L. H. de Figueiredo, and W. Celes, "The Evolution of Lua," 2005. Available online at *http://www.lua.org.*

[Microsoft05] Microsoft, "Methods and system for general skinning via hardware accelerators." U.S. Patent Application, 2005.

[Python05] Python, "Python Programming Language." 2005. Available online at *http://www.python.org.*

[Rene05] Rene, B., "Component Based Object Management." *Game Programming Gems 5,* Charles River Media, 2005: pp. 25–37.

[Schemenaur01] Schemenaur, N. and T. Peter, "Simple Generators." PEP, 2001.

[Tismer00] Tismer, C., "Continuations and Stackless Oython." *Proceedings of the 8th International Python Conference,* Arlington, VA, 2000.

4.5

Exposing Actor Properties Using Nonintrusive Proxies

Matthew Campbell and Curtiss Murphy, BMH Associates, Incorporated

campbell@bmh.com, murphy@bmh.com

At some point, every game engine tackles the problem of exposing actor properties. Even the simplest engine will eventually need the ability to expose the internal properties of game actors to external tools. Level editors need them so designers can build maps without relying on developers. Messaging frameworks need them so they can effectively build generic messages and send network updates. Load/save modules need them to facilitate state persistence. The need is clear, but unfortunately the solution is not always apparent, especially in C++.

This gem describes a flexible, loosely coupled architecture for exposing the properties of game actors. It also shows how to solve this problem with no modification to your game actor classes. Sometimes this is accomplished through introspection. However, in C++, this almost certainly requires a modification to your actors, which is not always possible. Therefore, this gem presents a nonintrusive solution for exposing the properties of game actors by creating a layer on top of your existing game objects. This is perfect when constructing level editors, game managers, and even messaging frameworks.

Actors and Proxies and Properties, Oh My!

The three primary elements of this solution are the actor, the `ActorProxy`, and the `ActorProperty`. This section describes the general definition of these three components.

Actor

Actors are all the unique objects in a game world. They are the meat of all games and contain much of the logic of how the world interacts. Vehicles, weather systems, emitters, triggers, and lights are all examples of actors. Actors can be simple, like a static tree, or complex, like an articulated, damageable tank complete with sound, weapons, and AI. For this discussion, the important thing is that actors have properties you want to expose. Vehicles have properties such as max speed and max damage. Weather objects have time-of-day, season, and cloud states. Triggers have collision range and event labels.

ActorProxy

An `ActorProxy` is a simple, data-oriented class that wraps each actor class. They are simple, but they play a pivotal role in this architecture by fulfilling two main jobs. First, they provide a common, uniform class that external tools, such as a level editor or game manager, can access and manipulate. Second, they know everything about the actor they wrap, especially the properties. Once defined, proxies can be used in place of actors, especially for the higher-level tools.

ActorProperty

An `ActorProperty` is a single, atomic piece of information about an actor. These are the nuggets of data you are trying to expose. It's what an editor will display and what the networking layer will send across the wire. As you can see in Figure 4.5.1, `ActorProperty` is defined by Set/Get methods, To/From string methods, and identifying information, such as name, description, and label.

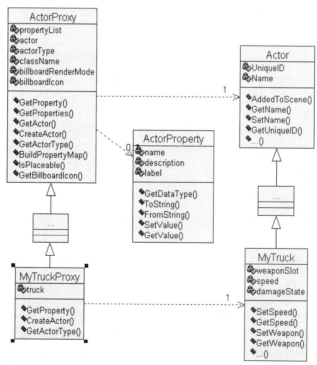

FIGURE 4.5.1 `ActorProxy` *class diagram.*

Although maintaining this information for every property in your system will add some slight processing overhead, it will vastly increase the flexibility, longevity, and usefulness of your game actors. This is especially true when your entire team buys into the concept and uniformly makes use of properties. Consider this: One of your teammates created a tessellated flag actor that was designed for the banners in a capture-the-flag map. It was very closed and served only one purpose. But if he had exposed the texture, period, phase, and amplitude as properties, he would have created a dynamic actor that could be used for quest NPCs, waypoints, housing decoration, and even inventory objects without changing any code!

Nonintrusive and Dynamic Architecture

So why use actor proxies? After all, the actor class is right there; why create more classes or add wrapper functionality? The answer is practicality. In an ideal world, you might not need this separation. However in the real world, there are dozens of engineers working on isolated modules across both physical and organizational boundaries. In other words, it might not be possible for every game object to uniformly support this behavior. Fortunately, actor proxies create a nonintrusive architecture that solves this problem and leaves the original objects clear of any property-related functionality.

The nonintrusive nature of this architecture is especially important when dealing with existing game engines or when integrating with legacy systems. "Did he just say legacy?" That's right, legacy, as in preexisting code. As games increase in size, cost, and complexity, the use of legacy modules becomes increasingly more important. The problem is that legacy modules can easily contain several hundred thousand lines of code that have no support for exposing properties. One way to fix this is to attempt to modify every object at the lowest levels of the engine. But that adds the much dreaded risk that existing code will become crippled. Instead, we recommend a nonintrusive property layer. Since this layer sits on top of the existing code, developers can add and manipulate properties without any of those nasty risks to the underlying code.

Another important attribute of this solution is the dynamic nature of `ActorProperty`. This is similar to the arguments in favor of aggregate-based design over inheritance-based design. In other words, any designs that are compile-time dependent could severely impact the longevity and flexibility of a given software system. Inheritance invokes compile-time dependencies that cannot be changed during runtime. The aggregate approach, on the other hand, allows behavior and attributes to be added and removed to an object during execution.

So, how does this concept relate to `ActorProperty`? In fact, they are one in the same. `ActorProxy` is, in many ways, an aggregate of the actor properties. In order to illustrate this concept, consider the following: A static mesh actor may want to change the number of texture properties it exposes whenever a mesh resource property is assigned. This would allow a level designer to assign individual textures to different faces of a cube or to the front and back of a door using the same base actor. Using a static, nonproxy solution would often lead to pointers directly pointing to their data elements. So to expose texture properties, pointers would be hard-registered in code at compile time. Such a system would not work for the above example, because the amount of texture properties changes at runtime. Fortunately, using the proposed property system, texture properties could be added and removed dynamically at runtime based on the static mesh that is currently loaded.

Actor Properties

Object-oriented designs should provide as much reuse and extensibility as possible. Components should communicate with each other in a simple, yet flexible manner, allowing the system to grow and adapt during its lifetime. This makes generic access to object data a necessity. In order to achieve generic data access in game engines, we introduce the ActorProperty. Actor properties are responsible for propagating data both to and from an actor. This section will build ActorProperty from the ground up, starting at the most basic building blocks.

Functors

The two most important attributes of ActorProperty are its "getter" and "setter" methods. In its simplest terms, a *getter* is a method for retrieving data, and a *setter* is a method for assigning data. When combined, they define everything needed to wrap each atomic data element. The question then is how to expose them in a generic way. Often, a technique known as reflection (or introspection) is used. Unfortunately, the C++ language does not natively support such a construct. This is where functors come into the picture. *Functors,* otherwise known as *function objects,* are a C++ mechanism for achieving the call-back function pointer behavior found in basic C code.

The following C++ code is a simple example of how a functor may be used. An extensive and in-depth discussion of functors can be found in [Hickey94]. The implementations for MakeFunctor, Functor0, and other functors are available at *http://www. delta3d.org.* For the purposes of this section, treat these objects as black boxes, and assume they function as described.

```
class MyClass {
public:
    void SayHi() { std::cout << "Hello!" << std::endl;
};

int main(int argc, char *argv[])
{
    MyClass test;
    Functor0 doHello = MakeFunctor(test,&MyClass::SayHi);

    //Prints "Hello!" to the console.
    doHello();

    return 0;
}
```

Getters/Setters

Now that we have explored the use of functors, let's use them to build the getter and setter functionality for ActorProperty. What does it mean to be a setter or getter function? In other words, what are the parameters and return values of a getter and a setter? Well, a setter function sets some data. Therefore, it takes one parameter—the new data. The getter function, on the other hand, returns the value of a property. Therefore, it takes no parameters and has one return value. Furthermore, to keep the method signatures simple, the getter and setter should support the use of exceptions to track errors.

The following code illustrates how to incorporate getter and setter functors into a base property class. Since the basic job of the property class is to work with functors (i.e., function objects), the class will need to hold onto those. This class also shows how templates come into play. Templates are a key part of generically supporting the many different data types in your system, such as integers, floats, and strings. Therefore, the property class is parameterized on two types, the SetType and the GetType. Subclasses can then specify what data type they support with the GetPropertyType method and by defining the SetType and GetType.

```
template <class SetType, class GetType>
class GenericActorProperty : public ActorProperty {
public:

    GenericActorProperty (Functor1<SetType> &set,
        Functor2<GetType> &get)
    {
        SetPropFunctor = set;
        GetPropFunctor = get;
    }

    //Subclasses return a specific datatype.
    virtual DataType &GetPropertyType() const = 0;

    //Sets the value of this property by calling the set functors.
    virtual void SetValue(SetType value)
    {
        SetPropFunctor(value);
    }

    //Gets the value of this property be calling the get functors.
    virtual GetType GetValue() const
    {
        return GetPropFunctor();
    }

private:
    Functor1<SetType> SetPropFunctor;
    Functor2<GetType> GetPropFunctor;
};
```

Property Design

The previous section defined functors and showed how they can be used in the base actor property class. However, there is a bit more to the story. After all, the GenericActorProperty class is just the base. This architecture needs to support a huge range of types, from simple integers and floats to complex types, such as textures, meshes, and sounds. To do that, you need a subclass for every property type, where each class supports one and only one type of data. Figure 4.5.2 below shows a subset of the property class.

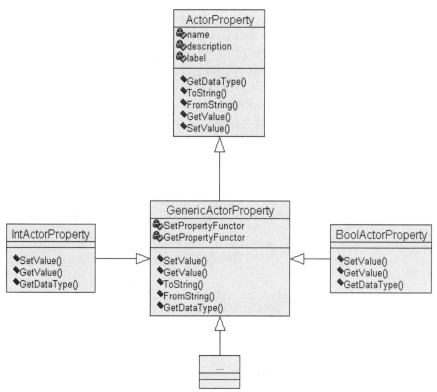

FIGURE 4.5.2 ActorProperty *class diagram*

This design is fairly straightforward. ActorProperty is a base class that contains important metadata (e.g., name, description, label). It also provides an interface for converting the property to and from a string. This is helpful for operations that require text parsing, such as saving and loading properties to and from an XML file.

Although not represented in the figure, ActorProperty should probably support serialization to and from a binary stream for operations like network communication.

Finally, we conclude this section with a code snippet illustrating the implementation of the IntActorProperty class. The ToString and FromString methods are not given in this example, as they are not relevant to our discussion. Those two methods are quite simple and merely convert an integer to and from a string.

```
//The integer property class . . .
class IntActorProperty : public GenericActorProperty<int,int> {
public:

    IntActorProperty(Functor1<int> set, FunctorORet<int> get) :
        GenericActorProperty<int,int>(set,get) { }

    const DataType &GetDataType() const
    {
        return DataType::INT;
    }
}

///A test class for our integer property…
class MyClass {
public:

    MyClass(int initialValue) { myValue=initialValue; }
    void Setter(int newValue) { myValue=newValue; }
    int Getter() const { return myValue; }

private:
    int myValue;
};

int main(int argc, char *argv[])
{
    MyClass test(25);

    //Example of creating an integer property. In an actual
    //implementation, this is stored on ActorProxy which
    //manages its list of actor properties.
    IntegerActorProperty prop(MakeFunctor(test,&MyClass::Setter),
        MakeFunctorRet(test,&MyClass::Getter));

    //Prints the value 25
    std::cout << "Value = " << prop.GetValue() << std::endl;
    prop.SetValue(10);
    //Prints the value 10
    std::cout << "Value = " << prop.GetValue() << std::endl;

    return 0;
}
```

Actor Proxies

Now that you understand the mechanics of `ActorProperty`, it is time to put them to use in `ActorProxy`. Fortunately, `ActorProxy` is extremely simple. Each proxy builds a list of the properties that expose the getter and setter methods. In addition to the properties, each proxy has a reference to its underlying actor. This allows high-level tools to use `ActorProxy` in place of actor object. Once initialized, `ActorProxy` provides a uniform layer of behavior that can be used throughout your game engine for object creation, file input/output (I/O), and even message passing.

The following segment shows an example of the `BuildPropertyMap()` method for `BaseLightActorProxy`. Each proxy overrides this method to build its property list.

```
void BaseLightActorProxy::BuildPropertyMap()
{
    const std::string GROUPNAME = "Light";

    // Get the actor that this proxy wraps.
    Light *light = dynamic_cast <Light *> (mActor.get());
    if (NULL == light)
        //Throw an exception!

    // Example of a simple Boolean property on Light Actor
    AddProperty(new BooleanActorProperty("enable","Enabled",
        MakeFunctor(*light,&Light::SetEnabled),
        MakeFunctorRet(*light,& Light::GetEnabled),
        "Sets whether this light is enabled", GROUPNAME));

    // Example of an int property that does not have a matching
    // setter on the wrapped Actor. Therefore, we added a
    // setter on the Proxy to convert data. Note the property
    // is flexible enough to use functors on different objects.
    AddProperty(new IntActorProperty("LightNum","Light Number",
        MakeFunctor(*this,&BaseLightActorProxy::SetNumber),
        MakeFunctorRet(*light,& Light::GetNumber),
        "Sets the light number", GROUPNAME));

    // Example – enumeration is a templated property
    // type that lets users assign one value from a list.
    AddProperty(new EnumActorProperty<LightModeEnum>(
    "Lighting Mode","Lighting Mode",
        MakeFunctor(*this,&BaseLightActorProxy::SetLightMode),
        MakeFunctorRet(*this,&BaseLightActorProxy::GetLightMode),
        "Sets the lighting mode", GROUPNAME));

    // Example of a complex resource property. Texture
    // resources store the resource path on the proxy itself.
    // When the setter is called on the proxy, it converts
    // the resource path, loads data, and calls the Actor's setter.
    AddProperty(new ResourceProperty(*this,
        DataType::TEXTURE, "BloomTex", "Bloom Texture",
        MakeFunctor(*this, &BaseLightActorProxy::SetBloomTexture),
        "Sets the bloom filter texture", GROUPNAME));
    ...
}
```

There are several things to note about this snippet. The first is that each proxy has complete control over its own properties to do with as it sees fit. This allows behavior like property-grouping, as seen by the Light group name. The second is that proxies can be more than just simple wrappers. The proxy can do whatever it wants, so long as it does not intrude on the underlying actor. In this case, Lighting Mode doesn't exist on Light. What actually exists on the real actor doesn't matter, so long as the proxy can create one or more properties, or behaviors to handle the difference.

Figure 4.5.3 shows how these properties can look when the BaseLightActorProxy is exposed in a level editor.

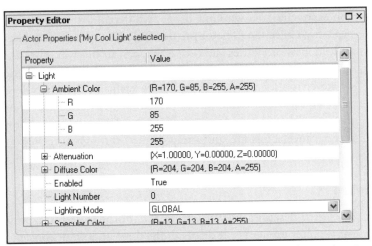

FIGURE 4.5.3   *Properties for* LightActorProxy *exposed in Delta3D.*

From Theory to Practice

This architecture is more than just theory. It's a very real and completely functional system. In fact, it is the basis of the Dynamic Actor Layer found in the Open Source Delta3D game engine [BMH05]. See Color Plate 7.

Early on, we were tasked to build a level editor on top of the existing engine. When we initially began work, we wanted to set up a base actor class and just put the properties directly on actors. Unfortunately, Delta3D was already being used by a variety of applications, and it became impossible to maintain the integrity of the core engine if we imposed a new uniform base class. This was further complicated, because the core engine actors were closely integrated with the scene graph. Fortunately, the proxy solution solved both of these problems while also creating a huge new capability for the engine. Old projects would remain unaffected, and new projects would get an incredibly flexible tool.

Although this article focuses on `ActorProperty`, this is not the only way to leverage `ActorProxy`. In fact, the Delta3D engine makes extensive use of this new architecture. As an example, the level editor needs a 2D billboard representation for all actors. Since the core actor class has no knowledge of properties and certainly knows nothing about level editors, we put that behavior in `ActorProxy`. In addition, we have added basic object messaging, logging, and even invokable message-handling methods to the original `ActorProxy` design. This entire suite of new behaviors required no additional modifications to the underlying actors.

Another thing happened based on the design of `ActorProxy` and `ActorProperty`. Since proxies could be used interchangeably and universally, it became evident that we could abstract that one level higher. So, we created a Dynamic Actor Layer that lets you expose libraries with one or many different actor proxies. Each library generically exposes a collection of actor proxies and actor types, much like `ActorProxy` exposes a collection of properties and property types. In this way, libraries of actors can be built in isolation by remote teams and then loaded dynamically into a game, editor, or whatever tools you want. Each library works at the proxy level, so it never matters what types of actors are under the covers. The final evolution of this design is to dynamically load separate libraries, depending on whether you are the client or the server. Since actors are uniformly defined through `ActorProxy`, base game logic will never know the difference.

Conclusion

This gem describes how to create a uniform layer for exposing and manipulating game object properties. It discusses the three important concepts of actor, `ActorProxy`, and `ActorProperty`, and why a nonintrusive and dynamic way of accessing actors' properties is important. It describes how to create the `ActorProperty` class using functors for the getter and setter, and how to use that to create a hierarchy of property classes. Finally, this gem explains how to pull properties together to create an `ActorProxy` for each of your actors to give you uniform access throughout your game. For more examples of this concept, a complete and fully working implementation of this design is available as part of the Open Source Delta3D project (Web site: *http://www.delta3d.org*).

References

[BMH05] BMH Associates, "The Dynamic Actor Layer." July 2005. Available online at *http://www.delta3d.org*.

[Hickey94] Hickey, Rich, "Callbacks in C++ Using Template Functors." 1994. Available online at *http://www.tutok.sk/fastgl/callback.html*.

4.6

Game Object Component System

Chris Stoy, Red Storm Entertainment

cstoy@nc.rr.com

Game objects are the basic things that exist in the virtual game world, providing the data and functions needed for that object to exist in the simulation. In C++, this is usually done by having a base `Object` class that is then subclassed to provide specific functionality and data. The problems with this approach are the explosion of subclasses that are required to implement each type of object, the duplication of functionality in objects that are not entirely related, and the requirement of every game object to fit within one of the predefined object types. This article proposes a solution to these problems by defining a *component-based game object system* where objects are a collection of components, with each component supplying specific functionality and data. This system also allows for runtime composition of objects and provides a data-driven system for composing a game object.

Game Objects

A game object represents the basic entity that can exist in the game world. At the most general level, it consists of a transform representing the location and orientation of the object, a unique identifier, some state information defining the properties of the object, and methods used to modify and query the state. Some examples of entities that can be represented as game objects are AIs, cars, trees, buildings, weapons, and anything else that represents an individual object in the game world. The problem with traditional hierarchical game object systems is that the amount of state data and the number of methods required to access that data grows to an unmanageable size as the required functionality grows more complex. As complexity increases, it becomes more difficult to understand exactly what all the code is doing, which increases the likelihood that some functionality will be duplicated and errors will crop up.

The Game Object Component System (GOCS) attempts to solve the problems related to class explosion and confusion by forcing functionality out of the game object itself and into components that supply very specific functionality and interfaces. Although initially this may seem like a more complex way of implementing features, it forces the use of proper interfaces for accessing data and compartmentalizes functionality into more-manageable pieces, making maintenance much easier.

At the core of the GOCS is the Game Object (GO). It consists of a transform (i.e., position and orientation in world space), a unique identifier, and a set of Game Object Components (GOCs), as shown in Listing 4.6.1:

Listing 4.6.1   Basic Definition of a Game Object

```
typedef std::string go_id_type;

class GameObject
{
public:
    GameObject( const go_id_type& id );

    const Transform& getTransform() const { return mTransform; }
    void SetTransform( const Transform& xform )
    {
      mTransform = xform;
    }

    const go_id_type& getID() const { return mGOID; }
    void setID( const go_id_type& id } { mGOID = id; }

    GOComponent* getGOC( const goc_id_type& familyID );
    GOComponent* setGOC( GOComponent* newGOC );
    void clearGOCs();

private:

    Transform mTransform; // local to world transform for obj
    go_id_type mGOID;     // unique identifier for this object

    typedef std::map<const GOComponent::goc_id_type, GOComponent*>
        component_table_t;

    component_table_t mComponents;     // map of all the components
};
```

From this basic definition, we can now create a unique object and place it into the scene-management system; however, it doesn't do anything interesting yet. In order to give our new object some functionality, we need to create some GOCs.

Base Game Object Components

The base GOC provides us a common interface that all GOCs must utilize. This allows the GO to manage the components and facilitate their use. Each GOC defines specific data and behaviors related to a specific set of functionality. Some examples of GOCs are health, visual representations, physics management, inventory, and AI functions. The base GOC is defined in Listing 4.6.2.

Listing 4.6.2 The GOC Interface

```
class GOComponent
{
    // GOComponent interface
public:
    typedef std::string goc_id_type;

    GOComponent() : mOwnerGO(0) {}
    virtual ~GOComponent() = 0 {}

    virtual const goc_id_type& componentID() const = 0;
    virtual const goc_id_type& familyID() const = 0;

    virtual void update() {}

    void setOwnerGO( GameObject* go ) { mOwnerGO = go; }
    GameObject* getOwnerGO() const { return mOwnerGO; }

private:
    GameObject* mOwnerGO; // The game object this
                          // component is a member of
};
```

Components are organized into class hierarchies based on the general functionality of the component. These groups of related components are called "families." Every component is derived from a base family component that supplies the common interface for that family of components. The family of a component is obtained with the familyID() method. The root interface class for a family of components must supply this ID, and it must be unique among all other families. One way of doing this is by using the name of the class itself as the family ID.

For example, say we wish to define a family of components used for rendering the visual part of a GO. We could do that as follows:

```
class gocVisual : public GOComponent
{
    // GOComponent interface
public:
    virtual const goc_id_type& familyID() const
        { return goc_id_type("gocVisual"); }

    // gocVisual interface
public:
    virtual void render() const = 0;
};
```

Here we simply override the `familyID()` pure-virtual method to return the ID of this family of components. We also provide a new interface specific to this family of components, consisting of a single new method, `render()`, which is used to render the visual representation of this component. You may think we could use the virtual `update()` method from `GOComponent` to render. However, the update method is meant to be used to update the state of the component. For example, we might need to update the position of bones in a human model before we actually render it.

Now that we can define a family of components, we need to define specific implementations of components in that family. This is done by deriving components from the family GOC interface class. Referring to our `gocVisual` example above, we can define a concrete implementation of the visual that will render a sphere as the visual representation of the object:

```
class gocVisualSphere : public gocVisual
{
    // GOComponent interface
public:
    virtual const goc_id_type& componentID() const
        { return goc_id_type("gocVisualSphere"); }

    // gocVisual interface
public:
    virtual void render() const;


    // gocVisualSphere interface
public:
    gocVisualSphere(float radius );

    const float getRadius() conse { return mRadius; }
    void setRadius( const float r ) { mRadius = r; }

private:
    float    mRadius;    // radius of the sphere
};
```

We have implemented the `componentID()` method from `GOComponent` as well as the `render()` method from `gocVisual`. Although we can now create an instance of this component, we still need to define how we manage the components in a GO.

Component Management in Game Objects

The interface for managing the components in a GO is simple. We need to be able to add components, remove components, and get a component. Doing all of this efficiently can be tricky, but for now we will deal with simply implementing these functions.

One rule that GOs observe when dealing with GOCs is that no two GOCs of the same family can exist within an instance of the GO. Since every GOC provides a specific functionality, having more than one of the same family would require the GO, or higher-level code, to have more knowledge of the GOCs than it needs to.

For instance, if we had two `gocVisual` components in a GO, a `gocVisualSphere` and `gocVisualCube`, someone outside the components would need to decide which visual to use when rendering. This would expose too much information and increase the dependencies throughout the code. In this case, a better solution would be to provide a `gocVisualContainer` component that could contain other `gocVisual` components, and decide which one to use when the `render()` method is called. The interface for accessing components is simple:

```
GOComponent* getGOC( const goc_id_type& familyID );
GOComponent* setGOC( GOComponent* newGOC );
void clearGOCs();
```

The `getGOC()` method will return the GOC with the passed `familyID`, or `NULL` if no such GOC exists. Likewise, `setGOC()` will set the component in the GO to the passed GOC, and if a GOC of that family already existed, returns the pointer to the replaced GOC. Finally, the `clearGOCs()` method will delete all of the GOCs in the GO. Notice that you need to pay attention to ownership of the component so that you do not leak memory. The simplest way to do this is by using a reference counted pointer class, such as `boost::shared_ptr`. However, use whatever method makes sense in your project. As an example, let's create a GO that contains a `gocVisual` and then render using that visual, as shown in Listing 4.6.3:

Listing 4.6.3 Creating and Using Game Objects and Components

```
void init()
{
    // DO INITIALIZATION
    // Assume we have a scene management class with a global
    // instance at gSceneMgr.
    gSceneMgr.clear();

    // create 10 GameObjects with random visual component
    for ( int ii = 0; ii < 10; ++ii )
    {
        GameObject* go = new GameObject( go_id_type( ii ) );
        go->setTransform( /*some random transform*/ );
        GOComponent* gvis = 0;

        // randomly decide which visual representation to use
        if ( rand()%2 )
        {
            gvis = new gocVisualSphere(5.0f);
```

```
        }
        else
        {
            gvis = new gocVisualCube();
        }

        go->setGOC( gvsphere );
    }

    // add the GameObject to our scene manager
    gSceneMgr.add( go );

    // FINISH INITILIZATION AND START MAIN LOOP
}

void renderFunc()
{
    // Assume this is called by the framework to render the scene.
    // Iterate over the scene and render all the game objects
    GameObject* go = gSceneMgr.beginIteration();
    while ( go )
    {
        // render the object
        GOComponent* goc = go->getGOC( goc_id_type("gocVisual") );
        gocVisual* gvis = static_cast<gocVisual*>(goc);
        if ( gvis )
        {
            // we don't need to know what gocVisual this is.
            gvis->render();
        }
        go = gSceneMgr.nextIteration();
    }
}
```

Communication Between Components

Although GOCs are designed to be as independent as possible, it is sometimes necessary for components to communicate with other components in the same GO. For example, a gocAI component may need to access data stored in a gocHealth component in order to make decisions. This is why the base GOC defines an "owner" GO for the component instance. When a component is added to a GO, the owner GO (ownerGO) is set in the component, and when the component is removed, ownerGO is cleared. Using this, a GOC can request another GOC from its owner GO. Care must be taken, however, since referring to a GOC from within another GOC increases coupling between components. In practice, this shouldn't be an issue if care is taken, since the interface requires more thought in accessing the data between GOCs. Let's take the gocAI example mentioned above and show how it would work:

```
#include "gocHealth.h"

gocAI::update()
{
    // see if we are really wounded and, if so, run away
    GameObject* go = getOwnerGO();
    GOComponent* goc = go->getGOC( goc_id_type("gocHealth") );
    gocHealth* health = static_cast<gocHealth*>(goc);
    if ( health )
    {
        if ( health->isWounded() )
        {
            setBehavior( cFleeBehavior );
        }
    }
}
```

Here we see the `gocAI` requests a `gocHealth` from its owner GO. If that component exists, then it uses it to check the wounded state and decides what to do from there.

Game Component Templates

GOs consist of GOCs. So far, the examples we have seen have been fairly simple. In practice, however, the components can become quite complex, and they can manage large amounts of data. For example, let's expand on the `gocHealth` component mentioned above—see Listing 4.6.4.

Listing 4.6.4   Definition of a `gocHealth` Component

```
class gocHealth : public GOComponent
{
    // GOComponent interface
public:
    virtual const goc_id_type& familyID() const
        { return goc_id_type("gocHealth"); }

    // gocHealth interface
public:
    typedef int health_value_t;
    enum bodyPart_e { head=0, torso, leftArm, rightArm,
                      leftLeg, rightLeg, cNumBodyParts };

    gocHealth();

    health_value_t getInitialHealthAt(const bodyPart_e part) const;
    void setInitialHealthAt(const bodyPart_e part,
                            const health_value_t hp);
```

```
    health_value_t getHealthAt(const bodyPart_e part) const;
    void setHealthAt(const bodyPart_e part, const health_value_t hp);

    bool isWounded() const;
    void reset();

private:
    health_value_t mCurrentHPs[cNumBodyParts];
    health_value_t mInitialHPs[cNumBodyParts];
};
```

Using this definition, we can create a new GO with gocHealth properties, as follows:

```
GameObject* go = new GameObject( go_id_type( "Human" ) );
go->setTransform( /*some random transform*/ );

// Create a human visual component
GOComponent* gcvis = new gocVisualHuman();
go->setGOC( gcvis );

// Create and initialize a health component
GOComponent* gchealth = new gocHealth();
gcHealth->setInitialHealthAt( gocHealth::head, 7 );
gcHealth->setInitialHealthAt( gocHealth::torso, 50 );
gcHealth->setInitialHealthAt( gocHealth::leftArm, 20 );
gcHealth->setInitialHealthAt( gocHealth::rightArm, 20 );
gcHealth->setInitialHealthAt( gocHealth::leftLeg, 30 );
gcHealth->setInitialHealthAt( gocHealth::rightLeg, 30 );
gcHealth->reset();
go->setGOC( gchealth );
```

Although this example is manageable, imagine having to code much-more-complex components with large numbers of initialization values. Also, we will most likely want to create more then one instance of a type of GO that all share the same components—for example, a set of AI enemies for your hero to fight. Not only will initializing each component when you create it become a chore, but you will also waste a lot of memory repeating common data in each component instance. In the gocHealth example, the mInitialHPs is constant across all component instances.

The Game Component Template (GCTemplate) solves these issues by defining how to initialize a component of a specific type. It also provides a storehouse for all common data and methods, allowing the actual GOC instance to manage only the changing data. Like GOCs, GCTemplates all inherit from a base interface class:

```
class GCTemplate
{
public:
    GCTemplate() { }
    virtual ~GCTemplate() = 0 { };
```

```
    // returns the GOComponent ID that, by default, we should register
    // created GOComponents as
    virtual const goc_id_type& componentID() const = 0;
    virtual const goc_id_type& familyID() const = 0;

    virtual GOComponent* makeComponent( GameObject* go ) = 0;

};
```

We can then create templates for each GOComponent we use. For example:

```
class gctHealth : public GCTemplate
{
    // GCTemplate interface
public:
    // returns the GOComponent ID that this template can create
    virtual const goc_id_type& componentID() const
        { return goc_id_type("gocHealth"); }
    virtual const goc_id_type& familyID() const
        { return goc_id_type("gocHealth"); }

    virtual GOComponent* makeComponent()
    {
        gocHealth* goc = new gocHealth(this);
        goc->reset();
        return goc;
    }

    // gctHealth interface
public:
    typedef int health_value_t;
    enum bodyPart_e { head=0, torso, leftArm, rightArm,
            leftLeg, rightLeg, cNumBodyParts };

    health_value_t getInitialHealthAt(const bodyPart_e part) const;
    void setInitialHealthAt(const bodyPart_e part,
        const health_value_t hp);

private:
    health_value_t mInitialHPs[cNumBodyParts];

};
```

Note in the gctHealth::makeComponent() method, we call a special constructor of gocHealth that takes the gctHealth template as a parameter. In this constructor, we store the pointer to the gctHealth template we are using to create the gocHealth component. Then, in the gocHealth::reset() method, we refer to the gctHealth template to get the initial hit points. Depending on the amount of data that is constant between component instances, this reference can save us some memory.

By storing these templates in a manager (a GCTemplate manager with a method createGOC() stored in a global singleton, for instance), we can create and initialize a GO, like so:

```
GameObject* go = new GameObject( go_id_type( "Human" ) );
go->setTransform( /*some transform*/ );

// Create a human visual component
GOComponent* gcvis = gTempltMgr->createGOC( "gocVisualHuman" );
go->setGOC( gcvis );

// Create and initialize a health component
GOComponent* gchealth = gTempltMgr->createGOC( "gocHealth" );
go->setGOC( gchealth );
```

Game Object Templates

The GCTemplates simplify the creation of the GO from the hard-coded format we saw before—but we can do better. By storing the set of component templates that we want to make up the GO in a template itself, we make the creation process even easier:

```
class GOTemplate
{
public:
    // type used for the GCTemplate list
    typedef std::list<GCTemplate*> gct_list_t;

    ~GOTemplate();

    // data access
    void clear();

    const std::string& name() const { return m_name; }
    void setName( const std::string& name ) { m_name = name; }

    gct_list_t& components() { return m_components; }

    void addGCTemplate( const GCTemplate* gcTemplate );
    GCTemplate* getGCTemplate( const goc_id_type& id ) const;

protected:
    GOTemplate( const std::string& name );
    std::string m_name;      // name of this template
    gct_list_t m_components;
};
```

Using this template definition, we can create a global manager (GOTemplMgr) that stores the available templates and provides a factory method, createGO(). This allows us to simply create a new instance of a GO:

```
GameObject* go = gGOTemplMgr->createGO( "GO Template Name" );
go->setTransform( /*some transform*/ );
```

Data-Driven Game Object Creation

One of the most powerful features of the game object component system presented is
that we can now define the composition of a particular GO in data. This depends on
the type of data files you wish to create and your resource system. For example, we
could define the above GO in XML using the following data:

```xml
<?xml version="1.0"?>
<game_object_template name="Ped_Female ">
    <components>
        <goc component="gocVisualHuman">
            <model name="Ped_Female"/>
            <scale value="1.1"/>
        </goc>
        <goc component="gocHealth">
            <hitpoints
                head="7"
                torso="50"
                leftArm="20"
                rightArm="20"
                leftLeg="30"
                rightLeg="30"/>
        </goc>
        <goc component="gocAIPedestrian"/>
    </components>
</game_object_template>
```

Assuming the game object template manager (and all supporting classes) implements the parsing functionality, you could easily create any number of GOTemplate
files that define the various objects you wish to use in your game.

Conclusion

This article presented a means of abstracting the component functionality that makes
up the various GOs used in a game. This allows us to create new types of GOs on the
fly by combining the different component functionalities. Using GCTemplates, we
can simplify the process of creating new GOCs, as well as save a little memory. Similarly, we can use a GOTemplate to define what components make up a specific GO
type. Finally, by providing the proper input methods, we can define the GO type
entirely in a data file (such as XML), allowing us to combine the various GOCs to
create unique GO types, all without changing any code.

GRAPHICS

Introduction

Paul Rowan, Rho, Incorporated

paul@rowandell.com

When I started programming games, it was my first chance to see how the professionals did it. I was initially charged with converting games that had made their mark as DOS games, retooling them for fancy GUI interfaces. This was the perfect opportunity to peek inside and get a glimpse at the magic that makes games happen. I remember on frequent occasions looking at a section of code, carefully deciphering its contents and function, and saying to myself, "That's it?" Viewed after the fact, it was obvious, straightforward, even simple. I remember seeing the entire magic processes melt away into believable and understandable pieces that were almost trivial when viewed in isolation. It was then that I began to realize that the magic was in the whole—the sum total of simple mechanics that created a complex and living thing— the game.

Magicians are bound by a code to never reveal the secrets of their profession. To do so would destroy the mystery of their performance and reveal it for what it is—a simple collection of diversions and offstage trickery that, when viewed from the audience, is indistinguishable from magic. I suggest that the magic is in the presentation and the willful suspension of the audience's disbelief, not the secret machinations that bring it about. Giving these secrets away does not break the magicians' code. In fact, it only heightens the mystery. It is the long study, expert skill, and clever performance that creates the magic, not the trickery itself.

This volume of *Game Programming Gems's* graphics section has a mixture of gems ranging from scene and geometry preprocessing to high-end GPU techniques, like per-pixel lighting and high-dynamic range rendering. We have a technique for rendering a wide variety of idle motions on human characters, using only a few basic animations. It is always a challenge to convincingly animate characters when they are not performing some previously prescribed action. Here is a solid approach to doing so. A couple of articles are devoted to scene preprocessing. One is an approach to generating binary trees of bounding volumes that adaptively tunes its heuristic criteria to choose optimal split planes, given the source geometry. Another is a twist on standard bounding-box determination using almost-oriented bounding boxes that compute best-fit approximations to geometry by orienting bounding boxes along a single axis. Additionally, there is an article describing techniques for optimizing the splitting of skinned and animated geometry for efficient GPU processing.

Several articles present approaches to creative uses of the GPU made possible recently via a more-unified shader model and high-precision frame buffers. Though certainly hardware-dependent, these gems will hopefully illustrate creative approaches to problems, even as GPU capabilities advance over the next several years. A couple of articles present uses for the newer vertex-texturing capabilities of modern graphics cards. Long relegated to cooperative work done by the CPU and GPU, now the video card can handle the entire technique. We have an in-depth treatise on a tough problem faced by many developers who attempt to create unified per-pixel lighting engines. This gem presents a solution for handling a large number of lights in a scene without rendering geometry more than once.

One of the most creative gems in this section is an approach to rendering textures that have line-drawn features that never come across effectively when stored on a low-resolution texture. This article provides a way to render road signs and similar features sharply at all scales, using a low-resolution texture and a pixel shader that works much like a font renderer. We also have an efficient approach to rendering dynamic skies, as well as a discussion of high dynamic range rendering techniques.

Here, then, is a piece of the magicians' tome. The following gems are a few of the tricks and sleights-of-hand that, when viewed as pieces, are simple stage tricks and misdirection. Herein you may find solutions that, when viewed in the harsh fluorescent light, create no more stirring a response than "Oh. That's how it's done." The magic is in combining these pieces into a performance that will challenge minds and whiten knuckles. The techniques on their own are simply tools of the trade: the magic is the *performance*.

5.1

Synthesis of Realistic Idle Motion for Interactive Characters

Arjan Egges, Thomas Di Giacomo, and
Nadia Magnenat-Thalmann
MIRALab, University of Geneva

egges@miralab.unige.ch,
thomas@miralab.unige.ch, and
thalmann@miralab.unige.ch

In this gem, we will discuss a class of motions that is often ignored in game development, but that is crucial for creating realistic character movement: *idle motions*. In nature, motionless characters do not exist, while in games we often encounter cases where no planned action (such as waiting for another character finishing their part) is implemented as a stop/frozen animation. We will present an architecture that will allow you to automatically generate idle motions as a part of the character animation engine in your game. Our approach overcomes the limitations of using a small set of existing clips as a basis for synthesizing idle motions. Direct use of a small set of animations results in unnatural repetition of movements and difficulties when inserting idle motions into an animation without breaking its continuity.

Our animation engine uses an exponential map representation for rotations, on which we apply a Principal Component Analysis (PCA). The PCA significantly reduces the dimension of the animation space and therefore allows for faster transfer of animation data, which is very useful for online gaming. Because of the reduced dimensionality, different motions can be generated very quickly while still retaining the dependence between different joints. The result is a wide variety of animations that are consistently realistic.

Introduction

Although virtual models of humans continue to improve both in real-time and nonreal-time applications, controlling and animating them realistically still remains a difficult task. Human beings are moving all the time and in unique ways. When animating a character, one first has to solve the problem of the lack of animation between different animation clips. This prevents an unnatural-looking frozen posture between motions. We will call the motions that occur in waiting/idle states between animation clips *idle motions*. We have identified three categories of idle motions:

Posture shifts: This type of idle behavior concerns the shifting from one resting posture to another. Examples of posture shifts are changing balance while standing, or switching to a different lying or sitting position.

Continuous, small posture variations: Because of breathing, maintaining equilibrium, and so on, the human body constantly makes small movements. When such movements are lacking in characters, they look significantly less lively.

Supplemental idle motions: These types of motions generally concern interacting with one's own body, for example touching of the face or hair, or putting a hand in a pocket.

There has been very little work done on realistically simulating idle motions, with the exception of work by [Perlin95] describing a motion generator (based on a noise function) for a few joints. However, human idle motions affect all joints and cannot easily be solved by using noise functions. Apart from generating random movements for separate joints, another possibility is to take captured animation files as a basis for generating idle motions. This results in idle motions that affect all joints; however, they are very repetitive and inflexible. Second, this approach generates transition problems between different animation clips.

Our method uses a database of existing animations. In our case, these animations are recorded using a motion-capture system, but they can of course also be designed by hand. There are a lot of techniques that generate new animations from an animation database, but they are seldom used to create idle motions. Kovar, et al. [Kovar02] proposes motion graphs for generating animations and transitions based on a motion database. This method could possibly be applied to specific problems other than the demonstrated locomotion; however, this technique relies on a closed database of motions that goes through a preprocessing stage. We want to smoothly adapt it to any animation scheme being motion-captured or computed on the fly. This is a key aspect, since idle motion is rarely the end goal of animators, but rather a convenient way to build a transition between different active movements.

It is therefore desirable to have activate/deactivate functionalities that can be triggered at the AI or script level. Li, et al. [Li02] divided the motion into textons modeled using a linear dynamic system. Additionally, Kim, et al. [Kim03] proposes a method that analyses sound, and that can generate rhythmic motions based on beats that are recognized in the audio stream. These techniques are best suited for motions consisting of rhythmic patterns, such as disco dancing. Pullen, et al. [Pullen02] proposed helping the process of building key-frame animation by automatically generating the overall motion of the character based on a subset of joints animated by the user. In this case, the motion-capture data is used to synthesize motion for joints not animated by the user and to extract a texture (similar to noise) that can be applied to the user-controlled joints.

Our method tries to minimize user intervention, and it is specifically oriented toward real-time applications. Lee, et al. [Lee02] proposes a motion-synthesis method based on example motions that can be obtained through motion capture. Relevant work has also been done by Arikan, et al. [Arikan02] [Arikan03] that defines motion graphs based on an annotated motion database.

Principal Components of Body Animations

Many techniques exist for animating virtual characters. Two very commonly used techniques are:

Key frames: An animation is constructed from a set of key frames (manually designed by an animator or generated automatically) by using interpolation techniques. Although this method results in very flexible animations, the realism of the animations is low, unless a lot of time is invested by the artists.

Pre-recorded animations: An animation is recorded using a motion-capture/tracking system. The animation realism is high, but the resulting animation is usually not very flexible. Methods have been developed to overcome part of this problem [Bruderlin95].

A method like PCA can determine dependencies between variables in a data set. The result of PCA is a matrix (constructed from a set of eigenvectors) that converts a set of partially dependent variables into another set of variables that have maximum independence. The PC variables are ordered corresponding to their occurrence in the data set. Low PC indices indicate a high occurrence in the data set; higher PC indices indicate a lower occurrence in the data set. As such, PCA is also used to reduce the dimension of a set of variables, by removing the higher PC indices from the variable set. As we are focusing on humanoid animations, and we want to be as independent from the geometry as possible, we perform the PCA on the underlying joint skeleton, according to the H-Anim standard [H-Anim05], which specifies a standard skeleton for humanoids.

In order to perform a PCA, we need to convert each frame of the animation sequence in the data set into an n-dimensional vector. In our case, one posture/keyframe is represented by 25 joint rotations (including one root joint) and one root joint translation. Directly applying the PCA on the rotation matrix values does not give a desirable result, since the rotation space has a non-Euclidean geometry. However, a linear version of the (orthogonal) rotation matrix can be constructed, which is called the "exponential map." The exponential map representation of rotations can be obtained by applying a matrix logarithm on an orthogonal rotation matrix. This representation of a rotation is very useful for motion interpolation [Alexa02] [Park97], because it allows applying linear operations on rotations. The matrix logarithm of a rotation results in a skewed symmetric matrix, which can be represented as a vector. In our case, we use 25 joint rotations plus one global translation to define a posture, so this results in a vector of dimension 78.

Although the exponential map representation of orientation allows for easy manipulation and interpolation, there are singularities in the domain. A log map can map each orientation to an infinite number of points corresponding to rotations of $2n\pi + \theta$ about axis v and $2n\pi - \theta$ about axis $-v$ for any $aX + bY + cZ + d = 0$ [Grassia98]. Consequently, measures have to be taken to ensure that these singularities do not interfere with the interpolation. (Please see [Grassia98] for a more detailed discussion.)

We have applied a Principal Component (PC) analysis on the posture vectors, which results in a PC matrix of 78×78. The conversion from a posture represented by a set of quaternions for rotations and one global translation can be converted into a PC vector as follows:

```
void toPC(Posture* p, PCPosture* g) {

    // the vector to be multiplied with the PC matrix
    // PCSIZE = 78
    float* quatTransVector = new float[PCSIZE];

    // get the global translation value
    translation root_trans;
    p->getTranslation(root, root_trans);
    quatTransVector[0] = root_trans.x;
    quatTransVector[1] = root_trans.y;
    quatTransVector[2] = root_trans.z;

    // now put all the joints (PCJOINTS = 25)
    // the getRotation method calculates the exponential map
    // representation of the joint rotation
    for (int joint = 0; joint < PCJOINTS; joint++) {
        skewSymTp rot;
        p->getRotation(joint,rot);
        int location = joint*3 + 3;
        quatTransVector[location] = rot.a;
        quatTransVector[location+1] = rot.b;
        quatTransVector[location+2] = rot.c;
    }

    // calculate product of transposed pcmatrix with //quatTransVector
    for (int row=0; row<PCSIZE; row++) {
```

```
                    float currPC = 0.0f;
                    for (int column=0; column<PCSIZE; column++)
                        currPC += globalpcmatrix_[column][row]
                            * quatTransVector[column];
                    g->setValue(row,currPC);
                }

                // clean up memory
                delete [] quatTransVector;
            }
```

ON THE CD

The conversion from a PC representation to quaternion posture is similar, and it is included on the accompanying CD-ROM. Once you have obtained the PC representation of a posture, you can profit from the dimension reduction due to the structure of the principal components.

In our case, components with an index greater than 25 are mostly zero, and can thus be removed. Although it can in some cases produce some motion errors, removing components greatly reduces the amount of data to be handled as well as the bandwidth required in the case of sending it over a network. As an extension, the dimension reduction can be directly linked to a level-of-detail algorithm that reduces the posture dimension according to the distance from the character in the scene.

Posture Shifting

In this section, we will propose a way to create an animation database from recorded clips. From this database, we can then automatically generate new, realistic animations. These animations can be activated and deactivated on the fly in order to avoid unrealistic static postures between different animation clips. In the following section, we will explain how posture-shifting idle motions can be added to your character's motions. As an example to illustrate our techniques, we use recordings of people standing.

The Basic Animation Structure

When a human is standing, their posture needs to change once in a while due to factors such as fatigue. Between these posture changes, the figure is in a resting posture. We can identify different categories of resting postures, such as balance on the left foot, balance on the right foot, or rest on both feet. As such, given a recording of someone standing, we can extract the animation segments that form the transitions between each of these categories. These animation segments, together, form a *database* that is used to synthesize balancing animations. In order for the database to be usable, at least one animation is needed for every possible category transition. However, more than one animation for each transition is better, since this creates more variation in the motions later on. In order to generate new animations, recorded clips from the database are blended and modified to ensure a smooth transition.

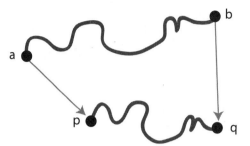

FIGURE 5.1.1 *A simplified example of fitting an animation from postures (a, b) to postures (p, q).*

Each animation segment in the database will have a beginning posture and an ending posture. When we want to chain these segments together, we first need to solve the problem of having a smooth transition between the different animation segments. In order to achieve this, we extend the database with all the possible transitions between beginning and ending postures. We create these "new" animations by adapting the animations that are already in the database, using a process called *animation fitting* (see Figure 5.1.1). In order for this technique to be as realistic as possible, we have to determine which animation in the database would fit best with the beginning posture p and ending posture q. In order to determine this, the system must choose the animation that has a first frame and last frame closest to p and q, respectively. Suppose that the postures are represented by a vector of PC values. We then define the distance between two postures as a weighted Euclidean distance between the two PC vectors. This is illustrated in the following code example:

```
float distance(PCPosture* p, PCPosture* q, int* weight) {
    float dist = 0.0f;
    for (int i=0; i<PCSIZE; i++) {
        float distComp = p->getValue(i) - q->getValue(i);
        dist += weight[i]*(distComp*distComp);
    }
    return dist;
}
```

Using these weights allows us to assign more importance to parts of the posture that occur frequently in the data. As a result, less-relevant parts of the posture contribute least to the distance between postures. The problem of estimating the distance between postures has also been addressed by Kovar, et al. [Kovar02], who uses point clouds that are driven by the skeletons. In our system, we choose these weights so that low PC indices have a higher weight than high PC indices. This way, the most relevant parts of the posture also form the most important factor in the distance calculation. Given the closest animation, we fit it so that it starts and ends at the desired postures:

```
void KeyFrameBodyAnimation::fit(KeyFrame* newkf0, KeyFrame* newkf1) {
    PCPosture* newkf0_pc = newkf0->getPCPosture();
    PCPosture* newkf1_pc = newkf1->getPCPosture();

    PCPosture* oldkf0_pc = keyframes_->begin()->getPCPosture();
    PCPosture* oldkf1_pc = keyframes_->end()->getPCPosture();

    float* offset0 = new float[PCSIZE];
    float* offset1 = new float[PCSIZE];

    for (int u=0; u<PCSIZE;u++) {
        offset0[u] = newkf0_pc->getValue(u)-oldkf0_pc->getValue(u);
        offset1[u] = oldkf1_pc->getValue(u)-newkf1_pc->getValue(u);
    }

    int size = keyframes_->size();
    for (int f=0; f<size; f++) {
        PCPosture* currFrame = keyframes_->at(f)->getPCPosture();
        for (int x=0; x<PCSIZE; x++) {

            // get the old pc value
            float pcval = currFrame->getValue(x);

            // apply the offset
            pcval += (offset0[x]*float(size-f)/float(size);
            pcval += (offset1[x]*float(f)/float(size);
            currFrame->setValue(x,pcval);
        }
    }
}
```

Extending the database using this technique is very fast, since we only perform linear operations on the animations. In order to further improve the speed, the nature of the PCs can be exploited by only applying the fitting procedure to a subset of principal components. The only thing to consider is that this animation-fitting technique only works for animations that differ little in their amount of displacement. For idle motions, this is fortunately the case.

Removing the Translation Offset

Since we will use the animations from the database later to create balance-shifting sequences, it is necessary to apply a normalization step so that the relative translations between the animations are minimized. We estimate the translation offset for each of the animation sequences to the origin (0, 0, 0) by the mean value of the first and last frames of the animation (see Figure 5.1.2).

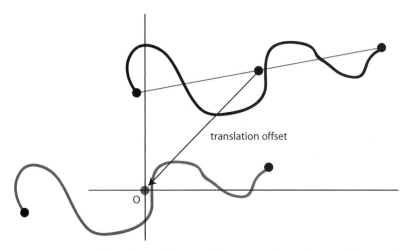

translation offset

O

FIGURE 5.1.2   *This figure illustrates the estimated translation offset in the (x, z)-plane (frontal-lateral plane) for an animation sequence.*

In order to remove this offset from the animation, for each frame we subtract the translation offset from the root translation for each frame. This is illustrated in the following code example:

```
void KeyFrameBodyAnimation::removeTransOffset() {
    // calculate the offset
    translation firstTrans, lastTrans, offsetTrans;
    keyframes_->begin()->getPosture()->getTrans (root,firstTrans);
    keyframes_->back()->getPosture()->getTrans (root,lastTrans);
    offsetTrans = -(firstTrans+lastTrans)/2.0f;

    // apply the offset
    for (int i=0; i<keyframes_->size(); i++) {
        Posture* p = keyframes_->at(i)->getPosture();
        translation currTrans;
        p->getTranslation(root,currTrans);
        currTrans += offsetTrans;
        p->setTranslation(root,currTrans);
    }
}
```

There are other possibilities to estimate the translation offset. For example, one could search the most-central key posture in the animation, or use the timing information to determine the middle of the posture shift.

Constructing a New Animation

Using the techniques previously described, we can now extend the database so that an animation exists between any beginning and ending posture. This extended database is then used to create new animations by sequencing the posture-shift segments. A pause is placed between each posture-shift segment so that the character waits an amount of time between each posture shift. Figure 5.1.3 shows some example postures of an animation that we have created using this system. More demonstration movies are available on the CD-ROM.

ON THE CD

FIGURE 5.1.3 *Some examples of postures created with the idle-motion engine.*

Although in our examples the PCA was performed on a database of standing people, this technique is not limited to only synthesizing standing humans. A more extensive database can be constructed that contains not only balance shifts of standing people, but also animations of sitting people that change their posture, or changes in the postures of reclining people. A problem that arises is the fact that these types of postures are relative to one or more objects—a chair or a bed, for example. However, the idle motion can be played relative to the human's position in space after performing the normalization procedure, as previously described.

Continuous Small Variations in Posture

Apart from the balance-shifting postures that were discussed in the previous section, small posture variations also greatly improve the realism of an animation. Due to factors such as breathing or small muscle contractions, humans can never exactly maintain the same posture as a robot would. As a basis for the synthesis of these small posture variations, we use the principal component representation for each key frame. Since the variations apply to the PCs and not directly to the joint parameters, it generates random variations that still take into account the dependencies between joints. Additionally, because the PCs represent dependencies between variables in the data, the PCs are variables that have maximum independency. As such, we can treat them separately for generating posture variations.

One method to generate variations is to apply a Perlin noise function [Perlin85] for each of the principal components or a subset thereof. Here, we propose another method that generates these small variations based on the shape of the curves in the motion-capture data. This method applies a statistical model to generate similar (random) curves. This approach also allows keeping certain existing tendencies in the variations that are specific to certain persons, such as typical head movements. An additional advantage over using Perlin noise is that this approach is fully automatic, and it does not require defining frequencies and amplitudes to generate noise. We analyze animation segments that do not contain any balance shifts or other motions other than the small variations. The results of the analysis will then be used to generate similar variations on top of other postures.

The selected animation segments need to be normalized so that only the variations persist and the base postures are removed. This is necessary because these variations will be synthesized on top of the balance-shifting postures. In order to normalize an animation segment, we calculate the mean value of each PC in the segment and subtract it from the PC values in each key frame. This removes the base posture and retains only the variations (see Figure 5.1.4). Clearly, this approach only works when dealing with animation sequences where the base posture does not change significantly during the sequence.

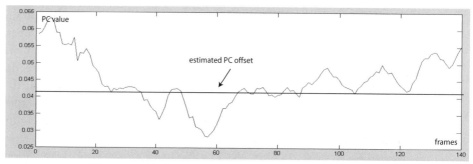

FIGURE 5.1.4   *This example shows the values of a principal component for an animation segment. The offset is estimated by the mean value, which is around 0.045.*

Variation Prediction

Now we describe how to predict the variations according to motion-capture data. To illustrate this process, we use the PC values of the animation segment in Figure 5.1.4. In order to reduce the number of points in the PC curve while retaining its global shape, the PC values are converted to a set of maxima and minima (see Figure 5.1.5). Then we will show a technique to predict the next maximum/minimum, given its predecessor point. For estimating the maximum and minimum, a simple algorithm can walk through the points and, given an error value *e*, determine if a point is a maximum or a minimum.

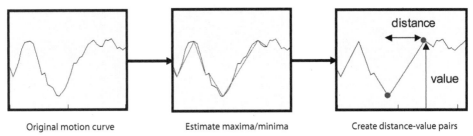

Original motion curve   Estimate maxima/minima   Create distance-value pairs

FIGURE 5.1.5   *Analysis and segmentation of an existing stream of small posture varia-tions for one PC into distance-value pairs.*

In order to remove the absolute timing from the data, we specify each maximum/minimum by defining its distance (in milliseconds) from the previous maximum/minimum and the corresponding PC value (see Figure 5.1.5). The next step is to construct a system that can, given a distance-value pair, predict the next distance-value pair. The generated distance-value pairs then form a new animation sequence.

In order to add some randomness to the system, we do not use the points directly, but we apply a point-clustering algorithm. In our application, we have applied a minimal spanning tree clustering algorithm [Jain99]. The algorithm is applied on the distance-value space, resulting in a set of clusters of nearby distance-value pairs (see Figure 5.1.6). From the motion-capture data, we know the successor for each distance-value pair. Using this information, we can define the probability of any transition between two clusters, resulting in a *probability transition matrix*. In order to ensure that there is always a transition possible, we keep merging clusters until there is no cluster from which there is no transition to another cluster possible—which basically means: no dead ends. The probabilistic model can be used to generate new animations, according to the following algorithm:

1. Add the neutral position at time $t = 0$.
2. Randomly select a cluster of points.
3. Randomly choose a point (i.e., a distance-value pair) within the cluster.
4. Add a key frame to the animation at time $t + distance$, with the specified PC value.
5. Based on the last selected cluster, choose the next cluster according to the probability transition matrix.
6. Randomly choose a point (i.e., distance-value pair) within the cluster.
7. Go to Step 4 and repeat until the desired length of the animation is reached.

Because the animations are not produced from the original points, but from randomly chosen points in the clusters, the variations show very little repetition. However, the PC value curve over the animation still has a very similar structure to the animation

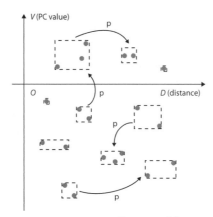

FIGURE 5.1.6   *A collection of distance-value pairs obtained from motion-capture data and clustered by the minimal spanning tree algorithm. The arrows represent the probability that a transition takes place from one cluster to another.*

samples that were analyzed. In order to have a variation synthesis, the process of generation of animation segments, which is described in this section, is applied to a subset of PC values. For each principal component, the variations are generated independently. This does not give unrealistic results, since the dependency between principal components is relatively small. The final result of the variation synthesis shows little to no repetition. This is due to the random choice of points in each cluster and because of the separate treatment of PCs. The method presented here to generate similar curves from a given curve is not limited to idle-motion synthesis. You can apply it to any problem you have where you need something more or less random, but still following a certain pattern—for example, when you want to generate textures or sounds from existing data that look and sound the same, but still are different.

Integration into a Real-Time System

In order to integrate the idle motions into a game where other animations might be playing, an infrastructure is needed that governs how the animations are mixed with the existing animations. The existing animations can be key-frame gestures, head movements, walking, and so on. The idle motions are blended relative to the other animations so that the idle motions can be played independently of the location and rotation of the corresponding virtual human. You can link every virtual human with an idle-motion engine that uses animation segments from different databases. In that way, you can place several virtual humans in one scene and have them all display different idle-motion behavior. A more precise description of how to blend the idle motions with other motions is given in [Egges04a] and [Egges04b].

Mixing idle motions with other animations happens in two steps (see Figure 5.1.7). First, the balance-shifting motions are blended with the other animations, using a weight factor. This blending happens at the joint level, which allows defining joint masks that specify which parts of the animations should be discarded in the final animation. Using these masks is crucial, since there are certain animations, such as walking or running, which should not be blended with any balance-shifting motions. Also, the masks indicate which part of the motion should not be changed. For example, in a gesture animation, the moving arms should not be blended with the static arm posture in the idle motions. This would result in a less pronounced gesture.

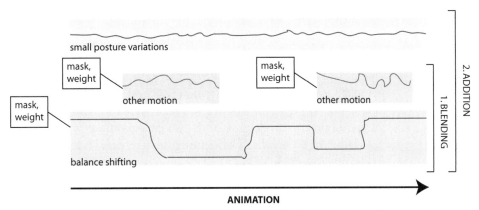

FIGURE 5.1.7   *Integration of idle motions into a real-time animation framework.*

After blending the balance-shifting motions with the other animations, the small posture variations are added to the animation. The addition of small posture variations happens in PC space. For each frame of the animation, the PC values of the blended animation and the variation animation are summed, resulting in the final animation. This approach works because, although the variations add to the realism of the virtual human during static postures, their presence during the animation segments is hardly noticeable.

Conclusion

The techniques that are described in this article allow creation of a system that, based on a database of animations and postures, can realistically reconstruct idle motions that are coherent with the animations and postures in the database. The animations can be generated and played in real time on any standard, 2-GHz desktop PC, since the most time-consuming calculations are precomputed during the data-analysis part. Additionally, the conversion between PC values and rotation matrices follows the real-time operation constraints, as it consists of applying a logarithm/exponential of a 3×3 matrix (or quaternion) and a matrix multiplication for each key frame.

References

[Alexa02] Alexa, M., "Linear combination of transformations." *SIGGRAPH 2002,* 2002: pp. 380–387.

[Arikan02] Arikan, O., et al., "Interactive motion generation from examples." *Proceedings of ACM SIGGRAPH 2002,* 2002.

[Arikan03] Arikan, O., et al., "Motion synthesis from annotations." *ACM Transactions on Graphics,* 22(3), pp. 392–401, 2003.

[Bruderlin95] Bruderlin, A., et al., "Motion signal processing." *Computer Graphics,* Vol. 29 (Annual Conference Series), 1995: pp. 97–104.

[Egges04a] Egges, A., et al., "Personalised Real-Time Idle Motion Synthesis." *Pacific Graphics 2004,* Seoul, Korea: pp. 121–130, October 2004.

[Egges04b] Egges, A., et al., "Example-based idle motion synthesis in a real-time application." *CAPTECH Workshop,* 2004: pp. 13–19.

[Grassia98] Grassia, F. S., "Practical parameterization of rotations using the exponential map." *Journal of Graphics Tools,* 3(3): 29–48, 1998.

[H-Anim05] H-ANIM Humanoid Animation Working Group, "Specification for a standard humanoid." August 2005. Available online at *http://www.h-anim.org/*.

[Jain99] Jain, A. K., et al., "Data clustering: a review." *ACM Computing Surveys,* 31(3): pp. 264–323, 1999.

[Kim03] Kim, T. H., et al., "Rhythmic-motion synthesis based on motion-beat analysis." *ACM Transactions on Graphics,* 22(3): pp. 392–401, 2003.

[Kovar02] Kovar, L., et al., "Motion graphs." *Proceedings of SIGGRAPH 2002,* 2002.

[Lee02] Lee, J., et al., "Interactive control of avatars animated with human motion data." *Proceedings of SIGGRAPH 2002,* July 2002.

[Li02] Li, Y., et al., "Motion texture: A two-level statistical model for character motion synthesis." *Proceedings of SIGGRAPH 2002,* 2002.

[Park97] Park, F., et al., "Smooth invariant interpolation of rotations." *ACM Transactions on Graphics,* 16(3): pp. 277–295, July 1997.

[Perlin85] Perlin, K., "An image synthesizer." *Proceedings of the 12th Annual Conference on Computer Graphics and Interactive Techniques,* ACM Press, 1985: pp. 287–296.

[Perlin95] Perlin, K., "Real time responsive animation with personality." *IEEE Transactions on Visualization and Computer Graphics,* 1(1), 1995.

[Pullen02] Pullen, K., et al., "Motion capture assisted animation: Texturing and synthesis." *Proceedings of SIGGRAPH 2002,* 2002.

5.2

Spatial Partitioning Using an Adaptive Binary Tree

Martin Fleisz

There are various techniques available for spatial partitioning; all of them have their merits and drawbacks. In most cases, the disadvantages depend on the properties of the processed geometry. For instance, certain techniques are very efficient for indoor scenes while being totally useless when applied on vast landscapes.

Therefore, Yann Lombard introduced the concept of Adaptive Binary Trees (ABTs) as an alternative partitioning method [Lombard02]. ABTs differ from other available techniques in that the ABT splits the space based on the scene geometry. Split volumes can be dynamically resized and can overlap to reduce the number of split faces. The split plane is determined by using a scoring system that takes different parameters into account, like the number of split faces and the splitting plane's location in space. Because of this adaptive behavior, the ABT is very well suited for partitioning any kind of scene.

How To Build an Adaptive Binary Tree

First, we create the root node of the tree. This is done easily by spanning an axis-aligned bounding box over the whole scene. Then we start a recursive subdivision function where in each step, the box is divided by a splitting plane that is perpendicular to one of the three major axes. As a result, two child nodes are created. Both are surrounded again by axis-aligned bounding boxes that can easily be tested against the viewing frustum. The function is stopped if the number of surfaces in a node reaches a predefined limit or if the tree becomes too deep.

So far, creating an ABT sounds relatively easy; however there is still one question left: How does one determine what plane is to be used to split a node efficiently? In his first ABT description, Lombard described the process of finding this plane as a mathematical minimization of different criteria (and their respective functions) [Lombard02]. Let us take a closer look at these criteria now:

Good Localization of Space

Our primary goal is to minimize the largest axis of the resulting child bounding boxes. This function will favor a plane that cuts the largest axis of the current node's bounding box.

$$f_1(pos) = \max\left(split\_x\_axis, split\_y\_axis, split\_z\_axis\right) \qquad (5.2.1)$$

Volume of Child Nodes

Both resulting child nodes should have nearly the same volume. This function favors planes that divide the current node into equal-size volumes.

$$f_2(pos) = abs\left(volume\_child1 - volume\_child2\right) \qquad (5.2.2)$$

Number of Faces

Surfaces should be evenly distributed over all leaves.

$$f_3(pos) = abs\left(numfaces\_child1 - numfaces\_child2\right) \qquad (5.2.3)$$

Number of Split Faces

This function evaluates the plane's face-splitting. The more faces the plane splits, the less appropriate it is as a division plane.

$$f_4(pos) = total\_number\_of\_split\_faces \qquad (5.2.4)$$

To find the best partitioning plane, all the functions above must be minimized. This is not as trivial as it may sound at first, because functions f_3 and f_4 both exhibit discrete behavior, which means that they can have many local minima (depending on the topology of the geometry). Additionally, each function is weighted by a factor, which provides even more control over the creation process. Using all this information, we end up with the following equation that has to be minimized to get a viable plane.

$$f(pos) = f_1(pos) \cdot w1 + f_2(pos) \cdot w2 + f_3(pos) \cdot w3 + f_4(pos) \cdot w4 \qquad (5.2.5)$$

The ideal distribution of the weighting factors depends on the requirements of the engine. If a scene already has a high polygon count, creating more rendering data should be avoided due to face splits; therefore, function f_4 should attract a higher weight than the others.

After a splitting plane is found, the node is split in two parts. Although function f_4 was minimized for the plane evaluation, many faces are still split. The ABT overcomes this problem simply by overgrowing the node's bounding boxes. The idea behind this behavior is that an ABT node does not need to represent a distinct region of space, but an approximate one [Lombard02]. To keep the tree's hierarchy efficient, the two child nodes should not grow too much. Lombard advises that the growth factor should be made a maximal percentage of a child box's volume. Using a factor between 5%–10% should eliminate nearly 90% of the split faces.

We have now finished the creation of our tree. Under certain circumstances, we would have to optimize the bounding volumes of the ABT, as Lombard suggests. However, this is rarely the case. In the end, you will get a perfectly balanced tree containing all the geometry data ready to be rendered.

ABT Implementation Details

The Search for a Splitting Plane

At first glance, the concepts behind an ABT seem very easy and logical. However, when implementing one, things might not be as straightforward as they first seemed. The most difficult step during creation is undoubtedly the determination of a splitting plane. At the same time, it is the most important part in building an ABT. The more perfectly the chosen plane splits the current geometry set, the better the final tree will perform when used for frustum culling. Let us now take a closer look at the implementation of the plane-selection part (see Figure 5.2.1).

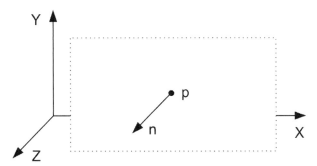

FIGURE 5.2.1 *Splitting plane defined by its normal* n *and the point* p, *perpendicular to the* z *axis.*

As mentioned earlier, the splitting plane's orientation is always perpendicular to the *x-*, *y-*, or *z*-axis. A plane can be simply determined by its normal vector and a point where it is passing through. Before starting with our search, we already have much information about the plane we are looking for. First, we know the normal vector—we can simply take the major axis perpendicular to our plane. Second, we need a point that lies on our plane or, to be more specific, we only need to know one coordinate of this point, namely the one that lies along the normal major axis. This is because our plane can be spanning infinitely into the other two dimensions, which means that we can chose any value for the associated coordinates. Here is a simplified outline of how to implement a plane-searching function:

```
Plane getBestSplitter(AABB curAABB, Surfaces *pSurfaceList,
    int iNumSurfaces)
{
    Plane bestPlane;
    float fBestPlaneScore = 1000000.0f;

    // we scan along each axis
    for(int iCurAxis = 0; iCurAxis < 3; iCurAxis++)
    {
        // curPlane's normal and point are both initialized
        // with 0/0/0
        Plane curPlane;

        // init plane's normal (parallel to scanning axis)
        curPlane.Normal.xyz[iCurAxis] = 1.0f;

        // sample a few planes along the current axis
        for(int i = 0; i < SAMPLES; i++)
        {
            // get the missing coordinate to finalize our plane
            curPlane.Point.xyz[iCurAxis] = getSample(i);

            // calculate the plane's score
            float fScore = getPlaneScore(curAABB, curPlane,
                                        pSurfaceList);

            // check if we got a better plane
            if(fScore < fBestPlaneScore)
            {
                bestPlane = curPlane;
                fBestPlaneScore = fScore;
            }
        }
    }
    return bestPlane;
}
```

ON THE CD

If you are looking for more detailed information on this topic, please refer to the ABT demo source code on the CD-ROM.

Determining a Plane's Score

After we have chosen a plane as a potential splitter candidate, we must calculate its score, using the evaluation functions already described. Because their definitions might seem somewhat vague, here is one possible way to implement them [Campbell03]:

$$f_1 = 1 - Length\big(ThisAxis\big)\big/Length\big(LargestAxis\big) \qquad (5.2.6)$$

Function f_1 calculates the ratio of the current scanning axis's length and the largest axis of the bounding box. If we split the largest axis, the result will be zero. If we split an axis that has nearly the same size as the longest one, the function will return a smaller value than for a much shorter axis.

$$f_2 = 2 * fabs\big(0.5 - SplitPercent\big) \qquad (5.2.7)$$

The *SplitPercent* parameter for f_2 in Equation 5.2.7 indicates how far into the volume the split reaches (e.g., 0.25 at a quarter, 0.5 in the middle, and so on) [Campbell03]. The equation will return higher values when the splitting plane's distance to the center of the current bounding box increases.

$$f_3 = fabs\big(NumFrontFaces - NumBackFaces\big)\big/NumFaces \qquad (5.2.8)$$

NumFrontFaces and *NumBackFaces* specify the number of faces in front of and behind the splitting plane, respectively. The higher the difference, the worse the result for f_3 will be.

$$f_4 = NumSplitFaces\big/NumFaces \qquad (5.2.9)$$

Equation 5.2.9 evaluates the proportion of split faces (given by the *NumSplitFaces* parameter) to the total number of faces in the current geometry set.

Controlling the Plane Selection

One question that often arises when implementing an ABT relates to the distribution of the different weighting factors. The short answer to this question is: There are no standard values that work well in all situations. If you have a lot of geometry data, you want to avoid the creation of further geometry due to splitting. Therefore, you will give function f_4 a higher weight than the others. Or, say you want to partition a terrain created from a height map where the geometry is evenly laid out. In this case, you won't have to care about function f_4, because there will be hardly any splits. (Even if the plane is not perfectly aligned with the geometry, splits will be avoided thanks to the relaxed bounding boxes.) You can use this information to give the function a very low or even zero weight, making the other parameters more important.

Actually, the weighting factors in the plane's scoring function provide an important feature to the user. With their help, you can gain total control over the tree creation without modifying any code. You can apply different weightings for different scene types and tweak them to get the best performance out of your ABT.

Dealing with "Critical Faces"

If you take a closer look at the ABT you have created, you may notice the following problem: Several leaves contain a small subset of faces with a certain material attached. Rendering such small data sets has a negative impact on performance and therefore should be avoided. To avoid these "critical faces" there are three solutions [Lombard03], (see Figure 5.2.2).

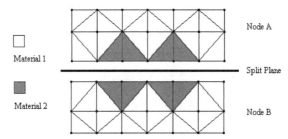

FIGURE 5.2.2   *Critical faces (using material 1) after splitting a node into two children.*

The first possibility is to deal with this problem directly by extending the plane score equation with a function that takes material boundaries into account. However, as Lombard states, the applicability of this approach depends on the way the material management is implemented in the engine.

Another way to overcome this problem is to reinsert critical faces. After identifying the faces, you can try adding them to a nearby node that already contains faces with the specified material. However, because of this process, the other node grows, which has an adverse impact on the tree's localization. One small side note: This is also a case where you have to optimize the bounding boxes of the tree, as described at the end of the ABT creation process.

The third option that Lombard used works completely differently from the other ones. When critical faces are identified, they are simply dumped in a "quarantine list" and removed from the leaf. After completion of the build process, we have our primary ABT along with a list of faces that are difficult to localize, which are distributed all over the scene. Now we run a second ABT creation over the critical faces. The resulting tree will be much shallower than the primary ABT and will contain much fewer faces. Faces sharing the same material will now be merged into a single node, since the nodes will have much larger volumes. Of course now we have to traverse two trees during rendering, which will cost a little bit in terms of performance. On the other hand, the rendering data is much more hardware-friendly now, and the result is an overall increase in performance.

Finding a Suitable Splitting Plane

The most difficult part when creating an ABT is finding the best candidate for a splitting plane. The number of possible planes is infinite; hence we have to select a small subset of them. Lombard's first ABT implementation used a neural network to find a suitable plane. However, one drawback of this approach is that it performs poorly, especially on large data sets [Lombard03]. Because the split plane selection is an important part in the ABT creation process, the following sections describe a number of approaches to identifying a suitable set of planes.

Linear Sampling

Linear sampling is a straightforward and fast way to find a splitting plane. Such a set could include planes that split the current volume at 10%, 20%, or whatever percentage of the length of one axis that you desire. While this method is very easy to implement, it is not recommended for building ABTs. Most nodes will contain "hotspots," which means that they concentrate their geometry in some small subvolume that will be most certainly missed with this approach [Lombard03].

Successive Approximation

A different way to obtain a splitting plane is to use successive approximations. We first select a plane that splits the volume in the middle, along one of the three major axes, and calculate its score. Now we select two subplanes where each one is one-quarter of the volume's size, away from the first plane in each direction. The plane with the best score is chosen as the next center plane, and the previous step is repeated, with the only difference that the distance to the new subplanes is now cut in half (only one-eighth of the volume's size). To illustrate, Figure 5.2.3 shows the first five steps of this approach. The approximation can be stopped after a few iterations, or if both subplanes have a worse score than the center plane. You may have already noticed that this process is like a binary search.

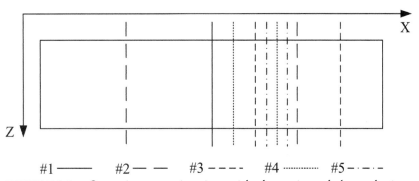

FIGURE 5.2.3 *Successive approximations with alternating subplane selection, starting on the right-hand side.*

Stochastic Sampling

Another method that is easy to implement is to use a stochastic sampler that simply chooses planes at random locations in the volume and calculates their scores. Finally, the plane with the best score is chosen as the splitter. One disadvantage of this technique is that geometry hotspots can be missed—as is the case when using linear sampling. Using a good random-number generator and enough samples is one way to avoid this problem.

Nonuniform Sampling

As already mentioned, using uniform sampling strategies is not the best way to find a splitting plane. Mirko Teran-Ravniker uses a nonuniform sampling approach that is based on a sinus for his ABT creation [Teran-Ravniker04]. With this method, the test planes become denser in the middle, which provides quite good results.

All-Vertices Approach

During his research, Lombard came up with the following approach that represents the mathematically perfect solution to this problem. If we take a closer look, we can distinguish between two different types of functions used in our scoring equation. First, we have ordinary linear functions, like the "location in space" and "child volume" functions (f_1 and f_2). The second type is called a "piecewise-defined" function— for example, the "child faces" and "split faces" functions (f_3 and f_4). If you graph these functions over all possible positions within the axis of interest, you will get a quantized graph. This means that you will only get integer numbers that remain constant over a certain length and then suddenly leap to another integer. Refer to Figures 5.2.4 and 5.2.5 for illustrations of the piecewise-defined function f_4.

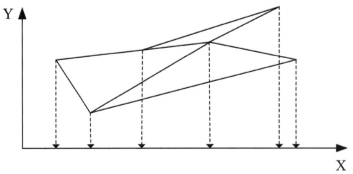

FIGURE 5.2.4   *A set of triangles with their vertices projected onto the x-axis.*

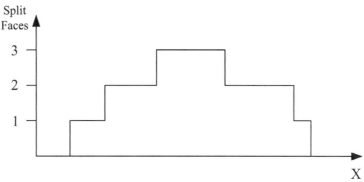

FIGURE 5.2.5   *The corresponding graph of the piecewise-defined function f_4.*

As can be seen in Figure 5.2.5, the leaps in the graph of function f_4 are not random; they always coincide with the vertex position of a face, projected onto the scanning axis. This means that between two points, the number of split faces is constant, and f_4 will always return the same result. If we now analytically solve the linear functions between two points, we will get the local minimum. If we repeat this operation for all other vertices, we will yield the perfect global minimum.

Using this method will create a perfect ABT. However it has one drawback; it is very time consuming. In the worst-case scenario, if you have a scene containing n vertices, you will have to calculate the score of $3 \times (n-1)$ planes. The number will usually be smaller, because there are a few vertices that project onto the same point on the scanning axis. One way to further decrease this number would be to scan just the longest axis for a division plane. In this case, keep in mind when selecting the weighting factors that the f_1 parameter from the plane equation will be rendered useless, as it is going to be zero all the time.

Statistically Weighted Multisampling

Andy Campbell came up with a very fast method that works amazingly well to find a suitable plane for splitting. First, we have to calculate the mean point of our current geometry set. Then we calculate the standard deviation to get the statistical spread of the vertices in space. In the next step, we sample 10 planes within one standard deviation on each side of the mean. Planes can be sampled either uniformly separated from each other or by increasing the distance as the samples get farther away from the mean.

The advantage of this method over the all-vertices approach is that it requires much fewer plane evaluations. It is also possible to combine this method with any of the other techniques. Instead of sampling the whole volume for planes, you would only sample in the area within one standard deviation from the mean. The results with this technique are almost as good as the ones returned by the all-vertices approach.

Using an ABT for Dynamic Scenes

The ABT in its current state is almost perfect for rendering static geometry. However, in modern games, users expect a certain amount of dynamics. This requires game developers to include dynamic objects in the engine that, in contrast to static geometry, can change their positions each frame. If we apply a few slight modifications, we can also use an ABT for dynamic objects [Lombard02].

Let's assume each dynamic geometry chunk has an axis-aligned bounding box assigned to it that follows the object wherever it moves. All we have to do now is to reunify the bounding volumes of all nodes between the leaf and the root, as can be seen in Figure 5.2.6.

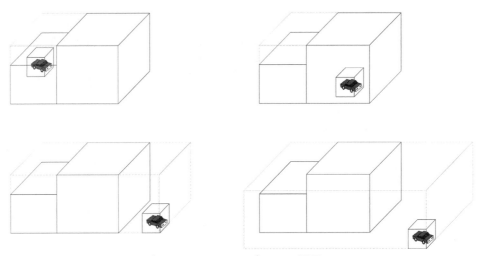

FIGURE 5.2.6 *Dynamic object moving around in an ABT.*

You'll immediately notice how the size of the parent node's bounding box increases when the object moves. The problem with this technique is that over time, if an object moves over a long distance, the ABT will slowly degenerate. This means that the tree's culling efficiency will be decreased further, resulting in a performance hit. One solution Lombard came up with is to introduce a degeneracy factor for each node that indicates to what extent the current node differs from its original volume. If this factor passes a certain threshold, the whole branch is rebuilt on the fly [Lombard02].

Another way of dealing with dynamic objects is to move the objects to higher tree levels so that they fit inside the bounding volume of a node. The problem with this method is that objects will quickly move up the tree, making the tree useless. This is because two locally near nodes must not be near in the hierarchical tree structure. Therefore, if an object crosses the border of two such nodes, it will slide up the tree and end up in the root node. As a result, a large percentage of objects will be located in the upper regions of the tree [Lombard03].

As you can see, ABTs can be used to manage scenes that contain dynamic objects. However, there is still some room for improvement in this area. Usually it is a good idea to separate these objects from their static counterparts and put them in their own spatial tree, although this requires processing and managing of a second tree.

Rendering an ABT

Rendering an ABT is very simple and extremely efficient. Starting at the root node, all you have to do is to check if the two children's bounding boxes are inside the viewing frustum. For each child that passes this test, repeat this step until either a child is not visible (i.e., its bounding box is outside the viewing frustum) or you hit a leaf. In the second case, you simply render the stored geometry data.

However, rendering does not only involve sending rendering data to the GPU, but also incorporates state changes. A leaf will most certainly contain geometry that uses several different textures, and vertex or pixel shaders for rendering. All these state changes are expensive, and therefore should be kept to an absolute minimum. Lombard gave a good example of how to increase the rendering efficiency of an ABT [Lombard02]. Let's assume we have, as shown in Table 5.2.1, a set of sorted faces after the tree was created, where several state changes are referenced by a shader state ID.

Table 5.2.1 Face List with Associated Leaves and Shaders

Face	Leaf ID	Shader State ID
1	123	0x12345678
2	123	0xABCDEF00
3	123	0xABCDEF00
4	123	0xABCDEF00
5	200	0x12345678
6	200	0x12345678
7	200	0xABCDEF00

From this list, we can build the list of faces in Table 5.2.2, attached to a specific node.

Table 5.2.2 Node List with Attached Faces

Leaf ID	Start Face	Number of Faces	Shader State ID
123	1	1	0x12345678
	2	3	0xABCDEF00
200	5	2	0x12345678
	7	1	0xABCDEF00

If we normally traverse the tree and render each node, we have to make three state changes in the examples shown in the tables, although the same work could be done using only one change. Therefore, instead of traversing the tree and rendering each node immediately, we create a render-state list sorted on shader state ID (see Table 5.2.3).

Table 5.2.3 Final Render-State List Sorted on Shader ID

Start Face	Number of Faces	Shader State ID
1	1	0x12345678
5	2	0x12345678
2	3	0xABCDEF00
7	1	0xABCDEF00

In addition, it is advisable to store a reference to the vertex data in the list, as well, to further increase efficiency. The following pseudo code snippet shows how the final render-state list is used to render the ABT's data [Lombard02].

```
for(each entry in render state list)
{
    if(Entry->ShaderStateID != LastEntry->ShaderStateID)
    {
        SetNewState(Entry->ShaderStateID);
    }

    RenderVertexArray(Entry->VAPointer);
    LastEntry = Entry;
    Entry++;
}
```

Especially in scenes with many different materials, the performance gain from the reduced amount of API calls will far outweigh the overhead caused by the sorting of the list. Of course, this method requires some sort of materials management that allows comparing a surface's shading parameters easily.

Conclusion

The ABT is a very efficient spatial-partitioning technique because of the adaptive behavior during creation. Each node is split into two child nodes, until the number of faces in a node meets a predefined threshold. The plane that cuts the current node's volume in two can be determined using different approaches. This includes simple linear sampling as well as successive approximation, or even more-sophisticated methods. The ABT can also handle dynamic objects. However, there are a few things to consider in this case. Although the implementation seems complicated at first, it is actually quite easy, and almost every graphics engine will benefit from using this type of spatial data structure.

Acknowledgments

Thank you to Anthony Whitaker and Yann Lombard for their help with this article.

References

[Campbell03] Campbell, Andy, "ABT questions: construction and use." June 16, 2003. Available online at *http://www.gamedev.net/community/forums/topic.asp?topic_id=163240*.

[Lombard02] Lombard, Yann, "ABT—What it is, and how to build them." November 14, 2002. Available online at *http://www.gamedev.net/community/forums/viewreply.asp?ID=675554*.

[Lombard03] Lombard, Yann, "Answers to ABT questions." June 21, 2003. Available online at *http://www.gamedev.net/community/forums/viewreply.asp?ID=961492*.

[Teran-Ravniker04] Teran-Ravniker, Mirko, "Tranquility Demo" February 23, 2004. Available online at *http://fly.to/teran*.

5.3

Enhanced Object Culling with (Almost) Oriented Bounding Boxes

Ben St. John, Siemens

ben.stjohn@siemens.com

Object level culling is the recognition that an entire object is not visible from the camera, without checking each triangle or point of the object. This ability is an important part of any graphics system that hopes to efficiently display complex scenes. The value of a culling system lies in the relation between the cost of calculating the visibility of an object to that of it continuing further down the render pipeline; this generally means finding the right tradeoff between the accuracy and complexity of the visibility calculation. Historically, this has meant very simple (if somewhat inaccurate) tests.

This gem presents a technique for improving the accuracy of object-bounding, which is useful for all manner of operations, including collision detection, lines of sight, picking, occlusion, and view frustum culling. We will focus specifically on view frustum culling, and how a hierarchical method culminating in fairly tight, oriented bounding boxes results in fast and accurate visibility calculations. We construct a semi-oriented bounding box that is oriented in the x- and y-dimensions, but only axis-aligned in z. This allows a dramatic simplification in the work necessary to calculate the bounding box without (for many cases) a significant degradation in culling quality.

Method Overview

The core idea is to calculate a bounding box that is "exact" for the x- and y-axes, but simply axis-aligned for the z-axis. When the bounding box is actually used to determine intersection with the view frustum, it will be handled as a normal, oriented bounding box. As objects can in general rotate freely, this avoids introducing the extra volume that can occur with axis-aligned testing. Basically, we assume that the bounding box can be found by rotating the object only about the z-axis.

How bad is this assumption? In general, it's not bad at all. As most objects on this planet are subject to gravity, they tend to have a nice, stable vertical component, which in turn means a vertical bounding box fits them pretty well. Only objects such as the one shown in Figure 5.3.1, which has a significant vertical skew, would benefit from having more freedom in choosing the bounding-box axes. And even if your models are from outer space, your artists (probably) aren't, so you should be okay. As our method is combined with bounding spheres, in the worst-case scenario a somewhat suboptimal fit is generated, but only for the z-direction.

FIGURE 5.3.1   *A case where projecting to the* x-y *plane yields a poor bounding box.*

We'll make a second assumption that the object is more or less centered about the origin. This is usually the case. It simplifies the equations, and at the end of the article, we can see how to correct for it if needed; so it's a fairly harmless assumption, as well.

Traditional Techniques

In the literature, there are generally two approaches used to generating the bounding box of an object. The first comes from statistics [VanVerth04], and is called the *covariance matrix*. The basic idea is to determine the axes, or directions, which have the largest and smallest variation in data. The covariance matrix for a set of 2D points is:

$$\text{cov} = \begin{bmatrix} S_{xx} & S_{xy} \\ S_{xy} & S_{yy} \end{bmatrix}, \text{ and} \qquad (5.3.1)$$

$$S_{yy} = \sum_{pts} \left(p_y^{\,2} - \overline{p}_y \right). \qquad (5.3.2)$$

Here, $\overline{p}_y$ is the average y-value of the points, and since we made the assumption that our object is centered about the origin, we approximate this with zero. Thus, the terms in the covariance matrix simplify to:

$$S_{xx} = \sum_{pts} p_x^{\,2}, \; S_{yy} = \sum_{pts} p_y^{\,2}, \; S_{xy} = \sum_{pts} p_x * p_y. \qquad (5.3.3)$$

The other approach comes from physics, where the *principal axes* are calculated for an object. The principal axes can be thought of as the preferred rotational axes of an object—or, more accurately, as the orientation that minimizes the moment of inertia for the object. The moment-of-inertia tensor is defined in Equation 5.3.4, and is the integration of mass times the square of the distance from the axis of rotation. It's like the mass of an object, but for rotation.

$$\mathbf{I} = \begin{bmatrix} S_{yy} & -S_{xy} \\ -S_{xy} & S_{xx} \end{bmatrix} \qquad (5.3.4)$$

Here the subterms are the same as for the covariance matrix, except that they should be multiplied by the mass at each point. In the simple case, the mass for each point is the same (and arbitrary), so we set it to one and ignore it. Later, we return to this simplification and see how we can improve our model.

The goal of both approaches is to *diagonalize* the matrix—that is, to find an orientation for the points so that the terms off the diagonal (S_{xy}) become equal to zero. This orientation can be represented by a rotation matrix, which transforms the world x- and y-axes so that they line up with the principal axes of the object. Both the physical and statistical techniques use diagonalization to minimize or maximize the distance from one of the axes.

Efficient Solution for Two Dimensions

In fact, for two dimensions, both the statistics and physics approaches actually end up calculating the same thing. One matrix is simply the scaled inverse of the other, and the solution for one is just the solution for the other. There's a fair bit of math coming, mainly some linear algebra. You can skip over it if you want and just trust the results. In the end we calculate an angle of rotation, for which the box around the points is nice and tight. But for the brave souls who want to see where this all comes from, read on. . . .

Both approaches take a symmetric matrix and try to diagonalize it. There's a handy theory in linear algebra that says this is *always* possible when your matrix is symmetrical and has positive values on the diagonal. In our case, the matrices in Equations 5.3.1 and 5.3.4 are defined as symmetric, and the diagonal terms are the sum of squares, so they're positive—so we're in luck.

Diagonalizing a matrix means solving Equation 5.3.5:

$$I = RDR^{-1} = RDR^{T},$$ (5.3.5)

where **I** is our inertia tensor, **R** is a rotation matrix, and **D** is a diagonal matrix.

Since **R** represents a rotation in two dimensions, it can also be written as:

$$R = \begin{bmatrix} c & -s \\ s & c \end{bmatrix} \text{ where } c = \cos\theta,\ s = \sin\theta.$$ (5.3.6)

And since rotations are generally *orthogonal*, its inverse is just its transpose. Expanding all of the matrices gives us:

$$\begin{bmatrix} c & -s \\ s & c \end{bmatrix}\begin{bmatrix} D_x & 0 \\ 0 & D_y \end{bmatrix}\begin{bmatrix} c & s \\ -s & c \end{bmatrix} = \begin{bmatrix} S_{yy} & -S_{xy} \\ -S_{xy} & S_{xx} \end{bmatrix},$$ (5.3.7)

which, with some algebraic manipulation, we can solve to yield:

$$\theta = \frac{1}{2}\tan^{-1}\left(\frac{2S_{xy}}{S_{xx} - S_{yy}}\right).$$ (5.3.8)

In the three-dimensional case, we would need to solve for the eigenvectors of a 3×3 matrix, which means first solving a cubic equation and then solving for the eigenvectors, both of which are fairly complicated and costly mathematical operations [Eberly02]. Furthermore, the simple connection between the covariance matrix and inertia tensor becomes more complicated.

Since we actually want the final rotation matrix rather than the angle itself, we can avoid costly trigonometric functions and their inverses, and solve directly for the sine and cosine of θ. First, we solve Equation 5.3.7 for $\cos 2\theta$, and then use the half-angle identities:

$$\cos 2\theta = \frac{S_{xx} - S_{yy}}{D_y - D_x} = \frac{S_{xx} - S_{yy}}{\sqrt{\left(S_{xx} - S_{yy}\right)^2 + 4S_{xy}^2}}, \text{ and}$$ (5.3.9)

$$\cos\theta = \sqrt{\frac{1 + \cos 2\theta}{2}},\quad \sin\theta = \sqrt{\frac{1 - \cos 2\theta}{2}}.$$ (5.3.10)

Thus, the whole system can be solved with just three square roots—a comparatively cheap operation, even on systems without floating point.

One final important note: We have now solved for the rotation that transforms from the world x- and y-axes to the primary axes of our object. To rotate our points correctly, we need to transform them by the inverse/transpose of this matrix in order to map our points back onto the x- and y-axes. An example should help make this clear.

Example

We'll apply our technique to the following simple problem. We take a rectangular box, rotate it, and then shave a corner off it, just to make it a little more complex (see Table 5.3.1). Thus, we know the solution we should get.

Table 5.3.1 A Chipped Box Rotated 30°

Original Points	Rotated Points
(4.0, 0.7)	(3.11, 2.61)
(3.0, 1.0)	(2.10, 2.37)
(−4.0, 1.0)	(−3.96, −1.13)
(−4.0, −1.0)	(−2.96, −2.87)
(4.9, −1.0)	(3.96, 1.13)
Bounding Box Area	16.00
Bounding Radius	4.12
Bound Sphere Area	53.41
AABB Area	43.40
Theta	31.5°
Calculated Bounding Box Area	17.75

It's worth noting that the bounding sphere is pretty big, more than three times larger than the true bounding box, and that while an axis-aligned box improves the situation, it doesn't help much. The volume for the calculated bounding box is pretty good, although it's still 11% more than the absolute minimum. The most important fact is that our solution is 31.5°—which is close, but further off than we might expect. Where does the error come from?

Improvements on Traditional Techniques

There are two sources of error, one of which we can do something about, whereas the other error turns out to be relatively unimportant. The error source that we cannot do anything about occurs because we are, in a sense, solving a different problem than we actually hoped to solve. We are solving the covariance, or moment-of-inertia, problem rather than actually calculating the minimum bounds of our point set. Both of these techniques use all the points in the object, finding a rotation that balances *something* for all of them. This means, for example, that if one choice of rotation results in many points slightly closer to the axes and a single point significantly further away, it will still be favored, since the total sum is minimized. For the minimum bounding box, we actually care only about the extreme values. While this perhaps sounds like a damning flaw in the technique, in our final version it will have only minimal effects.

The second flaw is the more important one; in correcting it, we develop a technique that delivers better results and delivers them faster. It also essentially eliminates the error introduced by the first flaw. Currently, both our models consider all of the points, and all equally. In the moment-of-inertia model, each point has the same weight. However, since we want only the bounding box, all internal points are not just useless information, they are error-inducing information. So, we don't want internal points.

Second, multiple points occurring at or near the same place on the x-y plane will also skew the results because they have more influence than they should. One point is enough to define the maximum x- or y-value; additional nearby ones just result in a rotation that tries to bring them closer to an axis, possibly at the expense of moving other single points further away.

So what can we do? For the three-dimensional case, Haines and Akenine-Möller [Moeller02] suggest using Gottschalk's method [Gottschalk99] of taking the convex hull of the object, and then using each face of the convex hull by weighting its midpoint according to its surface area. This means we solve the problem of finding the moment of inertia of a hollow shape with thin walls, which maps nicely to finding the bounding box. It also removes the error introduced by multiple points near each other, because the nearer they are, the smaller the triangle faces they belong to will be. However, it is also obviously a complex process. Determining the convex hull alone is $O(n \log n)$, and this doesn't address the more difficult problem of determining how the faces are constructed from these points and actually doing these calculations.

This is where our key simplification of only considering the projection in the x-y plane really comes into its own. This is because we only need to consider the lengths of the lines connecting the bounding points, rather than faces, and the points have a clear order. For example, we can just proceed clockwise around the border. We still have the problem of determining the convex hull in the first place, and we get around this with a simple approximation.

One can think of the convex hull of a point set as being composed of the minimal and maximal points relative to all possible axes. This means each point on the convex hull is the maximum in a particular direction. By limiting the number of directions, we can reduce the work considerably, while only reducing the accuracy to a limited extent. Since we can also bound this error, we can just increase the resulting bounding box accordingly, and can then be certain that all points fall within it.

The Simplified Convex Hull

What will we do? We consider only four axes, which result in eight points. These are the x- and y-axes, and the axes formed by the lines $x + y = 0$ and $x - y = 0$. On the number plane, this just corresponds to finding the points farthest away on the x- and y-axes, and along the diagonals (see Figure 5.3.2).

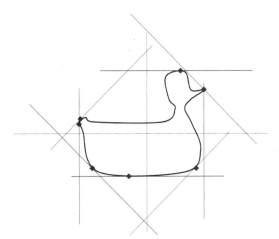

FIGURE 5.3.2   *The simplified convex hull of a duck.*

This calculation is very quick:

```
For each point:
    x = p.x
    y = p.y
    z = p.z
    r2 = x*x + y*y + z*z
    if (r2 > rMax)
        rMax = r2
    For x, y, z, x+y, and x-y
        if ([x] > [xMax])
            record point's index and update [xMax]
```

The maximum error in this case is $(1 - \cos 22.5)/\cos 22.5$, or roughly 8%. To be certain our volume includes all of the points, we need to scale both our x- and y-bounds by this amount, and end up with a volume increase of ~16%. If desired, we could transform all of the points into the bounding box's orientation, and find the exact maximum and minimum values, but this is unlikely to be worthwhile.

It is also be possible to reduce this error considerably by taking into account axes of the form $x +/- 2y$ and $2x +/- y$, but the additional complexity this brings makes its value questionable. It does reduce the maximum error to $(1 - \cos 11.25)/\cos 11.25$, or 2%, which is a considerable gain.

In the literature, such a bounding volume is called a *k-polytope* or *k-DOP* (Discrete Oriented Polytope), where k is the number of minimax points calculated—in our case, eight. Typically, bounding planes are used, which are exact, rather than bounding points, which aren't. However, using points is simpler and requires less storage space, too. This technique brings a number of advantages with it. First, we have an O(n) technique to get the (more or less) convex hull. Second, the operations used (representing the constant in the big O notation) are very simple—just comparisons and additions, which are very cheap, even on hardware without floating-point support. Third, for later and more-complex calculations, we need only consider these eight (or fewer) points. Finally, we get the order of the points for free, so calculating the line segments we use for weighting is fairly trivial.

Bringing It All Together

Let's consider our entire process now. For all calculations, we assume that the origin of the points more or less coincides with their center.

First, we go through the complete list of points. For each point we calculate its distance (squared) from the origin and its "projection" along each axis (x, y, z, $x + y$, $x - y$). The minimum and maximum of all of these is recorded.

The eight (or fewer) x-y hull points are then used to construct the inertia tensor matrix, with the line segment lengths used to weight each of the points. Each point is weighted by the sum of the distances to its previous and next neighbor, which requires an unavoidable square-root operation.

We then solve for the rotation matrix and apply it to the eight bounding points. From these, we determine the maximum lengths in each axis direction. These lengths are usually called the "half-lengths," and we will represent them as h_a, h_b, and h_z. We then extend the length of the x-y vectors by 8%, our previously calculated error term. In general, it's useful to actually keep the half-lengths in the form of axis and length, as we'll use both and don't want to regularly recalculate the individual values.

When we apply this to our original problem, we get the solution: 29.7°, pleasingly close to the exact solution, with a resulting volume of 16.33. The remaining error actually comes from our assumption that the points are centered about the origin, which is not the case, since we've cut a corner off of our box.

At this point, we can be quite pleased with ourselves. We have a tight bounding box, and that at O(n) cost, with a quite very low constant. We've avoided all trigonometric functions, and only have a few square roots to deal with. The question remains, how do we use this information? How do we actually cull against this box?

Culling with the Bounding Box

First, we want to determine whether it's even worth using the oriented box as a bounding volume. For example, if the object is a sphere, its bounding box is actually *larger* (surprise, surprise) than its bounding sphere. This can be quickly determined. Since the bounding sphere check is so quick, we do it in any case and only perform the more costly bounding box test if necessary.

To determine whether the bounding box is actually a tighter fit, we simply compare the volumes of the two bounding shapes. If Equation 5.3.11 holds, then the sphere is a better fit.

$$\frac{4}{3}\pi r^3 \leq 8h_a h_b h_z \tag{5.3.11}$$

This can be recorded in various ways, depending on what your trade-offs are between code cleanliness and memory. We also note the shortest side. Its length corresponds to a *minimum sphere;* if the object's center is closer than this to the view frustum, we know the object intersects the view frustum; so performing the bounding box intersection test would be a waste of effort.

To check whether the box itself intersects the view frustum, we need to orient it properly. The axes and lengths are transformed exactly, as for the object itself (i.e., rotation, translation, and scaling). If desired, since we know the vectors have a particular form (one z-vector and two x-y vectors) this multiplication can be optimized, but this is probably unnecessary. We then have the three vectors in camera space (h_a', h_b', and h_z'). We then project each half-length onto the normal $\mathbf{n}_{fi}$ of the view frustum plane, which gives a distance toward the plane. For the corner nearest to the plane,

$$d_{\text{nearest}} = d_{\text{center}} - \left(\left| h_a' \cdot \mathbf{n}_f \right| + \left| h_b' \cdot \mathbf{n}_f \right| + \left| h_z' \cdot \mathbf{n}_f \right| \right). \tag{5.3.12}$$

If this is less than zero, then part of the box intersects with the view frustum. (Actually, at the corners this is slightly pessimistic.) Under most circumstances, and always when we are just calculating if the object is *outside* the view frustum, we only need to consider the three planes of the view frustum nearest to the object center (see [Moeller02]), one of which is either the near or far z-plane, so this whole calculation is fairly cheap.

Tying it all together, we have the following pseudocode segment for checking intersection with the bounding volume. In general, as soon as we know the object is *outside* the view volume, we can return; but if it's potentially inside, we need to apply increasingly more-exact tests.

```
// could do a sphere-sphere check first, but ignore that for now
// object is in camera coordinates
for zNear, zFar, and nearest of left/right and top/bottom plane pairs
    d = signed distance from plane
    if (d > radius) // sphere is outside
        return EOutside;
    if (d > innerRadius) // need to check vs. box
        record plane index and distance

if (BoxSmallerThanSphere() && (recorded plane indices != 0))
    transform half-lengths to camera space
    for all planes
        if (plane index)
```

```
dA = dot(n,hA) * lenA
dB = dot(n,hB) * lenB
dZ = dot(n,hZ) * lenZ
dCorner = fabs(dA) + fabs(dB) + fabs(dZ)
if (distanceToPlane > dCorner)
    return EOutside

return EIntersecting
```

It should be noted that since the near and far clip planes are very simple, the other planes are symmetric, and the view frustum is the same for all objects, there are a number of optimization opportunities in this routine.

Further Improvements

Although we have a quite accurate and fast technique for building a bounding volume and testing against it, there are a number of potential improvements.

Center Offset Vector

Should the origin of an object be significantly far away from its centroid, a *center offset vector* can be useful. This is simply the offset (in local object coordinates) from the origin to the center of mass. The center offset then must be stored as part of the culling data structure, but its transformation and use are fairly straightforward. It definitely introduces additional work and complexity into the culling calculation, so careful consideration should be made about whether to implement it.

Detection of Objects Completely Within the View Frustum

An important additional optimization has also been passed over in this article: the recognition of when an object is completely *within* the view frustum. In this case, we can skip clipping tests for individual triangles, which is often fairly costly. Performing this test makes the frustum algorithm somewhat more complicated, and it isn't as easy as determining whether an object is outside the view volume, since you need to make certain the object is completely within *all* planes. But the individual tests tend to be fairly similar, and the improvements described above (i.e., first sphere tests, then inner sphere tests, then oriented box tests) are still valid.

Project onto Different Planes

The choice of the x-y plane was fairly arbitrary. If models in general use a different axis as their vertical direction, this can also be used. Or, to automate the process, values for projection to the x-z or y-z planes could be calculated, and the best result taken. As a guideline, it is the cross-terms (in our case, S_{xy}) which indicate whether rotation will give a better bounding box. Using this information, it's not necessary to completely solve for each potential projection.

Other Culling-Enhancement Techniques

When an object is determined to be outside the viewing volume, [Assarsson99] generally got a respectable speed-up by recording which plane indicated this, and tested it first the next time the object's visibility was checked. He called this the *plane coherency* optimization. The idea is that from frame to frame, such a splitting plane is likely to remain constant. Whether the additional complexity this entails is worthwhile should be determined by profiling.

Conclusion

We've presented a technique for both efficiently calculating a bounding volume for an object, and for checking that bounding volume against the camera's view frustum. The bounding volume is a box rotated within the *x-y* plane. It is calculated by determining the principal inertial axes of an approximate convex hull of the object. The method presented has $O(n)$ complexity, with a small constant; avoids the use of any transcendental functions; and is quite robust in the face of irregularly shaped objects, as it only uses the convex hull (more or less) of the object.

We then described a hierarchical method for testing the visibility of the object. First, we attempt to exclude objects based on their bounding spheres. Then, if necessary and potentially successful, tests against the bounding box are performed. In this way, the conservative set of visible objects can be rapidly determined, without requiring the manual creation of bounding volumes.

These enhanced bounding volumes can then be used in additional ways, such as for collision detection, ray intersection, and occlusion culling, hopefully improving the efficiency of all of these tasks.

References

[Assarsson99] Assarsson, Ulf and Tomas Möller, "Optimized View Frustum Culling Algorithms." Technical Report 99-3, Department of Computer Engineering, Chalmers University of Technology. Available online at *http://www.ce.chalmers.se/~uffe/vfc.pdf*.

[Eberly02] Eberly, David, "Eigensystems for 3 × 3 Symmetric Matrices." Available online at *http://www.geometrictools.com/Documentation.html*.

[Gottschalk99] Gottschalk, Stefan, "Collision Queries using Oriented Bounding Boxes." Ph.D. Thesis, Department of Computer Science, University of North Carolina at Chapel Hill, 1999.

[Moeller02] Akenine-Möller, Tomas and Eric Haines, *Real-Time Rendering*, 2nd Ed. A. K. Peters, 2002.

[VanVerth04] Van Verth, Jim, "Using the Covariance Matrix for Better-Fitting Bounding Objects." *Game Programming Gems 4*, Charles River Media, 2004.

5.4

Skin Splitting for Optimal Rendering

Dominic Filion

dfilion@hotmail.com

Introduction

Rendering skinned meshes forms a central part of any modern 3D game engine. For some, such as Real-Time Strategy (RTS) games, skinned meshes actually form a large subset of all data being rendered on screens, and optimal rendering of skinned geometry becomes paramount. It is now customary to offload all vertex processing to the GPU subsystem, and skinned meshes are no exception. However, skinned meshes pose certain complications to the skinning process.

As a brief review of the skinning process, vertices in the skinned mesh have extra information attached to each vertex in the form of bone indices and bone weights. Bone matrices affecting the mesh are inserted into a finite-size bone *palette*, with each vertex specifying the bone palette indices that affect it. Bone matrices are then weighted by their respective weights, concatenated, and applied to each vertex.

One limitation any GPU skinning algorithm must deal with is the limited size of the bone palette. The 2.0 vertex shader specification has now enlarged the number of available vertex registers from 96 to 256. However, these bone matrices must generally coexist with other information, such as lighting parameters, material information, fog specification, and so forth. Each bone matrix consists of a 4×4 matrix from which the last column can be discarded, as it is always $[0 \ 0 \ 0 \ 1]^T$. Transposing the resulting 4×3 matrix yields a 3×4 matrix that occupies three vector registers per bone. In addition, at least nine registers will normally be reserved for the projection matrix, a material color and, for example, two omni lights (i.e., color and position for each light). Thus, the maximum practical allowable number of bones in the bone palette is 29 under vertex shader version 1.1 and 82 under vertex shader version 2.0. If many other parameters need to be used for nonskinning purposes, such as lighting, then the maximum bone palette size will be much reduced.

Restricting the maximum number of bones on a single character to such a low number will most often not be desirable, however; and this is where some form of mesh splitting becomes necessary. A mesh with a large number of bones will then be partitioned into several portions, each portion using a unique bone palette of the required maximum size. Although the process could be offloaded to the artist, it is much more desirable to have this process handled automatically.

Even in cases where the entire bone set on a character fits into a single bone palette, mesh splitting may still be desirable. This stems from the fact that the number of bones influencing a single vertex may vary from zero to four in most production pipelines. This could be handled by using a four-weight vertex shader and assigning a zero weight to any extra weight slots not currently being used. This is not an optimal solution, however; it wastes GPU-cycles processing weights that have no contribution. A more optimal solution will be to further split the mesh into sections that use the same number of weights and to switch between different types of vertex shaders that are each specifically designed to compute one, two, three, or four weights.

Note that whether this will result in a speed-up will depend on the specifics of your graphics pipeline. Under DirectX, for example, switching vertex shaders has some cost associated with it (although this cost tends to decrease with each new version of the API). On other platforms, like the PlayStation® 2 (PS2), new VU (Vector Unit) microcode will have to be uploaded to and/or be activated in the vector units whenever the shader type changes. Thus, splitting a low-detail mesh will not always result in a speed-up. The ideal conditions for both bone-palette splitting and bone-weight splitting will be high-detail, more-complex meshes where each bone influences many vertices.

Thus, what we have here is a splitting of the mesh, first according to the number of bones influencing each vertex, and then according to the number of bones that will fit into a bone palette. The focus of this article will be an exposition on good heuristics for doing this along, with a demonstration of how to implement the mesh-splitting algorithm.

Splitting Concepts

Because mesh splitting that depends on various parameters is actually a common occurrence in most graphics pipelines, a simple elaboration of splitting concepts is useful. Although the focus here is on splitting meshes based on skinning limits, other heuristics on which a mesh might be split could be:

- Split meshes that have more than a certain number of optimal vertices or triangles;
- Split meshes that have different materials or textures applied on different mesh subsections in the art editing tool;
- Split static meshes that are affected by different lights for static-lighting precomputation; or
- Split meshes along predefined physical fracture paths for breaking objects into debris at run-time.

Mesh splits within the context of this article always occur along the triangle edges. We are merely separating mesh triangles into different subsections; no new triangles will be added, removed, or changed by the splitting process.

The splitting process takes each triangle in the mesh and assigns it to one of several *buckets*. Each of these buckets becomes a subsection of the mesh, and will receive its own index and vertex buffer. A simple example of a mesh split can be seen in Figure 5.4.1, with relevant vertex and index buffer structures.

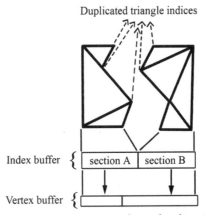

FIGURE 5.4.1 *A simple mesh split with relevant structures.*

Splitting the mesh generally takes up more memory, as some triangles are duplicated. Because vertexes shared between two bone palettes will use different local bone palette indices to address the same bones in different palettes, some vertices will also have to be duplicated.

During the splitting process, we will have to specify to which bucket each triangle will be put. For this, we define a structure called CTriBucketInfo, as follows:

Listing 5.4.1 CTriBucketInfo **Structure**

```
struct CTriBucketInfo
{
    CBonePalette*    pBonePalette;
    int              WeightCount;
};
```

This structure gives all information needed to know to which bucket a triangle belongs. Two triangles will be in the same bucket only if they have identical corresponding CTriBucketInfo structures.

During the setup phase of the mesh-splitting algorithm, we allocate an array of these `CTriBucketInfo` structures, creating a `CTriBucketInfo` for each triangle in our mesh. The main heuristic of the splitting algorithm will fill out each `CTriBucketInfo` structure.

Weight-Splitting Heuristic

Splitting according to the number of weight influences on each triangle is fairly simple.

Algorithm 5.4.1   Weight-Splitting Heuristic

```
For each triangle
    For each of the 3 vertices on the triangle
        Set triangle weight count to zero
        For each of the 4 weights on each vertex
            Set vertex weight count to zero
            If vertex weight is nonzero
                Then increment vertex weight count
        If vertex weight count > triangle weight count
            Then update triangle weight count with vertex
            weight count
    Store the triangle weight count in an array of
        CTriBucketInfo for future mesh split
```

Algorithm 5.4.1 is fairly straightforward. The two loops iterate over every vertex of every triangle, looking up each vertex to find the vertex with the highest number of skin weights. This number then gets stored in the `CTriBucketInfo` structure for that triangle.

Bone Palette Heuristic

The bone palette-splitting heuristic is a little more involved and requires a bit of careful analysis. Complex meshes may get split in two, three, four, or more bone palettes; there are many ways that these mesh sections could be arranged. It may not be immediately obvious why and under what conditions a certain mesh-splitting scheme might be more optimal than another one, so in this section we will go into a bit more detail about why the partition heuristic is important.

An incorrect partitioning of the skinned mesh will result in there being more partitions than is necessary. If not correctly analyzed, a mesh that should have fit into two bone palettes will spawn three or four bone palettes. More mesh sections means more rendering batches, more duplicates in the index and vertex buffers, and generally lower performance.

Once we assign a bone to a bone palette, we would expect to not have to assign it to any other bone palette; however, this is most often not the case. Take for example a typical game character's arm skeleton, as shown in Figure 5.4.2.

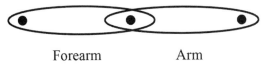

Forearm   Arm

FIGURE 5.4.2 *Simple arm bone skeleton.*

If we assign the arm bone to one of the bone palettes, then this will allow us to use this bone palette to skin any vertices that are influenced by the arm bone only, as shown in the figure. However, to skin the elbow vertices, we need *both* the arm bone and the forearm bone, and these would need to appear on the same bone palette. As we move farther down the arm, we can see that skinning the wrist will require both the forearm and the hand bone in the same palette, and so forth.

Thus, assigning a bone to a palette does not mean we are done with that bone; it may overlap with another bone, and we may be unable to place the overlapping bone within the same bone palette, because the bone palette may already be full.

For every iteration of the splitting algorithm, we have to choose which bone we want to add to our current bone palette. As much as possible, once we add a bone to a bone palette, we would like to avoid having to insert that same bone in a different bone palette. It is this inclusion of bones into multiple palettes that makes for less-efficient partitioning. Some overlap of bones in multiple palettes is inevitable, as all the bones have influence zones that overlap with neighbor bones that have to be included within the same palette. Since we can't add the entire skeleton within a single palette, at some point a break must be made, and a bone will have to be reincluded into a different palette.

Any bone in the skeleton has an influence zone that overlaps with some of its neighbors. For every vertex that is influenced by the bone, we can note which other bones are also affecting this vertex. We call the set of bones that influence a particular vertex the *influence set*. Under most systems, the maximum number of bones affecting a particular vertex is limited to four; thus, influence sets will contain no more than four bones.

We can gather and note all possible influence sets where a particular bone appears. The arm bone, for instance, may appear with the following combinations: arm bone only, arm bone influence along with forearm influence, or arm bone influence along with hand bone influence. Everywhere a bone's influence zone overlaps a neighbor's, we get a new influence set combination. We will now refer to these possible sets as *bone combinations*, which are influences on the mesh. Thus, our arm bone has three combinations.

When building the bone palettes, we must ensure that all the possible bone combinations of the mesh appear within at least one of the bone palettes. For our arm bone, at least one palette must contain both the arm bone and the forearm bone, and at least one palette (perhaps the same one) must contain both the arm bone and the hand bone. Otherwise, we will be unable to render the region where both these bones overlap, as no palette would contain the required set of bones (and we would be forced to create another palette that contains both these bones).

Thus, to eliminate a bone from further processing, we must add the bone to the current bone palette along with all other bones that appear within the same bone combinations as the bone we are processing. In other words, all bone combinations containing that bone must be present within the same bone palette. It seems reasonable to look for a heuristic that allows us to eliminate bones from further processing as early as possible.

This finally gives us a hint toward a suitable heuristic: We would like to first add to our bone palettes those bones that have the *least* bone combinations. In this manner, we will have to add only a minimal number of other bones to the bone palette to be able to eliminate that bone from further processing.

This generally results in an *inward* bone-partitioning scheme. Bones on the outer limbs, like fingers, tend to get added first, while bones in the middle, like the torso (which normally overlaps with many other bones, such as legs, head, and arms), get added last. While we could have processed the bones by simply adding bones farther down the skeleton first, by basing our heuristic on the number of bone combinations, we have a more general algorithm that will not depend on the particular topology of the bone structure.

With that in mind, here is an overview of the heuristic based on bone combinations:

1. Compute all bone combinations for the mesh.
2. Find the bone with the least combinations.
3. Add the bone to the palette.
4. Add as many bones that share combinations with this bone as possible.
5. Remove any combinations that were completely included within this bone palette.
6. Repeat until all bone combinations for that mesh have been included within one of the palettes.

Heuristic Details

In this section, a sample implementation of the heuristic will be shown. We have reviewed some of the theory behind the heuristic, and the following section will now be more code-intensive.

The first step to finding the best bone candidate for inclusion in a palette is to record every possible bone combination with the skeleton. We will then be able to find out which bone uses the least amount of bone combinations. Thus, as in the example given previously, an arm bone will likely have three combinations: vertices that are affected only by the arm bone, vertices that are affected by both the arm and the forearm bone, and vertices that are affected by both the arm and the shoulder bone. As shown in Figure 5.4.3, if a bone is being used by vertices 1 and 2 of a triangle, and another bone is being used by vertex 3 on that triangle, then both bones must be present within the same bone palette to be able to render that single triangle.

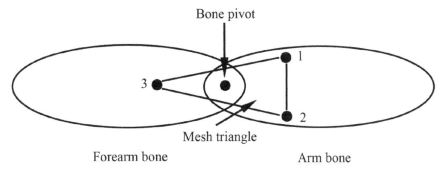

FIGURE 5.4.3 *Shared bones within a triangle.*

Thus, to figure out all of the used bone combinations, we first need to record which bones are used by each triangle. Since each triangle has three vertices, we have up to 12 bones used per triangle. This set of (up to 12) bone indices can then be stored as a unique combination. Algorithm 5.4.2 shows how to do this.

Algorithm 5.4.2 Initial Heuristic Setup

```
Const DWORD MAX_BONES = 256; // Maximum total bones allowed
struct BoneCombination
{
    DWORD BoneIndices[12];
};
BoneCombination AllBoneCombinations[TriangleCount];
set<BoneCombination> BoneCombinationSet;
bool BonesUsed[MAX_BONES];

For each triangle
Reset BonesUsed array to all zero
    Fill BoneCombination entries with special value FREE_SLOT

    For each of the 3 vertices on the triangle
        Retrieve vertex bone indices and weights
        For each of the 4 vertex weights
            If weight is nonzero then
    mark this index as used in the BonesUsed array

    For each entry in the BonesUsed array
        If bone index is used (BonesUsed entry is true)
            Store index in first available free slot in BoneCombination
            structure corresponding to this triangle in the AllBoneCom-
            binations array
            Insert BoneCombination structure for current triangle in
            the BoneCombinationSet
```

A few notes on the bottom half of this algorithm are worth mentioning. We first tag all bones that are being used by the particular triangle being processed. Then, in a second pass, we iterate through all bones and add them in order to a `BoneCombination` structure that records the bones being used by that triangle. The reason the bones are first marked up then added is to quickly sort the bone indices so that two identical bone combinations with the same indices appearing in the same order will use the same sequence of bone indices, as these are sorted within the `BoneCombination` structure. In C++, an STL set is used to record all bone combinations; using a set, we can add the same bone combination multiple times as we encounter it on different triangles, and the set will only record the combination once.

Having recorded all bone combinations, we can count in how many bone combinations each bone appears, as shown in Algorithm 5.4.3.

Algorithm 5.4.3   Counting Bone Combinations

```
// An array storing bone combination counts used in the algorithm
int BoneCombinationCount[MAX_BONES];

Fill BoneCombinationCount with zeroes
For each BoneCombination in BoneCombinationSet
    For each of the 12 bone indices within the BoneCombination
        Increment the BoneCombinationCount entry corresponding to the
        current bone index
    Ignore the entry if it is marked as FREE_SLOT
```

Here, we go over all combinations and increment the combination count for each bone that appears within a combination. With this information in hand, we can finally implement our heuristic, find the bone with the least combinations, and use it as our candidate for adding to our current bone palette, as shown in Algorithm 5.4.4.

Algorithm 5.4.4   Finding Best Candidate

```
int BonesInPalette = 0;
bool AddedBones[MAX_BONES];

For each bone palette
    Fill AddedBones array with zeroes
    While BonesInPalette is smaller then the maximum allowed number
    of bones within a palette
        Loop over all entries in BoneCombinationCount and find the
        lowest value in the array that is higher than zero; store the
        value and the array index for that value

        If all entries in BoneCombinationCount were zero
            We are done; exit

        Add bone

    Finalize bone palette
```

The steps in the algorithm are, for the most part, fairly obvious.

Having found our bone candidate, we can add all bones that share combinations with it to our bone palette. We do this by iterating over all bone combinations, spotting all combinations that contain our current bone being processed, and add to the bone palette any other bones that appear within the bone combination.

Algorithm 5.4.5 Adding the Bone

```
//  A handy container for bone palettes
list<DWORD>    BonePalette;


If bone is not currently marked as already added in the AddedBones
array
     Add bone to BonePalette
     Mark bone as added in AddedBones array
     Increment BonesInPalette

For each BoneCombination within BoneCombinationSet
     If current bone index is assigned to any of the 12 slots within
     BoneCombination
          For each of the 12 slots within BoneCombination
               If bone index in that slot is not marked as already added
               in the AddedBones array
                    Add that bone to BonePalette
                    Mark that bone as added in AddedBones array
                         Increment BonesInPalette
                         If BonesInPalette is equal to maximum allowed
                         number of bones in palette
          Exit current loop
```

Once this is done, we can loop over all bone combinations again, removing from the bone combination set any bone combinations that are now fully within the bone palette. This ensures that the heuristic is correct and ultimately ensures that every bone combination appears within one of the palettes.

Algorithm 5.4.6 Removing Processed Combinations

```
// This map will store, for each bone combination, in which bone
// palette it was stored
map< BoneCombination, BonePalette*> CombinationsMap;


For each BoneCombination in BoneCombinationSet
     If all bone indices within BoneCombination are marked as added in
     the AddedBones array (don't forget to ignore FREE_SLOTs!)
          For each slot within BoneCombination
               Decrement BoneCombinationCount for the bone index in that
               slot
```

```
Associate current BoneCombination with current palette index
in the CombinationsMap

Remove current BoneCombination from BoneCombinationSet
```

Once a bone palette is finished, either because it has been filled up or because there are no more bones to process, we must store some specific information associated with the palette to remap the bone indices. Since we are reducing from a large set of bones to a smaller palette, the global bone indices referenced by the mesh vertices will have to be remapped to indices that are valid within the local bone palette used by that vertex. The algorithm to store the information needed to do this goes as shown in Algorithm 5.4.7.

Algorithm 5.4.7   Bone Palette Finalization

```
// A useful structure for finalization
struct BonePalette
{
    int* BoneIndices;
    int* GlobalBoneIndexToPaletteBoneIndex;
}

Allocate space in the bone palette for the
    required number of indices.
Store bone indices.
Store original bone index in the unpaletted version of
    the skeleton for remapping of bone indices in the vertex buffer.
Add BonePalette to the global list of palettes.
```

The current palette's index is also stored in an STL map that used the current combination as its key. We will later use this map to find out which bone palette each bone combination uses.

The pGlobalBonesToLocal array contains the local bone index for each global bone index found within the palette. This can be used to remap the bone indices when the vertex buffer is rebuilt for the new bone palettes. Having assigned each bone combination to a bone palette, we can use this information to categorize each triangle to a different triangle bucket, depending on its assigned bone palette. For each triangle, we set the pBonePalette entry in the CTriBucketInfo structure for this triangle to the corresponding palette for this triangle.

With all CTriBucketInfo structures filled, it is now a trivial matter to reorganize the index buffer of the mesh and order triangle indices according to the CTriBucketInfo in which they are assigned, and store separate triangle batch information for each triangle bucket. The vertex buffer also needs to be rebuilt, as vertices that are shared by two or more bone palettes will certainly use different local bone indices to refer to the same bones in different palettes; in these cases, the vertices will have to be duplicated. The index and vertex buffer structures are highly specific to the application and will depend on your particular needs. The process for rebuilding the index and vertex buffers would be as shown in Algorithm 5.4.8.

Algorithm 5.4.8 Rebuilding Our Mesh—Better, Stronger, Faster

```
For each triangle
    Add triangles to index buffer — use a map to associate separate
    index buffers to corresponding CTriBucketInfo structures
    Add vertices to vertex buffer — again using a map
```

Conclusion

The heuristic presented here will provide for skin partitions that are often logically organized and that result in the least amount of total bone palettes. It works on arbitrarily complex skeletons and is not limited by any expectations as to the skeleton's layout. Its implementation is fast enough that it can be run at export time without any significant delay being added to the production pipeline.

5.5

GPU Terrain Rendering

Harald Vistnes

harald@vistnes.org

The task of most terrain-rendering algorithms is to generate a triangle mesh with high visual fidelity from a heightfield. To achieve this without generating too many triangles, view-dependent level of detail control is required. As the camera moves, the triangle mesh needs to be updated. In each update (often as frequently as once per frame), the new vertex positions must be calculated by looking up the elevations from the heightfield. This per-frame updating of vertices consumes a considerable amount of CPU time. By moving the heightfield lookup from the CPU to the GPU, the vertex positions can be calculated in the vertex shader. Thus, it is no longer necessary to perform per-frame vertex buffer updates.

This gem will present an easy-to-implement algorithm for rendering terrain on the GPU. The cornerstone of GPU terrain rendering is the vertex texture fetch capability in Shader Model 3.0. The presented algorithm reduces the memory requirements substantially by reusing a small vertex buffer containing only three floats per vertex. By storing the heightfield in a vertex texture, the elevation of a vertex can be looked up in the vertex shader, offloading the per-frame vertex buffer updates usually performed by the CPU.

Basic Algorithm

The general idea of the algorithm is as follows: The terrain is divided into a number of blocks, and each block contains a fixed number of triangles. The vertices of the blocks are organized in a $(2^k + 1) \times (2^k + 1)$ regular grid so that each vertex corresponds to one of the $(2^n + 1) \times (2^n + 1)$ elements in the heightfield. All blocks are flat squares as they are passed to the 3D API. The vertices are then displaced in the vertex shader by fetching corresponding elevations from the heightfield vertex texture. Since vertex positions are calculated in the vertex shader and not on the CPU, and since all blocks consist of an equal number of vertices, a single vertex buffer can be reused for all the blocks. In addition to the vertex buffer, a single index buffer is needed. The indices can be organized such that the entire block can be rendered as a single, long triangle strip.

461

Only a couple of uniform shader parameters are altered to render a different block using the same vertex buffer and index buffer. Depending on the block size, the memory savings are substantial compared to having one vertex buffer per block.

The uniform parameters that must be set for each block include a set of scale and bias factors. These are used to specify the area of the block and its location on the terrain.

Figure 5.5.1 shows a 33 × 33 heightfield and two 5 × 5 blocks with different scales and biases. The heightfield elements are indexed by the two parameters u and v, where $0 \le u \le 1$ and $0 \le v \le 1$. Similarly, the horizontal positions of the block vertices are given by the two parameters s and t, where $0 \le s \le 1$ and $0 \le t \le 1$. For a given block, the scale and bias represent the mapping $\{s,t\} \Rightarrow \{u,v\}$. The new $\{u,v\}$ pair is then used to sample the heightfield texture to get the elevation h, where $0 \le h \le 1$. The three-tuple $\{u,h,v\}$ is the local space vertex position[1]. Since the $\{s,t\}$ coordinate is used to calculate both the position and the texture coordinate of a vertex, we store s as the vertex's x-coordinate and t as the z-coordinate in the vertex buffer. In fact, we store only position data in the vertex buffer, and thus require only three floats per vertex.

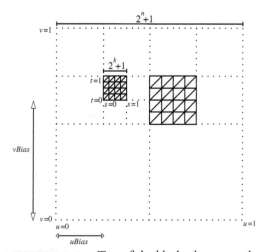

FIGURE 5.5.1   *Two of the blocks that cover the terrain. A scale and bias is all that is required to map a block to a specific region of the terrain. Notice the correspondence between block vertices and heightfield elements.*

---

[1]To get to world space, a non-uniform scaling matrix should be used to get the proper relationship between vertical and horizontal extents.

The following code lists a minimal vertex shader written in HLSL, which shows how to implement the vertex position transformation. uScale, vScale, uBias, vBias, heightfield, and matWorldViewProj are uniform parameters. Note that the input position's y-coordinate is not used at all. This will be used later.

```
float4 VS(float3 pos : POSITION) : POSITION
{
    float s = pos.x;
    float t = pos.z;
    float u = s * uScale + uBias;
    float v = t * vScale + vBias;
    float4 tex = float4(u, v, 0.0f, 0.0f);
    float h = tex2Dlod(heightfield, tex).x;
    pos = float3(u, h, v);
    float4 pos0 = mul(float4(pos,1.0f), matWorldViewProj);
    return pos0;
}
```

If a block were to cover the entire terrain, its scale parameters would be 1.0. For a block to cover a quarter of the terrain, both scale parameters should be set to 0.5. As can be seen from Figure 5.5.1, the scale parameters for the larger block are 0.25, and are 0.125 for the smaller block. The bias parameters for the larger block are both 0.5; but for the smaller block, uBias is 0.25 and vBias is 0.625.

Level of Detail

As noted earlier, by halving the scale parameters, the area covered by a block is reduced to a quarter. Thus, a block can be divided into four smaller blocks with half the scale. If we start with one block covering the entire terrain and then recursively divide it into four children until the blocks match the heightfield resolution, we have effectively created a quadtree of blocks.

As you have probably guessed, we will use this to control the level of detail (LOD) of the terrain. We recursively evaluate each block and decide whether to render it or to divide it into four smaller blocks. Depending on our evaluation criteria and the block size, we can reduce the total number of triangles rendered and still get a nice terrain.

In this gem we will use a simple distance-based evaluation criterion so that distant blocks cover more area than blocks closer to the camera. Thus, more detail will be shown in close proximity to the camera. A better alternative would be to use the maximum screen-space vertex error for a block, as this would also consider the roughness of the terrain, not only the distance to the camera. The approach used in [Ulrich02] can easily be adopted to accomplish this.

The distance-based evaluation criterion is given by the simple test:

$$\frac{l}{d} < C$$

If the test fails, the block is rendered. If the test succeeds, the block is divided into four smaller blocks and the recursion continues. The value l is the distance from the center of the block to the camera, and d is the world-space extent of a single triangle, as seen in Figure 5.5.2. This distance-based criterion is adapted from [Röttger98]. C is a tunable constant that controls the quality of the rendered terrain. By increasing C, more blocks will be refined, and thus more triangles will be rendered. In the accompanying demo on the CD-ROM, the quality parameter can easily be adjusted with a slider control.

ON THE CD

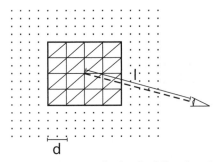

FIGURE 5.5.2   *The level of detail evaluation criterion is based on the distance from the camera to the center of the block, and on the world-space extent of a triangle.*

Listing 5.5.1 shows how the terrain can be rendered with level of detail control. The world matrix is used to get world-space distances. Here, the world matrix is assumed to be a scaling matrix. The initial values of the parameters are 0.0 for fMinU and fMinV; fMaxU, fMaxV, and fScale are initially 1.0; and iLevel is set to the depth of the quadtree.

Listing 5.5.1

```
void Render(float fMinU, float fMinV,
    float fMaxU, float fMaxV,
    int iLevel, float fScale)
{
    float fHalfU = (fMinU + fMaxU) * 0.5f;
    float fHalfV = (fMinV + fMaxV) * 0.5f;
```

```
        float d = (fMaxU-fMinU)*m_matWorld._11/(m_iBlockSize-1.0f);

        D3DXVECTOR3 c(fHalfU*m_matWorld._11,0,fHalfV*m_matWorld._33);
        D3DXVECTOR3 v = c - g_Camera.GetPos();
        float l = D3DXVec3Length(&v);

        float f = l / d;

        if (f > m_fLOD || iLevel < 1) {
            Draw(fMinU, fMinV, fMaxU, fMaxV, iLevel);
        } else {
            Render(fMinU, fMinV, fHalfU, fHalfV, iLevel-1, fScale/2);
            Render(fHalfU, fMinV, fMaxU, fHalfV, iLevel-1, fScale/2);
            Render(fMinU, fHalfV, fHalfU, fMaxV, iLevel-1, fScale/2);
            Render(fHalfU, fHalfV, fMaxU, fMaxV, iLevel-1, fScale/2);
        }
    }
```

The well-known problem of popping will occur as the camera moves, and is because of the sudden change in block refinements. Popping can be prevented by morphing the elevation of vertices between different levels of detail. To implement this, two vertex texture fetches would be required, and then a linear interpolation based on a morph parameter is performed.

Having the level of detail in place, we are finally ready for a discussion on block sizes. Generally, we want to batch a large number of triangles to reduce API render calls. However, smaller blocks allow for more variation in level of detail. If the blocks are too large, too-large areas are covered by equal-size triangles. This will result in either too coarse or too fine a triangulation, depending on the LOD constant. In addition, by having smaller blocks, they are more likely to be outside the viewing frustum, allowing more blocks to be culled during the quadtree traversal. In the test demo, we have found that block sizes 17 × 17 and 33 × 33 make a good compromise between render calls and varying triangle sizes.

Avoiding Cracks

Cracks will appear on the borders between blocks of different levels of detail. This is a problem that must be handled in all terrain LOD algorithms. A number of different approaches can be used to prevent the dreaded holes in the terrain. We have chosen to use the simple, yet elegant solution of vertical skirts along the block borders. The algorithm described in [Ulrich02] also uses this approach. As can be seen in Figure 5.5.3, each block is extended with a vertical border called a "skirt". When two blocks from different levels of detail meet, any potential crack will be filled by the skirt geometry. Even though the vertical skirts can cause some lighting problems and texture stretching, the crack fillings are typically too small to be distracting.

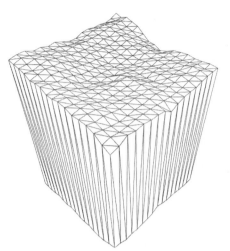

FIGURE 5.5.3   *Each block is extended with a vertical skirt along its border.*

We want to add the skirts without affecting the existing algorithm. A single vertex buffer is still used; the extra vertices are simply added at the end of the buffer. The extra vertices will be referred to as the *skirt vertices*, as opposed to the *terrain vertices*. The index buffer will still be able to represent all indices as a long triangle strip.

But how can we differentiate the skirt vertices from the terrain vertices in the vertex shader? As a matter of fact, we don't have to. As you saw in the vertex shader code listing, the vertex position's *y*-coordinate was not used. We'll make use of it now. When we initialize the vertex buffer, we set the terrain vertices' *y*-coordinate to 1.0 and the skirt vertices' *y*-coordinate to −1.0. In the vertex shader, we then modify the single line:

```
pos = float3(u, h, v);
```

to

```
pos = float3(u, h*pos.y, v);
```

This way, the skirt vertices will automatically get a negative elevation. The horizontal position of the skirt vertex is equal to its corresponding terrain border vertex. No special cases are required to handle the skirt vertices; the only expense is the extra triangles along the border.

Note that this trick assumes that the heightfield does not contain negative elevations. Negative elevations are typically used for terrain below sea level. This problem can easily be fixed by offsetting all elevations until none are negative, effectively raising the sea level.

Frustum Culling

We can test if the blocks are inside the viewing frustum during the quadtree traversal. If a block is completely outside the frustum, we skip it by aborting the recursion. This test can be performed at the beginning of the `Render()` function in Listing 5.5.1.

The easiest bounding volume to use in this case is an axis-aligned bounding box. The local-space horizontal extents are given by the minimum and maximum u and v coordinates of a block. The minimum and maximum elevations are, however, not so easily found. The most accurate solution would be to compute the minimum and maximum values for all blocks in the quadtree during initialization. In the accompanying demo on the CD-ROM, we chose simply to use the minimum and maximum elevations for the entire terrain for all bounding boxes. This will result in bounding boxes that are much higher than required and can result in invisible blocks not being culled. In a real-world implementation, you should go for the more accurate solution.

ON THE CD

Calculating Normals

If we want to add dynamic lighting or environment-mapping effects, we have to have the normals of the terrain. As shown in [Shankel02], the calculation of heightfield normals can be significantly optimized and require only four heightfield lookups and two subtractions. Exploiting this, the vertex normal can be calculated in the vertex shader by sampling four neighboring elevations in the vertex texture, in addition to the elevation for the vertex itself. On current hardware, vertex texture fetches are quite expensive, so this approach might be too costly. However, vertex texture fetches are likely to be optimized in future hardware generations, so this may not be a problem for long.

Given a vertex and its four nearest neighbors, as shown in Figure 5.5.4, the vertex normal is given by [Shankel02]:

$$\mathbf{N} = \{(w - e), 2d, (s - n)\},$$

where d equals the distance between the vertices, in the same units as the elevations.

A disadvantage with this approach, however, is that the normals depend on the level of detail. This results in visible changes in the lighting, as camera movement causes the level of detail to change.

To avoid this problem, all vertex normals for the entire terrain can be calculated offline and stored in a normal map. The normals can then be looked up in the pixel shader, enabling the terrain to be lighted independently on the underlying triangulation. This approach is also much faster than calculating the normals per vertex due to the expensive vertex texture fetches. The visual quality of the lighted terrain is also higher. On the downside, the normal map can require a significant amount of texture memory.

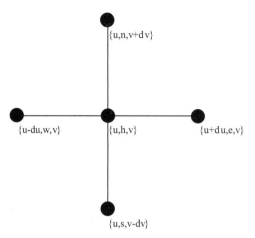

FIGURE 5.5.4   *The elevation at a vertex's four nearest neighbors are all that is required to calculate the vertex normal.*

ON THE CD

In the accompanying demo source, both techniques have been implemented, and you can switch between them by pressing F5. The effect of the different techniques is easily seen in Color Plate 8. In the top screenshot, the normals are calculated in the vertex shader; while in the middle, a normal map is sampled in the pixel shader. You can clearly see the difference in lighting between the different levels of detail in the first screenshot.

Collision Avoidance

A game that only consists of a nice terrain wouldn't be too exciting. We need to put objects on top of the terrain, such as trees, buildings, cars, enemies, and so on. And we never want the camera to intersect with the terrain and let the user see the backside of the triangles. To ensure this, we need to be able to find the elevation of the terrain at any given horizontal position.

Typically this is implemented by sampling the heightfield on the CPU—possibly by doing a bilinear interpolation of the four nearest points. This approach is not desirable in our case, as we don't have a copy of the heightfield in system memory.

There is an elegant solution that does not require a second copy of the heightfield. The trick is to render the result of a heightfield query to a texture. To prevent the camera from intersecting with the terrain, create a 1×1 texture that can be used as a render target. Then create a dynamic vertex buffer containing a single vertex with position data only. Each time we want to perform a heightfield query, we update the vertex buffer by setting the desired $\{u, v\}$ coordinates in the vertex's x- and z-coordinates. Set the texture as the render target, and render the vertex buffer as a pointlist. In the vertex shader, pass the position's x- and z-coordinates to the pixel shader as texture coordinates. Then in the pixel shader, sample the heightfield at the desired coordinates and return the height as the color of the pixel. The single pixel of the render-target texture will then contain the terrain elevation at the desired location.

ON THE CD

In the accompanying demo code, this approach has been used to prevent the camera from moving below the terrain. The heightfield query is performed once between each frame.

Of course, this approach is not restricted to a 1×1 query for the elevation at the camera position. You can generate a larger render target and vertex buffer, and query for several positions in the same call. This can be used to simultaneously query the elevation of lots of objects on the terrain. Utilizing hardware filtering, this can potentially be faster than the traditional CPU terrain sampling, even when using more-traditional terrain-rendering algorithms.

Implementation Issues

This gem is not a tutorial on how to use vertex textures. Information on how to set up your application to use vertex textures can be found in [Gerasimov05] or in the DirectX documentation [D3DX05]. The accompanying demo uses DirectX 9.0, but vertex textures are also supported in OpenGL, so there should be no problems implementing the algorithm in either 3D API. Here we will only cover DirectX 9.0.

One drawback to storing the heightfield in a texture is that the heightfield size is limited by the maximum texture size supported by the graphics hardware. The maximum texture size of a typical modern graphics card is 4096×4096. Thus, very large terrains, such as 16 K by 16 K, cannot be directly supported. One possibility is to split the terrain into several textures and load them when needed. For a typical game level, though, the maximum texture size will be large enough.

Vertex texture support is currently in its infancy, and graphics hardware does not yet support a wide range of texture formats to be used for vertex textures. As an example, NVIDIA GeForce 6800 only supports D3DFMT_R32F and D3DFMT_A32B32G32R32F texture formats for vertex textures. In the demo, D3DFMT_R32F was used. This implies that each pixel is a 32-bit floating point, while heightfields often only use an 8- or 16-bit integer for each elevation value. Thus, the vertex texture will require more memory than the accuracy of the heightfield demands. Future hardware generations will probably support more vertex texture formats, though.

On GeForce 6800, only nearest-neighbor filtering of the supported vertex texture formats is supported. If bilinear or trilinear filtering is required, you have to implement it in the vertex shader. This involves more vertex texture fetches and can become a performance hit.

Due to the currently limited support for vertex textures, it is necessary to be equipped with a fallback implementation for hardware without vertex texture support. Of course, any traditional terrain-rendering algorithm can be used in that case. One solution that requires little effort is to use one vertex buffer for each block and fill the elevations on the CPU. Except for the vertex texture fetches, most of what has already been discussed can be used on older hardware.

Results

ON THE CD

In the accompanying demo code on the CD-ROM, the GPU terrain-rendering algorithm is implemented with a few configurable settings. A procedurally generated 2049 × 2049 heightfield is read from a D3DFMT_R32F DDS texture. The normal map has been generated from the heightfield and stored in a D3DFMT_V8U8 signed texture format. The y-component of the normal is skipped from the normal map, and is instead calculated from the x- and z-components in the pixel shader.

Two of the parameters that can be altered in the demo are the block size and the normal calculation method. Table 5.5.1 and Table 5.5.2 list some timing results for different block sizes, using the normal map and vertex shader normals, respectively.

Table 5.5.1   Timing Results for Different Block Sizes When Using the Normal Map

	9 × 9	17 × 17	33 × 33	65 × 65
Fps:	43	85	78	89
Tris/sec:	35 M	70 M	73 M	78 M

The tests were performed running the application in window mode on a laptop with a NVIDIA GeForce 6800 GO graphics adapter. The LOD constant was set to its default value. As can be seen from the results, a block size of 9 × 9 is clearly too small, as it involves too many render calls. Although 65 × 65 yielded the best result in the normal map case in this test, it generally generates too-large areas of equal-size triangles. We have found that 17 × 17 is a good compromise between render calls and block areas.

Table 5.5.2   Timing Results for Different Block Sizes When Calculating the Normals in the Vertex Shader

	9 × 9	17 × 17	33 × 33	65 × 65
Fps:	43	54	37	40
Tris/sec:	35 M	45 M	34 M	34 M

In addition to the block size, we also see that using the normal map is roughly twice as fast as calculating the normals in the vertex shader. As it also results in superior visual quality, as seen in Color Plate 8, there should be little doubt in which method to use.

Conclusion

This gem has presented an easy-to-implement algorithm for rendering terrain on the GPU. The key point of the algorithm is to store a heightfield as a vertex texture and reuse a small vertex buffer for the entire terrain. The low memory requirements and the low CPU usage present great advantages, as it leaves more resources available for other important tasks in a game, such as physics and AI. The speed of the algorithm is comparable to other terrain algorithms. As Shader Model 3.0 becomes standard in graphics hardware, terrain rendering on the GPU is likely to retire some of the terrain-rendering algorithms commonly used in games today.

References

[D3DX05] Microsoft DirectX Developer Center, DirectX C++ documentation. Available online at *http://msdn.microsoft.com/directx/*.

[Gerasimov05] Gerasimov, Phillip, et al., "Shader Model 3.0—Using Vertex Textures." NVIDIA whitepaper, 2005. Available online at *http://developer.nvidia.com/object/using_vertex_textures.html*.

[Röttger98] Röttger, S., et. al., "Real-time Generation of Continuous Levels of Detail for Height Fields." *Proceedings of WSCG '98,* 1998: pp. 315–322.

[Shankel02] Shankel, Jason, "Fast Heightfield Normal Calculation." *Game Programming Gems 3,* Charles River Media, 2002.

[Ulrich02] Ulrich, Thatcher, "Rendering Massive Terrains using Chunked Level of Detail Control." April 2002. Available online at *http://cvs.sourceforge.net/viewcvs.py/*checkout*/tu-testbed/tu-testbed/docs/sig-notes.pdf?rev=HEAD*.

5.6

Interactive Fluid Dynamics and Rendering on the GPU

Frank Luna

frank@moon-labs.com

For shallow 3D fluid rendering, many techniques use a sum of sine waves approximation, such as those discussed in [Vlachos02] and [Finch04]. Because these techniques use static geometry animated in a vertex shader, they are fixed in the sense that the user cannot explicitly interact with and disturb the fluid. Interactive fluid effects can be achieved by doing the physics computations on the CPU and then using dynamic vertex buffers to update the geometry. This approach is discussed in [Lengyel02]. The disadvantage of this approach stems from having to do the physics calculations on the CPU and then having to transfer the new geometry back to the video card every time the simulation is updated.

Currently however, with Vertex Shader 3.0-capable graphics hardware, and in particular the vertex texture fetch functionality, both the physics and rendering of a fluid can be done completely on the GPU, using general-purpose computation techniques. By offloading the fluid dynamics to the GPU, applications avoid the dynamic vertex buffer update and take advantage of GPU power to handle a higher workload. Furthermore, it frees the CPU to do other tasks. In this gem we discuss in depth how to implement a dynamic fluid system that performs both the physics and the rendering on the GPU using DirectX 9.0c. Figure 5.6.1 and Color Plate 9 show screenshots from the demo provided on the CD-ROM, and illustrate how ripples are updated and rendered on the GPU.

ON THE CD

FIGURE 5.6.1   *Pond ripples are generated interactively by user input, and the simulation is done on the GPU.*

Mathematical Background

In this section, we state the necessary mathematical facts for implementing the simulation. Our discussion here is brief and we omit details, as the underlying mathematics is not the theme of this article.

2D Wave Equation

The Partial Differential Equation (PDE)

$$\frac{\partial^2 h}{\partial t^2}(x, z, t) = c^2 \left(\frac{\partial^2 h}{\partial x^2}(x, z, t) + \frac{\partial^2 h}{\partial z^2} \right) - \mu \frac{\partial h}{\partial t}(x, z, t) \qquad (5.6.1)$$

describes the motion of a 2D wave, with damping force $-bv$, based on the following assumptions:

1. Constant and uniform mass density
2. Constant and uniform surface tension (even during wave motion)

3. Perfectly flexible surface (i.e., no resistance to bending) so that the tension forces are always tangent to the surface

4. Small angles of inclination so that the approximation $\tan\theta = \sin\theta$ holds

Thus, the model works best for simulating fluids where the waves do not get too big, such as puddles, ponds, and relatively calm lakes. A good derivation of this PDE (without the damping) may be found in [Kreyszig62].

For artistic control of the wave, the parameters c and μ can be altered, which control the wave speed and damping, respectively. However, care must be taken to ensure that the values set satisfy the stability condition (see "Stability").

An Explicit, Finite Difference Scheme

The solution to Equation 5.6.1 is some function $y = h(x, z, t)$ that describes the height of each point on the membrane at some particular instant in time (i.e., the wave motion is transversal). To obtain an approximate solution to Equation 5.6.1, we assume a rectangular domain and lay a grid over it; these grid points correspond to the vertices of the triangle mesh representing the surface of the fluid. Once the grid is constructed, we already have the x- and z-coordinates for each vertex; our goal then is to find an approximation to $y = h(x, z, t)$ for each grid point so that we also have the vertex height (i.e., the y-coordinate). To do this, we approximate the partial derivatives with the following finite difference formulas:

$$\frac{\partial^2 h}{\partial t^2}\left(x_i, z_j, t_k\right) \approx \frac{h_{i,j}^{k+1} - 2h_{i,j}^{k} + h_{i,j}^{k-1}}{(\Delta t)^2} \tag{5.6.2}$$

$$\frac{\partial^2 h}{\partial x^2}\left(x_i, z_j, t_k\right) \approx \frac{h_{i+1,j}^{k} - 2h_{i,j}^{k} + h_{i-1,j}^{k}}{(\Delta x)^2} \tag{5.6.3}$$

$$\frac{\partial^2 h}{\partial z^2}\left(x_i, z_j, t_k\right) \approx \frac{h_{i,j+1}^{k} - 2h_{i,j}^{k} + h_{i,j-1}^{k}}{(\Delta z)^2} \tag{5.6.4}$$

$$\frac{\partial h}{\partial t}\left(x_i, z_j, t_k\right) \approx \frac{h_{i,j}^{k+1} - h_{i,j}^{k-1}}{2(\Delta t)} \tag{5.6.5}$$

Here we used the notation $h_{i,j}^{k} = h\left(x_i, z_j, t_k\right)$. For further simplicity, we stipulate that $\Delta x = \Delta z$. Substituting Equations 5.6.2, 5.6.3, 5.6.4, and 5.6.5 into Equation 5.6.1, and solving for $h_{i,j}^{k+1}$, yields the following explicit formula:

$$h_{i,j}^{k+1} = k_1 h_{i,j}^{k-1} + k_2 h_{i,j}^{k} + k_3 \left[h_{i+1,j}^{k} + h_{i-1,j}^{k} + h_{i,j+1}^{k} + h_{i,j-1}^{k} \right] \tag{5.6.6}$$

where

$$k_1 = \frac{\mu(\Delta t) - 2}{\mu(\Delta t) + 2}, \ k_2 = \frac{4 - 8 \times c^2 \dfrac{(\Delta t)^2}{(\Delta x)^2}}{2 + \mu(\Delta t)}, \text{ and } k_3 = \frac{2c^2(\Delta t)^2}{(\Delta x)^2(\mu(\Delta t) + 2)}.$$

In other words, we now have the solution function $y = h(x, z, t)$ for the ijth grid point at the next time step $k + 1$ in terms of values we already know—namely, the solutions from the previous two time steps. Figure 5.6.2 shows the previous grid point solutions the ijth grid point solution depends on at time step $k + 1$. So after Δt time units have passed, we simply apply Equation 5.6.6 to each grid point to generate the new height at time step t_{k+1}. Because Equation 5.6.6 depends on the two previous solutions of each grid point, we need to maintain two additional grid buffers to store the grid solutions at t_k and t_{k-1}.

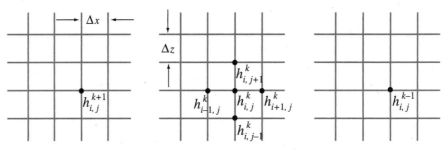

Next $k + 1$ Solution   Current k Solution   Previous $k - 1$ Solution

FIGURE 5.6.2   *The solution at the $t_k + 1$ time step depends on solutions from the t_k and $t_k - 1$ time steps.*

Of course, in order to begin using this scheme, we must already have available the first and second initial solutions. No matter—we simply specify the first and second initial solutions manually; this can be zero, if the fluid starts off undisturbed, or it could be filled with some initial wave data generated by some other means, such as an input heightmap or by summing sine waves.

A derivation (with error information) of the finite difference schemes given in Equations 5.6.2, 5.6.3, 5.6.4, and 5.6.5 can be found in [Burden01]. [Lengyel02] also provides an intuitive geometric derivation, but it lacks error information.

Stability

The explicit formula given by Equation 5.6.2 is not always stable; [Lengyel02] gives the following stability condition: The wave speed c and time step Δt must simultaneously satisfy the following inequalities:

$$0 < c < \frac{\Delta x}{2(\Delta t)} \sqrt{\mu(\Delta t) + 2} \text{ and } 0 < \Delta t < \frac{\mu + \sqrt{\mu^2 + 32 \frac{c^2}{(\Delta x)^2}}}{8 \frac{c^2}{(\Delta x)^2}}.$$

Tangents and Normal Vectors

For normal mapping, we require the tangent basis for each vertex of the fluid mesh. The function $h(x, z, t)$ describes the height of the surface at some point (x, z, t). Then, the partial derivatives

$$\frac{\partial h}{\partial x}(x, z, t) \text{ and } \frac{\partial h}{\partial z}(x, z, t)$$

specify the slopes of the tangent lines at the point in the x- and z-directions, respectively. Thus, the tangent vectors in the x- and z-directions are given, respectively, by

$$\mathbf{v} = \left(1, \frac{\partial h}{\partial x}(x, z, t), 0 \right) \tag{5.6.7}$$

and

$$\mathbf{u} = \left(0, \frac{\partial h}{\partial z}(x, z, t), 1 \right) \tag{5.6.8}$$

To see this, consider Figure 5.6.3.

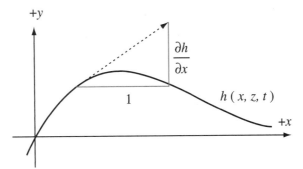

FIGURE 5.6.3 *The partial derivative gives the slope of the tangent line at some point on the curve. Then, using the "rise over run" definition of slope, if we run one unit, we rise ∂h/∂x units. The idea is analogous to the tangent vector in the z-direction.*

Observe from Figure 5.6.3 that **u** and **v** are not unit vectors. Given the tangent vectors, the normal vector is found by a simple application of the cross product:

$$\mathbf{n} = (\mathbf{u} \times \mathbf{v}) / \|\mathbf{u} \times \mathbf{v}\|$$

where we use a left-handed coordinate system.

The partial derivatives in Equations 5.6.7 and 5.6.8 may be approximated by the following finite difference formulas:

$$\frac{\partial h}{\partial x}\left(x_i, z_j, t_k\right) \approx \frac{h_{i+1,j}^k - h_{i-1,j}^k}{2(\Delta x)} \qquad (5.6.9)$$

and

$$\frac{\partial h}{\partial z}\left(x_i, z_j, t_k\right) \approx \frac{h_{i,j+1}^k - h_{i,j-1}^k}{2(\Delta z)} \qquad (5.6.10)$$

GPU Implementation

Textures Represent Grids

The GPU analogy of an array is a texture. We can write to a texture via render-to-texture functionality (the GPU equivalent is array write), and we can read from a texture by sampling it in a pixel shader (the GPU equivalent is array read). Note that rendering to and sampling from the same texture simultaneously is undefined [Harris04].

To implement the finite difference scheme given by Equation 5.6.6, we need three grids—a grid to store the next solution, a grid to store the current solution, and a grid to store the previous solution. Hence, we require three floating-point render-target textures.

```
DrawableTex2D* mPrevStepMap;
DrawableTex2D* mCurrStepMap;
DrawableTex2D* mNextStepMap;
```

Now, because each element in the grid only stores a height value, we could get away with a 1D element format, like D3DFMT_R16F; however, current hardware (e.g., GeForce 6800 GT) does not support rendering to a D3DFMT_R16F render target. We could instead use D3DFMT_R32F, but present hardware does not support alpha blending (i.e., D3DUSAGE_QUERY_POSTPIXELSHADER_BLENDING) with this format, which we need to disturb the waves. Consequently, we use the D3DFMT_A16B16G16R16F and waste space by only storing the height value in the red channel; the green, blue, and alpha channels are not used.

Doing the Simulation on the GPU

Every time Δt time units elapse, we need to update the simulation and compute the new height values for each point on the grid. Our goal is to do this completely on the GPU—that is, instead of using the GPU to output color information, it is going to be used for the general-purpose computation of updating our grid height values.

Given the grids `mPrevStepMap` and `mCurrStepMap` of the two previous solutions at time steps t_{k-1} and t_k, we want to compute the grid heights for the next solution (and store it in `mNextStepMap`) at time step t_{k+1}. In a CPU implementation, we would just iterate over each grid element and apply Equation 5.6.6. But how do we do this on the GPU? Well, the pixel shader gets executed for each pixel drawn to the render target; consequently, we can think of a pixel shader as a loop body:

For each pixel P_{ij}
    Execute Pixel Shader on P_{ij}

Therefore, we proceed as follows:

1. Set `mNextStepMap` as the render target.
2. Set `mPrevStepMap` and `mCurrStepMap` as texture effect parameters so that they can be sampled in a pixel shader (i.e., they consist of our input for computing the next solution).
3. Draw a unit quad directly over the entire projection window; this ensures the pixel shader will be executed for each pixel in the render target.
4. Apply Equation 5.6.6 in the pixel shader.
5. Update is done; prepare for the next update by cycling the render targets:

```
DrawableTex2D* temp = mPrevStepMap;
    mPrevStepMap = mCurrStepMap;
    mCurrStepMap = mNextStepMap;
    mNextStepMap = temp;
```

The actual vertex and pixel shader implementations to do this are given as follows:

```
// Texel size in texture space [0, 1] units.
uniform extern float gTexelSize;

// Precomputed constants from Equation 5.6.6.
uniform extern float gK1;
uniform extern float gK2;
uniform extern float gK3;

// Previous grid Solutions.
uniform extern texture gPrevStepTex;
uniform extern texture gCurrStepTex;
```

```
sampler gPrevStepSmplr = sampler_state
{
    Texture = <gPrevStepTex>;
    [...]
};

sampler gCurrStepSmplr = sampler_state
{
    Texture = <gCurrStepTex>;
    [...]
};

void PhysicsVS(float3 posH : POSITION0,
    out float4 oPosH : POSITION0,
    out float2 oUV : TEXCOORD0)
{
    // Vertices already specified on the projection window.
    oPosH = float4(posH, 1.0f);

    // Transform projection window coordinates [-1, 1] +y up
    // to texture coordinates [0, 1] +y down.
    oUV = float2(posH.x, posH.y) * float2(0.5, -0.5) + 0.5;
}

float4 PhysicsPS(float2 uv : TEXCOORD0) : COLOR
{
    // Zero out boundaries.
    if(uv.x < 0.001f || uv.x > 0.985f ||
        uv.y < 0.001f || uv.y > 0.985f)
        return float4(0.0f, 0.0f, 0.0f, 0.0f);
    else
    {
        // Sample grid points from previous and current time steps.
        float c0 = tex2D(gPrevStepSmplr, uv).r;
        float c1 = tex2D(gCurrStepSmplr, uv).r;
        float t = tex2D(gCurrStepSmplr,
            float2(uv.x, uv.y - gTexelSize)).r;
        float b = tex2D(gCurrStepSmplr,
            float2(uv.x, uv.y + gTexelSize)).r;
        float l = tex2D(gCurrStepSmplr,
            float2(uv.x - gTexelSize, uv.y)).r;
        float r = tex2D(gCurrStepSmplr,
            float2(uv.x + gTexelSize, uv.y)).r;

        // Return next solution at this
        // grid point (Equation 5.6.6).
        return float4(gK1*c0 + gK2*c1 + gK3*(t+b+l+r),
            0.0f, 0.0f, 0.0f);
    }
}
```

As you can see from the pixel shader PhysicsPS, we zero out the boundaries. (If you do not want zero-boundary conditions, you could draw lines on the edges of the projection window, which describe the boundary conditions.) Moreover, you may be concerned about sampling points off the texture map. There are different ways to handle this; for example, you could set a cylindrical texture wrap, or you can just clamp the value to the boundary values. Last, the parameter `gTexelSize` tells us how far to move up, down, left, or right on the texture map to sample the adjacent grid values (recall Figure 5.6.2); it is defined as 1/*TextureSize*. If your texture is not square, then you would move a different offset value for each of the horizontal and vertical directions—that is, 1/*TextureWidth* and 1/*TextureHeight*.

Calculating Tangents and Normal Vectors on the GPU

After we have updated the simulation, we can compute the new tangent vectors based on the new vertex heights. To do this, we first must add another grid data structure to store the tangent vector data:

```
DrawableTex2D* mTangentMap;
```

Observe that for the tangent vectors, we only need to store the partial derivatives (i.e., the *y*-coordinates of Equations 5.6.7 and 5.6.8), since given that data, we can easily reconstruct the tangent vectors when needed. Moreover, because we do not need blending operations for the tangent vectors' texture, we can get by with the `D3DFMT_G16R16F` format, where

1. The red component stores $\partial h/\partial x$, and
2. The green component stores $\partial h/\partial z$.

Now, to compute the tangent vector data, we simply iterate over each (updated) grid element, apply Equations 5.6.9 and 5.6.10, and write the result to `mTangentMap` (i.e., `mTangentMap` is the render target). This leads to the following pixel shader (the vertex shader just renders a quad, as in `PhysicsVS`) for computing the tangent vector data:

```
// Step size in local space
// (needed for Equations 5.6.9 and 5.6.10).
uniform extern float gStepSizeL;

// Heights of vertices we are computing tangent information for.
uniform extern texture gCurrStepTex;

sampler gCurrStepSmplr = sampler_state
{
    Texture = <gCurrStepTex>;
    [...]
};

float4 CalcTangentsPS(float2 uv : TEXCOORD0) : COLOR
{
// Zero out boundaries.
```

```
if(uv.x < 0.001f || uv.x > 0.985f ||
    uv.y < 0.001f || uv.y > 0.985f)
    return float4(0.0f, 0.0f, 0.0f, 0.0f);
else
{
    float t = tex2D(gCurrStepSmplr,
        float2(uv.x, uv.y - gTexelSize)).r;
    float b = tex2D(gCurrStepSmplr,
        float2(uv.x, uv.y + gTexelSize)).r;
    float l = tex2D(gCurrStepSmplr,
        float2(uv.x - gTexelSize, uv.y)).r;
    float r = tex2D(gCurrStepSmplr,
        float2(uv.x + gTexelSize, uv.y)).r;

    // Apply Equations 9 and 10.
    float xtanY = (r - l) / (2*gStepSizeL);
    float ztanY = (t - b) / (2*gStepSizeL);

    return float4(xtanY, ztanY, 0.0f, 0.0f);
}
}
```

Copying a Texture on the GPU

Recall that we have been using 16-bit floating-point render-target formats. However, current hardware (e.g., GeForce 6800 GT) that supports the vertex texture fetch functionality only works with 32-bit floating-point render-targets, like D3DFMT_R32F and D3DFMT_A32B32G32R32F. Thus, before we can do the displacement mapping, we need to copy our current grid data (i.e., heights and tangent partial derivatives) to a texture in the format D3DFMT_A32B32G32R32F. We lay the data out in the following way:

1. Red channel stores vertex height.
2. Green channel stores $\partial h/\partial x$.
3. Blue channel stores $\partial h/\partial z$.
4. Alpha channel is not used.

The following pixel shader does the copy (again, the vertex shader just renders a quad, as in PhysicsVS):

```
// Source Data for the copy.
uniform extern texture gHeightMap;
uniform extern texture gTangentMap;

sampler gHeightSmplr = sampler_state
{
    Texture = <gHeightMap>;
    [...]
};
```

```
sampler gTangentSmplr = sampler_state
{
    Texture = <gTangentMap>;
    [...]
};

float4 CopyTexPS(float2 uv : TEXCOORD0) : COLOR
{
    // (r1, 0, 0, 0) + (r2, g, 0, 0) = (r1, r2, g, 0).
    float height = tex2D(gHeightSmplr, uv).r;
    float2 tangents = tex2D(gTangentSmplr, uv).rg;
    return float4(height, tangents, 1.0f);
}
```

where the data is copied into a `D3DFMT_A32B32G32R32F` render target:

```
DrawableTex2D* mVertexDataMap;
```

Displacement Mapping

Let us review what we have done thus far. First, in a GPU implementation, textures replace arrays; we write to the texture by rendering to it, and we read from it by sampling it. Second, every time step (i.e., after Δt time units have passed), we compute the next solution to the wave equation at this new time step; we then cycle the solutions to prepare for the next update: The current solution becomes the previous solution, the next solution becomes the current solution, and the next solution points to the old previous render target, which is no longer needed and can be overwritten in the next step. Once the new vertex heights are computed, we proceed to compute the essential data of the tangent vectors (i.e., the partial derivatives for the y-coordinate). Because we cannot utilize the vertex texture fetch functionality with a 16-bit floating-point texture, we next copy the texture, storing the vertex height data and also the texture, storing the tangent vector data in 32-bit, floating-point texture format.

Thus, at this point we have the current vertex heights and essential tangent vector data all stored in a single texture identified by `mVertexDataMap`. We are now ready to feed this data into the vertex shader to actually set the height of the vertex and build its tangent basis. To do this, we set `mVertexDataMap` as a texture effect parameter and sample it in the vertex shader with the intrinsic `tex2Dlod` function, where we specify zero for the w component of the second parameter in order to access the topmost mip-map LOD (we actually only have one level, anyway). Then we extract the data from the RGB components:

```
OutVS GPUFluidRenderingVS(float3 posL : POSITION0,
    float2 uv : TEXCOORD0)
{
    OutVS outVS = (OutVS)0;
```

```
// Sample heightmap for displacement.
float4 data = tex2Dlod(gDispSmplr, float4(uv, 0.0f, 0.0f));

// r-component stores the height.
posL.y = data.r;
outVS.posH = mul(float4(posL, 1.0f), gWVP);

// Build tangents and normal vectors.
float3 xtan = normalize(float3(1.0f, data.g, 0.0f));
float3 ztan = normalize(float3(0.0f, data.b, 1.0f));
float3 normalL = normalize(cross(ztan, xtan));

... Do Other Vertex Shader Work.

}
```

Altering a vertex location based on an input texture is called *displacement mapping*, and the vertex texture fetch functionality is what allows us to do this. Previous hardware could not sample textures in a vertex shader.

Interacting with the Fluid

Disturbing the Wave on the GPU

So far, our system works by manually initializing the first and second solutions, and then applying Equation 5.6.6 to compute subsequent solutions. However, our real goal is to be able to disturb the fluid at runtime on the GPU. For example, for a fountain, you may want to dynamically generate ripples based on water drops; for a lake, you may want to dynamically generate waves based on a moving boat, or when game characters wade through the fluid.

We can view Equation 5.6.6 as solving a new problem at each time step—that is, it computes a new solution based on the two previous solutions, and it does not care about solutions prior to that. So the trick is to just manually modify the two previous solutions to add in the new disturbance (i.e., displace the grid heights of the vertices affected by the disturbance); and then, when the simulation is updated, the fluid will be updated with these new disturbances taken into account, since Equation 5.6.6 depends on these previous solution grids. Note that we do not simply want to override the previous wave motion over a particular area; we instead add/subtract displacement from it. In addition, when we disturb an area of grid points, we should disturb the surrounding grid points to a lesser degree so that there is not too much of an abrupt transition.

At first this seems very easy (and it actually is), but remember that our grids are textures stored in video memory, so we cannot just write to them from the CPU. Recall, though, that rendering to a texture is the GPU equivalent of writing to an array. Thus, we can set the previous two solutions as render targets and then draw triangles (circles, squares, or whatever shape you want the disturbances to be) onto the projection window covering only those pixels corresponding to the grid points that we want to disturb. Furthermore, because we are rendering these triangles directly onto the projection window, the z-coordinate is free; we use the z-coordinate to store the magnitude of the height displacement. The following shaders illustrate:

```
void DisturbVS(float3 posH : POSITION0,
    out float4 oPosH : POSITION0,
    out float oHeight : TEXCOORD0)
{
    // Vertices already specified on the projection window.
    oPosH = float4(posH.x, posH.y, 0.0f, 1.0f);
    oHeight = posH.z;
}

float4 DisturbPS(float height : TEXCOORD0) : COLOR
{
    return float4(height, 0.0f, 0.0f, 1.0f);
}
```

Moreover, we enable alpha blending, and set the source and destination blend flags to One;. This ensures the heights are accumulated, rather than overridden:

```
// f = src * srcBlend + dest + destBlend
// = src * 1 + dest * 1
// = src + dest (i.e., accumulate the heights)
AlphaBlendEnable = true;
SrcBlend = One;
DestBlend = One;
```

Recall from "Textures Represent Grids" that we used `D3DFMT_A16B16G16R16F` instead of `D3DFMT_R32F` for this blending support.

Barrier Maps

Presently, only the zeroed-out boundary conditions present barriers; that is, when the waves reach the boundary, they simply bounce off as if there was a wall. It is not difficult to come up with other instances of where barriers would be desirable. For example, the body of water may not be perfectly rectangular, but may exist in an irregularly shaped pond; when the water reaches the perimeter, it should bounce off. Or we may have small islands in the middle of our water, and the waves should bounce off the edges of these islands. Or we have other objects, like boats or bridge pillars that serve as barriers to the fluid.

To handle this, [Tessendorf04] suggests barrier maps to mask the grid points where obstacles occur. The idea is to assign a weight of [0, 1] to each grid point. If the grid point coincides with a barrier, its weight is zero, and its neighbors' weights should be some transitional value (unless also a barrier) to ensure a smooth fall-off. Then, when computing the height of the vertex, we factor in its corresponding weight from the barrier map, which can zero-out or lessen the height. If the barriers change (e.g., moving boats), then you can dynamically create the barrier map by rendering to it.

Further Reading

[Tessendorf04] uses a linearized Bernoulli PDE, from which an explicit formula is derived. This alternative equation can be programmed on the GPU using the same strategy this article discusses. On the other hand, [Zelsnack04] solves the same 2D wave equation that we do here, but employs a Verlet Integration numerical method instead of a finite difference scheme.

Our explicit scheme is not always stable. Unconditionally stable schemes exist (e.g., the Crank-Nicholson scheme), but are typically implicit and require solving a system of equations at each time step in order to obtain the solutions. [Krüger05] develops a framework for solving systems of linear equations on the GPU, which can then be used for implementing implicit schemes.

Good-looking static ocean waves can be made by scrolling heightmaps representing the wave heights and doing the displacement mapping via the vertex texture fetch functionality (see [Kryachko05]). A hybrid method may be devised by adding this technique for general ambient waves with dynamically generated waves as described in this article.

Typical water-rendering techniques include combining reflection and refraction maps via a Fresnel term, where scrolling normal maps are used to perturb the texture lookup (see [Vlachos02], [Pelzer04], and or [Sousa05] for implementation details). Caustics (i.e., concentrated light striking the underwater surface) may be implemented by scrolling caustic maps, or by a more sophisticated method as described in [Guardado04] or [Ernst05].

Finally, [Tessendorf02] provides an excellent general survey of ocean water rendering.

Conclusion

We have shown how to implement an interactive fluid simulation completely on the GPU. In doing so, we avoid the problems of a typical CPU implementation: the obvious CPU cost (games are primarily CPU-limited [Blythe05]), and the system-memory to video-memory transfer. The latter is particularly problematic for large grids, as uploading even a medium-size grid of vertices (e.g., 256×256) with position data, texture coordinates, normals, and tangent vectors is quite costly. More generally, the techniques described in this gem should provide further ideas for moving other simulation tasks, such as particle systems, from the CPU to the GPU.

References

[Blythe05] Blythe, David, "DirectX: The Next Step." Meltdown 2005 Presentation, 2005.

[Burden01] Burden, Richard L. and J. Douglas Faires, *Numerical Analysis*, 7th Ed. Brooks/Cole, 2001.

[Ernst05] Ernst, Manfred, Tomas Akenine-Möller, and Henrik Wann Jensen, "Interactive Rendering of Caustics using Interpolated Warped Volumes." *Graphics Interface*, 2005. Available online at *http://graphics.ucsd.edu/~henrik/papers/interactive_caustics/*.

[Finch04] Finch, Mark, "Effective Water Simulation from Physical Models." *GPU Gems: Programming Techniques, Tips, and Tricks for Real-Time Graphics*, Addison-Wesley, 2004.

[Guardado04] Guardado, Juan and Daniel Sánchez-Crespo, "Rendering Water Caustics." *GPU Gems: Programming Techniques, Tips, and Tricks for Real-Time Graphics*, Addison-Wesley, 2004.

[Harris04] Harris, Mark J., "Fast Fluid Dynamics Simulation on the GPU." *GPU Gems: Programming Techniques, Tips, and Tricks for Real-Time Graphics*, Addison-Wesley, 2004.

[Kreyszig62] Kreyszig, Erwin, *Advanced Engineering Mathematics,* John Wiley and Sons, 1962.

[Krüger05] Krüger, Jens and Rüdiger Westermann. "A GPU Framework for Solving Systems of Linear Equations." *GPU Gems 2: Programming Techniques for High-Performance Graphics and General Purpose Computation*, Addison-Wesley, 2005.

[Kryachko05] Kryachko, Yuri, "Using Vertex Texture Displacement for Realistic Water Rendering." *GPU Gems 2: Programming Techniques for High-Performance Graphics and General Purpose Computation*, Addison-Wesley, 2005.

[Lengyel02] Lengyel, Eric, *Mathematics for 3D Game Programming and Computer Graphics,* Charles River Media, 2002.

[Pelzer04] Pelzer, Kurt, "Advanced Water Effects." *ShaderX²: Shader Programming Tips & Tricks with DirectX 9*, Wordware Publishing, 2004.

[Sousa05] Sousa, Tiago, "Generic Refraction Simulation." *GPU Gems 2: Programming Techniques for High-Performance Graphics and General Purpose Computation*, Addison-Wesley, 2005.

[Tessendorf02] Tessendorf, Jerry, "Simulating Ocean Water." Simulating Nature, SIGGRAPH Course Notes, 2002. Available online at *http://users.adelphia.net/~tessendorf/docs/coursenotes2002.pdf*.

[Tessendorf04] Tessendorf, Jerry, "Interactive Water Surfaces." *Game Programming Gems 4,* Charles River Media, 2004.

[Vlachos02] Vlachos, Alex, John Isidoro, and Chris Oat, "Rippling Reflective and Refractive Water." *Direct3D ShaderX: Vertex and Pixel Shader Tips and Tricks*, Wordware Publishing, 2002.

[Zelsnack04] Zelsnack, Jeremy, "Vertex Texture Fetch Water." 2004. Available online at *http://download.developer.nvidia.com/developer/SDK/Individual_Samples/DEMOS/Direct3D9/src/VertexTextureFetchWater/docs/VertexTextureFetchWater.pdf*.

5.7

Fast Per-Pixel Lighting with Many Lights

Frank Puig Placeres, University of Informatic Sciences, Cuba

fpuig@fpuig.cjb.net

L ighting is one of the elements that has been greatly enhanced with the improvement of graphics hardware. A few years ago, a typical game only used static lighting through the implementation of light maps and a few per-vertex lit objects. However, game graphics has been moving into fully per-pixel lighted worlds in which most of the lights are dynamic.

Standard lighting solutions that handle dynamic lights often involve rendering objects affected by lights in several passes, each pass using a shader program that computes the influence of a few lights. In addition to the multipass penalty, the main disadvantage of this approach is that complicated shaders must be written for all light combinations, such as shaders for omni lights only, or for omni and spot lights.

Today, graphics materials also handle complex effects, like steep parallax mapping and multilayered texture coordinate animations. Several combinations of them can also be used, which only increases the number of passes. The shader instruction count required to describe those materials is high, and is increasing as the hardware power increases and allows more-complicated effects. Summing the code for handling several combinations of different lighting models and shadows clearly overwhelms the shader complexity allowed by the graphics hardware.

This gem presents an idea for improving the standard deferred lighting approach to reduce not only the hardware target and the number of shaders that must be written to represent complex scenes, but also to increase the power of post-processing effects like depth of view, head haze, and fog.

Deferred Solution

Traditional lighting solutions submit the object's geometry and apply the light's influence immediately. When dealing with a high number of lights that influence an object, the rendering process has to be split into several passes. On each pass the object's geometry is submitted to the graphic pipeline, and the contribution of a group of lights is computed. The results of those passes are combined in the fragment buffer, so finally the total lighting influence is produced.

Deferred rendering comes in handy as a solution for dealing with a high number of lights without submitting the object's geometry multiple times. As shown in Figure 5.7.1, deferred rendering allows processing of the scene in only two passes, independent of the number or complexity of lights. In the first pass, instead of storing the color of each screen pixel, the per-pixel surface attributes, like the normal, specularity, glow factor, and occlusion term, are stored in the fragment buffer.

In the second pass, for each light, this buffer is used as a texture, and a flat quad is drawn with a one-to-one mapping of texels to screen pixels. A fragment program unpacks the surface properties from the buffer of each screen pixel and, using the light's position, color, and so forth as parameters, evaluates the lighting equation and combines them in the fragment buffer to produce the fully lit scene.

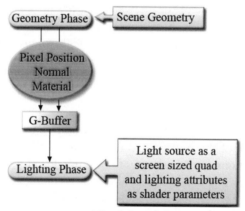

FIGURE 5.7.1   *The deferred shading pipeline.*

Deferred Shading Implementation for High-End Hardware

ON THE CD

As previously described, a classical deferred-shading implementation involves two main phases: the geometry phase and the lighting phase, which communicate through the Geometry Buffer (G-Buffer). A very simplified implementation of deferred rendering can be found in the included CD-ROM under the name "Deferred Shading MRT."

Geometry Buffer

One of the most important steps when planning a deferred rendering system is to determine which parameters are needed to compute the per-pixel lighting equations. In the first example, only the pixel position and its normal are, used since the example only shows point lights with diffuse components. Other parameters, like specular power and glow factor, can be additionally stored if the lighting equation will perform specular contribution or other advanced lighting effects.

Once the required parameters are defined, a geometry buffer is built. This buffer is the place where detailed information about each screen pixel is stored. Commonly, it is implemented as some render target textures, where the pixel shaders of the geometric phase store the selected parameters.

When dealing with medium- and high-end hardware, it is possible to use floating-point textures to hold the position and normal vectors. However, there are typically too many values to store them in only one texture, so several passes must be done to spread the values in different textures. If the graphics hardware supports Multiple Render Targets (MRT), it's possible to store all the needed parameters in just one pass. Figure 5.7.2 shows how the first example, included on the CD-ROM, organizes the necessary pixel values in two floating-point textures.

ON THE CD

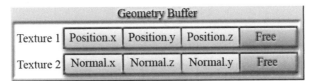

FIGURE 5.7.2 *Packing position and normal into two floating-point textures.*

Geometry Phase

In the geometry phase, the G-Buffer is placed as the render target, and the complete scene is submitted to the pipeline. The shaders executed in this stage pack all the needed pixel's geometrical and surface properties into the G-Buffer. The process could be as simple as presented in the first example, where the pixel world position and normal are sent to the pixel shader, which in turn packs them into the color output and stores them in the G-Buffer. In this first example, the G-Buffer consists of two textures, as presented in Figure 5.7.2.

```
PS_OUTPUT ps_main( PS_INPUT Input )
{
    PS_OUTPUT o;

    o.Color0.xyz = Input.WorldPos;
    o.Color1.xyz = normalize( Input.WorldNormal );

    o.Color0.w = 0; // these two values are unused in this example,
    o.Color1.w = 0; // but they could easily fit the specular power
                    // and occlusion term
    return o;
}
```

Effects like skinning and displacement mapping, which transform the scene geometry, are also set to be processed during this phase.

Lighting Phase

The lighting phase is the most important stage of deferred shading. For the moment, only the lighting influence is going to be computed. Further additional effects, like shadows and depth of view, would be applied in this phase, as well.

After all parameters are saved into the G-Buffer, the textures that comprise it are sent to this stage as input parameters to the shader programs. All light sources are iterated, and for each of them, the light equation that describes the light is evaluated for every screen pixel. This is done by drawing a quad that covers the screen and executing the shader program at each pixel.

```
float3 LightPos;
float InvSqrLightRange;
float4 DiffuseLightColor;

float4 ps_main( float2 texCoord : TEXCOORD0 ) : COLOR
{
    // screen pixel position and normal are extracted
    // from G-Buffer

    float3 Normal = tex2D(Texture_Normals, texCoord);
    float3 PixelPos = tex2D(Texture_Pos, texCoord);

    // Computes light attenuation and direction

    float3 LightDir = (LightPos - PixelPos) * InvSqrLightRange;
    float Attenuation = saturate(1-dot(LightDir, LightDir));
    LightDir = normalize(LightDir);

    // Lighting equation

    float DiffuseInfluence = dot(LightDir, Normal)*Attenuation;
    return DiffuseLightColor * DiffuseInfluence;
}
```

Once all the lights' quads are rendered and the shaded influence of each light is computed, they are blended in the frame buffer, so at the end the screen contains the complete scene with per-pixel lighting applied. It's worth mentioning that different combinations of lighting models can be used while using deferred shading, with no additional overhead. So far, only diffuse point lights have been shown; but it only requires writing other pixel shaders to perform spot light or specular omni lights, and then just rendering the screen-size quad with the correct pixel shader.

Basic Storage Optimizations

Multiple render targets are still not commonly supported. This implies that on systems lacking such support, a fallback solution must be implemented. That solution involves executing the geometry phase several times, each storing different parameters to the G-Buffer. As executing the geometrical phase several times implies processing the scene geometry over and over, the rendering system will suffer some performance impact that will be evident on the high-poly scenes that players expect for the next-generation games. Fortunately, there's a way to avoid the multipass approach: clever packing of the parameters into a single texture!

The following list has the parameters usually stored in the G-Buffer.

• Normal
• Position
• Material attributes, like emission, specular power, and so forth

Normal Packing

The pixel normal parameter is a three-dimensional vector, and therefore three values must be stored in the G-Buffer. However, normals are constrained to unit length vectors. That restriction allows discarding one of the values, to be recovered later by applying the equation:

$$z = \pm\sqrt{1 - x^2 - y^2}$$

The problem with using only this equation is that z can be a negative or positive value, so the original z sign has to be stored as well. Working around that extra bit, there is also a way to discard it. The example so far performs the lighting equation using world space vectors. Migrating to view space instead allows some extra benefits. For instance, if all screen pixels belong to front-faced polygons, then their normals will have the same sign. When some screen pixels belong to back-faced polygons and two-sided lighting is requested, it can be clever to store their normals during the geometry phase as if they belonged to front-faced polygons instead.

Packing the normal into two values as shown above saves some storage room, but it increases the number of instructions to be performed when unpacking the values. Luckily, when some extra memory is available, there's a way to overcome those extra lines. The normal x- and y-components are in the range of $[-1, 1]$, but when storing the normal x- and y-components in the G-Buffer, it's useful and some times necessary (as will be shown later on) to store them in the $[0, 1]$ range. Applying that transformation allows the use of a two-dimensional lookup texture that holds, at each pixel, the normalized normal with x- and y-components defined as the u- and v-texture components.

Using this texture and the x- and y-normal components from the G-Buffer, the normalized normal vector can be assembled with only one texture fetch instead of the unpacking math code, which can save up to five arithmetic instructions. An example of code to generate any size texture can be found on the CD-ROM (see "Compute Normal Texture"), as well as the second deferred texture example.

ON THE CD

Position Packing

As with the normal vector, the pixel position is also a three-dimensional vector. But contrary to normals, it is not a unit-length vector. Therefore, the Pythagorean trick cannot be applied to pixel positions. Nevertheless, there's a way to reduce the number of values needed to store the position in the G-Buffer.

Given the screen position of a pixel, a ray can be built from the eye to that position. If the distance from the eye to the pixel is known, then assembling the original position is only a matter of multiplying the normalized ray by the given distance, as shown in Figure 5.7.3. In the lighting phase, it's possible to create the ray from the camera position to the screen pixel so that the only value that really needs to be stored in the G-Buffer is the distance from the eye to the pixel. Storing how far the position from the camera is becomes as simple as computing the length of the vector that holds the view space position. However, building the screen-eye ray is a bit more complex.

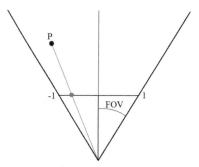

FIGURE 5.7.3   *Deriving the pixel's position, given only the distance.*

In the lighting phase, the pixel shader receives the texture coordinates of the pixel in the G-Buffer. Transforming the received texture coordinates from the [0, 1] texture space to the [−1, 1] normalized screen space allows derivation of the original projected pixel position.

At first glance, the normalized screen x-y coordinates can be assigned to the ray x- and y-components. The z-value is a bit trickier. When defining the perspective projection matrix, the field of view angle is used. As shown in Figure 5.7.3, it's possible to use the tangent of that angle to find the distance at which the half-screen is unit length. That is the value to be placed in the ray z-component.

Even when the ray components have been computed, it still doesn't take into account that the screen width and height are not the same. Overcoming that issue could be as simple as multiplying the ray x-component by the view aspect ratio used to build the projection matrix. The following code shows the process of building the eye-screen ray in the vertex and pixel shader of the lighting phase.

Geometry Phase Vertex Shader:

```
o.EyeRay = float3(inPos.x * ViewAspect, inPos.y, TanFOV);
o.Depth  = length( ViewSpacePosition );
```

Lighting Phase Pixel Shader:

```
float3 PixelPos = normalize(Input.EyeRay) * Depth;
```

ON THE CD

An example of the complete position-packing procedure can be found in the second deferred example in the CD-ROM.

Material Packing

Material attributes refers to a group of values that define the surface properties. Examples of these values are the emission color, the specular power, and the glow factor. Storing each of those attributes into the G-Buffer consumes a huge amount of storage space. One easy way to avoid that storage penalty is to discard some of those values and not use them in the lighting equation, although this means heavily decreasing the lighting quality, which is unavoidable.

Looking around the properties of the material attributes, it's obvious that in most cases those values are not changed per pixel, but per surface. Given that there are a limited number of materials, another way to pack the attributes could be to store them in an auxiliary material array containing all the needed attributes for each material, and use it as a material palette in the lighting pixel shader to unpack all material attributes. That way, the only value that needs to be stored in the G-Buffer is the position of the material in the array.

Depending on the number of materials allowed by the deferred rendering system, there are two ways to submit the material palette into the lighting shader. If the palette length fits into the shader constant register, the rendering system fills them so that the lighting pixel shader can access the desired material by doing indexed lookups. However, if the material array length exceeds the available constant register, then material attributes are saved in an auxiliary texture, where every vertical line represents a different material. When in the lighting shader, the surface properties are accessed through the use of texture fetches. If the material count or the attributes of any surface are not going to change during the simulation, the material texture doesn't need to be created at runtime, but only when compiling the game levels.

Shader Optimizations and Hardware Limitations

Reducing the number of values to be stored allows using a single texture in the G-Buffer. Floating-point textures, however, are not widely supported, so taking special care of the needed precision for each parameter allows reducing the target hardware. Next are some examples of how to reduce the number of bits to be stored.

The x- and y-components of the normal vector can be represented as an 8-bit integer without sacrificing too much quality. In fact, on some scenes they can even be stored as 5-bit or 6-bit without being noticed; however, 8-bit seems to be the common choice, since it matches the precision of the bump and normal textures.

As before, the position vector can be encoded as a single value that represents the distance from the eye to the pixel. Reducing the precision of that depth value has a noticeable impact on the scene quality; however, using from 24 to 16 bits to represent it can be supported as a fall-back solution for low- and medium-quality graphics options. See Figure 5.7.4 and Color Plates 10a and 10b for examples of the differences apparent with different depth precisions.

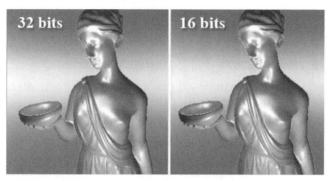

FIGURE 5.7.4 *Scene rendered using different depth precisions.*

ON THE CD
The third deferred example on the CD-ROM shows an implementation that uses 16 bits to store the pixel depth and a byte for each of the normal components, so that it fits a single A8R8B8G8 texture, which is widely supported. If there is a need to use different material configurations to store specular powers or diffuse colors, it is feasible to reduce the normal component precision down to 6–7-bit, which allows storing 4 to 15 different material combinations in the G-Buffer.

Now that it's possible to target low- and medium-end hardware, it's also necessary that the lighting be as fast as possible. A basic solution will be to optimize the shader code. For instance, some common lighting shader improvements can be applied. The attenuation factor can be precomputed in a 1D texture and then perform a simple texture fetch, thereby avoiding some arithmetic instructions. Also, the use of the half-data type instead of the float-one whenever the extra precision is not needed, as in the last example, can help improve the shader on some graphic cards. Rearranging the instruction order or reformulating some of them can also help the compiler produce faster programs. In general, most of the common shader optimizations fit into the deferred shading programs.

High-Level Deferred Shading Optimizations

Optimizing only the shaders involved in the different phases of the deferred shading framework helps support a wide range of graphic hardware and improves the performance of the whole system. However, if the render process is implemented exactly as described in this article, and every light source is sent to the lighting phase as a quad without supporting any high-level optimization, the system can suffer a fill-rate bottleneck.

In next sections, some high-level optimizations are shown concerning a light manager that works as a firewall between the render system and the lighting phase shaders, as shown in Figure 5.7.5. This light manager is implemented using two main phases: the social stage and the individual stage.

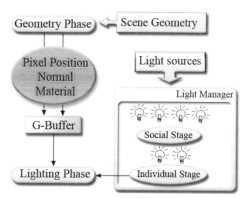

FIGURE 5.7.5   *Deferred shading pipeline with a high-level manager.*

Social Stage

In this first phase, the system accesses all the lighting sources and applies general optimizations in order to reduce the number of lights that are being processed. At first, some algorithms are used to find which lights are occluded by the scene geometry or are not in the visible range of the camera. These algorithms use the light-bounding objects and perform the culling with them. By that way, only the lights that make any contribution to the visible screen are used. However, not all the visible lights make a significant contribution to the scene. When the system requires losing a bit of quality and precision in order to get some performance, the lights that only affect a few pixels can be omitted. Other high-level optimizations avoid processing lights very close in screen space and that affect almost the same region. Those lights can be carefully combined into a big, bright one without introducing many errors. The above works better if the lights are far from the camera position.

While the steps presented so far greatly reduce the number of lights to be processed, the performance can still be too low. It's possible to adjust the maximum number of lights affecting each region to about 8–10. Similarly, if the number of lights grows too big, then only the biggest, brightest, or closest visible lights in the scene are processed.

Individual Stage

Once the social stage is applied, a list of source lights is determined. The individual stage iterates that list and optimizes the processing cost of each light. When creating the scene, lights are classified in two main groups: global lights and local lights.

Global lights are those that affect the entire scene. They are one of the most expensive type of lights because they need to process every screen pixel and commonly don't allow high-level optimizations. Those lights are implemented by drawing a screen-size quad with the proper light shaders. Contrary to those lights, a local light has position and shape. As locals only affect the pixels inside the light-bounding object, most of the time not all screen pixels get influenced by the light, so there is more room for improvement.

For instance, the scissors test can be configured to surround the light-bounding object and quickly discard pixels on the outside of the scissors rectangle. Even the bounding object itself can be rendered instead of the screen-size quad, as described. Dynamic branching can help discard unlit pixels by avoiding those with positions farther than a radius from the light source when using a sphere, or out of the bounding object when using a general mesh. [ATI05] describes a technique to implement dynamic branching using the stencil test on hardware that doesn't support it.

Light level of detail is another feature that can be implemented on the individual stage, which allows adjustment of how much quality versus how much performance the system brings. This way, lights that are too far away don't have to be computed with the same quality as lights that are near the camera. In Figure 5.7.6, three levels of detail are presented, including the "no light" level. As can be seen, the second level of detail includes multiplication by a t factor. This is performed in order to smoothly move from one level to the next by setting t to take values between 1 and 0, as shown in the figure. So the specular term is shown when at the start of the second level of detail and smoothly fades out until no specular term is returned when reaching the next level. That way, no hard lighting changes are noticeable when moving from one level of detail to the next.

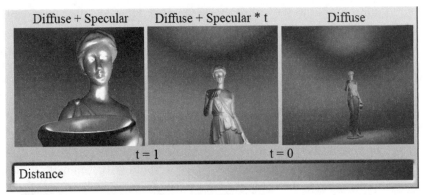

FIGURE 5.7.6 *Example of lighting level of detail.*

Extending Image-Space Post-Processing Effects

In this article, the terms *deferred shading* and *deferred lighting* have been used synonymously as the same technique. So far, only lighting has being discussed, but there's more to deferred shading than just lighting. Deferred solutions provide more power to image-space post-processing effects by giving them control of the in-screen geometry. That last feature is the one that allows performing lighting as a post-processing effect.

Adding other effects, like per-pixel fog or volumetric fog, becomes very simple and fast now that we know how far each screen pixel is by just accessing the G-Buffer. Fog becomes a special global light that, instead of illuminating, simply fades into a predefined color based on pixel depth. Forward shadow mapping and depth of field also fit very nicely into the deferred shading pipeline, while using them in standard rendering ways is not always straightforward.

The true power of deferred shading lies not only in the ability to perform a wide range of post-processing effects, but also in the possibility of mixing them. Introducing another effect to the rendering pipeline, such as heat haze distortion, no longer involves multipasses, but simply implements a clever shader that performs the effect using the G-Buffer, adding it to the system by introducing a new light source. The light can also be optimized to only affect a delimited region of the world by transforming it into a local light.

Deferred shading gives full power to the image-space post-processing effect and allows using several of them to render a scene without further geometry processing. Photo-realistic scenes require a large number of post-processing effects in order to accomplish the shades that give reality to the final image. With those rendering expectations in mind, deferred shading seems to be the technique that offers one of the fastest and simplest ways to implement a number of effects.

Conclusion

As has been described, deferred shading is a technique that allows rendering a scene with a high number of lights, without caring about how many lights per object or which light combinations are used. It also allows combining lights with other post-processing effects to give the scene a touch of reality, with no extra scene-processing penalties.

The real benefits of this technique are expected in the next-generation games where very complex shaders are going to be used in addition to a high number of lights affecting every single surface. So far, only deferred shading systems can deal with that requirement without being overwhelmed by scene complexity. No matter how real the scene is expected to look, deferred shading is the way to go.

Reference

[ATI05] ATI, "Dynamic branching using stencil test." *ATI Software Developer's Kit,* June 2005.

5.8

Rendering Road Signs Sharply

Jörn Loviscach, Hochschule Bremen, University of Applied Sciences

jlovisca@informatik.hs-bremen.de

Standard texturing does not handle images with sharp features well. Road signs, as well as road markings and lettering on billboards or labels, tend to blur as the viewer comes close. However, a short pixel shader applied to a specially preprocessed texture can produce an image quality that in many cases rivals vector graphics. The technique presented in this gem is based on thresholding a standard texture to produce a binary image. It can be employed for textures consisting of a small number of different colors such as text labels (black and white), no-smoking signs (black, red, and white), and road markings (white and transparent).

The blurriness of standard textures lies in the nature of bitmap images: No matter how highly resolved the texture image is, at some scale of magnification its pixels (i.e., texels) will become recognizable. Figure 5.8.1 and Color Plate 11 illustrate this. The bilinear interpolation typically applied in graphics hardware may suppress pixel staircasing (a.k.a., "jaggies") in such situations. However, it invariably washes out edges that should be infinitely sharp, such as the outlines of typeface characters.

If the texture contains only pure black and pure white, a simple method can solve this problem, at least in principle: Use a pixel shader to apply thresholding to the bilinearly interpolated texture; that is, if the retrieved grayscale level is darker than medium gray, turn it into perfect black, and if the level is above medium gray, turn it into perfect white. Thus, no gray pixels remain, and a sharp boundary between black and white regions is established.

However, it turns out that life is not that simple. The outline produced by such a process contains wiggles, shows jaggies, and reduces to a strange cloud of salt and pepper if viewed from some distance, as shown in Figure 5.8.2.

These three obstacles can be overcome without too much effort [Loviscach05], with no increase in the size of the texture, no additional texture requests per pixel, and inexpensive additions to the pixel shader. In this respect, this technique is different from related work. For instance, [Ramanarayanan04], [Sen04], [Tarini05], and [Tumblin04] treat full-color textures with embedded sharp features. This leads to techniques that are computationally much more expensive.

FIGURE 5.8.1   *Standard textures with bilinear interpolation tend to produce blurry lettering (top, 64 × 64 texels). The technique presented in this gem uses a short pixel shader and a preprocessed texture to yield sharp textures (bottom, same texture size).*

FIGURE 5.8.2   *Subjecting a standard texture (top left) to hard thresholding (top right) leads to jaggies (inset top right with eightfold magnification), oscillations (bottom left), and salt-and-pepper effects at distant view (bottom right and inset).*

In contrast, [Loviscach04] and [Loop05] build shapes bounded by cubic curves, using comparably efficient pixel shaders. However, both works rely on triangles being placed along the boundary curves—possibly hundreds or thousands of triangles for complex lettering. This does not seem to be an option with today's consumer-level graphics cards, which clearly favor textures over geometry.

Antialiasing Thresholded Textures

Special measures are necessary to guarantee high texturing quality both on magnification (screen pixels are smaller than texels) and minification (screen pixels are larger than texels). On magnification, jaggies have to be suppressed; on minification, the texture should be reduced to a coarser, smeared-out version with no pixels at all that are perfectly black or perfectly white.

Soft Thresholding

Thresholding immediately leads to jaggies, as no grayscale pixels appear that could soften the staircases of the black and white pixels. One easy way to cope with this is to abandon pure thresholding, but rather amplify the contrast. In this case, the grayscale value t retrieved from the texture by bilinear interpolation is subjected not to thresholding:

```
float c = 0.0;
if(t > 0.5)
    c = 1.0;
```

but rather to contrast enhancement:

```
float c = clamp(0.5 + a*(t-0.5), 0.0, 1.0);
```

where a controls the amount of amplification. A value of 1 reproduces the input; as a goes to infinity, contrast enhancement melts into thresholding. Note that the clamp instruction can often be left out because the graphics hardware will clamp colors on its own.

The value of a now controls the sharpness of the edges. The objective is to set a in such a way that jaggies are smeared out, but at the same time the sharpness appears consistently high. Thus, transitions between black to white should always have the same width in screen space, no matter what the scale. In experiments with the described method, a width of one-third pixel turned out to offer the optimal trade-off between sharpness and jaggedness.

The change from black to white happens from one texel to the next. If the view is close to the texture, the texture is magnified. Those two texels may be mapped to pixels that lie, say, 10 screen-space pixels apart. Setting a to 1 would result in a transition from black to white that extends over all of these 10 pixels. However, what is wanted is $4\frac{5}{6}$ pixels of black, a transition region of $\frac{1}{3}$ pixel, and $4\frac{5}{6}$ pixels of white. Thus, one has to set a to 10×3: After $4\frac{5}{6}$ pixels, t equals $\frac{29}{60}$, and the grayscale value just starts to grow beyond black (see Figure 5.8.3). In general, this means to set a to $3 \times s$, where s is the screen-space size of a texel.

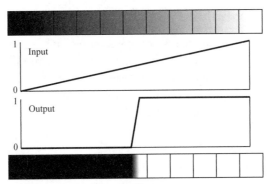

FIGURE 5.8.3   *To transform a screen-space distance of 10 pixels into a transition region of $\frac{1}{3}$ pixel, the amplification has to be set to 30.*

Texel Size

To scale the colors correctly, one needs to determine the screen-space distance between adjacent texels at runtime. Pixel shaders offer special instructions that come to help. In HLSL, these are called ddx and ddy. They compute the derivatives of their arguments with respect to screen-space x and y. To use these instructions in this setting, one can equip the objects with additional texture coordinates, uvScaled, that do not have a range of 1×1, but of width $\times$ height. Alternatively, one could also form uv*float2(width, height) using the standard texture coordinates uv at the cost of one additional 2D-vector multiply.

The two 2D-vectors ddx(uvScaled) and ddy(uvScaled) span the ellipse that is the footprint of a screen-space pixel in texture space, measured in units of texels (see Figure 5.8.4). Under oblique view or with deformed texture coordinates, the footprint may turn into a strongly elongated ellipse that spans many more texels along its major axis than along its minor axis.

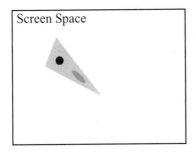
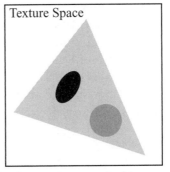

FIGURE 5.8.4   *The footprint of a circular screen-space pixel in texture space is an ellipse, and vice versa.*

To compute the amplification factor a, the number of pixels per texel is needed—that is, the footprint of a texel in screen space must be known. This is the inverse setting, as shown by the medium gray circle and disk in Figure 5.8.4. For brevity let's call the components of ddx(uvScaled) e, f; and those of ddy(uvScaled) g, h. Hence, the matrix that takes local changes of x-y screen coordinates to changes of the scaled texture coordinates is:

$$\begin{pmatrix} e & g \\ f & h \end{pmatrix}$$

A texel can be approximated by a circular disk of radius $\frac{1}{2}$ in uvScaled texture space, and a texel's footprint in screen space can be approximated by an elliptical disk. This disk is composed of all points that are offset from its center by $(\Delta x, \Delta y)$ such that

$$\left\| \begin{pmatrix} e & g \\ f & h \end{pmatrix} \begin{pmatrix} \Delta x \\ \Delta y \end{pmatrix} \right\| \leq \frac{1}{2}$$

This can be written:

$$\begin{pmatrix} \Delta x \\ \Delta y \end{pmatrix} \cdot \begin{pmatrix} e & g \\ f & h \end{pmatrix}^{\mathrm{T}} \begin{pmatrix} e & g \\ f & h \end{pmatrix} \begin{pmatrix} \Delta x \\ \Delta y \end{pmatrix} \leq \frac{1}{4} \tag{5.8.1}$$

The shape of the disk is determined by the eigenvalues of the matrix

$$\begin{pmatrix} e & g \\ f & h \end{pmatrix}^{\mathrm{T}} \begin{pmatrix} e & g \\ f & h \end{pmatrix} = \begin{pmatrix} e^2 + f^2 & eg + fh \\ eg + fh & g^2 + h^2 \end{pmatrix}$$

which are given by

$$\lambda_{1,2} = \frac{1}{2} \left(e^2 + f^2 + g^2 + h^2 \right) \pm \sqrt{\frac{1}{4} \left(e^2 + f^2 + g^2 + h^2 \right)^2 - e^2 h^2 - f^2 g^2 + 2efgh} \tag{5.8.2}$$

A vector along one of the two principal axes in x-y screen space is multiplied by the corresponding λ. Let $\mathbf{v}$ be a vector along a principal axis that extends from the center to the boundary of the ellipse. Then its length $|\mathbf{v}|$ equals that of either the minor or major radius. Equation 5.8.1 results in:

$$\lambda_{1,2} |\mathbf{v}|^2 = \frac{1}{4}$$

and hence

$$|\mathbf{v}| = \frac{1}{2\sqrt{\lambda_{1,2}}}$$

Thus, the minor and major diameters of the ellipse are twice that, respectively, namely:

$$\frac{1}{\sqrt{\lambda_1}} \text{ and } \frac{1}{\sqrt{\lambda_2}}$$

The square-root term in Equation 5.8.2 appears with a plus sign in the first solution and with a minus sign in the second. Thus, to come up with a simple, but approximate formula of the size of a texel, we discard that term altogether:

$$s = \frac{\sqrt{2}}{\sqrt{e^2 + f^2 + g^2 + h^2}}$$

This can be quickly computed through a 4D vector, and hence we set:

```
float s = 1.4/length(float4(ddx(uvScaled), ddy(uvScaled)));
```

However, if one wanted to use the arithmetic mean or always use the major diameter, so as to favor sharpness, this would incur a rather long computation of the square root term in Equation 5.8.2.

The Transition to Mip-Mapping

If the texture is viewed from a distance, it should turn into a mass of gray pixels—as with standard mip-mapping. If one sticks to the main idea of controllable contrast enhancement via:

```
float c = clamp(0.5 + a*(t-0.5), 0.0, 1.0)
```

this can easily be implemented by using a mip-mapped texture to retrieve t and let a go to 1.0 as texels in screen space become much smaller than the pixels themselves.

Given the texel size s as computed in the previously, one can simply set:

```
a = max(1.0, 3.0*s);
```

Thus, as the size falls below one-third of a pixel, the result of the pixel shader is identical to a standard mip-map request. Figure 5.8.5 shows the dependency between s and a.

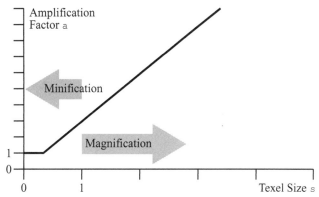

FIGURE 5.8.5   *On magnification, the amplification factor*
a *is three times the texel's size. On strong minifaction, the*
original value of the texture is returned.

In total (and after some optimization), the pixel shader looks like this:

```
half4 t = tex2D(mySampler, IN.uv);
float2 ef = ddx(IN.uvScaled);
float2 gh = ddy(IN.uvScaled);
half sInv = length(float4(ef, gh));
half a = max(1.0, (3*1.4)/sInv);
half c = 0.5 + a*(t.r-0.5);
OUT.color = half4(c, c, c, 1.0);
return OUT;
```

It compiles to 11 instructions of pixel-shader assembler version ps_2_x.

To achieve a clean transition between thresholding on magnification and standard mip-mapping on minification, it is not enough to control the amplification. In the transition range, a is on the order of 1.0 so that medium-gray levels in the texture will not change much. This effect results in objectionable gray blotches close to the boundaries between black and white, as shown in Figure 5.8.6.

This problem can be overcome if the finest level of the mip-map does not contain medium-gray levels. Experimentally, it turns out that it suffices to forbid the middle 32 of all 256 levels possible with the standard 8-bit representation (i.e., the subrange 112 to 143 of the range 0 to 255). The optimization process employed to fill mip-map level 0 (to be discussed in the next section) takes care of that.

FIGURE 5.8.6　*If the stored texture (left) contains gray values close to medium gray, the contrast-enhanced image may show gray halos or holes (right) if the amplification* a *is close to 1.0.*

Optimal Textures for Thresholding

The textures that this gem deals with are typically generated from vector graphics, for instance via bitmap export functions of illustration software. Subjected to thresholding, however, such bitmaps lead to dents and humps in the outlines. By generating the texture image differently, one can use this behavior to one's advantage.

Geometry

One may expect that the shapes formed by thresholding a bilinearly interpolated texture are bounded by polylines: What else should result from linear operations? Whereas this is true for a triangular grid, it is false for the square grid used in standard texture mapping (see Figure 5.8.7).

If *a*, *b*, and *c* are the values at the corners of a triangle, bilinear interpolation results in:

$$(1 - u - v)a + ub + vc,$$

where *u*, *v*, and $(1 - u - v)$ are the barycentric coordinates on the triangle. If, however, *a*, *b*, *c*, and *d* are the values at the corners of a square, bilinear interpolation results in:

$$(1 - u)(1 - v)a + u(1 - v)b + uvc + (1 - u)vd,$$

which can be written as:

$$a + u(-a + b) + v(-a + d) + uv(a - b + c - d).$$

Note the product *uv* that appears in this formula, which turns it into a nonlinear expression.

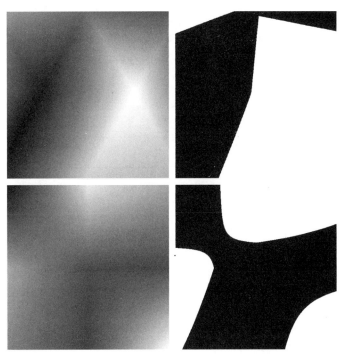

FIGURE 5.8.7   *On a triangular grid, thresholded bilinear interpolation leads to shapes bounded by polylines (top right). On a square grid, however, the outlines become rational curves (bottom).*

The contour of the thresholded texture passes through the points (u,v), at which the expression above equals $\tfrac{1}{2}$. For this curve, we find a rational dependency of v on u:

$$v = \frac{\dfrac{1}{2} - a - u\left(-a + b\right)}{\left(-a + d\right) + u\left(a - b + c - d\right)} \tag{5.8.3}$$

if the denominator does not equal zero.

One can extract precise data about the geometry. Assume that the outline intersects the edge between the texel with value b and the texel with value c. This means that b is less than $\tfrac{1}{2}$ and c is greater than $\tfrac{1}{2}$, or vice versa. The outline intersects the edge at the point (u,v) with

$$u = 1, \quad v = \frac{b - \dfrac{1}{2}}{b - c}.$$

By taking the derivative of Equation 5.8.3 with respect to u, one can compute the angle at which the outline intersects the edge. The derivative equals the tangent of the angle between the curve and the horizontal direction. The derivative's value at $u = 1$ is given by

$$\frac{ac - bd - \frac{1}{2}(a - b + c - d)}{(b-c)^2} = \frac{\left(a - \frac{1}{2}\right)\left(c - \frac{1}{2}\right) - \left(b - \frac{1}{2}\right)\left(d - \frac{1}{2}\right)}{(b-c)^2}.$$

Similar equations apply to intersections along other edges.

Optimization

As the outlines are rational curves, they are not easy to control. Two sets of parameters offer themselves for this task: first, the positions of the intersections between the outline and the edges of the texel grid; and second, the directions of the outline curve at these intersections. Both types of parameters can be computed easily from the texture, as previously described. As a basis for comparison, the same data are extracted from the original vector graphics. To this end, standard image-processing techniques can be applied to a high-resolution bitmap version of the original graphics.

The objective is to compute the texture in such a way that both the position and the angle data of the original image are reproduced well after thresholding. Since the details of the outlines are only of interest in a magnified view, the higher (i.e., coarser) mip-map levels can be filled by box filtering, as usual. Only the finest one, mip-map level zero, is changed.

As it turns out, only in exceptional cases is it not possible to construct a texture in such a way that all position and angle constraints are fulfilled. If an outline intersects n interior edges of the texel grid, then there are n position and n angle conditions. The variables that can effectively be adjusted are the grayscale values at the adjacent texels. If the outline does not take too-sharp a turn, the number of these texels is $2n$ (see Figure 5.8.8). Otherwise, it is slightly lower. Effectively, one loses one more degree of freedom because the thresholded image does not change if all grayscale values are scaled around the value of $\frac{1}{2}$.

These figures demonstrate that the constraints typically cannot be obeyed completely. One has to employ an optimization process that is guided by some appropriate error metric, as demonstrated in the next section. This optimization can proceed quite fast, since it only has to affect texels adjacent to the outline. The vast majority of texels can remain fixed at either pure black or pure white.

Most prominently, the optimization leads to sharper corners. It automatically handles corners with counterbalancing texels, as shown in Figure 5.8.9.

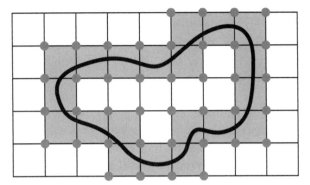

FIGURE 5.8.8 *Typically, nearly* n *texels influence an outline that intersects* n *edges. In this example* n = 20, *and the number of contributing texels is 40.*

FIGURE 5.8.9 *In the vicinity of corners, the optimization leads to complex patterns so as to allow sharp turns (top: unoptimized and thresholded; bottom: optimized and thresholded). Note the huge size of the texels.*

Error Metric

Two simple choices offer themselves for the error metric: first, the sum of squared differences between the actual and the intended positions of the intersections between the outline and the edges of the texel grid; and second, the sum of squared differences between the actual and the intended angles of the outline at the intersections.

As experiments reveal, both metrics lead to objectionable errors in the outline (see Figure 5.8.10). While the first metric ensures that all intended intersection points are hit precisely, it leads to strong zigzag patterns in-between. The second metric leads to outlines that reproduce soft curvature very well; however, typeface characters appear bulged and with irregular stem width.

Thus, the proposed solution is a mixed metric. Generally, it favors the precision of the angles. However, the more perpendicular the angle is to the edge of the texel grid, the more the precision of the position is taken into account. This leads to outlines that are quite smooth, but at the same time mimic the horizontal and vertical lines of typeface characters very well, as seen in Figure 5.8.10.

isito isito
isito

FIGURE 5.8.10   *Metrics solely based on the positions (upper left) or on the angles (upper right) of the intersections lead to objectionable errors. A mixed metric (bottom) can suppress most of these.*

In program code, this boils down to the following additive contribution to the error metric per intersection:

```
double r = Math.Min(1.0, Math.Abs(angleOriginal));
return r*angleDistance2 + (1.0-r)*positionDistance2;
```

where `angleOriginal` is the intended angle (measured in radians), `angleDistance2` is the sum of the squares between the differences of the intended angle and the actual ingoing and outgoing angles at the intersection, and `positionDistance2` is the squared difference between the intended and the actual position.

The Authoring Application

ON THE CD

On the CD-ROM, you will find an authoring application, including its source code (see Figure 5.8.11). It generates DirectDraw® Surface (.dds) texture files optimized for thresholding and offers a 3D preview through a pixel shader. It is based on .NET 1.1 and (Managed) DirectX 9.0c, using the languages C# and HLSL.

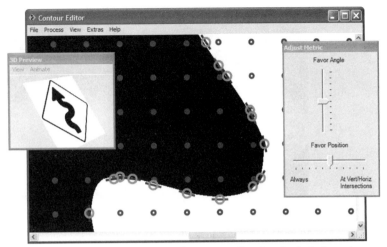

FIGURE 5.8.11   *The texture authoring application included on the CD-ROM allows you to interactively adjust the metric and to edit the position and angle constraints. These are automatically extracted up front.*

The software allows the user to load high-resolution bitmap files, select the desired coarseness of the results (downsampling factor), and save the results to .dds files. The user can interactively change the error metric to favor the precision of positions or angles, or to combine an angle-based metric with position-error terms for intersections that are nearly perpendicular to an edge of the texel grid. On top of that, users can use the mouse to select edges and edit the position/angle constraints, with the cursor and Page Up/Down keys.

Constraint editing turns out to be of much help when an intersection between the outline and an edge of the texel grid happens almost parallel to the edge, or if several intersections lie in close proximity. To reduce oscillations of the outline in this case, the user can shift the position constraints and rotate the angle constraints. The optimization runs in a background thread to provide an interactive preview of the actual outline resulting from the edits. In its current version, the authoring application does not allow direct editing of the grayscale values of the resulting texture: This would often lead to complex changes due to the rational nature of the boundary curves. See Figure 5.8.12 and Color Plate 12 for an example of the results achieved through editing.

The optimization process runs indefinitely and concurrently with the editing. The software randomly picks a texel near the boundary, computes the error metric in its surroundings, and changes the grayscale level of the texel by up to ±5 of the 256 possible steps (but avoids the medium range of 112 to 143, as discussed above). If the error metric is lowered by this replacement, the new value remains in the texture. If

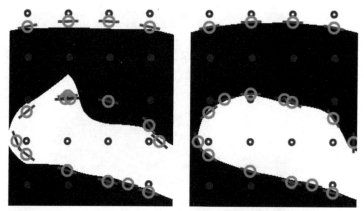

FIGURE 5.8.12 *The user may edit position and angle constraints to solve critical situations, such as nearly tangential intersections that overtax the optimizer (left: before, right: after). The constraints are displayed circles for the positions and lines of the angles.*

not, the change only remains with a small probability, which quickly goes to zero with the amount of error. This behavior allows us to escape local minima in the error metric. It is a variant of simulated annealing [Wikipedia05], without temperature decrease.

ON THE CD

Finally, the authoring software offers the function "Multicolor Combine," which combines two or four .dds files into one, to be used for multicolor images. The CD-ROM includes an .fx file that demonstrates the use of such textures. A simple choice to mix several color layers, such as a black and a red layer for a no-smoking sign, would be:

```
OUT.color = float4(black*red, black, black, 1.0);
```

However, this leads to objectionable image errors as shown in Figure 5.8.13 and Color Plate 13. The black cigarette would have to end precisely where the red strike-through begins. This cannot be ensured. Rather, we can mask black by red:

```
OUT.color = float4(1.0-(1.0-black)*red, black*red, black*red, 1.0);
```

and put a complete cigarette shape in the black layer—so to speak, "below" the red strike-through.

The pixel shader is as cheap for four-color layers as it is for one layer, because the thresholding computations can be done in parallel with `float4` instead of `float`. Note, however, that expressions such as `black*red` require that the clamping of the

ON THE CD

colors after contrast enhancement be done explicitly in the pixel shader. See the example files on the CD-ROM.

FIGURE 5.8.13 *Multicolor images used naively (top) show objectionable errors at points where several colors meet (see the magnified portion). Reverse engineering of such images into a stack of one-color images solves the problem (bottom: 64 × 64 texels).*

Another authoring application of Multicolor Combine joins a texture optimized for thresholding and a standard texture. The thresholded texture can be used as stencil on the other texture—for instance, to create road markings (see Figure 5.8.14).

FIGURE 5.8.14 *A thresholded texture can also be used as a stencil for a standard texture (size: 128 × 128 texels).*

Conclusion and Outlook

Road signs and markings use visually robust typefaces and shapes. The presented thresholding technique can reproduce these well with textures in the range of 64×64 to 256×256 texels. The processed textures behave correctly both on minification as well as magnification. They can be magnified indefinitely without losing sharpness. Rendering speed is only affected marginally, since the pixel shader code is extremely short and uses only one texture request. Thus, current graphics cards achieve fill rates of approximately one billion pixels per second with this technique.

The presented method is not able to resolve two outline curves within a single texel. Thus, intricate shapes, such as typefaces with serifs or sharply pointed shapes, require much higher texture resolutions to be represented faithfully. Sometimes, however, even tiny features below the scale of a texel may be reproduced if the user adjusts appropriate settings for the position and angle constraints.

It is obvious how to include lighting and other standard effects, such as depth-map shadows with thresholded textures. But the idea can be carried further; for instance, 3D textures may be used to create animated outlines. Another avenue for extension would be to apply the idea to full-color textures. One could try to represent such a texture as a combination of an image with only soft-color gradients and an image with sharp edges. The former could be stored directly at a low resolution. The latter could be converted to employ thresholding.

References

[Loop05] Loop, Charles and Jim Blinn, "Resolution Independent Curve Rendering Using Programmable Graphics Hardware." *ACM Transactions on Graphics,* Vol. 4, No. 3 (SIGGRAPH 2005): pp. 1000–1009.

[Loviscach04] Loviscach, Jörn, "Paving Roads with Pixel Shaders." WSCG 2004 Full Papers: pp. 39–46.

[Loviscach05] Loviscach, Jörn, "Efficient Magnification of Bi-Level Textures." SIGGRAPH 2005 Sketch.

[Ramanarayanan04] Ramanarayanan, Ganesh, et al., "Feature-Based Textures." Eurographics Workshop on Rendering 2004: pp. 265–274.

[Sen04] Pradeep, Sen, "Silhouette Maps for Improved Texture Magnification." ACM SIGGRAPH/Eurographics Conference on Graphics Hardware 2004: pp. 65–73.

[Tarini05] Tarini, Marco and Paolo Cignoni, "Pinchmaps: Textures with Customizable Discontinuities." *Computer Graphics Forum,* Vol. 24, No. 3 (Eurographics 2005), pp. 557–568.

[Tumblin04] Tumblin, Jack and Prason Choudhury, "Bixels: Picture Samples with Sharp Embedded Boundaries." Eurographics Workshop on Rendering 2004: pp. 186–196.

[Wikipedia05] Wikipedia contributors, "Simulated Annealing." Wikipedia: The Free Encyclopedia. Accessed August 12, 2005. Available online at *http://en.wikipedia. org/wiki/Simulated_annealing.*

5.9

Practical Sky Rendering for Games

Aurelio Reis, Raven Software

AurelioReis@gmail.com

As more games shift toward expansive outdoor environments, the sky has become a much more visible part of every scene. When you consider the fact that sky-rendering techniques can be very computationally expensive, you can see the importance of efficient approaches to sky rendering. In this gem, we examine a number of intelligent generic and specific optimizations that can be applied to various sky implementations. These optimizations can be used to ensure that the user has a consistent frame rate, even with the sky in full view at high resolutions.

What We Want Versus What We Get

For a foundation in approaches to dynamic sky rendering, we recommend reading some of the research done by [Nishita00], [Preetham99], or [Jensen01]. Most of the available methods are quite complex, which relates to the fact that they try to emulate real-world physical phenomena. Taking into account a number of atmospheric parameters to simulate the sky is certainly not an easy task, and until just recently has been an approach strictly reserved for offline renderers; but as we continue the move to fully accelerated graphics environments, these techniques have become much more accessible.

Up until a few years ago, sky boxes textured using pre-rendered skies (using an offline renderer like [Terragen]) were the most common way to represent the sky at interactive frame rates. Constrained to advanced flight simulators, dynamic skies were far outside the grasp of most games. However, with the welcome arrival of MMOGs (Massively Multiplayer Online Games) and games like *Grand Theft Auto 3*, which required full day and night cycles, developers delved even further into increasing the realism of the natural environment. Striking a balance between visual quality and performance has been a challenge, and presentation quality has certainly suffered.

There is a stark contrast between what is possible on modern graphics hardware and what should be used in a game. In most demos of sky rendering, you see a very strong presentation highlighting the sky technique itself; but for developers, this isn't as useful a sight as it may seem. The [ATI Atmosphere demo], for instance, while being quite an impressive display of atmospheric scattering, does not present a fully interactive scene, and when coupled with an interactive scene is sure to be restrictively expensive due to the high number of shader instructions used.

The problem is that most demos of these techniques use a sparse world and don't show as detailed a scene as you might find in a real game. This type of scene is an environment populated by other interactive 3D objects that require their own processing power from the CPU or GPU. In a real game, you often have skinned 3D characters, multiple blending operations on the frame buffer, a large triangle count, and heavy per-pixel use.

This gem does not present a new or better sky-modeling technique, but instead describes a number of ways to make the existing techniques work better for you and your game. The main point is to cut through the technical and theoretical specifics, and delve into what bottlenecks are specifically hampering a real-game implementation, and how we can overcome them. The optimizations presented here are completely feasible and easily implemented for use in a real, commercial product. Although this article will delve mostly into the subject of rendering the sky color and clouds efficiently, also it will briefly touch upon such things as efficient lighting techniques for the ever-changing lights emitted by stellar objects. In summary, the end goal is a sky technique that is not only aesthetically pleasing, but which is also efficient to render, leaving enough clock cycles for us to insert a game into our nifty rendering engine.

What's That in the Sky?

Let's first examine the components that make up a dynamic sky, as well as review the terminology we'll be using. First, we have the sky color, which is commonly represented using a sky dome—for us, a hemispherical 3D model. Computations are broken down into discrete points that are performed over the surface of the dome, either per-vertex or per-pixel.

Methods available to determine the sky color at that point can either be a statistical (i.e., using observed and reproduced data) or analytical (i.e., physically based) approach. An analytical model, for instance, might actually calculate the Mie and Rayleigh scattering, as well as ozone and radiant contributions to a particular point. However, it should be noted that most implementations simplify the equations down to the strongest contributing factors, which are usually Mie and Rayleigh scattering. The physics of atmospheric conditions has been well documented, and as mentioned in the previous section, representing it graphically is not a mystery. We will use a few base sources for the sky implementation presented here, which were inspired by other authors.

For the sky color rendering, we will use the optimizations presented by [Spoerl04], which essentially simplified the equations presented by [Nishita00] to only take into account a simplified sky-color algorithm. In this algorithm, only the Rayleigh and Mie scattering terms are calculated (and in a simplified form), and the optical depth is essentially replaced by a scaling factor based on the height of the current sampling point. This is also suggested by [Nielsen03], except that he supplements this approximation with the ability to dynamically change the optical depth to simulate atmospheric darkening for views at varying altitudes. To find the position of the sun in the sky, relative to the observer's position, we'll be using the algorithms outlined by [Jensen01]. To derive an accurate sun color for a specific time of day, the equations outlined by [Preetham99] will be used.

An important aspect of the atmosphere that will not be covered is clouds. A large amount of research has been done on high-quality cloud rendering; however most of the proposed algorithms just aren't fast enough for real-time use. [Dube05] presented an impressive implementation using what is essentially a ray tracer within a pixel shader to calculate the amount of light absorbed by the clouds at varying depths. The only limitation was that an explicit sunlight direction could not be specified. [Reis05] presented a similar implementation based on the work of [McGuire05], which takes the light direction into account. An efficient solution would be to use the traditional scrolling-sky plane trick, where a texture is mapped to a plane whose texture coordinates are scrolled to simulate movement. This texture could also be projected onto the ground to simulate cloud shadowing.

And last, but just as integral, are the sun and moon. Since we'll only be talking about the sky dome method, the easiest way to get a moving sun and moon is by projecting a sun or moon image onto the geometry using a projective texture matrix. Calculating this matrix takes quite a bit of work, and caching the results for certain times of day could potentially take up quite a bit of memory (depending on the sampling frequency). A possible optimization would be to draw your sun and moon onto a cube map that is then loaded by the game, and rotated based on the current time of day. Rotating a cube map within a shader takes quite a few instructions though, so a cost-effect way of drawing the sun and moon is difficult to find.

The Bottlenecks

When rendering your sky, there are a number of performance-related issues that may arise, depending on the technique you are using. If your approach is done exclusively or even partially on the CPU, you may run into a number of CPU-related bottlenecks that need to be resolved. On the other hand, if you're taking complete advantage of 3D hardware acceleration, you may have an entirely different set of performance bottlenecks.

With the next generation of games making extensive use of pixel shaders, it's quite possible that the majority of them could become pixel-bound. The number of vertices in a scene is variable and based on how the triangles in a scene are constructed (i.e., via triangle lists or strips); and although the number of pixels on the screen is proportional to the screen resolution, the number of times a pixel shader executes for a physical pixel on the screen is also variable because of overdraw. When a mesh is sent to the video card to be drawn, its vertices are projected onto the screen and must be filled. Even though the video card tries to be relatively intelligent about rejecting pixels that aren't visible, the fact that the video card must consider them alone can warrant performance penalty. Although a pixel is not drawn, it can still affect performance; some pixels (due to blending) are always considered, and extreme care must be taken to optimize their shaders. Early depth rejection (through the pre-z pass) and reducing instruction counts through texture lookups (which can be very speedy) are often the way to go to reduce shader expense and complexity.

So let's talk about where a sky implementation may be bound. In the "old" days of sky boxes, one of the biggest concerns was what resolution to use. Pretend we were using a cube map that is 512×512 texels in resolution. Depending on the distance to or size of that part of the sky, as well as the texture-filtering method used, you could potentially be drawing either more or less than 512×512 pixels. This leads to fill-rate issues, where a large number of texture samples could potentially eat up your performance at high-resolution settings (where there are more pixels to fill in).

Weighing the Benefits of a Vertex- or Pixel-Based Sky

In our situation, where we could be doing quite a number of computations per-pixel, this could really hurt us. The obvious solution would be transfer the possible calculations per-vertex and only take the texture sample hit in the pixel shader. This has its own unique set of issues, however. Assuming we're at least using bilinear filtering, the color values are interpolated across the surface of a triangle between all of its triangles; and although this helps to simulate a smooth range of values, it will also leave you with harsh artifacting due to the low sampling frequency of a low-polygon mesh. This can definitely ruin any chance of nice color gradients across the sky.

So where does this leave us? Well, we could either bite the bullet and eat the potential cost in favor of higher quality, and go with a very low-resolution mesh but do our work per-pixel, or we could use a medium- to high-polygon mesh and do the computations per vertex. The choice is really yours and is based on where your main bottlenecks lie (either vertex or pixel). When talking about the generalized equations, however, we'll assume we're talking about the vertex shader version (for simplicity's sake). In practice, both methods are usable, because they scale effectively for different hardware configurations. Presenting each option individually to the user is way too complex and is certainly not the way to go, so a generic "sky detail" slider as a graphics option could easily toggle between any of the available methods invisibly, with a default value set based on the hardware detected.

Another thing to consider is how you've decided to present precalculated constants and lookup tables for your shaders. In the accompanying demo provided on the CD-ROM, we show how to precalculate a pseudo-optical depth needed by the shader to simulate the intense color of the atmosphere near the horizon and the darkening of the sky as the user gains altitude. (The implementation is meant to be very simple, so it forgoes calculating the altitude change to the pseudo-optical depth. [Nielsen03], however, does describe an effective method to simulate this.)

ON THE CD

The vertex format for the dome vertex buffer must be prepared to take the optical depth as an additional texture coordinate uniform parameter. The dome vertex declaration is listed below:

```
const D3DVERTEXELEMENT9 g_DomeVertexDecl[] =
{
    { 0, 0, D3DDECLTYPE_FLOAT3, D3DDECLMETHOD_DEFAULT,
    D3DDECLUSAGE_POSITION, 0 },
    { 0, 12, D3DDECLTYPE_FLOAT3, D3DDECLMETHOD_DEFAULT,
    D3DDECLUSAGE_NORMAL, 0 },
    { 0, 24, D3DDECLTYPE_FLOAT3, D3DDECLMETHOD_DEFAULT,
    D3DDECLUSAGE_TANGENT, 0 },
    { 0, 36, D3DDECLTYPE_FLOAT3, D3DDECLMETHOD_DEFAULT,
    D3DDECLUSAGE_BINORMAL, 0 },
    { 0, 48, D3DDECLTYPE_FLOAT2, D3DDECLMETHOD_DEFAULT,
    D3DDECLUSAGE_TEXCOORD, 0 },
    { 0, 56, D3DDECLTYPE_FLOAT1, D3DDECLMETHOD_DEFAULT,
    D3DDECLUSAGE_TEXCOORD, 1 },
    D3DDECL_END()
};
```

Specifying additional vertex elements through vertex streams is probably a better way to add the additional elements to the vertex format, but we choose to just use a different usage index. Below you can see how the values are filled in for the model vertex buffers:

```
// Precalculate any constants for the Dome Models.
const float fInv = 1.0f / 5.0f;
for ( int i = 0; i < 3; i++ )
{
    DomeVertex *pVertices;
    g_DomeModels[ i ].LockVertices( (void **) &pVertices );

    int iNumVerts = g_DomeModels[ i ].GetNumVerts();
    for ( int j = 0; j < iNumVerts; j++, ++pVertices )
    {
        pVertices->fOpticalDepth
            = 1.7f - powf( fabs( pVertices->vNormal.y ), fInv );
    }

    g_DomeModels[ i ].UnlockVertices();
}
```

In the shader, the vertex input structure has the optical depth as an input parameter:

```
float OpticalDepth : TEXCOORD1;
```

Finally, in the vertex shader, the optical depth is directly read and either used there or sent to the pixel shader as a texture coordinate, where it will be interpolated per pixel. This brings up a good point. Originally this value was calculated as needed in the vertex program, using the vertex position directly. But passing the vertex position to the pixel shader and then calculating this value there often results in much smoother values. The answer as to why should be obvious. Whenever you pass a value from the vertex program to the pixel shader through texture coordinates, that value is interpolated using the graphics hardware. This is why you need to renormalize light or eye vectors when passed there for per-pixel lighting. We need to take this fact into consideration whenever dealing with any data we get on a per-vertex basis. Using this optimization, for instance, leaves us with a low-polygon mesh (100 polygons or less) that will not give us enough range of values to present the sky effectively using the vertex shader technique.

Although we've given quite a few suggestions on ways to increase performance for your sky implementations, as stated previously, the most intensive operations that are being done are those done every frame, either per vertex or per pixel. What we ultimately need to do is find some way of caching a specific state-of-the-sky dome in a way that we can use for at least a few frames. The problem, of course, is that our scene is vibrant and interactive, so the view is changing constantly. The most direct option would be to directly capture the 3D environment to a texture, and project it into the scene in a realistic fashion. How do we do this?

Introducing the Cubic Sky Map

The cubic sky map is essentially a cube map that represents the sky, cached at a specific point in time. By rendering the sky dome onto the six faces of the cube map, we're essentially able to capture its current state and reuse it over a number of frames. Although we still do incur the fill-rate texture sampling cost, this is far better than the cost of all the computations that would have been done each frame either per vertex or per pixel. After the dome has been rendered to the cube map, it is mapped to a very simple box and rendered with the following pass-through vertex shader:

```
VS_OUTPUT_CUBEPASSTHROUGH RenderCubeMapPassthroughVP(VS_INPUT IN)
{
    VS_OUTPUT_CUBEPASSTHROUGH OUT;

    // Transform the position from object space to homogeneous
    // projection space.
    OUT.Position = mul( IN.Position, g_mWorldViewProjection );

    // Pass through the eye vector.
    OUT.TexCoord0 = g_vLocalEyePos - IN.Position;

    return OUT;
}
```

And here is the pixel shader:

```
PS_OUTPUT RenderCubeMapPassthruPS( VS_OUTPUT_CUBEPASSTHROUGH IN )
{
    PS_OUTPUT OUT;
```

```
        // Directly sample using the given vector (normalization is
        // implicit through the cube map).
        OUT.Color = texCUBE( CubeMapSampler, IN.TexCoord0 );

        return OUT;
    }
```

As you can see, we call this a "pass-through" cube map shader because all it does is calculate the eye vector ray (i.e., the vector from the viewer's eye position to the vertex position) and passes it as an interpolated vector that samples directly into the cube map in that direction. Since the cube map by nature normalizes vectors, you don't even need to renormalize it.

As far as the cube map resolution goes—a high of 512 is imperceptible, while 256 down to 128 are acceptable and certainly worth scaling to, based on the user's hardware specs. At around 64, you start to notice severe banding and artifacts along the sky-color gradients, so quality is severely degraded. This happens most noticeably around the dome borders, but the player should never see them anyway, so it doesn't matter. Anything higher than 512 incurs a pretty hefty cost, so we recommend around 256—and if you've got the horsepower, 512.

Now, although caching the results is a fine optimization, it hardly helps if we need to render to a cube map every frame—the expense, of course, being that we have to render the dome six times for every cube face (five, actually, if you're smart and don't bother with the ground face). So how do we efficiently keep the cube map up to date? We render it sporadically. Depending on what time scale your time-of-day implementation works on (assuming you're using dynamic skies because of its ability for this), you'll want to have an update rate that refreshes the cube map whenever the time changes enough to be perceivable.

Time, on Our Conditions

A reasonable time scale would be about one game minute per one real second—so one game hour every minute, and one game day every 24 real minutes. At this rate, time changes would probably be perceptible around every 30 game minutes or so, possibly even more around dusk or dawn, so let's say every 15 game minutes to be safe. At this rate, you'd need to update your cube map every quarter of a game hour, so about every 15 real-world seconds. Honestly, this is plenty of time to do it, but we're presented with another problem here. Updating six faces of a cube map, never mind the actual scene view itself, can cause quite a chug on your frame rate. What we need to be able to do is spread the cost out. We do this by updating each cube face over a number of frames.

Now, we can either do them successively or sporadically over a fixed amount of time. The former method would involve just rendering each cube view, frame after frame. The latter (and preferred) method would actually calculate the times within the 15-second intervals for us to spread out the computations. Assuming we are only updating five of the faces (as we should be), that gives us a cube face update every three seconds. This definitely spreads out the cost very nicely, but there's still one more issue. Although we're not trying to update the time while rendering out the current time of day, we are rendering a different state for the sky onto separate faces at different times. This can be very obvious, as previously stated, for the times of day when the sky has a lot of perceptible changes. Unfortunately, the only option is to use a swap chain of sorts, where one cube map is being rendered to while the other is being drawn to the sky box, then switching jobs at the next time update. Doing this ensures we won't get any weird color shifting from the updated cube faces.

Dawn of a Demo

ON THE CD

The demo and accompanying source code that are included with this gem show off a number of the methods and techniques discussed thus far. The code is highly documented and should be relatively easy to navigate through. Although it's not meant to be a focal point of the demo, a normal mapped terrain is used to make the ground a little more interesting.

The terrain height map was generated by World Machine Basic (Web site: *http://www.world-machine.com*), the low- and high-polygon meshes and diffuse texture by T2 Terrain Texture Generator (Web site: *http://www.toymaker.info/html/texgen.html*), and finally the normal map by nVIDIA Melody. (For those unfamiliar with the process of normal mapping, visit the Melody homepage at *http://developer.nvidia.com/object/melody_home.html*.) We use three sky domes to present the potential aliasing artifacts from using either the per-vertex or per-pixel techniques. In practice, if you've chosen to use a strictly vertex-based implementation, it can help to generate a dome where the number of vertices near the edges is exponentially greater than those at the top of the dome. This can help because although there is not much color variation near the top of the dome, the edges may have very stark color contrasts during dusk and dawn hours, which can be better represented if there are more vertices to simulate these values. This would also help for the pseudo-optical depth described earlier.

ON THE CD

Of particular interest in the code on the CD-ROM: You may want to look at how the CSceneView class works, and how the main view is generated and cube map render subview attaches to it. The scene view system basically has one main view and any number of child views that could be attached to it in any order or hierarchy (although a limit is enforced). Each view contains a number of parameters that describe how it will be rendered. Included with values like the view transform and projection matrices is the view target type, which describes where the view will be drawn to. This allows the dependent subviews, or even the main view, to be drawn to any number of textures, which can be used for things like planar water reflections, cube map reflections, (orthographic) GUI views, or even post-process effects over the scene.

As the time of day changes, so does the position and color of our sun or moon. In our scene, we only take into account global illumination from these sky objects. The lighting on the terrain is basic per-pixel phong shading, although a simple ambient term is approximated based on the color of the shadowed pixel. An interesting technique would be to take the cube sky map that we've already generated and use it as a color guide for our ambient. For instance, at dusk when the sky is many different colors, the unlit portion of the terrain might take on some faint color from the sky in its direction, instead of just the globally defined ambient color. We may even want to convolute the cube map to simulate a more proper light diffusion. Doing so, however, can be pretty expensive, as it requires either sampling multiple points and summing their average result at run-time, or downloading and convoluting the cube map on the CPU (which is incredibly expensive).

Sampling the cube map in world space alone is not something you do lightly, and we recommend this merely as an advanced-technique suggestion (i.e., it's probably not practical for games). Using some clever heuristics, it's possible to alter the ambient light values based on the time of day. This could help to "normalize" the lighting contributions over the course of the day so at the sun's highest point, the scene is not too bright, but at night the scene is not too dark. Also, calculating pseudo bump-mapped lighting using some kind of constant light term can help to retain the increased level of detail when using normal mapping with low-polygon models.

For haze/fog, we implemented a simple extinction model that is evaluated for all the objects in the scene. We considered implementing the single scattering model presented by [Sun05] but decided against it, as haze is expensive enough on its own. The haze density value along with a number of other graphics options can be easily toggled from the GUI. We implore the reader, however, to explore any method that may increase the visual realism of aerial perspective, while maintaining reasonable performance.

Down the Horizon

One last thing we'll touch on from the demo is high dynamic range rendering. A real-world scene has an incredible dynamic range—according to [Reinhard02], approximately 10 orders of absolute range and 4 orders of dynamic range from shadows to highlights. Simulating this in an outdoor environment is incredibly important, especially if you want to apply post-processing effects like glare to very bright parts of the scene, like the sun during the day or even the moon at night, when those objects are the brightest parts of the sky. Using tone-mapping with floating-point buffers (and even a floating-point cube map) can be expensive, however, so we urge caution. Using standard glow or intensity-ranged glare (stored in the alpha channel for instance) over a scene can certainly wash out and blur important detail; but at the very least, it can offer better performance in the long run. Also, make sure to choose a standardized range that is able to represent all possible objects in a scene. Although during the day there won't be any objects brighter than the sun, going inside will drastically alter how the values are mapped, so special care must be taken when applying high-intensity lighting values.

Although the demo was made as close to a game environment as possible, there was just no way to present all the elements of a game without actually making one, which is quite an intensive process, as is well known. You can try to be as practical as you like, but in the long run, breathing life into a moving, vibrant environment will definitely require an incredible amount of performance. And as we continue to strive for more-immersive and realistic environments, we must try to balance our graphics pipeline and techniques to take full advantage of the hardware. Although we tried to show how high-level objects might affect performance, there are a multitude of small performance killers left unaddressed. In the long run it pays to be safe, so the special care taken to optimize your sky implementation should definitely take precedence over any additional features that might have been present.

Conclusion

In this gem we went over a number of practical and generic optimizations, and special tricks you may use to increase performance in your sky implementation, and showed them in the sky implementation provided. We also examined some parts of the graphics pipeline and sky rendering techniques to explain why we may be getting unacceptable performance, and how to identify where the bottlenecks may be coming from.

We hope you enjoyed the article and are able to take something from it for your sky implementation. Although we stress performance over visual aesthetics, more-realistic dynamic skies are a noble goal for our games, and we believe they are definitely attainable if modest care is taken to intelligently optimize for best performance on modern systems. Thank you, and best of luck on your sky implementations!

References

[ATI Atmosphere demo] Available online at *http://www.ati.com/developer/demos/r8000.html.*

[Dube05] Dube, Jean-Francois, "Realistic Cloud Rendering on Modern GPUs." *Game Programming Gems 5,* Kim Pallister, Ed., Charles River Media, 2005.

Intel Vtune™. Available online at *http://www.intel.com/cd/software/products/asmo-na/eng/vtune/index.htm.*

[Jensen01] Jensen, Henrik Wann., et al., "A Physically-Based Nightsky Model." Available online at *http://graphics.stanford.edu/~henrik/papers/nightsky/.*

[McGuire05] McGuire, Morgan and Max McGuire, "Steep Parallax Mapping." Available online at *http://graphics.cs.brown.edu/games/SteepParallax/.*

[Nielsen03] Nielsen, Ralf Stokholm, "Real Time Rendering of Atmospheric Scattering Effects for Flight Simulators." Available online at *http://www2.imm.dtu.dk/pubdb/views/publication_details.php?id=2554.*

[Nishita00] Nishita, Tomoyuki., et al. "Display Method of the Sky Color Taking into Account Multiple Scattering." Available online at *http://nis-lab.is.s.u-tokyo.ac.jp/~nis/abs_cgi.html*.

[Preetham99] Preetham, A. J., Peter Shirley, and Brian Smits, "Practical Analytic Model for Daylight." Available online at *http://www.cs.utah.edu/vissim/papers/sunsky/*.

[Reinhard02] Reinhard, Erik., et al., "Photographic Tone Reproduction for Digital Images." Available online at *http://www.cs.utah.edu/~reinhard/cdrom/*.

[Reis05] Reis, Aurelio, Clouds-rendering demo. Available online at *http://www.codefortress.com*.

[Spoerl04] Spoerl, Marco and Kurt Perlzer, "Advanced Sky Dome Rendering." *ShaderX²*, Wolfgang F. Engel, Ed. Wordware Publishing, 2004.

[Sun05] Sun, Bo., et al., "A Practical Analytic Single Scattering Model for Real Time Rendering." Proceedings of SIGGRAPH 2005. Available online at *http://www1.cs.columbia.edu/~bosun/sig05.htm*.

[Terragen] Terragen™, Scenery Generator. Available online at *http://www.planetside.co.uk/terragen/*.

5.10

High Dynamic Range Rendering Using OpenGL Frame Buffer Objects

Allen Sherrod,
Ultimate Game Programming

ProgrammingAce@UltimateGameProgramming.com

In game development these days, there are many different effects that can be produced in real time that rely on post-processing. As graphics become increasingly more complex, so does the code and hardware that is required to produce it. As more effects are added to a rendered scene, more off-screen rendering and processing is taking place. The purpose of this gem is to present a new, efficient, and fast way to perform off-screen rendering in an OpenGL application, using the recent addition of frame buffer objects. On the accompanying CD-ROM is a demo application that performs a high dynamic range post-processing effect to demonstrate how to use the OpenGL frame buffer objects.

Introduction to Frame Buffer Objects

There are a number of ways that we can render to an off-screen surface in OpenGL. Each of these methods has its own set of pros and cons that should be taken into account when choosing the method that is right for us. The top issues that often affect our decision when choosing an off-screen rendering method concern the technique's memory consumption and performance.

The first option we have is to use the OpenGL functions `glReadPixels()` and `glTexImage*D()`. The problem with this method is that it is very slow and would be inefficient to implement in a game engine, therefore making it the least recommended way of trying to render to a surface or texture. Another option would be to use `glCopyTexSubImage2D()`, which is faster than using `glReadPixels()`. The problem here is that we are still not processing our effects at an exceptional rate. The third method we can use to render to an off-screen surface is to use what are known as *pixel buffers,* or *p-buffers* for short. P-buffers are a great option, because they are faster in terms of speed over the previous choices. They are also great because you can create an off-screen surface with different dimensions than the original screen resolution, use a different pixel format than the original window, and we don't have to deal with a lot of OpenGL state juggling. Although p-buffers are a good solution, they do offer their fair share of problems and issues, which can include high memory consumption, expensive context switching, difficult code management, and complications when porting to other operating systems.

In spite of these issues, p-buffers do have one benefit: We can abstract the code to set up and use a p-buffer as a reusable class. This fits in nicely for any developer using object-oriented programming, since all you have to do is to create one class with the necessary code to handle the p-buffer creation, maintenance, and cleanup for every platform you wish to support. The problem with this is the extra work that we would have to be bothered with.

The question now is how do we resolve our issues efficiently? P-buffers are fast enough, but they suffer from a few problems and issues that we can't just overlook. Luckily, the answers to our questions come in the form of the OpenGL Frame Buffer Objects (FBOs). FBOs are great to use for a number of reasons and can make life much easier than the previous methods discussed. For example:

- FBOs allow the results of a rendering to be directly read as a texture.
- They require a single context, which makes switching between them fast.
- Less memory is used by sharing textures and buffers between objects.
- FBOs will work on all hardware that has the necessary driver support.
- It is easy to set up, use, and clean up.
- No extra steps are necessary to port code to other operating systems.

OpenGL FBOs use the `EXT_framebuffer_object` extension. There are two new objects that are being introduced with this extension, which include frame buffers and render buffers. Frame buffers are a collection of buffers (e.g., color, stencil, and depth), while render buffers are simple 2D images that store the result of a rendering. When you bind a frame buffer, its attached images are the source and destination of all fragment operations until you unbind it or bind another frame buffer. You can have a frame buffer without creating a render buffer, but you can't have a render buffer without creating a frame buffer. Keep this in mind.

As we know, there are quite a number of ways we can perform off-screen rendering, but when it comes to portability, ease of use, and performance, we will be using FBOs. For nVIDIA users, you will need to have a minimal driver version of 77.72. At the time of this writing, however, ATI users will need to wait a little longer until driver support is added to their products (since FBOs are pretty new, it is doubtful that ATI users will be waiting long). Be sure to update to the latest drivers for your hardware.

Setting Up FBOs

In order to code an application using FBOs, we must check and make sure we support the `EXT_framebuffer_object` extension as well as have the latest version of glext.h. This is necessary, since we need to get function pointers to the necessary functions when dealing with the Windows operating system. Once all the requirements are in place, we can start to code our applications.

Creating, using, and destroying frame buffer objects is a lot like textures and shader objects, and requires the OpenGL functions shown in Listing 5.10.1, where *n* is the number of objects that are being created or deleted, `framebuffers` is an unsigned integer variable (or array) that will store the ID(s) of the object(s), and `target` is `GL_FRAME-BUFFER_EXT`.

Listing 5.10.1   Functions Used to Create, Make Use Of, and Delete Frame Buffers

```
void GenFramebuffersEXT(sizei n, uint *framebuffers);
void DeleteFramebuffersEXT(sizei n, const uint *framebuffers);
void BindFramebufferEXT(enum target, uint framebuffer);
bool IsFramebufferEXT(uint framebuffer);
```

The `GenFramebuffersEXT()` and `DeleteFramebuffersEXT()` functions work in a similar manner as the functions `glGenTextures()` and `glDeleteTextures()` by allowing you to create/delete frame buffer object(s). When you bind an FBO using `BindFramebufferEXT()`, all operations will occur on the images attached to that object. Sending `0` or `NULL` to this function will return OpenGL to its default buffer and stop the rendering to the current frame buffer object. You can check if an object is a valid frame buffer object with a call to `IsFramebufferEXT()`.

Textures can be attached to a frame buffer object with a call to void `Framebuffer-Texture2DEXT(enum target, enum attachment, enum textarget, uint texture, int level)`, where:

- `target` is `GL_FRAMEBUFFER_EXT`,
- `attachment` is `GL_COLOR_ATTACHMENT0_EXT` . . . `GL_COLOR_ATTACHMENTn_EXT`, `GL_DEPTH_ATTACHMENT_EXT`, or `GL_STENCIL_ATTACHMENT_EXT`,
- `textarget` is either `GL_TEXTURE_2D`, `GL_TEXTURE_RECTANGLE`, `GL_TEXTURE_CUBE_MAP_POSITIVE_X`, or `GL_TEXTURE_CUBE_MAP_NEGATIVE_X`, etc.
- `texture` is the texture object that was created with a call to `glGenTextures()`, and
- `level` is the mip-map level of the texture that is being attached.

The status of a frame buffer object can be checked with a call to enum `CheckFramebufferStatusEXT(enum target)`. This function can only be called after a frame buffer was created. `CheckFramebufferStatusEXT()` will return one of the following values:

- `GL_FRAMEBUFFER_COMPLETE`
- `GL_FRAMEBUFFER_INCOMPLETE_ATTACHMENT`
- `GL_FRAMEBUFFER_INCOMPLETE_MISSING_ATTACHMENT`
- `GL_FRAMEBUFFER_INCOMPLETE_DUPLICATE_ATTACHMENT`

- `GL_FRAMEBUFFER_INCOMPLETE_DIMENSIONS_EXT`
- `GL_FRAMEBUFFER_INCOMPLETE_FORMATS_EXT`
- `GL_FRAMEBUFFER_INCOMPLETE_DRAW_BUFFER_EXT`
- `GL_FRAMEBUFFER_INCOMPLETE_READ_BUFFER_EXT`
- `GL_FRAMEBUFFER_UNSUPPORTED`
- `GL_FRAMEBUFFER_STATUS_ERROR`

Next is the render buffer API. The render buffer API looks similar to the frame buffer API and is made up of the functions listed in Listing 5.10.2, where

- `n` is the number of objects you are creating or deleting,
- `renderbuffers` is a unsigned integer/array of unsigned integers,
- `target` must be the value `GL_RENDERBUFFER_EXT`,
- `internalformat` can be any normal texture formats (e.g., `GL_RGB`, `GL_RGBA`, etc.),
- `width` and `height` are the buffer's dimensions,
- `pname` can be `GL_RENDERBUFFER_WIDTH_EXT`, `GL_RENDERBUFFER_HEIGHT_EXT`, or `GL_RENDERBUFFER_INTERNAL_FORMAT_EXT`,
- the `params` value is based on what `pname` is. If `pname` is `GL_RENDERBUFFER_WIDTH_EXT`, then after the call, params will have the width of the buffer's dimension; if it is `GL_RENDERBUFFER_HEIGHT_EXT`, then params will have the height.

Listing 5.10.2 Render Buffer API Functions

- `void GenRenderbuffersEXT(sizei n, uint *renderbuffers);`
- `void DeleteRenderbuffersEXT(sizei n, const uint *renderbuffers);`
- `void BindRenderbufferEXT(enum target, uint renderbuffers);`
- `boolean IsRenderbufferEXT(uint renderbuffer);`
- `void RenderbufferStorageEXT(enum target, enum internalformat, sizei width, sizei height);`
- `void GetRenderbufferParameterivEXT(enum target, enum pname, int *params);`

The `GenRenderbuffersEXT()` and `DeleteRenderbuffersEXT()` functions are used to create and delete render buffer objects. `BindRenderbufferEXT()` is used to bind a render buffer, much like `glBindTexture()` is used to bind a texture object. `IsRenderbufferEXT()` is used to check if the object ID that is passed into the function is a valid render buffer object. `RenderbufferStorageEXT()` is used to define the format and dimensions of the render buffer. And `GetRenderbufferParameterivEXT()` is used to get a parameter that defines the render buffer. If you wanted to know the width of the render buffer, you would call `GetRenderbufferParameterivEXT()` with the parameter `GL_RENDERBUFFER_WIDTH_EXT` passed into it.

The next thing we need to cover is how to attach a render buffer to a frame buffer. This is done with a call to `void FramebufferRenderbufferEXT(enum target, enum attachment, enum renderbuffertarget, uint renderbuffer)`, where:

- `target` must be `GL_FRAMEBUFFER_EXT`,
- `attachment` is `GL_COLOR_ATTACHMENT0_EXT ... GL_COLOR_ATTACHMENTn_EXT`,
- `renderbuffertarget` must be `GL_RENDERBUFFER_EXT`, and
- `renderbuffer` is the ID of the render buffer object you are trying to bind to the currently bound frame buffer.

Mip-maps can also be generated on all texture images attached to a target, using the function `void GenerateMipmapEXT(enum target)`. The `target` parameter can have a value of either `GL_FRAMEBUFFER_EXT` or `GL_RENDERBUFFER_EXT`.

High Dynamic Range Rendering with FBOs

ON THE CD

To demonstrate the use of OpenGL FBOs, this gem comes with a simple, high dynamic range-rendering application. In computer graphics, the scenes that are displayed to the screen are limited to a low dynamic range of luminance values between 0.0 and 1.0. In reality there is a much higher range of luminance values that our eyes can detect, which is normally lost in photos and computer graphics. In video games and other graphical applications, we have a limited number of bits for each color component used when rendering the scene.

The fewer bits we use, the lower the precision of values. Previous generations of graphics hardware had access to only integer formats with a limited number of bits for each color component. Now we have access to more bits, which allows us to store much higher-precision values. This leads us to a higher dynamic range of luminance colors. Using floating-point buffers instead of integer buffers allows us to have more precision, since floats can store a higher precision than integers.

High Dynamic Range (HDR) rendering typically starts by rendering a scene into a floating-point buffer. The high precision of the floating-point buffer allows us to store a higher range of values than our normal integer buffers could. With the HDR scene in a floating-point buffer, we can now add various post-processing effects to enhance the scene. For example, we can add flares, blooms, and more to give the impression of realism and increased detail in the scene. These post-processing effects are typically done by rendering a full-screen quad with the HDR-rendered scene applied to it as a texture image. Doing this allows us to perform a nearly unlimited number of effects in real time.

We are usually required to use some number of passes in order to create a desired effect. The bloom effect, for example, is used to create a halo around bright areas of the scene, and requires us to perform a number of steps: First, the scene is rendered into a floating-point buffer. Second, a full-screen quad is rendered as a texture image into another buffer that is one-sixteenth the original size. Next, horizontal and vertical blur filters are applied to the down-sampled scene. Finally, the results of the first render and the end results of the final (blurred) render are tone-mapped and displayed on the screen.

What we've described here would take about five passes to complete and doesn't even include all the other effects we might want to have in our scene, such as flares or depth of field.

Once we are done with the scene, we can display it on the screen. Since the scene is using a high dynamic range of values, we must tone map the results so our computer monitors or television screens are capable of displaying them. This is done in order to keep our rendered scenes from looking like an overexposed image, since our display hardware does not expect our data to be in a HDR format.

Although HDR rendering can be done on older hardware using integer buffers, and by performing different tricks and short cuts, there is a loss of precision and the performance is often terrible. With a lack of precision we get a lack of quality. There are techniques and formats that allow us to perform HDR rendering with integer buffers, like the Radiance RGBE8 format. The RGBE8 format stores 8 bits for each Red (R), Green (G), and Blue (B) color component in the image. The E component of the image is a common Exponent value that is used to pack three floating-point values into the R, G, and B components. These 32-bit images are loaded, decoded by the application, then used to perform HDR rendering in a scene. There is still a loss of precision with these images, but they can be used without giving up too much quality.

You have probably guessed by now that we tend to do a lot of off-screen rendering per frame when it comes to HDR rendering. The more advanced we want our HDR scene to look, the more processing we will be doing. If you want to add other, non-HDR effects to the scene, like depth of field, for example, then even more off-screen rendering passes will be taking place. Speed is everything, of course; so if we are to take advantage of modern rendering techniques, we will have to get as much performance as possible. Also, the memory footprint comes into question; and luckily for us, FBOs are the best option in all cases. FBOs also work well with systems set up for SLI (nVIDIA's Scalable Link Interface) multiple GPU setups, rather than p-buffers or any of the other techniques mentioned in this article. In fact, using FBOs is highly recommended when dealing with systems that take advantage of off-screen rendering.

ON THE CD

The basic, high dynamic range demo that comes with the CD-ROM accompanying this article works by rendering a scene to an off-screen floating-point buffer, then tone mapping the results while being displayed to the screen. The scene is made up of a 3D object that is textured with an HDR image called a "light probe." Light probes are images that store scene information, such as a cube map or a sphere map, using a high dynamic range of values. These images can be created with a tool called HDR Shop, assuming you have a bunch of images you want converted into a HDR cube/sphere map. Although not a must, HDR images can help you perform very realistic and high-quality reflection mapping in a 3D scene.

Once the scene is rendered to the floating-point buffer, it will need to be tone mapped before being displayed on the screen. Tone mapping maps a high dynamic range image into a low dynamic one so that it can be rendered on the screen without looking like an over-exposed display. The tone-mapping technique described here is a simple one. It works by multiplying the color values by an exposure level that is reduced exponentially.

ON THE CD

The demo applications also use the OpenGL shading language for high-level, programmable vertex and pixel shaders. When you run the application, you can control the exposure level with the U and D keyboard keys to see the different results. You can also rotate the object with the Arrow keys on your keyboard and exit the application using the Escape key.

Conclusion

ON THE CD

The OpenGL frame buffer extension is a great addition to the OpenGL graphics API. All things considered, using FBOs will not hurt your application in any way, and could actually aid you in development and implementation. There is a demo to go along with this gem that performs HDR rendering in an OpenGL GLUT window. The demo was tested on a Windows XP desktop running a GeForce 6800 GT graphics card.

Things To Keep in Mind

There are a few things that you should keep in mind when working with OpenGL FBOs:

- Do not create and destroy frame buffer objects each frame, or you can hurt your performance and efficiency.
- Avoid using functions like `glTexCopy()` or `glCopyTexImage()` when modifying the contents of textures used as rendering destinations.
- Frame buffer objects allow for switching between multiple rendering destinations quickly.
- You can use a single frame buffer object with multiple texture attachments, or you can use a different frame buffer object for every texture to which you wish to render.
- You don't need to create a render buffer in order to use frame buffer objects, but you do need a frame buffer in order to use a render buffer.

Further Information

For further information on OpenGL frame buffer objects please feel free to take a look at a presentation created by Simon Green (nVIDIA Corporation) at *http://download.nvidia.com/developer/presentations/2005/GDC/OpenGL_Day/OpenGL_FrameBuffer_Object.pdf*. The nVIDIA SDK 9.5 comes with a demo that uses OpenGL FBOs in a simple and straightforward manner.

Also in the nVIDIA SDK, there is a demo application and a white paper on SLI. The white paper, "SLI Best Practices," can be viewed online at *http://download. developer.nvidia.com/developer/SDK/Individual_Samples/DEMOS/Direct3D9/src/ slibestpract/docs/slibestpract.pdf.*

You can download high dynamic range texture images from Paul Debevec's Web site at *http://www.debevec.org.* You can also create your own HDR images using a application called HDR Shop, which you can download from *http://www.ict.usc. edu/graphics/HDRShop.*

For more information on high dynamic range rendering, the book *Programming Vertex and Pixel Shaders* by Wolfgang Engel (Charles River Media, 2004) is recommended.

Further Reading

Green, Simon, "The OpenGL Frame Buffer Object Extension." August 8, 2005. Available online at *http://download.nvidia.com/developer/presentations/2005/GDC/ OpenGL_Day/OpenGL_FrameBuffer_Object.pdf.*

Young, Paul, "SLI Best Practices." August 25, 2005. Available online at *http:// download.developer.nvidia.com/developer/SDK/Individual_Samples/DEMOS/ Direct3D9/src/slibestpract/docs/slibestpract.pdf.*

AUDIO

Introduction

Alexander Brandon,
Midway Home Entertainment

abrandon@midway.com

The field of audio programming has grown by an order of magnitude in the past three years alone. One can equate simple polyshapes and low-res textures with simply "playing a sound" from a point source. With the advent of realistic physics technology, massive asset resource management, and more-realistic expectations from consumers, major publishers worldwide are hiring audio programmers full time to tackle these new challenges. The gems presented here range from simple concepts that yield new methodologies to completely new and advanced ideas, and all of them will help take your game audio engine to the next level.

The operative phrase in these articles is "real time." Most titles traditionally do not use much (if any) synthesis in which graphics are rendered in real time constantly (save for textures). This is going to slowly change, starting with next-generation audio engines, and being on the forefront of this means using more audio subsystems to attach to AI and physics, as well as rendering.

"Real-Time Sound Generation from Deformable Meshes" by Marq Singer takes a giant leap into sound synthesis specifically for games and presents an idea that quite possibly no one has thought of yet. Imagine slamming a car into another car and having the sounds generated realistically as well as in real time. While deformable meshes are still proving problematic to fit into a tightly budgeted and scheduled game pipeline, they will be commonplace for next-generation titles that demand any kind of realistic simulation beyond standard physics through engines like Havok. But just as with Havok, at first no one really considered sound. Marq's consideration and presentation is a welcome addition to audio-programming bibles, and if it can find its way into your next title, you'll be breaking new ground; only a handful of games have used just physics sound systems.

"A Lightweight Synthesizer for Real-Time Sound Effects" by Frank Luchs tackles in-game real-time synthesis. This is not a new concept; for a long time, SoundMAX® (Analog Devices) was touted as being the greatest in-game synthesizer engine ever made. But this time Frank's code samples stand a good chance of being used in next-generation products. Real-time effects and generation are the hallmark of a great graphics engine, and sound can no longer take a back seat to graphics—at least to the level that it once did. Going beyond ambient sounds, such as water and crickets, Frank opens real-time synthesis to other regularly used sounds, such as footsteps, lightning, and fire. Need to use memory more intelligently, even with 24 MB at your disposal on Xbox 360? Give this one a shot.

"Real-Time Mixing Busses" by James Boer takes the current "real-time mix" craze and delves a step deeper. Allowing an engineer the same tools as film post-production houses is going to be a requirement for next-generation games if their audio is to compete with the quality level of films, and the process presented by James illustrates many excellent techniques to provide game audio engineers those tools. One would hope that such tools would eventually be developed commercially, as well.

"Potentially Audible Sets" by Dominic Filion is to audio what hidden surface removal is to a rendering engine. It paves the way for "load-on-demand" functionality, conserving precious memory and buffer sizes to concentrate chiefly on what is in the player's field of aural perception. The real kicker with potentially audible sets is their use of occlusion and obstruction, which is becoming a staple of first-person perspective titles.

"A Cheap Doppler Effect" by Julien Hamaide is a gift. Why? Remember the use of Doppler in *Half-Life® 2?* The sound of trains approaching and passing by? The terrifying hum of the manhacks as they whizzed far away and then got closer, missing your head by inches? Now that power is in your hands. Julien's article provides perhaps the most comprehensive article in the series, with its extensive code, math, and samples. He practically writes everything for you and hands it to you on a silver platter. Go implement it.

"Faking Real-Time DSP Effects" by Robert Sparks isn't so much a work of code genius as a very clever alternative to adding too much in the way of streaming code that will choke your DVD buffer and cause those skips and pops we're so familiar with. Using multichannel files, you can effect any sound you like in any number of ways. Do you want a Lexicon reverb in your game? Now you can have that, and we don't know anyone who has tried it yet.

6.1

Real-Time Sound Generation from Deformable Meshes

Marq Singer, Red Storm Entertainment

marqs@redstorm.com

In this gem, we will explore a technique for the generation of realistic sounds based on the deformation of volumetric meshes. Objects are modeled in the same fashion as those used to simulate deformation and fracture, in which a tetrahedral mesh is created to approximate a solid internal structure. Using a technique known as "modal analysis," the meshes are processed offline into discreet vibrational modes. In the real-time simulation, a force is applied to the model, causing movement and internal deformation. The collision forces are projected onto the precomputed frequency modes. All of the modes are then scaled, based on their contributions, and summed together. The result is a complex waveform that can be sent to an audio renderer as the simulation runs, producing highly realistic sounds that correspond to the in-game forces being applied to the model.

A Review from *Gems 4*

In *Game Programming Gems 4,* [O'Brien04] describes the use of modal analysis in producing real-time deformations in complex models. We'll review some of those techniques here. Using the data from those methods and a few simple manipulations, the vibrational modes of deformation will be combined into a complex waveform and processed by a sound renderer. This rather striking and realistic effect can be obtained with very little overhead beyond that needed for the former deformation calculations.

Like many applications in the world of computer games, the process described will draw on a number of existing techniques and combine them in a novel fashion. The models used in the simulations are volumetrically tessellated into tetrahedra to produce functional units. A system of constraints is determined for these units, much in the same way as those used in soft-body simulations. The combination of these techniques has already been described in a number of references for calculation of objects that fracture dynamically. See [O'Brien99] for a detailed description of the use and calculation of these tetrahedral meshes.

In this gem, there is a good deal of discussion of modal analysis and modal synthesis being used to predetermine the states of our objects. Previous work has been done using modal techniques and precalculated modes with objects that deform dynamically but do not fracture. In one example in *Game Programming Gems 4*, this was employed to model a rubber ducky (the author calls it a "dodo") in a rather realistic simulation. We can make some assumptions by imposing the restriction that the objects do not break or fracture. Objects modeled this way will eventually return to some sort of resting state after forces have been applied. If no breaking occurs, then the mesh need not be retessellated. Such a refactoring will require many more calculations to be run on the new pieces of the object, and none of the previous offline calculations will be applicable. Also, if an object is constrained to return to its original shape, we can assume that there are a finite number of possible subshapes it can move through before it returns to rest. These "modes," as they are referred to in the rest of the text, will form the basis for creating the waveforms that will become our final sound.

Overview

Briefly, the process is straightforward. For an object we wish to simulate, precalculate its vibrational modes. Force applied to a model will cause an oscillation through the mesh points. The collection of modes is analyzed and culled. Since the goal is to produce an audible sound, we can discard any vibrational modes that fall outside of the normal range of human hearing (20–20,000 Hz). In addition, we can disregard any modes involving forces outside of a reasonable range for the simulation. For example, a simulated wind chime is probably not going to have to contend with the explosive force of a grenade. A separate rigid body simulation is used to move the object about and resolve collisions. When an object in the simulation collides with something, extract the modes that cross the point of collision. Sum the resulting amplitudes and frequencies of the collision into a complex waveform. The new data generated from the collision is then sent to an audio renderer and played as a sound.

Modal Analysis, A Brief Review

Game Programming Gems 5 and the References at the end of this gem contain articles that describe the process of modal decomposition and modal simulation in far greater detail than presented here. Nevertheless, it is important to have some understanding of how a nonlinear system is transformed into a matrix of independent oscillators. This section is a partial review provided for completeness.

To complete the deformation portion of our simulation, we will utilize modal decomposition, in which the system is linearized and decomposed into discreet modes and modal synthesis, the production of a weighted combination of relevant modes.

For a given physical system discretized with a technique such as the finite element method, we can generically describe it in the following form:

$$K(d) + C(d, \dot{d}) + M(\ddot{d}) = f \qquad (6.1.1)$$

where d is a vector of parameters that describe the configuration of the simulation (e.g., node positions), and the over-dots are the first and second derivatives with respect to time. K is a nonlinear function that takes d as input and returns elastic forces. If this were a spring-mass system, K would compute the forces exerted on all nodes. C is a nonlinear function that takes the velocities and returns dampening forces, and f is a vector of external forces on the system—for example, collisions or user input. M is a function that takes the accelerations ($\ddot{d}$) and returns the forces required to generate them. Recall Newton's Second Law, $f = ma$.

Although Equation 6.1.1 is generally nonlinear, if we assume displacements are relatively small, we can linearize from the system's rest configuration with:

$$Kd + C\dot{d} + M\ddot{d} = f \qquad (6.1.2)$$

where K, C, and M are referred to as the system's stiffness, dampening, and mass matrices, respectively.

The next step is to diagonalize Equation 6.1.2. Using a technique called "Raleigh Dampening," C can be expressed as a linear combination of the mass and stiffness matrices, such that

$$C = \alpha_1 K + \alpha_2 M \qquad (6.1.3)$$

for some value of alpha one and alpha two. [O'Brien02] notes that this is not the only possible dampening technique available, and that others could be applied. The advantage here is that Raleigh Dampening is relatively straightforward and simple.

Substituting in our new value for C, we have

$$K(d + \alpha_1 \dot{d}) + M(\alpha_2 \dot{d} + \ddot{d}) = f. \qquad (6.1.4)$$

M is symmetric and positive definite. We can use a Cholesky factorization to decompose M such that $M = LL^T$ $M = LL^T$. If we define an additional variable $y = L^T d$, premultiply Equation 6.1.4 by L^{-1}, and express M in terms of y, we now have

$$L^{-1} K L^{-T} (y + \alpha_1 \dot{y}) + (\alpha_2 \dot{y} + \ddot{y}) = L^{-1} f. \qquad (6.1.5)$$

The matrix $L^{-1} K L^{-T}$ $L^{-1} K L^{-T}$ can be further decomposed such that $L^{-1} K L^{-T} = V \Lambda V^T$, where V is an orthogonal matrix with columns that are the eigenvectors of $L^{-1} K L^{-T}$ $L^{-1} K L^{-T}$ and V^T is the diagonal matrix of eigenvalues. Another variable, z, can be defined in terms of y, where $z = V^T y$, and another premultiply of Equation 6.1.5 by V^T results in

$$\Lambda(z + \alpha_1 \dot{z}) + (\alpha_2 \dot{z} + \ddot{z}) = V L^{-1} f. \qquad (6.1.6)$$

A quick manipulation gives us

$$\Lambda z + (\alpha_1 \Lambda + \alpha_2 I)\dot{z} + \ddot{z} = g \qquad (6.1.7)$$

where $g = V^T L^{-1} f$.

Although the steps are a little complicated, the end result is relatively straightforward. The linearized Equation 6.1.4 has been converted to a diagonal matrix containing a set of decoupled oscillators. The ith row of the system presented in Equation 6.1.7 is a scalar, second-order differential equation:

$$\lambda_i z_i + (\alpha_1 \lambda_i + \alpha_2)\dot{z}_i + \ddot{z}_i = g_i \qquad (6.1.8)$$

where λ_i is the ith entry in the matrix Λ. Equation 6.1.8 can be solved in a number of ways, but for this article, we'll concentrate on the analytic solution

$$z_i = c_1 e^{t\omega_i^+} + c_2 e^{t\omega_i^-}. \qquad (6.1.9)$$

The c_1 and c_2 are arbitrary complex constants, and ω is the complex frequency, where

$$\omega_i^{\pm} = \frac{-(\alpha_1 \lambda_i + \alpha_2) \pm \sqrt{(\alpha_1 \lambda_i + \alpha_2)^2 - 4\lambda_i}}{2}. \qquad (6.1.10)$$

The absolute value of the imaginary component of ω is the frequency (in radians per second) of one mode. The real component is the mode's rate of decay.

The columns of $L^{-T}V$ are the vibrational modes of our object. Individual modes do not interact with one another. This property allows us to decouple the system into independent oscillators. The eigenvalue for each mode is the ratio of the mode's elastic stiffness to the mode's mass, and it is the square of the mode's natural frequency.

For a discussion on deformation methods and the selection of the K, C, and M matrices, see [O'Brien02].

Requirements for Sound

We have to take a number of factors into account when determining what is required for sound production. A few of these are going to work in our favor in terms of computation expense.

Any sound simulation is going to be limited by the range of human hearing. Frequencies from 20 Hz to about 20,000 Hz can generate audible sounds. This is to our advantage, as mentioned previously, in that we can disregard modes outside of this range. This also means the simulation will have to use an integration time step small enough to account for the high end of this spectrum (i.e., approximately 10^{-5} s). This is a fairly small step and may prove too discrete for most real-time systems. Sounds produced in simulations with a larger time scale may still prove adequate, but the results will have a dull, muddy quality with the absence of higher frequencies.

This technique takes advantage of the oscillations that occur when modeling deformation. In real life, as in the model, most of the sounds that an object generates arise from vibrations driven by elastic deformation. Because of this, we have to apply some technique (e.g., modal synthesis) that reproduces these internal deformations. Rigid-body simulators or inertialess techniques are not suited for this type of simulation. This is not to say that a rigid body engine is unnecessary. Most simulations of this sort employ some sort of classical physics engine to move the objects about and resolve collision. One benefit of this approach is that the rigid-body calculations for the whole models are invariant to the particle calculations used in deformation.

If we are already employing a physics engine that models dynamic deformation of objects, then the actual production of sound comes virtually for free. The techniques for deformation already describe modes that are discrete vibrational states and can be additively combined. The complex wave that is produced can easily be expressed as a sound wave without much additional manipulation. Because we are modeling only the object's vibrations, and not how those vibrations transfer into the air or reflect off other bodies, our modeled sound is basically omnidirectional. Increasing the realism of the sound (e.g., adding falloff or reflection) can be done using existing audio techniques, but at increased cost.

From Deformation to Sound

All the parts are now in place to perform our audio simulation. The objects' modes have been precalculated offline, and we have a rigid-body simulation in place to apply forces. In this portion of the simulation, deformable objects will be treated as rigid bodies, possibly as separate representations, until a collision occurs.

For every object of interest in the simulation, we'll precalculate the matrices presented in the section on modal decomposition. The vibrational modes of the object (i.e., the columns of $L^{-T}V$) are retained for use in the real-time system.

Recall from the definition of Equation 6.1.10 that the absolute value of the imaginary component is the mode's frequency. The columns of $L^{-T}V$ are parsed for values of $|Im(\omega^i)|$ that fall in the range of 20–20,000 Hz (3.18–3,180 Rad/s). All other values are discarded. Even though a large number of modes are discarded in this step, the count is still somewhat large. In practice, some have found that a small number of modes (the first 800 or less) are reasonably sufficient for sound production.

The real-time rigid-body simulation is run normally. When collisions occur, the forces are projected on the modes from the previous step. The response is determined using Equation 6.1.9.

Surface vibrations are the essential component for transferring vibrations from an object to another medium, such as air. Modes are scaled based on how much they distort the surface of the object. All the scaled results are summed together. This summed result is then sent to the audio renderer, possibly after some additional processing for spatial sounds.

Back in the definition of Equation 6.1.9, c_1 and c_2 were referenced as arbitrary complex constants. Now, with all the parts in place, we can define a mode's response to a projected impulse by substituting

$$c_1 = \frac{2\Delta t g_i}{\omega_i^+ - \omega_i^-} \tag{6.1.11}$$

with

$$c_2 = \frac{2\Delta t g_i}{\omega_i^- - \omega_i^+} \tag{6.1.12}$$

where Δt is the interval over which the force is applied, and t is the time at which the impulse was applied. After simplifying, we have the equation

$$z_i = \frac{2\Delta t g_i}{|\text{Im}(\omega_i)|} e^{t\,\text{Re}(\omega_i)} \sin(t\,|\text{Im}(\omega_i)|). \tag{6.1.13}$$

Computing Equation 6.1.13 for every sample would be prohibitively expensive. Fortunately, a sample can be determined from the previous value, with a single complex multiply by applying the equality $e^{\omega(t+s)} = e^{\omega t} e^{\omega s}$.

From this point, it is simply a matter of taking the summed frequencies and sending them to an audio renderer (possibly with additional processing). Although sound production can be seen as a sort of by-product of deformation, it is possible to refocus our attention from the visual to the auditory. If the types of objects being modeled are relatively rigid, such as metal or wood, and the expected oscillations are fairly high in frequency, some savings may come from bypassing a rendering step. Frequencies that produce the most interesting sounds will probably not distort the models enough to be visually interesting. Given that, one might want to consider using this technique purely for sound production.

Conclusion

This technique for sound production is fairly elegant. If our simulation is already trying to model dynamic deformation, we can piggyback a sound production implementation at little additional cost. Despite the simplicity and the savings from pre-calculating the modes offline, the calculations required are costly and may not be feasible with lower-end hardware. As the trend in parallelism continues in newer consoles and PCs, some mathematical restrictions become less severe. It is very likely that this and other related techniques, such as dynamic fracture, will become commonplace in the next few years.

Further Reading

Hauser, K., C. Shen, and J. F. O'Brien, "Interactive Deformations Using Modal Analysis With Constraints." *Graphics Interface 2003* (June), Halifax, Nova Scotia: pp. 247–256.

O'Brien, J. F. and J. K. Hodgins, "Animating Fracture." *Communications of the ACM*, 43(7): pp. 68–75, July 2000.

O'Brien, J. and J. Hodgins, J., "Synthesizing Sounds from Physically Based Motion." *Proceedings of SIGGRAPH 2001*, Los Angeles, California, August 12–17. ACM Press, New York, 1999: pp. 529–536.

Pentland, A. and J. Williams, J., "Good vibrations: Modal dynamics for graphics and animation," 1989. *Proceedings of SIGGRAPH 89*, Computer Graphics Proceedings Annual Conference Series: pp. 215–222.

References

[O'Brien99] O'Brien, J. F. and J. K. Hodgins, "Graphical modeling and animation of brittle fracture." *Proceedings of SIGGRAPH 99*, Computer Graphics Proceedings Annual Conference Series: pp. 137–146.

[O'Brien02] O'Brien, J. F., C. Chen, and C. M. Gatchalian, "Synthesizing Sounds from Rigid-Body Simulations." *Proceedings of SIGGRAPH 2002*, Los Angeles, California, August 12–17. ACM Press, New York, 1999: pp. 529–536.

[O'Brien04] O'Brien, James F., "Modal Analysis for Fast, Stable Deformation." *Game Programming Gems 4*, Charles River Media, 2004.

6.2

A Lightweight Generator for Real-Time Sound Effects

Frank Luchs, Visiomedia, Ltd.

gameprogramminggems@visiomedia.com

In this gem, we demonstrate a method for efficiently rendering the ambient part of audio for scenes in interactive applications. Usually, a sonic environment consists of a large number of sound-generating objects, which leads to heavy computational load. We want to build a more economical model. This is achieved by using a single generator operating in stereo that is able to cover most of the audio stuff we find in natural and artificial sound textures. Rather than present an abstract solution, we will concentrate on mimicking a few natural sounds, such as those of a cricket and a bird.

We begin with a look at the structure of our engine, outline the synthesis method, and then describe how it differs from conventional approaches. Finally, we will dive deep into the problems of synthesizing a real-world example. We demonstrate the versatility of the engine by switching, in real-time, between prepared sequences of totally different sounds. A wide palette of parameters can be used to modify the audio interactively and in a manner directly related to the player's position and orientation.

The Ambient Engine

The topics covered in this article make use of an extended version of the PortAudio Library [Bencina05]. In order to define our synthesis methods as audio units, we built a small extension to the buffer processing of PortAudio. We also made an audio filter using the Freeverb source code [Wakefield00]. The engine has a grain sequencer with the ability to navigate between different parts, and a convenient sequence generation and filter system. We will see that the secret of building an efficient model with low processor load lies in the precalculation of this grain sequence.

Sound Synthesis

When computing sound waves that represent ambient sounds, we must distinguish between periodic and random components. Our particular approach is a synthesis based on sequencing grains of sounds that contain information about the random noise generator and the deterministic quasi-sinusoidal (semi-sine wave) generator.

Our grains have the following main properties:

- Frequency
- Duration
- Level
- Noise level
- Envelope
- Partials

For efficiency, the generator uses an integer accumulator instead of a floating-point phasor. This automatically wraps from a max at 2^{32} (4,294,967,296.0) to zero. The increment is precalculated from the duration in samples and stored in the grain. Inside the buffer loop, the increment is added to the phase. Then this phase is used for a lookup in a sine table for our sample.

For a wide range of sounds, concatenating simple sine waves is sufficient, but the grain allows for up to three additional partial definitions with their own ratio and level. When playing the chain of grains, the system interpolates between the pitch and level of the individual overtones. With partials, we are able to produce the sharper sounds mainly needed for the lower frequency range, as well as atonal metallic sounds and formants. For example, a spoken "a" will have formants at 800 Hz, 1150 Hz, 2900 Hz, and 3900 Hz. The addition of sine waves with integer ratios results in tonal sounds; using noninteger relationships leads to atonal sounds.

Complex frequency modulation, vibrato, and glide effects can be achieved by preparing the tracks with the desired pitch information. Our grains have a variable size with a default of 107 samples. At a sample rate of 44100 Hz, this corresponds to a resolution of 3.33 milliseconds. Repetition is easily detected by a human listener, but this is good enough to avoid audible steps. On the other side, we can produce elements that have a length of several seconds, which is more efficient for static sounds.

Figure 6.2.1 illustrates a high-level overview of the sound synthesis system. Contrary to conventional granular synthesis, we use no overlapping and no windowing. Also, we have only one grain at a time. In order to prevent artifacts at grain boundaries, we only switch on integral phases. With this method, it is easy to synthesize clear harmonic tones.

In addition to the master level, grain elements have an index to a lookup table with various unipolar normalized curves. This feature is mainly used by longer grains to produce soft envelopes without the need to slice a segment into smaller ones with individual amplitudes. Mostly, we will use quarter parts of a sine function or exponentials. Exponential functions are common curves, because they represent natural decay patterns in acoustical systems. In order to cover a group of grains with a single envelope, we have the option to set a scale and a section for each grain in the group. For instance, a group of four grains will have a scale of four and ascending section

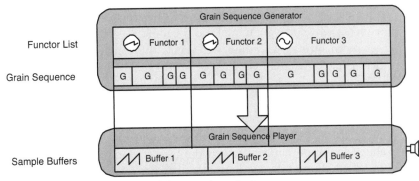

FIGURE 6.2.1   *Overview of the sound synthesis system.*

indices 0,1,2,3. A single grain with its own envelope would have a scale of one and section index zero.

What makes this method so fast? Instead of using a number of concurrent sound generators at the same time, we concentrate on the foreground events. With the small grains, we can switch rapidly between totally different sounds. This technique takes into account psychoacoustic considerations, namely the masking effect, in order to ignore the inaudible partials, thus saving a lot of computation time.

A nice sample of this effect is the ThunderLightningRain patch of the demo, which is available online at *http://www.visiomedia.com*. While you might have heard such sounds quite often, please note that you don't hear a prepared mix of three different tracks. What you hear is just one oscillator quickly switching between the elements thunder, lightning, and rain.

Using filter and a light reverb, we can give the impression of having multiple layers. We precalculate the audio for later use to prevent the unnecessary and resource-intensive process of sample calculation. We are able to synthesize an impressive number of sound textures in real time without stressing the processor. Most of the calculation is done when the tracks are created; thus, this generator is as efficient as a sample playback system, but offers more flexibility. It would be very difficult to achieve this scalability by other means, especially with multiple layers of static audio samples.

Real-World Examples

Cricket

Cricket sounds are a nice example for our synthesis system, because they are simple to understand but have some characteristics common to most sounds in nature. One of these characteristics is the fractal occurrence of random values. To generate a believable sequence of quasi-repeating tones, we have to vary pitch and amplitude on different layers. Our engine has five layers where we can alter the grain properties: sequence, envelope, grain, cycle, and sample.

By analyzing a recording, we came to this conclusion: Crickets produce short and clear triple tones at a frequency of 4200 Hz. The pulses inside the triple have 40-ms distance, and the silence between the triples lasts 240 ms. A single pulse has a ratio of 16-ms playing and 24-ms stopped.

Using the raw numbers above, our first try at resynthesis sounded a bit like a cheap alarm clock, so we improved our sound with some additions to make it believable. Most important was to vary the gap between the triples from 160 ms to 320 ms. Then we adjusted the loudness, because after further examination, we saw that triple groups had different levels, and also the pulses inside a triple have different, random levels.

We shaped the amplitude of the cricket pulse grain by using two envelopes in the form of a quarter of a sine. For the attack phase we used the first quarter, for the decay phase we took the third (negative) quarter normalized to the range 0–1. In comparison to the original, the synthetic cricket sounded a bit too clean. We compensated for this with a grain noise level of 10 percent, which added a light amplitude variation on each cycle. This adds an overall noise to the sound. The amount of noise can be adjusted per grain.

Our result sounded much better. But something was missing, and that was the most interesting fact. Our gaps were absolutely silent, but the original contained background noise. We added soft pink noise with a peak at 240 Hz, and that made the difference!

We can simulate a field of crickets by putting single triplets with a lower level at random places between the gaps and increase the random level of the original triplets. Here we have the masking effect again. Together, with a random balance per grain, this will sound like a handful crickets spread over the field.

Bird Song

Bird songs are fascinating acoustic phenomena. They are an important and unique part of a soundscape. The synthesis of a bird song follows the same principle as for the cricket, but is somewhat complicated by the fact that we have more melody and rhythm. Tones slightly overlap, and we have fast glides at the beginning of some chirps.

Our example bird song produces a sequence of 15 main chirps with a 330-ms length. The main pulse is 110-ms long and can have frequencies in the range of 2800 Hz to 5600 Hz. In the sequence, we also can find double pulses with 110 ± 50 ms, and triples having 3×50 ms. A typical single pulse has an attack phase with 15 ms and a decay phase of 95 ms. In the attack phase, the frequency glides from 7000 Hz to 4300 Hz, but not all pulses have this glide effect.

Following is the list of our 15 pulses with their frequencies:

1. 4331
2. 3340–4062
3. 3337–4071
4. 4290
5. 3399–3916
6. 4311
7. 5544–3989
8. 4371–4154
9. 5620–4007
10. 3707
11. 2910–3776
12. 4252
13. 5272–4044–3899
14. 3707–3899
15. 2767–3899

For the glide, we use eight tiny grains with a length of 15 ms. Because the grains are so small, we don't activate the elements envelope, but fade in grain by grain. With each grain, we lower the frequency, starting from 7000 Hz, until we reach the decay phase at 4331 Hz. The decay phase uses an exponential envelope and has a constant frequency for 90 ms. The characteristic bird sound is generated by the fast changes in the frequency of single chirps. Fast switching between the overlapping double pulses of the chirping produces the same result as combining different sound producers in the scene. Until the foreground element is dominant, you will not notice any breaks.

Conclusion

The synthesis method presented in this article can produce an enormous variety of ambient noises. Other applications are water, rain and bubbles, and weather effects such as thunder and lightning, as well as eruptions, magma, and fire. The ambient software synthesizer Saccara [Saccara05] is based on the sequencing of audio grains and specializes in wind and water effects.

Although we are interested in believable sounds and not scientific "truth," the resulting sounds are quite realistic—especially the more complex sounds that are very dense, but which still have the dynamics to allow individual elements to be heard. The complex and time-intensive process of manual sample selection, editing, and layering is eliminated by using a sequence of non-overlapping grains. Our technique allows complex sonic scenes to be simulated at interactive rates.

The Demo

The demo available at our Web site plays a nonrepeating stream of various ambient scenarios. We have prepared the following sequences: IntroSequence, TheCave, Flowing, Glass, RandomPartials, Magma, Footsteps, HowlingWind, Crickets, Chiff-Chaff, and ThunderAndLightning. The demo and its source code are available at *http://www. visiomedia.com.*

References

[Bencina05] Bencina, Ross and Phil Burk, PortAudio, 2005. Available online at *http://www.portaudio.com.*

[Saccara05] Saccara, 2005. Available at *http://www.visiomedia.com.*

[Wakefield00] Wakefield, Jezar, Freeverb, 2000. Available online at *http://ccrma. stanford.edu/~nando/clm/freeverb/.*

6.3

Real-Time Mixing Busses

James Boer, ArenaNet

author@boarslair.com

Controlling volume within an audio subsystem is not the kind of code a programmer is likely to implement often. And to most programmers, it probably seems like a reasonably simple task. However, once audio-content developers begin requesting volume controls to achieve faster production turnaround, it becomes easier to appreciate how a comprehensive and unified mechanism can benefit the developer. A more flexible approach will allow the programmer to add volume-related features to the engine long after the basic system has been put in place. We will discuss a basic technique for implementing volume controls in an audio library that allows complete customization of volume control through a simple "chained buss" mechanism.

Not Such an Unimportant Task

Audio libraries are pipelines that push digital waveform data through various controls, effects, and mixers. The ultimate destination of these waveforms is a digital-to-analog converter that transforms the signal from a digital approximation into a true physical waveform, after which it can be amplified and sent to speakers. There are various points along this virtual pipeline before the final mixer and converter, at which we would like to control the volume in some manner. Let's examine these points:

- Many audio systems make use of a per-source volume control, which can let sound designers tweak volume without having to edit the waveform data itself.
- Additionally, you may wish to provide per-source ADSR (Attack Decay Sustain Release) envelope control.
- Various sounds may be categorized and controlled as a group (e.g., sound fx, dialogue, music, etc.).
- Individual groups may need automated volume control, or ducking groups; for instance, it may be desirable to drop the music volume by some amount when spoken dialogue plays, and ramp the music back up to its original value later.
- Many games require some sort of master volume control; a manual volume function requires one control.

- If you wish to have an automated master volume function (such as a fader that operates on all currently playing sounds), then you will need a volume control for this.

You might be surprised to learn that there can easily be as many as six distinct points of volume control along a basic audio-rendering pipeline. But beyond the simple number of volume-control points is a more fundamental problem. Every game has a potentially different set of requirements for how these volume controls are arranged.

As a simple example, some games may require different logical groupings of audio channels than others. A baseball game may require distinct audio groups for the announcer, crowd and background sounds, in-game sound effects, and music; whereas a fighting game may just require music and sound effects volume controls. A musically themed game may require even more-sophisticated control, using numerous different volume busses.

One might ask, "Why not create a simple, hard-coded set of busses that encompasses as many volume controls as could potentially be needed?" Indeed, this has been the solution often observed in most libraries, if a solution has been attempted at all. Often these are labeled as audio channel "groups" or "categories" in an audio API— such as for music, sound effects, or dialogue. Additionally, a "master" volume control is also sometimes provided. Unfortunately, this presents a bit of a quandary if a game requires a different configuration of busses than the audio system provides by default.

One example of this might be if a game requires two distinct audio controls for a single "group." As we've explored to some degree earlier, this could occur for a "dialogue" channel. During critical dialogue exchanges, it is sometimes helpful to lower the volume of all nondialogue channels by some degree during the dialogue exchange, and raise the volume back up afterward. How would you go about doing this with a standard audio volume system? In many cases, this would be a complex affair to code and would require considerable modification at the audio-library level.

The simple answer to why hard coding volume controls is a bad idea is much the same as why it's a bad idea for other areas of game development: It's nearly impossible to anticipate the needs of a single game during its long development cycle, much less the needs of every game this library may have to service in the future. It's not much more work to build a flexible and nearly infinitely configurable system, so let's see how it would work.

Implementing a Volume Buss Chain

We've established that hard coding volume controls into fixed groups and busses is a bad idea for an audio library. But what is a good alternative?

The basic answer is fairly simple: Each volume control is a small object that simply acts like a link in a chain of volume controls. The volume controls are chained together in the same manner as the audio data moving down the pipeline from the source to the final mixing buffer. Any number of unique volume control busses can be created and linked to parent busses, forming something of a tree structure—albeit a tree that is traversed only from leaf to root. Parent busses have no knowledge of their children, unlike a typical tree. Figure 6.3.1 demonstrates how a set of volume busses might be configured.

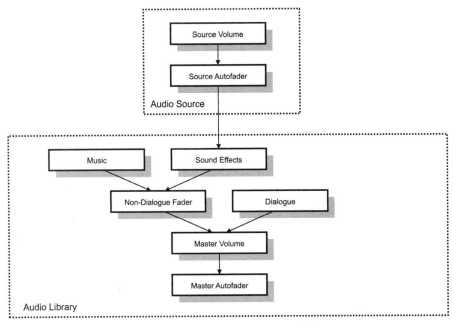

FIGURE 6.3.1 *A typical set of busses that might be used for a game.*

Each volume buss is created only with the knowledge of a single buss farther down the pipeline—or lower on the tree structure, as it were. This allows the creation of discrete "volume buss groups," such as the "dialogue," "music," and "sound effects" shown in Figure 6.3.1, as well as individual volume-control objects specific to individual audio sources. These controls are often exposed to end users directly through some sort of audio faders.

However, note that there is additional depth to the groups, such as a single buss called "Non-Dialogue" linked below the other nondialogue groups. This buss could be used to automatically lower the volume whenever dialogue appears. If desired, the game could also implement a group such as an "Incidental Dialogue" group that would not affect the volume of other channels. You can probably begin to see how a simple mechanism such as this affords a great deal of flexibility in configuring an audio system for your game.

Traversing the entire chain of volume-control objects allows a simple calculation of the final volume at which the currently playing buffer should be set. An interesting effect of combining these calculations is that we only end up applying volume once at the actual sound source. This works quite well, as many audio SDKs (such as Direct-Sound® or OpenAL) only have a single point (per sound channel) at which volume can be applied.

Although these volume busses can be created and used in any way you wish, there are some specific scenarios for which using them would make the most sense. One such scenario occurs when a set of busses is maintained within the core of the audio library, probably associated and managed through a unique ID, such as a string or integral value. When audio busses are created to control individual source sounds, this ID value is specified as a creation parameter of each individual sound, allowing the newly created volume buss to attach itself to a particular volume buss maintained by the audio system.

The code for implementing a volume buss is actually quite trivial. Generally speaking, a volume buss can be constructed of nothing more than a class containing a volume variable and a pointer to its own class (or structure). The pointer is used to link from child to parent in the tree, somewhat opposite of how trees are typically constructed. Listing 6.3.1 shows a basic implementation for a volume buss class:

Listing 6.3.1

```
class VolumeBuss
{
public:
    VolumeBuss()
    {
        m_Volume = 0.0f;
        m_DownstreamBuss = NULL;
    }
    void SetDownstreamBuss(VolumeBuss * buss)
    {
        m_DownstreamBuss = buss;
    }
    void SetVolume(float volume)
    {
        m_Volume = volume;
    }
    float GetVolume() const
    {
        float vol = m_Volume;
        if(m_DownstreamBuss)
            vol *= m_DownstreamBuss->GetVolume();
        return vol;
    }
```

```
private:
    float m_Volume;
    VolumeBuss * m_DownstreamBuss;
};
```

As you can see, a volume buss at its simplest is really nothing more than a single volume variable that can be chained to other similar variables.

Volume as Ratios or Decibels

In order to easily calculate the total results of each volume control along a given chain, we must first understand the nature of volume control in the digital world. In nearly every case with modern hardware and APIs, audio volume is a subtractive process. Waveforms are initially constructed at a volume level designed to provide a good signal-to-noise ratio (or sometimes a good dynamic range in relation to each other). Volume can only be reduced programmatically from these initial levels—in other words, amplification of the original waveform is not typically possible. Often, the nature of this reduction is given in terms of decibels (dB), which is a logarithmic scale, but sometimes the value is given as a ratio—a floating-point value between zero and one.

Whichever method is used, combining two volume values is a simple matter. For ratios, you simple multiply the values together. For logarithmic scales, you add the total reduction in decibels. For instance, if one volume control is set to –3 dB and the other is set to –4 dB, the total volume should be set at –7 dB.

Efficiency Concerns

If your audio mixing might be done in software, such as on the PC, you should consider that changing volume on each update might be very inefficient. As such, you should consider tracking the final volume value calculated by the volume buss chain, and comparing it to the last known value. In this manner, you can avoid having to change an active sound buffer's volume control unless it is actually necessary.

This may sound a bit more complex than it really is. In pseudo code, it would look something like Listing 6.3.2.

Listing 6.3.2

```
// Inside a timed update function
NewVolume = VolumeBuss.GetVolume();
if (NewVolume != CachedVolume)
{
    SoundBuffer.SetVolume(NewVolume);
    CachedVolume = NewVolume;
}
```

Alternatively, you could enhance the audio buss class to allow it to determine if the volume had changed since the last time the volume was checked.

Other Enhancements

One of the most practical uses of this system comes in the form of dedicated volume busses for fades and envelope-control systems. Indeed, it might be worthwhile to build such automated processes into the volume buss class itself. This way, any node in the chain can be designated as a mechanism for easily and automatically creating a simple fade-in or fade-out, or even something as sophisticated as a full ADSR envelope [Boer04]. Fading out all sounds could then be as simple as the following line of C++ code:

```
// Fades out all sounds over two seconds
AudioManager::getVolumeBuss(ID_MASTER)->fadeout(2.0);
```

Conclusion

Volume control in an audio library may seem like a reasonably trivial feature, but it can cause unnecessary limitations and compromises in your game's audio design if not enough thought is given to its design. The basic volume-control buss chain design can help to ensure your audio library can meet any design challenge in the future without having to be rewritten.

Moreover, this article demonstrates that it can even pay to give a bit of extra thought to the design of simple components, such as volume controls. A little bit of flexibility built into the system early on can save lots of work rewriting and reworking code in the future.

Reference

[Boer04] Boer, James, "Dynamic Variables and Audio Programming." *Game Programming Gems 4,* Charles River Media, 2004.

6.4

Potentially Audible Sets

Dominic Filion

dfilion@hotmail.com

If a tree falls in the forest and there is nobody around, does it make a sound?

Much progress has been made in recent years toward delivering a more refined sound experience for gamers, with the advent of EAX and game systems with 5.1 surround sound. As it stands, however, the richness of algorithms devoted to sound environments pales in comparison with the complexity of algorithms normally devoted to visual effects. Many of the algorithms, however, are adaptable in some way to the audio domain.

A vital technique often used by graphics developers is hidden surface removal. Objects in the scene are treated by a diverse array of algorithms to determine which objects stand a chance to actually be seen by the user. In the visual domain, hidden surface removal nowadays is mostly a matter of optimization: Videocard z-buffers ensure that the scene always renders correctly, no matter how poor the higher level hidden surface removal is. The counterpart of hidden surface removal in the audio domain would be hidden sound removal, a technique that can enhance the realism of sound environments in a meaningful way. Using such a technique, we can realistically model a sound environment with hundreds of sounds playing simultaneously within the environment, and have the algorithm figure out which sounds are relevant from the point of view of the player.

PVS Primer

We will touch briefly on the basics of one of the most common hidden surface removal algorithms—potentially visual sets—and then explore how the same algorithm can be adapted for the audio domain.

In a Potentially Visible Set (PVS), the level is divided into an arbitrary number of zones (regions), and for each region we precompute (at export time) some information that describes what other regions *might* be visible when the player is standing anywhere within that region; this is what we refer to when we speak of the PVS of a region. At rendering time, the system determines in which region the player is standing, and any regions that are not part of the current region's PVS are rapidly eliminated from further processing. We will see later how we can use the same concepts explained here to define a PAS (Potentially Audible Set).

A *PVS* is essentially a gross estimate of the visibility of objects. The player might be standing anywhere inside the volume of a region, and so an accurate assessment is impossible. What is important is that every object that *may* possibly be seen is put inside the PVS (see Figure 6.4.1).

The regions that comprise the PVS are normally convex regions. Because convex regions cannot hide themselves whenever the player is inside their boundaries, the restriction to convex regions for convex regions to be convex simplifies enormously the algorithm that precomputes PVSs enormously.

The regions that make up the PVS could be defined manually by a designer, but it is common to automate this process and let the level be automatically split into convex regions through the use of a BSP (Binary Space Partitioning).

One important limitation of PVSs that must be mentioned is that they are best used with static or semistatic environments. Doors can be handled well, as can be openings that may appear, such as crumbling walls and so forth, but if the sound environments consist of large occluders moving about, then the algorithm may not be suitable.

Basic PAS

There is much that we can adapt from PVS for sound environments. In Figure 6.4.1, we can observe the behavior of both light and sound within a similar environment.

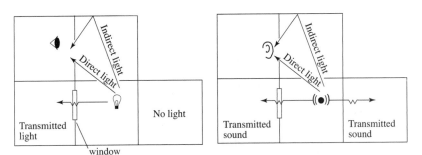

FIGURE 6.4.1   *Similarities between light and sound behaviors.*

Light in the environment can reach the eye directly or can bounce off of walls before it reaches the eye, producing such effects as reflections and ambient illumination. Light can also be transmitted through some types of mediums, such as glass (represented by the window in Figure 6.4.1), and can be tinted (i.e., its frequency shifted) by passing through such mediums.

Sounds have similar properties: they can reach the ear directly or bounce off of walls, producing reverberation and reflected sound waves. Sounds also transmits though a much wider range of materials, generally becoming low-pass filtered as they do so. Because the behavior and sonic properties of these different types of sound effects are so different, we will generally treat direct, indirect, and transmitted sound waves separately.

Direct Sound Paths

Sounds for which there is a direct path between the emitter and the receiver will generally reach the emitter without modification. Some effects can be applied for sound attenuation and dampening of high frequencies at large distances. To find out if we have a direct path between the sound and listener, we must trace a ray between the two and find out if there is an occlusion.

While we could trace a ray through each polygon of the sound geometry to find an intersection, we can rapidly eliminate the majority of cases where a direct path to the sound emitter is not possible even by using a direct-sound-path PAS. We will split the sound geometry into regions using a BSP, and for each region, we will determine what other regions *possibly* have a direct sound path with the current region. Thus, when the listener is in region A, the BSP needs only to test if there are sounds playing within any regions that are part of region A's potentially audible sets, and it can safely ignore all other regions.

Because with sound we can get away with less-precise shaping of the environment, it's generally a good idea to use a simplified version of the level geometry to model the sound environments. To make it easy, we can restrict the BSP geometry to axial planes that enclose the rooms and areas where the sounds will exist.

This gives us a set of cubes that represent our sound environment. The loss of minute detail in the environment will not affect the sound environment reproduction in any noticeable way. By using more-complicated shapes beside the cubes, we could design an algorithm that would cull out hidden sounds more precisely; but this would come at the cost of heavier computation to cull out these sounds, and it's quite likely we will lose more in performance than we gain by trying to get an "exact" solution.

The BSP process divides the sound geometry into recursive half-regions. We start by finding the global bounding box of the entire level's geometry, and split it into halves along the plane of one of the sound geometry polygons. The polygons are then categorized depending on which side of this plane they lie, and each half is further subdivided into halves along polygon planes until each region contains polygons only on its boundaries. A full explanation of the intricacies of BSPs is beyond the scope of this article; for more information, refer to [BSP01]. A good knowledge of BSP basics is required to fully grasp all of the material in this article, so if you need to brush up on your BSP knowledge, it is highly recommend to do so.

The BSP gives us a tree of planes that subdivide polygons of the sound environment. From this BSP, we can extract convex regions that describe the sound geometry.

Because we restricted the sound geometry to axial polygons, the BSP regions will all be cubes of different sizes, with each face of the cube defined by a quad polygon.

Each BSP region can be tagged as being solid or empty; this information will become useful when we calculate the potentially audible sets. All front BSP leaves of the tree can be considered empty regions, and conversely, all back BSP leaves will be solid regions.

The planes of the BSP are generally oriented according to the direction of the normal of the polygon they represent; thus, we can safely assume that any region behind a BSP splitting plane is solid space. This assumes that the sound level geometry was well formed without any seams, and is entirely closed.

Once we have correctly tagged regions, we will need to find *portals*—that is, polygons that define an opening between two regions. The task of finding portals between regions becomes trivial: Iterate over all the polygons that define a region, and tag all polygons that connect two empty regions as being portals. Conversely, polygons that connect an empty region to a solid region can be considered wall surfaces.

We now have a set of regions with information on the portals connecting these different regions. This is all we need to perform our PAS computation (see Figure 6.4.2).

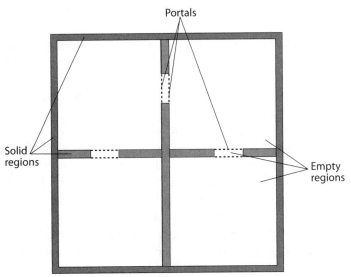

FIGURE 6.4.2   *Solid and empty regions, and portals.*

Let us consider an example. Refer to Figure 6.4.3. For a sound in region A to be heard in another region, it must pass through one of the portals of region A. Thus, if we can "see" a portal of region A from another region, then we certainly have a direct path to the sound within region A. The rules governing the potentially audible sets are laid down here. If a sound is playing within region A, then:

- It is heard inside region A.
- It may be heard inside all regions connected no more than two levels away from region A, through a portal.
- Given a set of regions S that does not include region A, it may be heard inside all regions of S that have a portal lying within the frustum defined by a portal of region A and a portal of a region connected to S.

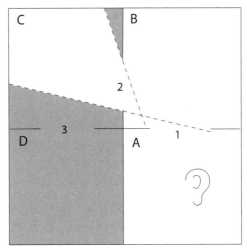

FIGURE 6.4.3   *Direct path frustum for region A.*

Ok, that was a mouthful. The first condition is easy enough: If you're in the same region as the sound, you will hear it through a direct path. The second condition isn't too bad either: If you are standing in region B right next to region A, or in region C right next to region B, there is a chance you may have a direct path. Remember, we are only interested in eliminating cases where it is *impossible* that there would be a direct path to the sound, no matter where within region A the sound is. Thus, it is easy to see that if the sound lies right next to an opening of region A, it will be heard directly from the regions B and C. The third condition is the hardest.

In Figure 6.4.3, the frustum is the region marked by the dotted lines. It is defined by portal 1 and portal 2. We find it by building a plane that goes through the left side of portal 1 and through the right side of portal 2, and through the right side of portal 1 and the left side of portal 2 (and similarly for top and bottom sides if this were a 3D illustration). This frustum defines the maximal extent of what you can see *through portal 1 and 2 when you are standing in region A.* You can't draw a direct line from region A to region C if the endpoint of the line in region C isn't somewhere within this frustum area.

Observing the Figure 6.4.3, notice that portal 3 is not within the frustum area. Thus, it is impossible for any object within region D to have a direct path to an object in region A with this configuration. We also have to take into account portals that may partially occlude other portals farther down a corridor, as in Figure 6.4.4.

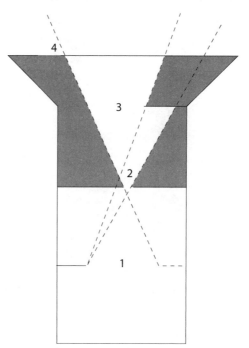

FIGURE 6.4.4   *Cumulative portal occlusion.*

Portal 2 is a small slit that allows only a small area to be seen/directly heard. This restricted frustum reduces the area of portal 3 that we can see through. (Observe that portal 3 should extend all the way to the left, but is clipped by the frustum of portal 2.) This reduces the frustum of portal 3. (The frustums of portals 2 and 3 share the same left boundary in this case.) Because portal 4 is not within the frustum, the region beyond portal 4 is not possibly visible from the region behind portal 1.

We treat this case by successively clipping portals by the frustums of the preceding portals as we go from one portal to the one beyond it. The pseudocode for building the PAS for a region is shown in Listing 6.4.1.

Listing 6.4.1 Pseudocode for PAS-building

```
for ( DWORD i = 0; i < regionCount; i++ )
{
    CRegion* pRegionA = regions[i];
    For ( DWORD j = 0; j < pRegionA->GetPortalCount(); j++ )
    {
        CPortal* pPortal = pRegionA->GetPortal( j );
        pPortal->BeingTested( true );
        CRegion* pRegionB = pPortal->GetOtherSideRegion();
        pRegionA->AddToPAS( pRegionB );

        for ( DWORD k = 0; k < pRegionB->GetPortalCount(); k++)
        {
            CPortal* pPortal2 = pRegionB->GetPortal( k );
            CRegion* pRegionC = pPortal2->GetOtherSideRegion();
            pPortal->BeingTested( true );
            pRegionA->AddToPAS( pRegionC );

            TestRecursivePortals( pPortal, pPortal2 );

            pPortal->BeingTested( false );
        }

        pPortal->BeingTested( false );
    }
}

void TestRecursivePortals( CPortal* pPortal, CPortal* pPortal2 )
{
    CRegion* pRegionA = pPortal->GetThisSideRegion();
    CRegion* pRegionC = pPortal2->GetOtherSideRegion();
    CFrustum* pFrustum = FormFrustum( pPortal, pPortal2 );

    for ( DWORD i = 0; i < pRegionC->GetPortalCount(); i++ )
    {
        CPortal* pPortal3 = pRegionC->GetPortal( i );
        if ( pPortal3->IsBeingTested() )
            continue;
        pPortal3->BeingTested( true );
        // Next function will return if portal clipping
        // does not entirely cull out the polygon
        CPortal* pClippedPortal;
        if ( pFrustum->ClipPortal( pPortal3, pClippedPortal ) )
        {
            CRegion* pRegionD = pPortal3->GetOtherSideRegion();
            pRegionA->AddToPAS( pRegionD );

            TestRecursivePortals( pPortal, pClippedPortal );
        }
        pPortal3->BeingTested( false );
    }
}
```

The end result of this algorithm is that we will have precomputed, for each region in our sound geometry, the set of all regions that could possibly have a direct sound path to that region. Thus, at runtime, we can find in which region the listener lies through the BSP and ignore any sounds that are not playing within the player's PAS. Herein lies the essence of the PAS algorithm. We can also make a number of useful extensions to the system for different sound behaviors.

Dynamic PAS for Doors and Windows

Although precomputed, the PAS does not have to remain static during the whole duration of the game. As doors and windows get closed or opened, this would open or close up different sound paths.

We can deal with these changes by first precomputing at export time the PAS for the level when a door is open. Again at export time, the door is then closed, and we can recompute the PAS for the case when the door is closed. We can avoid recomputing the entire PAS for the whole level by using the following rule: Everything that *sees* the door must have its PAS recomputed, and everything else stays the same. Every region that is within the PAS of either of the two regions on each side of the door must have its own PAS set recomputed.

We then end up with two sets of precomputed PAS for the entire level: one for the door open and one for the door closed. Since the two PAS sets will be very similar (most regions in the level are not affected by that particular door being closed or open), we can store the PAS for the open case and only store the sections of the PAS for the closed case that are different from the open case. At runtime, we can switch between the two PAS cases as the door opens or closes.

Extended PAS: Transmission

The basic PAS structure gives us a good base for quickly discovering regions that have possible direct paths to our current position. Sound can also travel through solid materials, however—a phenomenon known as *transmission*. Transmitted sounds have a filter applied to them so they will sound muffled.

Finding the sounds that might be transmitted can be done using the underlying region and portals structure used to generate the PAS. Each region contains a list of all portals (connections between empty regions). We can also generate a list of all walls (or solid portals) of that region from the same structures—that is, connections between empty and solid regions.

When a sound is played, it can be recursively propagated through all solid portals that connect to the originating region. As the sound passes through each solid portal, the sound can be muffled some more, until it decays to zero as shown in Listing 6.4.2.

Listing 6.4.2 Pseudocode for Sound Transmission

```
bool PropagateTransmittedSound( CRegion* pSrcRegion )
{
if ( pRegion->PlayerIsInPAS() )
    Return true;     // Direct path - no need to transmit
    for ( DWORD i = 0; i < pSrcRegion->GetSolidPortalCount();
    i++ )
    {
        CPortal* pSolidPortal =
            pSrcRegion->GetSolidPortal( i );
        CRegion* pRegion =
            pSolidPortal->GetOtherSideRegion();
        MuffleSound(
            pSolidPortal ->GetMufflingCoefficients() );

        if ( pRegion->PlayerIsInPAS() )
            {
                PlayMuffledSound();
                return true;
            }

        if ( pRegion->DistanceFromSource() <
            pSound->GetMaxDistance() &&
            PropagateTransmittedSound( pRegion ) )
                return true;

            UnMuffleSound( pPortal->GetMufflingCoefficients() );
    }
    return false;
}
```

The muffling of sounds from one region to another could also be precomputed and stored in a second, different PAS specifically made for sound transmission.

Extended PAS: Reflection

Reflections are the third and physically most complex type of sound effect. They encompass reverberation, such as sounds reflected off a wall. In a densely occluded environment, sound will reverberate through corridors easily, so we can generally approximate that sound will propagate in all directions through corridors when it plays.

We achieve this by "flood-filling" the regions surrounding the sound until we arrive at the listener or at the sound's attenuation threshold. This gives us an estimate of the shortest path that the sound will take as it bounces through the corridors. We can estimate the loudness of the reflected sound from the distance of the shortest path to the listener.

We also want to place reflected sounds properly. If a sound is turning corners as it bounces through a corridor, we need the sound to be played with current attenuation at the nearest portal to the listener, not at its point of origin. This is shown in Listing 6.4.3. Note that this code only needs to be run when a new sound starts playback or when the player changes zones, which is relatively infrequently. When the player doesn't change zones, the results of this function stay the same for several frames.

Listing 6.4.3 Pseudocode for Sound Reflection

```
Void FindShortestDistanceReflectedSound( CRegion* pSrcRegion )
{
CPortal* pClosestPortal = NULL;
    float fShortestDistance = FLT_MAX;
    if ( PropagateReflectedSound( pSrcRegion, NULL, 0.0f,
        fShortestDistance,
        pClosestPortal ) )
    {
        PlayReflectedSound(pClosestPortal, fShortestDistance );
    }
}

bool PropagateReflectedSound( CRegion* pSrcRegion, CPortal*
    pSrcPortal,
    float fCurrentDistance,
    float& fShortestDistance,
    CPortal*& pClosestPortal )
{
    if ( pSrcRegion->PlayerIsInRoom() )
        return true;
    if (fCurrentDistance < fShortestDistance )
    {
        fShortestDistance = fCurrentDistance;
        pClosestPortal = pSrcPortal;
    }
    if ( fCurrentDistance > pSound->GetMaxDistance() )
        return false;
    for ( DWORD i = 0; i < pSrcRegion->GetPortalCount(); i++ )
    {
        CPortal* pPortal = pSrcRegion->GetPortal( i );
        CRegion* pRegion = pPortal->GetOtherSideRegion();

        if ( !pSrcPortal )
        {
        if ( PropagateReflectedSound(pRegion, pPortal,
        fCurrentDistance +
        pSrcPortal->DistTo( pSound->GetPosition() )    ) )
        return true;
        }
        else
        {
        if ( PropagateReflectedSound(pRegion, pPortal,
            fCurrentDistance +
            pSrcPortal->DistTo( pPortal ) ) )
            return true;
        }
    }
}
```

Conclusion

The system described here provides a complete environment for the simulation of ambient effects on sounds playing within an arbitrarily complex environment. The use of a PVS, taken from computer graphics, can be successfully adapted to rapidly find which sounds can be directly heard within a sound environment. The PAS and its companion BSP structure can also be extended to account for effects such as transmission and reflection. This allows a complicated sound environment in which hundreds of sounds may be playing simultaneously, and the PAS system will rapidly find the ones relevant to the listener.

Reference

[BSP01] BSP Trees FAQ. Available online at *http://www.faqs.org/faqs/graphics/bsptree-faq*.

6.5

A Cheap Doppler Effect

Julien Hamaide,
Elsewhere Entertainment

julien.hamaide@gmail.com

The quality of 3D graphic-rendering engines continues to approach realistic quality. But this is not the case for other sectors of video games. The goal of this article is to illustrate a technique that will increase the realism of game audio. By simulating the Doppler effect, it is now possible to dynamically modify emitted and perceived sounds. Indications of movement are then given for sound-emitting entities. This technique can also be used offline—for example, for effect creation in video. The technique is quick and easy to implement.

The Doppler Effect

The Doppler effect is the apparent change in frequency of a sound emitted by a source when it exists in a relative translation between the source and the listener. This impression is caused by the change of perceived wavelength. Figure 6.5.1 represents the wave at a given time when the source is moving. If the listener and the source are approaching each other, the perceived wavelength is smaller; the observer then hears it at a higher pitch. This effect is very perceptible when an ambulance approaches with its howling siren. When the ambulance passes by and moves away, the wave has an increasing amount of distance to traverse. The listener now perceives a longer wavelength, giving the impression that the sound has a lower pitch.

We will continue with the equations necessary to compute a Doppler effect. In Figure 6.5.2, the source is moving toward the listener with a speed V_s. The source emits a wave of frequency f_0, wavelength λ_0, and period T_0. A first wave front is emitted, which moves with a speed v at ~340 m/s. The value of speed to use is equal to the speed of the moving object projected on the axis that connects the source and the listener. T_0 seconds later, the source emits another wave front. The first wave front then traverses a distance of $v * T_0 = \lambda_0$. But the source traverses a distance of $V_s * T_0$. The perceived wavelength is computed in Equation 6.5.1.

$$\lambda' = v * T_0 - V_s * T_0 = (v - V_s) * T_0 \qquad (6.5.1)$$

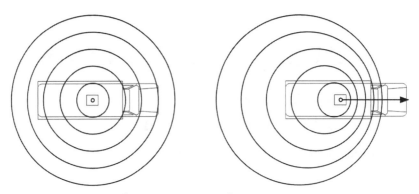

FIGURE 6.5.1   *Sound wave propagation for a moving source.*

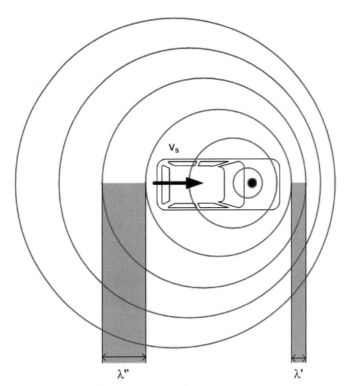

FIGURE 6.5.2   *Perceived frequency computation.*

By convention, the speed value is positive if the source and the listener approach each other, and is negative if they move apart. In the latter case, speed would have a negative sign; λ' will therefore be larger. If λ' is divided by v, Equation 6.5.2 and Equation 6.5.3 are obtained.

$$T' = T_0 \frac{v - V_s}{v} \tag{6.5.2}$$

$$f' = f_0 \frac{v}{v - V_s} \tag{6.5.3}$$

Equations 6.5.4 and 6.5.5 are obtained the same way if the source's speed is V_s and the observer's speed is V_o when the listener moves.

$$f' = \frac{v + V_o}{v - V_s} f_0 \tag{6.5.4}$$

$$T' = \frac{v - V_s}{v + V_o} T_0 \tag{6.5.5}$$

From a practical point of view, the Doppler effect corresponds to an increase or a decrease of sound reproduction speed, as with turntable discs. If it turns more quickly, the sound seems to have a higher pitch; if it turns more slowly, the sound seems to have a lower pitch. This is the same principle used to create the sound modified by the Doppler effect.

Example

To illustrate the theory, we will use a simple example. The configuration is represented in Figure 6.5.3. Only the source is moving. The speed to take into account in Equation 6.5.4 and Equation 6.5.5 is the amplitude of speed projection on the source-observer axis, using the convention described above. In our case, since only the source is moving, the speed is equal to the variation of the distance between the source and the listener. For the example, the speed is calculated from the distance, because it is then easier to find the analytical expression of speed. In a practical case, the projection of the speed vector on the axis is easier to use.

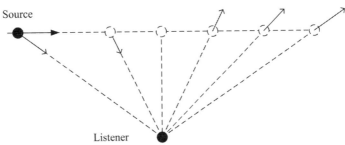

FIGURE 6.5.3 *Doppler effect with only the source in motion.*

The position of the source P_s and of the listener P_o are defined in Equation 6.5.6 and Equation 6.5.7.

$$P_s = (10 \cdot t, 1, 0) \tag{6.5.6}$$

$$P_o = (0, 0, 0) \tag{6.5.7}$$

The distance is computed with Equation 6.5.8.

$$D = \sqrt{(10 \cdot t)^2 + 1} \tag{6.5.8}$$

The calculated speed is then shown in Equation 6.5.9. The negative sign comes from the chosen rule. Actually, if the distance D decreases, its derivative will be negative. But the rule needs a positive speed if the source and the listener approach each other, thus the derivative of the distance is negative.

$$V_{s/o} = -\frac{dD}{dt} = \frac{100 \cdot t}{\sqrt{(10 \cdot t)^2 + 1}} \tag{6.5.9}$$

ON THE CD

The source's speed is shown in Figure 6.5.4a, the frequency ratio in Figure 6.5.4b. On the CD-ROM, WAV files with a Doppler effect can be found.

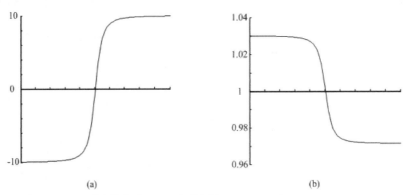

(a)   (b)

FIGURE 6.5.4   *(a) Relative speed. (b) Frequency ratio.*

Programming the Doppler Effect

An audio record is represented by a list of values kept in an array. These values are separated with a fixed lapse of time. This time is labeled T_s, a sampling period, which is the inverse of the sampling frequency F_s. Typical sampling frequencies are 44.1 kHz and 22.05 kHz. To apply the Doppler effect, the speed of reproduction of the emitted signal must be modified. That corresponds to a temporal dilation and erosion. The perceived signal must also be sampled at the original sample frequency. For a signal and a sampling frequency, there exists a simple relationship between the time of the sample and its index in the array containing the sampled value (see Equation 6.5.10). Here, i represents the index of the array, and it must be an integer.

$$t = i \cdot T_s \qquad (6.5.10)$$

As demonstrated earlier, we will apply a change of frequency corresponding to a temporal dilatation or erosion. Equation 6.5.5 shows that the ratio T'/T_0 is only dependent on v (speed of sound), V_s, and V_o. This frequency ratio and period ratio are then independent from the signal itself.

To apply a frequency change, a simple temporal modification is applied according to Equation 6.5.4. Equation 6.5.11 is used to carry out the transformation. According to Equation 6.5.10, t can be replaced by i if both signals (source and perceived) have the same sampling frequency, and if T_s is equal for both signals.

$$t_{src} = \frac{v + V_o}{v - V_s} \cdot t_{dst} \equiv i_{src} = \frac{v + V_o}{v - V_s} \cdot i_{dst} \equiv i_{src} = R \cdot i_{dst} \qquad (6.5.11)$$

The times and index variables suffixed by "src" refer to the emitted signal; the ones suffixed by "dst" refer to perceived signal. We now have enough to fill out the table of the signal perceived using the source values according to Equation 6.5.12.

$$S_{dst}\left(i_{dst}\right) = S_{src}\left(i_{src}\right) = S_{src}\left(i_{dst} \cdot R\right) \qquad (6.5.12)$$

Here, i_{dst} is an integer, but R is not. $i_{dst} \cdot R$ will therefore not be an integer, either. $S_{src}\left(i_{dst} \cdot R\right)$ does not always exist. To solve this, we will use interpolation. One of the available techniques is presented here. The chosen one is simple and cheap in computation, while giving excellent results.

The code equivalent to this algorithm is:

```
void apply_doppler( int * src_signal, int *dst_signal,
     float ratio, int frame_sample_count )
{
    for( int i=0; i< frame_sample_count; i++)
    {
        dst_signal[i] = src_signal[i*ratio];
    }
}
```

As mentioned, `i*ratio` is not always an integer. This problem is tackled later.

Linear Interpolation

In Figure 6.5.5a, the original signal is represented. The sampling instances are indicated with points in the graph. These are the only available values from the original signal.

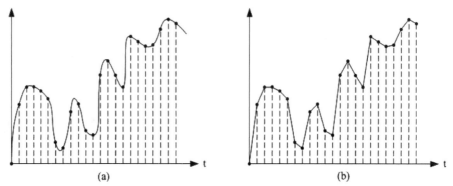

FIGURE 6.5.5   *Sampled signal (a) and linear interpolations (b).*

The desired value is interpolated with the help of the previous and following values. As the indices of the table are used, the index distance between two values is equal to one. The algorithm rounds the index up and down as needed. A value proportional to the position inside the interval is computed. Source code for this is as follows:

```
int interpolate( int* source_array, float wished_index )
{
    int index = (int) floor( wished_index );
    float delta = wished_index -index;

    return (int) ( source_array[index] * ( 1.0f - delta )
        + source_array[index+1] * ( delta ) );
}
```

In the code from the previous example,

```
dst_signal[i] = src_signal[ i*ratio];
```

becomes:

```
dst_signal[i] = interpolate( src_signal, i*ratio );
```

Calculation of the Index Starting from the Ratio *R*

According to Equation 6.5.11, i_{dst} is computed from i_{src} and R. This needs a multiplicative for each sample. The next sample, i_{dst}, is incremented by one. According to Equation 6.5.13, it is sufficient to add R to i_{src}. The multiplicative is then transformed into an additive.

$$(i+1)_{src} = R \cdot (i+1)_{dst} = R \cdot (i_{dst} + 1) = R \cdot i_{dst} + R = i_{src} + R \qquad (6.5.13)$$

The code then becomes:

```
void apply_doppler( int * src_signal, int *dst_signal,
    float ratio, int frame_sample_count )
{
    float isrc;
    for( int i=0, isrc=i; i< frame_sample_count; i++, isrc +=
        ratio)
    {
        dst_signal[i] = interpolate( src_signal, isrc );
    }
}
```

Variable Speed

There are cases when the relative speed between source and listener is constant, but often this is not the case. The relative speed of the source varies according to Figure 6.5.4a; thus, it is not constant. The frequency ratio changes continuously during the frame according to Equation 6.5.10. Computing the ratio for each new sample would give the best result. However, this solution is too CPU-expensive, because it needs a division for each sample.

The ratio in the previous example varies according to Figure 6.5.4b. To save a lot of computing power, the ratio function will be linearized into pieces. The function will be approximated by a suite of small linear segments. For each frame, the ratio at the beginning and at the end of the frame is computed. The value is then linearly interpolated between those two values. As the frame length is very short, this linearization does not introduce any problems, and will not be noticed from the listening point of view. Figure 6.5.6 shows the linearization by pieces of the curve from the Figure 6.5.4b. The length of the frame has been increased to show the phenomena. This also shows that the length of the frame is not constant, as can be the case in a game engine.

The code then becomes:

```
void apply_doppler( int * src_signal, int *dst_signal, float
ratio_start, float ratio_end, int frame_sample_count )
{
    float isrc;
    float delta_ratio = ( ratio_end - ratio_start )/
        (sample_count-1);
    float ratio = ratio_start;

    for( int i=0, isrc=i; i< frame_sample_count;
        i++, isrc += ratio)
    {
        dst_signal[i] = interpolate( src_signal, isrc );
        ratio += delta_ratio;
    }
}
```

ON THE CD

The complete source code is on the accompanying CD-ROM.

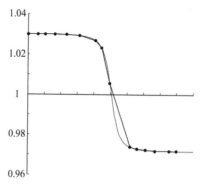

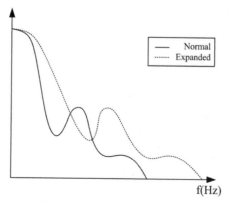

FIGURE 6.5.6 *Frequency ratio made linear by pieces.*

If you want to increase the precision of the transformation, you can decrease the number of points (frame_sample_count) per call to the function. For an offline treatment, the ideal is to compute the ratio for each new sample according to Equation 6.5.10.

Aliasing

The transformation of an aural signal is not without risk. The sampling theory still applies. By applying an expansion or erosion, frequential space also undergoes a transformation. An acceleration of the sound stretches the spectrum in the high frequencies. Figure 6.5.7 illustrates the frequencies of a sound; it also illustrates (with a dashed line) its frequencies after the calculation of acceleration. The same effect occurs when the signal is slowed down, but the spectrum shrinks.

FIGURE 6.5.7 *Expansion of the spectrum range.*

A problem can appear, though: the aliasing of the signal. According to Nyquist theory, if the signal has a part of its spectrum higher than the half of the sampling frequency, this part appears between zero hertz and half of the sampling frequency, adding abnormal sound (noise) to the signal. A practical example of aliasing and the mathematical background can be found in [Wiki05].

In our case, if the signal is accelerated to higher values, the frequency range is expanded and can reach the aliasing limit. It is important to ensure the maximum values of the ratio are never reached in order to prevent aliasing. It is a good idea to limit the spectrum of the signal to a known value to control this potential problem.

However, if the source is moving at 100 m/s (360 km/h), the ratio R become equal to 0.7 (see Equation 6.5.14). This ratio stays relatively near 1.0, and it needs a very fast object to reach limit conditions. If the sound does not have a spectrum close to the Nyquist, the problem should never occur.

$$R = \frac{v + V_o}{v - V_s} = \frac{340 + 0}{340 - 100} \approx 1.4$$

$$R = \frac{v + V_o}{v - V_s} = \frac{340 + 0}{340 + 100} \approx 0.8 \tag{6.5.14}$$

Implementation

ON THE CD

The implementation given on the CD-ROM tries to reproduce the real conditions of a game engine. The signal is treated by 40 ms/frame (25 FPS). A random value varies slightly the duration of each frame to simulate the variable duration of a real frame from a game engine. The principal method (`apply_doppler`) can be used as is in your game.

Conclusion

The Doppler effect is a physical phenomenon that modifies the perception of a sound when movement exists between the observer and the source. This phenomena is constantly present, but it is noticed only when speeds are high. This article presents a simple and efficient technique for simulating the effect. This technique allows you to increase the audio realism at low cost and can also be used offline to create sounds. Give it a try!

Resources

[Wiki05] Wikipedia, "Aliasing." December 2004. Available online at *http://en. wikipedia.org/wiki/Aliasing.*

6.6

Faking Real-Time DSP Effects

Robert Sparks, Radical Entertainment
sparks.robert@gmail.com

Consider a video game that features a radio playing music inside of a room. The radio sounds clear and loud when the player is inside the room with it. However, when the player is outside the room, the radio should realistically sound quieter and muffled. This muffling and attenuation is a dynamic, real-time effect called "occlusion" and is supported by next-generation consoles. But what do you do when your target hardware doesn't support the dynamic, real-time DSP effects that you want? What if you want something special?

Fake it.

This gem will show how to simulate any effect on any platform. The technique is simple to implement, yet extremely powerful.

Faking It

The key to faking dynamic real-time effects is that most of the work gets done offline, when the content is created. Instead of creating single-channel sound files as we normally would, we create specially designed sound files that contain multiple channels. One channel of the multichannel files contains the original unprocessed sound. All other channels contain processed variations of the original. So for example, one channel could sound like an unprocessed radio, one could sound like a radio playing through a wall, and another could sound like a radio playing underwater.

When we play the multichannel sound files back in the game, we treat each channel as a positional sound that exists at the position of the object to which we are attaching sound. Each channel is played back with its own overall volume. Because the individual channels are synchronized and are located at the same physical location, their sounds combine to produce an overall sound for the object. As we change the volumes of the channels, we change their combined sound. The result sounds astonishingly like a DSP effect is being applied by the hardware.

Example: A Radio Playing Music in Room

ON THE CD

To better understand this technique, we will return to the example introduced at the beginning of this article. In addition to the following description, sample code and source WAV files can be found on the CD-ROM and provide a more hands-on demonstration.

Consider a video game that features a radio playing music in a room (Figure 6.6.1). The listener begins in a room with the radio, and the radio sounds clear and loud. When the listener leaves the room, the sound of the radio quickly becomes quieter and muffled.

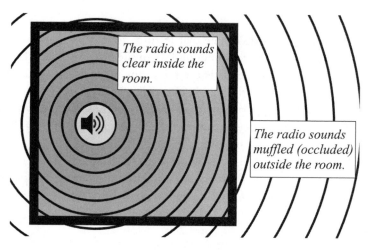

The radio sounds clear inside the room.

The radio sounds muffled (occluded) outside the room.

FIGURE 6.6.1   *A radio in a room sounds clear inside the room and occluded outside the room.*

To implement this example we require a sound file with two channels. In one channel, the file will contain the unfiltered sound of a radio from inside the room. In the other channel, the file will contain the sound of the radio from outside the room (see Figure 6.6.2).

When we play the multichannel radio file back in the game, we assign a positional voice to each of the channels and play them all from the position of the radio object. Since the listener begins inside the room with the radio, we turn up the volume of the unprocessed channel and turn down the volume of the processed channel (see Listener Position 1 in Figure 6.6.3). The radio sounds clear and loud, as we hear only the unprocessed channel of the file.

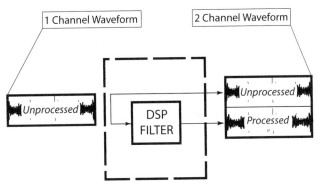

FIGURE 6.6.2 *Preparing a multichannel sound file.*

When the listener leaves the room, we fade the volume of the unprocessed channel out and fade the processed channel in (see Listener Position 2 in Figure 6.6.3). The overall sound of the radio changes as it quickly becomes occluded; the unprocessed channel becomes the only channel that we hear.

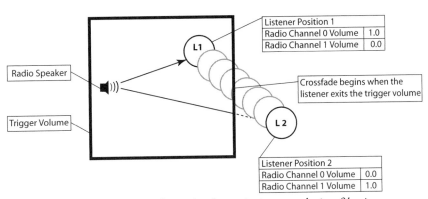

FIGURE 6.6.3 *Controlling channel volumes imitates occlusion filtering.*

The cross-fade from one channel to the other can occur over a fixed amount of time in the example and will sound extremely effective.

Constant Power Volume Curves

As we adjust the channel volumes of a multichannel file, we want the listener to hear a change in the overall sound of the file, but not be aware that we are substituting sounds. We hide this substitution by ensuring that the total power outputted by all the channels at any given time is equal to the maximum power that can be outputted by just a single channel on its own (see Figure 6.6.4). When implementing this gem, the reader should ensure that the total power of the channels remains constant.

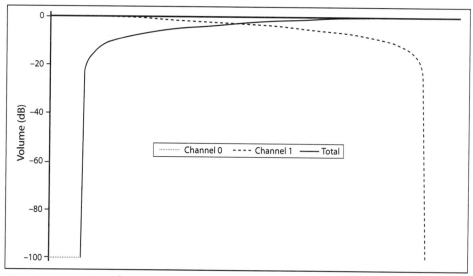

FIGURE 6.6.4   *Two channel volumes maintain a constant total power.*

Advanced Control of Channel Volumes

In our simple example, the extent of our volume control was limited to a fixed-rate cross-fade that began when the listener exited a trigger volume. It's a very simple and effective technique that particularly suits cases where the listener will cross a well-defined threshold from one environment to another.

A more subtle effect is created by mapping the listener's progress across a threshold to the progress of the cross-fade. This way, the cross-fade reflects other factors, such as how fast the listener is moving.

Anything can be used to control the volumes of channels, not just listener position. For example, listener health may control the volumes.

Multichannel Files and DirectSound

ON THE CD

Using DirectSound to implement this gem requires some special direction. Direct-Sound does not support playing multichannel files as positional sounds. The sample code included on the *Game Programming Gems 6* CD-ROM provides wrappers for the DirectSound classes that provide this additional functionality.

Costs and Benefits

The main benefit of this technique is that it brings any imaginable effect to any target hardware. The effect can be created in absolutely any way. For example, the effect could be created naturally. Sound effects can be recorded with a several microphones at once, each in a different acoustical environment.

It would be possible to implement this technique using multiple, single-channel files instead of a single multichannel file. However, the multichannel files allow long sounds to be streamed from a disk without additional seeks.

The cost of this technique is that multiple versions of sounds are in memory and are being played at the same time. As a result, memory and hardware voices are consumed more quickly than would otherwise be the case. The technique probably can't be applied to all sounds in a game at all times. Drawing attention to a few highlighted sounds with impossible-sounding DSP effects will likely create the most dramatic results.

Conclusion

Using the technique presented in this gem, any DSP effect can be faked on any target hardware. The result is flexibility in sound direction that might be impossible to implement in other ways.

Acknowledgments

Thanks go to Bill Gates, Corinna Hagel, and Borut Pfeifer for help with this article, and to Tim Hinds for much sound programming knowledge.

NETWORK AND MULTIPLAYER

Introduction

Scott Jacobs, Virtual Heroes

scott@escherichia.net

Sometimes the concerns of the networking/multiplayer specialist never seem to change. Ample bandwidth continually appears to be just around the corner; but when approached, it often turns out to be a mirage. Either new graphics or simulation techniques require increasing amounts of data, or games are deployed to platforms like cell phones, which reset expectations of how much bandwidth and processing power are available. Thomas Di Giacomo and his coauthors present methods for saving bandwidth and processing power when dealing with 3D animation data, while still obtaining maximum performance by scaling the data to the available bandwidth and computing potential.

Massively multiplayer online games continue to be an area of great interest to game networking professionals, and the scope of concerns in this area range from the design of complex systems to getting the best usage out of a few dozen bits. This section includes gems on both scales. Viknashvaran Narayanasamy and coauthors address complex systems by describing a high-level architecture for MMOGs, with the goal of creating complex, emergent behaviors. And Yongha Kim takes aim at working with bandwidth constraints, and gives us bit-utilization suggestions while describing an MMO-suitable technique for generating systemwide, unique game object identifiers.

Without minimizing the value of previous gems, Peter Smith suggests that we leave concerns of architecture and bit usage to others, particularly in order to get up to speed quickly during the early investigational phases of a game's development. He presents an MMO-prototyping scheme where system architecture, bit utilization, and a lot of other complicated details have already been handled by taking advantage of an existing, extensible MMO system: Linden Lab's *Second Life*®.

Design, architecture, prototyping, and development will not result in a minute of multiplayer gameplay fun if players cannot connect with each other. Complementing Jon Watte's article from *Game Programming Gems 5,* Larry Shi and Ying Sha present a gem that adds TCP to the family of protocols that can potentially be used through much of the currently available consumer NAT hardware.

The following gems address a wide variety of issues faced by game-development professionals. Whether approaching this section as a lead programmer, designer, or networking software engineer, you'll likely find a gem to help guide your thoughts or maybe to put directly to use!

7.1

Dynamically Adaptive Streaming of 3D Data for Animated Characters

Thomas Di Giacomo, HyungSeok Kim, Stephane Garchery, and Nadia Magnenat-Thalmann, MIRALab, C.U.I.; University of Geneva

thomas@miralab.unige.ch,
kim@miralab.unige.ch,
stephane@miralab.unige.ch,
thalmann@miralab.unige.ch

Chris Joslin, School of Information Technology, Carleton University, Ottawa

cjoslin@connect.carleton.ca

Introduction

While online games have been around for a long time, recent increases in network bandwidth have helped them become exponentially more popular. The size of games can now range from tens of concurrent users to hundreds of thousands in some cases, and this represents a large amount of 3D-data usage. Due to its bulk, exchange of 3D data has been limited, as most online games use prestored 3D models rather than transmit models dynamically. This constraint puts limitations on interactivity, which is a key property of 3D content. Similar to video and audio (although 3D data is usually smaller), adapting compressed content remains one of the key techniques for squeezing down the mass of exchanged data and, consequently, the overall required bandwidth.

Based on MPEG compression algorithms applied to 3D, this article discusses how to create scalable data for interactive characters, and how to appropriately and dynamically reduce transmitted mesh and animation data over time, according to specific contexts, such as available bandwidth, number of polygons supported by the client, or the importance of the character in the scene. Not only do we seek to control the size of the data to be sent with respect to visual quality, but we'll also attempt to control the rendering complexity for real-time performances with more characters, and for real-time performances on lightweight devices such as PDAs.

Background and Related Methods

First, we need some multiresolution methods to represent geometry and animation data in an adaptive way. Then, with this scalable content, adaptation and decision-making mechanisms will select the appropriate resolution dynamically according to a given context. We discuss below a few approaches used to represent multiresolution geometry and animation, as well as look at existing work in encoded data adaptation (particularly related to MPEG compression, where lots of activities focus on stream adaptation).

Local Computer Graphics LOD

From computer graphics academic literature, we could enumerate an impressive list of work on Level of Detail (LOD) for geometry, such as that used by [Hoppe96] to create multiresolution models. It consists of refining or simplifying the polygonal mesh according to certain criteria, such as the distance to the camera, in order to save computations during the rendering, and/or to meet some timing requirements. [Garland97] also proposes a method based on error quadrics to simplify surfaces of 3D objects. Some of these geometrical methods are even specifically geared toward characters; for instance, [Fei99] proposes LOD for virtual human body meshes, and [Seo00] for virtual human face meshes. The main consideration for characters (over other objects) is to retain a specific number of polygons at the joints (or near control points for the facial animation) to preserve a good quality when animated. Another approach for simplifying the real-time rendering of numerous characters is to convert 3D objects to 2D, as done with imposters by [Tecchia02].

Adaptation of Encoded Media

Though 3D data is often stored locally, stream-based delivery is a more appropriate solution for networked games. Therefore, data compression becomes a key component of the game system. We are not detailing compression schemes here; we are using standardized ones that provide tools and generic formats to allow for interoperable content. Several standards coexist for 3D graphics: VRML, X3D, and U3D. Even if MPEG was originally focused on video and audio, 3D graphics is now receiving a great deal of attention with BiFS (Binary Format for Scenes) integrated into the core of MPEG specifications (see [Walsh02] for details on MPEG-4), as well as with efforts by the SNHC (Synthetic and Natural Hybrid Coding) group to define an Animation Framework eXtension (AFX) in the standard. This extension specifies bone-based animation, as detailed in [Preda04], while facial animation is included in MPEG-4 systems specifications. So we finally base this article on MPEG for the following reasons: uncompressed 3D representation in MPEG-4 is rougly similar VRML; MPEG provides a complete media framework and effective compression schemes; and MPEG-7 and MPEG-21 allow semantics for media objects, as well as processing mechanisms, such as their adaptation.

Bitstream adaptation is paramount when considering 3D graphics delivery, as it offers a wide range of possibilities, such as driving single-content delivery toward multiple devices, or scaling the content complexity and size according to a specific context (e.g., network bandwidth or terminal capabilities). Bitstream adaptation requires a description of the scalable encoded data for bitstream modifications, descriptions often done by using gBSDL (generic Bitstream Description Language) explained by [Amielh02]. Adaptation can be processed for many different types of media, such as audio in [Aggarwal01] or video in [Kim03], with the specificity of each media considered in order to ensure an optimum adaptation, both for the quality of content provided and for the accuracy of the adaptation. Work on scalable 3D graphics in that direction has started to emerge—for example, [Van Raemdonck02] and [Di Giacomo04].

Preparation and Production of Scalable 3D Data

In this section, we discuss how scalable geometric and animation data can be prepared. This is the first needed step to be able to adapt data encoded from those scalable representations.

Scalable Representation of Mesh

We devise a method of adaptation using a clustered hierarchical model. The premise involves clustering all the data so that a specific complexity can be obtained by simply choosing a set of clusters. From the complex mesh $M_n(V_n, F_n)$ where V_n is a set of vertices and F_n is a set of faces, it is sequentially simplified to $M_{n-1}, \ldots, M_1, M_0$.

A multiresolution model of this simplification sequence has, or at least is able to generate, a set of vertices V and faces M, where union is denoted as "+" and intersection is denoted as "-":

$$V = \sum_{i=0}^{n} V_i, \quad M = \sum_{i=0}^{n} M_i \qquad (7.1.1)$$

V and M can be partitioned into a set of clusters. The first type is a set of vertices and faces that are removed from a mesh of the level i to make a mesh of the level $i-1$, denoted by $C(i)$. The other type is a set of vertices and faces that are newly generated by simplification, denoted by $N(i)$. Hence, a level i mesh is as follows:

$$M_i = M_0 + (\sum_{j=1}^{i} C(j) - \sum_{j=1}^{i} N(j)) \qquad (7.1.2)$$

There are many simplification operators, including decimation, region merging, and subdivision; here we use half-edge collapsing operators (see Figure 7.1.1) and quadric error metrics (see [Garland97]).

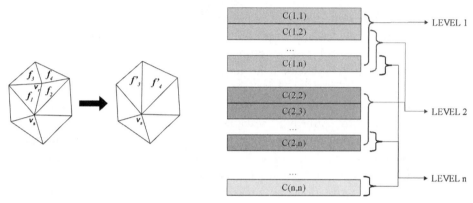

FIGURE 7.1.1   *Illustration of edge collapsing (left) and the cluster structure (right).*

Via an edge-collapsing operator, an edge (v_r, v_s) is collapsed to the vertex v_s. From the example in Figure 7.1.1, faces f_1, f_2 are removed from the mesh, and faces f_3, f_4 are modified into f'_3, f'_4. The clusters are defined as

$$C(i) = (f_1, f_2, f_3, f_4) \qquad (7.1.3)$$

and

$$N(i) = (f'_3, f'_4) \qquad (7.1.4)$$

Evaluating Equation 7.1.2 still requires relatively complex operations: set unions and intersections. From the properties of the simplification, it is ensured that $N(i)$ is a subset of unions of $M_0, C(1), \ldots, C(i-1)$. Using this property, the cluster $C(i)$ is sub-clustered into a set of $C(i,j)$, which belongs to $N(j)$, where $j > i$ and $C(i,i)$, which does not belong to any $N(j)$. It is the same for M_0 where $M_0 = C(0)$. Thus, the level-i mesh is represented with the following equation, which requires simple set selections.

$$M_i = \sum_{k=0}^{i} (C(k,k) + \sum_{j=i+1}^{n} C(k,j)) \qquad (7.1.5)$$

The last step is the ordering to reduce the number of selections during the adaptation process. Ordering the vertex data is rather straightforward, because the edge-collapsing operator (v_i,v_s) ensures that every $C(i)$ has a single instance of the vertex, v_i $C(i,i)$. By ordering vertices of $C(i,i)$ in the ascending order of i, the vertex data for level i can be selected by a continuous block of data, $v_0, v_1, \ldots, v_i$. For the indexed face set, each $C(i)$ is ordered with $C(i,j)$ in the ascending order of j. Thus, an adaptation to level i consists of at most $3i+1$ selections, or at most $2n$ removals, where n is the number of levels.

So far we have described the process using only the vertex positions and face information. In the mesh, there are other properties that have to be taken into account, such as normal, color, and texture coordinates. Because these properties inherently belong to vertices, a process similar to that used on vertex positions is applied. Exceptional cases are: 1) two or more vertices that use the same value for a property, or 2) a single vertex that has more than two values for the same property. In both cases, there is a unique mapping from a pair of vertex/face to a property's value. The properties for the face/vertices of cluster $C(i)$ have a mapping from (v_i, f_j) where $v_i \in C(i)$. If a property p belongs to more than one vertex, such as $(v_i, f_1) \rightarrow p$ and $(v_j, f_2) \rightarrow p$, p is assigned to the cluster of $C(j)$, where $j < i$. By ordering this, p remains active as long as there is one vertex that has p as its property. Therefore, we have a valid set of clusters for each level i.

The right-hand side of Figure 7.1.1 shows the idea of clustering. Each cluster has a set of vertices and vertex properties, such as vertex normal, colors, and texture coordinates. Along with vertex information, the cluster has a set of indexed faces, normal faces, color faces, and texture faces. Also, each cluster can consist of subsegments with their own materials and textures. Each level is selected by choosing blocks of clusters.

In real applications, it is often not necessary to generate all levels of detail. Differences by a few polygons do not usually result in significant differences either in performance or in quality. By using the proposed representation, the modeling system is able to generate a set of levels with any combination required by the model and application, and this scalable representation of geometry can be encoded using MPEG compression schemes.

Preparation of Scalable Animation Data

After geometry, we now need to represent our facial and body animations with scalability to allow for their adaptation when encoded.

For facial animation, we use the MPEG-4 Facial Animation Parameters (FAPs) to drive a facial animation engine. These parameters only provide information about the displacement of feature points of the face (e.g., for deforming the face shape when animated), though they do not provide any information for the displacement of neighboring vertices. From the FAP information, you can define each displacement—that is, which vertices are influenced and in which directions, according to FAP intensity.

There are basically two ways to animate faces with FAP information. The first is with a piece-wise linear interpolation of the FAP control points. This technique requires low computational cost during animation, but the modeling stage is rather complex, since one has to define an influence region for each feature point of the face. In addition, this needs to be done for each model and for each level of detail.

Another technique is to use geometric deformation algorithms to compute an FAP's influence (see [Magnenat-Thalmann04] Chapter 6, for details). This technique allows for an automatic processing of influenced vertices according to Facial Definition Parameters (FDP). In a few seconds, the facial animation engine is able to animate a facial model with only this information and produce a Facial Animation Table (FAT) describing influences of FAP points and interpolation information—and at runtime. The FAT is automatically constructed from the high-resolution model. Since the vertices of the model were ordered by FDP and its influences, we can easily extract the corresponding FAT information from a high-level FAT table for each model; therefore, only the corresponding part of the global FAT table is then transmitted to the client.

Different areas on the face are predefined, with different levels of detail for each of these areas. A high-resolution animated face is shown in Color Plate 14. The different parts of the face, shown in Figure 7.1.2 and Color Plate 15, are initially specified. Later on we will discuss in more detail the different Level of Articulation (LOA) values for the face before introducing the applications of these definitions—such as in networked games.

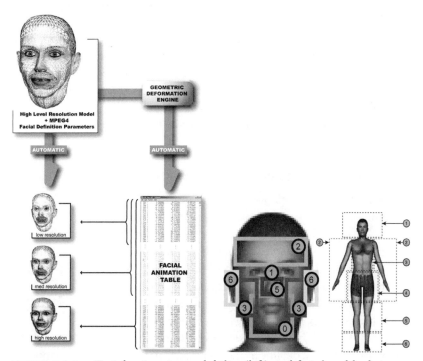

FIGURE 7.1.2 *Facial animation scalability (left) and facial and body interest zones for adaptation (right).*

The face is segmented into different interest zones, as shown in Figure 7.1.2. This segmentation makes it possible to group the FAPs according to their influence zones with regard to deformation. For each zone, we also define different levels of complexity. The zone segmentation is based on MPEG-4 FAP grouping, although we have grouped the tongue and inner/outer lips together, because these displacements are very much linked. The zones are defined as shown in Table 7.1.1.

Note that the LOA does not influence the head rotation value. Depending on the user's interest, we can further increase or reduce complexity in specific zones. For example, a specific scene in the game based on speech requires precise animation around the area of the lips and less animation in other parts of the face. In this case, the complexity can be reduced to a very low level for the zones containing eyeballs, eyebrows, nose, and ears zones, and have a medium level for the cheek zones, and a very high level in the jaw zone.

Table 7.1.1 Facial Elementary Zones: Listed are zones from which one can derive global zones, such as "eyes" composed of elementary zones 2 + 3, or "lower part" composed of 1 + 4 + 5, or "all."

Elementary Zone	Number of Joints	Description
1	31	Jaw (jaw, chin, lips, and tongue)
2	12	Eyeballs (eyeballs and eyelids)
3	8	Eyebrow
4	4	Cheeks
5	3	Head rotation
6	4	Nose
7	4	Ears

Four different levels of complexity are defined for facial animation (see Table 7.1.2), with the direct hierarchy as defined for the body below, but based on the FAP influence according to the desired complexity or game context. Two different paths can be followed to reduce the level of complexity: The first consists of grouping FAP values together (i.e., all upper lip values can be grouped into one value), and the second is a removal of feature points already influenced by neighboring facial features.

Table 7.1.2 Predefined Levels of Articulation Profiles for Facial Animation

Level of Articulation	Number of FAPs	Description
Very low	14	Suppressing unimportant FAP and full symmetry
Low	26	No symmetry and group medium-level FAPs together
Medium	44	Group equivalent FAP values together two by two
High	68	All FAP values

Finally, adapted FAP streams can be used in two different ways. The first is by decoding the stream and reconstructing all FAP values according to the level of articulation rules. In this case, we have just reduced the bitstream. The second way consists of also simplifying the deformation processing. In MPEG-4 facial animation engines, deformations are computed for each FAP value and they are grouped. To reduce that processing, the adapted FAP stream can be directly used by the deformation engine by explicitly designing the deformation area for each level of complexity. This work of regrouping can be done automatically during the preprocessing step or be can be transmitted with the model.

For body animation, we also use MPEG to represent and compress animation data as Bone-Based Animation (BBA). BBA is generic in terms of hierarchy, but our body animation engine is based on the H-Anim 1.1 hierarchy (i.e., defining specific joints and bones for skeleton-driven animation).

Body animation is commonly performed by skeleton-based animation where the hierarchical structure of the bones and joints allows a rather straightforward level of complexity that corresponds to the level of depth in this hierarchy.

Following the H-Anim specifications, LOA can be defined as needed for adaptation (see Table 7.1.3). For instance, the lower level includes shoulders and hips to enable minimalist motions even at this level. The medium level is also a simplification of the spine compared to the primary H-Anim definition.

Such levels of complexity are used to select an adapted level of detail for the animation of the virtual human. For instance, some virtual humans that are part of an audience in a stadium do not require a high level of articulation. Thus, using a very low LOA is for them enough; while the main player's character, who is moving, talking and is the focus of the player, requires a high level of articulation—thus using a medium or high LOA. Though it is not such a significant gain for a single virtual human, this feature provides efficient control for the animation of a whole crowd, or for adapting animations according to terminal and network capabilities.

Table 7.1.3   Predefined Level of Articulation Profiles for Body Animation

Level of Articulation	Number of Joints	Description
Very low	5	Shoulders, hips and the root joints
Low	10	Very low joints, plus neck, elbow, and knee joints
Medium	35	Low joints, plus fingers, toes and spine joints merged into a single joint
High	88	Full hierarchy—all joints

The main purpose of defining interest zones is to allow the user or game engine to select the parts they are most interested in, as shown in Table 7.1.4. For instance, if the character is presenting a complete script on how to do cooking, but the user is only interested in listening to the presentation and not observing motions, then the animation can be adapted to either the upper body, or even just the face and the shoulders. Another example would be a tourist guide pointing at several locations, such as theaters or parks. The user may only wish to focus on the arms and hands of the presenter. The lower-level interest zones, consisting of six zones (Figure 7.1.2), can be composed into higher-level ones.

Table 7.1.4 Level of Articulation: Listed are elementary zones from which one can derive global zones, such as "upper body" composed of elementary zones 1 + 2 + 3 + 4, or "face-shoulder" composed of 1 + 2 + 3, or "lower body," or "all."

Elementary Zone	Number of Joints	Description
1	2	Face only
2	49	Right and left arms
3	25	Torso
4	4	Pelvis
5	4	Legs
6	4	Feet

Adaptive Delivery Driven by Context

The previous section presented the construction of scalable data for geometry and animation of characters. Figure 7.1.3 and Color Plate 16 illustrate one specific use case of such scalable content; now we'll explain the adaptation process itself.

Stream adaptation basically consists of modifications of the bitstream when being delivered. Given a bitstream containing the highest resolution of content, we can reduce it to meet network or client constraints, as illustrated by Figure 7.1.4.

The principles of adaptation in MPEG-21 are based on XML schemas (gBDSL, as introduced previously) used to describe the encoded data. Your encoder, outputting a compressed geometry or animation, will also generate a gBSD file that describes the produced stream. One example for a two-frame body animation is included on the accompanying CD-ROM. The adaptation engine can then transform the bitstream with an appropriate XML style sheet (also on the CD-ROM) that contains information on how to adapt the stream according to a set of parameters passed by the adaptation engine. These parameters define a given context for the adaptation to occur, and can consist of a variety of things, such as the network bandwidth, the player frame rate, and so forth. The information and methods for adapting the bitstream must be in line with the scalability defined in the previous sections, since the schema is defined on a low level in order to take into account those scalable features.

ON THE CD

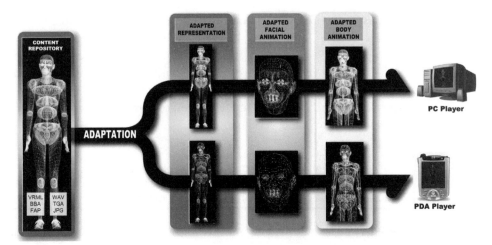

FIGURE 7.1.3   *Data flow with adaptation from the content database to the user.*

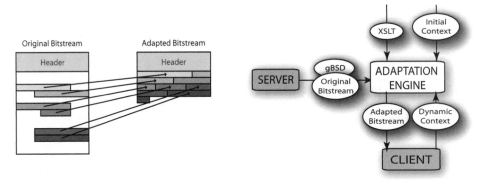

FIGURE 7.1.4   *Bitstream adaptation principle (left) and the networked architecture (right). Note that the adaptation engine can also be part of the server, or that different adaptation engines can coexist for distributed adaptation.*

The original FAP and BBA MPEG codecs do not exhibit very advanced scalability. Though the grouping of parameters for the encoding is suitable for the zones previously discussed, it is not suitable for the LOA. This means that we must define our schemas on quite a low level to perform adaptation with LOA.

What to Use as Adaptation Context

As many things as you would like! Well, we have to restrain ourselves a bit, and here we'll discuss contexts defined by client capabilities (especially rendering performance), network capacity, and user or scene preferences.

There are many different target contexts to which the mesh and animation can be adapted. The main consideration is to make sure that the mesh and animation is adapted to satisfy all contexts. In the context of the network, you could use bandwidth measurements and figures in order to determine the available capacity. The user's preferences or real-time constraints generally consist of selecting the LOD explicitly (if the application allows). The terminal's capability is the most complex, and is dependant on many factors. In this case, device benchmarking can be performed to match the client capabilities to the levels of the scalable content.

The following procedure can be used in order to approximate the level of complexity to which the content should be adapted. First, the content is executed on a standard test device at its highest resolution. The test device is expected to decode and render the content, at a suitable frame rate, which provides the value F_N (greater than 25 fps, for instance). Then the test device is benchmarked under normal test conditions, which involves reducing the number of concurrently running applications to a minimum. The most appropriate benchmark is used—more than one if possible—which provides us with a value B_N. Finally, as part of the runtime execution, the target device is benchmarked (either prior to runtime or as part of the initialization process) and provides us with a value B_T. B_N and B_T should be of the same type, either for a specific matching benchmark, or a weighted sum (again with corresponding elements). We can then compute an adaptation ratio: If the target device is required to run at a value of F_T, the mesh and animation should be adapted by using a ratio R_A (you can also directly reduce the number of polygons by this factor, using the closest approximation). In all cases, we need to account for the test machine's excess and the target machine's possible limitations; we therefore use Equation 7.1.6 to compute the mesh and animation reduction ratio.

$$R_A = \frac{F_N}{F_T} \times \frac{B_T}{B_N} \times C_R \qquad (7.1.6)$$

Then, for all cases where R_A is less than 1.0, adaptation is required. For all other cases, the mesh and animation representations remain unchanged. C_R is an additional factor that can remain at 1.0, but can be used to allow the user to specify how much computational power should be taken by the processing of a specific content. An additional factor is that lots of content might be decoded and rendered on the same device at the same time—a graphics animation and audio stream, for example. Using this method, it is simple to account for two or more pieces of content on the same machine. The value C_R can also be used for the ratios attributed to each digital item as long as the sum of all C_R values is equal to 1.0. This method is quite effective, because it permits adaptation without the need to: a) comprehend the various performance factors within a computer (e.g., CPU type or frequency, which require knowledge of the hardware architecture), or b) reduce the process to a simple linear approximation.

The adaptation in terms of the network capacity is directly governed by the available bandwidth C_B, the encoded file size F_S, and the download time T (for the mesh, as it is not dynamically downloaded) that a user is prepared to wait, or which you believe is reasonable; see Equation 7.1.7.

$$\frac{C_B}{F_S} \times T = R_A \qquad (7.1.7)$$

R_A provides the ratio of the original file to the adapted file; and as the main element contributing to this size (assuming that the encoding process is well balanced) is the mesh size, for instance, then the size of the stream is reduced. Values for F_S, C_B, and even T are easily obtained, and therefore the value for R_A is also easily determined.

Finally, the adaptation process for geometry does not require additional memory other than the storage for clusters to be processed and for adapted mesh data. A "client-side adaptation" can generate a set of clusters with lower levels of detail that can be dynamically adapted during rendering time, in a way very similar to how traditional LOD systems work.

Conclusion

Our global results showed a gain of approximately 30% for general performance and 25% to 40% for the data size. The bit rate is always important in networked applications and for online games. Therefore, the size of 3D transmitted data should be considered, controlled, and reduced when possible. Adaptation is a way to achieve this. Working at a different level than compression schemes, adaptation and compression can be coupled together for better results.

Not only is stream adaptation a benefit for managing the bit rate, it also (especially in the case of 3D) provides an intelligent way to manage rendering complexity according to the client's capabilities and the requirements of the current scene to be rendered.

References

[Aggarwal01] Aggarwal, Ashish, et al., "Compander Domain Approach to Scalable AAC." *110th Audio Engineering Society Convention,* 2001.

[Amielh02] Amielh, Myriam, et al., "Bitstream Syntax Description Language: Application of XML-Schema to Multimedia Content Adaptation." International World Wide Web Conference (WWW 2002).

[Di Giacomo04] Di Giacomo, Thomas, et al., "Adaptation of Virtual Human Animation and Representation for MPEG." *Elsevier Computer & Graphics,* 2004, Vol. 28, No. 4: pp. 65–74.

[Fei99] Fei, Guangzheng, et al., "A Real-Time Generation Algorithm of Progressive Mesh with Multiple Properties." ACM Symposium on Virtual Reality Software and Technology, 1999: pp. 178–179.

[Garland97] Garland, Michael, et al., "Surface Simplification Using Quadric Error Metrics." SIGGRAPH 1997: pp. 209–216.

[Hoppe96] Hoppe, Hugues, "Progressive Meshes." SIGGRAPH 1996: pp. 99–108.

[Kim03] Kim, Jae-Gon, et al., "Content-Adaptive Utility Based Video Adaptation." IEEE International Conference on Multimedia & Expo (ICME 2003): pp. 85–94.

[Magnenat-Thalmann04] Magnenat-Thalmann, Nadia, et al., *Handbook of Virtual Human,* John Wiley & Sons, 2004.

[Preda04] Preda, Marius, et al., "Virtual Character within MPEG-4 Animation Framework eXtension." IEEE Transactions on Circuits and Systems for Video Technology, 2004, Vol. 14, No. 7: pp. 975–988.

[Seo00] Seo, Hyewon, et al., "LoD Management on Animating Face Models." IEEE Virtual Reality 2000: pp. 161–168.

[Tecchia02] Tecchia, Franco, et al., "Image-Based Crowd Rendering." IEEE Computer Graphics & Applications, 2002: pp. 36–43.

[Van Raemdonck02] Van Raemdonck, Wolfgang, et al., "Content-Adaptive Utility Based Video Adaptation." IEEE International Conference on Multimedia & Expo (ICME 2002): pp. 369–372.

[Walsh02] Walsh, Aaron, et al., *The MPEG-4 Jump-Start.* Prentice Hall PTR, 2002.

7.2

Complex Systems-Based High-Level Architecture for Massively Multiplayer Games

Viknashvaran Narayanasamy, Kok-Wai Wong, and Chun Che Fung, Murdoch University

viknash@hobbiz.com, k.wong@ieee.org, lanceccfung@ieee.org

Designing exciting Massively Multiplayer (MMP) games increasingly involves a greater level of complexity that grows exponentially along with rising expectations from game players. This is mainly due to the massively connected nature of MMP games that allows thousands of players to play the game online simultaneously. Current game architectures do not extend well to MMP games, as they are based on predetermined behavior. This gem introduces an architecture based on the emergent properties of complex systems to minimize deterministic behavior in MMP games. A bottom-up design approach that relies on heterogeneous agents, self-organization, heavy interaction, feedback, and emergence within game objects was used to design a multitiered architecture that will scale well for next-generation MMP games.

As the entire architecture is extensive and incorporates a number of common features found in other game architectures, this gem will only highlight the unique features that this architecture introduces. This gem will take a software engineering approach to provide a high-level abstraction of the architecture that will enable anyone to implement it in their MMP game.

Complex Systems and Emergence

Complex systems are highly structured systems that have a number of interacting elements that are organized into structures that vary in depth and size. These structures are subject to processes of change that cannot be described by a single rule or reduced to only one level of explanation [Kirschbaum98]. Complex systems were originally intended to study the combinatorial problems of parasitism, symbiosis, reproduction, genetics, mitosis, and survival-of-the-fittest strategies in nature and biology [Odell02]. Systems that can be studied as complex systems have a number of identifying characteristics, namely self-organizing structures, nonlinear relationships, order/chaos dynamics, and emergent properties [Kirschbaum98]. Contributors to Wikipedia [Wikipedia05] have noted that complex systems can also be distinguished by the presence of feedback loops, open environments, and indeterminate system boundaries.

Massively multiplayer games exhibit many of the properties and behaviors that can be found in industrial applications of complex systems. This can be attributed to the highly interactive environment with thousands of human and AI-based Non-Player Characters (NPCs), large persistent worlds, a nondeterministic number of game states, and multiple unpredictable inputs from human players from different socioeconomic, ethnic, and cultural backgrounds.

The game architecture based on complex systems that is presented in this gem facilitates the incorporation of some of the desirable features of massively multiplayer games that have not been possible in recent years. The architecture facilitates the creation of truly infinite worlds that exhibit emergent behavior. The unique, emergent properties of the architecture enable actions that were not originally intended in the original game design to emerge throughout the lifetime of the game. These actions introduce a level of unpredictability and randomness in game behavior that is paramount for the next generation of massively multiplayer games.

The Multitiered Architecture

The complex systems-based multitiered architecture consists of four unique tiers: the environment tier, object tier, agent tier, and overseer tier (see Figure 7.2.1). Traditional multitiered and layered architectures exhibit orthogonality between the layers or tiers to reduce coupling between the various layers/tiers. Orthogonality in this architecture is present between the environment tier and the other tiers. This was done to ensure that the stability of the environment is independent of the evolving nature of the other tiers. On the other hand, object, agent, and overseer tiers were designed to work synergistically and cohesively together to allow for increased interactivity and emergence within game objects.

The object tier consists of the component and composite layers. Emergence starts in the component layer of the object tier and propagates upward through the interaction and aggregation of component objects. The agent tier represents all game objects that have higher-level functions in the game. This includes the NPCs, human players, and other game objects that exhibit a significant level of artificial intelligence. The object tier and agent tier enable designers to make use of simple game rules for component objects, to produce organized and structured high-level behavior. The overseer tier is the last and most significant tier in the architecture. It makes use of agents to implement multiple artificial game governors that exhibit policy-based controls that have varying influences over all game objects in the game environment.

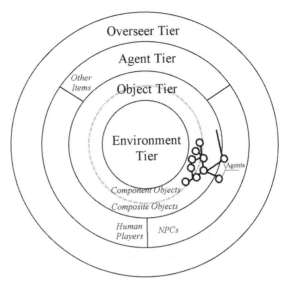

FIGURE 7.2.1   *The Multitiered architecture.*

Environment Tier

The game environment defines the global properties of the virtual game world being simulated. The environment tier includes these global properties as well as an implementation of the game engine. The *game engine* in the environment tier consists of the simulation, graphics, audio, physics and AI engines, the event and input handlers, and the resource and hardware abstraction layers. However, unlike other game architectures, direct access to the game engine resources and game data resources is disallowed. This is done to allow the objects (see Object Tier) in the MMP game to run on different client and server machines simultaneously without client-specific knowledge of the platform it is running on. This also allows the game to be implemented on different platforms (e.g., console, PC, Web, mobile, etc.), as only the implementation of the environment tier has to change for each platform. The client machine downloads only a relevant subset of objects required for the client's view of the game environment and maintains the object states to be consistent with the server. The client's environment tier communicates with the server's environment tier only to retrieve and update game data (e.g., level, graphics, etc.) during the operation of the MMP game. Figure 7.2.2 illustrates the operation of the client/server architecture.

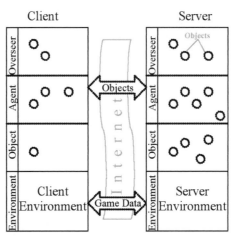

FIGURE 7.2.2   *Client/Server MMP game architecture.*

The game objects in the other tiers can interact with the environment tier only through the event handler, AI engine, and the resource abstraction layer, as shown in Figure 7.2.3. The *AI engine* employs a number of overseers (see Overseer Tier) to implement an essential set of rules to define the capabilities and the limitations of the client-specific environment. It also implements an essential set of game rules for things like in-game economics, physics, and environmental boundaries. The *input handler* retrieves user inputs and generates events to let the game engine handle the inputs.

Unlike conventional game architectures, the *physics engine* is placed at the same functional level as the other engines that interface with hardware to reflect the upcoming trend of off-loading physics computation to dedicated PPUs (Physics Processing Units) [Ageia05]. The *graphics engine, audio engine,* and *game data module* mirror the functionality of their counterparts in common game architectures, so details of these functional components will not be described. The *event handler* works hand in hand with the simulation engine to translate object and user events to admissible events for the simulation engine. The event handler also routes events as they happen to objects that have subscribed to specific event types.

The simulation engine is synonymous to a game loop. It makes use of the Discrete-Event Simulation (DES) model [Garcia 04]. The DES model was originally designed for executing simulations in complex systems where the order of execution of events is unknown and unpredictable due to the large number of objects present. In such a scenario, the continuous simulation model used in the majority of games that rely on the sequential polling and execution of events does not preserve the causality of the system. As the simulation processes in a discrete-event simulator are executed the moment they happen, the time-order execution of events is preserved. This immedi-

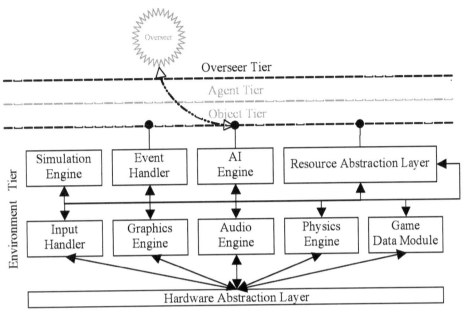

FIGURE 7.2.3 *Environment tier.*

ate execution of events also increases the sensitivity of the system's response to simulation events.

As shown in Figure 7.2.4, both the graphics and simulation processes are simultaneously executed. This allows the graphics-rendering rate to be independent of the simulation speed. This is especially realizable in the latest generation of gaming hardware architectures that support parallelism.

Events generated by the user and events generated by the program will be queued for processing. When there are no events queued, the system will go into sleep mode until preempted by new events in the queue. Dynamic simulations that require constant updates can generate periodic events with the help of the system clock to perform updates at a user-definable frequency that is independent of other simulation processes and the rendering subsystem—for example, simulation of a person constantly walking. The simulation process is ordered, and prioritization of events can occur with the aid of the queue.

Resource allocation and servicing is done through the *Resource Abstraction Layer* (RAL). It is often the case that multiple objects will concurrently seek the same resources to perform identical or different tasks. Resource allocation and prioritization in games is especially tricky, as there are real-time requirements in some resource types (e.g., graphics or networking). Simple rule-based algorithms implemented in the RAL to avoid unfair conditions will not suffice, as the continuous addition of emerging types of game objects will quickly lead to rapid explosion in the number of

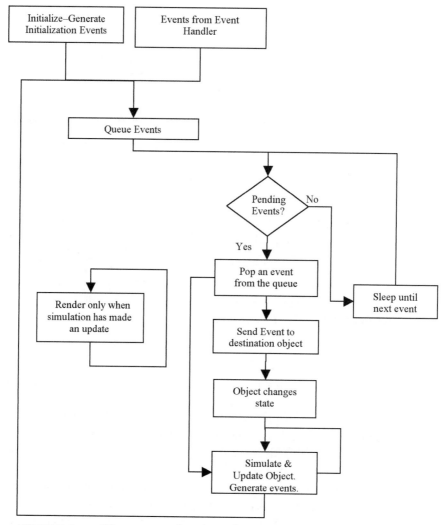

FIGURE 7.2.4   *Discrete event-based simulation engine.*

rules in this layer. To address these resource contention issues, a distributed agent algorithm was used together with *collaborative assignment agents* [Seow02].

The distributed-agent algorithm used is based on the Multi-Agent Assignment (MA[3]) algorithm by [Seow03]. In the algorithm, each game object possesses only localized knowledge of the resources it requires and performs BDI (Belief, Desire, Intention) [Geiss99] reasoning before advertising resource exchange intentions. The arbitrating agent (see Figure 7.2.5) for the particular resources required then performs arbitrations with the intentions and assigns resources accordingly. The MA[3] algorithm is highly suitable for this application because it speeds up the lengthy arbitration by

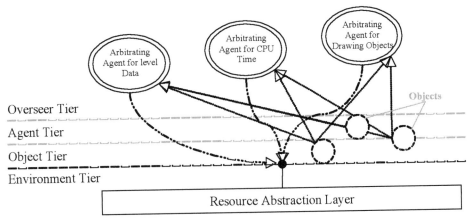

FIGURE 7.2.5 *Arbitrating agents perform collaborative resource assignment using MA³.*

making use of a heuristics selection process to choose near-optimal heuristics. Also, the algorithm allows game objects to work in parallel, retrieving resources as collaborative resource negotiations are done, using distributed, decentralized agent reasoning.

The game objects will carry out negotiations collaboratively by working out an agreement interactively that is acceptable to all agents. This is done by having each game object select and reselect different resources through proposed resource exchanges that are done in the presence of an arbitration agent. *Self-organization* is evident when each of the game objects attempts to achieve the common goal of maximizing the total number of resource-exchange intentions being serviced accordingly.

Object Tier

The object tier consists of the component and composite layers. This section will describe how emergent properties can be coded into game objects by taking a bottom-up approach to build objects upon objects, forming composite objects, and eventually intelligent agent objects that exhibit emergent behavior.

It can be said that the complexity involved in implementing a game is the result of the complex structure of game objects and the inter-relationships between them [Wilkinson93]. Designing game objects to have a varying number of operations and attributes to express a number of different relationships will easily increase the complexity involved in development when MMP games are extended to include *emerging properties*. In response to that, the architecture utilizes the composite design pattern in software engineering to implement game objects so that game objects, as well as collective structures of game objects, can be treated identically.

Design patterns are proven software engineering tools that enable the successful reuse of designs and architectures. A good reference for the composite design pattern and other design patterns is [Gamma94]. Here we make use of UML (Unified Modeling Language) class diagrams to illustrate the organization of attributes, operations, constraints, and relationships within composite objects. A good reference for UML class diagrams is [Booch98].

Many of the game objects can be viewed as components and aggregations of components that form higher-level structures or composite game objects. These objects are called "composite objects" in object-oriented programming [Rumbaugh94]. Static interconnections and behavioral interactions of components, as well as global constraints imposed on the composite objects, closely resemble the workings of complex systems and the complex systems MMP architecture in this gem [Ramazani94]. Figure 7.2.6 shows a simplified class diagram representation of how game objects were implemented as composite objects in the architecture. Composite game objects allow all the game objects to interact uniformly through recursive composition. Figure 7.2.7 illustrates the higher-level structures that form from the simpler component objects.

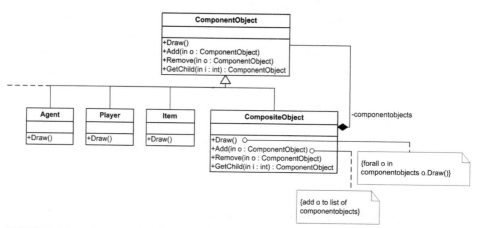

FIGURE 7.2.6   *A composite object in the MMP architecture.*

Composite objects offer a way to structure game objects and their semantic relationships in an organized manner. It is essential to identify how attributes, operations, and relationships propagate up from simple component objects to more-complex composite objects, so that effective emergence can be implemented.

Attributes and operations propagate upward in different ways. For example, when the physical weight of the object is a common attribute in all the objects, the weight of the composite object will be a sum of the weight of its components. However, in another example, when we consider the ambient lighting in a room with a lamp (i.e., the room being the composite object and the lamp being the component

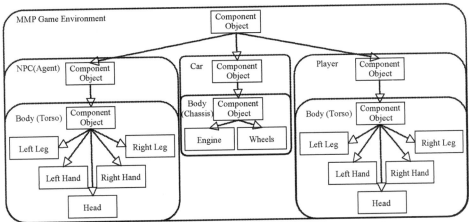

FIGURE 7.2.7   *Higher-level structures of composite game objects from other component game objects.*

object), the room inherits the ambient lighting conditions from the lamp, as it is. To distinguish between how attributes, operations, and relationships propagate from component objects, and to provide a framework to facilitate this propagation in a complex environment, it is necessary to partition the attributes, operations, and relationships by their inherent, aggregate, and emergent properties [Ramazani94].

Inherent attributes of a game object in the architecture are attributes that have logical meaning when accessed directly from the composite game object itself. From the example in Figure 7.2.8, the inherent attribute of the color of the car is selected from a pool of similar inherent attributes. In the example, the car game object derives its color from the chassis. To retrieve the inherent attribute, the operation GetColor() from the Chassis component object of the car composite object is used as it is. This makes the GetColor() operation in the car object an *inherent operation* of the composite car object, because it is an operation defined by one of its component objects. The fact that only some of the components (i.e., in this case, only the chassis) in the composite object participate in this relationship makes it an *inherent relationship*. Inherent relationships are common in the implementation of games because they are very simple to implement; however, they don't allow each of the components to contribute toward the final make-up of the higher-level structure (i.e., the car). This is of little value in the MMP game architecture, as the emergent properties in the higher-level structures can be easily predicted.

Aggregate relationships, on the other hand, are of more value to the game architecture, as the constraints in the relationship affect all component objects. In Figure 7.2.8, the *aggregate attribute* Weight and the aggregate operation GetWeight() are used to illustrate this. A new GetWeight() *aggregate operation* has to be created to derive the sum of the Weight attributes in the components of the composite car object. Similarly,

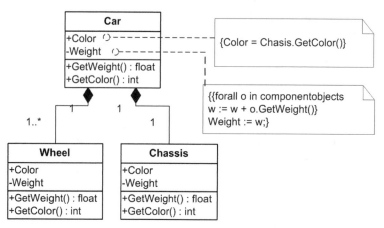

FIGURE 7.2.8   *A composite car object exhibiting inherent and aggregate properties.*

a new `Weight` aggregate attribute value is derived from this process. Changes made to the aggregate attributes in the components will require a change in the aggregate attribute of the composite object, while changes made to the aggregate attributes in the composite object might propagate down to its constituent components. It is important to understand that the new aggregation relationship emerges *only* when the component objects are associated together with a composite object (i.e., the car has weight only when the wheels, chassis, engine, etc., are attached). The aggregation relationship is highly beneficial to the complex systems-based MMP game architecture. However, with aggregate relationships, new behaviors emerge from the aggregation of existing properties of the component objects, but new properties do not emerge in the composite objects.

In Figure 7.2.9, when the `Car` composite object enlists a new `Engine` component object, new *emergent attributes* of speed and direction are introduced. The `move()` operation that appears out of this *emergent relationship* is then termed an *emergent operation*. Emergent attributes are unique, as they identify specific properties that characterize the composite object as a whole and not as just a combination of its parts. The emergent operation, on the other hand, is unique, because it introduces a new operation that does not rely on the component objects. For example, the car is capable of movement only if the engine, wheels, chassis, and other relevant parts are present.

Emergent relationships make the implementation of a complex systems-based MMP architecture feasible, as they support the bottom-up creation of game objects. Emergent relationships enable the encapsulation of the components of the composite objects, as client objects only interact with the composite object that exhibits emergent properties. Emergent relationships reduce the complexity involved in development, because they enable developers to treat composite objects as if they were individual objects.

However, the challenge in this architecture is to maintain the functional validity of the emergent properties during gameplay. This is done by ensuring that the func-

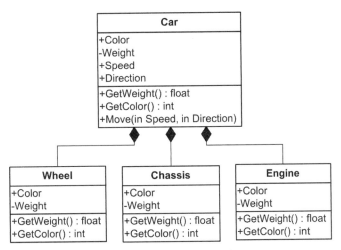

FIGURE 7.2.9 *A composite car object exhibiting emergent properties.*

tional meaning of the emergent relationships between component and composite objects are valid. As shown in Figure 7.2.10, this can be easily implemented as a table of emergent relationships. For example, if the engine of a car is damaged after hitting a wall, the particular relationship can be marked as invalid, and access to the emergent properties of Speed, Direction, and Move() can be denied. The observer design pattern can then be used in conjunction with the emergent relationship table to implement an Observer object for each component. The Observer object maintains a one-to-many dependency between objects, so that changes in the component observed will be communicated to the appropriate composite objects [Gamma94].

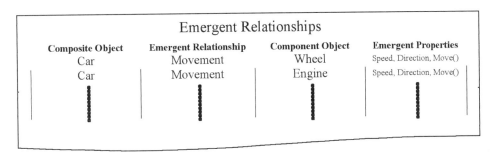

FIGURE 7.2.10 *The emergent relationship table.*

Agent Tier

The agent tier hosts the NPCs, human players, and other game objects that exhibit a significant level of artificial intelligence in the MMP architecture. Each agent object embodies a micro game engine (see Figure 7.2.11) that contains attributes of the agent and agent-specific routines of the game engine. Conceptually, each agent stores its own game data within itself. The actual implementation differs, as game data and other resources are pooled together and stored in a central location to facilitate efficient memory management. Initially, agents negotiate for resources through the arbitration agents. After resources are allocated, the agents communicate directly with the resource abstraction layer to access allocated resources. Resources include processes and threads to run custom game loops and operations within each agent object. An event handler in the agent object processes events routed to it by the event handler in the environment tier. Agents can create events to perform updates and other operations through the event generator. This will prompt the simulation engine or other engines to act accordingly.

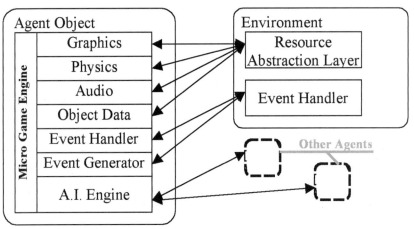

FIGURE 7.2.11   *Components of an agent.*

The AI engine communicates with other engines to effect its decision-making process (see Feedback-Based Decision-Making System). The agent tier was designed to be platform-independent so that high-level concepts found in complex systems can be easily extended to improve the MMP game experience.

Overseer Tier

The decentralized approach to control adopted by most complex systems is also present in this architecture. Agents with the means to influence the actions of other agents directly were introduced to exercise policy-based control of game objects in the virtual game environment. These agents have been termed *overseers*. The overseers play a major role in administering policies so that emergent properties in the game environment that can potentially cause the system to behave absurdly are removed.

However, great care must be taken to ensure that the policies introduced are not overly dominant so as to not suppress emergence.

Multiple overseers allow different policies from different policymakers to affect different player niche markets. The segregation and grouping of players can be done in many ways. Grouping can be done by cultural diversity to allow overseers to ensure that cultural values are represented faithfully. It can also be done by age group to prevent certain content from reaching younger players. To allow multiple individual policymakers to influence the behavior of agents, and to sustain the many-to-many relationship in the complex environment, overseers are used to influence the behavior of agents to varying degrees.

In Figure 7.2.12, the overseers' influence on other game objects decreases with increasing spatial differences. NPC E is largely affected by Overseer 1's game policies and partially affected by Overseer 2's game policies. NPC F is partially affected by both overseers' policies. NPC D is only affected by Overseer 2's policies. The spatial partitioning can occur in a number of different ways.

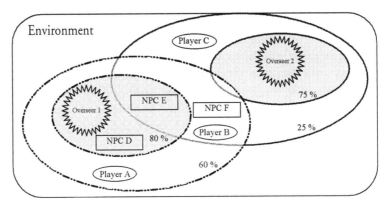

FIGURE 7.2.12   *Overseers influence agent behavior via policy-based control.*

For example, Overseer 1 can be used to govern Army A in a MMORTS, while Overseer 2 can govern Army B. Both overseers will then implement policies that are common to both armies. When a battle occurs between both armies, a spatial partitioning can be made with the length of service of each soldier (i.e., agent) to determine the probability of defection for each soldier. As the physical distance between the overseers becomes increasingly smaller (when the armies approach each other), each of the overseers will attempt to force agents on the opposing team to defect.

In another example, overseers can be used to implement in-game economic policies. We might then observe that Player B's economic model is governed more by Overseer 1 than Overseer 2, because Player B falls in between an influence level of 60%–80% from Overseer 1, in contrast to the 25%–75% influence level from Overseer 2.

Other game rules have also been implemented as overseer policies. These include policies to encourage fair play, prevent collusion between players, track abnormal behavior, and employ cheat detection.

Feedback-Based Decision-Making System

The *feedback-based decision-making system* is part of the AI engine in the agents and overseers. Most game designs have a feedback system in place to allow agents in the game to make decisions based on only the current game state at the time the decision is made. This architecture is rigid and supports few evolving characteristics for the game objects, as they are only influenced by non-evolving game rules. There have been many efforts to break this rule-based paradigm. Machine learning [Alexander02] and neural networks [Manslow02] have been used to provide some level of randomness in systems. The feedback model used in this architecture, when used in unison with these techniques, improves the emergent behavior of the system. In the feedback-based agent-agent interaction model presented in Figure 7.2.13, agent behavior is no longer influenced by just its AI engine and feedback from its actions, but is also influenced by the actions of other agents, who are in turn influenced by other agents, thus introducing *cross-term inducing features* [LeBlanc00] into the environment.

The game state holds the state of all attributes in the virtual world. When the agents make decisions, they require a view of the current state of the world, the external inputs that triggered the decision-making process, and the responses to similar actions taken by other agents. When heterogeneous agents with varying decision-making processes interact with each other, the unpredictability of the decisions that are made increases.

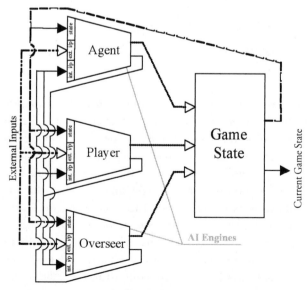

FIGURE 7.2.13   *A feedback decision-making model.*

It is assumed that human players learn only from the behaviors of other agents in addition to the game responses to their actions, just like the other agents in the architecture. However, this is not entirely true, as human players also take into account their real-world experiences before making decisions. This allows a form of natural randomness to emerge in the virtual game environment, as human responses are also fed back into the system. Overseers are also part of the feedback model. Their main role is to allow only desirable agent behavior to propagate among other agents over time. There are a number of methods to implement the feedback-based decision-making model in Figure 7.2.13. The one used in the MMP architecture is quite complex and beyond the scope of this gem. [Norlig00] and [Rogova03] offer insight into these particularly complex decision-making processes. [Evans02] presents a much simpler architecture that makes use of BDI (Belief-Desire-Intention) reasoning [Geiss99], together with a perceptron model that make use of the weighted average of the feedback and inputs received for effective decision making.

Conclusion

Developing massively multiplayer games that can present players with new and interesting challenges, behavior, and content is not a trivial task. The architecture presented in this gem can be used as a foundation to develop online games that exhibit the emergent properties and behavior that are much needed by next-generation massively multiplayer games.

References

[Ageia05] Ageia, "A White Paper: Physics, Gameplay and the Physics Processing Unit." March 2005. Available online at *http://www.ageia.com/pdf/wp_2005_3_physics_gameplay.pdf.*

[Alexander02] Alexander, Thor, "GoCap: Game Observation Capture." *AI Programming Wisdom,* Charles River Media, 2002.

[Booch98] Booch, Grady, *The Unified Modeling Language User Guide.* Addison Wesley, 1998.

[Evans02] Evans, Richard, "Varieties of Learning." *AI Programming Wisdom,* Charles River Media, 2002.

[Gamma94] Gamma, Erich, et al., *Design Patterns.* Addison-Wesley Longman, 1994.

[Garcia04] Garcia, Inmaculada, Ramon Molla, and Toni Barella, "GDESK: Game Discrete Event Simulation Kernel." *Proceedings of the 12th International Conference in Central Europe on Computer Graphics, Visualization and Computer Vision 2004* (WSCG 2004). Available online at *http://wscg.zcu.cz/wscg2004/Papers_2004_Full/E67.pdf.*

[Geiss99] Geiss, W., *Multiagent System: A Modern Approach to Distributed Artificial Intelligence.* The MIT Press, 1999.

[Kirschbaum98] Kirschbaum, David, "Introduction to Complex Systems." October 1998. Available online at *http://www.calresco.org/intro.htm.*

[LeBlanc00] LeBlanc, Marc, "Formal Design Tools—Emergent Complexity & Emergent Narrative." *Proceedings of the Game Developer's Conference* (GDC 2000).

[Manslow02] Manslow, John, "Imitating Random Variables in Behavior Using a Neural Network." *AI Programming Wisdom,* Charles River Media, 2002.

[Norlig00] Norling, E., L. Sonenberg, and R. Ronnquitst, R., "Enhancing Multi-Agent Based Simulation with Human-Like Decision Making Strategies." *Proceedings of the Second International Workshop on Multi-Agent-Based Simulation 2000,* Boston. Available online at *http://citeseer.ist.psu.edu/norling00enhancing. html.*

[Odell02] Odell, James, "Agents and Complex Systems." *Journal of Object Technology,* Vol. 1, No. 2: pp. 35–45, July 2002. Available online at *http://www.jot.fm/issues/ issue_2002_07/column3.*

[Ramazani94] Ramazani, Dunia, "Contribution of Object-Oriented Methodologies to the Specification of Complex Systems." *IEEE Engineering of Complex Computer Systems* (ECCS 1995): pp. 183–186.

[Rogova03] Rogova, G., C. Lollett, and P. Scott, "Utility-Based Sequential Decision-Making In Evidential Cooperative Multi-Agent Systems." *Proceedings of the Sixth International Conference of Information Fusion,* 2003.

[Rumbaugh94] Rumbaugh, J., "Building boxes: Composite Objects." *JOOP,* Vol. 7, No. 7: pp. 12–22, November 1994.

[Seow02] Seow, Kiam Tian and Khee Yin How, "Collaborative Assignment: A Multi-agent Negotiation Approach Using BDI Concepts." *Proceedings of the First International Conference on Autonomous Agents and Multiagent Systems: Part 1* (ICAA 2002): pp. 256–263.

[Seow03] Seow, Kiam Tian and Kok-Wai Wong, "Collaborative Assignment: Using Arbitrated Self-Optimal Initializations for Faster Negotiation." *Proceedings of the International Conference on Computational Intelligence, Robotics and Autonomous Systems* (CIRAS'03), 2003.

[Wikipedia05] Wikipedia, "Complex system." July 20, 2005. Available online at *http://en.wikipedia.org/wiki/Complex_system.*

[Wilkinson93] Wilkinson, M. and P. Byers, "The Engineering of Complex Systems," *IEEE Computing & Control Engineering Journal,* August 1993: pp. 187–189.

7.3

Generating Globally Unique Identifiers for Game Objects

Yongha Kim, Nexon Corporation

ysoyax@gmail.com

Game objects that synchronize across the network need identifiers (IDs) to discriminate each other. On increasingly common multiserver systems that have massive user access [Svarovsky02], millions of game objects are potentially generated and destroyed every minute, and some of them need to be stored in, or synchronized with, a database. If each game object is not identified uniquely, the objects may conflict, and duplication of data is possible. This results in difficult synchronization of game objects between the game servers.

Because of this problem, generation of Globally Unique Identifiers (GUIDs) is a required feature for game object systems of online games. Additionally, if these GUIDs can contain useful information, such as the type of object and the time of object creation, the GUIDs can be effectively utilized for tracing and managing objects. This article suggests a method for generating 64-bit GUIDs safely and efficiently using an ID server and object factories.

Requirements for Game Object GUIDs

First, let's look over what requirements we have for game object GUIDs and in what ways we can satisfy those requirements.

Sufficient GUID Space

To manage game objects, issuing an ID as a handle to the game object's pointer is common not just in online games, but also in standalone games. Generally, 32-bit unsigned integer data types are used, which on most platforms can create approximately 4 billion IDs. In most standalone games, this is more than enough IDs to accommodate all the objects that will be created. Some developers even divide the 32 bits into two 16-bit words, using the upper 16 bits to classify the object's type and the lower 16 bits to store the ID of actual object instance. But for online games, especially MMORPGs where persistent worlds need to be maintained, a GUID space of 4 billion isn't sufficiently large. In extreme cases, 10,000 game objects requiring GUIDs can be created every second, filling the 4 billion ID maximum within five days.

Since Nexon, Incorporated released *Nexus TK* in 1996 (the first MMORPG), they have released numerous games that require large numbers of unique object identifiers. Some of them used 32-bit IDs; and in time periods that ranged from a few months to three years, these games exhausted their entire 32-bit space. Some that used 64-bit IDs also exhausted their potential space when bits were improperly utilized. When ID systems filled up during service, it was necessary to change ID-issuing methods and replace every ID issued in the past, which was really painful. It was realized that when issuing IDs, a secure space was needed that could be used for at least 10 years.

Efficiency

Creating a 128-bit GUID with compounded time or a MAC address is already widely known [ITU-T X.667]. However, using 16 bytes for an ID is expensive in processing, persistent storage space, and network bandwidth. In addition, existing 128-bit GUID creation methods are too complicated to use in object factories expected to produce 10,000 objects per second. For game object IDs, there needs to be a more affordable data type and simple creation methods.

Globally Unique Characteristics

Since game objects move and synchronize across numerous systems in online games, IDs that are locally unique on the creating system can clash during synchronization. If two different game objects own the same ID, different parts of the system may be using different object properties or even entirely different object types in their processing! The real problem here is that when those errors occur, they are very difficult to detect and even harder to fix.

Let's remember the following requirements of a good GUID system:

- Uniqueness of past and future IDs must be guaranteed.
- Uniqueness of IDs created by different object factories must be guaranteed.
- If IDs are synchronized across databases or systems, the uniqueness of the ID must be guaranteed across those databases and consistently refer to the same game object.

Information About Objects

An ID that contains information about the game object it identifies offers a number of advantages over one that doesn't. For example, in most circumstances, system logs only write IDs, and not additional information about the game object itself. Semantic information in an ID can increase the usefulness of these logs in diagnosing errors. It can also be helpful for data-mining trends, such as item popularity and other user-influenced emergent properties of the persistent world. Examples of information that could be contained within an ID are creation time, the factory from which it was created, and the type of game object.

Generating GUIDs

Now we explain how to generate 64-bit GUIDs that satisfy the requirements above. As shown in Figure 7.3.1, the 64-bit GUID is constructed from two 32-bit parts that are created by separate processes. The upper 32-bit time tag is generated by a globally owned system called the "ID server" and is then supplied to the object factory. The object factory generates the lower 32-bit serial number. The time tag and serial number are combined to create the final 64-bit GUID.

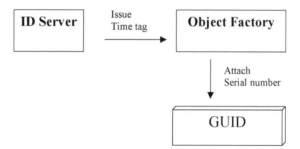

FIGURE 7.3.1   *GUID generation. A global ID server generates a time tag and supplies it to the object factory. A serial number is then generated by the object factory, which is combined with the time tag, and the final 64-bit GUID is issued.*

While the time tag's uniqueness is guaranteed globally, the local uniqueness of the serial number completes the final global GUID. Also, the ID server takes responsibility for the time tag's generation, and object factories bear responsibility for generation of serial numbers. As a result, the structure becomes simple, roles are clear, and managing ID generation is efficient.

Generating Time Tags

As shown in Figure 7.3.2, time tags are formed with 20-bit time stamps and 12-bit chunk numbers. Time stamps use January 1, 2005 as 0x00001. The value is incremented every 10 minutes and can be used for 20 years.

$$0 \times \underline{\text{T T T T T}} \,\underline{\text{C C C}}$$

20bits   12bits

T : Time stamp

C : Chunk number

FIGURE 7.3.2   *Time tag formation. In hexadecimal notation, T is the time stamp, C is the chunk number.*

If the game is expected to be in service even longer, lowering granularity so the time stamp is increased every 20 minutes will allow you to use it for 40 years. The chunk number is the cumulative count of time tags issued with the same time stamp. It increases every time an object factory asks for a time tag from the ID server. When the time stamp increments, the chunk number resets to 0x000.

Using the above method will allow the generation of 4,096 unique time tags every 10 minutes for 20 years. It is important that time tags be globally unique, so there should be only one ID server issuing them. If that is difficult in reality, one solution is to reserve some bits from the chunk number and use them as a unique identifier for each ID server.

Generating Serial Numbers

The serial number is issued from object factories and is composed of 8 bits for object type, 8 bits of reserved portion, and 16 bits of instance number (see Figure 7.3.3). The object type bits allow the GUID to reflect the type of game object to which the GUID refers. You can assign object types for every class of game object, but it's not necessary. In MMORPGs, the most troubling, frequently generated game objects are items, so it may be helpful to manage these by subdividing them, even if they share the same class. The reserved portion is for dealing with exceptions or future requirements. If not needed, it can hold the object factory's unique number or type.

$$0 \times \underline{\text{O O}} \,\underline{\text{R R}} \,\underline{\text{I I I I}}$$

8bits   8bits   16bits

O : Object type

R : Reserved

I : Instance number

FIGURE 7.3.3   *Serial number generation. In hexadecimal notation, C is the object type, R is reserved, and I is the instance number.*

The instance number, like the time tag's chunk number, is a value increased every time a serial number has been issued. When an object factory acquires a new time tag from the ID server, the instance number resets to zero. If there is a separate instance number counter for each type of game object, object factories can generate $n \times 65536$ serial numbers with one time tag, where n is the number of object types.

Handling Exceptions

A variety of problems can arise with a global GUID system if needs are not properly anticipated and handled, including overflow and security issues. Here we briefly discuss how such problems can be addressed.

Generating Temporary IDs for Use in Client Object Factories

A game player's client might have object factories to replicate (synchronize) and control game objects, but for security reasons, the client's object factories usually shouldn't have the authority to create new game objects that can affect the global state. Sometimes, though, there's a need to make temporary game objects that do not synchronize with other processes—for example, to manage the UI or respond to local events with a game object. Giving the object factory restricted authorization to generate IDs would be one solution. For these types of game objects, set the time tag's time stamp to 0x00000 and declare the serial number's object type as different from the global objects that need synchronization.

Chunk Number Overflow

Chunk number overflow occurs when the chunk number reaches 0xFFF. It occurs when object factories exhaust their instance numbers too rapidly, or when there are too many object factories requesting time tags from the ID server. It's important that this exception never occurs; and if necessary, the number of object factories accessing the ID server should be restricted. For example, the normal users' client object factories should not access the ID server. The number of object factories using time tags supplied by the ID server should probably be kept under 100.

If this exception occasionally cannot be avoided, increase the time stamp and reset the chunk number. If the time stamp was already incremented when the appropriate time comes to update it, then it's not necessary to increase it again.

Instance Number Overflow

Object factories can only combine serial numbers with given time tags, so when the instance number reaches the maximum, no more GUIDs can be generated. When this happens, object factories can request a new time tag from the ID server. This process may not be instantaneous, so to generate GUIDs right away, use the reserved portion of the serial number for the instance number overflow. To prevent this, when object factories exceed a certain instance number, for example 0x8000, they can preacquire the next time tag from the ID server.

Conclusion

Naive generation of IDs isn't much of a problem, but designing an ID-issuing system that doesn't have to be modified during service is a little tricky. We hope that our experience, learned through mistakes, comes in handy for you.

References

[ITU-T X.667] ISO/IEC 9834-8:2004 Information Technology, "Procedures for the operation of OSI Registration Authorities: Generation and Registration of Universally Unique Identifiers (UUIDs) and their use as ASN.1 Object Identifier Components." ITU-T Rec. X.667, 2004.

[Svarovsky02] Svarovsky, Jan, "Minimizing Latency in Real-Time Strategy Games." *Game Programming Gems 3,* Charles River Media, 2002.

7.4

Massively Multiplayer Online Prototype Utilizing *Second Life* for Game Concept Prototyping

Peter A. Smith,
University of Central Florida

peter@smithpa.com

Introduction

With the introduction of Massively Multiplayer Online Games (MMOGs), the size and complexity of the average game is becoming increasingly larger as players demand greater and more-immersive experiences within these virtual worlds. With the new subscription-based service model being utilized by most of these games, the constant infusion of funding should be creating the perfect environment for creativity and innovation to flourish. However, this is not the case. The Catch-22 of MMOGs is that they are expensive to develop and maintain, and therefore publishers are becoming ever more cautious about how they invest money into these projects. So, how does a developer without an MMOG infrastructure prototype their new innovative approach to the MMOG genre without already having significant financial backing? They can leverage the technology of other companies, such as Linden Labs's MMOG environment *Second Life*.

Why Use *Second Life*?

Second Life, at its core, is a MMOG environment. *Second Life* uses "Linden Dollars" to fund its internal economy and provides players with a unique experience unlike most other MMOGs. The main feature that sets *Second Life* apart from its more commercialized counterparts is that the world relies on user-created content—so much so, that Linden Labs decided to allow users to be able to keep Intellectual Property (IP) rights to the content they create within the world [Ondrejka04a]. This is virtually never seen in the game development community. Most companies even retain the rights to mods created with their software. This strategy has helped Linden Labs maintain constant growth in a crowded field of fledgling MMOGs. *Second Life* hit 40,000 users in August of 2005 [SecondLife05b]. See Figure 7.4.1 for a graphical representation of where *Second Life* stands in the market.

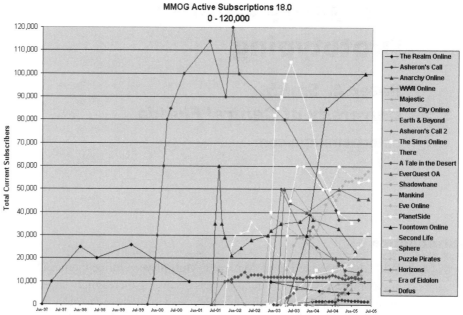

FIGURE 7.4.1   *MMOG active subscriptions [Woodcock05].*

Second Life even provides the economic mechanisms for the creator to buy, sell, give, or trade their items without usurping any control of the process. This feature has led to a much more consistent economic system than what is found in other popular MMOGs. At the time of this writing, every thousand Linden Dollars are worth about four dollars on the Gaming Open Market [GOM05]. More detailed information, such as the current rate, can be found at *www.gamingopenmarket.com*. This has led to a very unique, waking dream feel. *Second Life* has become a place where you never know what to expect next. Of course, *Second Life* is not the only MMOG to provide tools for user-created content.

Available Alternatives

Some available alternatives to using *Second Life* are *There* and *Active Worlds*. *There* (*www.there.com*) was launched late in 2003 and has many of the same benefits as

Second Life. Users are able to create their own content in *There.com.* The drawback is that content needs to be run through an approval process, which could eat up valuable development time. This is to ensure that inappropriate content is not put into the world. *Second Life* does not have this limitation. Consequently, *There.com* seems more like *The Sims* than *Second Life* [Book05].

Active Worlds (www.activeworlds.com) has a longer history than most MMOGs. Starting in 1997, *Active Worlds* has gained a lot of ground in the academic community. The main draw is the ability to develop your own world that stands on its own server. Of course, the pricing model for that is similar to any dedicated server pricing. In this model you are able to create content in your own world or universe with only approved players accessing the content. While this helps add a level of privacy not found in *Second Life,* it also removes the benefit of having "built-in" game testing performed by the public. The number of users available in a virtual world is important because they will be able to beta-test creations [Book05].

When evaluating options for MMOG prototyping, a great place to find more information is the Virtual Worlds Review. You can consult it online at *www.virtual worldreview.com* to get the most up-to-date information. A brief inspection will reveal that currently, *Second Life* has a broad range of powerful features and user benefits that make it stand out as the best choice.

Features of *Second Life*

Second Life provides an impressive number of features that make it a great tool for the aspiring MMOG developer. The core of *Second Life* is a real-time, streaming 3D world that is endlessly expandable. The underlying network technology is a proprietary grid-based network configuration. What this means to the developer is that as the player moves about the world, he is seamlessly transported from one server to the next without interruption or loading, so huge environments are possible. In Figure 7.4.2 you can see squares breaking up the map of a section of *Second Life.* Each square represents a different region. Each region equates to 16 square meters in the real world, or on one dedicated server. You can get a feel for how large *Second Life* really is, both geographically and technically, by counting the number of regions on the whole world map [Ondrejka04b].

Avatars in *Second Life* are infinitely customizable. Not only are there simple tools for modifying the shape of the player's Avatar, you can also provide them with custom clothes and animations. Furthermore, you can import the animations and clothes from popular development tools, such as Poser™ and Photoshop. As with customizing the player character, developers can also create and modify their own objects for characters to interact with. Easy-to-use geometric building tools are provided right in the player's console. If these tools are not robust enough, models can also be loaded from popular modeling packages as well [SecondLife04].

Everything in *Second Life* can be made to look and behave as the content creator wishes. Included with the customizable characters and objects is a powerful scripting language structured loosely on the C++ programming language [Brashears03]. With

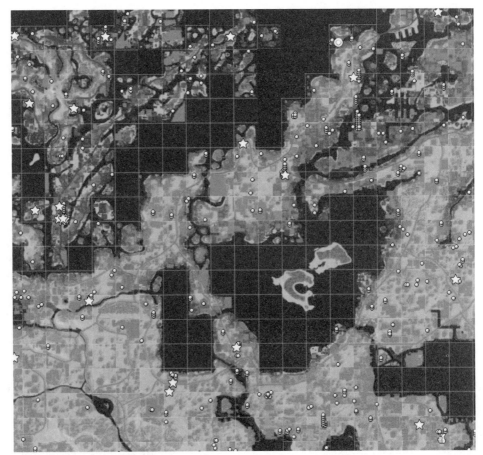

FIGURE 7.4.2   *A random section of the* Second Life *world map reveals locations of people and events.* Screenshot from Second Life *(www.secondlife.com), a service of Linden Research, Inc.*

the Linden scripting language, developers can assign complex behaviors to every object in the world. From simple pose balls to vehicles—if you can dream it, you can script it in *Second Life*. The most powerful feature provided in *Second Life* is the integration of the Havok physics engine. This standalone middleware provides extremely accurate physics to many popular games like *Half-Life 2* and *Full Spectrum Warrior* [Havok05]. Getting access to this technology for development teams would normally be rather expensive. More information on Havok is available at *www.havok.com.*

Getting Started in *Second Life*

Getting started in *Second Life* can be a daunting task. The first step is to go to *www.secondlife.com,* sign up for an account, and download the software. The first time a player enters the world they are presented with a tutorial to help them get started. Unfortunately, this does not cover where to go or how to learn about development in

Second Life. Much like user content, Linden Labs has deferred user training to *Second Life* residents, as well. Fortunately, the user base is a very dedicated and passionate group that has stepped up to the challenge in spades. Multiple resources exist that will help new users get up to speed in the way that is best for them. Be it video, text, live courses, or mentor programs, multiple training options are available in *Second Life* [SecondLife04].

Initially, it is best to go through the beginner's guide, which is a great overview of how to use *Second Life*. After using the beginner's guide, move on to the "Beginning Guide to Scripting." Then, it is best to go though the Wiki and possibly take classes offered by the Learning Center, a location in the virtual world shown in Figure 7.4.3. Both options are supported heavily by the user community. Beyond these resources, people tend to be very open to helping others within the *Second Life* community. Just start talking to people in the virtual world and ask them for the information you need.

FIGURE 7.4.3 *The author standing in front of the Learning Center. Screenshot from* Second Life *(www.secondlife.com), a service of Linden Research, Inc.*

Design Considerations in *Second Life*

When designing a game, the designer should take into account the strengths and constraints of the development platform. Not every game will translate well into every system, and this holds true in *Second Life*, as well.

Strengths

Second Life is a unique development environment that can be used for all manners of 3D games. From simple games of chance to complex role-playing games, *Second Life* can be made to fit almost any game genre. The major strengths of *Second Life* are its ability to support massive numbers of players in the environment, its physics simulation, its ability to scale for player size, and the built-in economic model.

Many successful *Second Life* games have concentrated on casino-style games, FPS-style games, and puzzle games. *Second Life* has provided some of the first massively multiplayer casual games on the market. The social aspects of these games are the greatest draw for *Second Life* players; you can even spend your time fishing if you want, as shown in Figure 7.4.4.

FIGURE 7.4.4   *Even fishing in* Second Life *can be a unique experience. Screenshot from* Second Life *(www.secondlife.com), a service of Linden Research, Inc.*

The physics simulation in *Second Life,* powered by Havok, allows for realistic vehicle mechanics, guns, and toys. From launching a man out of a cannon to racing a car, to a *Second Life* version of *Unreal, Second Life's* physics simulation allows these events to be as realistic as possible. One of the more popular sites in *Second Life* allows the players to sky dive, a remarkably fun virtual experience that relies heavily on the physics simulation.

One of the interesting strengths is that games can be scaled to support groups of any size. If 10,000 people want to play the same game, it can be run in different regions. All objects can be copied and reused without affecting the development cost.

Constraints

Although *Second Life* may seem like a perfect solution to MMOG prototyping, it is not without its limitations. Like most online environments, *Second Life* can suffer from lag. When entering new regions of the map, it is not uncommon to see buildings pop onto the screen. Sometimes people will appear naked and moments later are fully clothed. Images on walls may initially appear fuzzy and become vivid only after they are in the scene for a short time. Lag is a necessary evil that must be designed around, as failure to do so can result in the significant placement discrepancies shown in Figure 7.4.5. Any game that requires fast updates, large numbers of physics routines, complex scripts, or lots of objects can cause undue lag [SecondLife05a].

FIGURE 7.4.5   *Lag can cause major issues for game developers in* Second Life. *Screenshot from* Second Life *(www.secondlife.com), a service of Linden Research, Inc.*

Designing around lag can be a difficult process, but it can be done. *Second Life* handles it quite well, and the user is generally unaffected. In fact, the way buildings pop into the scene one primitive object at a time adds to the waking-dream feel of the overall environment. A comprehensive list of ways to manage lag is available on the Wiki home page [SecondLife05a].

Developing a Prototype

When creating a prototype, it is best to begin with simple objects and build up to full games in *Second Life*. Games can combine any number of scripts, primitives, and textures. This example is a walkthrough of how to create a simple toy, the Infinity Ball (not to be confused with a popular trademarked toy). Take a look at Figure 7.4.6 to see the Infinity Ball being created.

The main benefit of *Second Life* development is that everything can be viewed and created in-world. In Figure 7.4.6, there are windows open for textures, geometry, files, and scripts. Many other windows are available to you, as well. Especially useful is the debug menu, which is normally unseen. To turn on the debug menu, hit Ctrl+Alt+Shift+D. The Debug Menu has the ability to open the error message window. It can be used to toggle off the terrain so that lost geometry can be more easily found. It can also be used to monitor environment variables, such as wind.

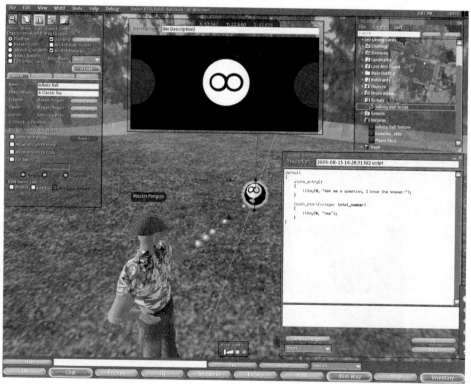

FIGURE 7.4.6   *Creation of the "Infinity Ball." The UI allows full access to all parts of the development, directly in-world. Screenshot from* Second Life *(www.secondlife.com), a service of Linden Research, Inc.*

To create your own Infinity Ball, follow these steps:

- First, go to a location on the map that has open Create permissions. This may be a public sandbox (there are many), or you can purchase land for this project.
- Right-click on the terrain and choose the Create button on the window that pops up. This will present you with a set of primitive objects you can create. Primitive objects range from cubes to trees.
- Select Sphere, and the cursor will turn into a magic wand.
- Click on the terrain. This will create a sphere.
- Now it is time to get a texture for the Infinity Ball. To do this, select Upload Image... from the File menu.

ON THE CD

- Find the Infinity_Ball_Texture.tga file on the accompanying CD-ROM and select it.
- Select Inventory from the View menu.
- Click on the Textures folder and drag Infinity_Ball_Texture onto the sphere, and the sphere should appear with the texture applied to it.
- Now, reposition the Sphere using the Move tool in the Create window.
- Go back to the Inventory window and select Create, and then New Script.
- The new script should be in the Scripts folder in the Inventory window.
- Right-click on New Script and rename it Infinity Ball Script.
- Double-click Infinity Ball Script to open the Script Editor window.
- In the Script Editor window, paste the following code:

```
float max = 8.0;
default
{
    // This code runs when a player touches the object
    touch_start(integer total_number)
    {
        float choice;
        integer result;
        // llFrand creates a random number
        choice = llFrand(max);
        // Casting the float as an integer
        // truncates the decimal
        result = (integer)choice;

        if(result == 0) llSay(0, "Yes, of course");
        else if(result == 1) llSay(0, "Can not predict now");
        else if(result == 2) llSay(0, "Signs point to yes");
        else if(result == 3) llSay(0, "Not looking good");
        else if(result == 4) llSay(0, "You can count on it");
        else if(result == 5) llSay(0, "It is certain");
        else if(result == 6) llSay(0, "No");
        else if(result == 7) llSay(0, "YES");
    }
}
```

- Finally, drag the Infinity Ball Script from the Inventory window onto the Infinity Ball.

Using this script, if the player touches the ball, the ball will randomly reply with one of the eight responses, much like the popular toy. This is a simple experiment, but it covers the basics of creating interactive objects in *Second Life*. With practice, anything is possible.

A Success Story

Probably the biggest success in the *Second Life* gaming community is *Tringo*. *Tringo* is a surprising mix of bingo and *Tetris*®. It has become such a success that it was licensed for commercial release in the real world. Designed by 30-year-old Australian programmer Nathan Keir over a Christmas break from college, no one expected *Tringo* to be the hit it has become. Donnerwood Media is preparing to publish *Tringo* as a mobile and Internet game [Grimes05].

FIGURE 7.4.7   *The author playing a game of* Tringo. *Screenshot from* Second Life (www.secondlife.com*), a service of Linden Research, Inc.*

Tringo manages to utilize the strengths and weaknesses of the *Second Life* environment perfectly. After paying to join the game, the player has a score card similar to a bingo card, only covered in *Tetris*-like pieces. The game calls out pieces, which cannot be rotated. The first player to fill their card calls "Tringo!" and they win the pot. It is simple and addictive, especially since you can socialize with other players as you play [Grimes05].

Conclusion

The simple genius of *Tringo* is a testament of what can be accomplished in *Second Life*. *Second Life* is in the early stages of its development, and even with a success story like *Tringo*, only a small fraction of what can be accomplished with *Second Life* has been realized. The next multimillion-dollar epic game may be designed within *Second Life*. Possibly the next big-hit casual game will be created inside its world. Being on the brink of something new, and having virtually unlimited resources to experiment and be creative with may give birth to the next big thing in the history of MMOGs. So all that is left is the big question: How will you spend your *Second Life*?

References

[Book05] Book, Betsy, "Virtual Worlds Review." August 15, 2005. Available online at *http://www.virtualworldsreview.com*.

[Brashears03] Brashears, Aaron, et al., "Linden Scripting Language Guide." 2003. Available online at *https://secondlife.com/download/guides/LSLGuide.pdf*.

[GOM05] Gaming Open Market, "Gaming Open Market Homepage." August 15, 2005. Available online at *http://www.gamingopenmarket.com/*.

[Grimes05] Grimes, Ann, "Tetris Meets Bingo." *The Wall Street Journal*, March 3, 2006: p. B3.

[Havok05] Havok.com, "Havok: Dynamic Gameplay." August 15, 2005. Available online at *http://www.havok.com*.

[Ondrejka04a] Ondrejka, Cory, "Aviators, Moguls, Fashionistas and Barons: Economics and Ownership in Second Life." September 23, 2004. Available online at *http://www.gamasutra.com/resource_guide/20040920/ondrejka_01.shtml*.

[Ondrejka04b] Ondrejka, Cory, "A Piece of Place: Modeling the Digital on the Real in Second Life." June 7, 2004. Available online at *http://papers.ssrn.com/sol3/papers.cfm?abstract_id=555883*.

[SecondLife04] "Second Life Starter Guide." June, 2004. Available online at *https://secondlife.com/download/guides/starter_guide.pdf*.

[SecondLife05a] Second Life Community, "LSL Wiki: Home Page." August 15, 2005. Available online at *http://secondlife.com/badgeo/wakka.php?wakka=HomePage*.

[SecondLife05b] Linden Labs, Incorporated, "Second Life Home Page." August 15, 2005. Available online at *http://www.secondlife.com*.

[Woodcock05] Woodcock, Bruce Sterling, "MMOG Active Subscriptions 0–150,000." August 15, 2005. Available online at *http://www.mmogchart.com/*.

7.5

Reliable Peer-to-Peer Gaming TCP Connections Penetrating NAT

Larry Shi

ai_shaying@hotmail.com

In this Internet gaming gem, we will describe a useful technique for creating peer-to-peer network sessions between workstations that are behind home or ISP Network Address Translators (NATs). The technique is applicable to many client-server architecture-based online games as well, because a separate peer-to-peer connection between currently interacting clients can alleviate some of the network burden on the servers. Game developers can use the peer-to-peer channel to carry data such as voice, chat text, and real-time video to enhance gameplay experience. We will discuss how NAT affects peer-to-peer connections, tricks to reliably create connections between computers behind NAT, and provide source code that can be used directly by game developers. The hope is that with this enhanced connectivity, games will not only be more fun, but also be able to reach more customers.

The Problem

As a game developer, if you want your game applications to be able to connect with each other in peer-to-peer mode without consuming costly server bandwidth, no matter how you design the solution, you will inevitably face the wall of NAT. Almost every commercial home network router, such as Linksys, Netgear, and many ISPs, rely on NAT to connect home computers to the Internet. Using NAT, ISPs avoid allocating a fixed static IP address to each customer. It allows ISPs to extend their IP addressing and support a lot more customers than the number of static IP addresses they own. NAT also allows home users to configure their home network using a separate private network address space, hiding the network's topology from the outside world. NAT achieves this through dynamic address and port translation. A four-tuple (local IP address, local port number, remote IP address, remote port number) uniquely identifies to the NAT each network connection or session. To bridge a home network with an external network, such as the ISP's network or the global Internet, a NAT device allocates a port from its own port space to each outbound connection passing through it. The NAT device automatically replaces each outbound packet's source IP address with the NAT device's IP address, and the source port with the allocated external port number.

Figure 7.5.1 illustrates a typical home network consisting of a home router acting as a NAT device for a set of home computers and other computing devices. The NAT device has an ISP-assigned, globally routable IP address, 172.168.5.23. Behind the NAT device is a private network using local IP address space 10.0.1.*x*. Assume that the home computer, 10.0.1.3, wants to connect to a service at global address 23.34.1.2, port number 1234. The NAT device will intercept the connection request (TCP SYN packet). According to the NAT protocol, it will allocate a new port number—for example, 5462—for this new connection. Then it replaces the outbound packet's source IP address with its own global IP, and the local source port number with the newly allocated port number, 5462. The NAT device uses the tuple (10.0.1.3, 31420, 172.168.5.23, 5462) to uniquely identify this connection and the translations required to maintain it. As Figure 7.5.1 shows, for every outbound packet with source address 10.0.1.3:31420, the NAT device translates the source address to 172.168.5.23:5462. For every inbound packet with destination address 172.168.5.23:5462, the NAT device translates the destination address to 10.0.1.3:31420.

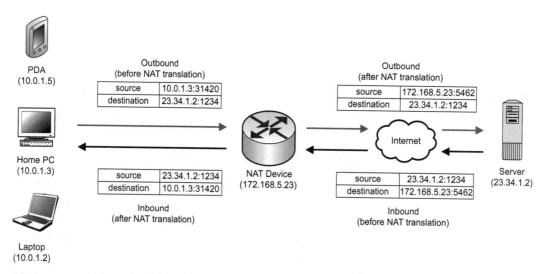

FIGURE 7.5.1   *Network address translation device.*

One of the complications NAT introduces to online games is that only connections originating from within the internal network can be established. A NAT device drops all inbound connection requests from the external network for which there is no translation tuple already recorded. Those dropped requests are called "unsolicited connection attempts." In other words, the problem is that a computer behind a NAT device cannot connect to another computer that is also behind a NAT device. Typically, this is not an issue for pure client-server-based games, as the server often uses a global IP address and does not use NAT.

State-of-the-Art

Due to the increasing popularity of applications such as peer-to-peer file sharing, Voice over IP (VoIP) teleconferencing, and online gaming, there is tremendous need to overcome the connection restriction imposed by NAT. Fortunately, there have been a number of solutions and hacks devised recently. One of the techniques that establishes peer-to-peer connections for computers that are both behind NAT devices is "hole punching." Hole punching can work for both UDP [Guha05] and TCP connections [Biggadike05] [Eppinger05] [Ford05]. In hole punching, computers at both ends try to initiate outbound connection attempts to the other end, using both the other end's private (internal) address and public (external, translated) address. The outbound requests will effectively punch holes in—or, in other words, add translation entries to—the NAT devices on the path, thus enabling the NAT devices to accept the inbound connection from the other end. Hole punching is simple and transparent to the applications. It works very robustly and reliably for most well-behaved commercial NAT devices.

There are several different ways of performing TCP hole-punching. The NAT-BLASTER paper [Biggadike05] describes a TCP hole-punching approach that uses a source IP spoof server and sequence number coordination tricks to establish TCP connections between two NATed computers. [Eppinger05] presents a method that uses regular socket programming and a sequence of orchestrated events to connect two NATed end computers. A more recent paper [Ford05] discusses how to establish peer-to-peer TCP connections using the special SO_REUSEADDR and SO_REUSEPORT socket options. We will describe in detail how to do TCP hole-punching based on [Ford05]. Understanding the technique requires familiarity with TCP/IP networking, NAT operating principles, and socket programming.

Approach

Figure 7.5.2 illustrates the configuration of a target network system. Without loss of generality, assume that there are two client computers, node A and node B. Both are networked and behind the NAT devices NA and NB, respectively. Furthermore, assume that node A resides in a private home network, 10.0.1.x, and its internal IP

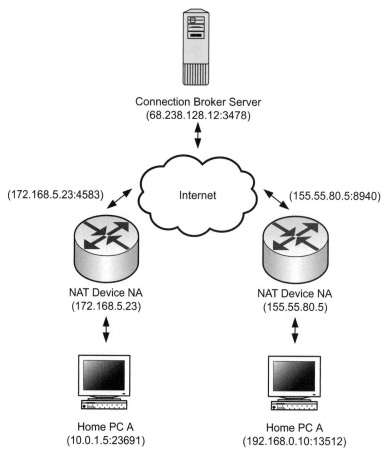

FIGURE 7.5.2 *Example setup of two client machines and a connection server.*

address is 10.0.1.5. B is at address 192.168.0.10 on internal network 192.168.0.*x*. NA's globally routable address is 172.168.5.23, and NB's globally routable address is 155.55.80.5. The goal is to use NAT hole-punching to establish a TCP connection between node A and node B for transmitting online gaming data. The procedure uses typical socket programming and involves the steps described in Figure 7.5.3.

As Figure 7.5.2 shows, for the hole-punching approach to work, it requires a Connection Broker Server (C) to facilitate connection establishment between A and B. C must have a globally routable IP address and use a known port number as the brokering service entry point. Assume that C's global IP address is 68.238.128.12 and it publicizes port number 3478 as the brokering service port. The steps for hole punching are illustrated in Figure 7.5.3.

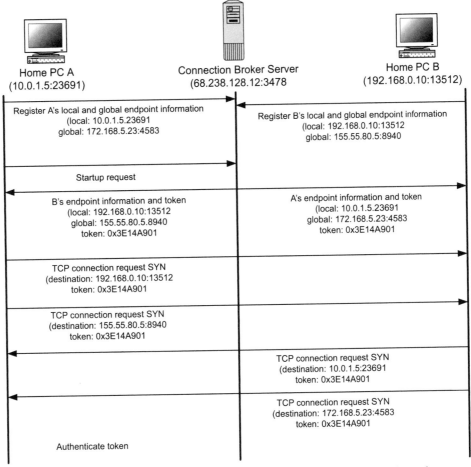

FIGURE 7.5.3 *The steps for hole punching. The procedure consists of 1) the end-point registration stage, 2) the startup stage, 3) the connection stage, and 4) the authentication stage.*

To enable a NAT device to accept inbound connection attempts targeting a particular client machine and service connection port behind the NAT device from a particular source address in front of the NAT device, a client machine first establishes a translation entry in the NAT device's end-point translation table. This translation entry maps an internal IP address and port number to an external IP address and an unused NAT device port number. To do this, the client machine sends a preemptive outbound packet using the expected inbound packet's global source address and port number as the destination address and port number.

As we have described earlier, a tuple of local address, local port number, remote address, and remote port number uniquely identifies a network connection or session. The NAT device will record the tuple of every outbound attempt. Later, when it sees inbound packets matching one of the recorded connections or sessions, it will replace the packet's destination address and port number with the local private address and port number routable in the private network behind the NAT device, and pass the packet on to the internal destination. The preemptive outbound packet creates a new connection (or session record) in the NAT device, and when the NAT device encounters the packets from the expected connection attempt, it thinks they are part of an already active connection, and therefore should be accepted. This is the basic principle of hole punching.

End-Point Registration Stage

In the end-point registration stage, each client machine initiates a TCP connection to the connection broker server and registers both its internal pair of address and port number and its external public address and port number. A client machine can retrieve its local IP address and port number through the getsockname() socket API call. If successful, the call returns both a 16-bit port number and a 32-bit IP address. Then the client machine obfuscates the IP address by doing a bitwise XOR with a four-byte magic number that both the connection server and the client machines agree on. Obfuscation of the IP address is necessary to avoid the corner case where a naive NAT device blindly scans payloads, translating IP addresses. After that, it constructs a packet payload as defined below, connects to the connection broker server, and sends the constructed payload.

```
typedef struct {
    unsigned long port;
    unsigned char address[4];
} local_end_point_info_t;

local_end_point_info_t payload;
unsigned char magic[4] = { 0xde, 0xad, 0xbe, 0xef };
struct sockaddr_in sin;
int server_tcp_conn_sock;

// allocate and bind server_tcp_conn_sock ...
int sinlen = sizeof(sin);
getsockname(server_tcp_conn_sock,(struct sockaddr*)&sin, &sinlen);
payload.port = sin.sin_port;
// XORing each byte obfuscates IP addresses in order to thwart
// NAT devices which replace IP addresses
// found in packet payloads.
payload.address[0] = BYTE0(sin.sin_addr) ^ magic[0];
payload.address[1] = BYTE1(sin.sin_addr) ^ magic[1];
payload.address[2] = BYTE2(sin.sin_addr) ^ magic[2];
payload.address[3] = BYTE3(sin.sin_addr) ^ magic[3];
```

The broker server knows a client machine's public address and port number (after one or possibly multiple NAT translations) once it accepts the client's connection. And it extracts the client machine's private address and port number from the packet payload:

```
typedef struct {
    unsigned long local_port;
    unsigned char local_address[4];
    unsigned long remote_port;
    unsigned char remote_address[4];
} end_point_info_t;

end_point_info_t        end_point;
struct sockaddr_in      sin;
socklen_t               sinlen;
int                     server_sock;
local_end_point_info_t payload;
//...
sinlen = sizeof(sin);
accept(server_sock, (struct sockaddr*)&sin, &sinlen);
end_point.remote_port = sin.port;
end_point.remote_address[0] = BYTE0(sin.sin_addr);
//...
point_point.remote_address[3] = BYTE3(sin.sin_addr);
GetPayload(server_sock, payload, sizeof(end_point_info_t));
end_point.local_port = payload.port;
end_point.local_address[0] = payload.address[0] ^ magic[0];
//...
end_point.local_address[3] = payload.address[3] ^ magic[3];
```

Both client machines register their local and remote addresses with the connection broker server in this step, although not necessarily simultaneously.

Startup Stage

Assume that node A wants to establish a peer-to-peer connection with node B. In the startup stage, A sends a request to the connection broker server C indicating that it wants to connect to B. Upon receipt of the request, C responds by sending B's endpoint information (i.e., public address and port number observed by C and local address and port number reported by B) back to A. Similarly, it will also send the endpoint information for A to B. The connection broker also generates a unique token (a sequence number, time stamp, or simply a random number) and sends the token along with the other information to both A and B. In the next connection stage, both A and B will use the token to prove the authenticity of each other's connection request. Though rare, without any sort of authentication, spurious connections based on stale connection requests could be established. Erroneous connections may also be possible if both nodes, each behind a different NAT, share the same private address space. To make the connection approach more robust and trustworthy, it is also preferred to have the token digitally signed. A simple solution is to use a public/private key authentication scheme to sign the token. The connection server can compute a public/private key pair and release its public key to all of the client machines, including A and B. When the connection server replies to A's startup request, it also returns a private key signed statement. For example, the connection server could create a statement that reads "In response to the client (A) at 172.168.5.23's request (ID = 12345) to connect to the client (B) at 155.55.80.5, the server at 68.238.128.12 issues token 0x3E14A901 to both A and B." Then server C computes a hash digest of the statement, using a hashing algorithm like SHA-1, and digitally signs the hash using its private key. C sends the statement and the signed hash to both clients A and B. The signing procedure allows clients to authenticate the statement by computing their own hash and comparing that to the one decrypted using C's public key.

Connection Stage

The connection stage starts after A and B each receive the end-point information and token from server C. A and B extract the token value from the received statement. They can then verify the authenticity of the token by recomputing a hash digest using the same method as C, decrypting the hash signature using C's public key, and finally comparing the decrypted hash with the recomputed hash. If they match each other, the message from C is authenticated. Both clients record the 32-bit token value, 0x3E14A901.

Next, A creates a TCP socket, listening on the same port number it used for connecting to C. Then it allocates two more TCP sockets, also binding to the same port number as the connection to C, and attempts connections to both B's private local end-point (192.168.0.10:13532) and B's public end-point (155.55.80.5:8940). B repeats the same procedure. It creates a TCP socket, listening on the port it uses to connect to C, and issues TCP connection requests to both A's public and private local end-points using TCP sockets originating from the same port number as B's connection to C. The reason for attempting connections to both the private and public end-points is because A and B may reside behind the same NAT. In that case, the NAT may not be capable of recognizing that outbound connection request actually requires rerouting back to the private network. Both A's and B's connection requests include the token number received from C for authentication purposes. Node A and node B are both simultaneously trying to connect and are waiting for connections. The first connection to complete the authentication stage (see Authentication Stage) ends the process. The connected-to node can stop trying to connect, and the connecting node can stop waiting for connections. If the NAT devices on the path between A and B are all well-behaved NAT devices, after a few TCP connection attempts, clients A and B will be connected.

The described technique requires multiple TCP sockets binding to the same local port number. More than that, it also binds the same port both for listening for incoming TCP connection requests and issuing outgoing connection requests. Though not a regular way of programming a TCP socket, all of these operations are supported by most operating systems' socket APIs, because a five-tuple consisting of protocol, local IP, local port, remote IP, and remote port identifies a socket uniquely. This means that socket programming allows binding of the same local port to multiple TCP sockets as long as the destination IP address and port are different.

To enable sharing the same port number among TCP sockets, applications have to set the TCP socket option SO_REUSEADDR or SO_REUSEPORT. Applications can configure socket options through the setsockopt() API call. After configuring socket options, node A or node B can bind the socket to the shared port number by calling the bind() socket API function. Note that if the application does not set the socket option properly, binding to the shared port will fail and return with an "address already in use" error.

Authentication Stage

To prevent the pathological case that a machine accepts a stale connection request or spurious requests from other machines, connection requests are authenticated. Both A and B provide the unique token issued by C in their connection requests. Upon receipt of a connection request, a machine will verify that the request does not come from a stale session by comparing the received token with the one received from the connection broker. If they match, the intended connection is accepted.

Applications

This technique for establishing peer-to-peer TCP connections among multiple NATed home PCs has great implications for a wide range of gaming applications. First, it is directly applicable to a large number of peer-to-peer games. Many such games are casual games that establish peer-to-peer TCP connections among a small number of player PCs. They can benefit from the described method by extended network connectivity. Second, for other types of online games, such as client-server-based games, the described technique can facilitate establishing on-demand network connections between client machines in addition to the clients' connections to the server. Game applications can take advantage of the availability of such peer-to-peer connections to carry certain real-time information that does not require synchronization by the server. Such information may include player speech, real-time video from a source (e.g., a Web cam), and online chat text. Without the peer-to-peer connectivity, the server must relay every piece of information to each client, consuming valuable server resources.

Limitation

The described technique works for all the NAT devices belonging to the category of cone NAT [Rosenberg03]. In a cone NAT, the NAT device consistently translates a pair of internal private IP address and port number to a pair of external IP address and port number, regardless of the destination address and port number. Unfortunately, not every NAT device is a cone NAT. In contrast to cone NAT, so-called symmetric NAT does not consistently translate an internal computer's IP address and port number to the same unique external IP and port number.

To give an example, consider the setup in Figure 7.5.2. There is a client machine A with internal IP address 10.0.1.5 behind NAT device NA with global IP address 172.168.5.23, and a second client machine B with internal IP 192.168.0.10 behind another NAT device NB with global IP address 155.55.80.5. Assume that A wants to connect to B. First it connects to the connection broker server C at 68.238.128.12 with service entry port number 3478. Assume that A's socket binds to a local port number 23691. Upon receipt of the outbound request, NAT NA will find a free port number, 4583, and add a translation entry in its NAT table. For every outgoing packet with source IP address 10.0.1.5 and port 23691, NAT NA, regardless of the destination, always translates the source address and port pair to 172.168.5.23 and 4583; NAT NA is a cone NAT. In contrast to this behavior, if NAT NA is a symmetric NAT, it will allocate a new port number for every outbound request to a different target address. In this case, for the connection request to client B after connecting to server C, NAT NA will replace the request's source port number with another port number instead of the number 4583 used in the case of cone NAT.

For the technique described in this gem to work, both NAT NA and NAT NB must be cone NATs. Various studies show that most commercial NAT devices are cone-NAT compatible [Ford05], and the trend is that symmetric NAT is becoming less common among ISPs and NAT vendors as they strive to support popular peer-to-peer applications.

Conclusion

This article describes how to establish TCP connections between gaming PCs that are both behind NAT devices, using hole punching. The described technique can enhance connectivity of peer-to-peer games. For server-based games, the additional connection channels, if properly used, can potentially enrich online play experience.

References

[Biggadike05] Biggadike, A., D. Ferullo, G. Wilson, and A. Perrig. "NATBLASTER: Establishing TCP Connections Between Hosts Behind NATs." ACM SIG-COMM Asia Workshop, Beijing, China, April 2005.

[Eppinger05] J. Eppinger, "TCP Connections for P2P Apps. A Software Approach to Solving the NAT Problem." Technical Report CMU-ISRI-05-104, Carnegie Mellon University, January 2005.

[Ford05] Ford, B., P. Srisuresh, and D. Kegel, "Peer-to-Peer Communication Across Network Address Translator." Usenix Annual Report, February 2005.

[Guha05] Guha, S., and P. Francis, "Simple Traversal of UDP Through NATs and TCP too (STUNT)." 2005. Available online at *http://nutss.gforge.cis.cornell.edu*.

[Rosenberg 03] Rosenberg, J., J. Weinberger, C. Huitema, and R. Mahy, "RFC 3489 - STUN - Simple Traversal of User Datagram Protocol (UDP) Through Network Address Translators (NATs)." 2003. Available online at *http://www.faqs.org/rfcs/rfc3489.html*.

About the CD-ROM

About the *Game Programming Gems 6* CD-ROM

The accompanying CD-ROM contains source code and demos that demonstrate the techniques described in this book. Every attempt has been made to ensure that the source code is bug-free and will compile. Please refer to the Web site *http://www. gameprogramminggems.com/* for errata and updates.

CONTENTS

Code: The source code and demos contained on the CD-ROM are contained in a hierarchy of subdirectories based on section name, and gem title and author. Source code and listings from the book are included. At each author's discretion, a complete demo is sometimes included. Windows demos were compiled using either Microsoft Visual C++ 6.0 (projects with a .dsw file) or Microsoft Visual C++ 7.0 (projects with a .sln file).

Figures: All of the figures from the articles are included, as well as the color plates.

GLUT: In this directory you will find the GLUT v3.7.6 distribution for Windows. For Windows-specific information, please visit Nate Robins's Web site at *http://www.xmission.com/~nate/glut.html.*

GLEW: Here you'll find the GLEW v1.3.3 distribution for Windows and Linux. Additional information can be found at: *http://glew.sourceforge.net/.*

DirectX: If you're running on Windows, you're very likely using the DirectX API. For your convenience, this directory holds v9.0c of the DirectX SDK.

SYSTEM REQUIREMENTS

Windows: Intel Pentium series, AMD Athlon, or newer processor recommended. Windows XP (64 MB RAM) or Windows 2000 (128 MB RAM) or later required. 3D graphics card required for some of the sample applications; the DivX codec (*www.divx.com*) is required for some of the movies. DirectX 9 and GLUT 3.7 or newer are also required, and GLEW v1.3.3 may be required in some cases, as indicated in the article text.

Linux: Intel Pentium series, AMD Athlon, or newer processor recommended. Linux kernel 2.4.x or later required; 64 MB RAM recommended, as well as a 3D graphics card, which is required for some of the sample applications. The DivX codec (*www.divx.com*) is required for some of the movies. XFree86 4.0, GLUT 3.7, GLEW v1.3.3, OpenGL driver, glibc 2.1 or newer are also required. Mesa can be used in place of 3D hardware support.

INDEX

Numbers with "GPG" proceeding refer to previous editions of the Game Programming Gems Series.
Numbers without this notation refer to the current volume.

A

A* algorithm, GPG2: 250
  aesthetic optimizations, GPG1: 264–271
  Master Node List and Priority Queue
    Open List implementation, GPG1:
    285–286
  navigation meshes and, GPG1: 294–295
  path planning with, GPG1: 254–262
  pathfinding and, GPG1: 294, GPG2:
    315, GPG2: 325, GPG5: 367–382
  priority queues for speed, GPG1:
    281–286
  speed optimizations for, GPG1:
    272–287, GPG5: 367–382
  weaknesses of, GPG1: 261–262
  waypoints and, GPG2: 315
A Star Explorer program, A* tool, GPG3:
  305
  performance, GPG3: 301–302, GPG5:
    367–382
  costs, GPG3: 295–296, GPG3: 298–300,
    GPG3: 304–305
  tactical pathfinding, GPG3: 294–305
  stochastic maps and, GPG4: 325–326
  D* (dynamic A*), GPG5: 383–389
  derivative algorithm with improved
    functionality, GPG5: 367–382
  heuristic estimate function of, GPG5:
    367–368
  multiple solutions returned by, GPG5:
    381
  nodes, multiple start and stop nodes,
    GPG5: 371–381
  pseudocode listing for reference, GPG5:
    368–370
Abstract interfaces
  described and defined, GPG2: 20–22
  disadvantages of, GPG2: 26–27
  factories, GPG2: 22–23
  as traits, GPG2: 23–26
  virtual destructors, GPG2: 23
Abstract syntax trees (AST), for programmable vertex shader compiler, GPG3:
  410
ABT (Adaptive Binary Trees), 423–434
  building, 423–425
  dynamic scenes, 432–433
  implementation, 425–428
  rendering, 433–434
  splitting plane, 429–432
  vs. binary trees, GPG5: 162
  cache-oblivious implementation of,
    GPG5: 159–167
  complexity of, GPG5: 163
  creation of, GPG5: 161–162
  performance testing of, GPG5: 166–167

  redundancy and reduction of memory
    footprint, GPG5: 163–166
  van Emde Boas tree layout, GPG5: 160
Acceleration, GPG4: 221–225
  lookup tables and, GPG4: 229
  and velocity on splines, GPG4: 180
  minimal acceleration Hermit curves,
    GPG5: 225–231
Access-based file reordering, 105
  best practices, 107–108
  factors affecting results, 106
Accidental complexity, GPG2: 258–259
Accuracy
  far position (hybrid between fixed-point
    and floating-point numbers), GPG4:
    162–166
  large world coordinates and, GPG4:
    162–166
Action-selection algorithms, 263–264
Actions, chaining, 265–266
ActionState class
  GoCap, GPG3: 231–232, GPG5:
    233–234
  for MMPs, GPG3: 509
Actor class
  GoCap, GPG3: 232
  for MMPs, GPG3: 512–513
ActorProperty class, 384–385
ActorProxy class
  wrapping actor classes, 384
  for massively multiplayer games, GPG3:
    513
Actors, 383–385
  nonintrusive environment, 385–386
  properties, 386–389
  proxies, 390–391
Adabala, Neeharika
  article by, GPG5: 539–549
  contact and bio info, GPG5: *xxi*
Adaptive Binary Trees (ABT), 423–434
  building, 423–425
  dynamic scenes, 432–433
  implementation, 425–428
  rendering, 433–434
  splitting plane, 429–432
Address-space management of dynamic arrays,
  GPG4: 85–93
Adobe Photoshop CS Digimarc, 100–101
ADPCM audio compression format, GPG3:
  589, GPG3: 620–621
Aerodynamics, GPG5: 395–409
  aerodynamic primitives, GPG5:
    398–406
  of bluff bodies, GPG5: 399–403
  curve balls, GPG5: 407
  drag, GPG5: 404

  fluid properties and standard atmosphere,
    GPG5: 398
  Kutta-Joukowski theorem, GPG5: 401
  load quantities, GPG5: 396–398
  Navier-Stokes equation, GPG5:
    398–399, 401
  rigid body dynamics, GPG5: 396–397
  of slender bodies, GPG5: 406
  of streamlines bodies, GPG5: 403–406
  thin wing theory, GPG5: 403
  for wind-driven particle system storms,
    GPG5: 407–408
Agent tiers, massively multiplayer games
  (MMPs), 617–618
Ahmad, Anis
  article by, GPG1: 581–583
  contact information, GPG1: *xxv*
AI. *See* Artificial Intelligence (AI)
AIControlStates, for massively multiplayer
  games (MMPs), GPG3: 509–510
Aiming, tactical pathfinding and, GPG3: 298
Air, cellular automata to model currents and
  pressure, GPG3: 200, GPG3: 206
Aircraft, aerodynamics for, GPG5: 407–408
Alexander, Thor
  articles by, GPG3: 231–239, GPG3:
    506–519
  contact and bio info, GPG3: *xxiii*
Algorithms
  action-selection, 263–264
  computer vision game application, 26–36
  lock-free, 5–14
  Open Computer Vision Library
    (OpenCV), 26
  string matching, 69–77
  terrain-rendering, 461–471
  Cylinder-frustum intersection test,
    GPG1: 382–384
  Diamond-square algorithm, GPG1:
    505–507
  Dijkstra's algorithm, GPG1: 294
  Heuristic costs algorithm, GPG1:
    276–278
  for infinite universes, GPG1: 136–139
  for landscaping, GPG1: 485–490
  learning algorithms, GPG1: 345–350
  levels of detail (LOD) selection, GPG1:
    435–437
  mazes, GPG1: 492–493
  name generation, GPG1: 493–498
  negamax algorithm and game trees,
    GPG1: 250–251
  randomness, GPG1: 135–136, GPG3:
    453, GPG3: 623–624
  search algorithms, GPG1: 254–262,
    GPG4: 217–219

Collaborative work, UML game engine,
GPG3: 73–82
Collision detection, GPG1: 390–402
OpenMP, 19–20
bounding sphere, GPG1: 390–393
line-plane intersection, GPG1: 394–395
octree construction for culling, GPG1:
439–443
point-in-triangle test, GPG1: 396–397
triangle "flattening," GPG1: 395–396
triangle-to-triangle, GPG1: 390, GPG1:
393–397
altitude relative to collision plane, GPG2:
182–183
brute-force comparison algorithm for,
GPG2: 228
distance to collision point, GPG2:
184–185
finding pairs with RDC, GPG2: 234–235
kickback collisions, GPG2: 187–188
line / line intersections, GPG2: 191–204
location of collision point, GPG2:
183–184
Recursive Dimensional Clustering
(RDC), GPG2: 228–238
reflected vectors (bounces), GPG2:
185–187
vector / plane intersections, GPG2:
182–190
barycentric coordinates, GPG3: 427
character movement and, GPG3: 321
path-finding and, GPG3: 321–332
probes or sensory for, GPG3: 235
sphere trees for, GPG3: 532
bounding volumes (proxy geometry),
GPG4: 505–506
camera scene boundaries and collision
geometry, GPG4: 307–308
collision errors, GPG4: 159
collision meshes, GPG4: 505
contact points and, GPG4: 253–263
detection *vs.* resolution, GPG4: 503–504
message-based entity management
systems and, GPG4: 81
oriented bounding boxes, GPG4: 506
real-time game engines and, GPG4:
503–514
Verlet-based physics engine and, GPG4:
236–237
costs of, GPG5: 468
see also Bounding boxes; Collisions
Collision model path-finding
described, GPG3: 321–322
fault-tolerant AI for, GPG3: 322–325
implementing movement along the path,
GPG3: 329–331
layered collisions, GPG3: 328–329
unobstructed space, GPG3: 325–328
Collisions
with damping, GPG2: 188–190
pathfinding and, GPG2: 317–323
sphere-to-plane collisions, GPG2:
189–190
audio coordinated with, GPG4:
654–655
of 3D bones-based articulated characters,
GPG4: 503–514
see also Collision detection
Collision shapes, selecting, GPG2: 318–321
Color
polygon tinting method to apply color,
GPG4: 452, GPG4: 457
sepia tone conversions, GPG4: 461–463

team colors applied to 3D models,
GPG4: 451–459
Combat games
AI to adjust difficulty and dramatic
tension in, GPG4: 315–324
artillery duel scenario, GPG5: 322–325
automatic cover finding with navigation
meshes, GPG5: 299–305
boss scenario for RPGs, GPG5: 325–327
Lanchester Attrition models to predict
results, GPG5: 317–328
melee (orcs *vs.* humans) scenario, GPG5:
318–320
narrow staircase (orcs *vs.* humans)
scenario, GPG5: 320
Combinational sequences, 169–173
Combs, William, GPG2: 343
Combs Method for managing exponential
growth, GPG2: 343–349
proof for, GPG2: 348–349
COM interface search, alternatives to, GPG2:
46–50
Command audio design pattern, GPG2: 517
Command queues, audio design and, GPG2:
517
Command stream servers, GPG4: 547
Comments, macro to add to asserts, GPG3:
29
CompactableChunkPolicy allocation policy,
GPG5: 139
Compare and Swap (CAS)
ABA problem, 9–10
code listing, 6
Compare and Swap 2 (CAS2), 6
Compare and Swap N (CASN), 6
Compatibility issues
cross-platform compatibility, GPG3: 69
portable serialization for online games,
GPG3: 536–545
RTTI edit/save system and file compatibility, GPG4: 120–122
Compiled Vertex Arrays (CVA), GPG1:
356–360
Compilers and compiling
binary space partitioning (BSP) trees. See
Binary space partitioning
calling conventions of, GPG1: 61–62
limitations of, GPG1: 24, GPG1: 31
templates as virtual, GPG1: 20–22
floating-point exceptions and, GPG3: 70
programmable vertex shader compiler,
GPG3: 406–411
tokenizers for, GPG3: 40
bug prevention and, GPG4: 16
conditional compilation, GPG4: 40
internal compiler errors, GPG4: 13
IDL compiler, GPG5: 635–636
Compile-time asserts, macro for, GPG3: 30
Compile-time constants, macro for, GPG3:
28–29
Complex systems, massively multiplayer
games (MMPs), 607–608
Component-based object management,
GPG5: 25–37
Component-based software, multithreading,
371–372
Component technologies, pie menus, GPG3:
119–124
Composable controllers, GPG5: 450
Composite audio design pattern, GPG2:
515–516
Composition, GPG1: 12
Composition tag, XML audio tag, GPG4: 627

Compression
image compression, GPG1: 185–186
wavelets, GPG1: 182–186
audio compression, GPG3: 585–594,
GPG3: 613–621
latency and, GPG3: 578
of quaternions, GPG3: 187–191
voice compression with vocoder, GPG3:
613–621
bitpacking for network games, GPG4:
571–578
motion capture data compression, GPG4:
497–502
Computation, history and development of,
GPG2: 165–166
Computational Fluid Dynamics (CFD)
fluid simulation, 189–205
see also Cellular automata
Computer vision, 25–26
future, 36
game application, 26–36
Open Computer Vision Library
(OpenCV), 26
Concave solids and CGS, GPG5: 108–109
Concept stage of game development, GPG3:
16
Concurrent multitasking mode, Python
embedding, 377
Conditional compilation, GPG4: 40
Conditions
Boolean operators as connectors, GPG3:
287–288
defined and described, GPG3: 286
Conduction, modeling with cellular automata,
GPG3: 209–210
Consistency management, GPG4: 579–589
Console game systems
data loading, GPG1: 90–91
debugging, GPG1: 115–119
depth-of-play technique, GPG1:
133–140
online services for, GPG4: 531
physics and fast deformations, GPG4:
283–284
screenshots and memory usage, GPG4:
390–391
Constants, in data-driven design, GPG1: 3–4
Constraints
ball and socket constraints, GPG4: 246
brakes and rigid body dynamics, GPG4:
249
friction, GPG4: 249
Jacobian constraints, GPG4: 243
motors and, GPG4: 249
positional error corrections, GPG4:
249–250
rigid bodies and, GPG4: 241–250
rope-and-pulley constraints, GPG4:
245–246
rotation and, GPG4: 243–246
screw constraints, GPG4: 246
stacks with hard contacts, GPG4: 248
velocity constraints, GPG4: 242–243
Constructive Solid Geometry, BSP trees and,
GPG5: 103–113
ConstructOnceStack allocation policy, GPG5:
139
Constructors
explicit *vs.* implicit, GPG2: 8
optimization and, GPG2: 7–8
Contact points
clustering contacts, GPG4: 255, GPG4:
259–261

IEEE floating points, GPG2: 168–169,
GPG4: 157–158, GPG4: 574
initial state variations and, GPG2: 108
integer comparisons, GPG2: 173
Intel architecture and, GPG2: 261
linear quantization, GPG2: 178
logarithmic quantization, GPG2:
178–179
performance measurement after optimization, GPG2: 180
propagated influence values and, GPG2:
293
sign test for, GPG2: 172
square root optimization and, GPG2:
176–177
text parsers, GPG2: 115
accuracy problems and large world
coordinates, GPG4: 157–170
increasing size of, GPG4: 161
Floating-point optimizations, GPG3:
182–184
Floating-point representations, *vs.* vector
fractions, GPG3: 163–164
Floats. See Floating-point numbers
Flocking, GPG1: 305–318, GPG2: 330–336
alignment, GPG1: 305–306
avoidance, GPG1: 306
cohesion, GPG1: 305–306
memory and, GPG1: 306
separation, GPG1: 305–306
steering behaviors, GPG1: 305–306
boids, varieties of, GPG2: 332–333
demo, Flocking with Teeth, GPG2: 334
rules of, GPG2: 330–331
attraction and repulsion curves, GPG4:
358–359
Flow experience in game play, GPG4:
316–319
Fluid properties of atmosphere, GPG5:
401–402
Fluid simulation
basic approaches, 189–193
rendering on GPU, 473–485
smoothed particle hydrodynamics (SPH),
193–199
code listings, GPG3: 205
Flythrough paths
natural cubic splines and, GPG2:
221–222
quaternion-based flythrough paths,
GPG2: 220–227
Flyweight classes, GPG2: 53
Flyweight objects
described, GPG2: 52
State And Media Manager (SAMMy),
GPG2: 52–54
Fog, range-based, GPG1: 548
Fog-of-War (FOW)
defined, GPG2: 280
visibility and, GPG2: 279
Foliage
physics for wind effects on leaves, GPG5:
417–419
widgets to render fast and persistent
foliage, GPG5: 515–526
Fonts
characters for multiple-language games,
GPG3: 93–94
double and multi-byte character sets,
GPG3: 97
single-byte character sets, GPG3: 96–97
Foot-sliding, GPG3: 396–399
Footprints, exaggerating, 45–46

Force Strength (FS), Quantified Judgment
Model (QJM), 284
Foreign languages
fonts and, GPG3: 93
spaces in, GPG3: 93–94
see also Multiple-language games
Forests, GPG3: 270
Formats
floating-point code, 122–126
fast bit blitter for conversion of, GPG2:
92–99
MRC file format for exporting, GPG2:
142–143
Forsyth, Tom
articles by, GPG2: 363–376, GPG2:
488–496, GPG3: 459–466
contact and bio info, GPG2: *xxii,* GPG3:
xxvii
Fox, David
article by, GPG3: 573–581
contact and bio info, GPG3: *xxvii*
Fractal brownian motion (FBM) fractals
clouds created with, GPG2: 245
described, GPG2: 241–242
landscapes created with, GPG2: 245
noise generator implementation, GPG2:
242–245
turbulent noise function, GPG2: 467
Fractals
defined, GPG2: 239
fault fractals, GPG2: 240–241
multifractals, GPG2: 244–245
plasma fractals, GPG2: 240
programming, GPG2: 239–246
see also Fractal brownian motion (FBM)
fractals; Fractal terrain generation
Fractal terrain generation, GPG2: 239,
GPG2: 246
fault formation, GPG1: 499–502
midpoint displacement, GPG1: 503–507
Fractional errors, vector fractions for exact
geometry, GPG3: 160–161
Fragmentation, GPG1: 92–100, GPG4:
43–49
memory, asset hotloading, 115
Frame-based operation, *vs.* function-based
operation, GPG3: 18
Frame Buffer Objects (FBOs), 530–533
Frame events, GPG3: 8, GPG3: 11
Frame-locking, GPG3: 488–489
Frames
as handles, GPG1: 95
memory allocation, frame-based, GPG1:
92–100
Frameworks
game-independent *vs.* -dependent,
GPG3: 17
implementation, GPG3: 20–23
object-composition game framework,
GPG3: 15–24
platform-independent *vs.* -dependent,
GPG3: 17
Free(), GPG2: 9, GPG4: 37
Free form deformation, GPG5: 435
FreeLibrary, GPG2: 34
Free lists
lock-free algorithms, 13–14
memory management and, GPG2: 9,
GPG4: 43–49
defined and described, GPG5: 129–130,
GPG5: 133–134
implementation of, GPG5: 135–136
policy-based design and, GPG5: 129–141

Freese, Peter
article by, GPG4: 157–170
contact and bio info, GPG4: *xxv*
Freezable class, GPG5: 156
FreezeMgr class, GPG5: 150–157
FreezePtr Template class, GPG5: 156
Freitas, Jorge, contact information, GPG1:
xxv
Frenet Frames *vs.* parallel transport frames,
GPG2: 217–218
Fresnel term
for reflections, GPG1: 581–585
refraction mapping, GPG1: 594
Freudenburg, Bert
article by, GPG4: 443–449
contact and bio info, GPG4: *xxv*
Friction
Coulomb friction, GPG3: 215–219
curvature and, GPG3: 225
deceleration and, GPG3: 216
dry friction forces, GPG3: 215–216
dynamic (kinetic) friction, GPG3:
215–218, GPG3: 219
Euler's method to simulate, GPG3:
220–221
geometric issues and, GPG3: 225–226
gravity and, GPG3: 217
nonsmoothness and, GPG3: 222–223
numerical methods for simulation of,
GPG3: 219–224
reformulation method to simulate,
GPG3: 221
regularizing friction, GPG3: 221
smoothness and geometric issues, GPG3:
225
static friction (stiction), GPG3: 215,
GPG3: 218–219
surfaces in contact, GPG3: 217
Taylor method (Taylor series), GPG3:
222–223
three-dimensional formulation, GPG3:
224–225
transitioning between static and dynamic,
GPG3: 223–224
viscous damping and, GPG3: 221
constraints and rigid body dynamics,
GPG4: 249
Front-end processing for multiplayer games,
GPG3: 528–530
Frustums
culling, 467, GPG1: 422–423, GPG5:
65–77
cylinder-frustum intersection test, GPG1:
380–389
view frustums, GPG1: 381–382
extracting frustum and camera information, GPG4: 147–156
plane transformation and view frustum,
GPG4: 147–149
post-perspective space and, GPG4: 402
oblique view frustums for mirrors and
portals, GPG5: 281–294
projection matrix and, GPG5: 283–285
FS (Force Strength), Quantified Judgment
Model (QJM), 284
FSMs. *See* Finite State Machines (FSMs)
Functional decomposition, GPG5: 355–357
Functionality, exporting, GPG1: 56–67
Function-based operation, *vs.* frame-based
operation, GPG3: 18
Function binding, GPG3: 38–42
networking and, GPG3: 42
scripting and, GPG3: 42

COLOR PLATE 1 *(Top) Building the histogram via player skin sampling. (Center) HSV color space image of the author's face. (Bottom) Detection of the author's face. (From article 1.3.)*

COLOR PLATE 2 *The player's avatar leans left in response to the player's movement. (From article 1.3.)*

COLOR PLATE 3 *The player's avatar returns to center in response to the player's movement. (From article 1.3.)*

COLOR PLATE 4 *Perfect buoyancy for a typical boat. (From article 2.5.)*

COLOR PLATE 5 *An arbitrary, concave object floating in water. (From article 2.5.)*

COLOR PLATE 6 *A screen shot from the test application in article 3.9: A Fuzzy-Control Approach to Managing Scene Complexity.*

COLOR PLATE 7 *Manipulating actor properties in the Delta3D editor. (From article 4.5.)*

COLOR PLATE 8 *In the topmost screenshot, normals are calculated in the vertex shader. In the center screenshot a normal map is used. Notice the vertical skirts in the wireframe screenshot. (From article 5.5.)*

COLOR PLATE 9 *The pond ripples are generated interactively by user input, and the simulation is done on the GPU. (From article 5.6.)*

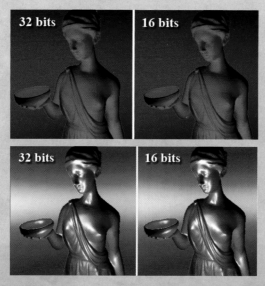

COLOR PLATE 10 *(a) Scene rendered using different depth precisions, showing diffuse lighting only. (b) Different depth precisions with diffuse and specular lighting combined. (From article 5.7.)*

COLOR PLATE 11 *Standard textures with bilinear interpolation tend to produce blurry lettering (top, 64 × 64 texels). The technique presented in this Gem uses a short pixel shader and a preprocessed texture to yield sharp textures (bottom, same texture size). (From article 5.8.)*

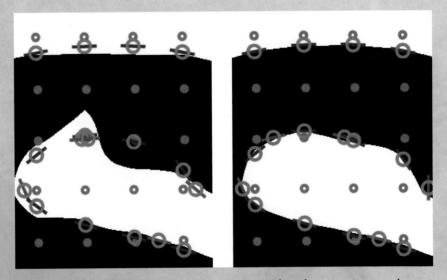

COLOR PLATE 12 *The user may edit position and angle constraints to solve critical situations such as nearly tangential intersections, which overtax the optimizer (left: before, right: after). The constraints are displayed as circles for the positions and lines for the angles. (From article 5.8.)*

COLOR PLATE 13 *Multicolor images used (top) show objectionable errors at points where several colors meet, see the magnified portion. Reverse engineering of such images into a stack of one-color images solves the problem (bottom, 64 × 64 texels). (From article 5.8.)*

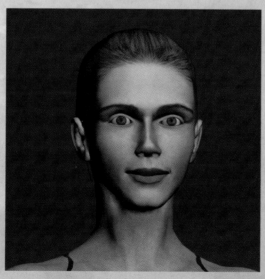

COLOR PLATE 14 *A high-resolution animated face contains 3D information to be streamed across a network. (From article 7.1.)*

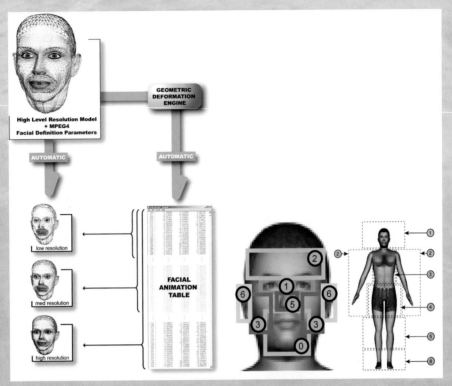

COLOR PLATE 15 *Facial animation scalability on the left and facial and body interest zones for adaptation on the right. (From article 7.1.)*

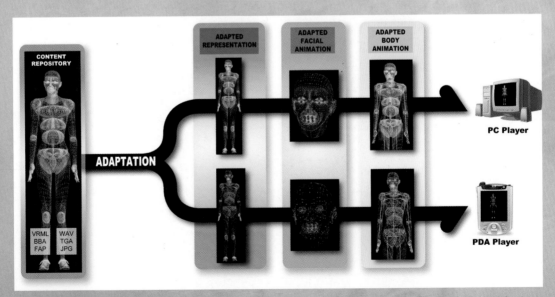

COLOR PLATE 16 *Data flow with adaptation from the content database to the user. (From article 7.1.)*